Gwynfor

PORTRAIT OF A PATRIOT

I Ruth, Gyda Chariad a Diolchgarwch

Gwynfor

PORTRAIT OF A PATRIOT

RHYS EVANS

Photographs: Ceridwen Pritchard; Geoff Charles; Meleri Mair; Bob Puw; Ken Davies; Arwel Davies; Marian Delyth; National Library of Wales; Hulton Deutsch; South Wales Evening Post; Media Wales Ltd; Professor Meic Stephens.

First impression: 2008

Cover photograph: Arwel Davies

ISBN: 978 086243 918 7

Printed on acid-free and partly recycled paper and published and bound in Wales by Y Lolfa Cyf., Talybont, Ceredigion SY24 5AP
e-mail ylolfa@ylolfa.com
website www.ylolfa.com
tel (01970) 832 304
fax 832 782

CONTENTS

A note on abbreviations 7

Introduction 9

Chapter 1 Conversion 1912-31 13

Chapter 2 Mission 1931–39 31

Chapter 3 The Great Storm 1939–45 57

Chapter 4 Stand Your Ground 1945–51 102

Chapter 5 'Soft Soap for the Voters' 1951–55 140

Chapter 6 Tryweryn 1955–59 161

Chapter 7 Civil War 1959–64 198

Chapter 8 A New Dawn 1964–66 241

Chapter 9 The Member for Wales 1966–70 267

Chapter 10 The Party's Over 1970–74 314

Chapter 11 Downfall 1974–79 341

Chapter 12 Any Other Business? 1979–83 392

Chapter 13 The Old Man of Pencarreg 1983–2005 440

Chapter 14 What Remains: the Legacy 452

Notes 457

Index 512

A NOTE ON ABBREVIATIONS

GE Gwynfor Evans Papers, National Library of Wales, Aberystwyth. The specific references contained in this version reflect the old categorisation in use before the papers were fully catalogued.

NLW National Library of Wales, Aberystwyth.

PCP Plaid Cymru Papers

PRO National Archives, Kew.

INTRODUCTION

PEOPLE, LIKE IDEAS, CAN BECOME SUBORDINATE to images of themselves. Subtle differences become polar opposites, rhetorical clarity is demanded even where it never existed and pieties are dutifully observed. Politicians are no exception to this rule but perhaps this truism is even more pronounced in the historically underdeveloped nations of which Wales is most definitely one. Indeed, only in Wales does a politician lose his (and it always is his) surname as a result of our supposed collective understanding of the subject. For Gwynfor, see Jim, Ron, Rhodri etc. It is within this context that the original Welsh language version of this book, *Gwynfor: Rhag Pob Brad*, literally translated as Gwynfor: Against All Treason was published in 2005.

The book then, as now, endeavoured to explain and demystify the myriad faces of Gwynfor. The first to be examined was the obvious one, that of Gwynfor the blessed, the nationalist icon who according to his acolytes, led Wales Moses-like out of her Egyptian captivity into the balmy airs of devolution. This school of thought was and is pervasive in Wales with encomium piled upon encomium leading to nothing but saccharine analysis. The second is the obverse of the first, Gwynfor the irrelevant. This intellectual tradition, largely but not exclusively Labourite in origin, while maintaining that Gwynfor's contribution to Welsh and British politics was marginal, reserved for him the 'enormous condescension of posterity'. The third part of this triptych was the ultra-nationalist analysis of Gwynfor which saw not so much great redeemer but quintessential quisling, particularly over that pivotal event in Welsh history, the drowning of Tryweryn.

The Welsh language version was an attempt to deconstruct these tribal attitudes and to create a subtler, fuller and more meaningful persona from the fragments of Gwynfor's life. What emerges, hopefully, is a coherent case for considering Gwynfor as one of the three Welsh architects of post-war Wales, along with Lloyd George and Aneurin Bevan. Although a lofty claim, my sincere hope is that this biography helps explains why modern Wales would not be what it is today were it not for Gwynfor. Put simply, Plaid Cymru would not exist but for Gwynfor; similarly, it is extremely doubtful whether a devolved Wales could have been forged if Gwynfor, by turns a complicated and simple man with a Messiah complex, had chosen a straightforward and more conventional path. A bilingual Wales would also, in all probability, be a forlorn hope. The same is true for modern Britain. Whilst Gwynfor was a consummate self-propagandist with a commensurate ego, it is undeniable that the British Isles are radically different because of the nationalist case which Gwynfor expounded so assiduously over so many decades.

This biography was written neither with malice aforethought nor with a sense of deference. I also endeavoured not to imbue each and every event with a Whiggish sense of inevitability, linking everything, despite my ultimate conclusions, with today's present. Important though Gwynfor is to understanding modern Wales, a constellation of factors, people and parties created this multi-faceted, small nation. It was also decidedly not an official biography though Gwynfor himself, and his family, collaborated generously. The central injunction at the heart of the Welsh language version was for Gwynfor's life to be debated and not shunted into the realms of either iconography or demonography, depending on the reader's viewpoint. But, alas, whilst the Welsh language version was generously received, Gwynfor did not, as I had hoped, become a contestable concept. Instead, the biography was seen for what it most definitely is not, the last word on Gwynfor. The English language version is, therefore, published more in hope than expectation that a different audience will meaningfully engage with such a vital figure. Indeed, it is one of the central paradoxes of Welsh life during the last dynamic decade that whilst devolution has continued apace, our understanding of how we came to be here is probably as shockingly incomplete as it ever was, militating against both good citizenship and policy making. Save for a few isolated practitioners, Welsh contemporary political history remains by and large a foreign country reserved for the idiosyncratic.

In many respects, the genesis of this book reflects this affliction because I never intended to write it. That it ever saw the light of day was a direct result of my father's horribly premature death. Writing Gwynfor was a very personal act, an attempt to banish despair and to give something back to the study of Welsh history, the field in which my father had so devotedly toiled. Those who aided the process of writing and researching the Welsh language version are acknowledged there, but a new host of debts were incurred in the process of publishing this one. Firstly, thanks are due to Dr T Robin Chapman who not only translated the Welsh language version but also elucidated some of the more recondite references to a different audience. I am also grateful to Professor Meic Stephens, Dewi Morris Jones and Carys Briddon for editorial support. Y Lolfa press in Tal-y-bont remained as supportive as ever, a model of cheerful laissez-faire publishing if ever there was one. Special thanks are owed to Penny Fishlock, a brilliantly incisive editor who excised innumerable idiocies and egregious slips with forbearance and good humour. Those which remain are obviously mine, warts and all. Last but not least, I must thank my family for having lived so long, indeed perhaps too long, with Gwynfor and all it entailed. My partner, Ruth, bore more than her rightful share of this burden and allowed Gwynfor to dominate a large part of our life. This version of Gwynfor also benefited greatly from her usual trenchant editorial insight and encouragement. Now, though, I'm glad to be able to tell her that a very personal ménage à trois is over, leaving others, I sincerely hope, to wrestle over the great man's legacy. With hope, love and gratitude, I dedicate this book to Ruth.

Rhys Evans
Cardiff
April 2008

Chapter 1

CONVERSION 1912–31

In the years between Gwynfor Evans's birth on Sunday 1 September 1912 and his death on Thursday 21 April 2005, the people of Wales began to think and behave as a Welsh people. For many, their Welsh identity took precedence over things British, and Welsh was spoken with pride and as a sign of a separate nationality. In the same way, the nation of Wales began to acquire, albeit hesitatingly, the apparatus of a state. This proto-state would have its own Assembly and a generation of politicians would define their political identity in Welsh terms. Some of those more emotionally inclined began to call their little country 'cool Cymru' – to use a word borrowed by Welsh-speakers towards the end of the twentieth century. Cardiff would become a capital city and a mecca for economic migrants drawn there by its bilingual institutions. The stable communities of Welsh-speaking Wales – *Y Fro Gymraeg* – fragmented and became random collections of individuals and families, many of whom had no knowledge of the language. In the valleys of the south, the process of de-industrialization would be completed. The last coal mines closed, and with them a unique way of life, leaving behind a lasting legacy of poor health and the economic sticking plaster of Objective One funding.

But the land that greeted Gwynfor on that first Sunday was one which today's Wales could scarcely have recognized. In 1912, the institutions that could justifiably be called Welsh were remarkably few, and the sun was setting on Liberal efforts to ensure some measure of Home Rule. Within a few years, all attempts to devolve power through Westminster were exhausted. The cultural circumstances of those who spoke Welsh were even more uncertain, as industrialism and population shift eroded the old Welsh way of life. For those who clung to this vision of Wales it looked likely that a virtuous, clean-living people faced extinction. In every sphere, there was a feeling – despite the existence of such Welsh institutions as the University and the Eisteddfod – that the Welsh identity was on the wane and the Welsh language in its death throes. However, by May 1999, and the opening of the National Assembly for Wales, another revolution had occurred. It was a very respectable patriotic revolution, and its victory was almost complete. In a bilingual ceremony, broadcast by an expensive, state-run Welsh-medium Fourth Channel, the Queen welcomed the birth of Wales's own Assembly. She was greeted at that Assembly by a former anti-monarchist rebel called Dafydd Elis Thomas, now a member of the House of Lords and the Assembly's Presiding Officer. He presided over the Assembly in a sharp suit under the banner of that formerly despised handful of hotheads, Plaid Cymru, the Party of Wales. For good or ill, Wales had been reborn. However, to understand the Wales of the twenty-first century we must go back to that foreign country of 1912 and tell the story of one of Wales's most remarkable sons, Gwynfor Evans.

Gwynfor occupies a central place in the creation of the new Wales, but it was the town of Barry that created him. The nationalist fire that burned in him for over nine decades was sparked by a place which had more in common with America than with Wales. In essence, Gwynfor's story is one of lost roots and a search to rediscover them, a process that left an indelible impression on contemporary Wales and Britain. Indeed, the Barry of 1912 was one of the most economically active places in the industrialized world. The 'Chicago of Wales' was created virtually out of nothing when the industrialist and philanthropist David Davies of Llandinam built a dock there in 1884. It had been an attempt to break the monopoly of Cardiff's docks over the export of coal – the 'black diamond' of the Rhondda – and it succeeded beyond the wildest dreams of these buccaneers. In 1881, Barry had 500 inhabitants; by 1911, 33,000 had made their way from every corner of Britain to the Welsh El Dorado, hoping to make their fortune in the 'magnetic south'. And unlike the other industrial towns of the region, Barry was a late arrival. In reality, the position of the Welsh language there was so precarious that there was little by way of Welsh culture to be threatened. Even today, one only needs to eavesdrop on the natives of Barry as proof of this. As the historian Peter Stead, himself a native of Barry, has commented, the local accent, like those of Cardiff and Newport, reflects the influence of incomers from Ireland and the west of England.[1] This was in complete contrast to valley towns like Aberdare and Merthyr. In Barry, these variegated beginnings meant the town would never have a clear or stable sense of identity.[2]

In the town itself there was a cultural divide. On the one hand, there was the working-class culture of the new arrivals: jazz, picture-palaces and public houses; on the other, the mores of the respectable Welsh-speaking middle classes, transplanted from outside but none the less prominent for that. Similar conflicts could be seen across Wales, leaving a feeling of resentment, as T Robin Chapman has written, 'that the familiar was in retreat, that everything previously assumed to be unchangeable was fast disappearing and being crushed under the feet of a surging crowd'.[3] In Barry, working-class culture was in the ascendant. This brought about a curious relationship between the town and the rest of Wales, and the majority of the inhabitants came to believe that Wales began some fifteen miles to the north in the 'Welshie' valleys, where the 'Shonis', a race of strangers, lived.[4] It was into this confusing world that Gwynfor Richard Evans was born, the first son of Dan and Catherine Evans.[5]

Like so many others in Barry, Dan and Catherine Evans were incomers. She was a native of Kidwelly, while Dan's family came from Velindre in the west of Glamorgan. By understanding this background one realises the importance of his father's family in Gwynfor's upbringing. Ben Evans, Gwynfor's grandfather, was a minister, the son of James Evans, a weaver who had somehow managed to earn a living and raise four sons in pretty adverse circumstances. James Evans is something of an enigma, but an elegy written for him strongly suggests he was a product of Victorian Nonconformist radicalism. As a chapel deacon, he had ensured that 'the lovely Sunday school/Would have the fragrance of a heavenly garden' at his death. It also appears from the same poem that he was a committed pacifist, active in 'all the movements of the kingdom of peace'.[6] But Nonconformist radicalism (and the world view that this entailed) was not the only influence. Ben and his brothers understood that the family library contained three great treasures: The Bible, *A History of the Madagascar Martyrs* and *Dr Adam Clarke's Commentary on the Scriptures*. These were weighty, not to say arid tomes, but their lasting influence was to set the brothers on the path of Nonconformism. Following a long struggle with what he described as 'Providence', Ben decided not to become a farmer. Rather than till the soil, he – and two of his brothers – resolved to turn hearts and souls to God as ministers.

But Providence or not, there was nothing providential in the inadequate education Ben Evans received. James Evans had decided to boycott the local National School as a protest against its ecclesiastical teaching. It was a principled stand, but a costly one, because it deprived his children of a formal education. Despite this unpromising start, Ben Evans overcame his difficulties and became a pillar of the community. The thirst for education never left him, however, and he eventually succeeded in gaining a place at a grammar school in Llangadog in the hope that he would learn enough to enter the ministry. This school provided him with far more than a formal education. In Llangadog, he met his future wife, Elizabeth 'Bess' James, the youngest daughter of Caeshenkin, and a member of a prominent local family. They married in 1882 and had three children, Dan, Idris and Ceridwen. This was the beginning of Gwynfor's connection with Carmarthenshire – a link that would provide him with both personal and political salvation in the decades ahead.

With his new wife, Ben set off for the Independents' college in Brecon, and then became a minister. His first calling was Siloh at Melincryddan near Neath, and before long he had built up a sizeable congregation. He also succeeded in reducing the chapel's debts before moving on in 1888 to a post at the newly-built chapel in Lloyd Street, Llanelli. He spent 11 years in Tinopolis, where the chapel thrived as thousands poured into the growing town. It was here that Gwynfor's father, Dan, was educated. Even so, his formal schooling was limited, and he was forced to leave at 14 to be apprenticed to an ironmonger. But in July 1899, as a new century dawned, Ben decided to face one final challenge – he moved with his family to the town of Barry and accepted a call to yet another new chapel, the Tabernacl. His decision was a tremendous blow to the Congregationalists of Llanelli, and a deputation of deacons was despatched in an attempt to prevent the move. Ben was determined, however. He insisted on moving and told the deacons at Lloyd Street that he was prompted by a sense of 'duty'.[7]

By the time Ben reached Barry, the town had broken all records, having grown more rapidly in the previous decade than any other town in Britain. The local paper claimed that nowhere else could boast so many 'enterprising spirits' as Barry and that it was impossible to predict what sort of town it would be in another ten years' time.[8] Barry was undoubtedly an exciting place for Ben to attempt to establish a new mission. But the town that did 'nothing by halves' also attracted Dan, who followed his father to the Vale of Glamorgan.[9] Dan found work at Hoopers, the ironmongers on the busiest street in Barry, Holton Road. Meanwhile, Ben was proving a huge success at the Tabernacl. He was also elected a local councillor and travelled Wales, eager to promote the cause of the Home

Rule movement, Young Wales or Cymru Fydd, and the broader values of Welsh Liberal Nonconformism. By 1905, the journalist and dramatist Beriah Gwynfe Evans, one of Young Wales's leading lights, was referring to him as one of 'the Men of the Age'.

Indeed, during 1905 Ben had risen to national prominence through his opposition to the funding of the Catholic school in Barry. The school had succeeded in convincing Barry Education Committee that it should receive money from the public purse while remaining free of Council control. Ben and his fellow-Liberals found the notion repugnant because of their staunch belief in the doctrine of 'No Control, No Cash!' He insisted, too, that Catholics should receive no preferential treatment. This battle over the implementation of the 1902 Education Act developed into a cause célèbre in Wales. Similar skirmishes were under way throughout the country, with Lloyd George, a particular idol of Ben Evans, leading the charge against the Established Church and Conservatism.[10]

In Barry, things were particularly heated. Ben and several other ministers threw off the shackles of respectability and refused to pay their rates. Twice he was hauled before the local magistrates for his pains. His belongings were sold to pay his debts – his wife's gold watch being sacrificed both times, with a kind friend buying it back for Mrs Evans. But Ben Evans was intent on doing more than protecting his wife's watch from the bailiffs. The minister of the Tabernacl decided that the only way to frustrate the Catholics was to gain control of the council. He stood for election against the Catholic Liberal and popular local GP, Dr O'Donnell. Despite being 'cursed by the priest', the minister topped the poll. In due course, Ben Evans was elected chair of the Education Committee. It was a resounding victory, and his fellow-Nonconformists could state with no small measure of self-satisfaction that the committee had been purged of 'all elements not in keeping with the principles of Welsh dissent and democracy'. A victory like this 'in a town both essentially anti-Nonconformist and typically non-Welsh' was all the sweeter for Ben and his supporters.[11]

The success, however, was soon tempered by a family tragedy. Ceridwen, Ben's daughter, died aged just 14. Tears flowed freely, it was said, on the day 'Ceri' was laid to rest, but the loss did nothing to dampen the family's faith that individuals had the ability to change their material circumstances.[12] Ben exercised his new authority on the council to promote the interests of Temperance and Young Wales – everything, as one contemporary wrote, 'that tended to uplift his fellow beings'.[13] It is curious to note, when one remembers how Gwynfor 'lost' his Welsh, that Ben Evans did more than virtually anyone else to support the language in Barry. The *Barry Herald* reported that he was the leader of the town's 'Welsh Nationalists' by virtue of his office as President of the Barry branch of the cultural society, the Cymmrodorion. In 1909, he attempted to make Welsh a compulsory subject in the town's schools – but failed by a whisker. Following this glorious defeat, he announced (to accompanying cheers and applause) that the enemies of the Welsh language had done their utmost to kill it but had failed.[14]

Ben was not the only member of the family to shine in the Edwardian Golden Age. By 1905, Dan had become disillusioned with his work at Hoopers and fed up with his meagre wage. He had a local reputation as a baritone, and toyed with the idea of singing professionally and joining the Carl Rosa Opera Company, but the whim did not last long. Aged 22, he decided to make his own way in the world and opened his ironmongers, Dan Evans, on Holton Road. Dan's guiding principle was to offer the best he could to the people of Barry at a fair price. His first advertisement in November of that year read 'One Trial And You'll Be Satisfied', and so it proved.[15] Before long the business began to expand, and he took on two apprentices: Edward Griffiths and Anthony Griffiths. They were talented workers, too. Edward Griffiths was later knighted after a successful directing career with Gaumont film studios, and Anthony Griffiths became the captain of one of the largest tankers in the world.[16] Dan was fortunate in both his staff and in the strong economic climate as Barry docks continued to expand during the first five years of the business.[17] His natural courtesy and industry were also vital and he earned a reputation as a man who knew exactly what the busy housewife needed most.

Dan was a canny businessman and he would travel around the chapels of the Vale, performing in countless concerts. Without exception, he refused any fee, telling his admirers: 'I haven't come here to receive payment but if you want to show your appreciation, I've opened in Holton Road, Barry, and you'll find a shop there you'll appreciate.'[18] To back him up he had a regiment of loyal staff who appreciated the decent working conditions in the shop. In the years that followed, the business grew substantially, and two more branches had opened by 1917.[19] Apart from Sundays, Dan worked for at least 14 hours every day, turning his hand to anything from serving behind the counter to ordering the latest gadgets from London and keeping the accounts. By the time Gwynfor was born, the shop was among the most important in the town and his father one of the pillars of Barry's chapel-going middle class. In 2005, as the Dan Evans company celebrated its centenary, the shop's survival was hailed as a rare example of the survival of a small business in an age of multinational capitalism.[20] However, the celebrations were short-lived. In August 2005, it was announced that the shop was to close in the face of unforgiving economic circumstances.

In 1911, Dan married Catherine Richard, daughter of William and Elizabeth Richard, landlords of the New Inn, Kidwelly. Details of Gwynfor's mother are scarce, but one thing is certain: her upbringing had been an unhappy one. Her father was a notorious drunkard who died when Catherine was only a year old. When she was 11, she lost her mother. Her aunt Sage and her husband Ben Jones, editor of the *Llanelly Mercury*, took on the responsibility of offering the orphan a home. Bereft of education and with no financial security, Catherine left Kidwelly in her teens and headed to London to work as a draper's assistant. She returned to Wales and found employment in a shop in Barry opposite Dan Evans's ironmongers. They courted for four years before marrying. Dan and Catherine worked in the shop together, where she showed the same readiness as her new husband to put in long hours in the china department. It was the start of a hugely successful partnership, both materially and spiritually. Catherine was alone in the world, and marrying Dan had been her salvation. But her father's drinking had left its mark. For the rest of her life she abhorred alcohol. In choosing a husband, it was said she sought three qualities: 'I wanted a teetotaller; I didn't want a sailor; I wanted a *capelwr* [chapel-goer]'.[21]

Gwynfor was born a year later, to the accompaniment of the hooters at Barry docks. His first home was Y Goedwig, 24 Somerset Road, and as the address suggests, he was raised in sight of the English Mendips. Indeed, it is one of the great ironies of Welsh geography that, as a child, the greatest patriot twentieth-century Wales produced could see more of England than of Wales. It was a fitting home for an ambitious businessman like Dan. Their neighbours were sea captains, men who were regarded as the middle-class élite of the town. Dan Evans's family (by 1918 Gwynfor had a sister, Ceridwen, and a younger brother, Alcwyn) were the only Welsh-speakers in the road, but that wasn't an impediment to their social integration. With so many young families in Somerset Road, Y Goedwig echoed to the laughter of children and to their parents' musical talents.

Gwynfor's first hazy memories were an amalgam of play and portents. The first thing he remembered was carrying a saucepan for his grandfather Ben, when he was two. His ambition was to be a train driver, and to his profound embarrassment in later life, he was fond of playing cowboys and Indians. Nor was he too shy to experience the ardour of first love when, at the age of four, he fell for Mary Rowlands. Even so, his was in many ways a difficult, dystopian childhood. The First World War was the shadow that hung over him and everyone else in Barry. It was an event that corrupted his innocence and destroyed the optimism which had made Barry so prosperous until 1914. If any town in Wales was conscious of the war, it was Barry. In 1914 it became a garrison town, and thousands of soldiers and refugees from Belgium made it their home. By the end of the war, a higher proportion of young men from Barry had enlisted in the army than from any other town in south Wales. Ben's chapel, the Tabernacl, played its part and the members took pride in the 'sizeable number' of brave men from its pews who set off to 'France, Salonika, East Africa and Egypt'.[22] In a special concert to honour the troops who were bound for foreign lands, Dan Evans sang 'The Drum Major' and the men themselves serenaded the audience with a performance of 'The Soldier's Chorus'.[23] In due course, this memory of how all the town's institutions had become branches of the military would have a profound effect on Gwynfor's pacifist brand of nationalism.

By the time Gwynfor enrolled at Gladstone Road Elementary School, in 1916, the war could no longer be ignored. In his autobiography he recalls seeing 'long columns of soldiers marching to the strident tones of a band down the slope a hundred yards from school … to board a ship that would take them to France'. The two things that left the most indelible impression on him were the goat leading the procession and the tears in some of the soldiers' eyes.[24] Both Welsh and British identities were fused at school and the children were encouraged to hero worship the troops in France. On Saint David's Day 1917, they gave a presentation on 'patriotic aims' and laid wreaths commemorating former pupils who had already fallen in battle. Six weeks later, the same pupils celebrated Saint George's Day with gusto.[25] But the war was not the only cloud to darken Gwynfor's childhood. Illness plagued him through his 'pretty unhappy' days at Gladstone Road. For many children in Barry, diphtheria was a common ailment because of the town's sewage system. At school, there was a 'vast amount of sickness',[26] and Gwynfor suffered two serious bouts when he was four and eight. On the second occasion, his Uncle Dudley came to his room following the doctor's visit and Gwynfor heard the word 'crisis' being used. He frequently believed he was about to die. He survived, but at a price. The years of ill health left their mark on him and well into his teens he suffered from lethargy and stunted growth.

As well as sickness, there was another complication in these early years that had a profound effect on Gwynfor's development: the language of the home switched from Welsh to English. Up until 1917, Dan and Catherine, Gwynfor's parents, would use a mixture of Welsh and English when they spoke to one another, even though Welsh was their mother tongue. They would use the same Anglo-Welsh hotchpotch when they spoke to their children, although Ceridwen never spoke anything but Welsh to her big brother 'Wo', as she called Gwynfor. Until he was five, they were both fluent Welsh speakers. Then, almost overnight, the language ceased to be used in the home. The first change was when the maid, Annie, a Welsh-speaker from Pontyberem, decided to leave. Dan and Catherine tried but failed to find a Welsh-speaking maid to succeed her, and in her place secured the services of Maggie, from Barrow-in-Furness, to look after the children. With Dan and Catherine in the shop from dawn until dusk, English was the language the children now heard at home.[27] There was also a further complication. At Gladstone Road, Gwynfor never heard a word of Welsh, and as a result decided he should start to speak English with his family. Dan and Catherine responded by speaking English to each other, as well as with the children, at all times.

At a time when the Welsh language was regarded as something of an inconvenience, there was nothing unusual in this. In 1911, a year before Gwynfor was born, the deacons at the Tabernacl had appealed 'urgently' to the Welsh-speakers of Barry to use the language with their children.[28] Ben, Gwynfor's grandfather, said something similar about Welsh two years later. 'It must be taken up on the hearth,'[29] he announced, but his own son chose to ignore his advice, and by 1921, the year of the Census, Welsh was in rapid decline in Barry. In Gwynfor's case, things were made worse by the dismissive attitude of the teachers at Gladstone Road to all things Welsh. Although the school enjoyed a reputation for its innovative curriculum, lessons in Welsh were an exception, and some staff took the infrequent Welsh lessons as an opportunity to 'read about horse-racing in the paper while hiding a bar of chocolate behind the paper and repeatedly asking what was the Welsh for this and that'.[30] In the schoolyard, the *lingua franca* was English – the common language of the Babel of Welsh-speakers (such as Gwynfor), English-speaking natives, and the children of incomers from England,

Italy, Greece and elsewhere.

But the idea that Gwynfor lost his Welsh entirely and had to re-learn the language from scratch when he was 18 is a myth. It is true that he had to brush up on his Welsh in his teens, but even in Anglicized, cosmopolitan Barry, Gwynfor heard plenty of the language. There is clear evidence of this. The most dependable source is his sister, Ceridwen. She was incensed by her brother's unwillingness to challenge newspaper reports which misleadingly claimed that Gwynfor had had to learn Welsh afresh. But by then the story had been repeated time after time by Gwynfor and his supporters and the romance of it suited his political ends. Gwynfor might well have been reluctant to speak Welsh after starting at Gladstone Road, but he could scarcely have avoided the language – at home and elsewhere. At Somerset Road, his great-aunt Jane, Ben Evans's only sister, had a considerable influence on Gwynfor, as she lived with them for eight years. Gwynfor would refer to her room in the house as 'The Welsh Room'. Here, on an almost daily basis, Gwynfor would speak Welsh with her. The same was true at the Tabernacl – the centrepiece of the family's cultural life. Three times every Sunday, and in meetings of the Band of Hope, Gwynfor would hear Welsh. Although the Sunday School was in English, that colourful throng of dockers, teachers and businessmen who attended the Tabernacl would converse in Welsh.

This was also the case with regard to the family's close connection to the Barry Cymmrodorion – a society which, through eisteddfodau and lectures, maintained some semblance of Welsh culture in adverse circumstances. As a boy, Gwynfor frequently went to Cymmrodorion meetings, and despite his efforts to avoid Arthen Evans, the society's energetic secretary, he too was determined that Gwynfor played his part. The result of all this contact with the language was that Gwynfor was sufficiently fluent to take first prize in the 'Barry Cymmrodorion Tests', a test in Welsh for those children who were considered to have Welsh as their first language.[31] This was not his only success: he won numerous prizes for his spoken Welsh too.[32] But perhaps the single most important cultural influence on Gwynfor in this period was the time he spent in Llangadog every summer with his great uncle Walter James, the village auctioneer. This was a community that the young Gwynfor perceived as an arcadian paradise; it was through the lens of Llangadog that he came to see the rest of the world.[33] Compared to the urban sprawl of Barry, Llangadog was Utopian. These were idyllic days of bike rides, pony round-ups and fishing. In time, this somewhat sentimental memory of Welsh rural stability would mould his nationalism.

But the countervailing influence was, of course, the war, and by 1918, it had also had a lasting effect on Gwynfor and every other child in Barry. When the armistice was announced on the wet Sunday morning of 11 November, the whole town celebrated, 'almost every house displaying bunting ... the whole day being one continued demonstration of rejoicing'.[34] The joy was premature, however, for the years that followed were difficult ones for the town. Dan's shop suffered like all the rest and Gwynfor remembered his shock at seeing his father in tears and hearing the word 'deflation' for the first time. He learned later that the shop's stock had declined in value to such an extent that the business itself was threatened. The effect on the children was immediate. When the family saw ships in dock they knew it would be a good day for the shop. Another family ritual each morning was to read the *Western Mail* in order to find out how many ships would be unloading that day.[35] The economic storm did not subside until the early 'thirties, but Dan Evans remained unbowed. In an echo of the Liberal message that inspired Gwynfor as a politician, Dan Evans believed that the small retailers of Barry should be entitled to run their businesses free of external interference and, during the 1920s, he devoted himself to the activities of the local Chamber of Trade. Throughout the decade he appealed to his customers in Barry not to be bewitched by the attractions of the large stores in Cardiff. The most important thing in the world to him (with the exception of the chapel) was that trade should prosper in Barry. Nothing, he insisted, should be allowed to undermine this, and when the miners went on strike in 1926, he praised his fellow-shopkeepers 'for the grand way in which they had supported the Government in the very disastrous period they had just passed through'.[36]

Politically, Lloyd George was Dan and Catherine's hero, and up until the 'thirties a picture of the 'Welsh Wizard' held pride of place on the wall of their home. This was not the family's only expression of Liberal principles – an upbringing that had an undoubted effect on Gwynfor's view of the world. Dan and Catherine despised alcohol and both were unstinting in their support of the Temperance cause in Barry. For Dan, signing the pledge meant that the good people of Barry would not be tempted into immorality. It was also a sign of the family's unwillingness to succumb to the accursed trinity of brewers, churchgoers and Tories. For her part, there is no doubt that her father's fondness for the demon drink fired Catherine's enthusiasm for the work of the town's 'Purity and

Protective League'.

In 1924, the year that saw the death of Lenin and the formation of the first Labour government, Gwynfor won a scholarship to Barry County School. He could hardly be described as an outstanding scholar and entering the BCS was a considerable achievement. He knew he had joined a social and intellectual élite.[37] Since its opening in 1896, its pupils had always considered it a Welsh Eton or Harrow.[38] The school magazine, *The Barrian*, contained a lively debate as to which fashion best suited boys of their standing – Bolshevik 'Oxford Bags' or the more subtle styles of Deauville and the great English universities. And with teachers as distinguished as the historian David Williams on the staff, the boys had good reason to feel confident about their abilities. Gwynfor found himself in a year group that was outstanding even by BCS standards: it included Ronnie Boone, who played rugby for Wales; Glyn Daniel, who became a world-famous archaeologist; and Alan Michell, a close friend of Gwynfor's, who later made his mark as a diplomat. The headmaster, Edgar Jones, was the architect of this success and 'The Boss', with his emphasis on creating the whole man, on the playing field and in the classroom, had a considerable influence on Gwynfor.

As the economic storm continued to rage, Gwynfor also sought sanctuary in his grandfather's chapel, the Tabernacl. Although the fire of the 1905 Revival had long since cooled, parts of Barry – despite some unruly elements – were still staunchly Christian. The commercial élite with whom Dan Evans identified so firmly was more God-fearing than any other, and living a virtuous life was considered just as important an indication of good character as success in business. From the outset, the Tabernacl, three times every Sunday, had been the bedrock of the family's cultural and spiritual life. As Dan was a respected deacon at the Tabernacl, Gwynfor had no choice but to embrace Nonconformism. But the son was never tempted by apostasy, and by his late teens he had come to appreciate Welsh Nonconformism as a bulwark against Anglicization and decadence. Another positive of the Tabernacl for Gwynfor was that it attracted such a wide cross-section of Welsh-speakers. Penuel, at the west end of town, was the natural choice for Barry's Welsh bourgeoisie, but the Tabernacl drew in the 'trimmers', or the coal levellers from the docks. For a young lad with his roots so deeply planted in Barry's middle class, these men held a curious fascination. As he watched them in prayer at the Tabernacl, Gwynfor was transfixed by the ability of the 'trimmers' to live blameless lives while continuing to work in the murkiest depths of the coal steamers. In Gwynfor's eyes, such men were a breed apart from the aimless, uncouth proletariat of the valleys. Rather, they represented the true Welsh *gwerin*, the cultured working class that he would come to consider as the foundation of Welsh-born, Welsh-speaking society.[39]

Even so, Gwynfor's misery from Gladstone Road continued to haunt him. He could not shake off his lethargy or his self-consciousness over his small stature. He was plagued, too, by morbid and melodramatic nightmares that prefigured the way he would write about Wales as an adult. In these nightmares he would almost invariably imagine himself close to death, before waking to find he had been spared. Up until his sixteenth birthday, too, his academic and social progress had been unremarkable – despite the outstanding education to which he had been exposed. Although he passed his Matriculation, he failed to gain a Distinction like the high-fliers in his class. There were compensations, however. Aged 16, he travelled abroad for the first time with his close friend, Alan Michell. They sailed in a small goods vessel from Barry to Spain, and spent six weeks walking in the Pyrenees. Gwynfor returned to Wales with a new interest in foreign countries, but another change was coming too.

The winter of 1928 was a dramatic one for Gwynfor. He began to grow, and within a year the familiar tall, dignified man had emerged. During this year of emotional upheaval he also fell in love for the first time, and for the next four years he courted the lively and beautiful Glenys Davies, a Barry girl. The pair had much in common: Ceridwen, Gwynfor's sister, was Glenys's best friend and she, like him, sang in the chapel choir. They grew so close over the following years that Ceridwen assumed it was only a matter of time before they would marry. It came as something of a shock to Ceridwen, then, when the relationship ended suddenly. Until he met his future wife, Rhiannon, his only serious relationship had been with Glenys, despite there being no shortage of female companions in the meantime.

As he reached his late teens, and with an attractive girl on his arm, Gwynfor's self-confidence flourished, enhanced by his feats on the hockey and cricket fields. By 1930, he was being described as the school's 'star medium pace bowler' and within the year he was school captain and had secured a place in the Welsh schools' eleven. As *The Barrian* put it: 'EVANS – Never gets rattled'.[40] The irony, of course, was that Gwynfor excelled in that most English of games, but he turned this to his own advantage. Playing the English gentleman's game, he said, taught him leadership skills and the value of 'esprit de corps'.[41]

It is no coincidence either that Gwynfor's attitude to Welsh changed too in 1929, the most significant year of his life. In his early teens, Welsh had been a source of irritation to him; indeed, at the beginning of 1929, he proposed (in English) at a debate in the Tabernacl's cultural society 'That the Tabernacl be changed into an English-medium chapel'. He lost the motion, and was advised by the chapel treasurer, John Davies, that it would be no bad thing for him to buy a Welsh dictionary and learn the language properly. He did so, but the real turning point came when he passed the Senior CWB and entered the sixth form. When he chose his specialist subjects for the next two years, he decided on Welsh rather than French – an unusual choice at BCS. He did so not out of any particular love for Wales but because he did not get on with the French master. He therefore, began his serious study of Welsh almost by accident, but its effect on him would prove to be profound.

Under the guidance of his young, enthusiastic Welsh teacher, Gwynallt Evans, Gwynfor warmed to the work of new and daring writers like Kate Roberts, R Williams Parry and T H Parry-Williams, as well as classic texts such as the medieval tales of the Mabinogi and the work of the eighteenth-century satirist and visionary, Ellis Wynne. His Welsh lessons were not the only formative influence. His history master, David Williams, perhaps the greatest Welsh historian of his generation, ensured that Gwynfor was aware of his country's rich heritage. His formal education was fed by long and frequent conversations with his friends Alan Michell and Glyn Daniel. At the same time he developed a passion for Welsh hymns, feeling a spiritual thrill as he accompanied his own lusty rendition of them on the piano. He felt a similar euphoria during his hikes through the Vale of Glamorgan, amazed by the natural beauty of Wales.[42] He visited certain parts of the Vale 'scores of times' as an escape from the mundane surroundings of Barry. 'There was never a place so lacking in tradition,' he concluded years later about his home town.[43] There was nothing out of the ordinary in this attitude. In his experiences and his reactions to them, Gwynfor was tapping into a more general Welsh aesthetic of cultural loss. This world-view had its roots in the determinedly anti-modernist periodical, O M Edwards's *Cymru*, which idealised the lyrical, the homely and the rural landscape. For Edwards and his disciples, the humble countryman in his whitewashed cottage was the true aristocrat. And as Gwynfor demonstrated throughout the rest of his life, there was no inconsistency in being both ascetic and romantic.[44]

These feelings were doubtless fuelled by a fair amount of adolescent angst, but Gwynfor was conscious too of a more general disenchantment with the politics of the time. His father's and his grandfather's generations had been convinced that Lloyd George could win a measure of Home Rule for Wales through the Westminster Parliament, and had no difficulty in supporting a mainstream British party. By 1929 (four years after the foundation of Plaid Cymru), a growing number of young Welsh-speakers were dismissive of the idea that one could serve Wales and at the same time remain loyal to the British political system. In the press, too, Plaid Cymru's growing influence was steadily becoming more apparent. When the firebrand nationalist Ambrose Bebb spoke about a Welsh-speaking renaissance or *Risorgimento* in 1929, he was in tune with the times. Nationalism was growing into a power which could no longer be ignored and was attracting, in Bebb's own words, 'a sufficient number of men and women to bring about the revolution they desire'.[45] The revolution would happen under the banner of Plaid Cymru, and the lesson for Gwynfor and his generation as they watched their fathers' disappointment was that one could not serve two masters.[46]

As this education in matters Welsh continued, Gwynfor's attitude to the Great War shifted, too. At 16, he had considered himself something of a socialist and, at school, he had been introduced to the *New Statesman and Nation* (much to the horror of the man who preceded him as Plaid Cymru's President, Saunders Lewis). It was a natural step, then, for him to join the Left Book Club and attend their meetings in Barry. But one could hardly describe these socialist leanings as fervent. His pacifism was far more entrenched, and the book that transformed his world-view in 1929 was Leyton Richards's *The Christian Alternative to War*, published that year. Richards and his colleagues in the Fellowship of Reconciliation were the subject of widespread press interest across Britain for their 'Christ and Peace' campaign. Reading Richards convinced Gwynfor that he too would be a Christian pacifist. The book's effect was almost immediate; while still a grammar school pupil, he resolved to show his colours, joining the League of Nations Union, a particularly influential movement at the time which sought to promote the principles contained in the Treaty of Versailles. In Barry and across Wales, branches of the LNU flourished, and its existence was for Gwynfor the surest guarantee that war would be no more.

In 1929, these two intellectual strands, Christian pacifism and patriotism, converged. It brought about what Gwynfor would later describe as a conversion. Overnight, he realized that he could bring together two sets of ideas – and this realization transformed him. In its own way, this conversion was just as far-reaching as those of the eighteenth-century mystic Ann Griffiths or the hymnwriter William Williams of Pantycelyn. From this point onwards, Gwynfor became a fervent Welshman and a committed Christian, seeing Wales as a series of stark contrasts. The ideal of a Welsh-speaking Christian Wales became a light to lead him through the darkness that followed the death of Welsh Liberalism. For Gwynfor, as for several nationalists of his generation, this 'Blessed Wales' had a 'soul'. The 'soul of the nation', the notion of that former Oxford don and editor of Welsh language popular magazines in the late Victorian and early Edwardian period, O M Edwards, beguiled Gwynfor. He began to think of Wales as an elect nation and the Welsh as latter-day Jews – a lost people in need of a Messiah. These ideas ran through Gwynfor's mind during the existential crisis that followed the collapse of Young Wales and his adoption of them was no coincidence.[47] In an address nearly a decade after his conversion, on 'The Aims and Ideals of Young Wales', Gwynfor attempted to rationalize the connection between upbringing and belief. Addressing the unlikely audience of the Barry Rotary Club in 1938, he spoke for the first time of the town that had made him what he was. This statement on his own generation was his confession of faith:

> They were cradled in a rocking world and never had known a stable one; the post-war years had seen social unrest, economic depression and the dissolution of moral codes and the accepted conventions. Two things characterised the period – rootlessness and ruthlessness. Society was drifting, without any sense of direction.

But out of this confusion came hope:

> In the midst of this chaos, the younger generation in Wales gradually became conscious of two traditions which met their needs in a very real way – religion and the national traditions. One gave life purpose and the other roots.[48]

The transformation that Gwynfor underwent from 1929 is nothing less than remarkable. The sickly boy gives way to the young patriot who believes that he has been 'called' to serve the nation. That nation, he sensed, stretched back to the Age of the Saints in a glorious, unbroken heritage. Even so, however intense the conversion, Gwynfor would not join Plaid Cymru for another five years, simply because he assumed that the '*Blaid Bach*', or 'Little Party', was too feeble to make any difference. Gwynfor's priority, rather, was emotional salvation from the difficulties he faced in Barry.[49] When he was asked in 1984 why he was a nationalist, his answer was simple: 'Most people will laugh at it as being in their eyes sentimental slush. Nevertheless for me it is basic. I love Wales.'[50] Until the end of his life, this desire to save people in the name of a Welsh-speaking, Christian Wales and to spare it the emotional 'damage' that he himself had suffered in his home town, would be his mission.[51]

His missionary work began at Barry County School. As secretary of the school eisteddfod, he harangued his fellow-pupils for being so indifferent to the competitions, and pleaded with them to show a little regard, 'if it is only out of respect for our patriotic students'.[52] His ambitions were not restricted to the school. In 1930 he applied for one of four Welsh scholarships awarded by the League of Nations so that he could travel to Geneva and see the League's work for himself. These scholarships were awarded by examination and Gwynfor threw himself into the preparatory work, reading and digesting dense volumes such as Hugh Dalton's *Peace of Nations* and Lord Cecil's *The Way of Peace*. His hard work was in vain, however. The adjudicator concluded that his grasp of the information was good but that his treatment of it was 'slight and superficial'.[53] The dream, however, did not end there; his father stepped into the breach and paid the substantial sum of £16 that allowed Gwynfor to join the successful candidates on their visit to Switzerland. This was the first time, but certainly not the last, that Dan would rescue his son financially.

Gwynfor left for Geneva on 1 September 1930. He was accompanied by the Reverend Gwilym Davies, secretary of the League of Nations Union and one of the most prominent public figures in Wales who was something of an idol for Gwynfor. Gwilym Davies showed him how European diplomats were undertaking disarmament talks that year. It was an exciting experience for such a young man, but overall the visit was a disappointment. The Alps and the Jura thrilled him, but he was mature enough to see that the treaty signed at Versailles was a source of contention in international relations, and that another war was a distinct possibility. As he listened to the delegates discussing the future of the Saar region, he detected indifference in their attitude. 'Members,' he commented, 'were continually walking to and fro, while the press-men seemed to vie with one another in making rustling noises with sheets of paper.' In the years that followed, Gwynfor's fears and those of his fellow-pacifists deepened: neither the LNU nor the diplomats in Geneva appeared to be capable of maintaining the peace. This disillusionment would unfold gradually. For the time being, Gwynfor felt more certain than ever that the answer lay with the LNU and that it was incumbent on him and others who thought the same to act as 'apostles in the cause of peace at home'.[54]

After the adventure in Switzerland, Gwynfor arrived home on 17 September to revise for his final exams. He had chosen Welsh, English and History, and although he was a conscientious scholar, his lack of fluency in written Welsh was a concern. He could only read a text like D J Williams's *Hen Dŷ Fferm* with the aid of a dictionary. But his fears of another failure were unfounded. In the summer of 1931, the good news arrived: he had sailed through the 'Higher' and won a Glamorgan scholarship to read Law at the University College of Wales, Aberystwyth. His home for the next three years would be another seaside town, but a very different one. He went to Aberystwyth as a boy and returned to Barry three years later as a man and a nationalist. But even in 1931 the foundations had been laid. Having lived with compromise for so long, Gwynfor had now made his choice: Wales.

Chapter 2

MISSION 1931–39

IN OCTOBER 1931, THE MONTH OF THAT YEAR'S GENERAL ELECTION, shortly after celebrating his nineteenth birthday, Gwynfor took the train from Barry to Aberystwyth for the first time. This was a pilgrimage, as he began the process of rediscovering his Welsh roots. The journey from Carmarthen through Cwm Gwili and on to Tregaron and the bustling station at Aberystwyth stirred him. His hopes were high at the end of that Indian summer; three years studying Law in one of the College's most prestigious departments stretched ahead of him. He knew, too, that although education in Aberystwyth was unashamedly English in character, he would have countless opportunities to improve his far-from-perfect Welsh. But from the very first day, Gwynfor found Aberystwyth a let-down. He was met at the station by Gwyn Humphries-Jones, from Bala, with whom he would share digs. Gwynfor had expected the young man to be his cultural guide; but it did not happen. When Gwynfor asked him in English to speak Welsh, he refused, saying he did not have the patience. Gwynfor's expectations about the language in its heartland were shattered; it was a lesson the fresher from Barry would never forget. It was his landlady at Ceinfan, his lodgings in Trefor Road, rather than his fellow-student from Welsh-speaking Wales, who helped him to master the language.[1]

His disappointment over Welsh had been a blow, but for an idealist like Gwynfor, Aberystwyth itself was a greater one. Whatever Barry's faults, there was no doubting that it was a vibrant place in which to live. Aberystwyth, and student life, was quite another matter. There were some 700 students living in the isolation of Cardigan Bay. The only way out of Aberystwyth was by train but students rarely had the chance to use it during term time. As a result, the academic community was close, but stultifyingly introspective, and somewhat unsophisticated.[2] And although 1931 was to be a turning-point – the year when the international crisis of the 'thirties began – students like Gwynfor, who took an interest in politics, were rare. For the first few days, he went with the flow, and within a week of arriving at College faced the traditional initiation ceremony. In his case, he, along with 80 other new students, were tricked into believing they had been invited to meet the College benefactor, Lord Davies of Llandinam. Having paid half a crown each, they were taken by charabanc to a remote house near Ponterwyd, before realizing that the whole thing was a practical joke. As the local paper, the *Welsh Gazette*, reported:

> Having realised the situation they accepted it with very good humour and immediately entered upon the tramp homeward, a distance of over twelve miles. They enlivened the journey with songs but it was long after midnight when, weary and footsore, they reached Aberystwyth.[3]

This was all part of student life at Aberystwyth, where young men revelled in this type of behaviour and threw themselves into homoerotic rituals and endless discussions about the 'Aber Spirit'. Gwynfor mentions it with apparent light-heartedness in his autobiography. At the time, however, the solemn young man from Barry certainly did not believe such levity was justifiable.[4] Gwynfor found it insufferable throughout his first year but held his tongue and channelled his energies into law and Christian pacifism.

In his search for sanctuary, the tiny lecture room in the Law Department, and the face of its eccentric professor, Thomas Levi, became familiar sights between 1931 and 1934. 'Tommy' Levi, by the time of Gwynfor's arrival in Aberystwyth, had become the stuff of legend, famous for his deafness and the Marconi ear trumpet he used as an aid to follow conversations. He was also renowned for his fondness for young ladies. That said, he was no clown; as a lecturer he was 'peerless, an artist' who believed 'a lecturer's job was to pave the way and stimulate an interest'.[5] By 1931, he had built up a strong department, and the 37 students under his care were known as 'the law aristocracy'. But although Gwynfor was a conscientious member of that aristocracy, his first year was not easy. Indeed, he only just succeeded in scraping through his exams. Even so, and despite the academic ordeals, the Liberal Levi taught him one lasting lesson, that 'Parliament is all-powerful'.[6] It was a political lesson which would guide Gwynfor and Plaid Cymru under his leadership in the years to come.

Another set of walls that became familiar to Gwynfor during that first year in

Aberystwyth were those of the meeting rooms of the SCM, or Student Christian Movement, the most popular society in College. Some 11,000 students were members of the SCM across Britain, but it was its Welsh wing, Urdd y Deyrnas ('Kingdom League'), that claimed Gwynfor's loyalty. In their meetings, under the secretaryship of the nationalist and pacifist Dr Gwenan Jones, Gwynfor's faith deepened, and he read the Urdd's publications with a passion. Their influence converted him to evangelism, and he was fired with a belief in Christianity and Utopianism. The Urdd's gatherings also taught him two things. First, and most important, was that the flame of hope is inextinguishable and that the creation of a new world order was possible, despite everything and everyone.[7] As a politician, he would depend heavily on this religious brand of Utopian idealism. The second lesson was how to behave in public. The Urdd's code of conduct placed a fervent emphasis on seriousness, and members were urged to try and live as saints in their communities, renouncing self-regard, gossip and alcohol. Gwynfor submitted utterly. He also dutifully attended Seion, the chapel where his funeral was held in 2005, but this, coupled with his inherent shyness, led some students to regard him as a pious snob.[8] No one at the time saw the makings of a national leader in him. His only concession to the jollity of student life at Aberystwyth was to play for the College hockey team, but despite his talents on the field, his seriousness made him a figure of fun. One day, as he was leaning over the balcony in the quad, Alun Lewis, the poet and a teammate, turned to him and stated categorically: 'You know what your trouble is, Gwyn? You're too bloody conventional.'[9]

This was not the only criticism levelled at the SCM and its members. Some leading nationalists, such as Saunders Lewis, regarded the SCM as a complete waste of time. He described it as 'another respectable and innocent [movement] that cannot fail because it has no objective'.[10] And if a label were needed for Gwynfor's politics at the time, then one could do worse than call him a sort of pacifist socialist product of the Left Book Club. For all his ardent patriotism, Gwynfor, according to his contemporaries, would have been the last man to buy a copy of Plaid Cymru's paper, *Y Ddraig Goch*. And although he attended meetings of the College Welsh Society, he still believed Plaid Cymru was an irrelevance with no hope of success – and with good reason. When a parliamentary by-election was called in Cardiganshire in September 1932, Plaid Cymru could not even raise enough money to pay the deposit. Another reason for his reluctance was his concern that self-government for Wales would do more harm than good to the depressed Welsh economy.

What Gwynfor found more relevant were the activities of the International Relations Club and the LNU. The club attracted several talented students, but they were in a minority. Most Aberystwyth students chose to ignore the events in Manchuria and elsewhere during Gwynfor's first year, hoping the whole business would just go away.[11] But this is perhaps not surprising when one considers how very much alive memories of the First World War still were. After all, the treaty signed at Versailles was founded on a belief that there would never be another war. Gwynfor, however, regarded such self-indulgence as reprehensible and, by 1932, decided something needed to be done. As a leading light in the International Relations Club and the LNU, he took the highly unusual step of lambasting student apathy in public. In an article for the student magazine, *The Dragon*, he outlined the danger of a breakdown of diplomacy, leading to anarchy in the Far East and disquiet in Europe. Gwynfor feared this could undermine the very credibility of the League of Nations. In outspoken terms, he accused the students of Aberystwyth of immaturity:

> It has been said that an enlightened Public Opinion is 'the life blood of a civilised community'. If other Universities are like Aber, we humbly suggest either we are not members of a 'civilised community' or this country is dying a bloodless death.[12]

This was hardly the best way to make friends, but he was unrepentant. There was no doubt either that the LNU – both in College and the town – was on the wane, so much so that one of the members of the town branch had called for an 'electric shock' to awaken it from its languor.[13] Gwynfor agreed, and after publishing his homily he arranged a series of talks called Crossroads. Although he could not have known it, it was a particularly appropriate title. On 30 January 1933, Gwynfor's faith in the ability of the League of Nations to ensure international peace was shattered when Hitler was elected Chancellor in Germany. On 9 February, students at the Oxford Union passed an historic motion stating that they would not fight for King and Country under any circumstances. The effect of this anti-militarist vote in Oxford – of all places – was sensational, and this sentiment swept through the other universities of Britain like a fever. In March of the same year, the Debating Society at Aberystwyth voted in a similar fashion. Naturally, Gwynfor was among those who spoke with fervour that evening in favour of the resolution 'That this House would not in any circumstances take part in armed conflict'.[14] Gradually, a generation began asking how it could best defend itself – a process that had a direct impact on the upper echelons of the LNU. The Union's fundamental principle, and one that Gwynfor had supported until 1933, was peace through reconciliation. Diplomacy, it was believed, was the answer and war could only be justified when all other methods had failed. But, increasingly, a number of Welsh men and women were coming to the conclusion that the only salvation lay in embracing absolute pacifism, and, little by little, the pacifist consensus unravelled. In June 1933, the Congregationalist Union, effectively the denomination's parliament, voted in favour of undiluted pacifism. Although the Congregationalists also voted to support the LNU, it was increasingly clear that they could not serve both masters. Gwilym Davies, who had accompanied Gwynfor to Geneva three years previously, was justified in speaking of a 'drift towards out and out pacifism in the big religious denominations of Wales'.[15]

Gwynfor was one of those doubters. Although he had been President of the Aberystwyth College branch of the LNU during 1933, he had gradually come to the conclusion that the League lacked teeth and that he would do better to throw in his lot with those who believed in outright pacifism. By November 1933, the month in which Germany left the League, Gwynfor joined a pacifist march around Aberystwyth on Remembrance Sunday under a banner bearing the slogan first heard in the Oxford Union: 'We will not fight for King and Country.' Such a pacifist statement was electrifying in a respectable, Liberal stronghold like Aberystwyth, and so incensed the local British Legion that some members attempted to tear the banner down. The local weekly, the *Cambrian News*, was convinced the students had been indoctrinated by 'communistic literature', but Gwynfor was unrepentant.[16] He held that it was the duty of his generation to speak out against a corrupt international system even more stridently. As the arguments raged Gwynfor, prompted by his tutor, Victor Evans, was offered a place at Oxford to study for a higher degree in Law – a well-trodden and prestigious path for Aberystwyth's brightest students. Its effect, however, was to make life more onerous still. He now knew he would need to spend more time in the library, even though he considered proselytizing his proper calling.

The nature of that calling had changed too. For years, he had channelled his efforts as a Christian pacifist into the LNU and the Kingdom League, but his patriotism since 1929, the year of his conversion, had been less focussed. At the beginning of 1934, his final year in Aberystwyth, he could see for the first time how pacifism and patriotism could be melded. He could also see that his patriotism needed political expression. It was this which turned him towards nationalism and the first stirrings of interest in Plaid Cymru. But the turning-point for him was seeing young Plaid members like Eic Davies and Hywel D Roberts selling copies of *Y Ddraig Goch* in the streets of Aberystwyth. The selfless look of these political pedlars selling certitude created a lasting impression on him. He was disappointed too during this time by the Labour Party's attitude to Wales. Keir Hardie, a convinced devolutionist, had been one of Gwynfor's heroes, and it came as a blow to him when he saw the Labour governments of 1924 and 1929 failing to carry out their devolution promises. All these factors led him to lean increasingly towards Plaid Cymru, but the pivotal moment, he wrote in his autobiography, came when he called in at Jac Edwards's shop in Aberystwyth and bought a dog-eared copy of the Plaid Cymru pamphlet *The Economics of Welsh Self-Government* by D J Davies,[17] an ex-miner, boxer, hobo, and remarkable intellectual force in Plaid politics.

Gwynfor had discovered D J Davies relatively late; *The Economics of Welsh Self-Government* had been published three years previously in 1931. For Gwynfor it was a remarkable revelation. He later wrote that things now made sense: here was a body of ideas that he could sell on the doorstep. Reading D J Davies led him to conclude that it was possible to support Plaid Cymru without the need to adopt the vague, medieval doctrines of its then-President Saunders Lewis on the foundations of Welsh economics. Equally important, Davies's pamphlet appeared to permit Gwynfor to reject both Marxism and Capitalism without being obliged to follow Saunders Lewis blindly into the Middle Ages. In essence, Davies argued for resisting Marxism and Capitalism, as far as was possible, through the distribution of private property. This would enable local communities to hold and control economic power. Although Gwynfor was a pragmatist in economic matters, Davies's influence on him cannot be overestimated. These principles of co-operation and devolved economic power became basic tenets of Gwynfor's nationalism.

Gwynfor may have warmed to Plaid Cymru through D J Davies, but in 1934 it was undoubtedly still Saunders Lewis's party. A genius even of D J Davies's calibre was marginal to the intellectual force that was Lewis. The same was true of the Welsh-speaking intelligentsia – figures such as W J Gruffydd, Kate Roberts and D J Williams – who were also party members. Saunders Lewis was the architect of *Deg Pwynt Polisi* ('Ten Policy Points'), published in 1934 – a document that became a ready manifesto for Plaid Cymru, with its ten simple, conservative principles.[18] It is difficult to imagine that Gwynfor had not heard of this outspoken statement and its vision of a Welsh-speaking rural Wales, shared ownership and a de-industrialised south. Constitutionally, the aim was to gain, not Welsh independence, but 'Dominion Status', as was the case in New Zealand and Australia – which would allow Wales to control its own affairs while simultaneously recognizing the Crown. It is doubtless true, then – despite the anecdote in his autobiography about the visit to Jac Edwards's bookshop – that the deepest influence on Gwynfor was Saunders Lewis's vision of an organic Welsh-speaking Wales. Indeed, it is strange (as Richard Wyn Jones has pointed out) how little acknowledgement Gwynfor gave to this indebtedness.[19] It is difficult to say whether this can be attributed to Gwynfor's later embarrassment at what happened between the two men. But this much is certain: it is a glaring omission in Gwynfor's account of his early life.

One need only glance at the Welsh press in 1934 to gain a sense of how influential Saunders Lewis was – for good and ill. In that year he called for Cardiff to be made a capital, for the BBC to have dedicated Welsh broadcasting, and for the establishment of a 'National Welsh Development Council'– the forerunner of what became the Welsh Development Agency or WDA.[20] It was Lewis, again, who urged Plaid Cymru to defend the Royal Welsh Agricultural Show against the decision of the Bath and West Show to visit Neath in 1936. These were noble aims, perhaps, but dissent and ill feeling followed Lewis throughout that year like a curse. Gwynfor must have been aware of Lewis's Catholicism and the difficulties provoked by his religious affiliation. He would also have heard of Lewis's passionate opposition to the new policy of allowing Plaid Cymru candidates to take their seats in Westminster if elected. But the great mystery in 1934 was the President's fundamental ambivalence to Fascism, and in particular his attitude towards Hitler, Mussolini and Mosley. On the one hand, Gwynfor would have read the press reports in March that year in which Lewis promised that his party would fight to the death to defend 'the popular masses of Wales against Fascist dictatorship'.[21] This was the acceptable face of Plaid Cymru's attitude towards Fascism – the only political question of any consequence in Wales and throughout Britain in 1934. On the other hand, Gwynfor must almost certainly have read Lewis waxing lyrical about the readiness of his party to go 'to the same source as the leaders of Fascism for living water to refresh the desert of our social life'.[22] No matter how one looks at his decision, nor how much emphasis Gwynfor placed in his autobiography on the far more reasonable and reasoned influence of D J Davies, the young idealist was joining an unpopular, irrelevant party wholly under maverick control.

In June 1934, Gwynfor gained a Second Class Honours degree in Law – good enough to allow him to take up the offer from Oxford. He left Aberystwyth for the last time with little regret, but rather than take the train back to Barry, he decided to walk home in the company of a friend, Dilwyn Davies. Gwynfor had seen a great deal of Wales during his time at Aberystwyth, but this particular four-day journey proved extremely stimulating. On the day after his arrival home, while the memory of the Welsh panorama was still fresh, Gwynfor went to visit Cassie Davies, the Plaid Cymru secretary in Barry, and asked to join the party. It was Cassie Davies's boast for the rest of her life that she was the one who accepted Gwynfor into Plaid Cymru's ranks. That said, not even a party enthusiast like Cassie Davies saw the makings of a national figure in Gwynfor. What struck her, rather, were his 'outstandingly good-looking' features and his 'Aberystwyth College blazer'.[23]

But Gwynfor was far more than a pretty face. From the day he joined Plaid Cymru, he had decided the party needed to combine nationalism with pacifism. During the summer of 1934, the relationship between the two ideologies was highly contentious, and the party was divided on the issue. On the one hand, there were Saunders Lewis's supporters, who believed in the 'force' of rebellion, as had happened in Ireland in 1916, to win self-government; on the other, there was a minority who held that the party should renounce violence because rebellion was contrary to Christian principles. But the debate over force or pacifism was largely a theoretical one. After all, Saunders Lewis never seriously considered calling for a rebellion or summoning an army. Indeed, the great divide within Plaid Cymru was not about methods, but rather attitude. The question was: did Plaid Cymru want to be a respectable party or a militant one? Plaid Cymru's militant wing in the early 'thirties feared that pacifism would undermine the whole party by making it too gentle and tame. It is this intellectual tension, rather than any desire for battle, that explains why Saunders Lewis was so wary of pacifism, and why pacifism was such an acutely sensitive issue. Lewis also mistrusted the LNU in Wales as a non-Welsh institution. It was a movement, he said, filled with 'the warm words and echoes of England'.[24] Indeed, when pacifism was discussed at the Plaid Cymru Summer School in 1934, the issue had to be left on the table. Lewis was firmly of the opinion that Plaid Cymru should not 'pass pointless proposals like those that emanated from Oxford'.[25] In an attempt to buy time, and prevent the split from widening, the decision was made to form a 'War Committee' to work on a more definite policy.

Gwynfor had missed the Summer School, but despite Saunders Lewis's clear warning, he was not prepared to let the matter rest. Not for the last time, the pacifist and the ex-South Wales Borderers lieutenant collided head-on. Although he had only been a member of Plaid Cymru for a couple of months, Gwynfor decided to write to J E Jones, the party organizer and Secretary, and state his case in a daringly frank letter. He hardly knew J E Jones, but insisted in his letter that 'working for peace' was an integral part of nationalism, and that Wales had 'a mission in that direction'. He added that it was the duty of 'an independent Wales' to 'lead the countries of the world to a more sensible attitude towards war'.[26] In due course, Gwynfor would fulfil his ambition to turn Plaid Cymru into a pacifist party, but at the price of a vendetta between himself and Saunders Lewis.

In October 1934 Gwynfor followed the well-trodden path from Aberystwyth to Oxford. Aberystwyth had been disappointing, but Oxford and St John's College entranced him. Meeting English students from English public schools on the hockey and cricket fields was a new and refreshing experience. He also found it stimulating to listen to famous preachers and lecturers such as Nathaniel Micklem and G D H Cole.[27] But it was the students' political maturity that captivated him most. In that year he found the city in ferment on the issue of socialism and pacifism; and although Oxford was as quintessentially English as ever and dominated by hearties from the major public schools, an eager pacifist like Gwynfor found it all breathtaking – just twenty months after the historic vote in the Oxford Union. As the editor of the student magazine, *Isis*, wrote, 'Oxford now, as then, regards war as the prerogative of the gorilla'.[28]

The first thing that struck him was the beauty of the ancient buildings and the enchanting quads. He strongly believed that Oxford's aesthetics, and sense of tradition, had a civilizing effect on its students. A revealing letter from Oxford published in *The Barrian* conveyed his mood:

> The hand of tradition is heavy on the place, restraining even the iconoclasm of the present generation. We study in libraries wherein is stored the learning of time immemorial; and when we dine, a mighty host of witnesses looks down on us from the walls of the college hall.

The chief virtue of Oxford's aristocratic students, for Gwynfor, was the consciousness 'that they will one day be among the leaders of the nation. This gives them an earnestness of outlook which pervades all their activities whether it be in religion or literature, politics or drama'.[29]

There is no doubt that Gwynfor was referring to himself here, and to the part he believed he was about to play in the national life of Wales. For him, Oxford surpassed Aberystwyth in all respects, and the University had a dignity that the University of Wales could not match. In that year, he found himself surrounded by such able Welshmen as philosophers J R Jones and Hywel D Lewis, the sociologist Huw Morris-Jones and the theologians Harri Williams and G O Williams, later archbishop of Wales. He also met the saintly George M Ll Davies, and the gifted polymath, Pennar Davies, although he had no opportunity to be better aquainted with them. When he compared the Oxford gatherings with the childish antics at Aberystwyth, his conclusion in *The Barrian* was unsparing:

> I did not find this seriousness in Welsh colleges; the debates at Aberystwyth were too often opportunities for a 'night out' for the rougher element, and cultural societies and clubs were supported only by a small majority. It is true the life at Aberystwyth had a gaiety which one misses here and that a real feeling of *esprit-de-corps* would be engendered by the inter-collegiate contests, but it does not yet turn its students to fill the position which is their duty and their privilege.

The reason for this immaturity, he supposed, was the failure of students in Wales to realize that they too had a role to play in their country's national life. He looked glumly over Offa's Dyke at a generation of young Welshmen and women with only one goal: 'to get a degree, with as much pleasure as possible thrown in, and they might be Zulus for all the interest most of them take in their own country'.[30]

Unlike the students at Aberystwyth, Gwynfor's obsessions during his time at Oxford were politics and the preservation of the Welsh language. He neglected his studies, spending hours perfecting his grasp of the language, with the help of some 80 second-hand condensed paperback classics, *Cyfres y Fil*, which he had discovered at Blackwells, the University bookshop. When he considered that his

Welsh was sufficiently correct, and at the request of J E Jones, he approached Edwin Pryce Jones with the intention of establishing a branch of Plaid Cymru. The meeting was a success, and shortly afterwards, Pryce Jones and Gwynfor met two other nationalists, Harri Williams and Tudno Williams. By February 1935 Plaid Cymru had its first branch in Oxford. Despite Saunders Lewis's warning in the same month that no one 'who wishes for a political career' should join the party, Gwynfor chose to take on the branch Presidency. In truth, few attended the meetings but it was a start of sorts. At the second meeting, he read a paper on 'Nationalist Ideals' and some of the invited guests 'were almost convinced' as they listened to him.[31]

From his very first contact with Plaid Cymru, Gwynfor knew how difficult his political struggle would be, and he understood that a life of thankless labour lay ahead. As his work for the branch continued, he encountered an endless series of problems: there was virtually no literature available, and even less guidance from the party leadership. However, he did not lose heart. Indeed, his two years at Oxford served to deepen his idealistic view of Wales and the supreme importance of the ordinary rural Welsh. As his second year in Oxford began, in October 1935, he came to believe (like Saunders Lewis) that the Welsh language was the bedrock of Welshness, and that 'the Welshman's spiritual genius' would disappear if it were lost. In tandem with this, he argued in his first major published article that the culture of Wales was morally richer than that of the English proletariat. Its popular culture was 'England's trash … dog racing, betting and gambling … the talkies and amoral, immoral novels'. From his Oxonian perch he contrasted the 'rottenness' of this working-class culture with the best of Welsh folk culture – the chapels, the miners who learned Welsh metrical verse at the coalface, and the ancient glories of the eisteddfod. For Gwynfor, the pity of it was that Welsh-language folk culture was being sacrificed at 'the altar of materialism'. The only salvation now, he argued, lay in Welshmen taking, as he had done, the leap of faith that Plaid Cymru represented.[32]

However, the Plaid Cymru group in Oxford was a minority within a minority. The heart of the University's Welsh-language activity was the 'Dafydd', or Dafydd ap Gwilym Society. For an expatriate nationalist, this cultural society was an oasis of warm, homely Welshness: a place of innocent humour, hymn-singing and chats over cups of coffee. Even reading racy medieval Welsh verses was considered a daring thing to do. It was also a thoroughly apolitical society

– with one exception. One evening, Gwynfor argued publicly for the rights of 'Welsh nationalism', leading to a heated exchange with the socialist members of the 'Dafydd'. Nor did he show any shame when he delivered a paper to the Society in March 1936. The unwritten rule among members was to speak on safe, apolitical topics, but Gwynfor (now Secretary) thumbed his nose at convention and spoke on the preservation of the language. He struck out at the underhand tactics of the Tudors for leaving Welsh in such a parlous state as it was in 1936 – at a time, he believed, when the language question was about to be settled 'finally'. Only one option remained, Gwynfor concluded: his 'brethren' in the 'Dafydd' must devote themselves 'to the battle for the continuance and development of the language'. [33]

Meanwhile, international relations were growing increasingly tense. Welsh Nonconformists (and Gwynfor with them) 'drifted gradually towards the Christian pacifist position'.[34] At the Plaid Cymru Summer School in 1935, D J Williams argued again, as Gwynfor had done the previous year, for nationalist pacifism, and for Plaid Cymru to remain neutral in the event of war.[35] Step by stumbling step, Plaid Cymru was reinventing itself as a pacifist party, as the peace negotiated at Versailles began to disintegrate, and a pacifist brand of nationalism gained ground. It is an indication of the force of this intellectual shift that even Saunders Lewis was powerless to withstand it as Plaid Cymru entered its second decade. By March 1936, when Hitler reoccupied the Rhineland, Gwynfor's fragile confidence in the LNU was finally shattered and he, along with scores of other Plaid Cymru members, moved towards pacifism – so much so that the editor of the north Wales weekly *Yr Herald Cymraeg* could claim, with some justification, that 'a higher proportion of Plaid members are outright pacifists than in any other political party'.[36]

With Hitler's troops in the Rhineland, in breach of the Versailles Treaty, the Prime Minister, Stanley Baldwin, was driven to publish a White Paper on rearmament – a statement which meant that Wales would have to accept its share of new military bases. For Gwynfor, the statement signalled that the government had 'lost all hope of ensuring peace through the League of Nations' and that the consequence would be an 'arms race' in Wales with 'thousands of English-speaking workers in our midst'. Although there had been talk since May 1935 of locating an airforce training establishment at Penyberth on the Llŷn peninsula in north-west Wales, it was only in March 1936 that Gwynfor realized the government was intent on pursuing its plans. Faced with what he regarded as a crisis, he called (echoing his private letter to J E Jones in August 1934) for a united front between nationalists and pacifists to alert the nation. He declared that what was needed now was not 'lukewarm sympathy' but 'hot-headedness'.[37] In short, Gwynfor, the soon-to-be lawyer, was calling for unlawful action to prevent military development in Penyberth – something the Plaid Cymru Executive had been considering since the end of the previous year.

The bitter struggle over Penyberth continued throughout the spring of 1936. More than once, Plaid Cymru's peaceful protests erupted into violence as disaffected youths in Caernarvonshire attacked the defenceless nationalists. If the *Daily Despatch* is to be believed, 'Professors, schoolmasters and ministers of the Gospel fought barefist' on the square in Pwllheli 'for their right to proclaim the cause of peace'.[38] Welsh politics was in turmoil and, despite the unfortunate headlines, the events had their significance for the party Gwynfor would lead nine years later. For the first time in its history, Plaid Cymru was a topic of discussion throughout Britain and the press was eager to know how the party's 'Gandhi-like' protest methods would be applied. But these exciting events were a vicarious experience for Gwynfor, still in Oxford and preparing for his finals. In June 1936, he gained another Second Class degree in Law, soon to be followed by the good news that he had been accepted as a trainee solicitor in Cardiff. In the normal course of events, this would have been a cause for celebration, but the students in Gwynfor's graduation year of 1936 felt that they stood at a crossroads. According to the editor of *Isis*, only two routes lay open to them: 'the attitude of the idealist or the attitude of the Hun warrior'.[39] True enough, because Gwynfor's idealism now deepened. After his final day in Oxford, he travelled back overnight to Wales with his brother Alcwyn in an ancient Singer car that Gwynfor had bought for £15. The highlight of the journey was leaving the car and climbing Pen-y-Fâl (Sugarloaf Mountain) to watch the sunrise. In that dawn, Gwynfor knew the only path he, and his country, could follow was that of the idealist. It remained now for him to redouble his efforts and persuade his countrymen that he was right.[40]

Gwynfor lived at the family home, now 35 St Nicholas Road, Barry – but the man who returned was very different from the boy who had set off for Aberystwyth. As Pennar Davies, Gwynfor's biographer and close friend, remarked, this was when the mission began 'in earnest'.[41] His day-to-day work at W B Francis's offices in Cardiff was an unwelcome distraction for the eager pacifist and nationalist. From the very outset, Gwynfor found it a waste of time, and he was largely ignored by the three partners who worked there. They succeeded in stifling any interest he might have had in the law, and the more he bought and sold houses for other people, the faster his enthusiasm evaporated.[42] Evenings and weekends were another matter as he seized every opportunity to further the twin causes of nationalism and Christian pacifism. Because pacifism was still a thorny subject, unresolved within Plaid Cymru, Gwynfor channelled his energies through a new radical movement established in May 1936: the Peace Pledge Union. The PPU's straightforward aim was to withstand militarism by rejecting war of any kind; the organization had none of the consensual mentality of the old LNU. During the next few years, Gwynfor worked tirelessly for the PPU. This almost inevitably caused considerable embarrassment to his father Dan, now a councillor in Barry and a leading public figure in the Vale of Glamorgan. Indeed, it was not unusual for Dan to leave a town council meeting to see Gwynfor addressing a crowd of pacifists from the back of a cart in King's Square. On several occasions, he found himself having to hold his tongue and learn to live with the actions of his wayward offspring.

If the activities of the PPU were regarded as marginal in Barry, working simultaneously for Plaid Cymru and the PPU was a dangerous, if not explosive combination. From 1936 until 1945, Gwynfor had to face this double unpopularity constantly. In Barry, Plaid Cymru's support was minute and it was suspected of being a breeding ground for Fascists and Papists. Gwynfor was only too aware of the situation. As he went from door to door selling *Y Ddraig Goch* and the *Welsh Nationalist*, it was an achievement to persuade a handful to subscribe and a miracle if any could be prevailed upon to renew their subscription.[43] The same opposition to nationalism was evident in the local *Barry and District News*. When the Barry branch of Plaid Cymru passed a resolution condemning the Air Ministry's plans for Penyberth, the paper expressed its horror that 'such cranks … wasting their time in futile opposition to the War Departments', were living among them.[44]

But at half past one on the morning of 8 September 1936, Plaid Cymru's profile in Barry, and everywhere else, was transformed when the contractors' huts at Penyberth were burned to the ground. In Saunders Lewis's memorable words: 'It was a splendid fire: we didn't need a light.'[45] The following day, when Gwynfor heard the news, he was euphoric. At last, Plaid Cymru, a trivial, inconsequential party throughout its short history, had made its mark. He wrote to J E Jones on the same day, praising the 'marvellous [action] and selfless bravery' of 'the Three', Saunders Lewis, D J Williams and Lewis Valentine, in an event that was 'bound to reawaken the spirit of those who think of Wales'. The action was also sure to divide Wales, he knew, and he called for 'enthusiastic work, without delay, throughout the country, to show the inhabitants of Wales and England we are proud of the lead that has been given to us'.[46] Within the same month, Gwynfor was using the triumph of Penyberth in an attempt to prevent the government from building a 'hideous' armoury near Bridgend.[47]

However, as with Penyberth, the War Office had its way in Bridgend. There is no doubt either that the year following Penyberth taught Gwynfor that success can be fleeting. The problem, after the three arsonists were jailed in January 1937, was that Plaid Cymru was essentially leaderless for eight months. As Saunders Lewis served out his sentence in Wormwood Scrubs, Gwynfor seized the opportunity to enact his own agenda for Plaid Cymru, calling publicly for nationalism to embrace pacifism. In an outstandingly outspoken piece for *Y Ddraig Goch*, he put forward a 'Policy Suggestion' on how Plaid Cymru should act when war came. He emphasised two points in particular: first, that 'a great war is approaching with depressing speed'; and second, that the next war would mean 'the destruction of civilization' with attacks from the air. Gwynfor's remedy was that there were 'thousands' who believed in uncompromising pacifism, enough to convince England's enemies that Wales was a different country. In that way, Gwynfor believed, Wales could be spared from Hitler, and he directed this appeal to his fellow Plaid Cymru members: 'Here is the vision: that the Nationalist Party makes peace the most important item on its agenda'.[48] There is no record of Saunders Lewis's response to Gwynfor's call, but it would certainly have made him choke on his porridge. Unlike Lewis Valentine and D J Williams, Saunders Lewis had had no pacifist motive for setting fire to the buildings at Penyberth – he had been driven by a hatred of English militarism.

No attempt was made to settle this difficult issue while 'the three heroes' languished in prison. The party concerned itself rather with how it should respond to the impending coronation of George VI. Logically, Plaid Cymru should have supported the coronation. After all, its constitutional policy of calling for Dominion Status implicitly acknowledged the existence and function of the Crown. Before his imprisonment, Saunders Lewis's advice as party President had been that the King should be cautiously welcomed on his visit to Wales.[49] But the Plaid Cymru

Executive chose to ignore Lewis's rare show of pragmatism, and called for Welsh councils to boycott the celebrations. The decision to do so was largely that of the party's acting Vice-President, W J Gruffydd, but within days the costly error became apparent; in Barry, Gwynfor saw what goodwill there was towards Plaid Cymru evaporate. In panic, he wrote to J E Jones to inform him that the Barry Cymmrodorion had voted to support the three martyrs but had rejected the Plaid Cymru appeal to boycott the Coronation.[50] Three weeks later, Barry's streets were packed with revellers. It was Gwynfor's own father, Dan Evans, who led the councillors in hearty renditions of 'God Bless Our Native Land' and the Welsh patriotic hymn, '*Cofia'n Gwlad*'.[51] For Gwynfor and J E Jones, it was a salutary lesson: the less said about the Coronation the better. Gwynfor never forgot it, and this partially explains why his objection to the Investiture of 1969 was so muted.

In the meantime, building continued uninterrupted at Penyberth. The press reported that the site at Penrhos was a hive of activity, 'where everybody works 12 hours and twelve'. Neat buildings were constructed for the RAF pilots, and the fire and its effects were dismissed as 'a mere blister in a corner'.[52] Reports like these were indisputable proof to Gwynfor that Plaid Cymru's magic had been lost under the de facto leadership of the maverick W J Gruffydd. Gwynfor's worries did not end there. As the debate over the Coronation continued, he feared the party was about to repeat 'the mistake made in Ireland of favouring politics to the detriment of language and culture'.[53] Although the Welsh language had been the original impetus behind the establishment of Plaid Cymru, incredibly, as late as 1937, the party had no clear policy on the matter. Some, like Saunders Lewis, dreamed of creating a monoglot Welsh Wales; others, such as J E Jones, regarded this as absurd.[54] As his party stumbled on without any clear direction Gwynfor watched the decline of the language in the east of Glamorgan with despair. In Barry, he claimed, 'only a dozen aged under twenty can speak Welsh'. In the valleys too, things looked bleak; the 'cancer', he said, had reached the Rhondda, Ogmore, Rhymney, Aberdare and Merthyr Tydfil, and Welsh was no longer heard on 'the lips of children playing in the street'.[55] The obvious solution, Gwynfor concluded, was to make Welsh the official language and oblige Plaid Cymru to acknowledge for the first time that Wales was a bilingual nation. It would also, he supposed, present the party with a new and practical campaign.

In May 1937, Gwynfor saw no point in complaining to anti-Welsh local authorities; that method had already been tried without success. The answer for

Gwynfor lay in persuading Plaid Cymru to lead a broad front, with support from the Welsh MPs. This would win sympathy, 'awaken Wales', and draw attention to the party.[56] It was also a fact, in his opinion, that a large number of 'national movements had drawn strength from a campaign to gain recognition for the language'. But within days of calling for such a broad, constitutional campaign to win the battle for the language, he clearly had second thoughts about tactics. In June, he wrote again to J E Jones to argue that the battle needed to be radicalized and that a 'non-co-operative' campaign was needed which would insist that Welsh should be used to send telegrams and address letters. Income tax returns should also be completed in Welsh.[57] The trainee solicitor was treading a dangerous path but, after Penyberth, unlawful action was essentially the party's preferred course. After all, W J Gruffydd himself had insisted after the 'three heroes' had been imprisoned that 'open or surreptitious rebellion' was the only way forward for Plaid Cymru.[58]

Two months after he had first aired his 'language scheme', Gwynfor revealed his ideas at the Plaid Cymru conference in Bala. It was a tense occasion. Students who belonged to the Gwerin movement, which wanted a popular front between socialism and nationalism, were unhappy at what they regarded as Plaid Cymru's obscurantism. Gwynfor turned a blind eye; his priority was a language plan for the party. In Bala, he proposed that Plaid Cymru should 'start a non-co-operation movement' to gain official status for Welsh. The motion was passed, and it was agreed that party leaders should take the initiative, with the Executive urging Plaid Cymru members to refuse to fill forms in English. The goal was for a dozen or so prominent members to refuse to complete their income tax returns, and be brought, in due course, before the courts.[59] As the year came to an end, things were progressing well, but then, early in 1938, the ardent desire to challenge the English legal system dissolved. It is not clear exactly why this happened but, from then on, Plaid Cymru directed its efforts towards supporting the Welsh Language Petition, under the vigorous leadership of the young Carmarthen-based barrister Dafydd Jenkins.[60] In one sense Gwynfor's law-breaking strategy had failed; in another, it had been a stunning success. For one thing, Gwynfor had forced Plaid Cymru to create a Welsh-language policy. It is also doubtful whether the Petition Committee would have received such support from Plaid Cymru in 1938 had Gwynfor not decided to put the language on the agenda. The outcome of this joint effort was the Welsh Courts Act of 1942 – a small but significant step in the battle for equality for Welsh-speakers.

The Bala conference left Gwynfor as the acknowledged leader of the younger wing within Plaid Cymru, but his new-found fame did not diminish his readiness to continue with the thankless task of canvassing for the party in the south. He took on the responsibility of editing a Welsh-language column for the *Barry Herald*, and also acted as treasurer to the Barry branch of the party. When called upon, he served as a lay preacher. But his major contribution during this period was his work in the valleys. This, Gwynfor believed, was the 'most difficult' region in Wales for the nationalist cause, 'chiefly because the English language and Marxism have taken hold of the people'.[61] During the summer of 1937, he addressed countless meetings in the depressed Taff, Rhymney, Rhondda and Cynon valleys. As a rule, he would travel up from Cardiff with Vic Jones, Gwyn Daniel and Griff Jones, and the established pattern was for one of them to address a crowd through a loud-hailer as the others went around selling party literature.[62] At the outset, Gwynfor had a reputation for conscientiousness combined with a certain meekness. When he agreed to address a meeting of Communists on the square in Tonypandy, Oliver Evans, Plaid Cymru's south Wales organizer, wrote to one young party stalwart, Wynne Samuel, to express his concern that Gwynfor was 'a little too gentle for a meeting of this sort'. At the meeting itself, someone in the crowd aimed a brick at local activist Kitchener Davies.[63] These meetings were a crash course in practical politics for Gwynfor; by the outbreak of war, he had hardened to such an extent that a close friend, Dewi Watkin Powell, nicknamed him Stalin.

Gwynfor's social conscience had been pricked by these visits to the recession-hit valleys. After his return from Oxford in 1936, he spent several summer holidays doing voluntary work at the Malthouse, a settlement for the unemployed in the Vale of Glamorgan. Some two thousand men, women and children from the Rhondda would spend time at the disused brewery every year, a welcome respite from unremitting poverty in the valley. Gwynfor was assigned potato-peeling duties, and although the work was hard and repetitive, the surroundings lent even that 'a certain romance'.[64] The warden of the Malthouse was George M Ll Davies, a leading pacifist and an outstanding figure in twentieth-century Wales. Gwynfor had already met him at Oxford, and during these stays at the Malthouse they developed a lasting bond. George Davies taught him one lasting political lesson too. Gwynfor saw how happy the children from the Rhondda were in the company of this godly and charismatic older man, and he decided that the way forward for him too was to emulate George Davies's 'Politics of Grace'. In practical terms, it would mean 'convincing men one by one in personal encounters' and rejecting 'the politics of foundations' – the Communist line of winning men's minds by mass action.[65]

Gwynfor's middle-class qualms were further eased by his membership of Plaid Cymru's Thursday Lunch Club. The club had been established at the behest of Saunders Lewis and, for several years, leading Plaid Cymru members would go without a meal every Thursday, sending its cash equivalent to unemployed families. In all honesty, this was a small sacrifice for most party members but Gwynfor was among the most enthusiastic and generous supporters of the scheme. He also tried, without success, to bring his fellow-Congregationalists into the debate on poverty. In 1938, he opened a can of worms when he put a motion before the Congregationalist Union which stated that it was futile to expect any 'definite economic policy for Wales' from a London government.[66] Even the Congregationalists, that most radical and socially aware of denominations, saw this as a step too far.[67] The matter was left on the table, and Professor Joseph Jones, the leader of the conservative wing of Welsh Congregationalism, was heard to remark that Gwynfor was advocating 'a kind of separation from England'.[68] But, however genuine his concern and however vigorous his activity in the Hungry 'Thirties, it would be wrong to ignore the fact that Gwynfor enjoyed considerable personal comfort at home in Barry. It is a measure of the success of Dan Evans's business by the end of the decade that Marks & Spencer offered him £11,250 for it in June 1937 – a vast amount at the time.[69] Negotiations continued until the eve of the Second World War, before Dan decided not to sell. He clearly had no need to do so. By 1939, he was the owner of two large farms: one in the Vale of Glamorgan and the other, Wernellyn, with its 250 acres, in Llangadog, Carmarthenshire.

Gwynfor's thoughts, meanwhile, were on the three nationalists in Wormwood Scrubs who, in September 1937, emerged to what the *Western Mail* called 'an orgy of crazy sentiment and self-adulation'.[70] Gwynfor did not indulge. His goal remained the formation of a pacifist policy for the party. In this respect, other leading Welsh pacifists had prepared the ground for him. In June 1937, within days of the bombing of Guernica in the Basque Country, two Nonconformist ministers from Eifionydd, J P Davies and J W Jones, called for the establishment of a union for pacifists in Wales, with a more distinctive Welsh flavour than the PPU.[71] This was the incentive behind the creation of the 'Welsh Pacifist Movement', and it proved to be a significant step because it dealt the final blow to any lingering faith in international mutuality. By the time June arrived, it was reported that the LNU in Wales faced a crisis as its membership and finances drained away.[72] The structure evidently existed for a distinctly Welsh brand of pacifism, and with the eager support of the Welsh weekly *Y Brython* the movement grew rapidly, attracting 'a host of Welshmen and women'.[73] Although there had been rapid success, its founders knew it would be foolhardy for such a movement to exist independently of such a popular organization as the PPU. In April 1938, therefore, the decision was taken to establish Welsh Pacifists as a Welsh and Welsh-speaking wing of the PPU, with Gwynfor's idol, George M Ll Davies, as President. The goal, as revealed in the *Heddychwyr Cymru* manifesto, was 'to reject war and never support or suffer another'.[74] That June, Welsh Pacifists met for the first time and Gwynfor was listed among the guest speakers. But his contribution did not end there: he played a pivotal role in laying the foundations for Welsh Pacifists throughout the rest of 1938. It may have been a minority movement, but its birth was a critical development. Now the Welsh could state that traditional Welsh pacifism, with its well-established tradition, was as vital as ever in the face of the increasing likelihood of war.

The establishment of the Welsh Pacifists also had political implications. Its existence imbued the pacifists within Plaid Cymru with renewed morale and assurance. Given Saunders Lewis's passionate dislike of pacifism, the skirmish between the two camps – pacifists and 'Saundersites' – during that summer's party conference could have been devastating. However, Gwynfor and his fellow-lobbyists within Plaid were fortunate. The spring of 1938 had seen Saunders Lewis under continual fire from members of Gwerin, Young Turks who, as mentioned, sought an accommodation between nationalism and socialism. Saunders Lewis had also faced criticism in the press for his failure to condemn Fascism and his reluctance to support the plight of the Basques under Franco. Gwynfor thought the accusation of Fascism was 'easily refuted', but Lewis reacted very differently.[75] His growing conviction by that summer was that his earlier decision not to stand again for the Presidency in 1939, was the right one.

By the time of the annual conference in Swansea in 1938, Saunders Lewis was politically a spent force. Plaid Cymru was divided over economics and pacifism, but Lewis chose instead to take on the left of the party. He did not dare challenge the pacifists – a far more powerful group than Gwerin. The international crisis and the uncertainty in Czechoslovakia added to the feeling that the party could break up. It was a stormy conference. Plaid Cymru was torn on economic policy and, although Saunders Lewis managed to flush the young socialists out of his party, the pacifists took full advantage of the political vacuum. J P Davies and Ben Owen passed a resolution calling on Plaid Cymru to reject violence in the fight for self-determination. For a party inspired by the Easter Rising of 1916, the effect would be profound. It meant the party would need to re-think its tactics and its nationalist narrative. Saunders Lewis ended his final speech as President with a warning to Gwynfor and those of a like mind: if Plaid Cymru was to follow the path of peace, it would need to frustrate the British government in Wales, as Gandhi had done in India, by continuously flouting its laws. Without that willingness to break the law, he said, 'the whole programme and objective of the Welsh Nationalist Party' would only amount to 'child's play'. His closing remarks were equally barbed: 'Only one path leads to the gates of a Welsh Parliament. It is the path that leads unswervingly through the prison cells of England'.[76] Saunders Lewis could not have known it at the time, but his proclamation would ring in Gwynfor's ears throughout his own Presidency of the party. It was the beginning of a split in Welsh nationalism that would last for half a century.

Gwynfor's interpretation of the Swansea resolution contrasted sharply with that of Saunders Lewis. For Gwynfor, four years of organizing, lobbying and campaigning had borne fruit; the unity of nationalism and pacifism for which he had called in 1934 had been achieved. In a jubilant article for the PPU weekly paper, *Peace News*, he announced to pacifists throughout Britain that Plaid Cymru had passed a resolution 'of great significance in Welsh politics'. Now, he wrote, the party could give a clear lead to the workers of Wales against war. In return, he believed that those who espoused peace in Wales should now expect the support of English pacifists in the struggle 'for the recognition of the rights of Welsh nationality'.[77] A week later, at the National Eisteddfod in Cardiff, Welsh Pacifists found themselves more popular than ever, and thousands flocked to their stand on the field, where 2,000 copies of *Peace News* were sold. Their activity was not confined to the Eisteddfod; in the autumn of 1938, Gwynfor hosted joint meetings between Plaid Cymru and Welsh Pacifists.[78] But if Welsh-speakers, generally, seemed at ease with the marriage of nationalism and pacifism, the response from England was rather different, where the majority of those in favour of international peace had little sympathy with the concept of Welsh pacifist nationalism. Gwynfor's contribution to *Peace News* prompted a sniffy riposte from a certain Marjorie Fenn of Sevenoaks, who expressed her surprise at 'your special correspondent Mr Gwynfor Evans claiming that the President of the Welsh Nationalist Party, Mr Saunders Lewis, had adopted the methods of Gandhi'. After all, she added, 'setting fire to other people's property cannot be considered as non-violent resistance'. [79]

Gwynfor did not publish a reply, but it is unlikely he would have been too concerned about the views of Mrs Fenn and her sort – for two reasons. First, Welsh Pacifists had grown rapidly during the summer of 1938 and claimed over 10,000 members by 1939. Second, the international climate had changed considerably between August and October 1938. In the summer of 1938, Gwynfor and Alcwyn went on a walking tour of Germany and saw for themselves the upsurge of Nazism and 'young people who liked to sing at the top of their voices as they marched in step'.[80] On their return in September, they found a Wales convinced that a serious war with Germany was unavoidable. The foundations were being dug for air-raid shelters in Cardiff and Gwynfor, like everyone else, was issued with a gas mask. Then, suddenly and without warning, the threat receded. On 30 September, Chamberlain flew back from Munich and waved that famous sheet of paper. His 'appeasement' policy appeared to have succeeded, and Hitler was tamed. Although Welsh MPs voted 20 to 13 against the Munich accord, the news was electrifying for a generation that had feared war was inevitable. The weekly *Y Cymro* enthused that Chamberlain had 'given us new hope for the future' while the *Western Mail* argued that Chamberlain deserved a Nobel Prize. In Cardiff, the Swastika was hoisted over the city hall.[81]

Welsh Pacifists joined in the general rejoicing, supporting wholeheartedly the policy of negotiation with Hitler. At a public meeting a few days after the Munich agreement, the pacifists ratified a motion thanking Chamberlain for his efforts in the cause of peace, and Gwynfor declared from the platform that 'Hitler's control of the continent does not mean the end of peace'. He expressed the hope too that the door was still 'open' to international understanding.[82] Those like Emrys O Roberts, who resigned from Welsh Pacifists because of the policy of appeasement, were exceptions. As with the Munich agreement, Gwynfor did not think that the pacifists had any reason to apologise, and voiced his public regret at Emrys O Roberts's decision to leave the movement.[83] Gwynfor's message throughout was that Hitler's ambitions were the result of English imperialism and the iniquitous treaty signed at Versailles. The solution was to travel 'half-way to meet the grievances of other nations'.[84] To this extent, Welsh Pacifists were no different from the PPU in England; the PPU was also ready to forgive Hitler's actions, both before and after Munich.[85]

The belief that there would be no war lasted until the beginning of 1939. The editor of *Yr Herald Cymraeg*, for example, wrote that there would be no conflict in 1939 because 'the way of conciliation offers certainty'.[86] In Barry, the new year was greeted with high spirits. As the town clock in King's Square struck twelve, there was a cheer and the crowds sang and danced but, within three months, the revelry had been replaced by a *danse macabre*. In March 1939, German tanks roared into what remained of independent Czechoslovakia and attitudes in Wales towards war and Neville Chamberlain's policy of appeasement changed utterly. From then on, the only answer, on the right and on the left, was to arm and get ready for an inevitable war. Gwynfor spent the first months of 1939 in London studying for his final law exams, but with conscription now a reality, professional considerations were shelved. As he watched the preparations in London, he could not conceive how the war could be called a war for 'freedom'. As he pointed out to J E Jones, no one uttered a word about 'the Welshman's freedom to speak his own language in his own country, or to live like a lord on the means test'.[87]

From March to May 1939, Gwynfor led the opposition within Plaid Cymru to conscription. His rather naïve hope was that the party could co-operate with Labour to ensure a parliamentary exception which would excuse young Welshmen from the draft, as had happened in Northern Ireland. Privately, he supposed it would be 'a feather in our cap' if the impetus could come from Plaid Cymru.[88] There was one huge rally in May 1939 where Saunders Lewis appeared alongside R W Williams, the Secretary of the North Wales Quarrymen's Union, to oppose compulsory military service, but the idea of a united front was always a vain hope. Gwynfor had met Labour sympathizers at PPU meetings in London and Cardiff, but he was an exception. By and large, mutual understanding between pacifists within Plaid Cymru and Labour was very limited. What made things worse as war approached was the relationship between Plaid Cymru and the PPU. Even before the outbreak of the war, some PPU activists in north Wales refused to work alongside nationalists. They were candid too about their distrust of nationalism.[89] Another obstacle was the division within Plaid Cymru itself over its opposition to conscription. One group, represented by Saunders Lewis, disagreed with conscription on the basis that no Welshman should fight England's wars.[90] Gwynfor belonged to another whose objection to conscription was based purely on pacifism. When one adds to these an even smaller grouping within Plaid Cymru which supported the war, it gives some idea of the magnitude of the task Gwynfor faced.

The Act passed in May 1939 made conscription law, obliging those who opposed war to declare themselves conscientious objectors – a nightmarish step for those who knew how 'conchies' had been treated in the First World War. In the same month, Plaid Cymru declared itself neutral, arguing that it was the duty of Wales, like the other small nations of Europe, to stay 'out of the imperialist skirmish'.[91] The party knew that Wales had no hope of pursuing such a policy but considered it justifiable. Neutrality was more an attitude of mind, a declaration that Wales had the right 'to decide for itself whether it wished to take part in the war or not'.[92] Some like the Plaid co-founder Ambrose Bebb, disagreed completely with the policy but, for the most part, the party managed to unite behind it.

As war approached, Gwynfor's frustration with his personal circumstances intensified. The campaigning and his worries over the fate of the relationship between Plaid Cymru and Welsh Pacifists were having a detrimental effect on his law studies. That summer, Gwynfor sat the exam to qualify as a solicitor; but his attention was elsewhere. By June 1939, back once again in Barry, he despaired that the 'Fed', the South Wales Miners' Federation, had voted in favour of conscription. Indeed, he was astonished that the miners, men whom he considered the heirs of the heroic Keir Hardie, were so committed to war. He voiced his disappointment and bitterness in August 1939 in an unusually aggressive piece for the *Welsh Nationalist*, in which he claimed that the miners' traditional intellectual independence had been crushed by militarism. The miners had forgotten, he said, Britain's responsibility for Germany's humiliation and Hitler's actions; the colliers had abandoned their principles for 'a sordid and unheroic readiness to send their sons of twenty into the maw of English militarism'. All this stemmed, he added, from their families' dependence on the English press and their fellow-travellers at the *Western Mail*.[93]

Gwynfor's only consolation during these months, but a significant one, was meeting Rhiannon Thomas, the daughter of Elizabeth Thomas, who was secretary of Welsh Pacifists. The colourful Dan Thomas, Elizabeth's father, was a great influence on Gwynfor. By the time they met, Dan Thomas was living in Roath Park. His journey to this respectable middle-class Cardiff suburb had been an eventful one. During the First War, Dan Thomas had fought in the trenches of France, before becoming a recruiting officer. At the end of the war, he had been appointed to the headquarters of Martins Bank in Liverpool, where he earned the nickname 'Red Hot Dan' for his work for the ILP and the bank workers' union. Despite his socialist background, he had been drawn to Plaid Cymru by the end of the 'thirties. Rhiannon, who was working in a bank in Newport at the time, won Gwynfor's heart. The pair met for a second time two months later at Tynllidiart, the Thomas family's holiday retreat near Islaw'r Dref, Dolgellau, when she was 'wearing a very light, short frock'. The Barry boy was, by his own admission, 'smitten' and they started courting – Gwynfor's first serious relationship since he and Glenys had parted almost eight years previously.[94]

During August 1939, two events changed the course of Gwynfor's life. The first was his acceptance of the secretaryship of Welsh Pacifists at that year's National Eisteddfod in Denbigh – a post which would in due course cause him and his family innumerable practical and legal problems. The second was his decision to give up the legal profession for good and work on his father's farm at Wernellyn, Llangadog. In hindsight, it seems a curious decision when one considers his total lack of any agricultural background, and odder still because he had passed his final exams in the same month. But these were exceptional days, and Gwynfor regarded his decision as completely logical. Indeed, he thought it unseemly to continue as a solicitor when so many of his friends were likely to suffer heavy penalties for failing to enlist in the British armed forces. From then on, his time would be split between Barry and Llangadog.

By now, the pacifists were busily preparing themselves for the worst. That August, Gwynfor spent hours holding mock tribunals for Plaid Cymru and Welsh Pacifists. He also set about learning reams of literature by heart to sustain him during any possible imprisonment. This emotional darkness was illuminated by one 'splendid thing': a perilous journey at the end of the same month to Amsterdam where 1,500 young Christians gathered for a memorable conference.[95] Around them, Holland was frantically preparing for war. Traps were being laid for the German tanks, and there were also elaborate plans in hand to drown swathes of the country. For these young idealists, however, the conference was one final opportunity to make sense of a world on the verge of collapse. They spent ten days in discussion, prayer and contemplation before joining together to sing a hymn of victory:

> À toi la gloire, O ressuscité,
> À toi la victoire, pour l'éternité.[96]

This unshakeable faith would be tested in the years ahead. Gwynfor returned to Wales and made a final plea in *Y Faner* for his fellow-countrymen to embrace 'a spirit of peace'.[97] But in vain. Five days later, on 3 September, a second world war had begun.

Chapter 3

THE GREAT STORM 1939–45

SEPTEMBER 1939 WAS A MONTH OF CONTRASTS. In Barry, and throughout Wales, the late summer weather was glorious. And the sun was still shining – inappropriately enough – on the Sunday morning when Chamberlain declared war. No one was fooled by the beginning of the 'phoney war'; as *Y Cymro* put it, it was 'the calm before the storm', and Wales knew that the sun was about to be eclipsed. Every community was ready for the struggle and 'the sandbags, trenches and blacked-out windows' were portents of the dark times ahead.[1] The schools in the south closed for a week, as did the cinemas for a few days. Thousands of English evacuees poured into the Welsh-speaking heartlands. Montgomeryshire alone accommodated 3,000 of them, and a further 10,000 arrived in Anglesey within a week of the declaration of war. There were remarkable examples of hospitality towards these children and families, tempered by uncertainty across rural Wales as the country faced the greatest linguistic experiment in its history. And as the blackout curtains were drawn, ordinary people showed extraordinary bravery. The day after the declaration, on 4 September, the people of south Wales went about their business with the same unflappable dignity as they had shown before the onset of the 'supreme tragedy'. 'Cardiff and South Wales towns,' the *South Wales Echo* announced with pride, 'were this morning notable for the absence of any untoward excitement.'[2]

The coming of war plunged Plaid Cymru into indecision and realized the worst fears of many nationalists. Several believed that war would sound the party's death knell; indeed, as early as New Year's Day 1939, Saunders Lewis had warned the Plaid Cymru Executive that he doubted whether 'the party could survive a war'.[3] The party and its new President, J E Daniel, faced a number of quandaries. Did it have the guiding principles to ensure survival? Did it have the self-discipline? Would its neutral stance lead to the arrest of its leadership and the collapse of its fragile base? And, unlike the Irish, who had also adopted neutrality, Plaid Cymru did not have a state to defend it. Compared to the Scottish National Party, Plaid Cymru's neutrality was far more assertive, and was official party policy. In addition, there were cultural questions to be answered. How would the Welsh, in this new, strange world of spivs, spam and sacrifice in the name of Britain respond to nationalism? No one knew the answers. Plaid Cymru was adrift.[4]

Gwynfor suffered particularly in the first days of the war, experiencing bouts of depression that would haunt him throughout his time in public life. On the day of the declaration itself, from his parents' home in Barry, he wrote a despondent letter to J E Jones. Uppermost in his mind was the morbid obsession with death that he had already experienced during his youth; the difference this time was that it was the death of the nation. 'I wonder,' he wrote, 'whether this is the darkest hour that Wales has seen? Will she survive? Thinking about her future weighs me down more heavily than anything; yes, even more than the possibility that scores of thousands are about to die.'[5] But the initial panic did not last long; and the steeliness that would typify his personality throughout the war soon asserted itself. Some days later, he shared his vision with a friend, the theologian and writer Pennar Davies, who was something of a father confessor to Gwynfor throughout his life. 'We must,' he said, 'consecrate our energies to ensure that Wales is not lost nor the things to which the Wales of our dreams aspires. Surrendering now would mean not only the demise of our country but perhaps too our moral disintegration as well.' From then on, Gwynfor acknowledged and embraced despair; he believed that only by doing so could he confront it. These thoughts allowed him to make some sense of the chaos of war and continue to believe that he could 'save one here, one there'.[6]

His new-found resolve did not blind him, however, to the potential impact of the evacuees on Welsh-speaking communities. The first evacuees arrived in Llangadog on 5 September, and there were very few areas that did not extend a welcome – willing or otherwise – to these mothers and children. The press was full of reports on the kindness they received and there were harsh words for whoever in Wales dared refuse them. These people were 'snobs', to quote the *Amman Valley Chronicle*.[7] Even so, the arrival of the evacuees caused difficulties. Alarming reports appeared about the intolerable pressure placed on the education system, the health service and on the Welsh character of local families. The novelist Kate Roberts spoke for many nationalists when she wrote, 'The clean-living families of Wales have had forced upon them some of the dirtiest and most disgusting people Merseyside has to offer.'[8] This, without doubt, was the major political issue Plaid Cymru faced during these first days, and it split the party. Saunders Lewis advocated the setting up of holding camps for the evacuees.[9] In the meantime, he called for the collection of 'facts on lack of hygiene and illnesses, the condition of the bodies and clothing of children and women'. He also suggested gathering 'facts about misbehaviour of all sorts' for inclusion in a hard-hitting memorandum to be presented to the government.[10] In the context of the times it was a merciless, not to say impractical, policy. Far more constructive and significant was Gwynfor's and J E Daniel's idea of convening a national conference to discuss the cultural crisis in Wales.[11] This was, of course, a long-term scheme; in the short term, Gwynfor had no sympathy with Saunders Lewis's hard line. The only answer, as he wrote to J E Jones, was assimilation:

> They are here now, and all we can do is to decide our attitude towards them. I believe the negative attitude of opposing them is worthless ... So, I believe our policy should be to get the Welsh to conquer the English through their kindness towards them, and assimilate them as Welsh as far as possible. These children may look back on the days they spent in Wales with gratitude, and this may, perhaps, do us some good.[12]

There was, nevertheless, no united policy and the disharmony presaged the immense problems that would damage Plaid Cymru in the years to come. During that September, it published a statement on its policy towards the war. This was shown to the censor who blue-pencilled it.[13] But the little that the party was allowed to publish was 'insufferable insolence', as *Y Cymro* put it, and such attitudes went too far for most Welsh people.[14] It was no surprise then that many Plaid members lost heart and felt the wisest course was to close the party down for the duration.

This, as will be seen shortly, is what happened to a large extent between 1939 and 1943, but Gwynfor did his utmost to ensure that the party would survive the war. This can be seen most clearly in the debate held in October 1939 over *The Welsh Nationalist*, Plaid Cymru's English-language monthly. Some party members wanted to cease production, but Gwynfor was determined there should be no such move because it would be 'a sign of weakness and cowardice'. Indeed, he wished to go further and publish an 'outright rebellious' issue. If publication were refused, he urged J E Jones 'to get hold of a private printing press and move it from place to place if necessary'. He was also inspired by a letter from Dylan Thomas on the same day he wrote his advice for J E Jones. Dylan Thomas, he believed, was just the sort who should contribute to a daring issue like the one he had in mind. The scheme was never adopted, but he had even bolder plans up his sleeve despite the police being 'after us for virtually everything we do now'.[15] The most astonishing of these was his intention to travel to Ireland and broadcast nationalist propaganda from there back to Wales. Bearing in mind the suspicions over possible links between Sinn Fein and the Nazis, it would have been foolhardy beyond all reason and, eventually, he was prevailed upon not to cross the Irish Sea.[16]

If anything, it was easier to operate as a pacifist than a nationalist during the early days of the war. It was also true that pacifists could do more in a practical sense; after all, conventional party politics had ceased and would remain on hold for a further six years. In fact, there was a mountain of work ahead for both camps if they wished to prevent as many young men as possible from joining the forces. As the months passed, Gwynfor switched back and forth between party and pacifist activity, and amazed everyone – especially his fellow-pacifists – with his work-load. During one week, he organized 27 meetings across Wales and spoke in twenty of them.[17] He was also prominent in the mock tribunals jointly held up and down the country between members of Plaid Cymru and Welsh Pacifists. For the pacifists, these sessions were an 'outstanding success' and a source of 'splendid' propaganda for Plaid Cymru.[18] He was also careful to ensure that the pacifists' good name was not damaged by those who were too lazy or too cowardly to enlist. One who incurred his wrath was Dylan Thomas. In October 1939, just a week after he had effusively praised Dylan Thomas, the Rimbaud of Cwmdonkin Drive asked Gwynfor how he could avoid the draft. He was disappointed. As Gwynfor considered Dylan Thomas to be a wastrel totally bereft of any pacifist instinct; he refused to help. Years later, he disclosed what he had said in their conversation: 'Thought he was taking the easy line, far too easy line and didn't have a great deal of respect for it. Just told him I couldn't do anything to help him.'[19] This combination of caution and commitment proved highly effective. The pacifists were encouraged as the tribunals turned out to be far fairer than those held during the First World War.[20] By the end of October, *Y Faner* could report on 'extraordinary activity' among the pacifists, with new branches established from the Monmouthshire valleys to rural Pembrokeshire.[21] Indeed, if Saunders Lewis is to be believed, the pacifists were perhaps too successful. In November 1939, he complained to J E Jones that there was 'so much pacifism in the young men's objection and Welsh nationalism is a secondary issue for them'. In short, Lewis did not believe in the 'honesty' of any joint claim of pacifism and nationalism before the tribunals as a reason for refusing to fight.[22]

It was not the end of the debate over pacifism within Plaid Cymru – far from it – but Gwynfor was not unduly worried. After all, his mission had been to bring nationalism and pacifism together. Moreover, life was already so hectic that he had little time to pay full attention to Saunders Lewis's misgivings. As the year ended, Gwynfor moved to Llangadog and set up home at Wernellyn, the family's sizeable farmhouse. Llangadog's only disadvantage, he confided to Pennar Davies, was the village's 'intellectual torpor' and its distance from a decent bookshop.[23] It was some compensation, however, that he now sensed himself to be part of a truly rooted community, very different from Barry. Gwynfor was not the only nationalist in the 'forties to make such a move, but its effect on him was lasting. As he surveyed the landscape at Wernellyn, he felt in communion with the ancient civilization of a free Wales, with the striking hill-fort of Garn Goch, and Dinefwr Castle, the chief court of the twelfth-century Lord Rhys, before him.[24]

Here, at last, he could live among naturally cultured people and Welsh-speaking institutions such as the local eisteddfod, the Gravelle Choir and the Cadogian Philharmonic Society – the type of gatherings that offered a permanence he had never known in Barry. Going to Providence chapel in the village and seeing hundreds paying rapt attention to giants of the Nonconformist pulpit like Jubilee Young and Dyfnallt Owen was pure pleasure. The other thing that struck him in 1939 was that Llangadog, at its two extremes, chapel and pub, was a welcoming village whose inhabitants, in the early months of the year at least, were surprisingly tolerant of this pacifist nationalist newcomer in their midst.[25] The great disappointment, however, as he soon discovered, was that the ordinary people of Carmarthenshire were so indifferent to using Welsh as an official language. Every public meeting, carnival and gathering of the parish council was held through the medium of English – even though there were only two people in Llangadog in 1939 who were unable to speak Welsh.

Gwynfor had come to Llangadog to work on his father's farm – the tomato-growing business that would sustain him financially in later life did not begin until 1942 – becoming manager of 'Conchies' Corner' as Wernellyn came to be called. Financially, his situation was healthy thanks to the monthly wage and free accommodation he received from Dan Evans. All things considered, it was a benevolent act because Gwynfor's father was neither a pacifist nor a nationalist. It was also a generous gesture to Welsh pacifism, given that so many conscientious objectors found work at 'Conchies' Corner'. This generosity was all the more impressive as Gwynfor was frequently absent from Wernellyn. His father employed a bailiff to look after the land and livestock from day to day, leaving Gwynfor effectively free to campaign full-time for Plaid Cymru and Welsh Pacifists.[26] This considerable financial support continued until Gwynfor was elected an MP in 1966. Now, with the tedium of the solicitor's office behind him, he could concentrate on the passion that had driven him since 1929: saving Wales.

As that autumn progressed Wales seemed more in need of salvation than ever, as its future grew less and less certain. The Welsh Rugby Union announced that all fixtures had been cancelled, and there was even talk of abandoning the National Eisteddfod. Welsh programmes on the BBC, suspended on the first day of the war, did not return. Such petty deprivations between them created a mood of cultural crisis. But the greatest threat of all, for many, was the number of evacuees. Even though some had already made their way back to Liverpool and London, it was increasingly clear that the situation was unsustainable.[27] W J Gruffydd called from the editor's chair at *Y Llenor*[28] for a committee in every village to safeguard 'the essential Welsh life of the inhabitants themselves' while Gwyn Jones, editor of *The Welsh Review*, insisted that the answer lay in special camps.[29] In the same spirit, Dyfnallt and Tecwyn Evans, secretaries of the University-based Union of Welsh Societies, issued a statement demanding 'a firm and steady stand for the Welsh Language in the stronghold'.[30]

These appeals were important in themselves, but the most important of all was the decision taken at the National Eisteddfod to appoint a committee 'to approach the religious denominations of Wales and other national institutions with a view to forming immediately a national consultative committee to safeguard Welsh cultures'.[31] The outcome of these endeavours was a conference of leaders on 1 December 1939 to discuss the way ahead. This gathering, in Shrewsbury, was the nearest thing to 'a Parliament that Wales has ever seen', according to *Y Cymro*, and it proved to be a turning-point for the Welsh language during the war.[32] Indeed, it is no exaggeration to describe it as one of the most important landmarks in the language's history. The meeting led to the formation of the Committee for the Defence of Welsh Culture. This committee attracted figures as diverse as Saunders Lewis, W J Gruffydd and the Urdd's Ifan ab Owen Edwards, and although they did not always agree, this was an enormous step forward. T I Ellis, head of Rhyl County School and son of the Liberal idol, Tom Ellis, was appointed secretary. From this point onwards, in the virtual absence of Plaid Cymru, hundreds of patriots with Wales's cultural interests at heart now had a focus.

The decision to form the committee would have an enormous impact on Gwynfor's life in due course, but throughout early 1940, his chosen channel was Plaid Cymru. It is true that the committee published a memorandum on evacuees, but its effect in Gwynfor's corner of Wales was minimal. He contented himself, rather, with a series of suggestions to J E Jones. In the valleys, he felt the Communists were overtaking Plaid Cymru as the main party of opposition to the war, and he attempted to urge Jones to lead a propaganda campaign in the miners' lodges but, in practical terms, this was fantasy.[33] The pacifists' standing had also suffered, as a combination of prejudice and official interference began to bite.[34] The nationalists' situation was made even worse when the tribunals ruled that nationalism was not a valid reason to refuse call-up.[35] Looking at the bigger picture, Gwynfor was afraid militarism was so rampant that the Welsh education system would soon begin to train pupils not only in 'the art of living, but also in the art of killing'.[36] These were dark words, but within days of writing them in January 1940, his worst fears were realized when he heard that Epynt, one of the last strongholds of the language in Breconshire, was to be turned into a firing range. One of the major battles in Gwynfor's life was about to begin but, by summer of the same year, a 'delightful community in the heart of the country', as the author and anthropologist Iorwerth Peate called it, had been destroyed.[37]

In reality, the War Office's announcement on Epynt was not a bolt from the blue. Its plans had been the stuff of rumour since October 1939. Even so, the official confirmation in February 1940 was a blow. Across an area of some 60,000 acres, there was talk that 79 farms would be requisitioned; in addition, a further 41 farms would lose land. The notice to quit, 57 days, was also utterly inadequate; and to add insult to injury, it would happen at the trickiest time in the husbandry calendar. A feeling of utter helplessness enveloped a whole community, but no one reacted with more forthright eloquence than William Williams, the NFU county secretary for Breconshire: 'Where are these beggars going to go? – Not a vacant house for them to shelter!!!... Poor fellows, they are nearly going out of their minds'. He feared it would need 'a terrible hard fight' if Epynt was to be saved.[38]

The struggle began in earnest on 9 March when 200 patriots (representing the Committee for the Defence of Welsh Culture), local politicians and farmers came together to discuss strategy.[39] Gwynfor joined the fray a fortnight later, spending a heartbreaking day visiting the 'Valleys of Mourning'. In the first community he visited in the Epynt hills, 'beautiful in appearance and Welsh in speech', he was taken aback. There were already signs that the army had begun preparations and one inhabitant issued a doleful prophecy: 'Yes, this place will have changed completely before long.' Gwynfor and his companion, John Thomas from Llanddeusant, trekked across the mountain to a neighbouring valley to meet an old man and his son-in-law. In an agonizing meeting, the pair, David Price and George Evans, showed Gwynfor the Babell chapel that was about to be demolished. Faced with this quintessential piece of Welsh Nonconformism, Gwynfor felt overwhelmed: 'The heart beat faster knowing that this was the true Wales'; but the blood boiled, too, knowing what would happen here within a few short months, and that, as the poet Ceiriog said, 'there will be new shepherds on these old hills'.[40] The sight enraged him; here was a community facing oblivion, in the name of 'English totalitarianism'. Within a month, Gwynfor had reached the conclusion that the real menace to communities in Wales in 1940 came not from Germany but from England. It was, as he commented later, 'Hitler's method – to present people with a fait accompli'.[41]

On his return from Epynt, on 14 March 1940, he wrote a forlorn letter to T I Ellis, secretary of the Committee. What he had seen there, he admitted, 'almost broke one's heart' and was clear evidence that there would be 'no Wales left at all by the end of the war' unless a strong campaign were mounted to save it. To this end, he promised to devote 'every night of the week' to prevent the villainy.[42] Gwynfor set to work with vigour, addressing dozens of meetings with Dyfnallt in the darkness of the blackout. By the end of March, there were hopeful signs as Welsh MPs like Will John, Clement Davies and Jim Griffiths campaigned alongside the farmers and the Defence Committee. What counted now was momentum and not leaving the farmers, as Saunders Lewis warned, 'to the mercy of the NFU and timid people like them'.[43]

However, Saunders Lewis's fears were well founded and the struggle to protect Epynt fell apart. On 2 April, Gwynfor went with J E Jones to Sennybridge and Cwm Cilienni. In the farmhouse at Cefn Bryn, 'they received a splendid welcome' and witnessed 'the spirit which will turn the battle into a complete success'. The farmer there, a Mr Lewis, said 'that most of the farmers were ready to fight to the last'. The only cloud on the horizon was a warning he heard about William Williams: it suggested he was 'doing his level best to persuade the farmers that there would be no objecting' and urging them to accept the War Office's compensation offer.[44] But persuading farmers not to object was not William Williams's only tactic. Williams wrote to T I Ellis on behalf of the 'Mynydd Eppynt and Bwlch-y-Groes Commoners Protection Committee' to say that he had had enough of working with the Defence Committee, and issued a clear warning:

> ... no outsiders should come to the area to make capital out of the unfortunate business to promote any principles they may hold... would strongly advise not holding meetings in Breconshire.[45]

The following day, Williams wrote to T I Ellis again to make his point more clearly still:

> ... your organisation and the Welsh Nationalist Party were doing tremendous harm for the affected farmers to have the War Office to purchase the farms, extend the time for clearing out and to pay fair and just compensations.[46]

William Williams's pragmatic intervention was instrumental in destroying the campaign. Not a single family could be persuaded to stay on as a protest in the hope that they would be physically evicted by the authorities.[47] Although the Defence Committee met on 4 April and established a sub-committee to act 'as they see fit on the issue', it was evident that the battle was over.[48] Within three weeks, the local paper was saluting William Williams as a hero, the man who had won fair compensation for the farmers of Epynt.[49]

These events left a bitter taste in Gwynfor's mouth. He may have overstated the extent of the opposition but he was right when he predicted that the evictions would be utterly devastating. The community was destroyed, some of the farmers' spirits were broken and the linguistic barrier shifted twelve miles to the west. Clwyd Bwlch y Groes was renamed 'Dixie's Corner', the road to Merthyr Cynog became 'The Burma Road' and Hirllwyn was rechristened 'Piccadilly Circus'.[50]

The sound of gunfire was a sure sign too that Gwynfor's lyrical ideal of a principled Welsh Wales had been corrupted. After all, it was William Williams, the farmers' leader, who had urged his colleagues to accept the compensation. And even the passage of time did nothing to assuage Gwynfor's bitterness at what Williams had done. Years after the war, he would describe Williams as a traitor and when he revisited the site where Babell chapel once stood to make a documentary in 1990, he was moved to tears.[51]

What happened at Epynt may have been an outrage, but it received very little attention outside the pages of *Y Faner* and *Y Ddraig Goch*. There was scant sympathy because by late April 1940 the whole of Wales was preoccupied with preparing for a possible Nazi invasion. This spectre served to drive Gwynfor closer still to Plaid Cymru and pacifism. At the end of April, his father awarded him a pay rise, but the money went straight into the party's coffers. When he wrote to plead with J E Jones not to draw attention to his contribution, he expressed the opinion that the least he could do was 'what one can' for Wales in the face of 'such a serious crisis'.[52] Such a sacrifice was consistent with Gwynfor's belief that nothing would come of nationalist aspirations until nationalists themselves were ready 'to compromise our standard of living for the cause (I refer to our middle-class members)'.[53] It was perhaps easy enough for Gwynfor to speak in such terms, given his financial situation, but it would be a serious mistake to assume that this would be an easy war for him. In May 1940, he had to pay a heavy price: relationships with some members of his family broke down.

May saw Wales paralysed with fear as the news broke of the fall of the Netherlands. As a result, the last remnants of tolerance for nationalism and pacifism disappeared. The German invasion of France spread paranoia throughout Wales. MI5 was convinced that Plaid Cymru's leadership had made contact with enemy spies, in the wake of a visit by a German agent called Gerhard von Teffenar. The secret service's main target was Saunders Lewis – a man who it was believed might side with the Germans if the opportunity arose. In the same way, M15 assumed there had been contacts between Plaid Cymru and the IRA in 1939. Although there were very good reasons to doubt the veracity of these assertions, for good or ill, men like Saunders Lewis, J E Daniel and Gwynfor were regarded as open to the charge of 'unreliability' in the event of a British defeat.[54]

The Fifth Column Bill was passed in May to deal with collaborators and those suspected of being less than totally loyal. The PPU leadership in England was a particular target. In the minds of the population there was a fear that covert Fascists might be lurking in their midst. All expatriate Germans and Italians in Wales were despatched to holding camps and the authorities did their utmost to make life as unpleasant as possible for pacifists. Welsh Pacifists were prevented from opening a stall at the central market in Cardiff which had been crucial to their activity for the previous three years.[55] The same thing happened in Swansea;[56] within a month, local authorities in Wales began to dismiss employees – especially teachers – for their pacifism. Swansea was the first, but not the last, of the Welsh councils to undertake such a purge.[57] And such moves were well received; in Swansea, thousands of women demonstrated in favour of the sackings.[58] Things were no better in the north, where J P Davies, one of the most prominent pacifists in Wales, was pelted with tomatoes and oranges, and the wall of his chapel in Porthmadog daubed with the slogan 'Cowards, Traitors... You Ought to Face a Firing Squad'.[59] The words reflected the common perception that the Home Office was not doing enough to protect the people from these 'collaborators'. Faced with this onslaught, all Gwynfor and the other members of Welsh Pacifists could do was appeal for 'a proper attitude and a generous spirit in the face of injustice'.[60]

In such a climate – where he embodied two things that were anathema to his fellow-Welshmen, pacifism and nationalism – it was almost inevitable that Gwynfor himself would be persecuted. It was, after all, the most intense period of widespread fear that Wales had suffered since the days of Napoleon and the French landings in the eighteenth century. In Barry, Dan Evans's vans and shop windows were painted with the words 'Spy', 'Traitor', 'Fifth Columnist'. One warehouse was burned and an attempt made on another.[61] This caused obvious tension within the family, so much so that Idris, Dan's brother, wrote to Gwynfor begging him to renounce his unconventional beliefs because of the damage they were doing to Dan Evans's image. As Idris Evans saw it, the time had come for Gwynfor to be less selfish. He insisted that Gwynfor should realize he was a member of a family, 'not only an individual'. He must renounce his pacifism as a charitable, Christian act.[62] But Gwynfor turned a deaf ear to his uncle's plea: he had begun to delight in the notion of sacrifice. As he wrote to Pennar Davies in May 1940:

> My hope, if we emerge from this war at all, is that we shall come through it purged of the things that corrupt us – comfort and a good standard of living and so on – these

> are the things of the world, material things, and we can never hope to build an independent, cultured, Welsh, Christian, living Wales if we persist in our old ways.

And, at the same time, he admitted to his friend that he was happy to be able to pursue a mission:

> These are full, busy days for those who take a different course from the government – yes, and joyful days too in their own curious way. At least these days give us a chance to live; but I do not know whether some of us will be allowed to live freely for much longer.[63]

He had good grounds for thinking that way. He knew he would have to face a military tribunal in due course – and the possibility of imprisonment. And, in the shorter term, he also feared he would be jailed for his candour as a pacifist. Gwynfor, like all other pacifists in Britain, was being closely watched by the authorities but, in Wales, there was a further complication. The secret service believed pacifism was inextricably linked to 'Welsh Nationalism of a very violent character'.[64] This, no doubt, was what lay behind the intention of the police in Barry to prosecute him after he had been overheard, when leaving the Tabernacl one Sunday evening, saying that his friends would soon need to learn German. As a consequence, his father was called into the local police station and shown a pile of papers noting every intemperate statement made by his wayward son. It was only thanks to his Uncle Dudley, it appears, that the police were dissuaded from bringing a case against Gwynfor.[65]

Even so, there was, and is, room to doubt Gwynfor's loyalty. As the war slipped away from the allies, he was evidently in two minds about what might happen if England fell. It was, he wrote to J E Jones, 'a heartfelt shame' to see a liberal country like England in such a position despite 'all its shortcomings'. But even in these dark days, he was unsure which fate would be better for Wales: an English or a German victory. Indeed, he confessed to the Plaid Cymru General Secretary he was not 'certain that it might be better for Wales (from the point of view of her continued existence) whether the Allies or the Germans won'. The only certainty was that pacifists and nationalists in Wales faced 'pretty grim treatment'.[66]

After the fall of Dunkirk, things took a turn for the worse. On 14 June, the Nazis reached Paris, 'one of the dark-red letter days of the twentieth century', according to Dyfnallt, editor of the Congregationalist newspaper, *Y Tyst*. As Hitler's troops swaggered along the Champs Elysées, it looked likely, even inevitable, that Britain itself would fall before the month was out. The evacuees streamed back to Wales and all those who were not behind the British war effort were objects of suspicion. The appeal in *Y Cymro* for the Welsh to lay aside 'all complaints'[67] was typical, and W J Gruffydd made a similar call for national unity in the pages of *Y Llenor*.[68] In the middle of June 1940, J E Daniel found himself forced to deny that Plaid Cymru was full of 'fifth columnists'[69] and by the end of the month, *Y Cymro* had published pictures to help its readers tell the difference between Junkers JU 52 and Junkers 86 aircraft.[70] The announcement at the beginning of July that the National Eisteddfod would not be held that year was, to some, irrefutable evidence that society itself was about to implode.

During these dark times, Gwynfor was sustained by faith if nothing else and, increasingly, saw a return to the land as a bulwark against international breakdown. The major question for him now was how a Christian society could be created in the wake of the pathetic failure of conventional methods. He believed he had found the answer in the rich soil of Llangadog, and urged his fellow-Christians to slay the beast through co-operative farming and 'collect money among friends' to buy land where 'a start might be made on this new communistic life'.[71] He did not confine his appeal to Christians; he tried to convince nationalists to buy a farm in the name of Plaid Cymru and offer work to those, like Wynne Samuel, who had been sacked because of their attitude to war. Privately, Gwynfor believed that members had enough money between them 'to buy or rent a dozen' farms if they were serious about it.[72] His idea was largely ignored, however. By July 1940, even in Carmarthenshire, the imperative uppermost in everyone's mind was survival and these elaborate schemes seemed sheer fantasy. When Gwynfor saw two aircraft in combat over Brynamman one July afternoon, he realized that retreat to the countryside was no guarantee of escape from the 'accursed folly' which now threatened the Welsh heartland.[73]

Although there was no assurance of safety in Llangadog, Gwynfor, like many in the Defence Committee, was eager to see children from the south Wales towns being moved to rural areas to spare them from the nightly air raids.[74] Unlike the cities of England, none of the Welsh towns had been designated as evacuation areas – a situation that left families utterly vulnerable as the bombs fell. It was Gwynfor, more than anyone, who began to draw attention to this in the hope that what he regarded as a basic injustice could be alleviated, if only a little. As he told T I Ellis that July:

> Events every day strengthen the argument for moving children from some of the southern towns into the Welsh-speaking Counties. For instance, as of yesterday Barry had suffered 41 air raids. I heard from my uncle Idris in London yesterday, who said that they have only had one alarm. In Barry hundreds of children are sleeping in dugouts every night and thousands are regularly losing sleep. There may be worse to follow... What makes things even more unjust is that there is plenty of space for London and Liverpool children in England. Only about one in every five or six of those expected to leave has done so; so there was room for five or six times the number who went. If the desire existed, safe places could by found in England for the children who are now in the Welsh Counties and have children from Cardiff, Barry etc in their stead.[75]

Gwynfor's letter was an important contribution to the intellectual argument in favour of moving children from the towns of south Wales to safety. In due course, this call would be taken up by some Welsh Labour MPs. But important as it was, Gwynfor's priority that July was to prepare himself for his tribunal – the hearing which would decide his fate for the remainder of the war. Although he had already prepared dozens of young men for similar occasions, the experience did little to calm his own fears. He continued to learn vast screeds of poetry by heart in case he might be jailed. He did so even though it was common knowledge by this time that the tribunals were rather civilized gatherings. For Gwynfor and his generation, the memory of the dreadful treatment meted out to conscientious objectors in the First World War was stronger than any evidence to the contrary. When the tribunal convened on 12 July, Gwynfor had in his pocket the most glowing array of testimonials ever presented to such a gathering. Among them were letters from Saunders Lewis and George M Ll Davies pointing out the perfectly obvious fact that Gwynfor's objection to war was genuine and unbending.

The tribunal was held at the Guildhall in Carmarthen, and began with questions from Oliver Harris, secretary of the South Wales Miners' Federation, as follows:

Oliver Harris: What if everyone adopted your attitude and Germany was successful in this war, do you think that would be to the advantage of Wales?

Gwynfor Evans: I do not think it would be to the advantage of Wales. I cannot see good ever coming from war. I feel very strongly that, even if this war continues to a British victory, the hope of a Welsh survival and of Wales making any contribution will be dead, because the processes now in full swing will have destroyed all life too fully for it ever to recover.

But Harris did not leave it there:

Oliver Harris: But you are content to let other people fight against them?

Gwynfor Evans: No. I am opposed to the Nazi and Totalitarian principle more than anyone who is in the armed forces. I have fought against the principle the whole of my life, but not in the same way as the Government now fight it. The only way to destroy Nazism is to stand up to it with all the moral strength we can muster.

Oliver Harris: Do you really believe that our moral influence can change the disposition of Germany?

Gwynfor Evans: Yes.

After that, it was the turn of the chair, Judge Frank Davies, to put his questions.

Judge Frank Davies: What would you do to save women and children if bombs fell at Llangadock?

Gwynfor Evans: My advice to them would be to make themselves as safe as they could.

Judge Frank Davies: And urge the fathers and brothers of these children not to bomb the enemy?

Gwynfor Evans: Yes, not to bomb them in return.

Judge Frank Davies: Other Welsh Nationalists who have appeared before this Tribunal, when asked if they would fight for Wales, say "Yes", but you say "No"?

Gwynfor Evans: Quite. I am a pacifist first and a Welsh Nationalist afterwards.

Mr J H Williams (member of the tribunal): It is one of the minor tragedies of Wales that young men of your character could not take the larger view in the present situation and co-operate with us. I think you could do so much for Wales, which is in need of men of your ability.[76]

Within the week Gwynfor heard that he had been given an unconditional discharge – a decision that meant he could do as he pleased, within reason, for the rest of the war.

This generous ruling applied to about fifteen per cent of the 'very religious objectors' who appeared before Judge Frank Davies. Although Gwynfor clearly belonged to that category, his expressions of relief were nonetheless genuine.[77] He wrote in joy to Pennar Davies that the bench had been 'particularly kind' to him.[78] But freedom brought new responsibilities. From now on, as George M Ll Davies warned him, everyone – from the most ardent pacifist to the most rabid warmonger – would expect great things of him now that he had achieved such prominent status.[79] As the Battle of Britain reached its climax, there was nothing easy about being 'a free man', but Gwynfor had little time to reflect on his situation. As the summer progressed, the number of Welsh pacifists dismissed from their jobs grew and other work had to be found for them.[80] Gwynfor played a major part in these largely fruitless attempts that summer – in the same year as he found himself elected to the Plaid Cymru Sanhedrin, the party's Executive.[81]

His discharge also meant that Gwynfor could now take steps to sort out his life. Among his first actions, in September 1940, was to get engaged to Rhiannon, naming Saint David's Day 1941 as the date of the wedding. Within a month of the engagement, Gwynfor offered his services to the Pacifist Service Units who were active in London's East End offering shelter to the poor – a courageous offer when one remembers that the Blitz was by then in full force. Fortunately for Welsh Pacifists (and perhaps for Gwynfor), the proposal was rejected by Nancy Richardson, on behalf of the PPU, because there was so much work to be done in Wales.[82]

She was right. Support for pacifism in Wales had ebbed since September 1940. If MI5 figures are to be believed, around seven in every thousand would register as conscientious objectors and of these a number would withdraw their objection before they faced a tribunal. MI5 officers with responsibility for Wales were justified in their assertion that: 'it would be safe to say that pacifism is not a menace to the war effort'.[83] The position was particularly difficult in the north that autumn as several pacifists wavered, influenced by wireless propaganda.[84] In the south, things were equally problematic and the arrangements made by the Forestry Unit in Pencader that employed sacked pacifists proved especially trying for Gwynfor.[85] Somewhat ironically, given their connections, members of Welsh Pacifists were very fond of attacking one another. The most difficult relationship for Gwynfor was the one between him as secretary and the chair, Richard Bishop, a Falstaffian figure with an unpredictable streak. Bishop would frequently neglect his duties in Wales to pursue 'his numerous wanderings in England'.[86] One practical problem facing Gwynfor was a shortage of petrol which restricted travel around Wales; another was the attitude towards pacifists in the Welsh press. As George M Ll Davies told Gwynfor, the *Western Mail* was 'whipping up hatred towards the minority … *Y Goleuad* was timorous, *Y Cymro* ran with the hares and the hounds, *Y Faner* was too ready to wave the red rag in front of John Bull, *Y Ddraig Goch* was always keen to put the knife into something or someone English'.[87]

To all intents and purposes, Gwynfor found himself trying to hold Welsh Pacifists together with no apparatus or instruments of propaganda – a huge task. Even so, he did not escape harsh criticism at the end of 1940. One common complaint was that he mixed politics and pacifism;[88] another was that the pacifists were effectively mute and that they had not held a conference or published a word in months. According to one sniping correspondent in *Y Tyst*: 'At best, it's a branch of the PPU'.[89] Such criticism would no doubt have hurt Gwynfor, but he was well aware of these problems. He spent Christmas 1940 leafing through back issues of *Y Deyrnas*, the pacifist periodical published during the First World War which had held the faithful together in difficult times. The experience left a deep impression on him and he bolstered his belief that the only way to save the pacifists from sinking into obscurity was for them to publish their own material.[90] This conviction led to the publication of a series of pamphlets under the name of Welsh Pacifists.

While all this was going on, Gwynfor did two things that proved vital to Welshness in Carmarthenshire. The first was a decision by a small group, meeting in the Rowlands Café in Llandeilo at the end of November 1940, to set up a local branch of the Defence Committee. Inevitably, Gwynfor was made secretary of the North and East Myrddin district.[91] From then on he wore three hats: those of Plaid Cymru, the Pacifists and the Defence Council. Even by his Stakhanovite standards, working like this on three fronts was astonishing. The second important development was his decision in December 1940 to establish a branch of Plaid Cymru in Llangadog. As with the Pacifists, however, it was a slog. Despite spending time and money on advertising the meeting, only seven turned up.[92] It was no surprise then that Gwynfor longed for the nightmarish year to end.

Christmas at Wernellyn was quiet and peaceful with all the family – including his Uncle Idris. There was another reason to celebrate, too. As the New Year dawned, Gwynfor was paid a fulsome tribute in the *Amman Valley Chronicle* for his efforts to protect the Welsh character of the area in the name of the Defence Committee. As 'Cerddetwr', the paper's Welsh-language columnist, wrote:

> He is a young, vigorous, cultured man and it is easy to see that his arrival in the Tywi Valley is a great asset to local life.

'Cerddetwr's one concern was that only the middle classes had attended the Committee's first meeting in Llandeilo:

> What a fine thing it would be to have cultured miners, and alcam workers too, and a thoughtful farmhand from the north of the county on the committee, if only out of respect for 'the horny-handed sons of toil'. There was a lot of talk about Welsh traditions and about the roots and branches of those traditions. What a shame that we did not remember that there is a close relationship between the soil of our country – the earth – and every tradition we possess.[93]

But this comparative contentment did not last long. Shortly after the New Year, the towns in the south were bombarded more intensely than ever; Llandaff and its cathedral were particularly badly hit, and 103 people were killed. By the middle of the month it was Swansea's turn to face the deadly onslaught. A month later, the same town suffered the war's worst attack on Wales. Faced with such a situation, calls by those including Gwynfor and Saunders Lewis for a ceasefire seemed almost idiotic.[94] Their message was extremely unpopular and bodies like the Congregationalists in Carmarthenshire and Llŷn who favoured a ceasefire were the exception. Far more representative of Welsh-speaking Wales was the view taken by the editor of the *Carmarthen Journal*. He judged the call for an early cessation of hostilities to be a 'very deplorable thing' and the action of 'a small number of cranks'.[95]

Gwynfor's efforts on Plaid Cymru's behalf at the beginning of 1941 created problems: lack of support, suspicion and haphazard organization. The quandary he faced during January 1941 was whether he should allow his name to go forward as Plaid Cymru candidate at the Carmarthen by-election – recently called following the retirement of Daniel Hopkin. The wartime convention was not to challenge the party defending the seat, but several Plaid Cymru members believed this was an undemocratic, English practice. Gwynfor agreed with them in principle, but the whole by-election issue caused him considerable unease. On the one hand, he thought Plaid Cymru should stand up for Wales in a parliamentary election, and not to contest the seat would be a sign of cowardice. On the other, he could see numerous difficulties. Carmarthen, to his mind, was 'the most hopeless seat in Wales' from Plaid Cymru's point of view because money was so scarce. The other stumbling block was that 'whoever stood would ruin his chances of doing anything of value in the future'. The only other option he could see was to follow the example of the nationalists in Scotland and ask the other parties to state that they would fight for Home Rule after the war.[96]

Gwynfor's friends were well aware of his qualms about fighting a by-election in the middle of a war but, in two minds, he came under tremendous pressure to stand. Eventually he agreed that his name could go forward on one condition, that his candidature was acceptable to his family. He left the matter with his future father-in-law, Dan Thomas, and went to discuss the issue himself with Dan and Catherine Evans in Barry. Their answer was unambiguous. Gwynfor's parents thought contesting an election under the prevailing circumstances – during heavy bombing and at a time when wedding arrangements needed to be made – was madness. They also thought that standing would be even more inadvisable since the other parties had agreed not to stand in wartime. Faced with this advice, Gwynfor decided to submit to his family's wishes, but it was not an easy decision. He confessed to J E Jones that 'this clash' of loyalties was 'a severe disappointment' to him.[97] In the end, Plaid Cymru did not put up a candidate.

Gwynfor and Rhiannon were married a week later, on Saint David's Day 1941, in an emotional ceremony. Three days previously, a bomb had landed within two hundred yards of Rhiannon's home in Roath Park, shattering the front windows and showering the pair's wedding presents with glass.[98] On the morning of the wedding itself, south Wales woke to familiar devastation: more destruction and deaths after another night of relentless air raids. Fortunately for the newly-weds, there was no bombing in Cardiff and the ceremony at Crwys Road Chapel proceeded without disturbance. The pair were married by Gwynfor's uncle, Idris, in a service full of nationalist symbolism. It was something of a society wedding in Welsh-speaking Wales – important enough to merit a report in *Y Faner* (the nationalists' 'house publication') and the undoubted high point, it was said, was an address by George M Ll Davies.[99] Davies said the couple were embarking on a great adventure and leaving a city of destruction behind in pursuit of love. The fact that love could be found amid the rubble of Cardiff was proof, the President of Welsh Pacifists asserted, that the flame of hope had not yet been extinguished. Sentimental words, no doubt, but powerful too given the context. With that, Gwynfor and Rhiannon left for their honeymoon: a couple of days at Tynllidiart, Dan and Elizabeth Thomas's holiday home.

They went on to Wernellyn, a dramatic change of circumstances for Rhiannon. Raised in a city, she found herself thrown, like Gwynfor himself eighteen months earlier, into rural Wales and the mysteries of agricultural life. She coped remarkably well, learning to milk, muck out and feed the stock.[100] Within weeks, they had settled into the way of life that would continue for nearly half a century – Gwynfor would pursue his mission, and Rhiannon would look after the home and live the life of a political widow. From the beginning of their marriage, her contribution to Gwynfor's public life was enormous. His dependence on her was total; he became a man who never chose a shirt or pair of shoes for himself. Rhiannon also shouldered many of Gwynfor's professional burdens, typing and taking shorthand notes. Important as this all was, her biggest contribution was being 'Rhiannon Gwynfor' – the gentle mother, and perfect companion to a public figure. In this respect, her own intelligence was secondary to her persona as 'Rhiannon Gwynfor'. She endured this without complaint, even though her husband's frequent absences from home put an unavoidable strain on their union.

Gwynfor wasted no time after his return from Dolgellau. In April 1941, he joined the executive of the Defence Committee for Welsh Culture – adding considerably to his already heavy workload. From then on until the end of the war, along with T I Ellis, he was crucial to the Committee's success. Moreover, in comparison with all his other activities, the Defence Committee was well regarded and beginning to win significant victories. In May 1941, following a long campaign involving parents in Swansea and some MPs, children from the town began to be moved to safety. Two girls came to stay at Wernellyn for a time – much to Gwynfor's approval and delight.[101] It is doubtful whether this did much to help their marriage, but the Evans's home life, like that of so many others in Wales, was driven by the rhythms of war. The same month saw Gwynfor realize his ambition to publish Welsh-language pacifist pamphlets – no mean feat given the privations of war. Vital to this was the support of the writer Kate Roberts and her husband Morris Williams, owners of the Gee Press in Denbigh. Without their readiness to publish pamphlets at threepence each, it is unlikely the scheme would ever have succeeded, given the refusal of several other presses to undertake such work. Gwilym R Jones, a Gee employee, generously offered help with the editing, but the censor was not always so accommodating. Indeed, the three series editors – Gwynfor, Gwilym R Jones and George M Ll Davies – deliberately appealed to 'the faith of Christ' in an attempt to avoid the blue pencil.[102] By June, the first of these pamphlets, Iorwerth Peate's *Y Traddodiad Heddwch yng Nghymru* ('The Peace Tradition in Wales'), was ready. The pamphlets proved a huge success and, by October 1941, the first three were out of print.[103] They appeared monthly from then on until 1944, 31 in total, and attracted some of the most talented and radical writers in Wales: Pennar Davies, J Gwyn Griffiths and T Gwynn Jones. Gwynfor himself edited the twelfth in the series, *Tystiolaeth y Plant* ('The Evidence of Children'), statements by 14 young people explaining why they were pacifists. Given the reluctance of the Welsh-language press to publish material by pacifists, these pamphlets proved vital in bringing together the scattered pacifist community. The Christian poet Gwenallt was right to describe them as 'a lonely lamp in a vast darkness'.[104]

When he looked back on his work with Welsh Pacifists, it was appropriate for Gwynfor to reflect on these pamphlets but, influential though they were, he chose to ignore the fact that the movement was in turmoil in 1941. The poet and pacifist Waldo Williams described the membership as 'split', and it was a widely-held perception.[105] One factor which undermined unity in some areas was the Welsh language. Some of the branches in the south were suspicious of it and the PPU's British Council was openly dismissive. When John Barclay, a leading member of the PPU, went to listen to Gwynfor addressing a meeting in the north, he felt distanced from the Welsh-speaking audience by 'impossible barriers of tongue and tradition'. But rather than keep his comments to himself, Barclay fanned the flames by publishing an impudent article in *Peace News* arguing that the solution was for Welsh Pacifists and those in England to begin to speak the same language.[106] Indeed, it was one of the great paradoxes of the PPU that its members were open-minded on almost everything except the Welsh language. For many of them, nationalism, and minority languages, were little better than intellectual obscurantism. As one correspondent in *Peace News* argued, they should learn Esperanto as had some members of the Fellowship for Reconciliation.[107] For a beleaguered group like the Welsh Pacifists, arguments such as this over the language were significant because, increasingly, they found themselves deprived of support from the PPU centrally. When the Forestry Units at Pontrhydyfen and Pencader closed during the year, Gwynfor discovered there was no help available for the men who had worked there to find employment. Shortly afterwards, Richard Bishop 'resigned' from his work in Wales. No one replaced him and Gwynfor and George M Ll Davies were obliged to deal with the resulting chaos.[108] It was some measure of compensation, but not much, when Gwynfor was elected that July to the PPU's British Council.

At least things were more promising with the Defence Committee, which was by then going from strength to strength. In August 1941, it joined forces with the National Union of Welsh Societies – a movement first established in 1913. Both organizations had ceased to exist as separate entities, but there was a general feeling that united they were stronger. At Gwynfor's suggestion, the new body was christened Undeb Cymru Fydd (New Wales Union) – echoing the name of Cymru Fydd, the Liberal Home Rule movement of the late nineteenth century which he considered 'the most popular national movement that modern Wales has seen'.[109] It was a crucial step for the survival of the Welsh language; thereafter, it had an effective organization to fight its cause. Moreover, Undeb Cymru Fydd ensured that there were people ready to work for the language in their communities in wartime. Its existence was important, but it did little to calm Gwynfor's more general concerns about its status. As he admitted in *Y Faner* that summer: 'Months are vital in these hectic times; indeed, days are vital when those days can bring events that are destructive to the Welsh heritage.'[110]

As harvest began that autumn, Gwynfor faced uneasy times. He had begun to hate the war and its effects. As he wrote to Pennar Davies: 'When I see men trampling my country, throwing her children onto the streets (e.g. from Epynt) I feel as if I could shoot the devils. But in the meantime I try to stay on the path that my conscience tells me in my quiet hours is the right one.'[111] His dejection was exacerbated by the lack of direction from Plaid Cymru at a time when politicians and commentators were thinking about the future of post-war Britain. In October 1941, he was asked to write a memorandum for Plaid Cymru outlining his own vision of Wales. As he worked on it, he soon realized that the party had no grasp of modern economics. Writing to J E Jones, he called it a 'terrible condemnation' that no member of the executive, himself included, had the least idea about 'Plaid's policy, indeed whether it had an industrial policy at all'. In a piece of uncompromising criticism, he listed the shortcomings in industrial policy: 'Who would control the industries? The capitalists? The capitalists and the workers?' Unless it could answer these questions, he said, Plaid Cymru had no right to expect the support of the workers 'when it preaches a politics without any economic hope'.[112]

The same indignation coloured his correspondence with T I Ellis. Gwynfor knew he was in favour of nationalizing the coal industry and the railways 'for the nation' and that full compensation should be paid. He also knew that he wished to nationalize monopolies such as electricity but, beyond those simple principles, he could see little more than a thick fog:

> When I venture into the heavy industries I am completely out of my depth … I know nothing about the subject [economics] and would welcome enlightenment … It is a terrifying flaw in us as the Nationalist Party that we haven't given more thought to these issues, and in my opinion, it's the main reason for our failure to appeal to the workers; we have nothing to offer them … Talk of deindustrialization etc will scare them, however true and important it may be… Unless we face up to these problems, the cultured Welsh will remain an academic body; or at least, their activities will not be relevant to the lives of most Welsh people, who live in the industrial areas.[113]

Gwynfor proposed that Saunders Lewis should turn his mind to these matters, and this is precisely what happened. Even so, it was a muted end to a grim year for both pacifism and Welsh nationalism. At least they had survived, and 1942 saw fresh hope for the Welsh language as the New Wales Union began to make its mark. Gwynfor now had an organisation behind him and he made full use of it. America's decision to enter the war in December 1941 also marked a substantial shift; from then on, it was clear the conflict would not last indefinitely. Throughout 1942, the popular press spoke of the need for Churchill to open a second front – not simply of survival.[114]

This new confidence was reflected in Gwynfor's own methods. Having been comparatively silent for so long, he began to insist on being heard. When it was announced that women were to be conscripted, he argued that civil unrest was the only way of ensuring Welsh Christian society remained intact. He called, for instance, on the Congregationalist Union to do far more, and reprimanded it for being 'dumb and cowardly' while the government was stealing away its young adherents. It was an outspoken criticism from someone not yet 30 years old, but the vision behind it was a call to action; his grand scheme was for Congregationalists to unite and formulate a policy of opposition to the new measure.[115] There is no evidence that any such gathering was held, but his efforts were supported by the New Wales Union; that January, they held three conferences to publicise the effects of compulsory war service on women.[116]

By the end of January, Gwynfor was being hailed by the Welsh-language press as 'the Welsh leader who is fast coming to prominence'. Not without reason. His public speeches were ever more messianic with their talk of 'giving ourselves to the new Wales' as 'a whole life's work'. He also, from then until the end of the war, associated the desire to wage war with immorality and Anglicization. Here, for example, is the picture he painted at a New Wales Union meeting on the effect of war on morality and Welshness close to home:

> Before the war the children in the Amman Valley played in Welsh; today one hears English everywhere – because of the arrival of evacuees. Welsh girls under 18 years old in the Swansea Valley go to pubs with English women. And as it sends these English people to Wales, the government at the same time calls our girls and boys away.[117]

There was, nevertheless, a price to pay for this new-found fame. In the wake of the essay Gwynfor published in *Y Tyst*, he suffered the most sustained attack he had experienced throughout the war. Llewelyn Evans, a fellow-member and a deacon at Providence chapel, wrote to the paper to thank the Lord that 'most in our country are ... so loyal to the authorities'. In his neighbour's eyes, Gwynfor was an 'agitator'– whose cowardly pacifism would hasten the death of all decency.[118] The great irony in this quarrel was that Llewelyn Evans had chosen to stay at home on his farm, Glasallt, in Llangadog for the duration. But in his response, published in the same paper, Gwynfor chose not to draw attention to that fact and stuck to his argument that it was through non-violent action – the way of Gandhi in India and Kagawa in Japan – that nationhood could best be defended.[119] This was not the end of the public row between the two – exchanges continued in *Y Tyst* for another month before a truce was called between the pacifist and the farmer from Llangadog.[120] His neighbours at Glasallt represented what Gwynfor later described in his autobiography as a 'particularly opposed' minority. The problem, however, was that the protagonists were both prominent in the Llangadog community. It was no coincidence that the 'Llandovery and Llangadock War Week' in 1941 raised seven times more than its original target – the highest total of any village in Wales.[121] The Evans family had to endure the enmity of this minority from 1942 until they left Llangadog in 1984 – partly because of a fundamental loathing of their politics.

Despite the malice of these assaults, there were brighter moments too. The first was the birth of Alcwyn Deiniol in January 1942. Six other children followed with metronomic regularity. Alcwyn Deiniol came into the world just as his father was beginning to see the anti-Welsh tide slowly turn. As the year began, the New Wales Union had gained attention and support for its stance in favour of two farmers who had been forced by Llangadog magistrates' court to pay for the translation of their evidence from Welsh into English. For Gwynfor, and many others, this amounted to 'a serious denial of justice' and the Union did more than anyone to seek redress.[122] As the fight continued, Gwynfor sensed that the 'nationalist cause' in the area had gained ground and that he had become 'surprisingly popular' as a result.[123] Protests were voiced by some Welsh MPs, and by April 1942 the Home Secretary, Herbert Morrison, had announced that no monoglot Welsh-speaker should have to pay for translation. Before the month was out, the Lord Chancellor, Lord Simon, had called for an inquiry into the status of the language as a direct result of the Llangadog case. The end of the year witnessed the passage of the Welsh Courts Act, benefiting – despite its major shortcomings – from the attention given to the Llangadog case.

Gwynfor saw other gains too. He arranged a meeting with Rhys Hopkin Morris, head of the BBC in Wales, to 'press upon him the wishes of Wales in [these] difficult days'.[124] And if things looked brighter for the New Wales Union, the same was true of the pacifists. In March 1942, reports appeared that the activity of peace groups in the south was on the rise 'after a fairly unexceptional period'. The response to pacifist literature was equally encouraging, with the first eight published pamphlets selling well.[125] Even Plaid Cymru succeeded in holding a one-day conference to discuss policy on social reorganization after the war. It led to the adoption of many of Gwynfor's and Saunders Lewis's ideas on nationalization through the establishment of co-operative boards.[126] But this fresh activity and sympathy was, of course, only comparative. Given what had gone before, any progress was welcome but, even so, the hatred towards nationalism and pacifism had not waned.

On a national level, Gwynfor worried how men like Dr Thomas Jones, Lloyd George's former Deputy Secretary, could demean nationalists by describing them as 'Hitlerians'.[127] He found Jones's words 'nasty and childish', but nonetheless deserving of 'serious consideration'.[128] Locally too, the same mentality was evident in the views of Carmarthenshire Education Committee. In May, a bitter dispute erupted after the New Wales Union and Carmarthenshire Congregationalists objected to the Cadet Corps' recruitment drive in the county's schools. The Education Committee called it 'Adolescent Education' and Gwynfor and his supporters were outraged. In their eyes, allowing 14-year-old boys to dress in military uniform was proof that militarism could become even more entrenched in Welsh public life. Gwynfor looked to Norway for inspiration – a country whose teachers had chosen exile and poverty rather than collaborate with the Nazi machine.[129] But the Education Committee completely ignored the lobbying; although a majority in Carmarthenshire, as early as 1942, had begun to voice concern at the status of the Welsh language, there was barely any popular support for an agenda that reeked of pacifism. As one E Harries, writing to the *Carmarthen Journal*, put it, Gwynfor was a 'Rip van Winkle', exhibiting 'a startling incongruity towards the needs of the hour'.[130] The criticism in the *Amman Valley Chronicle* – the same paper that had voiced its admiration of him a few months before – was similar. According to one correspondent, Gwynfor was suffering from some sort of 'kink'.[131] And, almost without exception, the people of Carmarthenshire felt the same antagonism towards this pacifist and nationalist agenda.

If pacifism was unpopular in the Wales of 1942, then Plaid Cymru was odious. Gwynfor was well aware of this hostility and he was continually frustrated by his country's unwillingness to understand – never mind appreciate – what nationalism had to offer. Privately, he would curse 'our people', the Welsh, as often as he would reproach the English. These lukewarm Welsh people – the MPs, councillors and officials – as well as 'the indifference of the ordinary people' were responsible, in his view, for Plaid Cymru's failure.[132] He also believed the chief motivation that drove Welsh MPs to Westminster was self-interest.[133] In the early summer of 1942, he felt the frustration keenly. Gwynfor was an irritated man. It was no surprise, then, that his anger boiled over.

The man who brought about the explosion was Gwilym Davies, his hero from the days of the LNU who had escorted him around Geneva when he was 18. On 6 July 1942, Gwynfor read in that morning's *Western Mail* that Gwilym Davies was about to publish a scathing piece in the Welsh literary and theological monthly *Y Traethodydd* accusing Plaid Cymru of seeking an independent, Fascist, totalitarian and Catholic Wales.[134] These were familiar accusations, but Gwynfor was afraid that an essay of this sort by such a respected figure would be hugely damaging. That morning, Gwynfor wrote to him begging him not to publish. If the article appeared, he argued, it would do 'more harm than virtually anything that has been written about us in the last ten years'. How, Gwynfor asked, could Plaid Cymru be totalitarian, Fascist and Catholic when these values were so contrary to one another. He went further: Saunders Lewis was 'completely anti-totalitarian'; the only member of Plaid Cymru who had made 'unwise' comments in recent times, according to Gwynfor, was Ambrose Bebb, who had spoken out 'once in anger'. The charge that Plaid Cymru was riddled with Papists was equally absurd:

> Only one has converted since S. L.– Cathrin Huws. No party has, on average, so many keen Nonconformists in its ranks... I cannot express how great this blow is to me. I have respected you ever since I had the privilege of going to Geneva with you. What makes this a mystery and a sorrow is that I know you are a friend to us; and yet no enemy could say anything worse. Of course, no enemy could do the same damage. The mud thrown by a friend sticks more, somehow.[135]

Gwynfor's letter made no difference. Gwilym Davies published his article in *Y Traethodydd* and plunged the leadership and the ordinary members of Plaid Cymru into crisis. Two days later, Gwynfor wrote to T I Ellis to reveal the full extent of his anger:

> What's come over him? Is he being paid for this? I've never read such nonsense in my life. It strikes me as repulsively dishonest, and I had always taken him to be an honest man. It will no doubt do great damage to the party, because that sort of mud is sure to stick and we will be labelled by the people of Wales with their most vile names.[136]

Gwynfor was right. Gwilym Davies, one of the pillars of the Welsh Nonconformist establishment, was responsible for the criticism – and not one of the usual suspects. As *Y Goleuad* put it, the article was 'a bombshell'.[137] And the pressure on Plaid Cymru to renew its campaign, in earnest, was all the greater because there were rumours that a new party, 'Group 1942', was about to be formed. This party, it was claimed, would bring together those nationalist elements within Plaid Cymru, the Labour Party and the Communists.[138] 'Group 1942' however came to nothing – it limited itself to collecting facts about the state of Wales – but Gwynfor, seeing his own party in trouble, was insistent that Plaid Cymru needed to restate its principles in order to kill off the insinuation that it was a Fascist party. In light of the government's announcement that there would be a Welsh

Consultative Committee to discuss reorganization, he wanted his own party to behave more pragmatically. The important thing, he told J E Jones, was:

> ... to earn the sympathy of the lads in the Forces. What about addressing them like this, 'That we, members of the Nationalist Party annual conference, send our warmest greetings to the Welsh in the Armed Forces and welcome them cordially to join us in the battle for a free and better Wales as soon as they have the opportunity'.[139]

His suggestion was accepted, in part, and during a stormy conference in 1942, Plaid Cymru announced that it was not a Fascist party. Even so, it had to wait a further year before it could begin to exhibit a more sympathetic attitude towards Welsh servicemen. Meanwhile, some younger members – like John Legonna and Trefor Morgan – were growing increasingly impatient with what they considered to be Plaid Cymru's dictatorial and impractical approach.[140]

As autumn 1942 arrived, Gwynfor struggled on diligently: work with the pacifists, the party, and the New Wales Union – not to mention his family concerns at Wernellyn. The anxiety about 'Group 1942' did not disappear completely and many in the party suspected that the Labour MP Jim Griffiths was busy behind the scenes.[141] Then, in November 1942, Welsh politics and Plaid Cymru were transformed when a by-election was called in the University of Wales seat. Although he had no great desire to win the poll, Saunders Lewis leapt back into practical politics with the grace of a gazelle. He viewed the election as a wonderful opportunity to win sympathy for Plaid Cymru in a seat that was not completely beyond reach. After all, only graduates had a vote and Plaid Cymru, in spite of the war, could still count on the support of a large proportion of educated people.

Saunders Lewis's candidacy was a major event in itself but the Welsh middle-class intelligentsia was thrilled even further when it emerged that none other than that former Plaid stalwart, W J Gruffydd, would be representing the Liberals.[142] In an instant, Welsh-speaking Wales split into two factions: Plaid Cymru supporters on the one hand; and others who despised Saunders Lewis's Papist, Fascist obscurantism. It also became an epic struggle between two ideologies: nationalism and Welsh liberalism. Gwynfor, T Gwynn Jones, J E Daniel, D J Williams and Lewis Valentine aligned themselves with Saunders Lewis; the Welsh establishment – Lloyd George, T J Morgan, J E Lloyd and R T Jenkins – threw in their hand with Gruffydd.

The election proved to be an education and something of a relief for

Gwynfor; at last, Plaid Cymru could be seen and heard in the context of war. As he told *Y Faner*:

> ... the place of every thoughtful Welshman today was in politics. There were encouraging signs in Wales, and the University of Wales would now have a marvellous opportunity to strike another blow for Wales by electing Mr Saunders Lewis as MP... There could be no second interpretation on such an event; and there would be no significance in electing anyone else.[143]

Gwynfor went out into the highways and byways to campaign for Saunders Lewis, his speeches echoing the diametrically opposed ideas that were so much part of the political idiom of the day. In Gwynfor's mind, those who would not campaign for Saunders Lewis were 'traitors'.[144] And despite the divisions, there was a general feeling by Christmas that the tide was turning, thanks to the resurgence of Plaid Cymru and the very public activity of the New Wales Union. The feeling was sensed locally too. 'Cerddetwr' used his column in the *Amman Valley Chronicle* to sing Gwynfor's praises again for his work for the Union:

> ... thanks are due above all to the young secretary from Llangadog. It was he who raised the thorny subject of paying the translator at Llangadog Court. He won a great victory in that discussion. Indeed, all that is best in Carmarthenshire has benefited greatly from Mr Evans's arrival in the Tywi Valley. Those who know him wish him continued strength in the fray.[145]

But, increasingly, it was Plaid Cymru which claimed the lion's share of Gwynfor's attention. As the New Year passed, between 'busy times with livestock and tomatoes',[146] Gwynfor sensed that 'one of the great struggles in our history' had already done 'great good'. His only disappointment, as the election campaign reached its conclusion, was that 'someone as harmless' as Gruffydd, of all people, had chosen to challenge Plaid Cymru. He attributed it to the unhealthy influence of Iorwerth Peate.[147] In the final days, Gwynfor threw himself into the campaign. He arranged an 'excellent' meeting for Saunders Lewis in Carmarthen, but the more he did, the more he feared that Lewis's Catholicism was poisoning Plaid Cymru's impact in Carmarthenshire.[148] 'Were it not for Saunders being a Catholic,' he told J E Jones, 'it would be pointless for anyone to stand against him. I know of several people in my immediate circle who cannot support him because of it. As a result, the vote will not reflect the full force of the Welsh nationalist cause.'[149]

The poll was held over five days at the end of January, and when W J Gruffydd was declared the victor with a clear majority over Saunders Lewis, Gwynfor, like many within Plaid Cymru, had mixed feelings. On the one hand, he believed that the 'awakening' had done 'great good';[150] on the other, he feared that the 'electoral storm' had wounded Plaid Cymru – especially so 'the tricks played by the Yellow Press' and its attempts to denigrate Lewis's Catholicism.[151] During the following month, Plaid Cymru propaganda attempted to portray the result as proof the party had 'arrived in Welsh politics'.[152] But, increasingly, Gwynfor, J E Jones and Saunders Lewis were concerned that the outcome would prove to be a double-edged sword – a ballot that would give heart to Plaid Cymru's faithful few, but would chill the blood of those who were less committed. The party's response was to issue a confidential memorandum entitled 'After the Election' based on a questionnaire sent to its leading members. The questions themselves hinted at the difficulties faced: 'Was Plaid too Catholic? Was its stance on the war an obstacle? From where had Gruffydd garnered his support?'[153]

Gwynfor and his party clearly learned a great deal from the election, and nationalist politics from then on took on a far more modern feel. In a sense, it had no choice, given that the topic of conversation in every pit and on every shopfloor was Sir William Beveridge's report on national insurance. It was a subject taken up by the editor of *Y Faner* who called on Plaid Cymru to face up to the new world order.[154] But even though there was an element of compulsion, Saunders Lewis and Gwynfor made a key contribution to the modernization of the party. There was a general feeling that a new age was dawning but, having spent so long leading an assault on Gruffydd, Plaid Cymru had no social programme to speak of. Gwynfor was especially aware of this and wrote to J E Jones (not the most profound thinker in party ranks) to alert him to the changes in the Welsh political landscape. 'The central question of the day', he told the party Secretary, was 'the organization, planning and totalitarianization of society', and insisted that the battle for freedom for Welsh workers must be fundamental to Plaid Cymru's activity. In the short term, he hoped this would be a means of countering the powers of the 'Bevs' – Beveridge and Bevin, the Minister for Labour.[155] Gwynfor was stating the obvious, perhaps, but Plaid members with such insights were rare.

Fortunately for him, he was presented with the ideal campaign to lead in the spring of 1943. That April there was concern, particularly in the south, about the government's 'transference' policy. Some Caernarvonshire quarrymen voiced similar fears. The policy allowed the government to move workers – including women – to wherever they were needed. It meant that, to all intents and purposes, unemployment had ceased to exist in Wales by 1943, but there was a real danger that the policy would have dire consequences. In practical terms, it meant women from Wales could be uprooted and sent to industrial centres like Dagenham, Slough and Wolverhampton.[156] A number of councils in the south convened a conference and MPs were persuaded to accept the principle of opposing transference.[157] For Plaid Cymru, it was a golden opportunity. Gwynfor, repeatedly, argued that transferring women on these 'budgie trains' was no better than Nazism. He also poured scorn on the trade unions in the south, arguing that their indifference was both surprising and sad. It was proof, he said, that their leaders were utterly under Communist control.[158]

This early venture into populist politics was certainly strong on rhetoric, but it had little impact. Worse still, tarring the whole Labour movement with the same brush was a tactical error because a number of Labour branches, and Welsh MPs like the member for Llanelli, Jim Griffiths, had indeed been outspoken critics of the policy. The cause in the south was further damaged by Gwynfor's and Saunders Lewis's decision to attack the trade unions.[159] It was, therefore, no surprise when Jim Griffiths rejected Gwynfor's suggestions out of hand. Plaid Cymru had 'no substance or constructive proposal'.[160] Similarly, Gwynfor and his party were censured by some local councils for having cynically used the situation 'to further their own interests'.[161] It should also be noted that by the end of the war many of these women had settled happily in England and were enjoying a comparatively high standard of living. The problem by then was getting them to return voluntarily from their enforced exile.[162]

It had been a shaky start, but at least Gwynfor was tackling practical politics – something that could not be said of all Plaid Cymru's leaders in the early months of 1943. Gwynfor, indeed, saw this period as a marvellous opportunity to challenge the socialists' claim that only they could build the new Jerusalem. But for the President of Plaid Cymru, J E Daniel, the idea of leading Plaid Cymru in post-war Britain was too much. For all his academic gifts, he felt he lacked technical expertise to steer the party through such a crucial time. The Catholicism of his wife Catherine was also a public impediment. J E Daniel therefore resolved to relinquish the leadership. It plunged the party into one of the greatest crises in its short history.

On 7 May 1943, J E Jones wrote to Gwynfor, informing him that Daniel no longer wished to be the President of Plaid Cymru, and added that of all the possible successors his was the only name that deserved serious consideration. He begged him to stand. He had, Jones added, all the qualifications and his pacifism was not considered to be an obstacle. Jones was convinced that Gwynfor as leader would eliminate the anti-Catholic prejudices which had plagued the party during Saunders Lewis's and J E Daniel's time at the helm. He promised in addition that he would receive substantial support as President; Jones envisaged a 'Presidential Committee' (which already existed) that could draw on Saunders Lewis's and J E Daniel's 'wide experience'.[163] But the brutal fact remained: Plaid Cymru was in a hole, and Jones's words of praise betrayed the truth that there was no one else available who was fit to run the party. Apart from Gwynfor, the only other names mentioned as credible successors to Daniel were Saunders Lewis, Moses Gruffydd and, perhaps, Lewis Valentine. Gwynfor allowed his name to go forward, but his hope was that Moses Gruffydd, a talented agriculturist and one of the party's most wealthy patriarchs, would stand. In all respects, Gwynfor was convinced that Gruffydd outshone him: 'He has specialist knowledge of an important field; he is experienced and loyal to the party'. His other great virtue, Gwynfor supposed, was that there would be no prejudices over 'religion or pacifism against him'.[164]

By June, there was huge uncertainty about the Presidency, and Gwynfor was beginning to feel the pressure. On 9 June, he agreed with J E Jones that he would stand if Moses Gruffydd refused and if he could allay the fears of his family in Barry who were, he said, 'hostile to Plaid'. He emphasised, however, that there was no certainty he could do so.[165] Although he had lived in Llangadog for four years, he was well aware that the Labour Party in Barry was undermining his father's grip on civic power, and using his son's high profile to damage him. Then, to cap it all, Moses Gruffydd confirmed that he did not want the Presidency because he was employed at the time by the Ministry of Agriculture. He also supposed that he would not be qualified for such an important position.[166] There was only one name in the frame, therefore, and everything depended on Gwynfor's decision. On 29 June, he attempted to explain the situation to J E Jones:

> The main difficulty I predicted was the attitude of my parents, but since I had not appeared on the streets of Barry since those unpleasant things had happened to my family after the fall of France, I believed that they could be persuaded to consider the matter judiciously. Last night my brother arrived here with a report on the situation. In

> short, here it is, that my father fumed at the suggestion and wanted me to know that it would split the family if I were to take the post. My brother fears that I would have to leave Wernellyn and look for another job. Maybe I shouldn't consider this as too great a demand, but there's more to it than finding work. For one thing, it is hard to imagine that the work wouldn't be such that I would have to devote all my time to it day in, day out – without any freedom to go here and there as the Presidency would require. I would have to find a job because I have no means to support the family. The other issue is how loyal a man should be to his family... My parents have suffered not a little because of me, and still do. Unfortunately, people are spreading stories about them all over town these days, and only yesterday my father went to see a solicitor to put a stop to some silly tittle-tattle about him – basically that he is a pacifist and a nationalist; and he is neither one nor the other; as a matter of fact he considers Plaid to be a bunch of stupid hotheads. (Did you see the story about the burning-down of Barry Memorial Hall – £75,000; the latest tale is that my father had a hand in the fire as a pacifist!) We'd take stories like that as a big joke, but four people came to my father one morning to say that they had heard them, and the whole thing worries him very much.

He warned J E Jones too that his father's health had begun to suffer and that he had fainted because of the strain:

> The choice that faces me is between accepting the post and tearing my family connections apart and harming my parents' health and peace of mind – and refusing the post in which I could possibly be of service to Wales. It's a fiendishly difficult choice. I cannot give a final answer without going to Barry to see my father; but if he continues in his current state of mind, I would not feel free to accept the post.[167]

As a compromise, Gwynfor suggested he would be willing to be nominated as Vice-President and that he would review the situation again 'in a year or two'. It is not known whether Gwynfor ever went to Barry but, on 2 July 1943, he received a sobering letter from his father begging him not to stand. It revealed at last the tensions that Dan had held in check for so long:

> These are very trying days for everyone and the trials and worries caused by the war are beginning to have their effect on people's nerves and tempers. I need not remind you that we have never by word or deed attempted to interfere with your position of Secretary to Welsh Pacifists... You are entitled to your opinion and you have never flinched in your attitude, but you should have regard for our feelings sometimes with regard to Undeb Cymru Fydd. I believe that this movement is trying to bring back the cultural values &c to Wales and her people. I am again very delighted... With regard to the Blaid, I feel that by accepting the position offered to you that the *Western Mail* will

> ... attempt to pour scorn upon you and the party. You know also that neither mam nor I are able to agree with their position... We know that Wales does not get her due attention but we believe that a movement like Undeb Cymru Fydd can do more and will attract more people than the Blaid and will in the end accomplish more for Wales... You know (not that I worry) that I lost the honour of J. P. through having a son as a CO [Conscientious Objector]... you see therefore that our attitude and work for these societies is having a very unfair reaction upon us.[168]

Even for someone as passionate in his nationalism as Gwynfor, this was a plea he could not ignore. Two days later, he wrote to J E Jones to share his ultimate decision with him:

> I do not need to say this is a blow for me too, because I believe I could do much for the cause if I were free from a stronger loyalty. I cannot face casting my parents to one side, and that is what allowing my nomination to stand would mean. I would have contempt for myself were I to do that. That is hardly worse than the shame I feel now in refusing responsibility at this difficult time.[169]

There is no doubt that this was a wise decision from a family point of view but, for the party, the side-effects were disastrous. When Plaid Cymru's members gathered in Caernarfon for their annual conference in August 1943, it was effectively a party that no one wished to lead. The poor unfortunate who agreed to fill the gap was Abi Williams – a fairly well-known figure within Plaid Cymru but completely unknown outside the narrow confines of the party. Although he was a good man, the Flintshire surveyor was totally unsuited to such a post for a variety of reasons.[170] First, despite his training as a minister, he hated public speaking and was a notoriously poor orator. Second, he had been the subject of unfair and malicious gossip about why he had left the ministry – one unfounded allegation was that he was a thief.[171] Third, he did not have an ounce of the vision that Plaid Cymru needed at such a crucial time. Despite these obvious disadvantages, Abi Williams was elected unopposed as President, and Gwynfor became his deputy.

Within weeks, it was clear to everyone that Plaid Cymru had made a huge mistake, as well as doing a disservice to a decent man, by allowing Abi Williams to step into the role. His first presidential address in *Y Ddraig Goch* revealed his pathological fear. In it, he confessed the call had been 'completely unexpected' and that 'he began the work with some trepidation'.[172] This, in essence, was the President's first and last meaningful contribution; only a few weeks after the Caernarfon conference, he was taken ill with something that disturbed his 'customary good health'.[173] It appears that the responsibility had exacerbated a pre-existing nervous condition. By the end of 1943, it was evident that Plaid Cymru had elected a no-hoper and this in turn affected Gwynfor. Traditionally, the post of Vice-President carried virtually no responsibility, but things were different now; Abi Williams's infirmity obliged Gwynfor – no matter what he had promised his father – to act as de facto President and become Plaid Cymru's back-seat driver until he took the wheel of the Presidency officially in 1945.

The great irony was that there was more opportunity for Welsh political patriotism to find expression in the summer of 1943 than at any other time since the outbreak of war. Italy had fallen to the Allies, and when the National Eisteddfod of 1943 opened, it was apparent, to quote *Y Cymro*, that 'some glimmer of hope' was visible in the eyes of the nation's leaders.[174] Politically, too, there was a perceptible momentum. The Deputy Prime Minister Clement Attlee's brusque announcement that he would not appoint a Secretary of State for Wales was hugely unpopular. It had also become clear that the Welsh Courts Act was a pig in a poke. These all offered considerable opportunities to Plaid Cymru, but Abi Williams did not respond. Lacking presidential leadership, Gwynfor stepped eagerly, if not confidently, into the breach. From the outset, he ignored the undertaking he had given his father, and set about the vital public work of outlining Plaid Cymru's policies for post-war Wales. In that year's annual conference, he spoke on 'Wales After the War', a piece that became something of a personal manifesto. In his speech, he insisted on two things: first, that his party realized the threat to Welsh moral life from outside influences such as the cinema and the public house. Like Saunders Lewis, he called for a specifically Welsh approach to social planning and for a national planning council. Secondly, he called on the party to appreciate that there was plenty 'of evidence of an increase in Welsh self-perception' among Welsh men and women serving in the forces. These people, he hoped, would represent the dawn of his new Wales.[175]

One of Gwynfor's first decisions during the two-year interregnum in the leadership was that the party needed to identify itself with Welsh people in the armed forces. Given Gwynfor's pacifism and the wider anti-war feeling within the party, this was never going to be easy, but the advantages appeared to outweigh the disadvantages to a considerable degree. The important thing for Gwynfor was that these young men knew the party was 'thinking about them, looking forward to their return, and counting on them in the battle for Wales – without being patronising or hypocritical'.[176] At his request in August 1943, thousands of copies of the newsletter *Cymru am Byth* were sent out to forces overseas. In addition, Gwynfor proved an important inspiration to T Elwyn Griffiths, an intelligence officer with the RAF in Cairo. Griffiths was the founder of *Seren y Dwyrain*, a publication for Welsh forces serving in North Africa, and Gwynfor's influence assured the project's success.[177] Behind the scenes he offered support to Griffiths and, on 16 September 1943, 'the first Welsh-language magazine ever published in the Middle East' appeared.[178] It quickly sold 1,500 copies from Tripoli to Baghdad. Buying it, Griffiths wrote, enabled Welsh exiles to forget 'their homesickness and low spirits' and 'to keep their patriotism alert and the language and culture of Wales alive'.[179] Without doubt, this cultural support was important and, in time, it was imitated by the publication of *Seren y Gogledd* – a Welsh-language paper for those serving in the colder climes of Iceland and beyond.

The success of this venture obscured Gwynfor's own isolation as he tried to drag Plaid Cymru towards the coming peace. Figures like Wynne Samuel, D J and Noëlle Davies, and Saunders Lewis, who took practical politics seriously, were exceptions. When Eisenhower announced over the New Year that the war in Europe would be won during 1944, Gwynfor was again driven to despair at his inability to offer economic solutions to Welsh problems. By 1944 the other parties, and the Welsh panel of the Reconstruction Ministry, already had schemes in place, but Plaid Cymru hesitated. Although the party had been working on a 'TVA scheme for Wales' – similar in nature to the co-operative venture of the Tennessee Valley Authority – since 1943, another six months would pass before the work of its architects, C F Matthews and Dewi Watkin Powell, would be presented to the public. As time ran out, Gwynfor could not hide his disquiet. He wrote to Pennar Davies in early January 1944:

> Having ventured to leave aside the basics, and think about our industrial society, I am at a loss. I can see some hope in the land and in rural communities; and I can see the superiority of the Co-operative principle over capitalism and Marxist Socialism, but after that – fog. I am trying to aim as openly as possible at a co-operative society that will restore agriculture to its true importance – and *good* farming, upon which man's physical health depends so much; that's the direction. We could do great things in Wales if we could remove the obstacles in our path to freedom and ensure the means of full liberty.[180]

Without a healthy economy, he knew there was no hope of creating a Christian Wales and that the Welsh people would face a dreadful future of 'Hollywood and greyhounds'.[181] But however conscious he was of the importance of economics, he could not shake off his private sense of inadequacy in such matters. In the crucial year of 1944, this deficiency was especially apparent, and in another letter to Pennar Davies, he touched again on this sense of failure:

> I have the feeling we are an eccentric minority, eager and irresponsible idealists ... when will our people become truly influential? What hope do we have against a power that offers insurance from the cradle to the grave?

Despite that, giving up was not an option:

> But woe betide us if we let our spirits drop; it would mean 'dropping out of history' as Middleton Murry is fond of saying. Quite literally, the fate of the nation rests on the next ten years. Can our generation rise above itself for a while? [182]

In January 1944 Gwynfor's anxieties about the future of Plaid Cymru grew as discussions began about creating a new party which would combine socialism and nationalism. The leading trade unionist Huw T Edwards set the cat among the pigeons when he called – not for the first or the last time – for a party which was not obsessed with the Welsh language nor with following the pacifist path.[183] Throughout that month, Gwynfor and J E Jones asked each other who exactly would want to join this proposed 'mongrel' party. Tecwyn Lloyd, John Aelod Jones [John Roberts Williams] and Goronwy Roberts were mentioned – three men, in Jones's opinion, who were either politically ambitious, prejudiced or unwilling to travel 'through the Plaid wilderness'.[184] In public, Plaid Cymru tried to claim that such a development was 'another sign of the party's enormous influence'[185] but, privately, Gwynfor was deeply apprehensive about what might happen and felt a new party was 'more likely to split and embitter those who work for Wales', leading to disaster for the nationalist movement.[186]

As with Gwerin and the '1942 Group', the demand for a united Green and Red front within Welsh politics was a damp squib. But Huw T Edwards's words reflected a perception that Plaid Cymru, weak though it was, could emerge from the war in better shape. That year's Saint David's Day Fund was well supported and, in March 1944, a new office opened in Cardiff. This event, as Gwynfor saw it, was proof not only that the party had made progress, but that nationalism in Wales had triumphed, despite a hostile press and a desire to 'reject responsibility and a host of other difficulties'.[187] Then, with signs of a political spring in the air, the party was shaken by Saunders Lewis's announcement on 18 April that he was severing his day-to-day contact with Plaid Cymru. He was doing so, he told D J Williams, for a number of related reasons.

> I can see that younger people than me, and more likely to succeed, are now ready to lead Plaid, and I am determined to give them their chance... That is the best thing for Plaid and for its goal. I have done my bit, and it is their turn now. If I continued to be prominent I would prevent their progress.

On that melodramatic note, Saunders Lewis promised to leave the arena to spend more time with his literary family: 'Virgil, À Kempis and the old Welsh writers.'[188] It is clear from the later correspondence between Saunders Lewis and D J Williams that Lewis had only two names in mind as future party leaders: Wynne Samuel and Gwynfor.[189] However, Lewis's declaration was shattering news. D J Williams called the letter 'a fateful one in the history of the Nationalist Party and Wales', and Gwynfor's reaction was similar.[190] By return of post, he wrote to Williams, describing Lewis's decision as historic:

> We must accept it for the time being, at least. Perhaps we shall see him return when times are more favourable to the movement – 'Hope springs eternal'. In the meantime, the burden will fall on people like J E and Wynne.[191]

Saunders Lewis did indeed return to the cut and thrust of political life, but the irony was that he returned at a time when the party was having even more difficulties, and came close to destroying Gwynfor's leadership.

It was a bitter blow, but Gwynfor responded positively and Saunders Lewis's announcement had the desired effect. He spent that spring working on countless projects: a pamphlet on the need for a Radio Corporation in Wales; and another, *They Cry Wolf*, on the continuing threat from English Totalitarianism.[192] News of the D-Day landings in June saw his level of activity increase still further. At the time, Gwynfor would rise at half past five each morning to do the milking and help with the hay harvest. However, this heavy manual work did nothing to curb his enthusiasm or his growing confidence that nationalism could prosper in Wales after the war. And there was no sense of shame either – even after D-Day – that he had embraced neutrality for so long.

On the contrary: what Plaid Cymru had done during the war was a source of pride to him because 'some have stood clearly and firmly in the name of the

Welsh nation and have done so without compromise'.[193] Saunders Lewis added to that confidence too. During July 1944, he published a highly significant article in *Y Faner* emphasising the need for Plaid Cymru to operate politically – especially in the valleys – through the medium of English.[194] But the vital development was the publication of the pamphlet *Plan Electricity for Wales* that summer.[195] Now, thanks to C F Matthews and Dewi Watkin Powell, there was a sound basis on which to argue for a TVA for Wales – a scheme which would provide co-operative management of natural resources like water, coal and steel. It was, in Dewi Watkin Powell's words, 'the Liberal tradition at its best'.[196] It also meant that Plaid Cymru could move away from Saunders Lewis's completely impractical policy of sharing property as widely as possible in the name of *perchentyaeth* or 'family ownership'.

Come the autumn, the military's grip on Welsh life loosened further. The requirement to take part in ARP (Air Raid Protection) exercises was dropped and the blackout regulations were less restrictive. At the same time, Gwynfor sensed more than ever the need for political leadership from Plaid Cymru and worried that his party was not prepared. He realized the war could come to an end that winter and an early General Election could follow; if that were to happen, he feared Plaid Cymru would 'face the most critical period' in its history. So much depended on its success and so little had been done to secure it. In his regular letters to J E Jones he expressed his anxiety that so few members of the party had thought about political strategy, nor were they seriously planning how to make a breakthrough. Indeed, he went so far as to formulate a timetable showing how long he was prepared to allow this to continue and warned Jones, 'If we haven't got somewhere in 10 years, we may as well give up.'[197]

His party was slow to respond to his warning and throughout the autumn of 1944 Gwynfor's frustration with some of the other leaders became increasingly evident. At meetings of the Executive, he found it impossible to understand the reluctance of men like J E Daniel to publish an election manifesto as soon as possible. Daniel's concern was to ensure a consistent policy, but for Gwynfor, the need to win over the returning soldiers and airmen was more pressing than intellectual niceties: 'Welshmen coming back to new things … Our job is to get them to join quickly'.[198] But with fewer than eight months before a likely General Election, the depth of ignorance about Plaid Cymru and the level of prejudice against it appeared insurmountable. The only way to overcome such hatred,

Gwynfor believed, was to fight parliamentary elections and take the message directly to the people. It was he, more than anyone, who pressed the party into fighting seven parliamentary seats in 1945 – a huge undertaking given its lack of resources. Other senior members of the party were far readier than Daniel to listen – including Saunders Lewis. In October 1944, Lewis argued that Gwynfor should 'have the chance to be President' and stay in the post for as long as he himself had (thirteen years) 'until he had won national authority'.[199]

All in all, it was a curious situation. On the one hand, there was Abi Williams, the President in name only, who was largely ignored; on the other, Gwynfor, the most politically astute of all Plaid Cymru's young leaders, with no seat to fight at the General Election. But late November saw a volte-face, when rumours emerged that Abi Williams was to stand in Merioneth, the party's most winnable seat. Broadly speaking, there were two problems with this: the first was Abi Williams's lack of 'presence' as a candidate; the second was the whispering campaign that still shrouded his decision to leave the ministry. By the end of 1944, things were so bad that prominent members in the constituency were begging Williams to withdraw and let Gwynfor, the party's rising star, step into the breach.[200] According to J E Jones, born and bred in Merioneth, Gwynfor would be regarded as a 'junior Tom Ellis', the man who could make the difference between merely doing well and actually winning the seat.[201] He suggested that Gwynfor's pacifism would not be a problem either; his supporters believed there to be a higher proportion of pacifists in Merioneth than in almost any other county in Wales.

Gwynfor had no part in these machinations, but Abi Williams soon heard rumours that there was a conspiracy against him and complained bitterly to J E Jones about the constituency party's dishonesty. In November 1944, Williams stood aside, with mixed emotions; bitterness at his betrayal, but relief that he would not have to face the likely electoral torture. On 13 November, the inevitable happened. The local Plaid Cymru organiser, Marion Eames, wrote to Gwynfor to inform him that Abi Williams had withdrawn and inviting him to stand.[202] Three weeks later, Plaid Cymru's Executive endorsed the invitation, making the most of Gwynfor's rather tenuous local credentials as a man 'with wide connections to families in many parts of Merioneth, and married to the grand-daughter of the late Mr John Jones, Tan-y-bwlch, Llanuwchllyn'.[203] In public, Plaid Cymru stated that it was Abi Williams's 'indisposition' which had led to the decision and, within the week, Gwynfor had accepted the invitation.[204] It is hardly necessary to add how delicate Gwynfor's position was, as Vice-President, in inheriting his superior's nomination; but as the election drew nearer, there was no time for bearing grudges. The Merioneth nomination transformed Gwynfor's life; accepting the offer added to his numerous responsibilities: Wernellyn, his work for pacifism and Plaid Cymru – not to mention campaigning in a constituency a hundred or so tortuous miles from his home in Llangadog.

But as a new chapter opened for Gwynfor, his dealings with his fellow-pacifists ended in acrimonious circumstances. The main reason was the perception of some pacifists in the south-east that Gwynfor, along with his father-in-law, Dan Thomas, regarded Welsh Pacifists as an extension of Plaid Cymru. The PPU in London agreed and the Union's development secretary, Donald Port, went so far as to inform Gwynfor of his suspicions that several non-Welsh-speaking members in the south-east had lost faith in the Welsh Pacifists' ability to represent them fairly.[205] In further letters, Port called on Gwynfor to provide him with a full account of the movement's activities 'both in connection with the Nationalist Party and its ordinary propaganda work',[206] suggesting to him that it would be a good idea to have a secretary 'who is not very preoccupied with Nationalism'.[207] By the spring of 1945, Gwynfor had had enough of the anti-Welsh bias of both the PPU in London and the pacifists in the south-east and he resigned as secretary. The movement's President, George M Ll Davies, was left feeling 'like a pelican in the wilderness', deprived of the partner who had kept 'the scribes and Pharisees in harmony'. Davies's only comfort was that he and Gwynfor had achieved the 'feat' of holding such a warring band of peace campaigners together for so long in trying times. [208]

It was a messy end to Gwynfor's work with the Pacifists, but his position was far from unique. As peace became ever more likely, similar pacifist groups in England were breaking up in the same way.[209] The discovery of the concentration camps at Auschwitz and Belsen hastened the process, undermining some enthusiasts' pacifism completely; but Gwynfor's resignation enabled him to work full-time for Plaid Cymru. At the turn of the year, he chaired Plaid Cymru's Executive for the first time 'in Mr Abi Williams's unavoidable absence'.[210] J E Jones thought Gwynfor had chaired the meeting 'most effectively and successfully' but, from then on, his sights were firmly set on the Merioneth seat.[211] At the beginning of January, he was formally adopted as the party's candidate in a euphoric meeting that sought to present Gwynfor to the county as the new heir to its radical tradition.

It was Gwynfor, one of his most fervent supporters claimed, who would wear the mantle of such nineteenth-century greats as Ieuan Gwynedd, R J Derfel and Michael D Jones. In the same vein, the now veteran D J Williams argued that voting for Plaid Cymru was not that bold a step. 'There was room in Plaid Cymru,' he said, 'for Socialists, Conservatives and Liberals – if they were ready to put Wales first.'[212]

Gwynfor echoed these sentiments in a conscious effort to dispel the idea that Plaid Cymru was a party of overly-radical hotheads. In Merioneth, it meant portraying himself as the natural heir to the Liberal crown. In talks to local groups he made frequent reference to local heroes, referring to Michael D Jones, R J Derfel and, of course, the Liberal MP Tom Ellis.[213] This propaganda had the desired effect. Within weeks of the adoption meeting, the Dolgellau weekly, *Y Dydd*, was drawing direct comparisons between Gwynfor and Tom Ellis: both had been educated in the University of Wales, before going on to Oxford; one had been the son of a farmer and the other was himself a farmer. 'Two young men with gentle and likeable natures, yet tough with it'.[214] Essentially, Gwynfor was merely serving up diluted nationalism for consumption in Liberal Welsh-speaking Wales; but many found it palatable.

This new credibility was not confined to Merioneth. Increasingly, political and social commentators were coming to realize that Plaid Cymru's economic plans, especially the TVA scheme, were workable. This won praise from three well-regarded experts: Julian Huxley, David Lilienthal (an acknowledged specialist on similar ventures), and Professor C H Reilly.[215] Electorally too, Plaid Cymru gained very encouraging support in two by-elections that spring. In the first, for Caernarfon Boroughs, Plaid Cymru portrayed itself as far more accommodating, leading the *Western Mail* to accuse its candidate, J E Daniel, of offering 'saccharine pills' and 'soothing syrup' to the electorate.[216] He eventually gained 25 per cent of the vote; three weeks later, Wynne Samuel won 16.2 per cent of the vote in Neath. These were excellent results, and confirmed the prevailing view within Plaid Cymru that the party's salvation lay in constitutional political activity. To this extent, Saunders Lewis gave the constitutional wing of the party his considerable moral support when he remarked that:

> ... the presence of just one independent Welsh nationalist member in the House of Commons would render the Welsh Parliamentary Party more Welsh, more robust, more brave, more eager than it has been for half a century.[217]

When the SNP won the Motherwell by-election, Plaid Cymru's leadership had every reason to hope that a hammering at the polls was not a foregone conclusion.

A fortnight after the Motherwell result, on 8 May, the war in Europe was over, but it seems that Plaid Cymru issued no statement whatsoever to mark VE Day. Across Britain, there were rapturous scenes – so much so that the pubs were allowed to stay open until midnight. But as Wales celebrated its survival and the heroic part it had played in 'the people's war', the nationalists were silent. However, Plaid Cymru's hopes were undiminished by this outpouring of pride in all things British. Indeed, when 5 July was named as Election Day, it could be said that some Plaid members' expectations were pretty much what they had been before VE Day. In Merioneth, hopes were, if not absurdly high then at least high enough for some in the party to suggest that they could win the seat. Gwynfor's ambition was far more realistic – to hold on to his deposit. Even so, as Gwynfor went canvassing (which he disliked), he soon learned it was possible to win hearts and minds by couching nationalism in less strident terms. After years of hearing about Saunders Lewis, the Papist extremist, this was a new experience for many electors. In Barmouth, for instance, Gwynfor made an unexpectedly favourable impression on the town's traders. More remarkable still was the response in Trawsfynydd where Gwynfor held an open-air meeting at half past eleven one night near the memorial to the soldier-poet Hedd Wyn. The scene reminded one rank-and-file party member in the county, Wmffra James, 'of the prophet Elias'. The party, it seemed, was becoming acceptable:

> We are now respectable people and have a status in the county's political life. The days of the leg-pulling and patronising and the Cinderella-calling are over and people are at last thinking that we have some brains.[218]

With Marion Eames and Elwyn Roberts – the former famed for her organizational skills and the latter for his proverbial toughness as an agent – to escort him around the constituency, the Plaid Cymru candidate was making a favourable impression. During the month-long campaign, Gwynfor addressed 120 meetings and filled village halls to overflowing in places like Llanfrothen and Croesor. But the campaign had its less inspiring moments too. In a Labour area like Blaenau Ffestiniog, there was open hostility to Plaid Cymru in general and to Gwynfor, the 'southern conchie', in particular.[219] In Blaenau, in broad daylight, he was threatened by a woman who ran after him wielding an axe.[220] The official Labour reaction was a little less frantic, but the party made a determined effort to undermine him nonetheless. D J Thomas, chair of the Labour committee in the county, claimed that Gwynfor had learned his politics from Ambrose Bebb – a 'fact' that made him a Fascist. He was also accused of Popery. Was it not the case, D J Thomas asked, that there was an astonishing similarity between the *Catholic Herald* and Saunders Lewis's current affairs column, '*Cwrs y Byd*', in *Y Faner*? But the most damning accusation was one of racism and the claim that Plaid Cymru was guilty of stirring up hatred in the name of patriotism: 'compare Hitler and the Jews in Germany. Remember that patriotism on its own is often a refuge for the insane and the angry'.[221]

On 5 July 1945, Wales went to the polls for the first time in a decade, but after the thrill of the campaign the vote itself was a personal disappointment for Gwynfor. He found, as he travelled around Merioneth, that people displayed less warmth towards him than they had in the public meetings. Polling day was followed by three weeks of speculation, while the ballot boxes remained sealed to allow time to count the votes of servicemen overseas. Gwynfor returned home to Wernellyn exhausted. The excitement of the campaign made it difficult 'to regain peace of mind'.[222] He found some respite with the hay harvest while all the parties waited to learn of their fate. The only information available was a series of opinion polls in the *News Chronicle* predicting a landslide win for Clement Attlee. Despite this, no one could quite believe the huge Labour majority the polls predicted. On 26 July, Gallup's forecast was proved correct – Labour had won a massive majority. Wales had a new hero instead of Lloyd George: Aneurin Bevan.[223]

In 1945, Labour could claim with conviction that it was the party of the people of Wales; it had won 58 per cent of the vote and 25 seats, and its hold over the country seemed unshakeable. Even so, Plaid Cymru had done surprisingly well in the seven seats where it had fielded candidates, and had made a respectable showing in such unlikely areas as Rhondda East and Ogmore. But Gwynfor was disappointed in his own result. Even though he had gained 2,448 votes – 10 per cent of the total – he was bottom of the poll in Merioneth, where the Liberal, Emrys Roberts, had just scraped home against Labour. Gwynfor believed that he, as well as Ambrose Bebb and J E Daniel (who had contested the two Caernarfon constituencies), had been 'squeezed out' in the contest between Labour and the

Liberals. This outcome in Welsh-speaking constituencies was 'the heaviest blow' because it revealed how suspicious the Welsh still were of nationalism. He took comfort, however, in the general decline in the Liberal vote, believing that Plaid Cymru, as heir to the Welsh radical tradition, would be the beneficiary.[224] His instinct in this respect would be the foundation of his electoral strategy until the 1970s.

Given the trials of war and the general loathing of both pacifism and nationalism, it is astonishing that Plaid Cymru was relatively unscathed. For six years, the vast majority of people in Wales had longed for the day when Hitler would be totally destroyed by the British war machine. Not so Plaid Cymru. Gwynfor's pacifist nationalist stance was undoubtedly principled, but he spoke only for an unpopular minority. Popular opinion held that Fascism should be defeated by the only possible means, war. In the decades to come Plaid Cymru would pay a high price for its failure to understand what the people of Wales were talking about in the pubs and praying for in the chapels. It would pay just as high a price for its ambiguity over who should win the war: Britain or Germany. Gwynfor's contribution during the war can only be assessed by stating this unpalatable truth, too long ignored by nationalists.

The other side of the coin, of course, is that the party's stand would not have been so clear cut and audible were it not for Gwynfor's tremendous commitment. For Plaid Cymru, keeping the message alive at all counted as a success. Neither is it an exaggeration to claim that the party could have disappeared altogether had Gwynfor not decided to 'rescue' Abi Williams as President between 1943 and 1945. The party benefited too from his insistence that it should operate as a political party using a language the people of Wales would understand. That he managed all this while continuing to work for the New Wales Union and the Welsh Pacifists makes his achievement all the more exceptional. Had Gwynfor Evans retired from Plaid Cymru at that very moment, aged 33, his place in the nationalist pantheon would have been secure. But the story had really only just begun. August 1945 saw the start of the longest and stormiest chapter: the Presidency of Plaid Cymru.

Chapter 4

STAND YOUR GROUND 1945–51

GWYNFOR FELT HE WAS FACING A NEW DAWN when he assumed the Presidency of Plaid Cymru on 6 August 1945. There was certainly a challenge ahead of him on that warm day in Llangollen, but he could be confident at least that everyone in his own party wanted him to succeed. Indeed, the sense that this was a fresh start was deeply and generally felt. The old guard greeted him with cheers and applause and Saunders Lewis advised them to vote for the new prospective President.[1] But this mood was not confined to senior party members – the rank and file found themselves attracted by Gwynfor's qualities too. For one thing, he was young and handsome – his commanding poise and wavy hair made women swoon.[2] This was not an insignificant matter; in the years to come, he would profit enormously from the fact that so many female party members were willing to fight to the last for their own personal matinée idol. This nationalist Clark Gable had the added advantage of being financially self-sufficient – meaning that he could devote himself wholeheartedly to the cause. His religious background counted in his favour as well. As a prominent Congregationalist, there would be less anti-Catholic and anti-nationalist 'Home Rule is Rome Rule' sniping. If anything, it was a case of 'Llanbrynmair Rule'. Respectable Congregationalists such as Gwynfor were now about to be in the ascendancy. D J Williams said it all when he wrote that this was 'the best [Summer School] ever for hope and promise' with '250 people present, most of them young'.[3]

Because the press considered Plaid Cymru irrelevant, the event was barely mentioned in the papers and there was only the odd stray reference to record the historic event for the party. For Gwynfor, on the other hand, it was the fulfilment of a mission; several decades after his election, he claimed he had been called to lead Plaid Cymru and that he felt 'like a minister' facing a new flock on that first day.[4] Having shadowed Abi Williams for so long, he could now lead Plaid Cymru openly, without causing his family or his community too much offence. Even so, despite feeling the post was his vocation, Gwynfor was not a fire-and-brimstone preacher: there were no great *ex cathedra* pronouncements, no laying down the law and, certainly, none of Saunders Lewis's histrionics. But the restraint was significant because Gwynfor's Presidency marked the end of the artist-as-politician within Plaid Cymru. From now on, the party would be led by respectable, semi-professional career politicians in Gwynfor's mould. For the time being, however, Gwynfor kept the change in leadership style a secret, and it was only in his private correspondence with J E Jones, Pennar Davies and D J and Noëlle Davies that he gave any indication of how he intended to attract sceptical voters into the Plaid Cymru fold.

On some things his mind was already made up. For one, following Labour's sweeping victory, he judged that it would be a mistake to 'make too obvious any hostility' towards it. Rather, he concluded that Plaid Cymru would do well to act as a pressure group and urge the new government to carry out 'a substantial programme for Wales'. The programme, he hoped, would include a Development Council for Wales and a Wales Radio Corporation within the next few years.[5] He was aware that it would be a long time before the Welsh people would begin to regard Labour with anything approaching objectivity, but was quietly confident the day would come when the enthusiasm waned and the electorate considered Labour 'more coolly and with a new poise'.[6] It was then, when the disillusionment with Labour had begun, that Plaid Cymru would seize the day.

The other fissure to exploit was the Liberal Party. Since the General Election, Gwynfor, in common with other Plaid Cymru intellectuals, was strongly of the opinion that the Welsh Liberal tradition was dying and that the party's strongholds in the west were there for the taking. His task now, to quote Saunders Lewis, was to attract to the nationalist cause those Welsh people raised on the Liberal tradition of Mabon, Tom Ellis and Llywelyn Williams.[7] Along with this, there was a feeling of confidence throughout Plaid Cymru that Britain's days as an imperial power were numbered. Gwynfor believed too that the dawn of the Nuclear Age in Hiroshima and Nagasaki that summer made arguing the nationalist case for a small country like Wales easier still. From now on, he concluded, no country could be safe from the bomb and its awful consequences.[8] Gwynfor was also an optimistic politician – over-optimistic at the outset, in fact – who was confident that Wales was more likely to give Plaid Cymru a fair hearing in 1945 than it had been in 1939. Now, he told Pennar Davies, the main difficulty was not 'complete disagreement' with Plaid Cymru as much as 'a failure to put Wales first'.[9] To gain the upper hand, he demanded major structural changes to Plaid Cymru that summer: the priorities were to move the head office to Cardiff, build an effective research department, and appoint Elwyn Roberts as Treasurer to clear the party's debts. Following this route map, Gwynfor set about making Plaid Cymru a real political party.

Gwynfor was not the only politician with firm ideas on how Wales could be re-born after the war. By October 1945, Attlee had begun to realize several of the promises made under Churchill's wartime coalition. South Wales was designated a development area and a series of industrial estates opened, bringing employment and real hope to deprived communities.[10] The work continued, too, to provide national insurance for all and, eventually, to create institutions such as the National Health Service and the National Coal Board. The people of Wales soon became attached to them, presenting Plaid Cymru with a new if not insurmountable challenge. From then on, it proved difficult, sometimes impossible, for the party to portray Labour as indifferent to the Welsh working class. The party needed to develop its own positive policies, and Gwynfor set about the task with the full backing of Saunders Lewis and others. As autumn approached, he argued for the merits of the TVA in an effort to give a Welsh dimension to Labour collectivism.[11] Similarly, Gwynfor made the need for a Welsh Coal Board and Radio Corporation central to the re-born party's programme.

But for all the talk – by both Labour and Plaid Cymru – of a 'New Age' in 1945, Wales found itself to some extent in a no-man's-land: in a period of peace overshadowed by preparations for the coming cold war. Curiously, then, Gwynfor's first five years as President were largely driven by militarism, as the realization dawned that life under Labour was not a paradise on earth and that the War Office would tighten its grip before it let go. Gwynfor had not given much attention to the effects of this conditional peace, but as soon as J E Jones received 'highly confidential' information in November 1945 of a plan to occupy 7,000 acres in Merioneth for military purposes, the army's land use became one of the party's main campaigns.[12] In time, this would become the campaign that demanded the lion's share of Plaid Cymru's attention. It did not get off to a good start. Gwynfor's suggestion of forming a defence committee to fight for the land in Trawsfynydd was rejected by local businessmen who were delighted with the announcement. After all, following the privations of war, this was a chance for them to make some money. But Gwynfor and some of the faithful in the New Wales Union persisted and succeeded in persuading some local landowners that their land was worth the struggle.[13] The campaign was favourably received and, by the beginning of 1946, some semblance of a pattern had developed, as the government seized more land and conscription continued. The prominence of these two topics – Welsh land and young Welsh men – was a golden opportunity for the nationalist cause, leading Gwynfor and J E Jones to the conclusion that the party was better placed to lead the fight than the New Wales Union.[14] This (by and large) is what happened, but the decision raised a thorny question: how could the party exercise any influence?

One answer was provided by the local elections in early 1946. Since the party had cleared its debts after the General Election, and had embarked on a membership drive from its new headquarters at 8 Queen Street in Cardiff, it found itself in a reasonably strong position. Gwynfor followed Saunders Lewis's advice and insisted that the party should fight elections on a far wider scale. Gwynfor judged that the poll – the first local elections since 1937 – would force people to become acquainted with nationalists.[15] Members set up a fund to support 'a Welsh freedom movement' and, as the elections drew closer, reports came in that young men returning from the forces were expressing interest in the party.[16] This confidence was increased by 'encouraging' stories that 'scores' of Plaid members would be standing, although it remained unclear quite how many would be doing so under the party banner. Nevertheless, the March elections were promising in many areas. At home, Gwynfor contested the Llangadog and Llansadwrn seat, and came within one vote of being elected.[17] At the time, it felt like a moral victory. Gwynfor was carried shoulder-high through Llangadog, before addressing a large crowd on the village square until well after midnight.[18] The result, central to the Gwynfor mythology, is crucial to understanding how he won hearts and minds in the county. It was also the beginning of a pattern, as the Labour honeymoon began to fade.

The elections were followed by other events that worked in Gwynfor's favour. The situation in the south Wales coalfields worsened, and unemployment became an issue once again. By Easter severe economic hardship had begun to bite in some parts of the valleys, forcing many workers to leave Wales for England as the wait for new peacetime factories became intolerable.[19] Wales was also outraged at Attlee's less than enthusiastic response to Welsh demands and the rumour that Wales was unlikely to have its own Secretary of State. There was confirmation that a 'central road' (between north and south Wales) would not proceed, undermining yet further the authority of '*Llais Llafur*' (Labour Voice), the Welsh-speaking wing of the party.[20] In the Llŷn peninsula, Billy Butlin received planning permission for his holiday camp. As the months passed, Gwynfor's image as the voice of moderate Welsh Wales grew. He crowned the first half of the year with a bravura performance before Welsh MPs, presenting a memorandum calling for an independent Radio Corporation for Wales. He did so in the name of the New Wales Union, but the striking fact was that other bodies including the National Eisteddfod, the Urdd and the National Farmers' Union[21] were beginning to echo the call for the BBC to relinquish its hold.

His success, however, gave rise to minor doubts about Plaid Cymru's methods. Although Saunders Lewis, back in August 1945, had called for the party to adopt practical politics, he still believed that unconstitutional methods had their place. He was cruelly disappointed, therefore, when Plaid Cymru decided not to break the law to prevent the Butlins development. J E Jones went so far as to place the matter before the party Executive, but it was clear that Gwynfor was not a supporter.[22] It was this decision, in all likelihood, that prompted Lewis to write to D J Williams, voicing his hope that: 'we shall see Gwynfor in Wormwood Scrubs one day – that's the one thing he needs to make him into a powerful leader. There is too little of the spirit of 1936 in Plaid Cymru in 1946, or Butlin's triumph would have been impossible'.[23] But for Saunders Lewis, the defining issue was compulsory conscription, and in *Y Faner*, he complained (having first praised Gwynfor's 'staunch and consistent perseverance') that young people needed to prepare themselves 'for tougher trials than facing lively meetings'.[24]

However, it would be wrong to assume that Plaid Cymru ignored conscription. Throughout April and May, there was evidently discussion within the party on the issue and the best way of opposing it. Consideration was given to an organized campaign of non-registration, but nothing came of the idea because of deep divisions over tactics and the appropriateness of defying the law. Typical were the misgivings of the young barrister Dewi Watkin Powell – the most decisive influence of all on Gwynfor's Presidency, perhaps – who warned the leadership openly that breaking the law would be a waste of time. He was also convinced that Plaid Cymru should resist the temptation 'to chase hares which have landed the Party in great unpopularity and which have left the movement, after 21 years' existence, with no MP to represent its views'.[25]

Gwynfor's instinct at this stage in his career was to do what was pragmatically possible, and although he sided with Watkin Powell, it was clear he was prepared to consider breaking the law if it could be shown it would not damage the party's parliamentary ambitions. On the subject of a Radio Corporation for Wales, for example, Gwynfor, in January 1946, expressed his willingness to lead a campaign of non-payment of licences, and the only obstacle preventing the move was a shortage of party members willing to go to court.[26] Indeed, it was only after Tryweryn that Gwynfor truly developed what could be described as a 'parliamentary' mentality, or an obsession with exclusively constitutional activity. This pragmatism is probably most evident in his private efforts to save Breton nationalists from persecution in France.

In early 1946, Plaid Cymru heard, mainly through Geraint Dyfnallt Owen and Dewi Watkin Powell, that a number of Breton nationalists were suffering ill treatment arising directly from the unwise decision of a minority to support the Germans during the war.[27] Following the defeat of the Nazis, the French government now had sufficient justification to seek to destroy Breton nationalism altogether. Plaid Cymru came out in support of the Bretons – without bothering to ask whether those it supported were Nazi sympathizers or not. Gwynfor realized it was a risky strategy, but said in retrospect 'we were pleased to face the danger'.[28]

This secret venture was co-ordinated by a sub-committee within Plaid Cymru comprising Delwyn Phillips, D J and Noëlle Davies, Dewi Watkin Powell and Gwynfor himself. The work began during the Summer School of 1946. However, covertly taking care of the refugees' needs was a tall order; the organizers needed a list of safe houses for them, arrangements to find them work, a fund to support them and regional agents – Dewi Watkin Powell in Cardiff and Delwyn Phillips in Birmingham. The model they adopted was that of *Clann na Saoirse* (The Celtic Freedom Union), and by October 1946, a network had been established that allowed Bretons to flee France for Wales.[29] The most popular route was for the Bretons to make for Paris, obtain false papers there, and catch the train to London, before heading to Abergavenny or Llangadog. The final destination for most of them was Ireland, a safe haven where hardly any questions were asked. During 1946, it is clear that many such nationalists spent at least one night at Wernellyn. More often than not, Gwynfor and Rhiannon did not know who they were or why exactly they were so keen to flee their homes; the fact that they were travelling under assumed names and that several spoke no English added to the confusion and sense of strain. The most famous of those who experienced Gwynfor's hospitality was Yann Fouéré – one of the architects of the Breton language movement.[30] He lived, under the name of Dr Moger, at Wernellyn for nearly ten months from October 1946 with his wife Marie Madeleine and their three children. Fouéré, like Gwynfor, was a committed pacifist and nationalist, and there is no evidence at all that he had sided with the Germans. Whether any members of Plaid Cymru offered sanctuary to Nazi collaborators is a moot point, but the fairest conclusion is that this probably did happen, especially given the reluctance of the hosts to ask for details.

Every effort was made to prevent this from becoming public knowledge and certainly most Plaid Cymru members had no idea what was happening at the end of 1946. Noëlle Davies, for example, pleaded with Gwynfor not to let the Bretons campaign in the Aberdare by-election in 1946 and warned him that revealing their presence would be 'disastrous, not only for the two concerned, but for all those now here and to come'.[31] But by mid-1947, Bretons like Fouéré who were living in Wales found their situation eased by changes in the international climate. They discovered that they could live relatively openly and Fouéré, for example, would attend Providence chapel in Llangadog with Gwynfor on Sundays. The French Embassy in London was well aware of what was happening, and the more it heard of the refugees' boldness, the angrier it grew with the unwillingness of the British authorities to arrest them. According to one civil servant in the British Foreign Office, Roche, the French chief counsellor in London, had told him he had seen a map where Brittany, Ireland and Wales had been shaded in the same colour:

> Monsieur Roche went on to say that this map looked to the French Embassy suspiciously like some of the maps put out before the war by the German Geopolitik experts. He then went on to hint that possibly behind this movement for Breton autonomy we might see some sinister Nazi plot.[32]

The Foreign Office rejected the suggestion out of hand and decided there were no grounds for pursuing Fouéré and the rest. In the words of the civil servant in charge:

> I see however no reason whatsoever for taking this question seriously. Neither the Breton Autonomist Movement nor the Welsh Nationalist Movement are in the least worthy of serious consideration and the whole thing is, I think, a rather bizarre form of Celtic nonsense.[33]

Fouéré was left in peace until 1948 when Gwynfor and some Welsh MPs had to intervene on his behalf once more to ensure that he was not returned to France.

The Breton episode, diverting though it was, was in truth an extended footnote to Gwynfor's efforts to develop his party into a political force. At the Ogmore by-election in June 1946, despite Labour attempts to denigrate the nationalists with posters claiming 'Welsh Nationalism Means Fascism', Plaid Cymru did surprisingly well.[34] The colourful Trefor Morgan succeeded in doubling his party's vote even though they had virtually no presence in the constituency. His achievement was all the more remarkable when one considers that Gwynfor had attempted to have Trefor Morgan's candidacy revoked because he considered him unreliable. Plaid Cymru's 29 per cent of the vote in a constituency where its prospects were thought to be negligible prompted observers and politicians from other parties to take it more seriously. There is evidence that the Liberals suggested an informal agreement with Plaid Cymru not to fight one another.[35] This tentative offer was refused outright by the Plaid Cymru leadership, but the political flirting was proof of what the *Observer* had noticed that summer: an appetite in Wales and in Scotland alike for 'a less extreme nationalism'.[36]

Attlee's government served to strengthen this perception, and as the summer progressed, the disaffection deepened in Wales with 'London Decisions'. Shortly before the National Eisteddfod in Mountain Ash, Attlee dropped his 'bombshell', announcing that there would be no Secretary of State for Wales.[37] It was made in the most peremptory fashion (by letter) and in defiance of the majority of Welsh MPs and councils. This diplomatic gaffe prompted *Y Cymro* to launch a campaign calling for the righting of this wrong shown to 'a Rejected Nation', providing a boost to Plaid Cymru (which, anyway, was not in favour of a Secretaryship).[38] For Gwynfor, there was no turning back and he spent the rest of that sodden summer harping on the same theme, that the Labour Party could never be made into a

Welsh party. Labour's disregard of Wales's administrative needs provided Plaid Cymru with ammunition for its argument that the only credible solution was self-government. This was again reflected in the press. 'Celt' (the veteran journalist E Morgan Humphreys) was an enthusiast for self-government and, as summer gave way to autumn,[39] some Fleet Street writers began to whisper about the possibility of Plaid Cymru capturing a seat in the event of another by-election.[40] The predictions were partly realized in December 1946 when Plaid Cymru's outstanding young candidate, Wynne Samuel, took 20 per cent of the vote at the Aberdare by-election. Gwynfor had canvassed, witnessing 'large meetings full to overflowing' and considerable sympathy for the party.[41]

However promising things might have been for Plaid Cymru in the valleys, they were arguably even better in rural Wales. That autumn, the harvest failed and it became increasingly obvious that Western Command was in no mood to loosen its grip on the land it controlled. In October 1946, the inhabitants of the Preseli region in north Pembrokeshire were outraged by the War Office's decision to seize 16,000 acres. It marked a severe blow to a Welsh-speaking area, but worse was to come. Gwynfor learned that there was also a plan afoot to occupy 5,000 acres in the Wye Valley – as part of a wider scheme to take over 50,000 acres across Carmarthenshire and Breconshire. He was horrified at the news, writing privately to J E Jones that 'the Welsh will have no land left – they will be like the Jews, scattered and lost in their own country'.[42] Gwynfor's fears about a Welsh diaspora were genuine enough, but he was well aware at the same time that the situation offered a political opportunity. He knew that a campaign against the War Office would be attractive – especially so in the Welsh-speaking strongholds of the west which he was so eager to win. In November 1946, therefore, he concluded that Plaid Cymru should create 'as much trouble as we can' on the land question. Even with this strategy in place, Gwynfor could not have dreamt in his darkest moments that the War Office's demands would be so voracious.[43]

As the year drew to a close there was significant news: shortly before Christmas, Gwynfor was nominated to be a member of the BBC's Consultative Committee in Wales. The body had no real power but membership was proof that Gwynfor was gradually becoming a major figure in Wales. It was important, but a dramatic point came a few days later on the eve of 1947, when the War Office confirmed that it was to occupy half a million acres in Wales. The revelation would transform Plaid Cymru's political priorities for the next three years.[44] In its attempt to explain the decision the War Office employed the 'moral' argument that thousands of young men had been killed in the Second World War because of the inadequate training they had received.[45] No doubt there was some truth in the claim. Nevertheless, from then on many Welsh people believed (with the exception of some within the Labour Party) that Wales was being asked to shoulder more than its fair share of the burden. Welsh MPs were stunned by the figure, and Saunders Lewis claimed apocalyptically that 'the next three years, the final three years of the first half of the twentieth century, will decide the fate of the Welsh language'.[46] In the political sphere, there was every expectation of a fierce fight. As *Yr Herald Cymraeg* put it: 'It is highly likely that the battle for Welsh land will be won or lost early in the new year'.[47] Similar pronouncements, coupled with a harsh economic climate, added to Plaid Cymru's determination that the party's duty in the year ahead was to redouble its efforts to lead the resistance to land claims and conscription.[48]

The first direct consequence was the protest at Llyn y Fan in the Carmarthenshire uplands on Saturday 11 January 1947. Although the War Office had stated on the previous day that Llyn y Fan would not be turned into a firing range, this was irrelevant by the time the protesters gathered. Similarly ignored was the supporting statement that the army would be claiming only 125,000 acres throughout the whole of Wales. Gwynfor and the party's leaders were adamant that the protest should continue because of the uncertainty that was felt across rural Wales. In the driving rain, 400 Plaid Cymru members climbed the treacherous slopes, 'like some ghostly column from Arthurian legend' according to the *Western Mail*, before reaching the banks of the lake.[49] They began by singing the National Anthem, followed by a patriotic hymn, '*Cofia'n Gwlad Benllywydd Tirion*', and ending with a prayer. But the undoubted highlight for the sodden pilgrims was hearing Gwynfor deliver a speech that would become part of his mythology. In it, he attacked Western Command for daring to set its sights on the land of Wales and for sowing the seeds of uncertainty in so many communities. He also dismissed as laughable the announcement that the original figure of 500,000 acres had been reduced to a quarter. The fact was, he said, that the War Office was as hungry for land as ever. It was a brief protest, but a successful one, and it was seen as a measure of Plaid Cymru's willingness to make land and language the central issues in its campaigns for the years to come. *Y Cymro*'s reporter had no doubts:

this, he wrote, was 'the most romantic, most uncomfortable, most colourful and shortest protest meeting ever held'.[50] To crown it all, Keidrych Rhys, editor of *Wales* and something of a literary *impresario*, even managed to include an account of the event in *Picture Post* – a considerable scoop for a party which found it difficult to attract any sort of attention at all.[51]

After the protest, Gwynfor was confident that Plaid Cymru had been more successful in a single day than it had been in years. First, press interest in the story remained high – so much so that *Y Cymro*, unlike *Y Faner*, no natural ally of Plaid Cymru, devoted a special issue to the land question. In the Commons, Welsh MPs also began to show a growing interest in the issue,[52] but the most important aspect was that triumphs like these underlined the extent to which Gwynfor had established himself as President. In a profile of Saunders Lewis that year, *Wales* could only express amazement at the quiet revolution that had happened within Plaid Cymru since the king had left the throne:

> It no longer scorns the idea of a Welsh Nationalist taking his seat at Westminster. It has at last abandoned the fratricidal notion that a Welshman who does not speak Welsh is 'untouchable'; its headquarters have been moved from Caernarvon to Cardiff and its campaign to convert the industrial south now rests on something more than a belief that the industrial south is a moral swamp which the wrath of God should long have delivered over to a sheep-run. It has begun to infiltrate into the field of local government.[53]

But Gwynfor did not rest on his laurels. Within a week of Llyn y Fan, he opened a second front in the assault on the military presence in Welsh life. He wrote to J E Jones to inform him that Plaid Cymru should oppose the Conscription Bill then going through Parliament. 'This,' he said, 'is our main task in these coming months.'[54] His tactic was to couple the campaigns against conscription and occupation with a wider opposition to power politics. It was a campaign, he hoped, that would force the Welsh to think of themselves as Welsh rather than English.[55] By the end of 1947, Gwynfor had developed his theme, combining it with Celticism as a means of defeating colonialism.[56] This campaign was yet to come, but his enthusiasm for the land issue led to new feats of endurance. At the end of January, he stayed up all night in Cardiff to finish his anti-militarist pamphlet, *Havoc in Wales*, before setting off for Llangadog at 6.30 the following morning.[57]

These efforts were not wasted. They culminated in a huge conference organized by the New Wales Union in Llandrindod in March 1947 to draw attention to land acquistion. In the same month, the army had announced it would not use land near Harlech and Preseli for training purposes. Nevertheless, as the military machine drew in its horns and as Plaid Cymru's profile rose, there was a price to pay. Some of the most consciously Welsh of the Labour MPs felt that Plaid Cymru was making political capital out of the situation, and the Caernarfon MP, Goronwy Roberts, went so far as to accuse 'nationalist Jesuits' of poking their 'long fingers' into 'non-party institutions'.[58] It was a sign of Labour's ill will towards Plaid Cymru that its members were prevented from attending the Llandrindod conference – one of the first national conferences to be held in Wales 'in generations'.[59] Other influential figures, like John Aelod Jones (the pseudonym of eminent journalist, John Roberts Williams), were critical of Gwynfor for complicating the debate by combining land and conscription because 'saving the peace' was of concern to the whole of Britain'.[60] But the most telling criticism came from within the party, from a faction who believed that it was Plaid Cymru's duty to break the law in order to keep the army at bay. Kate Roberts, for instance, complained that '... the military should be prevented from taking over farms through passive resistance... The time for talk is over. There has been plenty of talk in Wales for years but nothing has been done apart from burning down the Bombing School'.[61] Kate Roberts expressed her willingness to act to protect the Vale of Clwyd and she wasn't the only one to use such language. On the Plaid Cymru Executive, radicals like Wynne Samuel and Ithel Davies spoke of sending groups into the threatened areas 'to take action'.[62] Despite the intensity of the protests, Gwynfor demurred. As a first step he wanted to see defence committees established in the areas under threat.

The press found it hard to understand this 'respectability' too, believing that Plaid Cymru's rhetoric on conscription and land was vacuous idealism. The *Liverpool Daily Post* commented that everyone was expecting a campaign of civil disobedience from 'the enigmatic Nationalists... something swift and novel in the way of nuisance tactics' but noted that all that had happened was the painting of a few slogans.[63] Saunders Lewis rubbed salt into the wounds when he stressed the gap between rhetoric and reality in Gwynfor's politics. Plaid Cymru, he said, 'must choose before long between resolve and resolutions'.[64] For the time being, however, Gwynfor maintained that a 'Gandhi-like' campaign as proposed by Saunders Lewis was impossible. He continued to pursue the constitutional path

– and there were plenty of causes to occupy him.

Over the summer, fears spread of a winter food shortage, the government decided to refuse Wales an Electricity Board, and, in July, it was revealed that Wales was the worst unemployment blackspot in Britain. But for Plaid Cymru, Western Command's activities in rural Wales were still the hot topic. It dominated the annual conference, where influential figures like D J Williams and Wynne Samuel called for 'practical action'.[65] As the economy slumped that autumn, the people of Tregaron voiced concerns over the intention to occupy 28,000 acres of the surrounding land. Along with local farmers and the New Wales Union, Plaid Cymru led the protests against turning Tregaron into a garrison town. The party organized a march with posters announcing 'Butter not Guns'.[66] There were similar protests from the students at Aberystwyth and the pupils at Tregaron County School. Gwynfor called on the farmers not to abandon their homes and as the civil servant responsible for the scheme remarked, the campaign was 'a storm of protest, largely inspired by the Welsh Nationalist Party'.[67] The battle was finally won in the summer of 1948 and, increasingly, Plaid Cymru's enemies, like the *Western Mail*, argued that the War Office had presented 'a heaven-sent chance for the pacifists among the Welsh Nationalists to inveigh against the military hand desecrating the noble mountains and lovely vales of Gwalia'.[68]

With the political winds blowing in Plaid Cymru's favour, Gwynfor attempted to persuade as many young men as possible to break the law and oppose conscription through civil disobedience. It is difficult to be certain why Gwynfor was so ready to launch a law-breaking campaign against conscription. After all, as has been seen already, it was Gwynfor who had been chiefly responsible for reining in those radicals who had argued for unconstitutional methods to prevent the occupation of land by the military. The most likely explanation for the tactical switch was Plaid Cymru's attitude to unlawful protest of any kind. D J Williams mentions in his diary the thrill he felt when he heard of Gwynfor's intention to establish the 'Keir Hardie Society' – at arm's length from Plaid Cymru – which would break the law in order to frustrate conscription. This was the society, he hoped, that would make Gwynfor into 'a proper leader' in Saunders Lewis's eyes.[69] At Gwynfor's request, a plan was drawn up which aimed at widespread unlawful action. It was hoped that it would attract at least a hundred Plaid Cymru members, as well as pacifists and religious leaders, to picket registration centres and face any punishment arising. Had the plan been enacted, then other methods such as 'painting slogans and sitting in the middle of the road' would also have been employed to force the authorities, 'at the end of a huge campaign', to prosecute as many Plaid Cymru members as possible.[70] The plan's advantage was that it would allow the party to concentrate on constitutional politics – in the same way that the existence of Cymdeithas yr Iaith Gymraeg (The Welsh Language Society) did in the 'sixties and 'seventies. However, although private talks continued until 1949, nothing came of the scheme because of deep divisions over tactics and the appropriateness of law-breaking. R Tudur Jones, one of Gwynfor's main advisers, doubted there were a hundred party members willing to face prison. Unless this figure were achieved, he feared 'the plan would become a farce'.[71] Gwynfor was disappointed too by the attitude of nationalists in the north,[72] but the fundamental problem was with the response of the Welsh in general. There were those parents, *Y Faner* asserted, who would not see 'much harm in twelve months of military discipline' for eighteen-year-old boys.[73]

It was also the case that many party members themselves saw this policy of merging pacifism, land and language as a hindrance. By 1949 several of these would leave to form the Welsh Republican Movement but, even in 1947, this group – largely ex-servicemen from the south-east – already thought Gwynfor was making a mistake in concentrating so much on the west. One of the first to break ranks and criticise Gwynfor was Cliff Bere, who called for a popular front to break Labour's stranglehold. The goal, he said, was 'to unite the two long-established elements in south-east Wales – patriotism and socialism'.[74] He was supported by 'Hwntw' (Vic Jones) in *Y Faner*. He accused Plaid Cymru of having failed utterly in the south-east and of having ignored the critical situation in Gwent and the 'heartbreakingly ineffectual' branches in the east of Glamorgan.[75] These critics were buoyed up by Ireland's decision to claim the status of a republic in 1947 – a decision which made Plaid Cymru's policy of recognizing the Crown by calling for Dominion Status appear craven to some. Gwilym Prys Davies, the most respected member of the group, declared that he was bored by the lifelessness of publications like the *Welsh Nationalist* and *Y Ddraig Goch* and that it was 'high time' Plaid Cymru preached the nationalism of a republic rather than Dominion Status.[76]

Gwynfor ignored the critics. He knew that any talk of independence would stick in the craw of Welsh-speaking Nonconformist Wales. He gave short shrift, too, to Vic Jones's claim that Plaid Cymru was a club for Welsh-speakers. He refused to acknowledge that Jones's piece for *Y Faner* contained any substance and accused him in private of being a bundle of prejudice and 'self-importance'.[77] He insisted in addition that Cliff Bere's idea of raising a popular front to defeat Labour was 'out of the question'.[78] The price Gwynfor paid for his stance was the formation of the Republicans two years later, but he maintained that his role as leader was to nurture Plaid Cymru after the barren war years. Even the idea of a united front to campaign for a Welsh Parliament – something of a personal obsession by the end of the 'forties – was anathema at the time. When J E Jones suggested in late November 1947 that Plaid Cymru should convene a conference with Labour and the Liberals to discuss the issue, Gwynfor told him that such a move would be likely to 'darken counsel'. He was also fearful that Labour and the Liberals would 'use' such a conference because they were so much stronger than Plaid Cymru. In his mind, he imagined the trade unionist Huw T Edwards betraying an ecumenical offer of the sort 'with a passion'.[79] Meanwhile, Gwynfor restricted his multi-party activities to issuing invitations to other parties to discuss 'the Cultural, Industrial and Economic Freedom of Wales'.[80]

This was largely a publicity stunt, but it did Plaid Cymru no real harm. At the end of 1947, Gwynfor's instinct that his party should continue to pursue the land issue was justified when Western Command announced a plan to claim 10,000 extra acres in Trawsfynydd.[81] Initially, he was of the opinion that any hope of success there was 'weak' given that 70 per cent of the male workforce in the area was employed by the War Office but, despite his doubts, this was too good an opportunity to ignore.[82] After all, the setting was Merioneth, the focus of Plaid Cymru's electoral ambitions. As the New Year dawned, the party's Executive met and confirmed that they would not give an inch in Trawsfynydd. The decision reflected a more general feeling among nationalists that Plaid Cymru should not support elements within the New Wales Union, such as T I Ellis and W J Gruffydd, who argued that a better policy would be to strike a bargain with Western Command.[83] This, during the early months of 1948, had been the public message in innumerable Plaid Cymru meetings. But the new policy gave fresh encouragement to those who thought it was high time for Gwynfor to lead a campaign of civil disobedience on the issue. Wynne Samuel predicted that the time for 'taking practical action was near',[84] and another, younger member, Huw Davies, argued that the age of 'wordy resolutions and futile conferences' would be over if new military bases opened in Wales.[85] Saunders Lewis sounded an even more chilling warning. In a waspish piece for *Y Faner*, he made a point of not expressing his opinion 'on the effectiveness of the steps being taken in Wales to stop this occupation and expulsion'.[86]

Publicly, Gwynfor aligned himself with this militant rhetoric by suggesting that Trawsfynydd might one day see the return of the spirit of the Rebecca Riots. But, two and a half years into his Presidency, it was evident that Gwynfor was in no mood to see the inside of a prison cell.[87] What concerned him more than anything was the danger that a spectacular unlawful protest at the end of the 'forties – like Penyberth over a decade before – would damage Plaid Cymru's credibility as a party that would one day be in a position to win parliamentary seats like Caernarfon and Merioneth. A further complication was money, and also uncertainty about Plaid Cymru's ability to fund costly court cases and support unemployed leaders. By the summer of 1948, for instance, Plaid Cymru's financial position was dire and the party's finance committee warned that 'the collapse of the only organised political movement working for Welsh freedom' was a distinct possibility.[88]

The other factor that explains Gwynfor's reluctance to break the law was his genuine belief that Plaid Cymru – despite financial adversity – was a party that was still growing. A successful dinner held to welcome the Irish President, Eamon de Valera, to Cardiff in October 1948, was irrefutable proof to him that Plaid Cymru, ever since the protest at Llyn y Fan, had made great strides and was beginning to be taken seriously. Part of this shaky confidence was the perception that the Welsh political landscape was changing and that tactically, Plaid Cymru needed now more than ever to act as a constitutional party. The development which had transformed the situation was the decision to establish the Advisory Council for Wales and Monmouthshire in October 1948 – a powerless body of nominees devised by the Leader of the House of Commons, Herbert Morrison, to defeat Welsh devolutionists within the Labour Party. For Plaid Cymru, the existence of the 'Council of Despair' under the chairmanship of the prominent trade unionist, Huw T Edwards, was a terrific opportunity. Coupling the council's probable impotence with Attlee's decision to refuse Wales a Secretary of State, back in the summer of 1946, gave credence to Gwynfor's argument that the Labour leadership hated devolution. He could also claim convincingly that Labour devolutionists – like Jim Griffiths and Goronwy Roberts – had failed lamentably in their struggle to loosen London's grip. But disillusionment with the Wales Council and the anti-Welsh bias of the Labour Party were not the only developments. Following on from the establishment of the Council, the Liberals were forced to re-state their policy on a federal Parliament more clearly than ever. The political dough was also leavened by the decision of the Conservatives – the unionist party par excellence – to create a more Welsh image by promising a Minister for Wales.[89]

By Christmas 1948, Gwynfor was as cheerful as he had been in those thrilling days after the burning of Penyberth. Even the fact that the Republicans were now bold and organized enough to call themselves a 'republican circle' did nothing to dampen his intellectual energy. In his private correspondence with Dr Gwenan Jones, he sensed that Plaid Cymru 'had touched bottom' already and that there were signs it was beginning to rise again. Politically, he felt a remarkable buzz and a golden opportunity for 'a strong movement' to benefit from the imminent disappearance of the Liberal Party, and the Labour Party having 'exhausted its programme and lost its idealism and missionary zeal'. The future of the Welsh language also looked more certain than it had done for years, and he believed the pioneering work in Welsh-medium education and publishing during 1948 was proof of 'a new attitude towards the language, especially among the middle class'. Given these factors, he admitted to Gwenan Jones that he found it hard to see how things could fail to 'take an important turn' during the 'next two or three years'. All that was needed now, on the eve of 1949, was what Saunders Lewis called 'political imagination' – the imagination to turn 'a feeble little movement into a national one'.[90]

The first 'big' idea that Gwynfor tackled in 1949 was a policy for the language. Although the prospects were somewhat brighter, the wider picture was still grim, and his constant theme throughout the 'forties and 'fifties (despite his optimism) was the parlous state of Welsh.[91] Encouraged by Gwynfor, Plaid Cymru's Executive decided in favour of a campaign to seek official status for the language. Gwynfor's rather Machiavellian aim was to have the government 'reject' the campaign in the hope that this would evoke sympathy for Plaid Cymru as the General Election approached.[92] In this respect, he was not disappointed by the popular response in Wales nor the Attlee government's decision to ignore the campaign. On Saint David's Day 1949, the Welsh chapels and societies were invited to support the call, and by the end of March, the party had received positive responses from 600 institutions.[93] The government refused to discuss the matter, and Plaid Cymru's public expression of disappointment disguised an underlying sense of success.

This was important, but its significance was minor compared to Gwynfor's decision in early 1949 to campaign for a Parliament for Wales which then took precedence over everything else. Indeed, it is no exaggeration to say that these months were among the most important in his life. The undoubted inspiration was reading the Israeli President Chaim Weizman's *Trial and Error*. The book, he told Pennar Davies in May 1949, was 'loaded with lessons and inspiration', and the clearest lesson was that the Welsh language could not be protected without a state.[94] For Wales, this meant that securing a Parliament – or even a degree of devolution – was essential. That much was plain; clearer still was the method. In Scotland, the Covenanters had been remarkably successful with their petition; by the end of 1949, as many as half a million Scots had signed it and there were eventually some two million signatories.[95]

These were exciting months, which gave Plaid Cymru's politics a distinctive shape on the threshold of a new decade. As the idea of a Parliament, and a campaign to win it, emerged in Gwynfor's mind, he experienced his first electoral success. On 18 April, he was elected to represent Llangadog on Carmarthenshire Council. Two days before the poll, Gwynfor could hardly believe the 'overwhelming support' he was receiving, and it appears that Thomas Jones – who had won the seat by one vote in 1946 – decided not to stand because of the likely defeat he would suffer.[96] In the event, Gwynfor was elected unopposed, but the victory was just as sweet and significant for all that. At last, for the first time, he had an elected platform and the chance to see Labour in action; it was an experience that intensified his almost pathological hatred of that party. Gwynfor found himself elected to a council where Labour had won a majority for the first time ever. It meant that nothing and no one could challenge its popular mandate. 'We are the masters now,' the council leader, Douglas Hughes, declared at the opening session.[97] Gwynfor had difficulty coping with such an arena and experienced stomach cramps every time he rose to speak. Frequently, as he was about to begin an address, some Labour members would open newspapers or stroll around the chamber. They did not like his measured tones or his saint-like demeanour. However, this is only one side of the story. Gwynfor too made a deliberate effort to puncture Labour's pomposity on occasions. There is no doubt he was often treated shabbily, but the new representative for Llangadog was also wily enough to know how and when to milk public sympathy.

From the moment he took his seat, he provoked dissent by sitting, for tactical reasons, with the Independent members. His intention was to exercise some influence over this coalition of Liberals, Tories and the unaligned but, for Labour, the decision was an affront. Seeing the councillor for Llangadog seated with the Independents was clear proof in their eyes that the tomato-grower was a closet Tory gent.[98] The social chasm between Gwynfor and the Labour group added to the ill-feeling. Douglas Hughes, an ex-miner who had experienced considerable hardship, found it difficult to listen to the son of a successful Barry retailer preaching about principles. Gwynfor was also suspected (with some justification) of using the Council chamber as a national stage. And if all that were not enough, Gwynfor began that first meeting by insisting on his right to address the Council in Welsh – something he considered common sense because the majority of members were Welsh-speaking.[99] But the request was refused and, from April 1949 on, there was a continuous struggle between Gwynfor and the Labour group as he attempted to increase the use of the language in all Council activities – but especially in the field of education. In relation to the history of the language, these epic battles are significant; for the first time ever, someone had attempted to tackle the totally inadequate status of Welsh in local government.

Carmarthenshire Council could take pride in having opened the first Welsh-medium primary school, in Llanelli in 1947; however, there was also a large vein of anti-Welshnness and paranoia about the language within Labour ranks. Councillor Gwilym Thomas, Llandybïe, expressed a representative view when he refused to support Gwynfor's attempt to make Welsh the official language of the Council, because he was 'more worried about the interests of the working class, whichever language they spoke'.[100] One comfort, however, was that these battles won the admiration of nationalists more widely across Wales. Indeed, for many Plaid Cymru members at the time, Gwynfor's efforts in 1949 on Carmarthenshire Council were among the most important in the history of the language. Saunders Lewis, for instance, believed Gwynfor's successes (and failures) on the Council were positive proof of the moribund nature of Labourite, chapel-going Wales. In that respect, he saw Gwynfor's stand as evidence of of the need for a 'revolution' in the working class's attitude towards Wales and for the promotion of spirituality over socialist materialism.[101]

But as the stand-off continued, the Republicans within Plaid Cymru became more organised and confident and, by April 1949, Gwynfor had come to the conclusion that he needed to clip the wings of this group described by the *Liverpool Daily Post* as 'Cymric Bolsheviki with beards and bombs'.[102] Since the Republicans had first come together at the Dolwar Cafe in Carmarthen in February 1949, there had been a fundamental change in their nature and in the threat they posed to Gwynfor's leadership. At first, they had merely discussed tactics.[103] It is also clear that the original aim of men like Gwilym Prys Davies, Huw Davies and Cliff Bere had been to stay within Plaid Cymru in the hope they could prevent patriotic voters in the south from switching their allegiance to the Communists.[104] Gwilym Prys Davies went so far as to ask Gwynfor to permit a popular front between the Communists and Plaid Cymru, but the President dismissed this possibility out of hand on the basis that the non-Christian Communists denied 'that politics has anything to do with morality'.[105] Faced with such opposition, the Republicans were uneasy and their political options limited. From February 1949 on, some of their leaders – like Trefor Morgan and John Legonna – began to discuss two choices: a breakaway by the time of the annual conference in August 1949 or, more unlikely, the seizure of the leadership of Plaid Cymru.[106]

This is the context which explains why Gwynfor decided to challenge them by placing a motion before the Executive in April 1949 calling on the Republicans to resign unless they could show 'faith in the Party'. In one sense, Gwynfor was over-reacting to the Republican 'threat' for in reality they numbered no more than a handful, and enjoyed very little support. Even so, he believed the existence of small groups like this confused the public as had Gwerin back in 1938. He also thought their ideas contradicted those of Plaid Cymru and that recognizing the Crown was a small price to pay for Dominion Status. Plaid Cymru's President was also uncomfortable with the secularism, anti-pacifism and, from his perspective, a lack of respectability among the Republicans. His uncompromising stance on the matter led to a heated debate on the Executive. Trefor Beasley claimed the party was too weak to withstand a split, while J Gwyn Griffiths insisted that members of the Republican Movement were among Plaid Cymru's best workers. But Gwynfor had his way: by 12 votes to three, Plaid Cymru's Executive called on the Republicans to resign from the party or cease their activities.[107]

The Republicans decided not to give way and Gwynfor's chosen tactic proved to be the wrong one. If anything, the Executive's ultimatum gave the Republicans new heart and, from April on, they became a public and coordinated faction within Plaid Cymru, constantly attacking what they saw as Gwynfor's timid attitude towards the Monarchy.[108] It is obvious that the Republicans' attacks and disloyalty had a profound effect on his state of mind because, by the middle of 1949, he had informed J E Jones that he did not wish to be re-elected President of Plaid Cymru due to exhaustion. In retrospect, his reaction was probably more a cry for help than a genuine threat to resign but, at the time, Gwynfor's unease caused panic in the party's ranks. Jones wrote back insisting it was 'impossible' for him even to consider resigning, because he knew of no one of his calibre who could fulfil the role.[109] On the same day, Saunders Lewis made a similar appeal, saying he would be 'dreadfully sorry' were he to leave the post in this way, bearing in mind the trust and influence Plaid Cymru had earned during his four years as President.[110]

This was some succour. Within a month, Gwynfor renewed his engagement with the two major issues that faced him: the Parliament for Wales Campaign and the Republicans. In an important meeting of the Plaid Cymru Executive in June 1949, he outlined his ambitious vision of making the call for 'a Parliament for Wales in Five Years' Plaid Cymru's main platform. To succeed, Gwynfor used all the arguments that had been formulating in his mind since Christmas. The strongest of these was the political one, and his confidence that a campaign for a Welsh Parliament would 'provide a boost', forcing the other parties to state exactly where they stood. The position in Scotland formed part of his analysis and he emphasised that Plaid Cymru could not afford to lag behind. The other argument was the economic one, since he believed that 'practical politics' would be popular once recession hit the south as the Marshall Aid scheme ended.[111]

It is fair to say that Gwynfor might have anticipated substantial objections to his vision but he was pleasantly surprised. After all, Plaid Cymru had been established to protect Welsh culture but now, here was the President asking it to make a Parliament for Wales, along the lines of the Ulster Parliament, its main goal. A Parliament would bring a measure of devolution, not complete 'freedom', but Gwynfor's answer to the accusation that he was compromising was that Wales's need was too great 'to debate in academic terms what Wales should have in another thirty years'.[112] Even so, the implications were enormous: by accepting the slogan 'A Parliament for Wales in Five Years', Gwynfor was asking his party to turn its back on short-term politics and the romance of heroism. It was strange, however, that the 'Penyberth faction' of Plaid Cymru were silent, especially when one considers how outspoken they would be over Tryweryn. The only real criticism seen in the press was that the plan was overly-ambitious, and the *Liverpool Daily Post* argued that such a timetable was 'political suicide'.[113] It may have been that his threat to resign from the Presidency had gained him some sympathy, but Gwynfor had won a vital internal struggle. By force of conviction, he had managed to ensure that his brothers in the Plaid Cymru faith were safe in the fold as he undertook this new venture.

At last, Plaid Cymru, presentationally and politically, was moving away from Saunders Lewis's influence, and this gave Gwynfor a second wind in his efforts to counter the Republicans. On the day after that all-important meeting of the Executive, he heard that the Republicans were on the verge of leaving Plaid Cymru but not, he admitted to D J Williams, 'before kicking up a heck of a row in the Conference and trying to take as many as they can with them'. Gwynfor thought it 'irresponsible', but for all his disquiet about possibly losing talented young men like Gwilym Prys Davies and Huw Davies, compromise was the last thing on his mind. Faced with what he considered a betrayal (particularly in the case of Trefor Morgan), he believed the Republicans could be defeated by ensuring that the 'demonstration' on their behalf in the conference was turned into 'a demonstration of party unity'.[114] D J Williams egged Gwynfor on in his opposition to the Republicans. Their politics were 'childish heroics' in his view and, by the time the Plaid Cymru conference had gathered in Dyffryn Ardudwy in August 1949, the magic circle around Gwynfor were convinced that the issue had to be confronted head on.[115]

Given their mutual hostility, it was no surprise that the conference turned out to be one of the most fiery in the party's history. The Republicans won the first round of the contest by arguing that the goal of a Free Wales should be Republic rather than Dominion Status. From the platform, one of the leading Republicans, Ithel Davies, asserted that Plaid Cymru's policy compelled them to be British first and Welsh second. Cliff Bere was equally mordant. To cries of 'Nonsense!' from Gwynfor's supporters, he suggested that they could close the conference with 'God Save the King' bearing in mind Plaid Cymru policy.[116] Gwynfor's tactic in heated situations like this was to say nothing, and delegate the dirty work to his lieutenants – in particular J E Jones and Dewi Watkin Powell. Watkin Powell's counter-argument was that the English Empire was developing into a society of free countries, and that Wales would enjoy the status of a free nation, albeit under the Crown. When it came to a vote, it was plain that the deputies had carried out their work splendidly: only 10 voted for a Welsh Republic with 99 against.

It was an overwhelming victory for Gwynfor, but even afterwards, it was not inevitable that the Republicans would leave Plaid Cymru and establish their own movement. Some, like Gwilym Prys Davies, hoped to stay within Plaid Cymru, whilst at the same time feeling that J E Jones's 'petty' attitude made it abundantly clear they were no longer welcome.[117] Although there is no evidence that Gwynfor encouraged J E Jones, there is no evidence either that he sought to prevent this attitude, and it is hard to believe that a faithful servant like the party's General Secretary would have done anything to offend his superior. As a consequence, some fifty Republicans left Plaid Cymru to form their own party by Christmas 1949. Gwynfor did not give a fig for their existence outside Plaid Cymru, and believed that the 'ordinary man' would express his lack of interest by ignoring them.[118] Their radicalism, expressed most clearly in the publication *The Welsh Republican* between 1950 and 1957, also aided Plaid Cymru by making it appear more moderate. The movement limped towards its inevitable demise in 1957 and some of its adherents returned to the Plaid Cymru fold while others joined Labour. But this was an empty and unnecessary triumph for Gwynfor and J E Jones. The great irony, as John Davies has remarked, was that it was secular and anti-establishment ideas like those espoused by the Republicans which would win Plaid Cymru a measure of credibility in the valleys of the south in the 'sixties and 'seventies.[119]

The sound and fury at Dyffryn Ardudwy meant that the conference's most important resolution, to approve a campaign for a Parliament, gained virtually no attention, but from the summer of 1949 on, Plaid Cymru's energies were focussed almost exclusively in that direction. The campaign began unconvincingly with the press dismissing its invitation to Clement Attlee to meet the organizers as a childish 'stunt', but despite this, Plaid Cymru's fortunes took a turn for the better.[120] In Machynlleth, in early October 1949, the party organized one of its most ambitious rallies ever: the intention was to assemble over a thousand people in the town where Owain Glyndŵr's old parliament had met, to call for a new Parliament for Wales. If this rally had failed, Gwynfor's credibility would have been in shreds so soon after the antics at the August conference, but he need not have worried. Four thousand people gathered to call for a Parliament – an astonishing figure given that devolution had not been discussed publicly since the days of New Wales, half a century before. And if the figure was a surprise, then the composition of the crowd was more surprising still. Alongside the teachers and ministers of religion who were Plaid Cymru's core supporters, there were new faces: miners, quarrymen and railway workers. The day culminated in a barnstorming performance from Gwynfor. Following his speech, one over-generous reporter claimed that Gwynfor, not Aneurin Bevan, deserved the title of Wales's greatest orator.[121] Anthony Davies (Llygad Llwchwr), the *News Chronicle*'s renowned scribbler, was impressed too. He maintained that Plaid Cymru had held the most significant rally in Wales since the days of Lloyd George and Tom Ellis, and that its success was a reflection of Welsh discontent with London rule.[122]

The burning issues following the success in Machynlleth were how to carry Plaid Cymru's campaign forward, and whether to take the obvious step of coming to an understanding with the Welsh Liberals. They too had recently 'rediscovered' their enthusiasm for a Welsh Parliament. The speculation continued for three months, but Plaid Cymru and the Liberals were reluctant to take those first hesitant steps to the altar. In the absence of any clear agreement, Plaid Cymru decided to take the initiative from the Liberals by deciding on 31 December 1949 that they would launch a non-party petition for a Parliament. On the following day, the Liberals opted to follow a similar, but completely separate, course by setting up a Parliament for Wales campaign of their own.[123] For several people in Plaid Cymru, the Liberals' decision was a 'shock' and left the clear impression that a unique and absurd situation had developed: for half a century, devolution (with the occasional very rare exception) had been stone-dead, but now two campaigns for a Parliament had arrived at the same time but following different routes.[124] To confuse matters even further, a minority within Plaid Cymru were fearful that the Liberals' new-found zeal for a Parliament was an example of what Saunders Lewis called 'an electoral trick', and that Plaid Cymru should be very cautious in dealing with them.[125] It took the wisdom of Liberal elder statesman Alderman William George to prevent the situation becoming a farce. Prompted by him, the two parties were persuaded they would be better advised to campaign together under the banner of the New Wales Union. At last, therefore, there was agreement but it was decided to wait until after the General Election before engaging in any joint campaigning.

Unsurprisingly, Gwynfor wanted to make the need for a Parliament the cornerstone of his party's election campaign.[126] But if the policy itself was clear, the campaign did not begin well for him. Saunders Lewis used his column in *Y Faner* to undermine the whole campaign by attacking both the notion of a Parliament for Wales and Gwynfor's leadership style. What Plaid Cymru needed, he said, was more of the spirit of Gandhi and Mrs Pankhurst – in other words, unlawful action. In addition, Lewis openly sympathised with the Republicans' methods: 'When the Welsh Republicans say that Plaid Cymru has lost the spirit of its early days, has turned its back on Penyberth, it seems to me the accusation is a fair one. Welsh life today is typified by a lack of the venturesome spirit'.[127] Saunders Lewis's homily led to banner headlines in the press: 'Extremists in the Blaid' the *News Chronicle* concluded,[128] and although Lewis (in his consistently inconsistent way) paid Gwynfor a generous tribute the following week, the damage had already been done.[129] Not for the first time, Saunders Lewis – who still exercised a massive influence over Welsh nationalism – had placed Gwynfor in a difficult spot, and had done so publicly. The only route open to Gwynfor was stubborn diplomacy because he knew an assault on Saunders Lewis would cause a split. In public, then, all he could do was restate his belief that only a Parliament could save the nation.[130]

Equally as important as a Welsh Parliament, Gwynfor held it as an article of faith that the party should fight as many parliamentary seats as possible. In the teeth of savage opposition from Plaid Cymru veterans, he managed to persuade the executive that Plaid Cymru should contest seven seats. Even though such prominent figures as Saunders Lewis, R Tudur Jones and D J Davies argued that fielding so many candidates was folly, Gwynfor was convinced this was the only way the party could expand its support base.[131] The campaign itself was pretty unremarkable for all the parties but, for Labour in particular, it was evident that the idealism of 1945 had long since waned. In Wales, there was enormous respect for Attlee's social reforms, but little enthusiasm for the campaign. After five years of economic hardship, Gwynfor's constant theme throughout was disillusionment with socialism.

Nationally, and back in Merioneth, he tried to portray Labour as a party just as committed to war and the Empire as its predecessors. The choice, then, for the electors in Merioneth and elsewhere was this: more militaristic land-grabs by the English Labour Party, or the pacifist nationalism of Plaid Cymru.[132] As the campaign continued that February, Gwynfor appealed to the moral conscience of the electors in Merioneth, reminding them that the Welsh people 'have been called to special work' and to fulfil 'a mission'.[133] This inevitably, perhaps, led to tensions in the campaign. Some party activists in the county thought it was a grave mistake to place so much emphasis on the moral and so little on the material. Other critics felt it was a tactical error to have so many teachers and ministers of religion addressing his election meetings. What, one such critic asked, did these men 'with their guaranteed salaries' know about the needs of working people? [134] And if Gwynfor had a tendency to appeal to high-mindedness, his opponents were more than ready to play a dirtier game since the result in Merioneth seemed likely to depend on the expected increase in the Plaid Cymru vote.[135] In a tight contest between the Liberals and Labour, the Liberals suggested the voters should not trust an incomer who was likely to 'turn out to be Welsh Independent Labour'. More damaging, but less credible, was a Labour claim that Gwynfor was a Catholic.[136]

After a month's campaigning in appalling weather, the people of Wales traipsed into the polling stations on 23 February 1950. Attlee won a parliamentary majority by a hair's breadth, and despite losing numerous seats in England, the Welsh remained as true to his socialism as ever. In Merioneth, the verdict on five years' continuous activity was a huge disappointment for Plaid Cymru, and Gwynfor finished at the bottom of the poll once again. His vote had been squeezed in a close fight between the Liberal victor, Emrys Roberts, and his Labour opponent, Owen Parry. Gwynfor's vote rose by less than one per cent and, on a national level, Plaid Cymru had made no progress, attracting a little over one per cent of the vote.

The general feeling in the Welsh press was that Plaid Cymru should have done far better after all its hard work since 1945. The drop of three per cent in the Welsh Liberal vote was also interpreted as clear evidence that devolution, and the fledgling campaign for a Welsh Parliament, had failed to inspire the electorate.[137] 'John Aelod Jones' crystallised the indifference towards it when he commented that the only petition he had heard of during the election in Merioneth was one in Blaenau Ffestiniog to prevent the nationalization of Tate and Lyle.[138] In nationalist ranks, the apparent crushing defeat led to a detailed post mortem. According to Plaid Cymru's own research, there was a long list of reasons and prejudices that kept people from voting for the party. These included:

> Jobs for the boys, the University Clique – too academic – teachers and preachers (Plaid is all intellectuals, totalitarians and disgruntled ministers someone said); don't want to open pubs on Sundays; right-wing party; Catholicism; no good for working people; no English on the radio; no place for Welshmen who don't speak Welsh in a free Wales, everyone must speak Welsh.[139]

Gwynfor was well aware of the harm wrought by these perceptions, but he was certain that the main reason for Plaid Cymru's electoral failure was the lack of media attention. Every night during the campaign, he says he despaired when he realized that the radio reached 'almost every home whereas the party can only reach a village once or twice in a public meeting'.[140] Lacking coverage on the BBC, there were only two solutions: to work harder between elections, and to create more 'good nationalists' through 'mental and spiritual conversion'.[141] Gwynfor, however, was not broken. 'Are we down-hearted?' he asked D J Williams with a rhetorical flourish. 'No'. 'Will we wobble?' he asked then. 'No'. After all, as D J Williams said, 'We should know what sort of material we have to work with in Wales.'[142]

He faced down those critics inside and outside the party who insisted fighting elections and campaigning for a Welsh Parliament were a waste of time. During April 1950, Plaid Cymru resolved to stand again in the same seven constituencies[143] and Gwynfor redoubled his efforts for a Welsh Parliament as 1 July, the launch date for the cross-party campaign, drew closer. He addressed numerous meetings and wrote a substantial pamphlet, *Plaid Cymru and Wales*, in an attempt to argue a logical case for a Welsh Parliament.[144] Nationalist enthusiasm was aided by growing agitation within the Welsh Labour Party. From the moment Cliff Prothero, Secretary of the Labour Party's Welsh Council, called the idea of a Parliament 'a frivolous demand', adding that his party would boycott the launch, there was considerable speculation over which Labour members would be brave enough to ignore him. The Welsh-language press speculated that David Thomas, Huw T Edwards and Goronwy Roberts might – men who, as Gwynfor put it, would be willing to challenge 'London's word'.[145] Gwynfor's anticipation was that a Labour presence within the Parliament campaign would split the party. It was an indication of his high, if not wildly optimistic, hopes that he warned Plaid Cymru members to prepare to welcome 'the Welshest section' of the Labour Party into 'the Nationalist movement'.[146] Gwynfor undoubtedly enjoyed commentating on the impending rift; after all, for the first time in his political career, he thought he had discovered a flaw in the Welsh Labour Party machine. But playing to the gallery in this manner was disastrous for the devolution campaign because it weakened the position of those Welsh members of the Labour Party – like Cledwyn Hughes and Goronwy Roberts – who were seriously considering whether or not they should join the Parliament for Wales Campaign.

There was also a price to pay for having been so busy since 1945. It was not unusual for Gwynfor to address half a dozen or so public meetings each week, travelling to every corner of Wales in his Morris Minor before returning to Wernellyn in the early hours of the morning. Then, more often than not, he would check the boilers in the greenhouses and bank up the fires before going to bed as dawn was breaking. This, five years into his Presidency, had become his way of life and he would adhere to the same ascetic timetable for decades to come. In short, his life consisted of campaigning, writing, endless travel and fish-and-chip suppers. He would only read what he needed to read, and playing the piano was his only relaxation. But even someone with Gwynfor's inexhaustible energy could not remain unaffected by these efforts. In May 1950, he underwent surgery for a burst appendix at Morriston hospital, and although it was a fairly routine operation, those closest to him took it as an ominous sign. His father-in-law, Dan Thomas, wrote to him begging him 'not to be so hard' on himself and warning him that it was only too easy for one man to do too much and 'deprive his age and his generation of the best of his service'.[147] D J Williams had similar anxieties and privately thought Gwynfor was working 'unreasonably hard'.[148] Gwynfor's young son Alcwyn heard the phrase 'Daddy's in a meeting' so often that he believed that 'Ameeting' was the name of a place. And although Gwynfor loved his family passionately, his priority was Wales. Once, he told another son, Dafydd, that he regretted having had a family because being single would have allowed him to work even harder for his country. Inevitably, his lifestyle also placed a strain on his marriage to Rhiannon, leading Dafydd to conclude it was a difficult relationship given the constant demands of Plaid Cymru.[149]

His health recovered sufficiently, however, for him to travel to Llandrindod and take part in the official launch of the Parliament for Wales Campaign on 1 July 1950. Devolutionists turned out in their hundreds to a gathering which resembled a revivalist meeting. Speaking from the stage, Gwynfor argued that the campaign for a Parliament was something spiritual and embodied 'one of the great ideals'.[150] But this was a minority opinion. In a hint at the tensions at the heart of the campaign that would surface later on, other speakers – like Ifan ab Owen Edwards and the main attraction, the capricious and brilliant Megan Lloyd George, Liberal MP for Anglesey – chose to emphasise the administrative benefits of such a Parliament, rather than any spiritual aspects. Factional disunity was evident when it came to appointing an executive and the whole campaign was nearly reduced to a 'parish pump shambles' as the parties (including the Communists) attempted to appoint their own favourites.[151] Others complained that the north was being treated more favourably than the south. Some of the older ones at the launch thought history was repeating itself as they recalled the disunity which had killed off the original New Wales movement fifty years previously. To add to the difficulties, there was not a single Labour MP present apart from the member for Merthyr, S O Davies. The Liberals, too, were divided and according to one leading party member, Glyn Tegai Hughes, the whole thing was an unholy mess: 'It went off at half cock from the beginning... I've never seen anything so abysmally organised'.[152] But whatever the opinions and divisions within the other parties, Gwynfor himself was delighted with the launch in Llandrindod, and as the first real campaign for devolution in two generations began, he was confident that a new chapter in Welsh history was opening.[153]

As the summer of 1950 progressed, Gwynfor skilfully linked the argument for a Parliament with an expression of the shortcomings of Welsh administration from Whitehall. Fortunately for him, two events incensed Welsh-speaking Wales at the same time. The first was the government's decision to ignore the findings of a public inquiry and allow the firing range at Trawsfynydd to be extended. The second was the Forestry Commission's high-handed scheme to plant trees on 20,000 acres between Cwrtycadno and Llanddewibrefi – thereby forcing 46 families to leave their homes. Worse still, were the Commission to have its way, intensive planting would eventually swallow up thousands of acres across mid and west Wales. In Carmarthenshire, Gwynfor and some local farmers made a stand, challenging the body that he liked to refer to as 'the lone wolf'.[154] During the ensuing battle, Gwynfor seized every opportunity to remind the communities under threat that only a Parliament could offer real relief. It was clearly a successful tactic and, in panic, Goronwy Roberts, the Labour MP for Caernarfon, wrote to his party leadership pleading for a change of policy:

> The Nationalist Party is growing… Many of our people are dispirited and frustrated. They find it so difficult to counter the arguments of the separatists. The facts are so positive… Unless we change our attitude we shall reap an inevitable whirlwind.[155]

As another General Election approached, Goronwy Roberts had grounds to feel uneasy. Although Plaid Cymru was unlikely to win any seats, a growth in support would adversely affect Labour's chances – particularly in Welsh-speaking constituencies. But as Plaid Cymru's appeal increased, Gwynfor was preoccupied not so much by his party as by the Parliament for Wales campaign. From the very outset, Gwynfor had been on the campaign's Executive, and the minutes clearly show that the whole thing would have ended in confusion were it not for his support. One indication of the chaos was that the campaign had to wait until New Year's Day 1951 before it had an office and an organizer – Dafydd Miles – eight months after the colourful pageant in Llandrindod. The committee met only twice during 1950.[156] In the meantime, there were no names on the petition and, as the campaign's shortcomings became increasingly obvious, the situation began to trouble Gwynfor. By the new year, he was fast reaching the contentious conclusion that the only way to kick-start the campaign would be to refrain from nominating candidates in constituences where the MPs supported it.

During the first quarter of 1951, he kept the idea to himself but influential figures within Plaid Cymru like Dr Gwenan Jones, Dan Thomas and – curiously enough – Saunders Lewis too, were of like mind. At the beginning of March, Saunders Lewis announced, outright, that the damage to Wales would be 'appalling' were the campaign to 'languish and die'.[157] There is also evidence that Emrys Roberts, the Liberal MP for Merioneth, a man greatly respected by Gwynfor, was beginning to think along similar lines as well.[158] Another consideration – though not the main one by any means – was that the party would save money by putting up fewer candidates.[159] What decided the issue, however, was Labour confusion over the petition. Despite the outspoken opposition of leading members like Cliff Prothero and Huw T Edwards to those 'who went to Llandrindod', the petition was beginning to attract the support of some of the most gifted Welsh-speakers in the Labour Party. On Saint David's Day 1951, the leader of this faction raised his head above the parapet: his name was Cledwyn Hughes, the prospective Labour candidate for Anglesey, an unlikely rebel, a talented solicitor and, according to some contemporaries, a former member of Plaid Cymru. Ten days later, the movement looked even more powerful when there were two meetings – in Rhyl and Caernarfon – where members of the Labour Party, Plaid Cymru and the Liberals shared a platform. In the middle of a period described by the historian Peter Stead as a political 'cold war', the significance of this thaw cannot be overemphasised.[160]

On 22 March, Gwynfor made the case for not contesting certain seats. After a discussion that lasted two hours, the Executive accepted his suggestion that the petition should come first. Even so, Gwynfor knew that justifying the change would obviously be 'difficult', to quote J E Jones.[161] Wynne Samuel, for instance, could not believe what had happened, and described the policy as 'utterly unworkable' in constituencies like Caernarfon and Merioneth, where there were Labour and Liberal candidates in favour of a Parliament. The effect, Samuel said, would be to ensure that a Parliament for Wales would not be the major issue in either party's programme.[162] And these were not the only difficult questions raised. There was confusion too about Plaid Cymru's role during the election campaign. Another concern was how to ensure that a candidate given a clear run was 'genuinely supportive' of the campaign. On 20 April 1951, the confidential 'President's Committee' of Gwynfor loyalists met to discuss these worries. Despite calls for further consultation, Gwynfor and J E Jones insisted this was the only course. As Aneurin Bevan had just resigned, Gwynfor was certain that the future of the Labour Party was at stake, and that the possibility of a split in the Labour ranks created an opportunity for Plaid Cymru. By Gwynfor's own admission, the spring of 1951 was 'wonderfully sunny' and these were 'exciting' days in Welsh politics .[163]

The change of election policy was announced on 1 May and Gwynfor sought to present it as 'a costly sacrifice' for Plaid Cymru. In *Y Ddraig Goch* that month, he wrote that it was about time Plaid Cymru realized Wales was not Ireland and that the Welsh could not take support for granted to the extent that the Irish could.[164] But however strenuous his efforts, his party's reaction was lukewarm at best. In Merioneth, there was considerable dissatisfaction when members heard that Gwynfor would not stand as candidate. Tecwyn Lloyd Owen, the local organizer, wrote to Gwynfor to warn him that 'a number of members in the county are unhappy with the latest decision' and that some of them 'are threatening to leave Plaid'.[165] *Y Cymro*'s verdict was equally damning, calling the announcement 'surprising' and suggesting that it left Plaid Cymru looking more like a pressure group than a national party.[166] For months, Gwynfor had to live with vociferous criticism of the way he was leading the party, and it was only at the last minute that the West Glamorgan district decided not to challenge the policy at the annual conference. Their motion was withdrawn, according to Wynne Samuel, 'solely out of respect for Gwynfor'. But, respect or not, Samuel was part of that influential faction who believed, in his words, that the President of Plaid Cymru had staged a 'political farce'.[167]

During these months of tactical manoeuvring, Gwynfor was more successful outside his party than within it. As a member of the University Court, he succeeded in using that rather unpromising institution to discuss the need for a Welsh-medium College. Presenting his case to the Court in July, he portrayed Wales as a country where thousands of farmers, clerics and ministers of religion were able to live their lives entirely in English. Was that not a shameful situation, he asked, proof of the need for a Welsh-medium College that would give the language the dignity it deserved? He acknowledged there would be problems in establishing such an institution, but was not the Irish achievement an example of how it could be done? This radical speech did not elicit a single objection, so great was the amazement 'after Mr Gwynfor Evans resumed his seat'.[168] The motion was passed by an overwhelming majority and, as a result, a committee was convened to examine the issue for the next four years. However, there was little support after that. Even Alwyn D Rees, who was to be so unswerving in his support for the idea of a Welsh-medium College during the 'sixties, doubted whether Wales could maintain such a body in the 'fifties.[169] In 1955, the sub-committee reported back, and although the idea of a Welsh-medium College was rejected, there was some progress and a recommendation was accepted calling on the University to extend Welsh-language provision in all Colleges. The greatest progress was seen in Aberystwyth and Bangor. Moves were also afoot, prompted above all by Gwynfor, to promote subjects like Welsh and Welsh History in the constituent colleges.[170] These successes consoled him. So too did the eventual launch of the petition at the National Eisteddfod in Llanrwst. The nonagenarian poet Elfed was the first to sign and, despite heavy criticism of the whole scheme from Labour, the general view was that the Parliament for Wales Campaign, after months of prevarication, was fully up and running by August 1951.[171]

Nevertheless, the great irony during this period of comparative growth in constitutional politics was that some of the leading figures within Plaid Cymru still felt the party would need to break the law in one final effort to thwart the War Office plans for Trawsfynydd. Since April 1951, the party leadership had been discussing the possibility of a mass protest at Trawsfynydd that would, perhaps, lead to several arrests. There was nothing new in this; after all, the memory of Penyberth was still fresh and a generation of party activists still believed – despite Gwynfor's pacifism – that direct action was the only way forward. The debate simmered for months before boiling over in the early summer of 1951. In June that year, Saunders Lewis launched a vicious assault on Gwynfor, not so much for any deficiencies of leadership – he believed he 'consistently spoke with the force and substance of a national leader' – but rather for his weaknesses as a tactician. In his column in *Y Faner*, Saunders Lewis was openly critical of the endless anodyne protest meetings that Gwynfor addressed. Having heard that Gwynfor had addressed such a meeting opposing the Forestry Commission in Llanbryn-mair,[172] Lewis decided that he could no longer hold back:

> ... protest meetings are child's play if all you have are protest meetings. Mr Gwynfor Evans cannot be effective and powerful as a leader in the defence of Wales because there are not fifty men in Wales who dare resist violence and oppression. It cannot be done without provoking opprobrium and hatred from most of the people of Wales themselves. It cannot be done without causing trauma within families and uproar in communities.[173]

It was a commanding piece, and a portent in many respects of Lewis's famous radio lecture on the state of the Welsh language, *Tynged yr Iaith*, eleven years later. Meanwhile, the Republicans were responding to Lewis's call; busily creating 'some trouble or other every day', as one columnist put it.[174] They had daubed the Mayor of Swansea's official car and were considered the true representatives of radicalism. The intelligence services had begun to take an interest in them too, adding to the pressure on Gwynfor to show similar decisivness.[175] Just weeks after Saunders Lewis's piece, D J Davies, the man who had charmed Gwynfor into Plaid Cymru, launched an even more vituperative attack on him. In two articles for *Y Faner*, Davies condemned almost everything that Gwynfor had ever done; from the slow growth of the party to the over-emphasis on the Welsh language, Davies saw a movement that was slowly sinking into obscurity. He contrasted the attractive radicalism of the Republicans with what Gwynfor had to offer – a petition for a Welsh Parliament. But for D J Davies, the greatest weakness was Gwynfor's pacifism and his unwillingness to adopt Gandhi's protest methods ever since 1938. He closed with a stinging salvo about the Swansea conference and what he judged to be the political disaster of 1938:

> And this was the beginning of the end for Plaid Cymru as an aggressive national movement. It became prissy and over-respectable and attracted into its ranks those Welshmen who wish to protect their own comfort and salve their conscience about the pitiful condition of their country at the same time! [176]

Between them, the two men whom Gwynfor most admired had publicly poured scorn on his whole approach since 1945. They had also done so in the cruellest way imaginable. Although there is no record of Gwynfor's response, it is likely that reading the three articles would have shaken him to the core because they underlined his dilemma more clearly than ever. On the one hand, there was his instinctive sympathy with constitutional politics and the petition. On the other, he still had some sympathy for those who believed constitutional protest had been exhausted following the decision of Hugh Dalton, the Minister for Planning, to ignore the findings of the 1950 public inquiry. It is impossible to know whether the newspaper pieces were an 'organized' conspiracy between Saunders Lewis and D J Davies but, shortly afterwards, there was a noticeable shift in the party's attitude towards law-breaking. In a 'dramatic' meeting of the Executive, it was decided that Plaid Cymru would attempt to close the Trawsfynydd camp by a sit-down protest in the road.[177]

The arrangements for the first protest on 30 August were strictly confidential and the protesters assembled by invitation only: a sober grouping of students, teachers and ministers of religion. Their ranks included some of the leading lights of Welsh nationalism – such as D J Williams, Waldo Williams and Lewis Valentine; along with these were younger, more tempestuous characters like Glyn James, Kitchener Davies and the poet R S Thomas. Their one uniting factor was their readiness to break the law – the least socially acceptable protest method in the Wales of the 1950s. On the morning of the protest, Gwynfor and J E Jones rose early to address the 75 activists who were uncertain of the techniques of non-violent protest. Gwynfor's message was clear: 'The time has come for us to do something other than talk. The time has come for us to act… We do not know what is going to happen to us. This is an experiment that may lead to other experiments.'[178] That said, the group set off from Bronaber in the direction of the camp and sat down on the dew-wet tarmacadam. Soon after, two army officers got out of their cars to ask why they were there. One of them expressed his disappointment that he would be unable to go for a haircut. Then a large military truck approached the demonstrators and braked as closely to them as possible.

Some of them were rammed by its front bumper – the first time, but not the last, that day the protesters would come into contact with cars and heavier vehicles. The police asked the protesters to move, but they refused.[179] As the protest got under way, Gwynfor took charge of events, deciding who or what would be allowed to leave the camp. For several of those present, Gwynfor's dignity and determination in new and difficult circumstances were impressive. Then, after presenting a letter to the commanding officer, Lieutenant Cudmore, explaining their reason for being there, the demonstrators decided to leave an hour early as a token of goodwill towards the police.

However, the reaction to the first protest was very mixed. Gwynfor believed Plaid Cymru had won a moral victory, and Saunders Lewis wrote to party headquarters to congratulate the demonstrators 'heartily' on their action.[180] At the same time, there were those in the party who were alarmed that Welsh nationalism had ventured into dangerous territory. Among the doubters were two young ministers, Islwyn Ffowc Elis and Huw Jones, who did not believe that Welsh-speaking Nonconformist Wales would ever be comfortable with such stunts.[181] The press in Wales shared their view. According to the *Liverpool Daily Post*, these 'Plaid Fanatics' had betrayed any goodwill that existed towards the Parliament for Wales Campaign from 'Welsh people of broad outlook'.[182] The *Western Mail* and the Labour MP for Rhondda West, Iorwerth Thomas, were even less sympathetic, accusing Gwynfor of behaving like a Welsh *Gauleiter*: 'The squatting act is a prelude to many acts of folly that will surely lead to the spilling of blood in the future.' On top of this, Thomas (in a statement which can only be described as paranoia even by his exacting standards) suspected that the whole protest had a whiff of Popery about it: 'Where is the clear voice of Nonconformist Wales warning people about the dangers of Rome?' [183] The Welsh newspapers were not alone in pouring cold water on the action. Immediately after the first protest, D J Davies again drew attention to the fact that a large number of those present had broken the law because they were pacifists rather than nationalists. 'It appears,' he said, 'that it is the Republicans who have the clearest vision in the politics of freedom in Wales today.'[184]

Meanwhile, there was widespread speculation about what would happen next and whether there would be prosecutions or not. Although a file on the matter reached the desk of the Director of Public Prosecutions, the private advice from the Chief Constable of Gwynedd, W Jones-Williams, was that the protest was just a 'silly prank' and that some of the demonstrators were disappointed that they had not been arrested.[185] Jones-Williams's assessment was astute and, in the absence of prosecutions, Gwynfor decided to hold a second protest. This time, he wanted demonstrators to trespass on War Office land 'as a symbol that we are reclaiming it as Welsh land'. Then he told J E Jones the protesters should 'plant a Red Dragon flag prominently on a hilltop as a sign that it is Welsh land' before occupying the main road.[186] The protest duly took place but, unlike the first one, the arrangements were made completely public, thereby increasing the numbers and the anticipation when a crowd of over a hundred met in Abergeirw on 29 September. Since the police knew there was a large protest on the way, J E Jones despatched eleven of them to march to the main entrance in an attempt to distract the authorities. The tactic worked well because, unknown to the police, the majority of the demonstrators reached the main entrance by the back road.[187] Once they were on Western Command territory, a flag was planted firmly on land that was seen as an integral part of Welsh heritage. That done, they sat down across the road and found themselves hemmed in once again by military vehicles.[188]

The demonstrators returned home after giving their names to the police, and although Gwynfor announced triumphantly that it was 'an important day in the history of Welsh freedom',[189] the doubts among some of the more respectable elements within Plaid Cymru continued. Once again, these were reflected in the Welsh secular and denominational press. The editor of *Y Goleuad,* the Calvinistic Methodist weekly, complained that the protests were fundamentally un-Christian[190] while the *Western Mail* urged that commemorative medals should be struck for 'Gwynfor's Squatters' and worn on their backsides – the most suitable place for nationalists to wear them![191] Faced with these mixed messages, Gwynfor's enthusiasm for direct action was tempered and in reality the Trawsfynydd protests, like the action at Penyberth, generated more heat than light. Although the two protests laid important intellectual foundations for the Welsh Language Society's protests a decade later, this would be the last mass protest by Plaid Cymru and Gwynfor until the Fourth Channel campaign in 1980. As will be seen shortly, Plaid Cymru's campaign for the non-payment of radio licences in 1955 was far less controversial for Gwynfor's party and the communities in which they lived.

At the height of this campaign, Clement Attlee called another General Election – an announcement which also explains why the Plaid Cymru leadership was not inclined to hold any more protests at Trawsfynydd. For the party, the election was a leap in the dark; it fielded only four candidates, and all in Labour strongholds – Llanelli, Rhondda West, Aberdare and Wrexham. In the west, where Plaid Cymru's support was strongest, all the party could do was watch and wait in the hope that allowing the supporters of the Parliament for Wales Campaign a clear run would bear fruit. On 25 October 1951, Winston Churchill was returned to 10 Downing Street by a slim majority, but the result was a calamity for Plaid Cymru. Megan Lloyd George and Emrys Roberts, two of the petition's most ardent supporters, lost their respective seats in Anglesey and Merioneth. Although the two Labour members who succeeded them, Cledwyn Hughes and T W Jones, were patriotic Welshmen, many in Plaid Cymru believed Gwynfor had gambled everything and lost. The post-mortem that followed the Election was a difficult one for him, with several of the party faithful openly criticising his political acumen. The journalist Mathonwy Hughes asked how he could justify a decision which meant Plaid Cymru had put its 'faith and hope in English Parties, only to see the members in whom they had placed their trust thrown out of Parliament'.[192] Kate Roberts agreed. In her typically peppery tone she spoke of 'huge dissatisfaction within Plaid at its lack of progress' with its oldest [members] very disgruntled with things'.[193] But the criticism was not confined to the Welsh intelligentsia. In Merioneth, a number of ordinary members were outraged because they believed Plaid Cymru had caused a patriotic Welsh Liberal to lose his seat. As a consequence, J E Jones was warned of bitter feelings that existed towards the party leadership.

For the first time during his career as President, Gwynfor had to cope with real failure. It had been his decision, more than anyone's, to give those candidates supportive of the petition a clear run in the Election but now he had to live with the consequences. To all intents and purposes, Wales found itself under Conservative and Labour control after the 1951 General Election. The Liberals had been virtually wiped out, but Plaid Cymru's situation was also dire. Even though Gwynfor could look back with some pride at what had been done in 1945, he had precious little to show for his efforts. Equally worrying was the continuing confusion within the party regarding its methods. Without any electoral successes, there were serious doubts about Gwynfor's apparent obsession with the Parliament for Wales Campaign. What many wanted was to see Plaid Cymru rediscover its roots and set aside pacifist respectability. They were, however, to be disappointed:

there would be no new Penyberth. At the end of 1951, Gwynfor wrote to D J Williams to tell him that something more significant would be needed in 1952 other than working for the party. That something for Gwynfor was the petition. 'We must,' he said, 'make the petition a success' in the year ahead.[194] The simple question, however, was almost impossible to answer: how?

Chapter 5

'SOFT SOAP FOR THE VOTERS' 1951–55

THE PARLIAMENT FOR WALES CAMPAIGN was under siege by the beginning of 1952. Its financial situation, according to its organizer, Dafydd Miles, was 'very serious' and he had not received a salary in over two months.[1] Miles was warned by the campaign treasurer, J R Jones, that 'the ugly shadow of bankruptcy' hung over everything, but Miles insisted on pressing ahead.[2] Just days into the New Year, it was clear that a public appeal for more funds had failed and that the sum collected was pitiful.[3] Megan Lloyd George's vital support disappeared for a while too as she retreated to America after losing her seat.[4] Inevitably, some of the campaign's supporters lost heart altogether. One of them, Sir Ifan ab Owen Edwards, wrote to Miles to suggest that 'soldiering on with the petition, and failing to get a huge number of names, could do more harm than good'.[5] Sir Ifan was not the only one who thought in this way. Meanwhile, in the north, other supporters lost heart because they 'were having some difficulty in countering the argument that there was a danger the counties of Glamorgan and Monmouthshire would dominate any Welsh Parliament'.[6] Faced with all this, Gwynfor's decision to put all Plaid Cymru's eggs in the 'Parliament for Wales' campaign basket looked increasingly reckless.

In truth, both Plaid Cymru and the campaign were going through a phase of political stagnation, brought about by other factors as well as the organisational difficulties. Following the election of a Conservative government, Churchill had kept his word and appointed a Minister for Welsh Affairs for the first time. For a while at least, Sir David Maxwell-Fyfe succeeded in defusing the numerous complaints from Welsh-speakers about how they were governed from London. Within a week of his appointment, Maxwell-Fyfe had announced that the

Forestry Commission would not be proceeding with its unpopular plans in Carmarthenshire; by February, he had shelved the War Office's plan to acquire over 11,000 acres of the Llŷn peninsula. In addition, Maxwell-Fyfe devolved some limited powers to the Departments of Agriculture and Education in Cardiff and, within a very short time, 'Dai Bananas' had earned the extra nickname of 'Dai Fair Play'. Indeed, after years of a centralized Labour administration, many in Wales were pleased with the Scot in Whitehall who expressed a willingness to listen to them. This caused substantial problems for the petition and some of its foremost supporters came to believe the whole thing was a waste of time. It was a heavy blow for Gwynfor when he received a letter from Sir Ifan ab Owen Edwards in the middle of January informing him that Maxwell-Fyfe had created such an impression on him that he had come to the conclusion there was no need 'for a movement to unite us on the vague matter which we used to call "a Parliament for Wales" '.[7] This was new territory for Gwynfor. After all, Plaid Cymru's rhetoric had been founded on the belief that London hated Wales. All that Gwynfor could do now was warn the people of Wales not to be seduced by the charms of a diplomatic Tory,[8] but the respect for Maxwell-Fyfe was so widespread that it reached the furthest shores of the Labour Party. Typical was the reaction of Huw T Edwards, chair of the Council for Wales and Monmouthshire, when he complimented Maxwell-Fyfe on 'a splendid start'.[9]

As the Parliament for Wales Campaign ran out of steam, the doubts within Plaid Cymru over the value of such an enterprise grew and Gwynfor's detractors began to severly criticize his pacifism – which they considered the most visible symbol of the 'niceness' of Welsh nationalism. The Reverend Fred Jones, a regular contributor to the Welsh press, led the assault in an article for *Y Faner* where he begged his party to dissociate its pacifism from its nationalism. According to Jones, Plaid Cymru came across as a 'pacifist society' and he claimed that he knew people who were not pacifists who felt that there was 'no room for them in the party'.[10] This opinion was supported by D J Davies. He, like Fred Jones, was convinced that the pacifists in Plaid Cymru had betrayed the party's principles, and had behaved much like the Communists by seizing the levers of power within the party – including its two monthly publications, the *Welsh Nation* and *Y Ddraig Goch*. He too regretted that the spirit of Penyberth had been lost and revealed that Gwynfor had confided in him that he would prefer Wales to remain 'captive' if the only option were to win freedom through violence.[11]

This criticism opened the floodgates to a torrent of censure by the allies of Saunders Lewis. Kate Roberts found the present state of Plaid Cymru a source of sadness, now that the panache and venturesome spirit of the early leaders was no more. O T L Huws was more angry than sad. He made an unsuccessful bid to convene a conference to discuss the 1938 resolution on pacifism. He was supported by the Catholic country squire, R O F Wynne, who went so far as to assert that pacifism was a 'heresy' for the Christian who was not a pacifist.[12] And although Saunders Lewis himself did not make public capital out of the affair he, like his colleagues, was ready to undermine the pacifism of both Plaid Cymru and its President. He refused to contribute to the *Welsh Nation* under the editorship of Pennar Davies, sending him this curt response to his request:

> I do hope that Plaid Cymru is not going to waste time and energy debating pacifism. The only thing worth discussing within the ranks of Plaid Cymru is how practically, effectively, constantly, to create a consciousness of Welsh nationhood and of the Welsh inheritance in the people of Wales. Our enemy no.1 is not English Government but our own apathy and inertia.[13]

The quarrel affected Pennar Davies deeply and, by mid-February 1952, the atmosphere within Plaid Cymru had become poisonous. Unlike Davies, however, Gwynfor remained intransigent, mocking the political naivety of the romantically minded. As he wrote to Pennar Davies: 'I don't know what these people would expect Plaid to *do* by adopting a militaristic policy – shoot Churchill, or raise a Welsh army or what?' For Gwynfor, his critics were guilty of misrepresenting the past, forgetting that Plaid Cymru had done 'little more than hold meetings (with the exception of the Bombing School)' in the 'good' old days.[14] He was also afraid – not for the first time – that the criticism was part of an organized conspiracy by Catholics within the party. 'I wonder,' he asked Pennar Davies, 'whether they have reached an agreement? Looks like it.'[15] There is no evidence such a conspiracy ever existed but, by 1952, Gwynfor was certainly considered a traitor by many Catholics. In turn, this fed the anti-Catholic paranoia that was prevalent among his Nonconformist friends. When the dispute was at its height, J E Jones had to defend the leadership publicly, comparing the activity under Gwynfor's Presidency with what had happened before Penyberth.[16] This proved enough to suppress the disagreements for a while, but it was abundantly clear that pacifism had the potential to tear Plaid Cymru apart – especially with the party experiencing more difficult times than usual.

Without doubt, life by the spring of 1952 was 'a little restless' for Gwynfor.[17] The petition had ground to a halt, and this meant the party had to create an impression in the County Council elections. In Llangadog work on the greenhouses also added to his burdens and, without any clear political agenda, he was forced to resort once again to bread-and-butter politics. However genuine his declaration to D J Williams a few months before that the Parliament for Wales Campaign would be his priority, there appeared to be no campaign to prioritize. He was disappointed as well by the government's White Paper on broadcasting, since he did not believe it gave meaningful powers to the BBC in Wales. In addition, he had lost all patience with his membership of the ineffectual BBC consultative committee. As he wrote to T I Ellis:

> The Welsh Council and its powers are most disappointing. Eight unpaid men who are unable to give much time to the task (with Parri Bach [the Aberystwyth Professor of Welsh, T H Parry-Williams] – the weakest of the weak– as paid Chairman) with no more say over programmes than Wales has already … e.g. it cannot make a decision on a subject like political broadcasts in Wales. No financial self-government. The power to appoint – to quote Alun Oldfield-Davies himself only 'Commissionaires and cleaners'… no ability to develop.[18]

In such unpromising times, being re-elected as councillor for Llangadog was a great comfort, and proof that he retained credibility as a voice for his community. But the undoubted high-point of this miserable year came when he unveiled a very significant stone at Pencader in late September. On an unseasonably hot day, thousands came to Pencader to view the stone that had been carried there all the way from Trefor in Caernarvonshire.[19] At a time when Plaid Cymru found it almost impossible to exercise any influence over the mass media – particularly the BBC – such a gathering was like gold dust for the party's leadership. After a series of speeches, the stone was unveiled to reveal the prophecy made by the Old Man of Pencader to Henry II eight hundred years before. Gwynfor's aim (it was he who had arranged the whole event) was to encourage Welsh people to think of themselves as Welsh, not British, and 'to make the Welsh into good nationalists'.[20] Indeed, when one assesses his contribution to Welsh social thought, it is difficult to overestimate the profound effect of this continual message – especially in Welsh-speaking Wales. Gradually, he, and a handful of others, were beginning to convince thousands of people in Wales that Britishness was rotten to the core and that they should look to countries like Denmark and

Israel for inspiration. By means of rallies, conversations and propaganda, Gwynfor shifted the course of Welsh intellectual history by persuading Welsh-speakers of the real value of the ideas of Emrys ap Iwan and Saunders Lewis. It was at meetings like the one in Pencader that the seeds of 1960s nationalism were sown and, in many ways, this 'victory' was just as important as the by-election triumph at Carmarthen in 1966.

But another decade would pass before these efforts bore fruit. As 1952 dragged to a close, Plaid Cymru was as insignificant as ever, and the Parliament for Wales Campaign was on its last legs. The support of the Labour Party was vital if that campaign was to succeed but, since May 1952, its leadership had threatened rebels like Cledwyn Hughes and S O Davies, who supported the petition, with fire and brimstone. Jim Callaghan's comment was typical. He insisted at his party's Welsh conference that socialists 'should accept the challenge and withstand the senseless nonsense of the Welsh Nationalists'.[21] At the same meeting, Merioneth Labour Party's call for an inquiry into devolution was rejected.[22] To complicate matters, the relationship between some Labour devolutionists and Gwynfor was strained – leading to further divisions among the petitioners. Cledwyn Hughes, for instance, could not understand why Plaid Cymru was so hostile to Labour. In a clear swipe at Gwynfor, Hughes said publicly that he was at times 'dreadfully disappointed to see so many Nationalist Party members criticizing our party with such bitterness'.[23] On top of all this, the Liberals were lukewarm, and lazier than ever in their support for the campaign.

Organizationally, the campaign remained in disarray, and there was very little evidence that work was actually being done to collect names – even in Gwynfor's favourite county of Merioneth.[24] The year ended disastrously for the campaign when Dafydd Miles announced that he wished to leave his post after months of thankless effort. It is easy to understand why Ambrose Bebb wrote to T I Ellis some weeks later to ask whether the campaign was still a going concern: 'we would like to know for certain that [the Central Committee] is still in the land of the living, and that it is really organising activity across the whole of Wales... So!! A pig's ear indeed'.[25] Bebb was right: the venture was about to end, leaving 'Home Rule Chaos', as the *News Chronicle* described it, in its wake.[26] But even negative coverage in the popular press was limited and Welsh patriotism waned as 1953 approached. Wales, like the rest of Britain, was caught up in Coronation fever. During the opening months of 1953, the Welsh-language press was full of stories about people in Wales eagerly buying their first television sets so as not to miss out on the experience.

For Plaid Cymru, the royal pomp meant that the campaign for a Parliament was largely ignored and significant tensions surfaced over its attitude to the monarchy. Gwynfor had learned his lesson in 1937 and was determined that Plaid Cymru should not shoot itself in the foot again. When George VI died in February 1952, Gwynfor had advised J E Jones that Plaid Cymru would be 'asking for trouble' if it made any statement on the matter, and he refused a request to speak in Welsh on the issue in Carmarthenshire County Council.[27] Nationally, too, the policy adopted was to say nothing but it became increasingly difficult to maintain such a policy of deliberate indifference. It was the bright young star of the party, Jennie Eirian Davies, who muddied the waters by calling on members to 'reject the royalist nonsense' that would be 'rampant throughout Wales' during 1953. What she wanted was for 1953 to be 'a year of vision' for Plaid Cymru – in other words, a year of anti-royalist protest.[28]

Jennie Eirian Davies's speech had an immediate impact. On 2 January 1953, when Plaid Cymru's Executive met, it was clear that some party members were baying for her blood. Hywel Heulyn Roberts alleged that several prospective Plaid Cymru candidates in Cardiganshire had reconsidered their membership after hearing her remarks, and Dewi Watkin Powell went as far as to say that she should be disciplined for her 'impetuosity'.[29] For once, Gwynfor rejected Watkin Powell's advice, telling him that 'it would take a brave man to do the disciplining' and that whoever did so would in turn be accused of being 'a little dictator'.[30] No disciplinary hearing was held, but Gwynfor was wrong to think that would be the end of the matter. *Y Faner* over the following weeks asserted that Plaid Cymru had deliberately ignored a central plank of its constitutional policy. One faction of the party was made up of members who wanted to extend the new Queen a warm Welsh welcome.[31] Its most prominent spokesman was Saunders Lewis, who accused his fellow-nationalists of 'standing to one side with Pharisaic long faces' as the Irish and 'negroes' of Cardiff enjoyed the colourful pageantry of the Coronation.[32] Another group comprised the Republican element as well as that smaller contingent under the quixotic leadership of D J Davies who believed that a family such as the 'Scudamores of Kentchurch' should be adopted and the Welsh people educated to think of them as a home-grown royal family. [33]

As the discussion continued, it was quite clear that Gwynfor was deeply alarmed at the damage it might do, since so many party members supported the Monarchy and because the Welsh in general, after the privations and misery of war, were enjoying a little colour in their lives. In mid-January 1953, therefore, he prepared a revealing (but unpublished) statement:

> (1) Although there are within Plaid, as in the Labour Party and the Liberal Party, some republicans, the official party policy is not anti-royalist. From the point of view of dominion status, the Queen will be Queen of Wales as she is of New Zealand or Ceylon.
>
> (2) Plaid has not issued any instructions to its members about the Coronation.[34]

This statement was corroborated by a letter from J E Jones which was sent to the district committees. It placed Plaid Cymru firmly on the fence: the advice of the party's Secretary on the key issue of the Coronation was 'to say nothing'. Gwynfor avoided making any statement on the matter but, if anything, his silence only made matters worse. When Elizabeth II was crowned on 2 June 1953, many within Plaid Cymru felt confused. When D J Williams announced that he wasn't 'very clear' in his mind 'about the coronation business',[35] he spoke for many in Gwynfor's party. Further, it was rumoured that the Union Jack had been flown at the Plaid Cymru office in Queen Street, Cardiff on Coronation Day.[36] Gwynfor's own family weren't exactly uninterested in the pageant. Gwynfor's wife, Rhiannon, and the children got up early on the morning of the Coronation to go to a neighbour's house to watch the historic event on television.[37]

After the Coronation, Gwynfor's life and that of his party returned to something approaching normality. It was no coincidence that in May a last-ditch effort was made to revive the moribund campaign for a Welsh Parliament. That month, Plaid Cymru received a request from the campaign's central committee to release Elwyn Roberts, the party's organizer in Gwynedd, to put the campaign back on track. Plaid Cymru agreed to let him go for two years on condition that he would work for the party in the event of a General Election or by-election in the meantime.[38] For Gwynfor, lending his best organizer was a fairly easy decision. After all, since Plaid Cymru had invested so much in the petition, offering Elwyn Roberts was merely an extension of the only political strategy it proclaimed. Roberts was due to start in his new role that September, but he took advantage of the National Eisteddfod in Rhyl that year to re-launch the petition. This was done successfully and the campaign was presented as a practical means of bringing a Welsh Parliament to a wide spectrum of society. The highlight of the launch was the decision by Huw T Edwards, who had been so dismissive at the time of the Llandrindod launch three years previously, to join the campaign. In his own words: 'His heart and head had at last come together'.[39] It was now hoped, as the columnist 'Celt' wrote in the *Liverpool Daily Post*, that Huw T Edwards and others in the Labour Party would acknowledge that giving Wales her own Parliament would be no bad thing.[40]

Gwynfor was encouraged by developments during the summer of 1953. A little over a fortnight after the Rhyl Eisteddfod, his growing family moved from Wernellyn to Talar Wen – a splendid house designed by the celebrated architect, and Gwynfor's brother-in-law, Dewi Prys Thomas. Although the new home stood on Wernellyn's land, it could hardly have been more different from the old one. Wernellyn represented Victorian solidity; Talar Wen was an expression of Gwynfor's confidence that Wales could plan a brighter future for herself. It was a modern home constructed entirely from Welsh materials. Gwynfor was lucky in that his father paid for the house and much of the furniture as a belated wedding present.[41] Gwynfor was truly happy in his new home, and the study with its sweeping views across the Tywi Valley became a refuge for him during the stormy times ahead. There was, nevertheless, a price to pay for living in a close-knit community: once the house was built, some of his opponents appeared to be jealous of it. Similarly, his decision to send two of his sons to the prestigious Llandovery College did little to dispel the perception locally that he was a closet Welsh Tory.[42]

As the family settled in at Talar Wen, Gwynfor threw himself wholeheartedly into the petition campaign. In September 1953, Plaid Cymru chose to take the initiative and decided to hold a rally in the party's name alone. It could have turned out badly, but the event proved a huge success. People flocked to Cardiff in their thousands, among them the Labour MP for Merthyr, S O Davies.[43] But the undoubted high-point was the team of runners who carried a flaming torch from Owain Glyndŵr's parliament house in Machynlleth into the midst of a crowd of three thousand at Sophia Gardens. A spectacular display of this sort was a completely new campaign technique for a party used to the meagre gruel of public meetings in chapel vestries, but it was no less effective for that. For Gwynfor, it was also a means of re-igniting the campaign and associating the party with demands for Cardiff, the city he thought of as 'a bastion of Englishness', to become capital of Wales.[44] And in the opinion of the press, Plaid Cymru was a quarter of the way there already. According to Anthony Davies, writing in the *News Chronicle*,[45] nothing like this had been seen in Cardiff before, while Paul Ferris for *The Observer* saw the event as evidence of Plaid Cymru's practicality and courage.[46]

Although this was strictly a Plaid Cymru rally, it had a definite influence on the wider Parliament campaign as well. By October, when Elwyn Roberts had officially begun his work as organizer, the petitioners' optimism had been boosted greatly. Megan Lloyd George and Gwynfor allowed themselves to think a Parliament was inevitable as the support from ordinary Labour members in Wales increased.[47] And they were not the only ones who believed the petition's fortunes had changed. Just days later, Cliff Prothero wrote to Morgan Phillips, General Secretary of the Labour Party, urging him to spell out the opinion of the party as a whole: 'the Labour Party is having the ground taken underneath its feet because we do not make a declaration one way or the other'.[48] A few days later still, there was panic in the Labour ranks because of a fear that the Communists (who backed the petition) were exercising an influence over the miners' union in the south. At the beginning of November, it appeared that Cliff Prothero's worst fears had been realized, when the NUM asked for 250 copies of the leaflet outlining the petition's aims.[49] Meanwhile, the campaign mushroomed, and the report produced for the petition's central committee showed that names were being collected at over a hundred locations across Wales.

By the middle of the same month, however, the zealous anti-devolutionist Herbert Morrison began to crack the whip – a development which had profound consequences for Gwynfor. On 11 November 1953, first the British Labour Party and then the party's regional council in Wales ruled that a Parliament would be detrimental to Wales. As a result huge pressure was put on Labour rebels like Cledwyn Hughes and Goronwy Roberts to withdraw their support for the petition. Another aspect of the 'counter-attack' was Labour's decision to make an official complaint about the BBC in Wales, claiming that the Corporation was a hotbed of nationalists.[50] For weeks, the only topic in the press was Labour's position and the pressure this placed on the five Labour MPs who backed the petition.[51] Publicly, Gwynfor speculated about their fate, and fanned the flames by predicting that he could imagine 'those members of the Labour Party in Wales who refuse to renounce their country's rights at its behest, leaving the fold, and, perhaps forming an independent Welsh Labour Party'.[52]

Privately, Gwynfor went much further, rejoicing that the Labour Party was tearing itself apart. At last, he wrote to Pennar Davies, the 'little' that Plaid Cymru had done for the petition had been enough 'to throw the enemy camp into disarray'. There was evidence of this, he said, at the packed meetings in Aberdare, Llanelli and Swansea. What mattered to him now was that some were suggesting that a Welsh Labour Party should be formed – although he did not believe it would ever come about. In the meantime, he hoped the five Labour MPs who supported the petition would stand firm. He sensed that Goronwy Roberts was willing to challenge Herbert Morrison because he was 'not expected to get a front-bench seat'. Cledwyn Hughes too, according to Gwynfor, was unlikely to yield because the idea of being part of a national cause appealed to him. Another reason which might keep Cledwyn Hughes on side, Gwynfor supposed, was that he was 'hugely out of pocket by being an MP' and that it would not break his heart 'were he to lose his seat'. T W Jones, the member for Merioneth, had no real choice but to stand his ground because his own constituency party wanted a Parliament and, of course, Gwynfor was sure that S O Davies would not give an inch. The latter's particular problem was that hardly anyone took any notice of him. The only real doubt was Tudor Watkins, the member for Brecon and Radnor, who needed to be 'kept in line'.[53]

As Christmas approached, Gwynfor was in good spirits. For one thing, Maxwell-Fyfe's popularity was in decline, but best of all was what he described to D J Williams as a 'splendid row' in Labour ranks. From then on, there was no pretence of any difference between Plaid Cymru and the Parliament for Wales Campaign. His only worry was that Plaid Cymru was not 'in better shape to make more of it' as the party Secretary, J E Jones, was in poor health.[54] Gwynfor had heard a rumour that some Labour members in Cardiff were about to resign, and he had also heard from Huw T Edwards that he would rather leave the Labour movement than concede defeat to Herbert Morrison. It was therefore no surprise when he concluded that 'something major for Wales could grow out of it all'.[55] When the Plaid Cymru leadership met at the turn of the year, several of them, like Gwynfor, were confident 'the door was opening' and that the long-awaited breakthrough was imminent.[56] The question was how to convert enthusiasm into action, especially in the south Wales coalfield. For Gwynfor and his fellow-leaders, the trade unions were the key to any success, and they went so far as to give serious consideration to launching a Plaid Cymru paper called *Welsh Labour News*.[57] The publication would contrast the 'repression' of the current administration with the more enlightened tradition of Keir Hardie and Arthur Henderson.[58] The paper never saw the light of day, but the campaign did produce its own *Welsh Clarion* which promised to answer the criticisms of anti-devolutionists, 'stone upon stone until the Welsh Parliament'.[59] And as might be expected, Labour dissent gave Gwynfor new confidence. He could now take the message to places like Port Talbot in 'steel country' and assert with conviction that Labour and the Conservatives were as bad as each other when it came to devolution.[60]

In March 1954, after weeks of discussion, Labour announced officially that it would oppose the petition, and this was confirmed at the party conference in May. This was the final blow, leaving devolutionists like Cledwyn Hughes isolated within their own party. But Hughes was also embittered by the lack of practical support the 'five' had received from Plaid Cymru. Cledwyn Hughes's declaration that one of the main reasons his stand had failed was 'the deep resentment throughout the rank and file of the Labour movement in Wales at the persistent and abusive attacks made by certain elements in the Principality on some of the most highly respected Welsh Labour leaders' was obviously aimed at Gwynfor.[61] And there was some truth in it. The position of devolutionists within the Labour Party would have been far stronger had Gwynfor adopted a more diplomatic attitude.

But Gwynfor's perspective is vital here too. Although he was disappointed by the failure of men like Cledwyn Hughes, he hoped a generation of younger people in Wales would realize that it was only through a specifically Welsh party that self-government could come about. He also wanted that generation to understand, as he had done, that it was a myth to believe that 'good Welshmen and women' could mould the Labour Party in their image. As a result, he considered the Labour response as an unintended tribute to Plaid Cymru because it had forced Labour to debate the issue of devolution for the first time since 1946 and to give specific reasons for rejecting it.[62] It was a decision that thrilled him, and Gwynfor interpreted it in the context of other encouraging signs: a rich year in Welsh literary output from Plaid Cymru members like Saunders Lewis, Islwyn Ffowc Elis and D J Williams; a successful Welsh opera company; and the growth of Welsh-medium schools. As he told *Y Faner*, only one conclusion could be drawn, that his party was 'making the nation realize its potential' despite the efforts of Labour Party 'gamekeepers'. With such a huge 'crack' in the socialist machine, Gwynfor dreamed of the day when Wales would save itself as he, as a boy in Barry had saved himself.[63]

This sense that success was close at hand was further strengthened when Gwynfor was appointed chair of the Congregationalists in June 1954. Given his background and family history, it was a huge honour, and a substantial political boost too. It was this event, above all, that finally killed off the insinuation that he was a crypto-Catholic. So great was the interest in his installation that people began queuing outside the chapel in Pen-y-groes, Carmarthenshire, from eight o'clock in the morning. According to Anthony Davies, correspondent for the *News Chronicle*: 'even at Epsom a few hours later there could have been no greater eagerness to see the Derby'.[64] Gwynfor chose to speak on 'Christianity and Welsh Society', making a plea for Congregationalists to create their own society rather than bury their heads in what he called 'pietism'. In other words, he argued that his political life was an extension of his Christianity, and that he was following in the footsteps of Congregationalist greats like Henry Richard, Samuel Roberts and Michael D Jones in making his nation more Christian and more Welsh.

His inaugural speech – the nearest he ever came to a full confession of faith as an adult – is also striking for its tone of confidence. At its heart was the assurance that the 'state dinosaur' was dying out and that a new Welsh-speaking society was taking its place. The clearest proof of this, Gwynfor suggested, was hearing about a collier in the Rhondda who was sitting on his doorstep one evening. And then, Gwynfor continued: 'some children came by from the Welsh School, speaking the language nineteen to the dozen as they went. The old man wept with joy. He did not think he would ever hear children speaking Welsh in the streets of the Rhondda ever again. But it happens'.[65] The delivery was masterly, but not everyone was happy with his performance, despite his attempt to present his activities as the extension of an ancient tradition. Although there were cheers and applause during his address, there were also calls of 'rubbish' and 'tripe' from a minority in the congregation who thought mixing politics and religion was heresy.[66]

But if Gwynfor was a heretic, he was a happy one. Although action on the petition had slowed considerably by that summer, there was plenty of evidence that the campaign had won hearts and minds. By now, the target of 250,000 names did not seem over-optimistic. According to *The Manchester Guardian*, the Parliament for Wales Campaign was attracting 'the solid citizens' as well as the 'incendiary fringe' of nationalists.[67] The campaign's central committee records confirm this. In October 1954, it was revealed that the problem was not so much getting people to sign the petition – even in 'very difficult parts of south Wales' – but rather having enough people to collect signatures.[68] Bearing in mind how much time, energy and resources Gwynfor had invested in the petition, one cannot overestimate the importance to him of remarks like these. And above all, Plaid Cymru had a perfect opportunity to take its message to the heart of the south Wales coalfield following the death of Emlyn Thomas, the Labour MP for Aberdare, in July 1954.

Aberdare at the time had a sizeable Welsh-speaking population, but the campaign began unfavourably for both Plaid Cymru and Gwynfor. Despite his best efforts, he had failed to persuade Wynne Samuel to be the party's standard-bearer in the constituency, leaving Gwynfor himself to step into the breach in the absence of any other credible candidate.[69] It was an awkward situation, exacerbated by the belief of many constituency party members that Gwynfor would not be half as popular as Wynne Samuel.[70] The continuing objection of some members to the principle of fighting parliamentary by-elections at all added to the difficulties. Saunders Lewis refused outright to support any campaign, insisting that Gwynfor was 'killing the only spirit that could inspire the country' and that 'only through Wormwood Scrubs' could Wales win her freedom.[71] But Gwynfor persevered, fashioning a campaign (jointly with Glyn James) which would heavily influence his victory in Carmarthen twelve years later. From the very beginning, new and popular tactics were employed, with Gwynfor, chair of the '121,000 strong Congregational Union',[72] appealing to the inherent Welshness of the electors in an effort to win them 'for Wales'.[73] Much of the campaigning was conducted through the medium of English and every effort was made to associate Plaid Cymru with successes on the rugby field and the legendary boxer Dai Dower. Music was also used and, for the first time, singing became a central part of the Plaid Cymru armoury. As Gwynfor raced up and down the valley, he did so to the accompaniment of Hawys Williams singing:

This is my story, this is my song,
Working for Gwynfor all the day long;
He is our hero, he never fails,
When you are voting do so for Wales.[74]

As the campaign continued in relentless rain, it became obvious to the journalists who had ventured to the constituency that change was afoot and that the younger generation was turning to Plaid Cymru. In the process, they were casting aside some of their parents' prejudices about nationalism.[75] Gwynfor also made political capital out of the patriotic sentiment evoked by the petition. On the night of the poll, Labour had to warn the electors in Aberdare not to be fooled by the nationalist 'Trojan Horse' hiding within the Parliament for Wales Campaign.[76] The following day, as expected, Arthur Probert was elected for the Labour Party, but Plaid Cymru saw its vote increase by 3,000 as the Labour faithful stayed away in droves. Gwynfor took 16 per cent of the vote, a slightly poorer showing than Wynne Samuel's in the Aberdare by-election eight years before but, in the context of three years' campaigning and debating the petition, it was felt that Plaid Cymru had worked a small miracle. 'Welsh Home Rule Men Seize Votes. Socialists shocked',[77] the *Daily Express* reported, while even the *Western Mail* was forced to acknowledge the effectiveness of 'Nationalist propaganda'. It would continue, the paper said, for as long as the nationalists could show 'that Wales has her own special problems that are getting scant attention at Whitehall'.[78] Gwynfor himself interpreted the Aberdare result as a huge vote of confidence in Plaid Cymru. Some days after the poll, he wrote in a triumphant mood to D J Williams saying there were two clear conclusions to be drawn. The first was that Plaid members in Aberdare were strutting the valley 'like cockerels'. The second was that 'it was obvious to everyone' who had taken part in the campaign that 'the great majority of people in the valley support a Parliament for Wales' and that their sense of Welshness had increased 'remarkably'.[79]

Following the by-election, Gwynfor turned his attention increasingly to broadcasting. Plaid Cymru was not at the time entitled to make political broadcasts.[80] The rules stated that a party needed to contest fifty parliamentary seats, a twelfth of the total, in order to qualify. This seemed absurd to Plaid Cymru as there were only 36 seats in the whole of Wales and the party had contested four of those in the 1951 General Election.[81] But despite these special circumstances, the Conservative and Labour whips (who were the decision makers in these matters) were not going to change their attitude. Nevertheless, by late 1954, Gwynfor was busy writing and drawing attention to the refusal of the two major parties to acknowledge that the Welsh context was different. He sought to milk as much sympathy as possible from the situation and, by Christmas, a host of individuals and organizations who had little interest in Plaid Cymru had expressed public sympathy with this cause. But the big prize was the announcement that the Wales Broadcasting Council was going to defy the two major parties by promising to give Plaid Cymru party political broadcasts twice a year between elections.

The Broadcasting Council's decision in December 1954 was a notable victory for Plaid Cymru, and Gwynfor continued to focus on broadcasting for several months. In particular, he drew attention to the quality of reception of BBC programmes in many parts of Wales, particularly predominantly Welsh-speaking ones. For years, thousands in Wales had been driven to distraction because programmes produced in Wales by the BBC were being overpowered after six o'clock in the evenings by the stronger signals of the American Station and others in East Germany. Throughout 1954, the press in Wales had been flooded with complaints about screeching background noise and, in December, the nationalist Gwyneth Morgan was fined for having refused to pay her radio licence as a protest. Her stand was an individual one, but others were willing to follow her lead – including Roger Hughes, the rector of Bryneglwys, Denbighshire. He had already spoken out on the matter and had, like Gwyneth Morgan, come to the conclusion that only unlawful action would force the government into action. He called for an organized campaign of non-payment of licences to be known as the 'Listeners' Association'.[82]

Over Christmas, Gwynfor clearly warmed to Roger Hughes's suggestion, and when Plaid Cymru's leadership met in January 1955 he was keen to see the party supporting the Association. Gwynfor, like R Tudur Jones, believed that there was every justification for breaking an unjust law, and that demanding payment for such a poor service amounted, in Jones's words, to 'fraudulent appropriation'.[83] With commercial television on the increase, moreover, Gwynfor was afraid that Welsh-speakers would cease listening to the Welsh wavelength unless there were an improvement in the next three years. In his eyes the Listeners' Association was one step removed from Plaid Cymru itself, and, as such, the party's name would not be associated with unlawful methods in General Election year. Even so, some of the party's leaders were suspicious of Gwynfor's argument, fearing it would undermine all previous efforts to present Plaid Cymru as a moderate party. When the time came to make a decision, the party leadership was split, and it was only after ten hours of discussion, with Gwynfor's casting vote, that Plaid Cymru decided to support the Listeners' Association.[84]

Within days, the Association was formally established. Gwynfor was its first member and chair. He paid two shillings for the privilege, promising to pass on his licence fee to the Association rather than the Postmaster General. The long-term plan was that the Association would transfer licence fees to the Postmaster only if reception on the Welsh wavelength improved. After a slow start, close to a hundred respectable Welsh-speakers promised they would be willing to defy the law.[85] This caused something of a headache to the authorities since the last thing they wanted was to portray Gwynfor, of all people, as a martyr. The other problem facing the Post Office was the popular support that the campaign was attracting in Welsh-speaking Wales. John Roberts Williams, editor of *Y Cymro*, spoke for many: 'For all individuals and organizations in Wales fighting this outrage – good luck'.[86]

At first the authorities ignored the Association but, as the 'radio strike' grew, the Home Secretary, Gwilym Lloyd George, was forced to take the 'strikers' to court.[87] Over the following months, 151 members of the Association were summonsed and their cases provoked considerable sympathy for the cause if not for Plaid Cymru. Gwynfor himself appeared before the magistrates at Llangadog in August 1955 'with every sign of being in an evil temper', according to a Post Office representative, when he was not allowed to address the bench.[88] But he won a decisive moral victory. The fine of two pounds and three shillings was a small price to pay, because his case and others speeded the process of establishing a decent radio service in Wales from September 1955 onwards.[89] As a result the Association disbanded as a practical force in December 1955 when the 'radio heroes' decided they should resume paying their licences – much to the relief of the authorities.

This was not Gwynfor's only triumph during 1955. The petition continued to flourish – in spite of financial problems and bad weather. In February 1955, for example, it was signed by the occupants of 1,074 of the 1,092 houses visited in Merthyr Tydfil. There were similarly impressive figures in the Rhondda and Llanelli.[90] The difficulty, however, once again, was finding enough people to collect signatures. A month later, S O Davies presented a Bill in Westminster calling for a Welsh Parliament and although it was roundly defeated, *Y Cymro* rejoiced that Welsh MPs were being forced to think about devolution.[91] It was an attitude shared by Gwynfor, and it is no coincidence that his friend Dewi Watkin Powell was responsible for drafting S O Davies's Bill.

Events at Westminster and the petition's success were part of a minor patriotic renaissance. In April, Gwynfor was re-elected to Carmarthenshire Council and, for the first time, he was not alone – another Plaid Cymru member, Gwynfor S Evans from Betws was also elected. This in itself was a step forward for the party after Gwynfor's several thankless years in local government. But the real significance of the result was that the two nationalists held the balance of power, with Labour and the Independents having 29 seats each. Given Gwynfor's visceral hatred of the Labour Party, it was no surprise that he did not give a moment's thought to any alliance with the Labour group. Rather, the two Gwynfors made a formal agreement with the Independents – who, despite their name, were a loose grouping of Liberals and Tories. This in itself was a controversial step, but the real red rag for Gwynfor's critics was his decision to accept the group's offer to become an alderman. Being an alderman meant that he could not be challenged in an election for six years and that his place within the Independents' system of privileges was assured. For the Labour group (and for some in Plaid Cymru), Gwynfor's decision was final proof that he was a Welsh Tory and that his only ambition was personal respectability. The *Carmarthen Journal* compared him to Faust, who had famously sold his soul to the Devil.[92]

He was deeply wounded by the comparison, and the aldermanship would haunt him for a decade. Even so, there is some truth in the accusation that he was in league with the Devil. By making a formal pact with the Independents, Gwynfor had undertaken to work alongside a group who concealed their true allegiances. This became evident when they opposed Labour attempts to improve the lot of the working classes in Carmarthenshire.[93] Gwynfor certainly enjoyed the status that came with the title, but had accepted the position for sound political reasons. Plaid Cymru's pact with the Independents ensured that his party could squeeze as much as possible out of its new partners.[94] Given this power, the two Gwynfors managed to ensure the implementation of some forward-thinking policies on roads, social services and Welsh-language education in particular. There were also moves to ensure that the County Council operated more like a democratically elected body and less like a Soviet Politburo. That said, it is difficult to avoid the conclusion that this marriage of convenience was ill-advised. If there was one accusation which damaged Gwynfor's efforts in the valleys during the 'fifties and 'sixties, then it was the charge he was a closet Tory. And for all his vehement denials, the title was the only proof many in the south needed that Gwynfor was at heart a Welsh *poujadiste*, a mouthpiece of conservative populism.

April 1955 and the approaching General Election brought temporary relief. Plaid Cymru expended all its efforts on the campaign, largely forgetting the Parliament for Wales Campaign. Temporarily, Elwyn Roberts left it to work as the Plaid Cymru agent in Conwy, as had been agreed, but the move deprived the campaign of its only full-time worker. It also lost its most charismatic leader when Megan Lloyd George joined Labour in April 1955. Even so, 'political patriotism' thrived. It was already heightened following the announcement that Plaid Cymru would not be allowed any party political broadcasts. The Postmaster General, Charles Hill, had decided that no broadcasting time could be allocated to the 'Welsh Nationalist Party' between elections because he said it would set 'an especially dangerous precedent'. But even as he forced the Broadcasting Council to toe the line, Hill knew there would be a price to pay. He had warned his colleagues in the Churchill cabinet that there was 'a virtual certainty of a serious political blow-up if the present proposal is banned'. He was right.[95] When news of the broadcasting ban broke, there was widespread sympathy with Plaid Cymru and many agreed with Gwynfor's analysis that the sanction was proof of 'openly totalitarian tendencies in the old parties'.[96] Immediately, Plaid Cymru began a campaign to lift the ban, publishing pamphlets, painting slogans and organizing rallies with other smaller parties such as the Commonwealth Party and the ILP under the banner of 'The Five-Party Committee'.

In the longer term, the restriction on political broadcasts was a considerable handicap for Plaid Cymru, and it took a decade's hard campaigning, and the establishment of a pirate radio station, before the restriction was finally lifted in October 1965. But, ironically, it proved an advantage during the 1955 General Election given Plaid Cymru's failure to really ignite its campaign. The first problem was the highly ambitious number of seats – twelve – that it had decided to contest. Gwynfor chose to pursue a policy of fielding as many candidates as possible despite opposition from some party members who feared that such an enterprise would be a costly waste of time. Dewi Watkin Powell, for instance, thought fighting unwinnable seats like Carmarthen was nonsensical, and venturing into Monmouthshire constituencies such as Abertillery even more so. But, for Gwynfor, the important thing was for Plaid Cymru to be seen as a truly national party. Several doubted his wisdom, but Gwynfor was resolute. Justifying his decision to enter the electoral desert of Monmouthshire for the first time, he told J E Jones that 'a very small vote would not do too much harm' considering 'that the propaganda value would be enormous'.[97] Gwynfor was proved right, but finding suitable candidates was difficult. Six weeks before the ballot, Plaid Cymru had only selected seven and Gwynfor had no choice but to travel up and down the country imploring friends to stand. The final total was one short of the target of twelve, but his strategy of giving the party a national presence was intact. Although it was not obvious at the time, he was laying firm foundations for nationalist growth in the 'sixties and 'seventies.

Eleven candidates, then, stood for the party in May 1955, but they immediately faced a storm of criticism. The announcement that Plaid Cymru would not be repeating its agreement of 1951, namely refusing to oppose candidates from other parties who were in favour of devolution had not gone down well. Megan Lloyd George – by now a member of the Labour Party – was furious by Gwynfor's decision.[98] The same was true of Goronwy Roberts and Cledwyn Hughes. For the Welsh wing of the Labour Party and their supporters in the Welsh-language press, it was an insensitive tactic given the sacrifices made by socialist devolutionists over the previous five years.[99] This became the hot topic in the press during the early days of the campaign, but Gwynfor remained unmoved. He knew full well by then that the political battleground had been transformed since 1951, and that this was not a struggle between individuals as much as 'between parties and policies'.[100] He was also determined that Plaid Cymru should not have to apologize 'for standing in any part of the country'.[101]

Gwynfor stood for a third time in Merioneth, basing his campaign on the by now familiar combination of emotion and Welsh patriotism. Although he, like the other Plaid Cymru candidates, mentioned bread-and-butter issues such as the modernization of the railways and the establishment of an electricity board for Wales, in reality these were secondary considerations.[102] Increasingly, and in contrast to his tactics when he assumed the Presidency, he appealed to his electors' values rather than their party loyalty. In a statement for *Y Cymro*, for instance, he insisted that all Plaid Cymru candidates had one thing in common: their 'passionate' love for Wales: 'They believe in Wales and in her potential and they wish to see her live with all their heart'. In Merioneth itself, he paid for election literature that echoed – curiously enough, given his pacifism – recruitment posters from the First World War:

> Wales Needs You. We Are Welsh First. Whatever Our Political Beliefs, Let Us Unite to Save Wales. We Are Voting for Gwynfor Evans.[103]

On another occasion, he made a public appeal 'to marry the strength of our country's socialism and its liberalism and its healthy conservatism' to create a movement that would be 'invincible'.[104] Essentially, he was trying to persuade his electors that Plaid Cymru was a non-partisan party. This was a 'national movement' in the true sense of the word – and anyone could join. As a short-term tactic, this patriotic call proved highly successful. As the polls opened, many observers believed Gwynfor Evans had every reason to be confident and that he would hold the balance of power between Labour and the Liberals in the county. According to *The Times*, Plaid Cymru was thought of as the young people's party in Merioneth as Gwynfor, once again, addressed packed meetings. Fortunately for him, he was fighting a constituency where television had little influence – a situation that would be reversed within four years.[105] 'Hafren', political commentator for *Y Faner*, went a step further, predicting that 26 May would be 'the greatest day in Welsh history' when the electors in Merioneth would finally snub Labour.[106]

After all the speculation, Gwynfor doubled his vote in Merioneth to 22 per cent, while Plaid Cymru nationally enjoyed encouraging results. Despite all the doubts, the party made an impression in seats like Conwy and Gower. More astonishing still was the 4.1 per cent in Abertillery – a seat then seen by many as being part of England. Gwynfor was delighted by the result nationally and the substantial increase in the share of the vote gained – from 1.2 per cent in 1950 to 3.2 per cent in 1955. For Gwynfor, there was now a light in the darkness: 'the Little Party' was getting bigger, the sect was growing into a church, and the people of Wales, at long last, were beginning to embrace nationalism.[107] After five years of uncertainty pursuing the dual policy of supporting the petition and contesting seats at Westminster, he could now crow to J E Jones that it had been at least a partial success. The petition was due to be submitted the following year, Labour was split over devolution, and the election result was a 'complete' justification of the policy of 'fighting everywhere possible'.[108] Now, he told J E Jones, it was time to pursue the vision for his party for the next five years: to fight between eighteen and twenty seats at the next General Election while concentrating on the three held by the Liberals – Cardiganshire, Montgomeryshire and Carmarthen. So inflated was his confidence by the early summer of 1955 that he did not see human resources as a problem. The only problem that would prevent him challenging Labour and Anthony Eden's new Conservative government was 'finding the money'.[109] On a personal level too, he felt pride on hearing of the birth of son Rhys, his seventh and last child.[110] Then, suddenly, and without warning, a rumour spread that Liverpool Corporation had its eye on one of the most beautiful villages in Wales to satisfy its need for water. The village was Dolanog – and its fight for survival would be the prologue to the epic struggle for Tryweryn. Gwynfor's brief nationalist honeymoon was about to be shattered in the most dramatic of circumstances.

1915: Gwynfor aged three with his mother, Catherine, and his sister, Ceridwen.

The 'Barry Boy': Gwynfor, his mother Catherine, his sister Ceridwen, his father Dan and the younger brother Alcwyn.

'Evans – never gets rattled' – the youthful cricketer (far left, middle row) at the Barry County School.

Frankfurt, 1936: on holiday with Alcwyn.

A very temperate joy: Gwynfor (with a bottle in his hand), alongside his family on a Dan Evans staff outing, 1934.

The young idealist: Gwynfor in the early 'thirties.

The Welsh Brideshead, 1935: Gwynfor (back row, second from the right) among the student members of Oxford University's Dafydd ap Gwilym society.

An uncharacteristically flamboyant Gwynfor celebrating the end of his Oxford University exams, 1936.

Discovering *Y Fro Gymraeg*: Gwynfor in Tynllidiart near Dolgellau, 1939. The picture was taken by his future father-in-law, Dan Thomas.

Love in the time of war: Gwynfor and Rhiannon in Tynllidiart, 1940.

Rhiannon, or 'Nanon' as she was affectionately called, on her first visit to Wernellyn in 1940.

Gwynfor and the 'Bishop': Gwynfor in the company of Richard Bishop, Chairman of Welsh Pacifists.

Pledging peace, 1941: throughout the Second World War, Gwynfor worked for Plaid Cymru, Undeb Cymru Fydd and the Welsh Pacifists – a Herculean task.

1 March 1941: Rhiannon, alongside her father, Dan, on her wedding day.

The first year of married life: Gwynfor and Rhiannon in Wernellyn, 1941.

Follow my leader: a Plaid Cymru meeting c.1947.

'Like some ghostly column from Arthurian legend': the Llyn-y-Fan Fach protest, January 1947.

The long march through t
institutions: Gwynfor and his fello
members of the BBC's Adviso
Council for Wales, 194

'Stop War Office Havoc in Wales': A Plaid Cymru protest against the military requisition of Welsh land. Gwilym Prys Davies is seen at the very front of the photograph taken in January 1947.

Stand Your Ground: The Abergeirw protest of 1948.

The Machynlleth rally: the launch of Plaid Cymru's Parliament for Wales campaign, October 1949.

Chapter 6

TRYWERYN 1955–59

THE DECADE-LONG BATTLE FOR TRYWERYN between 1955 and 1965 was the most ambiguous and painful in Gwynfor's long career. He did more than any other Welsh politician in his struggle to prevent Liverpool Corporation drowning the village of Capel Celyn. And no one worked harder to show how parliamentary democracy disregarded Welsh public opinion. By drawing attention to this situation in the years to come, Gwynfor created thousands of constitutional nationalists – including Dafydd Wigley, who would succeed him as President. But that is only half the story. The parallel narrative is that of Gwynfor as a traitor – the man who was ready to compromise with Liverpool, the ambitious politician too cowardly and self-regarding to face imprisonment to save a Welsh-speaking community. It was this perception which led directly to the establishment of the Welsh Language Society and the more militant nationalism of the 'sixties. This view of him as a traitor would prove a turning-point for Welsh nationalism. It would also prove a decisive moment for Gwynfor as a man, to the extent that it would make him turn his back on Merioneth and offer his resignation as President of Plaid Cymru.

In a story full of paradoxes, it is somehow appropriate, given its twists and turns, that the story of Tryweryn did not start in Tryweryn itself at all, but in the village of Dolanog in Montgomeryshire. Since January 1955, Liverpool Corporation had been discussing its need for water with the Welsh section of the Department of Housing and Local Government. There were three areas under consideration for the construction of a dam: Haweswater in Greater Manchester, Dolanog, and Liverpool's favoured site at Cwm Tryweryn.[1] These discussions had taken place in private and the residents of Dolanog and Capel Celyn had no idea that their future was being weighed up so clinically in the corridors of Whitehall and Cardiff. After several months of confidential meetings, in August

1955, Plaid Cymru learned for the first time that such a scheme was afoot. J E Jones heard that Liverpool Corporation had its sights on Dolanog while Gwynfor heard a rumour that a site in Merioneth was the target.

There was no indication at the time, however, that the plans would lead to a crisis for Plaid Cymru and Capel Celyn. Gwynfor's rather vague response was to suggest that the party should make a statement 'on the land question in Wales and the rights of English authorities'.[2] His intention at the time had been to launch another campaign against compulsory conscription but, in September 1955, the news was made public: Liverpool was looking at Dolanog and considering creating a reservoir that would extend for four miles along the river Vyrnwy. It would involve the drowning of Dolanog, including the historic home of the Welsh hymnwriter Ann Griffiths at Dolwar Fach. Once the threat became public knowledge, a campaign began immediately to save Dolanog. *Y Cymro* called it the 'Last Days of Dolanog', consciously echoing the title of the popular film about the drowning of a fictional valley, *Last Days of Dolwyn*, released six years previously. Gwynfor warmed to the theme, claiming that Plaid Cymru's duty was to prevent a similar fate in the real world of Dolanog.[3] He was also determined that Plaid Cymru should never acknowledge the right of English local authorities to occupy and use 'any area of Wales' for a purpose that was not 'for the good of Wales'.[4] But Liverpool was shrewd. While admitting that Dolanog was under consideration, they confirmed, almost in passing, that they were also looking at two other sites – Frongoch and Tryweryn, both in Merioneth. In the heat of battle, this was the announcement that campaigners like Gwynfor and the press seized upon. Everyone, understandably enough, thought it would be a struggle to save Dolanog.

Four days before Christmas, the people of Tryweryn's fears suddenly intensified when they heard that Dolanog was safe. Based on the advice of Huw T Edwards, chair of the Council for Wales, the civil service realized there would be a storm of protest if Liverpool dared to drown 'Ann's country'.[5] Given the warning, they concluded that: '… Treweryn [*sic*] will cause less opposition than Dolanog'.[6] Thus Tryweryn's fate was sealed and it was only a small step then for Liverpool to accept the mandarins' recommendation and announce generously that Dolanog was safe. Liverpool was satisfied with the outcome: it had found a much larger valley, but at the same time it created the impression that the city was respecting Welsh public opinion. It is impossible to say whether this was all deliberate, but it was certainly a massive triumph for a city which genuinely believed it needed water to improve its slums and boost its industries. It was a strong moral argument and, in no time, it created a substantial momentum for Liverpool Corporation.

Gwynfor reacted furiously to the news, deriding Liverpool's Labour councillors for their scheming. All the talk about drowning 'the home of a genius and saint' before 'seizing somewhere else … just as vital to the life of the nation' was a blatant 'show of hypocrisy'.[7] And in Gwynfor's eyes, the attitude of the Welsh-speakers on Merseyside was also reprehensible as they refused to support the villagers of Dolanog and Capel Celyn simply because they believed Liverpool needed the water. For these people, Liverpool's contribution to Wales during the war gave the city a moral claim to Welsh resources, but Gwynfor dismissed these Welsh expatriates as 'cowards'.[8] Without doubt, another battle had begun and would demand 'a huge and costly effort'. But, however sincere his words, Gwynfor could scarcely have dreamed how costly and bitter the struggle would eventually become.

Plaid Cymru's Executive was similarly unaware of what lay ahead. At the end of 1955, the leadership met in Aberystwyth amid consternation about the impending fate of Capel Celyn. It was decided that Plaid Cymru should fight a constitutional campaign to save Tryweryn, emphasizing that the party's fundamental opposition to the scheme was based on economics. This was the beginning of the public struggle but, behind closed doors, an acrimonious clash between the constitutional and unconstitutional wings of Plaid Cymru had begun which would, in time, develop into an epic battle for the party's future. The constitutional wing was by far the stronger, and it was agreed that constitutional methods should be employed first. However, at that first meeting, it was also decided to draw up 'a confidential policy on the matter for the future'.[9] In other words, the party was drafting a policy on unlawful action.

The link between Plaid Cymru and the villagers in Capel Celyn was Elizabeth Watkin Jones, daughter of Watcyn o Feirion, considered to be the embodiment of folk culture in that corner of the county. As secretary of the Tryweryn Defence Committee, 'Lizzie May', jointly with Gwynfor, were the architects of the campaign. Without her contribution and Gwynfor's, it is doubtful whether the name Tryweryn would still be remembered more than half a century later. But in spite of Gwynfor's enthusiasm at the beginning of 1956, the fact is that many in Wales were reluctant if not downright unwilling to respond to the impending destruction of Capel Celyn.[10] Gwynfor and Elizabeth Watkin Jones co-ordinated a forceful campaign while, and this was a great achievement, holding internal tensions in check.

The first problem they faced was the stance taken by the people of Bala, the district's main town. In mid-January 1956, they heard that Bala Town Council had invited a member of the Corporation to explain the scheme to them. Elizabeth Watkin Jones was appalled when she heard this and realised that the first task she and Gwynfor faced was to 'convince in Jerusalem' and attempt to alert the 'Philistines in our midst' that Tryweryn was worth preserving.[11] The problem, however, was that several people in Penllyn agreed with the 'Philistines' in Bala that Capel Celyn was an unremarkable, unromantic backwater – which made it even harder to ignite their indignation. The farmers of Capel Celyn were aware of this, commenting in one of their meetings that public opinion was tepid and that 'Tryweryn is not a sacred place like the home of Ann Griffiths'.[12] The same indifference was also evident among the working classes of Merioneth. When T W Jones, the Merioneth MP, held public meetings, many of his Labour supporters would urge him not to 'waste our time talking about Tryweryn tonight', preferring him to 'give us a bit of politics'.[13] Elizabeth Watkin Jones's prime concern, however, was that the residents of Capel Celyn itself were so fearful of what lay ahead of them. In a heart-rending letter, she wrote to J E Jones:

> It's true that the people of Celyn have been slow in joining the fight but this was because they lacked a leader and we didn't like the idea of doing it for them… The truth is that their poetic/musical culture has made them too dreamy and slow to deal with the whole business of Liverpool's oppression.[14]

It was evident that anyone who wanted to save Capel Celyn would have to tread carefully.

Gwynfor's feat during these early months was to present the intellectual argument for preserving Tryweryn by combining patriotism and economics. In countless speeches and essays throughout 1956 and beyond, he reminded the Welsh people why the bleak acres of Capel Celyn were so special. As with the battles at Epynt and Trawsfynydd, he based his objection on the almost mystical quality of the land, arguing that Tryweryn was 'the heart of a part of the country that is acknowledged as somewhere where Welsh culture is seen at its best and strongest'.[15] But unlike Epynt and Trawsfynydd, making the case for Capel Celyn was more complicated. It was relatively simple to fight for Welsh land in the name of pacifism, but now he had to explain to English and international audiences why a big city like Liverpool should not have a share of the abundant rain that fell on Merioneth. The destruction that Liverpool had suffered in the war also clearly gave the city a moral credibility. It was virtually impossible to undermine the emotional argument, and, having met with little success, Gwynfor decided to counter the emotionalism by claiming that Liverpool's real motive was capitalist greed. He proposed that Liverpool should look to Manchester for water and not persist with the lie that the city's working classes were festering in filthy slums.[16] This, in essence, was the message he sent to Liverpool Council at the end of February, warning them that Welsh 'national consciousness' had developed greatly during the last few years.[17]

Little by little, the campaign for Capel Celyn would cast a shadow over all Plaid Cymru's activities. But, important though it was, Gwynfor tried to continue with the previous mission of expanding the party's appeal: in January, he addressed foreign journalists; in March, he completed his work on the petition;[18] in the same month, he held a series of meetings to discuss the possibility of establishing an independent Welsh-language television company.[19] However, very gradually, Tryweryn began to transform Plaid Cymru's activities as the party channelled more and more of its efforts into saving this remote valley. At the time, Gwynfor had no real choice; had he not led the battle, it is doubtful whether anyone else would have done anything meaningful to help. This is clearly illustrated by the disastrous story of the Capel Celyn Defence Committee. When the committee was first established, at the end of March 1956, Gwynfor and Elizabeth Watkin Jones became responsible for deciding its direction and tactics simply because no other member was willing to do so. This situation arose even though Gwynfor was not even a full member of the committee. Rather, he was appointed one of ten honorary presidents – the others included such prominent figures as Megan Lloyd George, Ifan ab Owen Edwards and T W Jones. However, the fact is that Gwynfor was the only one of them who actually did anything practical to defend Tryweryn.

He gave generously of his time despite profound doubts among some committee members that it was unwise for them to have the President of Plaid

Cymru in their ranks. They feared that his presence would lead to a bias against the Capel Celyn campaign among those whom Elizabeth Watkin Jones described to Gwynfor as 'the prejudiced Welsh'.[20] At the time, Plaid Cymru was more unpopular than usual because of its support for Archbishop Makarios in Cyprus who was fanning the flames of rebellion against British forces on the island.[21] But Gwynfor's problems as de facto leader of the committee were only beginning. With so many members suspicious of him, and others reluctant to take any action, it was never going to be plain sailing. John Roberts Williams wrote in *Y Cymro* that the Defence Committee's weakness seemed to be too much preaching and too little organization – unlike the struggle to save Dolanog.[22] Gwynfor also had to compete against the indifference of many eminent Welshmen and women towards Tryweryn. Typical was the historian R T Jenkins, who wrote to Elizabeth Watkin Jones that 'the advantages of the scheme for the area outweigh any disadvantage'.[23] As a result, he refused the request to write a pamphlet outlining the intellectual case for preserving Capel Celyn. No one else could be found to write it and, in the end, Gwynfor himself was obliged to do so.

It was yet another burden and further proof of the difficulties the campaign faced in the spring of 1956. There were only a few months left before Liverpool was due to submit its Bill to Parliament asking for the right to drown the valley and the village. But, meanwhile, convincing people in Wales of the urgency of the situation was proving to be a gruelling task. The editorial support of the *Western Mail* was an unanticipated fillip, but Gwynfor was driven to distraction by the continuing apathy – especially in Penllyn. He was devastated, though not surprised, when Bala Town Council voted against supporting the Capel Celyn Defence Committee and its campaign. Tryweryn, they explained, was not within their boundaries.[24] The councillors justified their decision by referring to concerns over the water supply to Bala itself, but commercial interests doubtless played a role too. Gwynfor tried in vain to convince Bala's traders that the shops could only expect a temporary boom and that there would be no prospects of a reduction in local taxation once the reservoir had been built.[25] Corwen was just as unsympathetic; its council saw fit to leave the request for support on the table.[26] So too Merioneth County Council. When the principle of supporting the people of Capel Celyn was discussed there, the councillors voted not to express an opinion. It was a close-run thing when the matter came before the council for the second time, and it was only in June, 'after a heated battle', that the formal vote was taken to oppose Liverpool.[27] This was six months after Liverpool had announced its plans. It comes as no surprise that Elizabeth Watkin Jones should sense 'a huge indifference on such an important issue'.[28]

As the local campaign limped on, there was growing pressure within Plaid Cymru for Gwynfor to carry out one great act of self-sacrifice. By April 1956, some members of the party Executive were keen to undertake law-breaking action without delay. J E Jones's notes on a meeting to discuss the issue reveal that Plaid Cymru's leadership were of the general opinion that 'people will be astounded if we do not do something'.[29] That 'something' meant the use of non-violent methods. The discussion continued for hours with some members suggesting that Plaid Cymru should consider actions as varied as a fortnight's picket of Liverpool, closing down one of the city's streets on a Saturday afternoon and plastering Wales with slogans. The Welsh authorities were also expecting some kind of action, and Blaise Gillie (chief civil servant of the Welsh department of the Housing and Local Government Ministry) ventured a prediction:

> The Central Office think it likely that if the Bill is passed, the Welsh Nationalists will proceed to at least token acts of physical resistance as has been done before the war, and obstruct the road at Trawsfynydd.[30]

There is no record of what Gwynfor said in that key meeting of the Executive, but it is obvious that he wished to be cautious and wait for the results of constitutional pressure. Following the meeting, a sub-committee was created, 'The Cwm Tryweryn Committee', to discuss methods. Gwynfor himself sat on the committee, along with leading figures such as R Tudur Jones, Tom Jones, Llanuwchllyn, and J E Jones.[31] By establishing such a body Gwynfor was buying time, without closing the door on the possibility of unconstitutional action in the future. However, the constitutional route was the most attractive one for political and personal reasons. From a personal perspective, his family circumstances made matters particularly difficult. With a family of seven children, Gwynfor was afraid that serving time in prison would force him to stop working for Plaid Cymru and mean he would be obliged to find employment as a solicitor.[32] It was for financial reasons, after all, that Saunders Lewis had withdrawn from frontline politics. In addition, he obviously had a responsibility towards Rhiannon. In September 1956, the couple had taken their first holiday together in five years. Her life throughout the 'fifties had been taken up with family concerns and her husband's almost perpetual absences.[33] Gwynfor hoped that he could escape prison and save his family any grief by frustrating Liverpool with the kind of political action that liberal Welsh Wales would understand. That was his goal, but as the Tryweryn affair continued, the demand for action similar to that at Penyberth weighed on his conscience like a ton of lead.[34]

Gwynfor's disinclination to face prison was not merely a question of personality. By the summer of 1956, the diplomatic chaos over Suez was uppermost in everyone's mind and many assumed there would be a General Election that autumn. Given Plaid Cymru's confidence that it could win Merioneth, there were those in the party who thought that it would be extremely foolish for Gwynfor to go to prison. There were other problems too. Although many Plaid Cymru activists were ready to break the law, in reality the campaign had failed to win hearts and minds. Party members in the county were not prepared to support a campaign that would upset sensibilities and bring the respectability of Plaid Cymru into disrepute at a local level.[35] The caginess is evident in records of the discussions held that summer on the relatively benign idea of picketing in Liverpool. Dewi Prys Thomas, Gwynfor's brother-in-law, tried to organize a march of 500 through the city centre but failed to persuade enough people to go.[36] Ordinary Plaid Cymru members had a variety of excuses for staying away, from gathering the hay harvest to organizing a garden party. In this regard, it is difficult to avoid the conclusion that these respectable patriots, the sort of people who had been attracted into Plaid Cymru by Gwynfor, found it hard to grasp the significance of Penyberth and the appeal of heroism. When all aspects of the situation are considered, it is far easier to understand why Gwynfor did not rush headlong into direct action.

However, Tryweryn was not the only irritant. Increasingly, J E Jones and Gwynfor's ambitious ideas to expand Plaid Cymru's organization faced difficulties. Although the party had been able to afford to fight the Newport by-election that year, it was in dire financial straits – mainly because of the cost of publishing the *Welsh Nation* every week. By September 1956, the paper itself was in a parlous state, leaving Gwynfor and Elwyn Roberts unsure about what course of action to take. Above all, they were eager to hear from the colourful expatriate Hywel Hughes, Bogota, who had promised to do 'something for Plaid'.[37] During 1956, Gwynfor met Hywel Hughes and explained to him that financial considerations were 'preventing the party's growth'. In this meeting, it appears that Gwynfor and Elwyn Roberts asked for a vast sum – £50,000.[38] Hywel Hughes said he could help but, crucially, he gave no indication of the amount he was likely to contribute. Meanwhile, Gwynfor and Elwyn Roberts were left to kick their heels as they waited for news from South America. As the days became weeks, the debt grew alarmingly, and Gwynfor was worried that Plaid Cymru's bank would refuse to process the party's cheques, thereby causing difficulties for its creditors. The situation was made a thousand times worse by J E Jones's deteriorating health, leading Gwynfor to hide the true state of affairs from him. When the situation was at its worst Gwynfor went cap in hand – unbeknown to the party's own organizer – to some businessmen in Cardiff, but with little success.[39] The crisis came to an end in November 1956 when Elwyn Roberts phoned with 'good news on the dollar front'.[40] It is not known exactly how much was received, but one thing is certain: even the cash injection from Colombia did not prevent the *Welsh Nation* from reverting to a monthly publication – a retrograde step and a heavy blow to Gwynfor and his party.[41]

Somehow or other, Plaid ensured the press were kept in the dark about the party's cash flow problems. However, in many ways, the financial crisis mirrored the increasingly desperate attempts to save Capel Celyn. Although Plaid Cymru had held a successful rally as part of its campaign in September 1956,[42] Gwynfor was gradually realizing that if Wales were to have any chance of defeating the hard-headed aldermen of Liverpool it would need to be united. Repeatedly, the city's Corporation refused the Defence Committee's attempts to open channels of communication.[43] So confident were the Liverpool councillors of victory that they considered any meetings with the committee would be a waste of time. And the same uncompromising attitude was now being publicly voiced by those within the Liverpool Welsh establishment as well. The editor of *Y Glannau*, the monthly newsletter of the Merseyside Welsh diaspora, took the view that drowning Capel Celyn was a splendid idea since there was 'no culture to boast of in the bleating of a sheep nor glory in brushwood'.[44] It is hardly surprising then that Gwynfor admitted to D J and Noëlle Davies in September 1956 that his spirits 'tended to go down into the cellar' over the whole Tryweryn affair.[45] It is probable too that Gwynfor was aware of the private criticism directed at him following the publication of his long-awaited statement, *Save Cwm Tryweryn for Wales*[46] – just a month before the Bill was presented to Parliament. This was meant to be the Defence Committee's strongest weapon but, when it appeared, it disappointed many as it was littered with technical errors. The sharp-witted Wynne Samuel remarked that there was 'no need to defend Treweryn [*sic*] with incorrect facts'.[47] And the response was similar from the civil servants in the Welsh department of the Housing and Local Government Ministry. One of them who had studied Gwynfor's pamphlet spoke in measured terms about the 'doubtful validity' of many of its factual conclusions.[48]

In practical terms, the first phase of the constitutional battle was unequivocally lost, hardly any pressure having been exerted on Liverpool Council. Although several Welsh organizations were willing to support the Capel Celyn cause, there was no unanimity. Indeed, *The Times* was able to state confidently (albeit misleadingly) that only five per cent of people in Wales opposed the drowning of the valley, and that the trade unions were strongly in favour.[49] This perception brought growing calls within Plaid Cymru for its President to take a more courageous, self-sacrificial stand. October 1956 saw the Plaid Cymru committee which had been charged six months previously with investigating the possibility of direct action, hold a vital meeting. But once again its members were hopelessly divided. Some, like Emrys Bennett Owen, favoured obstructing Liverpool Corporation's work on the dam by interfering with the contractors' equipment. Others, like Dr Elwynne Jones, saw that as a slippery slope leading to 'the use of force in the long run'.[50] For his own part, Gwynfor was prepared to consider civil disobedience, because he drew a distinction between the use of force in relation to property on the one hand and the use of force to people on the other. Even so, his lack of enthusiasm was evident. He bought time by delegating to Emrys Roberts, the *Welsh Nation*'s radical young editor (and full-time staff member of Plaid Cymru from 1957 onwards), the task of organising 'Gandhi-like tactics'.[51] With Emrys Roberts – a man considered by none other than Saunders Lewis as the 'most dangerous appointment' in Plaid Cymru's history – now responsible for formulating tactics, the activist wing of the party came to the fore.[52]

Time was running out, and Liverpool Council was about to submit its scheme for parliamentary approval. Plaid Cymru's response was to re-launch its protest. Elizabeth Watkin Jones had also heard rumours that Labour MPs were ready to support Liverpool and that even Megan Lloyd George, one of the Defence Committee's honorary presidents, was about to side with her new friends at Westminster.[53] She did not, in fact, do so but, in the prevailing climate, the next natural step for Gwynfor, Plaid Cymru, and the Defence Committee was to take the fight to the enemy – the chamber of Liverpool Council.

On 7 November 1956, Gwynfor, R Tudur Jones and David Roberts, vice-chair of the Defence Committee, visited St George's Hall, Liverpool, with the intention of addressing the Council. They knew full well they had little hope of presenting their arguments directly to the councillors, but they could not have anticipated the storm that ensued. It was the Welsh delegation's misfortune that their visit coincided with a memorably short-tempered day for the Council. The second item on the agenda was a motion of censure from Labour on the Tories' handling of Suez. When the motion was presented, the Conservatives stormed out of the chamber singing 'Land of Hope and Glory'. For ten minutes, all council business was suspended, and it was only after order had been restored that the matter of Capel Celyn was discussed. By then, everyone was in a foul mood and the atmosphere in the chamber was toxic as the councillors approved spending £30,000 on the preparatory work at Tryweryn. When Alderman Frank Cain presented the recommendations of the Water Committee, Gwynfor rose to his feet and began heckling him from the public gallery. Looking back on the Tryweryn campaign, Gwynfor would say that the most exciting moment in the whole affair was when he asked in his most courteous Oxford English for the right to address the assembled gathering: 'My Lord Mayor, will you accept a deputation from Wales?'[54] The councillors looked up at him dumbstruck, but Gwynfor proceeded, with his heart thumping loudly. The message was one audiences in Wales had heard countless times before, but being able to convey the 'deep opposition throughout Wales' to the scheme in such a forum was a gilt-edged opportunity. Within seconds, the Liverpool city fathers realized what was happening and apoplectic cries of 'Order, Order' and 'Go Back to Wales' echoed through the chamber. Bessie Braddock, a Liverpool MP (and wife of the Labour group leader, John Braddock), looked as if she were about to have a fit, and used every ounce of her twenty stone to beat her desk as she cursed Gwynfor. The Council chair vainly called for order, and it was only when the police intervened that the three Welshmen left. From Plaid Cymru's point of view, the point had been made – Capel Celyn would not be drowned without a fight – but for all the press attention, the protest did not make a jot of difference to attitudes in Liverpool. *The Liverpool Echo* described it dismissively as 'a scene', and considered the Suez protest to be far more significant than Gwynfor's.[55]

Plaid Cymru now needed a new tactic, and soon. Three days later, Gwynfor argued in an extraordinary meeting of the party's Executive that the Liverpool Council had not taken the objection to the drowning of Capel Celyn seriously. Other aspects worried him as well: the indifference of Welsh MPs and the claim in *The Times* a month before that only five per cent of the people of Wales gave tuppence for the fate of Tryweryn. The situation, he said, 'puts even greater pressure on Plaid'.[56] Gwynfor therefore persuaded those around the table that a new and different approach was needed, and it was decided to return to Liverpool with the people of Capel Celyn itself. The party leadership agreed this was the best way forward, but the villagers took some persuading. The Capel Celyn Defence Committee had already discussed the idea and rejected it. Some if its members thought it 'useless' and 'that a little group from Capel Celyn would not count in the big city'.[57] By now, however, Elizabeth Watkin Jones was working largely on her own initiative, 'often consulting no one but Gwynfor Evans'. In the teeth of considerable opposition from the more conservative wing of the Defence Committee, Gwynfor and Elizabeth Watkin Jones insisted on a protest in Liverpool. On 21 November, shortly after milking time, the entire community of Capel Celyn (with the exception of one or two farmers who were unable to make the journey) set off for Liverpool. It would be one of the most heart-wrenching and emotional protests in Welsh history.

Their buses displayed posters: 'Your homes are safe – why destroy ours? Please, Liverpool, be a great city not a big bully'.[58] It was one last attempt to stop the Council on the day of the vote on drowning their homes. The protest would never have taken place were it not for Gwynfor, and it was he who gave leadership to the anxious villagers as they reached the city. As they climbed down from their vehicles, their mood was as gloomy as the weather. Mrs Jennie Rowlands from Gelli farm doubted there was any point in protesting: 'Do you think the big council will listen to us, a few village people from Wales? We can't speak English well. We are Welsh and our land and language is Welsh.'[59] The situation was aggravated by the local constabulary's decision to provide 'enough police for Downing Street' to control the demonstrators, who were supported by Welsh students from the University of Liverpool. It was, however, to be a peaceful protest and their progress, to quote *The Manchester Guardian*, was 'rather orderly and hopeless and inescapably pathetic'.[60]

Gwynfor led the way through the grey streets. Behind him came the small band from rural Merioneth:

> … small boys in new boots, with the tags sticking out behind; bigger boys in the pride of long trousers; and girls; a group of women in neat winter coats who might have been part of a women's outing; farmers with tweed caps and faces under them tanned to the protuberant bones; a tiny girl with a fur muff staggering slightly.[61]

When they reached City Hall, Gwynfor asked to address the Council on behalf of the Capel Celyn Defence Committee. By then, Alderman John Braddock, the Council leader, was already in the process of presenting the application to drown Capel Celyn. But even through the thick chamber walls, councillors could clearly hear the hymns being sung by the villagers in the street below. Then, unexpectedly, John Braddock agreed that Gwynfor could address the full Council – just a fortnight after he had been summarily ejected from the same building. It was a prime moment for Gwynfor, and he seized his chance. According to *The Manchester Guardian*: 'Mr Evans made such a brilliant plea for the preservation of the valley's economic and cultural life that the council broke into spontaneous applause at the end'.[62] It was, however, a hollow, short-lived victory.

Gwynfor was answered by John Braddock, who accused Plaid Cymru of trying to make political capital at Capel Celyn's expense. He argued too that the party's statements on the villagers' rights were pure propaganda. It was also nonsense, he continued, that Liverpool had not consulted on the matter. Was it not the case, he asked, that Liverpool had discussed the issue with the 40 Welsh councils? His words carried the day, and when it came to a vote the nationalist objections were swept aside. By 95 votes to 1 (with three abstentions), Capel Celyn's fate was sealed. Even so, and surprisingly, the villagers were not downhearted. Gwynfor was now their hero and they warmly embraced him after his speech. Shortly after lunch, the protest came to an end, but Gwynfor left Liverpool with a clear promise : 'We will be back soon'.[63]

They did not return. The focus of the battle now switched from Merseyside to Westminster but, as the issue came before Parliament, there were doubts within Plaid Cymru about the best way forward. After all, the party had never fought a parliamentary campaign. Some members, it appears, wanted action immediately. On the day after the Liverpool protest, R Tudur Jones wrote to Gwynfor to warn him of 'a rumour that Elystan [Morgan] is seriously considering blowing up the water pipes from the Vyrnwy to Liverpool'.[64] In the midst of this confusion, the only certainty was that 'the longest and bitterest conflict in contemporary Welsh history', as the *Liverpool Daily Post*, called it, was about to begin.[65]

Gwynfor and Elizabeth Watkin Jones prioritised the parliamentary struggle rather than law-breaking, and for some three weeks after the Liverpool protest, both believed that the battle could still be won in the House of Commons. Buoyed by signs that MPs like Raymond Gower, the Conservative member for Barry, were ready to fight for Capel Celyn, they had some grounds for optimism. Seven Labour MPs had also presented a parliamentary motion asking Liverpool not to proceed. In early December 1956, Lizzie May wrote to Gwynfor to tell him that 'prospects are much improved' and that 'victory is certain if we work like lions to ensure it'.[66] Then, out of the blue, the situation changed completely. Just days after Elizabeth Watkin Jones's upbeat letter, Gwynfor received more sobering correspondence from his parliamentary observer in London, Dewi Watkin Powell. According to Watkin Powell, Cledwyn Hughes and Goronwy Roberts were 'furious' with Plaid Cymru because of its actions over Tryweryn. Both, it seemed, considered Plaid Cymru's stance on the matter to be unnecessary interference in north Wales politics. This was not the only bad news. Dewi Watkin Powell went on to warn Gwynfor that Welsh patriots within Labour were beginning to side with Liverpool Corporation. Watkin Powell's suggestion in this vitally important letter – signalling as it did that any shared campaign was out of the question – was that Wales 'should know about this'.[67]

Dewi Watkin Powell was right. The relationship between the Wales Labour Party and Liverpool's Labour Council was changing, as uncompromising opposition mellowed into something more pragmatic. Just a week later, Merioneth County Council, Liverpool Corporation and the Welsh Labour MPs held a meeting, and Liverpool undertook to allow Merioneth access to some of the water reserves. The chair of the Welsh Labour MPs' group, Walter Padley, confirmed the news when he said that the two authorities would meet shortly 'to seek agreement'.[68] In other words, the Labour MPs were seeking an accommodation between Liverpool and Merioneth while at the same time pursuing efforts to save Capel Celyn. It goes without saying that the two aims were contradictory.

Gwynfor could scarcely believe what was happening. On Christmas Day 1956, he wrote to D J Williams with his thoughts on the 'treachery that has destroyed all the good work done throughout the year to protect the valley, the people and the water'. Everything had changed. Because of this treachery, Gwynfor believed it was now 'difficult to see any hope of succeeding in the effort' and that all he could do was 'stick with it and seek as much benefit for Wales as possible'. This was not straightforward either. He was eager to tell the people of Wales that their MPs were 'hopeless', but the challenge for Gwynfor and Plaid Cymru was trying to operate politically in an age of emerging mass communication. Without the media, all he and his tiny party could do was rely on supportive writers: Waldo Williams, Kate Roberts, Leslie Richards and Islwyn Ffowc Elis. This was scant comfort and Gwynfor felt little Christmas cheer. Rather, he cursed the 'quislings' who were 'selling their birthright without even haggling over the price'.[69]

Three days after Christmas, Plaid Cymru's leadership met to discuss the crisis, with Gwynfor more convinced than ever that the Welsh Labour Party had betrayed Capel Celyn 'in cold blood'. They had two motivations, according to Gwynfor. The first was that Welsh Labour MPs felt greater loyalty to their fellow-socialists on Liverpool Council, and especially so to the council leader, John Braddock. Second, Gwynfor suspected that Plaid Cymru had developed into an 'obsession' for the Welsh Labour Party because the nationalists were the backbone of the Tryweryn struggle. Those guiltiest of this duplicity in Gwynfor's opinion were the three Labour MPs who were considered the most faithful in all things Welsh: Goronwy Roberts, Cledwyn Hughes and T W Jones.[70]

From this point onwards, Plaid Cymru set about depicting Welsh Labour MPs as a bunch of toadies. T W Jones was accused by Gwynfor of being an unofficial spokesman for Liverpool Council[71] – a charge described as utterly 'wicked' by the Member for Merioneth.[72] But how true were these accusations? There was no foundation to the claim that Cledwyn Hughes and Goronwy Roberts betrayed Capel Celyn, but, in the case of T W Jones, there is some evidence to support the criticism. In January 1957, for instance, Jones (while still a member of Capel Celyn Defence Committee) stated that the only way to attract an atomic power station and work for the county was by constructing a dam at Tryweryn and ensuring a sufficient supply of water.[73] At best, his conduct was inconsistent, as he found himself pulled in two directions, by conservation on the one hand and the need to create jobs on the other; at worst, he lacked principle.

The tragedy for Capel Celyn was that the dispute wrecked the campaign to save the community, giving John Braddock and his outspoken comments against the Welsh free rein.[74] As a result, the fragile unity was shattered. Undeb Cymru Fydd failed to act, and many of the organizations that had undertaken to correspond directly with Liverpool broke their promise. Elizabeth Watkin Jones herself felt that she was 'forced to work constantly against Labour tricks'.[75] The tension between the parties meant that the Conservative MP Raymond Gower was the only link Gwynfor had with the rest of the Commons. Gwynfor relied heavily on him and it was he who presented the county petitions from Wales; in the same way, he corresponded with Gwynfor, letting him know how the parliamentary wind was blowing.[76] But by late January 1957, the political turmoil was palpable. *Y Cymro*, for example, bemoaned the ill-feeling. In a damning article, its editor wrote: 'The battle over Capel Celyn is coming to the boil. And as usual, it is not one between Wales and someone else, but between the Welsh themselves.'[77] Gwynfor, however, was unapologetic. Deep down, he knew Capel Celyn was a lost cause and that the priority now was to prepare for a General Election – possibly as early as 1957.[78]

The relationship between Labour and Plaid Cymru was further soured by the Carmarthen by-election, held in late February following the death of Sir Rhys Hopkin Morris. At the time, Plaid Cymru's organization in Carmarthen – a constituency that Gwynfor considered not 'politically shrewd' – was in tatters.[79] But despite his private misgivings, he worked tirelessly for the party's candidate there, Jennie Eirian Davies. She, without doubt, was the star of the campaign, and addressed over one hundred meetings in the battle against Labour's Megan Lloyd George.[80] Although the impressive Megan Lloyd George won as expected, Gwynfor found it hard to conceal his disappointment at Jennie Eirian's failure to keep her deposit – in spite of an excellent campaign and the President's best efforts. The only comfort – crucial in seeking to understand how Gwynfor won the seat in 1966 – was what had happened to the Liberal vote. With the death of Hopkin Morris came the demise of Liberalism in Carmarthenshire.[81] Nine years later, Gwynfor would inherit this 'Whig-Liberal' bloc.

At the time, however, only the most hopelessly optimistic would have predicted that Gwynfor could ever win at Carmarthen. After all, he, according to Plaid Cymru propaganda, was to be the saviour of Merioneth and Tryweryn. But as spring approached, the constitutional doors were closing, one by one. The promise made by the Minister for Welsh Affairs, Henry Brooke, to conduct a survey of Wales's need for water before deciding on Capel Celyn's fate was of no value. As the Tryweryn Bill made its passage through the Lords, it became clear that Brooke was committed to drowning Capel Celyn without delay. Almost as disheartening was the indifference within Wales itself, and the withdrawal of previous objections made to Parliament, among them those from Denbighshire

County Council and the water boards for East Denbigh, Deeside and Clwyd. In Parliament, only two bodies eventually submitted formal objections: Merioneth County Council and the parish council of Llanfor and Llanycil. Gwynfor tried to counteract this by submitting a joint statement by the residents of Capel Celyn to the Lords. But in vain; there was upsetting news from the community. In early May 1957, Elizabeth Watkin Jones wrote to tell Gwynfor that 'difficulties had arisen' that would make it hard 'to get a stronger statement now'. She went on to explain:

> There has been some difference of opinion – the people of Celyn are beginning to show the effects of the stress and uncertainty of these last 1½ years… In my opinion (as one who knows everything about everybody in Celyn) it would be as well to leave everything as it is at present. The psychological effect is greater than anyone could guess.[82]

Gwynfor was shaken. What followed immediately was a characteristic bout of despair. In May 1957, he felt he had failed as President – not only on cultural issues such as Capel Celyn but also because of his inadequate knowledge of economics. Ever since the death of his economic guru, D J Davies, the previous October, Gwynfor felt he had been thrown headlong into a 'baffling and wholly unfamiliar world'. His private correspondence at the time finds him confessing that appearing on television programmes to discuss economics 'without knowing the subject' was a tremendous strain.[83] But the main problem was party morale. That May, so few conference motions were proposed that Gwynfor himself had to write extra ones. His annoyance prompted him to suggest to J E Jones that it would be no bad thing to 'leave such matters to those who call for more conferences'. He was also angry with party members who took his Presidency for granted. Although he had been nominated President again, no one had asked his permission, and he was in 'considerable doubt' about whether he should allow his name to go forward. He decided that the 1957–59 term would be his last as President. He informed J E Jones of this, telling him that 'the party should prepare for change'. His natural successor, Gwynfor thought, should be the church historian, R Tudur Jones – someone who would make a 'splendid' President.[84] No record exists of when exactly Gwynfor changed his mind, or of how serious was his threat to stand down. Given the lack of evidence, the only certainty is that his messianic political mission got the better of his cry for help. After all, politics was Gwynfor's life and the line between the personal and the political was for him a thin one.[85]

Even so, despite this sense of purpose, and the optimism that a new nationalist dawn was imminent, he could scarcely have foreseen events when the Tryweryn Bill received its second reading on 3 July 1957. This would be the vital parliamentary vote but, from the very outset, its opponents were in an impossible position. The Conservative government whipped its vote, and Henry Brooke was hugely supportive of what was, after all, a private member's bill – the lowest form of parliamentary legislative life. On the Labour benches, influential figures such as Barbara Castle and Harold Wilson voiced their backing for Liverpool Corporation. The final vote was 166 in favour and 117 against. Only one Welsh MP voted in favour, and the majority of 49 was smaller than expected; it was a victory of sorts. The third reading three weeks later would be a mere formality.

On the weekend following the vote, Gwynfor travelled to Tryweryn, having heard that the Liverpool City Housing Committee were due to visit the village. They did not as it transpired but the people of Capel Celyn were not interested in organizational niceties by then. In every window and on every gable-end, Gwynfor saw the posters begging Liverpool to change its mind: 'Please Do Not Drown The Homes That Welcomed Liverpool's Evacuees. Your Homes Are Safe – Do Not Drown Ours'.[86] It was a tragic sight, but for Gwynfor the slogans were a stark reminder that time was short. After the second reading, the pressure had grown on him to state Plaid Cymru's policy on unconstitutional action once the parliamentary battle was lost. Gwynfor had sought to avoid the issue, arguing that the majority of 49 was too small to allow the dam to be built, but this was considered by many within Plaid Cymru to be empty rhetoric. They thought the Rubicon had been crossed and that the only option was to defy the law. J E Jones supported passive resistance, so too Emrys Roberts; indeed, Roberts maintained that the Plaid Cymru conference of that year should pass a motion in favour of 'physical resistance' since no other option remained but 'constant sabotage'. It was time, Emrys Roberts continued, to show '... that this warning is no bluff'.[87]

Saunders Lewis saw things in much the same way. Before the second reading, he wrote to D J Williams that it was 'someone's duty to go back to that stench-ridden hole (Wormwood Scrubs)', while regretting that 'that spirit had died in Plaid Cymru'.[88] In July 1957, Saunders Lewis met Henry Brooke over lunch, and the likelihood is that during this meeting he warned Brooke that the Liverpool scheme was 'sufficient to warrant physical actions'.[89] This was not Lewis's only effort to change the party's policy before the third reading. He went so far as to phone J E Jones to request a meeting with Gwynfor and Dewi Watkin Powell. His aim was to urge the pair to embark on a policy of unlawful action but, at Watkin Powell's suggestion, Gwynfor decided not to meet Lewis.[90] Watkin Powell's advice (as usual) was vital and, in a letter to Gwynfor, he argued that Lewis had been out of front line politics for fourteen years and that the party's success since then was a result of constitutional campaigning. Watkin Powell continued:

> ... I am adamant that no action should be taken, however dramatic it might be, that is illegal or that threatens to sacrifice any member of Plaid.

And he pleaded with Gwynfor to realize that:

> ... the vast majority of the residents of Tryweryn... are more than satisfied with the compensation that they are getting now, indeed, satisfied for the scheme to proceed and give Plaid Cymru the credit for fighting so well to secure such terms for them.[91]

In their private conversations, too, Dewi Watkin Powell warned Gwynfor that an official policy of law-breaking by Plaid Cymru could be sufficient grounds for the police to bring a charge of conspiracy against the party. In short, it could become an offence to be a member.[92]

As the demands for a personal sacrifice intensified, Gwynfor stalled. The third reading on 31 July sealed Tryweryn's fate but, both before and after, Gwynfor sought ways of avoiding the issue. The first was to concentrate all Plaid Cymru's short-term campaign on Henry Brooke, portraying him as a 'Welsh Gauleiter'.[93] Part of the same strategy was to prevent Brooke from addressing that year's National Eisteddfod in Llangefni. In a 'stormy' meeting of the party Executive on the eve of the Eisteddfod, Plaid Cymru discussed how to achieve this. One suggestion was cutting the microphone cable on the stage.[94] Others were prepared to interrupt him with patriotic hymns from the auditorium.[95] Gwynfor was especially keen on such moves, and wrote to the chair of the Eisteddfod's executive committee to warn him that Brooke was sure to be given 'a tempestuous reception that would be awkward for him and the Eisteddfod alike'. He stressed too that 'his arrival after all the trouble over Tryweryn' might appear to some 'as the Eisteddfod Council's blessing on Henry Brooke's "actions"'.[96] Gwynfor's letter led to one of the bitterest clashes in the festival's history. The local MP, Cledwyn Hughes, was livid, and accused Gwynfor of behaving in a 'highly impertinent' manner, accusing him of making the Eisteddfod a platform for his 'political predilections'.

This was 'unforgivable'.[97] As the agitation continued, the Eisteddfod did all it could to isolate Gwynfor, and the festival's General Secretary assured the civil servant Blaise Gillie that they were united in their determination to see Brooke in Llangefni.[98]

On 1 August, as the Tryweryn Bill became law, Plaid Cymru gathered in Bangor for its annual conference, where the question on everyone's lips was whether or not Brooke would go to Llangefni. From the moment Blaise Gillie set foot on the Eisteddfod field the following week, the ill-feeling towards Brooke was evident, as was the split in the Eisteddfod Council. The respectable faction wished to leave matters as they were, while others, led by Thomas Parry, were convinced that the Eisteddfod, of all institutions, should not allow 'Babbling Brooke' to make an appearance. As tempers became more frayed, Thomas Parry and his supporters threatened to boycott the festival's showpiece events and the rebels carried the day. Brooke withdrew.[99]

The response was mixed. 'An ill mannered and discourteous act',[100] opined the *Liverpool Daily Post*, and a pillar of the London Welsh establishment prophesied that the Eisteddfod had become a 'Republican Nationalist Jamboree'.[101] Plaid Cymru, however, saw Brooke's decision as a miracle. D J Williams, for instance, asserted that 'Brooke's absence from Llangefni due to such circumstances, was the most important united blow that Wales has given to the English government in living memory'.[102] In the same vein, R Tudur Jones claimed that 'Liverpool will not hold Tryweryn for ever'.[103] However, these were empty threats by Gwynfor's followers. The constitutionalist wing of the party had no real interest in breaking the law – partly because of the wishes of Plaid Cymru members in Merioneth, partly because of their unshakeable belief in parliamentary politics, and partly because they doubted the practicability of such tactics. Secretly, Gwynfor was convinced that not enough people would be willing to face prison for the sake of Capel Celyn.[104] Basically, Gwynfor and his advisers were paying lip service to Penyberth. But half-hearted or not, their role in keeping Brooke away from Llangefni was enough to carry the day for the softly-softly wing of Plaid Cymru. In two meetings – one during a particularly lively Summer School and the other on 31 August – it was decided Plaid Cymru would stick to its constitutional methods.

Gwynfor's true nature exemplified his actions after the third reading. On 1 August, he went on his own initiative to see David Cole, editor of the *Western*

Mail – the establishment paper that had astonished many with its support for the people of Capel Celyn. Gwynfor spent some four hours with Cole, trying to win the paper's approval for a 'pretty idea' of his own that would give Liverpool its dam and its water supply but save Capel Celyn at the same time.[105] The plan involved drowning the upper portion of the Tryweryn valley. There is no doubt that Gwynfor was motivated by the interests of Capel Celyn and its residents, but such a scheme undermined Plaid Cymru's whole argument. After all, the party had spent the previous two years arguing that Liverpool did not need any more water. Now Gwynfor appeared to be conceding that very point. He was also betraying serious naivety by thinking he could persuade Liverpool to change its plans. Even so, David Cole was keen, and after Dewi Watkin Powell had explained things further, he agreed to support Gwynfor's proposal and convene a national conference on the issue. This had all taken place before that year's National Eisteddfod, but Gwynfor revealed nothing about the behind-the-scenes bargaining when he arrived in Llangefni to be greeted as a hero over the Henry Brooke affair.

In the months ahead, Tryweryn took up most of Gwynfor's time. He was asked by Plaid Cymru to write a pamphlet on what had taken place, subsequently published as *We Learn from Tryweryn* in October 1957. In it he asked that the outrage be taken as a warning: 'As things are, July 31st, 1957, can be repeated in 1958 and 1959 and through the years'.[106] The pamphlet gave English a new verb, ' "to Tryweryn" – to exploit the land or natural resources of a small nation, or to destroy its social life or language, in the interests of a big neighbouring country or part of it'.[107] And as part of the campaign to ensure that Tryweryn would be remembered, he asked every district branch of the party to organize at least a dozen public meetings on the lessons to be learned. A committee was formed to discuss the feasibility of buying a farm in the valley in an effort to frustrate the contractors.[108] In the meantime, the authorities feared worse was to come. David Cole wrote to Henry Brooke to alert him that 'the seeds of an Irish problem' had been planted in Wales.[109] A month later, in November 1957, Brooke presented a paper to the Cabinet asking for a bridge to be built across the Severn to alleviate the 'wide and deep distrust of the Government's attitude towards Wales'.[110] The decision, taken a year later, to divide the huge steelworks between Ravenscraig in Scotland and Llanwern near Newport was a smaller but significant expression of the same concern.[111]

Gwynfor's efforts to remind people about Tryweryn made a lasting contribution to Welsh intellectual history but, in the short term, he channelled his own energies into the national conference. He succeeded in winning the support of the Lord Mayor of Cardiff for the venture, and he agreed to preside. The response was similarly supportive from Penllyn Rural District Council and its chair, Emrys Bennett Owen – a man of great local influence. However, several people, both inside and outside Plaid Cymru, had deep reservations about the conference. A number of councils refused to send delegates – including Deudraeth, Penllyn's neighbour to the west. Councillors felt that the recommendation to submerge only part of the valley was every bit as odious as Liverpool's original intention, and inconsistent too. Merioneth County Council thought it was quite simply too late for such an enterprise.[112] In addition, Cardiff Council, the conference host, had little credibility since it was in the process of building its own controversial dam at Llandegfedd in Monmouthshire. The plan to flood only the upper pasture of Cwm Tryweryn also proved unpopular with Plaid members in Merioneth and with the residents of Capel Celyn, because it would have led to saving houses in the village at the expense of property belonging to two families higher up the valley.[113]

Tryweryn was not the only territorial battle that concerned Gwynfor in 1957. His conscience was pricked too by the situation in Anglesey. The County Council there had stirred up a hornet's nest by inviting Birmingham to relocate 9,500 of its citizens to the island. The Council's intention had been to halt depopulation, but friends of the Welsh language thought the idea disastrous. For Gwynfor, this threat, so soon after losing the parliamentary battle, was particularly difficult to bear. As he looked at Wales in 1957 he was desolate. He wrote to Pennar Davies insisting that the crisis in Wales was deepening – and that it filled him 'with a sense of helplessness and bitterness to see the betrayal and indifference all around him'. He felt that 'the flow of the most powerful currents' was against the nationalist cause, leaving its supporters 'like children trying to turn back the tide with buckets'. It was, he said, utterly 'nightmarish'.[114]

But despite his despondency, the national conference on Tryweryn went ahead in late October 1957. Over two hundred representatives met in Cardiff and the press reaction was favourable. This, according to the *Western Mail*, was '...The True Voice of Wales... Its Tone is Friendly, Reasonable'.[115] Gwynfor, striking a note of remarkable credulousness, declared that the conference offered 'a real chance of success' and that Liverpool could still be prevailed upon to proceed with the new, less damaging scheme.[116] There was, of course, no such hope at all. Merioneth County Council's decision not to send delegates had undermined the whole affair.[117] They were portrayed as traitors in the Plaid Cymru press – 'the sellers-in-chief of our national birthright' – but the truth was that the Council was merely bowing to the inevitable.[118] Hardly anyone (Gwynfor apart) expected success, and when Liverpool rejected any compromise in early 1958, it was seen by many as the merciful end to a sorry saga.[119] For Gwynfor's critics, too, it was proof positive of his wrong-headedness ever since the Llangefni Eisteddfod.

Liverpool's decision on Tryweryn was described as 'a deliberate slap in the face' by Gwynfor but he insisted, with a rhetorical flourish, that it was not the end of the matter.[120] Brave words, but he, like the majority of those who feared for the future of the language, did not know where to turn at the beginning of 1958. Looking back on the previous year, 'Daniel', writing in *Y Faner*, said that 1957 would be remembered for two things: first Sputnik, and second because it had been 'one of the years that saw more mortal blows to Welsh identity than usual'.[121] His analysis of the essence of 1957 was correct, and such attitudes tended to feed nationalist uncertainty over tactics. By the beginning of 1958, the Macmillan government felt more comfortable than ever, promising the Welsh a land of milk and honey. It meant there would be no immediate opportunity for Gwynfor to challenge T W Jones in the poll in Merioneth, in what Gwynfor hoped would be a ballot on Tryweryn. As it became ever more obvious that Plaid Cymru could do nothing to prevent Liverpool from proceeding, Gwynfor turned his attention to other matters.

In the year which saw CND founded, Plaid Cymru's campaign against the hydrogen bomb began under the slogan 'A lead back to sanity'. Meetings were held, but these proved uninspiring. Generally speaking, only language issues could ignite Plaid Cymru passions, and the greatest perceived threat in 1958 (and for years to come) was the arrival of commercial television. In January 1958, TWW began broadcasting from its studios at Pontcanna in Cardiff – the first time commercial television had been seen by viewers in south Wales. In the north, Granada was already up and running. Overnight, the viewing habits in Wales were being transformed. By 1957, ITV could claim 76 per cent of the entire television audience – a remarkable figure given that it had only begun in September 1955.[122] For the Welsh language, the effects of commercial television were calamitous. Although Granada broadcast two hours a week in Welsh, this could hardly be described as a firm commitment, despite the inspired work of producers like Rhydwen Williams and Warren Jenkins. On Easter Sunday 1959, for example, Granada's Welsh-language programme was shelved in favour of live wrestling.[123] TWW's loyalty to the Welsh language was equally flimsy. Despite the best efforts of individuals like Wyn Roberts and Meurig Jones, TWW's shareholders – including the impresario Jack Hylton and the *News of the World* – were more interested in profits.

It was with some justification, then, that Gwynfor anticipated the death of the Welsh language unless provision improved, and as the number of licences increased, he came to see a Welsh television service as one of the 'important conditions for the continuation of the nation and its language'.[124] But seeking the best way forward was a bone of contention for many at the forefront of Welsh life – including Gwynfor himself. Some TWW shareholders, such as Sir Ifan ab Owen Edwards and Huw T Edwards, argued that the answer lay in co-operation between commercial companies and the BBC. This was rejected out of hand by the BBC and its Controller in Wales, Alun Oldfield-Davies. However, Gwynfor (and Plaid Cymru) chose to side with those who believed the BBC and TWW could work together and share the new channel. It was a view commonly taken by others concerned for the language, and it appears that by adopting this stance Gwynfor was abandoning the idea he had two years before: the setting up of a Welsh-language commercial company. Throughout 1958, he spoke regularly on the matter, even producing a pamphlet jointly with J E Jones, *TV in Wales*. But, by and large, Plaid Cymru's efforts were received half-heartedly by those keen on an expansion of Welsh-language television services. By the spring of 1958, a joint committee of supporters of the Welsh language had been campaigning assiduously to make both the BBC and TWW more aware of the issue, and they felt Plaid Cymru was confusing matters with irrelevant arguments for the establishment of yet another talking shop. Some of the joint committee's most ardent members, such as Jac L Williams and R E Griffith, even refused to sign a Plaid Cymru petition on the subject.[125]

Gwynfor's decision to temporarily abandon the idea of setting up a commercial channel also marked an important tactical change on his part. One cannot be entirely sure what prompted him, but one possible explanation is that, since December 1957, he had been a member of the Wales Broadcasting Council

– the body responsible for regulating BBC Wales. As one might expect, his membership created its own tensions. The most tangible of these was between Gwynfor and Alun Oldfield-Davies, a man justifiably described by John Davies, the official historian of the BBC in Wales, as the father of Welsh-language television.[126] Oldfield-Davies was shrewd enough to know how to work the system and, basically, had little respect for Gwynfor's constant hectoring on what was best for Wales, as his letter to BBC headquarters amply illustrates:

> I question the propriety of having the leader of a political party as a member of the Council... [Evans] brushes aside technical difficulties, supposing them to be easily surmountable given the will... I find myself unsympathetic to his political approach to a question which seems to me to be one of constantly balancing competing tastes and demands in relation to available resources.[127]

But not all Gwynfor's suggestions fell on deaf ears. During 1959, some Home Office civil servants were of the opinion that Welsh MPs could develop the 'Welsh Nationalist Case' on broadcasting, and Gwynfor used his friendship with Raymond Gower and Tudor Watkins to this end. Both men were at the forefront of efforts to convince the Postmaster General of the value of a third channel for Wales.[128] The goal was not achieved but, by 1960, there was a more widespread awareness of the shortcomings of broadcasting in Welsh. However crude his tactics, Gwynfor (and members of the joint committee) had succeeded in alerting Welsh-speakers to the threat that broadcasting presented.

Everyone realized, of course, that it would be a long, attritional battle. In the meantime, Gwynfor had to carry on with the struggle which Plaid Cymru and the younger generation thought more important – the attempt to save Tryweryn. But after the failure of the national conference, Plaid Cymru had run out of practical ideas. During February 1958, the party's Executive sent a statement to the Lord Mayor of Cardiff calling for a one-day strike by miners and steelworkers in the south to save Capel Celyn. Plaid Cymru's leadership thought that such action could transform Tryweryn's plight overnight but, without union backing, it was an absurd idea. The only practical result was that Plaid Cymru lost the support of the *Western Mail*, the paper most in favour of the national conference. As its editorial commented: 'Such action as the Welsh Nationalists are now advocating would merely be a piece of futile industrial vandalism.'[129] Without any specific undertaking to embark on a campaign of law-breaking, Gwynfor could do nothing to challenge the perception that Plaid Cymru had failed on Capel Celyn.

As Liverpool Corporation began to purchase Tryweryn's farms, John Aelod Jones (John Roberts Williams) used his column in *Y Cymro* to point out what was fast becoming obvious to all: 'There is nothing more silent than silence. Just look at Tryweryn.'[130] The residents of Capel Celyn agreed, feeling there was nothing the Defence Committee could now do to save the village.[131]

There seemed to be a leadership vacuum, and all sections of Plaid Cymru were again calling for Gwynfor 'to act positively'. One rank-and-file member, Nest Lewis Jones, secretary of the Cardiff branch, wrote to Gwynfor pleading with him to take 'a courageous stand over Tryweryn... using any means he thinks fit'.[132] In the upper echelons of the party, there was further discussion on the appropriateness of breaking the law. In June 1958, a motion to act unlawfully was left on the table, with the more pragmatic members of the Executive arguing that any such action at this stage would be 'an action for the sake of sacrifice' – and not one for the sake of Tryweryn as such.[133] No vote was taken but the question of 'action' was causing an unprecedented divide in the party. Just days before the National Eisteddfod of 1958, a motion was put forward by the Cardiff branch to break the law over Tryweryn. But once again the Executive decided it could not be undertaken, and that unconstitutional action would have a disastrous effect on public opinion.[134] J E Jones's words during the annual conference in August 1958 were uncompromising. 'There remains,' said Jones, 'no practical method of freeing Tryweryn from the grasp of Liverpool Corporation. We have lost a battle; now we must win the war.'[135]

Gwynfor's own grasp on the Executive, Plaid Cymru's holiest of holies, was as firm as ever, but the general membership was less biddable; many were still enchanted by their idol, Saunders Lewis, and he was still in high dudgeon. During August 1958, he decided he could no longer hold his tongue, and used the platform of the National Eisteddfod at Ebbw Vale to tear a strip off Plaid Cymru for supporting the building of an atomic power station at Trawsfynydd. He also ridiculed the thousands from Dyffryn Nantlle who had marched in February 1958 in favour of a power station under banners calling for 'Bread Before Beauty' and 'Pylons Before Poverty'. It was a speech befitting a crashing snob:

> Let us not sell our future in the twentieth century for a mess of pottage. Take your banners to Tryweryn, and take more than banners. It is the duty of the young people of Wales to save Welsh rural life and they should be courageous in protecting their country for the twenty-first century. What matters is national self-respect and dignity.[136]

Following the speech, Saunders Lewis confessed to D J Williams that he hoped to see another Penyberth in Capel Celyn, and that he would have been ready to break the law were it not for his 'cares' and his wife, Margaret's opposition.[137]

This may well have been geriatric bravado, but Saunders Lewis's return to the political stage damaged Gwynfor. First, it fed the growing perception that Gwynfor was a coward – a man who was not prepared to get his hands dirty to save a Welsh-speaking community. Second, it undermined the work that Gwynfor and Plaid Cymru had been doing among the trade unions of Merioneth before a possible General Election. At the time, discussions were about to begin between Gwynfor and the Railwaymen's Union in the county. Given the context, the timing of Lewis's decision to attack the workers of Merioneth and Caernarvonshire was disastrous. This in any event was how R Tudur Jones, the party's Vice-President, interpreted the speech:

> I fear that Saunders is not in close enough contact with the state of mind in Gwynedd at the present time ... Certainly, it is important for us to make clear that we are not siding with the high-minded societies in England who make it their business to interfere in Welsh affairs not because they love Wales but because they like to take their holidays in Gwynedd.[138]

But the damage to Plaid Cymru in Merioneth, and to Gwynfor's image as the champion of the little man in nationalist politics, had been done. Saunders Lewis was not the only eminent figure in Welsh Wales who was urging nationalists to fight for Tryweryn. In October 1958, Huw T Edwards, chair of the Advisory Council for Wales and Monmouthshire, stated that Liverpool deserved all it got if the protests became militant. There was no mistaking his forthright message:

> Many thousands of Welshmen, I am convinced, will be prepared to make sacrifices to prevent Liverpool getting away with Tryweryn... many thousands would be willing to face gaol over this issue... I would remind you that threats have been made against the Mersey Tunnel. That is the kind of thing that might happen. The Welsh people will not forgive Liverpool.[139]

Days later, the political heat rose further when Edwards resigned the chairmanship – an act that the press interpreted as a 'bombshell'.[140]

It might have been expected that Plaid Cymru would benefit from Edwards's statement, but it was not the case. Indeed, the party's silence when the 'Prime Minister of Wales' stood down was deafening. Although Plaid Cymru welcomed any effort to undermine the Advisory Council's credibility, Edwards himself was a problem for the nationalist movement. In the first place, he continued to insist that he was a loyal Labourite – despite Gwynfor's best efforts to tempt him into the Plaid Cymru fold. This tended to draw attention to Gwynfor's failures. Secondly, he was seen as a far more charismatic and passionate politician than Gwynfor on the very topic that was fast becoming a nationalist obsession.

Gwynfor had good reason to remain silent in the days following Huw T Edwards's resignation. By the end of October, Plaid Cymru (and Elwyn Roberts) were busy organizing a highly ambitious trip for Gwynfor to the United States and Canada. Its very simple aim – regardless of what Gwynfor claimed in later years – was fundraising.[141] It was hoped was that the party could emulate what Irish and Jewish exiles had achieved in America, and turn patriotism into dollars to support Plaid Cymru for decades to come. That, at least, was the theory, but it became a logistical nightmare. Although 'Don Hywel' in Bogota had contributed the princely sum of £1,000 to pay for the venture, many within Plaid Cymru saw it as pointless, unable to believe that the Welsh in America were anywhere near as political as the Irish.[142] A further problem was the refusal of the British Government to help in any way. Plaid Cymru's request for the trip to be given official status was turned down, and Henry Brooke warned the American Embassy to keep an eye on Gwynfor – describing him as a 'prosperous farmer in Carmarthenshire'.[143] Despite the handicaps, Gwynfor sailed from Southampton on board the *SS America* on 3 November 1958. He left the troubles of Tryweryn behind him, but the trip was no junket. He knew that failure could play into the hands of his critics at home.

Eight days later, he reached the American mainland and saw the Red Dragon flying over New York harbour. Waiting to greet him were a group of supporters including two children wearing Welsh costume – even though their parents were from Yorkshire.[144] This set the tone for five weeks of flag-waving and attempts to stir up a feeling of Welsh patriotism among Americans. After changing his currency at a Wall Street bank, Gwynfor began his mission, and gave dozens of interviews to the American press.[145] On that first morning alone, he appeared on America's most popular television programme, *The Garroway Show* – watched by ten million. The interest in Gwynfor and what he had to say was astonishing, given Plaid Cymru's virtual total lack of profile back in Britain. With the help of the American journalist Colin Edwards he travelled widely and met many people.

From Washington, where he spoke to the renowned American trade unionist John L Lewis, to the snows of Utica and on to the warmth of San Francisco, Gwynfor was being acknowledged as someone of note, and the interest in him was reflected in the purple prose of the press. According to the *New York Times*: 'Mr Evans' ruddy face and his manner suggest the poet Dylan Thomas.'[146] The *Washington Post* painted a similar picture: 'Evans, a witty, soft-spoken Welsh revolutionary who wants Wales to get rid of England.'[147] Gwynfor was more than happy to play the game, suggesting that the Welsh were like their Celtic cousins: 'Perhaps we'll learn from the Irish', he told the *New York Times*, 'they're very good politically.'[148]

As the trip went on, the British authorities' concerns increased. Gwynfor managed, for instance, to concoct a wholly artificial dispute over his right to meet President Eisenhower. It was never going to happen, but he maintained that the British Ambassador in Washington had prevented it. Once again, it led to favourable coverage in both America and Wales.[149] The authorities responded by having individuals report back to Britain on what was happening. Peter Brooke, Henry Brooke's son, despatched to spy on Gwynfor at a meeting in Boston, found the Plaid Cymru President's words and behaviour 'mad, quite mad'.[150] But for all the attention paid to him, and despite his own efforts, the financial response to Gwynfor was far from generous and he managed to raise only 'a couple of thousand dollars'.[151] Short-lived, too, were Plaid Cymru's hopes of setting Welsh pulses racing across the Atlantic. Gwynfor left America believing he had brought about a fundamental change in attitudes, although he would write later in his autobiography that Welshness in the States was 'completely sentimental'.[152]

A few days before Christmas, Gwynfor arrived home to thunderous applause from his inner circle. Islwyn Ffowc Elis wrote to say the trip had 'given heart to every nationalist' he had met.[153] Gwynfor was in an excellent mood. The trip had been a tonic and, still buoyant, he decided to come down from the fence – he would lead a campaign of civil disobedience over Tryweryn. At the turn of the year, the Plaid Cymru Executive passed a resolution in favour of 'passive resistance at Tryweryn when the time comes'. To that end, a small group of members was chosen to consider methods and preparations.[154] Gwynfor told the party it was time to take action. 'I would feel a coward,' he said, 'if I were to do nothing to prove our sincerity. As with Trawsfynydd.' He also wanted to send a clear message to other English cities, especially Birmingham, that they would not be allowed to plunder Welsh communities. Gwynfor proceeded to lay out the conditions of unlawful action: 'Nothing physical at all; No sand in any machine; No tipping over of any cement mixer.' Nor, it appears, was Gwynfor too worried about the effect such action might have on Plaid Cymru's prospects in the pending General Election. 'Yes, election or no election,' he answered Executive member Dafydd Orwig when he warned that unlawful action could harm Gwynfor's hopes of taking Merioneth. Indeed, Gwynfor had already been preparing the ground by talking to party members in the county about the new tactic. The only concession to constitutional politics was that there would be a ban on any unlawful activities during the fortnight immediately before the ballot itself.[155]

Why then, the change of heart? It is evident that the reception in America had affected Gwynfor, and the rebel in him took over his more cautious solicitor's way of thinking. But there were other factors as well. At the beginning of 1959, as the contractors began to prepare the site at Capel Celyn, Plaid Cymru was at last forced to decide on its attitude to unconstitutional action. Another reason for the new-found radicalism was the support given to English pacifists following the 'Committee of 100' protests. The Reverend Michael Scott – whom Gwynfor had met, and who had previously addressed the party's Summer School – had led these protests against the rocket-firing range at Swaffham, Norfolk. Plaid Cymru's leadership was in close contact with Michael Scott at the time.[156] It would appear, then, that these factors were the reason behind the change of policy, thereby ending years of tactical uncertainty. A resolution was passed to establish a sub-committee to take the matter forward; the response, however, was very mixed and the party was divided on the issue. On the one hand, the more militant wing of Plaid Cymru was delighted. One member of that group, Elystan Morgan, insisted that the next step would be 'a strong, decisive and courageous act, characterized by self-sacrifice'. To Morgan's mind, there had already been enough talking because 'a large proportion of the nation has long since grown sick of hearing about Tryweryn'.[157] Others, however, were horrified by the new policy. Dewi Watkin Powell was particularly shaken, and sent a peevish letter to Gwynfor suggesting that the renewed discussion of lawbreaking was 'a sign of political immaturity'. He was of the opinion that talk of action was 'a pathetic, pathological fixation'. He also maintained that protests like those at Swaffham were perfectly alright for a small ginger group who wanted to exert pressure on the government of the day 'but not for a party that has its sights set on forming a government for Wales one day'. Worst of all, according to Watkin Powell, was the likely impact on Plaid Cymru's electoral hopes in Merioneth: 'An act seen as folly by these people could lose Merioneth for us.' Dewi Watkin Powell begged Gwynfor to restrain the sub-committee and strangle the scheme at birth.[158]

This vitally important letter was not the only correspondence Gwynfor received pleading with him to reconsider the impact that a Penyberth-like action might have. Some days after receiving Watkin Powell's letter, a similar one came from R Tudur Jones – a man every bit as influential as the cautious barrister. Tudur Jones was afraid that Plaid Cymru's political enemies – Labour MPs like Goronwy Roberts and T W Jones would be 'hoping to goodness that we make a mistake so that they can reap the benefits'. With this in mind, he pleaded with Gwynfor to give serious consideration to the wishes of Plaid members in Merioneth.[159] Similar messages came from the county itself. Ifor Owen, for instance, believed that taking action at Tryweryn 'could have an adverse effect on the fearful vote that we anticipate for Gwynfor in the election'.[160] It was also common knowledge that one of the most prominent party members in the county, Tom Jones of Llanuwchllyn, was busy arranging compensation for the villagers of Capel Celyn.

The pressure on Gwynfor was intense, and he faltered. At the end of January, when the sub-committee met at the Golden Lion in Dolgellau to discuss unlawful action, it was clear that Gwynfor had cold feet. This meeting, on 31 January 1959, it is fair to say, was a vital moment in Welsh nationalist history. Without any consultation, the committee decided to respect the President's U-turn and a motion was passed 'not to organize any action before an election if an election occurs during the summer'. There would be no new Penyberth. It left those favouring action speechless.[161] They could not believe that Gwynfor, in such an undemocratic manner, had overridden the party Executive's resolution on such a crucial issue. But far from healing the increasingly obvious split in the party, Gwynfor made a difficult situation a hundred times worse by unveiling a new scheme of his own that would ensure some profit for Merioneth once Capel Celyn was drowned. This action was, without question, the greatest political mistake of Gwynfor's career, for the plan involved a measure of compromise with Liverpool. Indeed, it was such a huge faux pas that Gwynfor, not the most self-effacing politician of his generation, was forced to admit in his autobiography that he had acted 'in a way which I later saw to have been unwise'.[162]

The controversial plan presented to Plaid Cymru at that Dolgellau meeting was called *Tryweryn – New Proposals*. Although Gwynfor and J E Jones had co-authored it, its architect was Dewi Watkin Powell. It contained three proposals: that the workers building the dam should be Welsh; that the workers employed on the Tryweryn site should be Welsh; and finally, that a Tryweryn Water Board should be established, with equal representation from Liverpool and Penllyn Rural District Council. This new board would have its headquarters in Bala and would have the right to sell any surplus water to industry or local authorities.[163] There is no doubt that *New Proposals* was an honest attempt by Dewi Watkin Powell to face what he considered an extremely difficult reality. Its aim was to offer a practical solution to a party that was split over unlawful action and knew deep down that the proposed development at Tryweryn would go ahead, come what may. After a brief discussion, the *New Proposals* document was accepted.

The basic problem with Watkin Powell's plan, however, was that it was the work of a clever London-based barrister with little political nous. There was no likelihood that Liverpool, after all the acrimonious arguments that had taken place, would be willing to share the water or any profit from selling it to other councils. Gwynfor and J E Jones's dream of seeing Penllyn grow rich 'just as very small states in the world profit from the presence of oil in their land' was a fantasy.[164] Inevitably, the scheme was rejected by Liverpool Corporation and by the Ministry of Housing and Local Government.[165] Its other great shortcoming was that it undermined all Plaid Cymru's rhetoric about the absolute right of the Welsh to manage their own land and natural resources. Tryweryn, as Harri Webb commented some years later, was Plaid Cymru's 'Munich'.[166]

The reaction both within the party and elsewhere was fairly hostile. Only *Y Faner* expressed praise. The *Western Mail* took delight in mocking Plaid Cymru's action with the headline 'Plaid Does About Turn Over Tryweryn'.[167] And there was astonishment in Merioneth too. Ifor Owen of Llanuwchllyn wrote to Emrys Roberts to voice his concern about the 'weaknesses', adding that 'people here in the north do not see the economic side of Tryweryn's water as clearly as those in the south'.[168] And although Gwynfor described the project as 'a gross affront to Wales', some members of his party were furious – an early sign of the far more damaging recriminations that would come close to destroying Plaid Cymru between 1959 and 1964.

The reaction of Gareth Miles, secretary of Plaid Cymru's University College branch in Bangor, summed up the feelings of the younger generation; he was, according to one report that reached party headquarters, 'in a complete sulk over Tryweryn'.[169] Similarly, the tireless language campaigner Eileen Beasley wrote to Gwynfor to castigate him for the compromise he had offered.[170] Some months later, at the annual conference, the Llangennech branch, where Eileen and Trefor Beasley were members, put forward a motion expressing regret 'that the Executive has failed to give due lead on the matter of the drowning of Tryweryn' and asking it to 'be prepared to organize passive resistance against Liverpool's plans in the valley'.[171] No vote was taken on the motion, but the Beasleys were not the only leading nationalists to show dissent. Saunders Lewis was outraged when Plaid Cymru's leadership published a piece in *Y Ddraig Goch* in May 1959 saying that 'the Welsh are not the Irish' and that 'it is now unseemly for anyone to talk like Elias before Ahab, unless he is totally convinced that his words will become deeds'.[172] The party's leadership was trying to close down debate but, having read the article, Lewis concluded that 'We are not Irish' would be become 'Plaid's epitaph'. [173] It is also clear that he had 'thought seriously' about severing all ties with Plaid Cymru as a result of 'the betrayal of Tryweryn'.[174]

Another sign of the party's inertia in the eyes of the 'activists' was its failure to support the stand taken by the eight who had resigned from the National Eisteddfod's executive committee in Cardiff. They had done so following the decision to invite the Queen to the festival, and included among the eight were prominent nationalists such as A O H Jarman and Griffith John Williams. However, even though they belonged to the Plaid Cymru high command, the party offered no support. Indeed, they were left isolated in a bitter argument that preoccupied the Welsh press for weeks on end. Gwynfor's concern was that Plaid Cymru would be drawn into an unnecessary dispute about the Crown.[175] But rather than join what was seen as a key battle for the Welshness of the Eisteddfod, he merely issued a statement expressing his disappointment that some individuals were fanning the flames. He added, somewhat optimistically perhaps, that his party was 'looking forward to the day when she will be the Queen of a Free Wales'.[176] But although his statement staunched criticism from British loyalist Eisteddfod supporters like Cynan and David James, it incensed the unconstitutional wing of Plaid Cymru. Reading the statement, Kate Roberts, for example, averred that 'an outsider might think... that Plaid Cymru does not believe in a Welsh-speaking

Wales' and she urged the party 'to come out in their true colours, whatever the outcome, and be more aggressive'.[177]

Even so, despite the infighting and the disgruntlement, it is important not to exaggerate Gwynfor's unpopularity in the wake of the *New Proposals*. At the time, Gwynfor was still a hero to many, and hopes were high as the General Election approached. The consensus within Plaid Cymru was that the 'breakthrough' was at last imminent, and that the party's struggle for Capel Celyn would be rewarded in the most important seat of all, Merioneth itself. To many, including Gwynfor, it would only be a matter of weeks before he would be known as Gwynfor Evans MP – a dramatic development which would open a new chapter in Plaid Cymru's history.

The pre-election campaigning got off to a flying start. After months of wooing, Huw T Edwards finally announced that he would be joining Plaid Cymru – the very party he'd excoriated a few years previously. Gwynfor chose to ignore the past, viewing the decision as significant. Even before he joined Plaid Cymru, Gwynfor had told Huw T Edwards it would be 'an historic event the significance of which future historians in Wales could not fail to appreciate' were he to dare to quit Labour.[178] When the news was announced at the National Eisteddfod in Caernarfon, Gwynfor was rapturous, believing that Labour's grasp on Welsh Wales was at last to be loosened.[179] He believed the chasm between the Labour movement and the nationalist movement was now being closed.[180] As it later transpired, Huw T Edwards's move was to be short-lived, and represented the act of a patriotic maverick. At the time, however, it threatened to re-draw the political map of Wales. Columnists in the Welsh press began to speculate on who would be next, so strong was Edwards's hold over the Welsh wing of his former party. The names mentioned included such well-respected Labour figures as Sir David Hughes Parry, Mary Silyn Roberts, David Thomas and Huw Morris-Jones.[181] All of these would have been important scalps for Plaid Cymru; however, Gwilym Prys Davies was *the* Labourite whom Gwynfor wished to see back in the fold.[182] But, in the event, the 'Huw T' conversion was a false dawn. Only Isaac Stephens[183] – a trade unionist whom Gwynfor had come to know well when Plaid Cymru had tried to save the colliery at Cwmllynfell – decided to follow suit.[184]

Even though few copied Huw T Edwards's lead, his very presence was sufficient to build the belief that Plaid Cymru was on the verge of a very good performance. Launching the party's manifesto, *Free Wales,* Gwynfor predicted that Plaid Cymru was sure to win at least 100,000 votes and the Welsh electorate appreciated the fact that it was the only party that wanted to see power devolved to the people at every level.[185] Every bit as important as devolution, Gwynfor believed that the broadcasting ban, and Plaid Cymru's inability to make party political broadcasts, would win them thousands of votes. A pirate radio station set up by Plaid Cymru became a central plank of the campaign to publicize the unjust 'ban'. Since March 1959, 'Radio Wales' had been broadcasting nationalist propaganda through television sets at the close of the day's official programmes. When the first broadcast was made, one Whitehall civil servant could not believe his ears:

> The transmission by 'Radio Free Wales' opened with extracts from a speech (language used not known) by Cynfor Evans [*sic*]... followed by a song in Welsh, an announcement that now that Plaid Cymru was on the air further broadcasts from different districts would be made and closed by a rousing chorus of Men of Harlech.[186]

Publicly, Gwynfor denied any connection with the station – a particularly misleading statement given that Plaid Cymru's Executive had organized the whole thing.[187] Gwynfor's position was all the more ambivalent when one recalls that he was a member of the Wales Broadcasting Council. Although the *Western Mail* accused Plaid Cymru of having 'stolen' this wavelength, Radio Wales was a huge success during the run-up to the election.[188] It received enormous coverage in the English press, and some younger Plaid members, like Glyn James and Elystan Morgan, regarded it as a means to challenge the authorities without harming the party's image.[189]

Across Wales, Plaid Cymru fielded 20 candidates – an enormously ambitious number given the financial burden involved – but it was consistent with Gwynfor's vision of creating a party for the whole of Wales. But Merioneth, 'Green, Golden and Glorious',[190] as *The Times* called it, was the big prize that October. As the campaign progressed, hundreds of young activists flooded into the county in the hope that they could contribute to an historic victory. David Rosser, of the *Western Mail*, sensed there was change in the air:

> This volunteer corps is stamping around the county with a fervour akin to a religious revival. Even the most outspoken critics of the Blaid agree that it is becoming a movement to be reckoned with in the area.[191]

Reading reports like this gave the nationalists renewed hopes about Tryweryn. According to Llwyd o'r Bryn, Gwynfor's stand for Capel Celyn was comparable to that taken by Tom Ellis during the Tithe Wars. Elizabeth Watkin Jones agreed, contrasting Gwynfor's stand with T W Jones's totally lethargic campaign. Gwynfor, she said, was 'the Moses of Tryweryn'.[192]

Labour reacted to the threat with an intense, often brutal, campaign. When reflecting on his political life, Gwynfor claimed that this was the most ferocious of the twelve elections he fought.[193] Labour sent one of its Carmarthenshire county councillors to Merioneth for ten days to spread the rumour that Gwynfor was a Tory.[194] The other tactic was to attack Gwynfor and his family for their middle-class background. With the blessing of the party centrally, Labour published ten questions with the sole intention of undermining him. One unjustifiable question asked why Rhiannon bought her clothes in Paris; another asked why Gwynfor sent his children to a public school in England. The Liberals posed a different, fairer threat; after all, they were in certain respects the establishment, and their candidate, Ben G Jones, was a solid, well-respected politician. Along with Emlyn Hooson, the pair fought to re-establish the Liberal ascendancy. It was a keen contest but, on the eve of the poll, the commentators were unanimous – there would only be a few hundred votes in it either way between Labour and Plaid Cymru.

The result, announced on 9 October 1959, was a dreadful blow to Plaid Cymru.[195] Not only had Gwynfor lost, he had lost by a large margin and the total number of votes for 'the Moses of Tryweryn' was 116 lower than the number he had received four years earlier. As for the other two parties, Labour's support had held up well and, much to the surprise of many, the Liberal vote had increased substantially. After all his efforts, Gwynfor received scant reward for what he had done for the people of Capel Celyn. T W Jones – having done precious little – was back at Westminster leaving Gwynfor in a political wilderness. The scenario across Wales was just as disappointing. Despite the occasional decent result in the valleys, Plaid Cymru's national total – 77,571 votes – was a good way short of the target of 100,000 that Gwynfor had set. Particularly disappointing to the party faithful were the results in previously promising seats like Carmarthenshire and Aberdare, where the nationalist vote had fallen. Gwynfor's whole-Wales strategy had failed, and his party now knew that success was not a foregone conclusion. All things considered, the goal of winning any parliamentary seat looked like a bad joke. Over the next five years, the party would tear itself to shreds as it argued over the best way forward. As the dream of saving Capel Celyn lay in tatters and the contractors from Liverpool set about destroying a Welsh community, the recriminations began. Gwynfor could not have done more for Capel Celyn, but the tactical confusion between 1956 and 1959 was his fault alone. He would now pay the price: the next five years would come close to destroying his whole career.

Chapter 7

CIVIL WAR 1959–64

In every respect, the devastating General Election results of 1959 were a severe jolt to Gwynfor's inner circle. D J Williams was rarely downhearted, but he was shattered by the outcome. In his diary, he described what had happened in Merioneth as 'a hideous disappointment', and a cruel disillusionment for Gwynfor more than anyone. This, he wrote, was 'a blow from which he will not easily recover' and his prediction proved accurate.[1] Politically, Gwynfor's world had fallen apart. After all, a significant proportion of Plaid's supporters had been certain he would win in 1959. Given the result, one could have imagined that Gwynfor would have been distressed but, surprisingly, he was not as dejected as those around him. Although his first instinct when he heard the news from Merioneth was to 'curse the people' and to call the electors 'small-minded', he soon rallied. Four days after the result, he wrote to D J Williams to share his vision for the future. Despite the disappointment, he believed that 'Plaid's strategic position [was] stronger than ever', because the Liberals had suffered 'a worse blow' than his own party. He also took comfort from the fact that Macmillan's Conservative Government had been re-elected. With Labour now powerless, Gwynfor concluded that devolution would be 'more attractive' and that it would be Plaid Cymru's task henceforth to turn socialists into Welsh Home Rulers. By meeting these Labour supporters 'personally and in groups', Gwynfor was sure that Plaid Cymru could steer a rather different political course from the one his party had taken between 1955 and 1959. Hope, he told D J Williams, 'still sprang eternal' under his 'wounded breast'.[2]

The implications were far-reaching. Gwynfor was calling on Plaid Cymru to reach out to the political left and operate in part as the Welsh conscience of the Labour Party. By this time, Labour was offering Wales a Secretary of State, and it was through this institution that Gwynfor saw some hope for a measure of devolution. Such a standpoint was ironical, as Gwynfor was the least ecumenical and least sympathetic to the Labour cause. The other irony was that Gwynfor had no idea how to reach the cultural nerve of the southern working class, because his animus towards bingo, bookies and working men's clubs was as strong in 1959 as it had been in Oxford thirty-five years previously. But given his difficult position he had no choice: he had to offer his party something new.

In late October 1959, he called a major meeting of the 'President's Committee' – a gathering of his most loyal political advisers – to discuss the way ahead.[3] Before they went on to debate the main business, those present cast a unanimous vote of confidence in his leadership. A public show of unanimity was unsurprising, but the fact a vote had been taken was an indication of the political pressure on Gwynfor. Having gained the committee's approval, he revealed his vision for the future in a memorandum. He began with the assumption that the party's growth had been too slow, and that it could not hope to benefit any more from undermining the Liberal vote. What was required, he said, was for nationalists to chase the Labour vote. This meant that Plaid Cymru faced three choices: to establish a new Labour Party; to unite Plaid Cymru and Labour; or to win support from within Labour. The first choice, of course, was impossible for Gwynfor: '… my emotional attachment to Plaid Cymru dictates this belief'. The second choice was equally impossible. How on earth, Gwynfor asked, could the party of Cliff Prothero, Ness Edwards and Aneurin Bevan have anything in common with Plaid Cymru? This left the third option: 'Win from LP [Labour Party] – to win substantial support from Labour ranks to PC'. But this had its problems too. According to Gwynfor, 'this cannot be done on an official or national level. And it cannot be done publicly, or it will arouse fatal antagonism'. Despite these challenges, he believed the party could reach out by targeting specific groups of individuals – including anti-nuclear campaigners and trade unionists. He also wanted Plaid Cymru to curb its enthusiasm for Dominion status for Wales: 'The opposition to our policy of Dominion status is so widespread that we have to say we are prepared to co-operate in establishing a limited measure of self-government.'[4]

This was all agreed, and Plaid Cymru tried to re-launch itself as a party of the left, a party that would not be unduly obsessed with the idea of freedom for Wales. There was no more talk, either, of a national movement floating, as Gwynfor described it, like some divine presence above the noise and fury of real politics. Instead, Gwynfor stated that Plaid Cymru was 'further to the left than the Communists', and that his party was the natural heir of the Welsh left-wing tradition.[5] There was some truth in this assertion, but Gwynfor had paid little more than lip-service to this tradition during his fifteen years as President. Be that as it may, between autumn 1959 and spring 1960, this was the rhetoric Gwynfor employed in an attempt to broaden Plaid Cymru's appeal and to divert attention from the never ending Tryweryn theme.

The gains were, however, very limited. Although Labour suffered a split in early 1960, Plaid Cymru failed to make any inroads into the socialist strongholds of the south, and for the bulk of the membership, all roads, both practical and emotional, still led to Capel Celyn.. This issue united the party: young and old; reactionary traditionalists and the new breed of socialist radicals in the south-east. Faced with this pressure, Gwynfor's grand scheme to move Plaid Cymru to the left disintegrated, and the party slipped back into a post-electoral torpor.

To a large degree, Gwynfor was a hostage to events in Tryweryn, and as the construction work proceeded apace, Plaid Cymru's failure became ever more apparent. At five to nine in the morning, on 2 January 1960, the last train chugged through Capel Celyn. Many local people wore black as a mark of respect; others wept openly as the Bala Silver Band played a popular funeral hymn, '*O fryniau Caersalem*'.[6] As it witnessed excruciating scenes like this, the younger generation's frustration with the leadership deepened, and some began to plan and conspire on their own account. Emrys Roberts drew up a confidential plan to hold a hunger strike in Liverpool, and wrote to a friend, Pedr Lewis:

> It would have good effect on the public I believe – far better than blowing anything up... Most important would be the effect on Plaid itself – I think it might give new heart to our members, silence the critics... All this would create greater public interest in the Blaid, and a willingness on the part of other people to throw in their lot with an organisation with some life and guts in it.[7]

Other members of Plaid Cymru were also thinking along the same lines. John Daniel, the most able of these young radicals, wrote an irritable letter to J E Jones asking what was being done in Tryweryn. Had the party, he wondered, 'given up the Tryweryn cause?'[8] In his reply, J E Jones had to admit that the compromise offer, the *New Proposals,* had not been accepted; 'hardly anyone expected it would'. As a response, this was not convincing. Jones's rather feeble undertaking to John Daniel was that the party was still keeping an eye on the site and that it would:

> ... look to see whether anything can be done when Liverpool starts work there ... I don't need to tell you that no one finds it easy to see precisely how to act effectively on work that will be carried out by contractors, but the desire remains strong in most of us.[9]

This was almost certainly empty talk. By April 1960, Gwynfor was more determined than ever that breaking the law over Tryweryn would be pointless. He attempted to re-ignite the constitutional battle by pressing on with his *New Proposals* – a scheme that, by his own private admission, was 'an utter defeat for us'.[10] But his effort failed. By the middle of 1960, the nationalists of Merioneth were eager to distance themselves from Capel Celyn. By then, developments at Tryweryn were bringing work to the area, and its residents were learning to live with the sad truth that the struggle was finally over. One local Plaid Cymru member, Vernon Jones, argued that any further protest would soon become 'a joke', especially in the local paper, *Y Seren*.[11] Gwynfor's problem, however, was that many of his party members refused to see it that way. For them, Tryweryn was a national issue – not a local problem in a remote valley.

He tried to direct his energies in other directions, but these failed too. One campaign that attracted Gwynfor and J E Jones was the courageous struggle waged by Eileen Beasley to have Welsh included on Llanelli District Council forms – a struggle that went on for so long that some leading nationalists like Saunders Lewis began to criticize Plaid Cymru's reluctance to support the family. Gwynfor decided to act and, in secret, he and J E Jones drafted a plan that would involve twenty party members joining Eileen Beasley in refusing to pay rates. The pair went as far as to send questionnaires to those most likely to support the campaign, but members in Llanelli were reticent. Although everyone supported Eileen and Trefor Beasley, few were willing to sacrifice property and face possible imprisonment for the language.[12]

The press were picking up on Plaid Cymru's obvious difficulties. For months, the *Western Mail* had been accusing Plaid Cymru of racism.[13] That in itself was hard to handle, but Gwynfor was more hurt by what was happening in the Welsh-language press. It seemed to have turned on Gwynfor from May 1960. The most outspoken critic was Huw T Edwards, who pleaded with his new party to be more energetic and militant.[14] This was a common perception; for many in the party and for commentators like 'Mignedd' in *Y Faner*, what was needed was 'something definite to kill off the idea that the Victorian crinoline is the most suitable dress for followers of Gwynfor Evans'.[15] Having spent so long fighting the nationalist cause, Gwynfor was beginning to doubt himself by mid-1960. In a strikingly candid letter to J E Jones, he confessed that his critics's tactics had succeeded, and that it was proving an almost impossible task to shake off the idea that Plaid Cymru was full of 'old-fashioned, out-of-touch people wanting to go back to the middle ages in some cases but usually no further back than Victorian times'. These critics, Gwynfor added, had had it 'their own way too easily in creating this image', because 'the main media in the country' were controlled by them. He regretted too that Plaid Cymru had not done more to present its case 'in modern terms and against a modern backdrop'.[16]

Gwynfor was not the only one in his immediate circle who thought this way. In the same period, he received a shocking, not to say bizarre, letter from R Tudur Jones in response to an anonymous call in *Y Faner* recommending the formation of a movement like Haganah – the terrorist organization that had fought for the establishment of an Israeli state. A movement of the sort, according to the unnamed correspondent in *Y Faner*, would prove that Plaid Cymru 'has failed to give a lead' as 'the main mouthpiece of the Welsh nation'.[17] Under normal circumstances, Plaid Cymru's leadership would have dismissed the letter as the ranting of a crank, but the party's standing was such that it was taken at face value. Tudur Jones warned Gwynfor that such a movement could be successful: 'I would not be surprised if some violent, secret organization came about with hundreds of Teddy Boys only too keen to help the cause with their razors and their knives.' To oppose any such move he proposed 'forming a non-violent army' at arm's length from Plaid Cymru that would 'act along Gandhi-like lines'. He suggested the new movement should be called the 'Freedom Army' and be organized into regional battalions from Arfon in the north to Uwch-Aeron in the south-west. It would then have the right to hold non-violent demonstrations on specific issues such as nuclear weapons or television provision in Welsh.[18]

Gwynfor did not act on R Tudur Jones's eccentric suggestion, but both were in search of a campaign, any campaign, which could reinvigorate Plaid Cymru. So it was manna from heaven when it was announced in the summer of 1960 that Rachel Jones, the non-Welsh-speaking wife of the Dean of Brecon, had been appointed chair of the Broadcasting Council for Wales, giving her the position, to all intents and purposes, of constitutional head of the BBC in Wales. In the event, she proved very effective in the role between 1960 and 1965 but, that summer, many in Wales considered her appointment distinctly odd. Rachel Jones had been living in Wales for only a decade after her return from Australia, and very few people outside Brecon even knew of her. In Plaid Cymru and Labour circles, it was generally believed that it was her friendship with Vivian Lewis, Henry Brooke's deputy, which had secured her the post.

Gwynfor immediately criticized the appointment, seeing it as a conspiracy devised by a clique of High Church Conservatives in the Brecon diocese. Her promotion, he told J E Jones, was 'a deliberate swipe at Wales by the Tories'. He suspected also that Henry Brooke had been determined 'for at least six months' that no Welsh-speaker should be appointed, and that the Conservatives had selected Rachel Jones so that she could be 'used by the government'.[19] Little by little, an institutional row became a national dispute, and various tactics were employed to block the appointment. The Broadcasting Council voted by six to one against giving the chair to Rachel Jones and sent a letter to the Prime Minister, Harold Macmillan, to express their disquiet. But in vain; on 28 June, Macmillan refused to pay any attention to this dramatic stand. The following day, there was a storm of protest in the Commons; George Thomas attacked the appointment, because it was, he believed, rank nepotism. As the wrangle continued, Gwynfor considered the possibility of bringing legal action against the government as a means of preventing the appointment. John Roberts Williams was also thinking along the same lines, and proposed opening a fund in *Y Cymro* to pay costs that 'may amount to a couple of thousand'.[20]

Rachel Jones was there to stay, however, and by mid-July Gwynfor had only two options – remaining within the Broadcasting Council or resigning. It was a real dilemma; although he was committed to the work of the Council, he felt he had no choice but to leave.[21] One of those who prevailed upon him to think again was Alun Oldfield-Davies, the Controller of BBC Wales. He wrote to Gwynfor when the crisis was at its most acute to remind him that his intention was 'to try the best I can to ensure the success of the Corporation in Wales'.[22] Within Plaid Cymru too, there were mixed views; some like Islwyn Ffowc Elis and Huw T Edwards were convinced that Gwynfor would fall into a trap by resigning. But the Rachel Jones issue was more than a disagreement about broadcasting. As with the battle for a Welsh Fourth Channel twenty years later, the debate was fuelled by wider political considerations. Many within Plaid Cymru urged Gwynfor to resign because it would, to quote R Tudur Jones, 'give you and Plaid a leading role again; nationally, it would give new heart to people in Wales'.[23] This was what Gwynfor probably wanted to hear. After the Tryweryn fiasco, Gwynfor was desperate to make a stand that would not prove too controversial. He was also of the opinion that his resignation would prove to the authorities that Plaid Cymru was stronger than the election result in Merioneth suggested.[24] On 18 July, he announced that he was resigning from the Broadcasting Council, along with another member, Huw Morris-Jones. Gwynfor continued to press Henry Brooke after his departure, and refused to meet him at a garden party organized by Brooke when the Queen visited the National Eisteddfod in Cardiff. Superficially, Gwynfor was as outspoken as any of the young radicals in his assertion that Brooke, who had been 'so discourteous to our nation' could not have expected to be greeted as 'a friendly guest'.[25]

Gwynfor might reasonably have expected a warm welcome at the party's annual conference in Cardiff, but it was not to be. For most of the younger generation, Plaid Cymru had lost its way. One young delegate, Gerald Morgan, could hardly believe his eyes as, with Soviet-like obedience, numerous resolutions were carried 'like sausages and emerged in hygienic plastic jackets full of breadcrumbs'. No one dared challenge the annual report and neither Gwynfor nor anyone from among his inner circle made the least attempt to explain why the election had been such a washout: 'The stinking fish of last October were shovelled into a corner and the Party turned away its respectable nose.' But what appalled Gerald Morgan more than anything was Plaid Cymru's putting propriety before protest: 'Instead, we have a *Noson Lawen* and a tent in the Eisteddfod. How respectable can we get[?]'.[26] Another young member, Cynog Dafis, saw things in the same light. In a private letter, he complained to J E Jones that 'Mr Gwynfor Evans' ignored 'completely the cruel beating that he took in the Merioneth election, and went straight for his usual target, Henry Brooke and his latest protégée, Mrs Rachel Jones… I greatly doubt whether condemnation of another party's actions, and another man's in particular, is a very dynamic way to open a conference'.[27]

Gwynfor made another mistake in publishing a pamphlet transforming Plaid Cymru policy on the constitution without consulting anyone. *Self Government for Wales and a Common Market for the Nations of Britain*[28] was written to attract Labour members and to kill off the accusation that self-government would be an economic disaster. From then on, Gwynfor hoped to see a Common Market based on the countries of the British Isles.[29] The clear intention was to bury the notion that Plaid Cymru wanted 'to dissociate the economic life of Wales from England' but, by doing so, he buried the policy of Dominion status at the same time.[30] In its place, Plaid Cymru demanded Commonwealth status. Gwynfor's intention had been to place Plaid Cymru's constitutional ambitions in a modern context but for purist nationalists this was further evidence that the party had jumped on the 'free trade bandwagon'.[31] Privately, some of the more independent-minded members of the Executive were far more damning. Harri Webb, for instance, believed all the talk of a 'British Customs Union' was intellectual hogwash and that the new idea was evidence of a party full of 'docile decorous language nationalists'.[32] Plaid Cymru's attitude to the language, and how best to protect it, was also central to this discussion of the party and its future. Following the 1960 annual conference, some of the younger members became increasingly critical of how the party saw its future direction, and since Gwynfor seemed so bereft of ideas they filled the vacuum with their own. The move caused alarm in the civil service. In October 1960, Blaise Gillie wrote to Henry Brooke to warn him there was 'a widespread impression that Alderman Gwynfor Evans, the present leader of the Party, is in danger of losing his grip over the party to an extreme and younger section'.[33]

Who, then, were these alleged 'extremists' who, for good or ill, lay behind this first real challenge to Gwynfor's leadership? When one looks at the period, what becomes clear is that a broad range of views were being expressed by the beginning of the new decade. There were those like John Davies, who would subsequently become first joint Secretary of the Welsh Language Society, who believed that an organized movement was needed to fight for official status for the Welsh language – the sort of body that could give moral and material support to a family like the Beasleys. For him, the answer was an organization whose members would refuse to pay television and dog licences.[34] By creating such a movement, John Davies hoped to relieve the pressure on Plaid Cymru, enabling it to face the future as a purely constitutional party. This, in due course, is what transpired with the creation of the Welsh Language Society, Cymdeithas yr Iaith Gymraeg, in August 1962.

John Davies's suggestion was both respectable and credible compared to some of the more fanciful notions entertained by other party members. A handful of Plaid members, including Harri Webb, who lived in Garth Newydd in Merthyr Tydfil, discussed law-breaking as a political weapon, as Gandhi and, later, the civil rights movement in the United States had done.[36] A programme of work was drawn up in order to achieve this and one of the habitués of Garth Newydd, Emrys Roberts, began to canvass opinion on the possibility of breaking the law at Tryweryn. The replies from Gwynfor's closest allies were not encouraging, and this would, in time, deepen the feeling of frustration with the President. Islwyn Ffowc Elis answered Emrys Roberts by saying that 'law-breaking, once started, would be difficult to end; that's the lesson of the IRA in Ireland'.[37] Another member, Meirion Lloyd Davies, thought that Emrys Roberts's suggestion made Gwynfor's position in Merioneth all the more difficult and pandered to the criticism heard during the campaign that 'Mr Gwynfor Evans' was 'a first rate-candidate' but that his supporters were 'too often juveniles, even juvenile delinquents'.[38]

Garth Newydd was not the only finishing school for radical dreamers. During the autumn of 1960, two separate groups began to meet to discuss the unconstitutional way forward. The first was the Belle Vue Group – a collection of individuals, many of them students at Aberystwyth, who decided to press Plaid Cymru to use unconstitutional methods in certain circumstances. The second gathering was altogether more exotic and colourful. This was the Garthewin Group – a collection of individuals who met under the auspices of the Celto-Catholic squire, R O F Wynne, to discuss armed rebellion and who had nothing but contempt for Gwynfor. The Garthewin Group was Catholic, idolized Saunders Lewis and some members were interested in right-wing ideas. J E Jones's name was mud. According to one of the younger members of the Group, Harri Pritchard Jones, Gwynfor's lieutenant was both 'insincere' and 'hypocritical'. There was discomfort too with R Tudur Jones's perceived 'arrogant' attitude towards Catholicism.[39] These ideas found voice from the summer of 1961 in *Cymru Ein Gwlad*, a house magazine for this vitriolic group, edited by Raymond Edwards. Another feature of the Garthewin Group was paranoia. Some members feared they were being pursued by the secret police and others searched for hidden listening devices at the beginning of each meeting.[40] Although only a handful of people attended these get-togethers at Garthewin, it was this group, given Saunders Lewis's influence over them, that Gwynfor feared most.

Little by little, the political pressure on Gwynfor was increasing, but he refused to give an inch to his critics, on the right or the left, as the troubles of 1960 threatened to spill over into the new year. He decided, for instance, that he should play a public role in the campaign to prevent pubs opening on a Sunday

– even though many in his party were eager to see the end of the traditional dry Welsh Sabbath. 'Patriotism,' as one put it, 'cannot be confined by the clasps of a prayer-book, nor is it measured out in pint pots.'[41] Within Plaid Cymru, there was a clear division over the issue, with Emrys Roberts and J E Jones against Plaid Cymru making a public statement on the matter. Officially, there would be no policy – but Gwynfor was determined it was his duty to defend what he saw as a 'Welsh institution'.[42] Despite objections from within his party, Gwynfor played a prominent role in the battle to save the Welsh Sunday, addressing over a dozen meetings prior to the referendum held at the end of 1961. It was a very principled stand but, from an electoral perspective, associating Plaid Cymru so closely with an antediluvian issue was thought unwise by many.

The same stubborn streak was evident in Gwynfor's determination to fight every by-election. In November 1960, the charismatic Emrys Roberts stood against Michael Foot in Ebbw Vale, gaining 2,091 votes – a remarkably good result given how hopeless a seat it was for Plaid Cymru. But to Gwynfor's critics, adhering to such a policy was idiotic given the failures of the past. The fact that Plaid Cymru's debts of £4,500 at the end of 1960 were greater than they had ever been preyed on many minds.[43] One such was Gwynfor's friend, Dr Gwenan Jones. *Y Faner* was savage, describing the Ebbw Vale result as 'a flea bite' and proof that the party's President was 'throwing money to the four winds'.[44] Islwyn Ffowc Elis was even more cutting, blaming the debt on a pervading atmosphere of 'blurred vision and ebbing enthusiasm'. The party's officers, he said, were 'weary' and the membership 'bored' by the constant effort to raise funds.[45]

Amazingly, perhaps, getting his party out of the red was not Gwynfor's first priority. Amid all the arguing about Plaid Cymru's political course and the advisability of fighting elections, Gwynfor was almost by stealth yoking Plaid Cymru's fortunes to one of the most high-minded – and disastrous – campaigns of the 1960s, the attempt to establish a commercial Welsh-language television channel. There had long been talk about the best way forward and, in September 1959, a national conference was convened on the subject.[46] It was decided to appoint a committee to pursue the issue but then, amid bitterness and misunderstanding, the committee split into two during the summer of 1960. One faction, comprising Jac L Williams and his supporters, argued that the only solution was to develop the BBC's Welsh-language service and that it was a waste of time – considering the enormity of the challenge – to create a commercial channel in Welsh. The other faction, led by Haydn Williams, the Director of Education for Flintshire, believed that Welsh could survive in a free market. By the end of 1960, this split between supporters of the BBC and those who backed a private sector solution had become entrenched. Gwynfor sided with Haydn Williams, and a small committee was established to apply for the right to run a Welsh station. In due course, this station would broadcast to the new south and west Wales region from the Llŷn peninsula to Pembrokeshire.[47]

The idea of creating a new company was 'the most important news in Wales for years', according to Gwynfor, and with his customary enthusiasm, he threw himself and his party into the work of raising the huge sum of £200,000 needed to obtain the licence.[48] The new company was named Teledu Cymru (Wales Television) – an abbreviation of is full name, Wales West and North Television Limited – and from December 1960, letters were sent from the Plaid Cymru offices in Bangor to potential investors using Gwynfor's reputation as an incentive. Use was made too of other names on the founding committee – including some with less obvious nationalist credentials – such as Colonel Williams Wynne and Colonel Traherne. Initial investment was promising and, by May 1961, Elwyn Roberts in Bangor had managed to raise £62,525. The subscribers included close friends of Gwynfor like Islwyn Ffowc Elis, who contributed £540 – a sum he could ill afford. Alcwyn, Gwynfor's brother, gave £5,000 – the largest donation of all the directors and irrefutable proof, if it were needed, of Gwynfor's confidence in the viability of the scheme.[49]

Those Plaid members who found the whole thing vague and over-ambitious were exceptions. Similarly, love of language proved stronger than common sense when the decision was made to begin broadcasting with just two transmitters – resulting in only a small proportion of the population being able to receive programmes. Gwynfor, however, judged that a little was better than nothing and that Welsh-language television would die out altogether if Teledu Cymru failed.[50] By June 1961, he and his fellow-directors heard the joyful news that the Independent Television Authority (ITA) had allocated the company its licence. But within two years, the dream turned to dust and Teledu Cymru's short life came to an end.

At the beginning of 1961 – one of most tempestuous years in Gwynfor's life – Teledu Cymru was his only ray of hope. Within Plaid Cymru, scepticism was rampant. D J Williams wrote in his diary that the Plaid Cymru Executive had spent hours 'discussing the new, mainly Catholic-led clique that is quite critical of Plaid and threatens its leadership to some degree'.[51] These fears were embodied in the figure of Catherine Daniel, the wife of the former leader J E Daniel, a Catholic herself and a close friend of Saunders Lewis. In February, Gwynfor received an alarming letter from Elwyn Roberts informing him of a meeting between himself and Catherine Daniel. Roberts listed her complaints one by one in a litany that Gwynfor must have found agonizing. The major complaint concerned the leadership, and his role as President. Catherine Daniel, Roberts reported, accused Gwynfor of having disappointed the younger element within the party – people like her son John Daniel, and Gareth Miles. In her view this had resulted in the party developing the knack of 'killing' its young leaders, the very people who could offer it hope. She also felt the Tryweryn episode to be a sad indictment of Plaid Cymru – believing that the party leaders should take action there, and surmising that they would only be sentenced to a few months' imprisonment if they did so, as opposed to the 10 to 15 years that any younger protesters would receive. She called on Plaid Cymru to throw out its Republican element and concentrate on 'land, water and language' and 'not a common market'.[52]

This letter undoubtedly shook Gwynfor's self-confidence. He was also worried that there was a plot among those who met at the Belle Vue in Aberystwyth to 'attempt to hold back money from the branches and not send it on' to the party centrally.[53] Two days after hearing about Catherine Daniel, Gwynfor took one of the most important decisions of his career: he left Merioneth and surrendered the parliamentary nomination. In short, he had had enough of both the constituency and the village in Cwm Tryweryn that had become a permanent symbol of betrayal. Although this was Gwynfor's own decision, and although Plaid Cymru in Merioneth begged him to reconsider, it is also true that 'various' nationalists in the county thought it was a good idea for him to leave, as the party was in the doldrums and there was continuing animosity over Tryweryn.[54] Gwynfor's decision was not made public until the end of the year, and the party was remarkably successful in keeping his real reasons a secret. Plaid Cymru's 'progress' and the growing demands on his time throughout Wales were Gwynfor's public justification, but there is no doubt having to leave Merioneth was a body blow for him.[55] Electorally, he had nowhere to turn, and although Carmarthen was eager for him to stand, he hesitated until April 1962 before accepting the nomination. His reluctance was justifiable in view of the party's disarray there; he also felt it would be 'a poor show' for the President to perform badly in an election.[56]

Gwynfor's problems were not confined to Catherine Daniel's list of grievances. In February 1961, it appeared the tide was turning in favour of those who wanted to break the law at Tryweryn, and take similar action on the site of the new reservoir that Birmingham Corporation intended to construct at Clywedog. Emrys Roberts warned Gwynfor by letter that there was talk of setting up a 'Direct Action Party' which would carry out acts such as stealing lorries from Tryweryn or breaking 'every window in Liverpool high street'.[57] Gwynfor's response to the warning is not known, but within days of his correspondence with Gwynfor, Emrys Roberts was canvassing for support for a major act at Tryweryn. He wrote to a select group of party members inviting them to join him in an act of civil disobedience. Roberts mentioned three options. The first was: 'Violent action of a destructive nature with the intention of causing such a disturbance that extra police and eventually troops would have to be called in to deal with it.' The second was to make the cost of building the dam so expensive for the contractors 'that they would either refuse to carry on or Liverpool find it impossible to raise enough money'. The final one – and the one favoured by Roberts – was to carry out a minor act, with a hunger strike in prison to follow.[58]

Gwynfor felt that Emrys Roberts was undermining him, and the firebrand's letter was not warmly welcomed in Merioneth either. Dafydd Orwig wrote to Gwynfor to inform him that local people had spoken of Roberts as a 'bloody Gandhi' when they heard of his proposal.[59] But there was worse to come. Although Gwynfor was thick-skinned and well used to personal criticism, *Y Faner* carried a piece in April 1961 that turned his world upside down. An article under the pseudonym 'Glyndŵr', made a damning comparison between 'The Two Gwynfors' – Gwynfor Evans, the party President, and Gwynfor S Evans, the Carmarthenshire county councillor who had fought for the right to have Welsh nomination papers accepted in local government elections. 'Glyndŵr' said that Gwynfor S Evans's stand was irrefutable proof that the pupil was 'greater than his teacher' simply because the teacher's tendency thus far had been 'to conform to the status quo'. Gwynfor came in for sustained criticism: he was attacked for having accepted the Congregationalist chairmanship as well as the aldermanship – proof, it was said, that he was a Tory.[60] The article was answered a fortnight later by Elystan Morgan and Tom Jones of Llanuwchllyn, who described all such claims as 'malicious'.[61]

But for Gwynfor the damage was already done and, on 20 April 1961, he shared his most private feelings with Elwyn Roberts. In a telephone call he found astounding, Roberts heard Gwynfor's voice, 'thoroughly depressed', saying he was desperate to share some extraordinary news with him; he was considering resigning the Presidency and saw the 'Glyndŵr' article as clear evidence that there was 'deep opposition to him'. Roberts tried to persuade him to change his mind, and promised he would speak to Gwilym R Jones, editor of *Y Faner*, about why he had published such a spiteful piece. Roberts took other steps during the coming days which he described as 'dark' ones for Gwynfor. He arranged for Gwynfor's friends to write to him in an effort to convince him that 'Glyndŵr' did not represent 'any group of members worth mentioning and that the accusations are without foundation'.[62] Roberts's appeal quickly materialised. By return of post, Gwynfor received a number of letters from some of his most faithful advisers, the 'Court of Llangadog'.

R Tudur Jones was the 'Godfather' of the Court. He set about ensuring that Gwynfor would not resign. He wrote to him insisting there was no reason why Tryweryn should weigh on his conscience. And there was another reason to stay, too:

> Only you can hold Plaid together. I know that it is often a thankless task and I have often had occasion to be astonished by your patience. But you should not think for a moment of letting the reins slip from your hands.

Tudur Jones went on to say that he sensed an 'organized conspiracy', and that Emrys Roberts was behind it – a man who would 'seize the real leadership' if his plan to take action at Tryweryn was realised. But there was something else, according to Tudur Jones, which was even more dangerous than 'feuding friends'. What he feared above all was the 'melancholy' that 'had spread throughout the movement recently'.[63]

In the short term, Tudur Jones's kind words soothed Gwynfor, but they did not solve the fundamental problem. And there were other challenges. Although no one else was likely to stand for the Presidency, there were several attempts to undermine the authority of Gwynfor's advisers and, by extension, his own leadership. In May 1961, for instance, Trefor Morgan was nominated by the

Belle Vue Group to stand against R Tudur Jones for the Vice-Presidency. Trefor Morgan failed, but Gwynfor thought the effort to weaken Tudur Jones was part of a wider conspiracy. He believed that Morgan was trying to get rid of J E Jones – who, according to D J Williams's diary, was 'ill and depressed' about the state of the party.[64] In private, Gwynfor referred to Trefor Morgan as 'a devil', and as he saw his friends facing their own difficulties, he decided to strike back. He insisted it was his duty and the duty of his friends to spare J E Jones 'any annoyance and persecution'.[65] The same determination was evident in Gwynfor's request for Plaid Cymru in Merioneth to release a statement to the press to prove he was not a coward and that it was the party members there who had refused his offer to act unlawfully over Tryweryn. When a statement was released, it stressed that Gwynfor had indeed made such an offer but that he had been frustrated by lack of support:

> … not only in our county, but also in the upper echelons of Plaid. We saw Mr Gwynfor Evans and other party officers being criticized on the subject of taking action, from some quarters. But let it be known that Plaid Cymru is a democratic political party. Its leaders are not dictators.'[66]

For the critics, however, such an explanation was neither here nor there and the Merioneth apologia was interpreted as a feeble attempt to paper over the cracks. It was answered in a waspish press release signed by prominent members of the Plaid Cymru Executive, namely Harri Webb, David Pritchard and Peter Hourahane, and included a stinging attack on the conservatism and smugness of Plaid Cymru in Merioneth. The title said it all: 'Tryweryn is in Merioneth, Tryweryn is also in Wales'.[67] In other words, some nationalists, especially from the industrial south-east, were determined that Plaid Cymru in Merioneth would not have the last word on action at Tryweryn. The atmosphere was venomous, and two distinct groups had emerged by the summer of 1961 – a Gwynfor faction and an 'activist' faction. Although an attempt was made to arrange a meeting between the two sides on 1 July 1961 to seek an accommodation, there is no evidence it ever took place. It would now take a stormy national conference to clear the air.

The conference was held the following month in Llangollen – the town where Gwynfor's Presidency had begun sixteen years previously. The atmosphere this time, however, was very different as the 'direct actionists' and the 'Gwynforites' came together for one of the most vital meetings in Welsh nationalist history. It was the first summer school for Dr Phil Williams, who would later play a leading role in the party, and he was astounded by the passion shown by the direct action camp: 'these felt total despair and an emotional need for some dramatic turning point. They quoted Penyberth and even Dublin Post Office'.[68] A motion had been put before the committee from the Merthyr branch calling on Plaid Cymru to take direct action against the proposed development at Clywedog. Everyone present at the conference understood its significance. Had the resolution been passed, the history of Plaid Cymru since 1945 would have been transformed, and Gwynfor's leadership would have become a serious issue. The atmosphere was dramatic enough even before the proposer, Catherine Daniel, stepped onto the stage.

In a speech which can be deservedly described as one of the most electrifying ever heard at a Plaid Cymru conference, she began to tear Gwynfor's leadership to shreds. She claimed that Plaid Cymru had no moral force and had become a left-wing school of 'dialectics'. In full flow, she accused the leadership of betraying the past, particularly the Penyberth tradition. Gwynfor sat through it all, listening intently but quietly through what was fast becoming the most ferocious assault ever on his authority. From the floor, there was constant shouting as the two sides heckled each other. But Gwynfor kept his counsel and refused to be drawn into the debate. In his own inimitable fashion, he left that thankless task to Roy Lewis, editor of *Y Ddraig Goch*; in his own speech, Lewis accused the direct action camp of being 'sentimental' and of having no idea what they meant when they constantly talked about taking action. The next to speak was Elystan Morgan. The accusation that the party had betrayed its supporters over Tryweryn, he said, was 'utterly false'. The booing was deafening by now but between them, Roy Lewis and Elystan Morgan succeeded in saving Gwynfor's skin.[69] The resolution was defeated by 51 votes to 30 – not a commanding majority but the result would have been closer still had Harri Webb kept his word and supported Catherine Daniel.[70]

In the long term, Llangollen proved to be a turning-point in Gwynfor's career – the cathartic moment when the 'constitutionalists' defeated the 'direct actionists'. But, in the short term, Llangollen provoked even more bitterness, especially from Saunders Lewis. A few days after the vote, he wrote to D J Williams to say that:

> … this pacifism is a microbe like tuberculosis; that's what killed Plaid Cymru three years ago… An exorcist priest should be called in to set its poor ghost to rest. RIP, say I.[71]

Catherine Daniel was equally embittered; she refused to contribute a penny to Plaid Cymru's coffers and blamed the party for wasting time on subjects 'like the H Bomb, race in Africa, a free market between Wales and England'.[72] Taking action at Tryweryn was still being discussed; Emrys Roberts also continued to talk of fasting in Liverpool. In response to this and other schemes, the leadership offered a compromise signed by J E Jones: from now on, there was to be no unlawful action in the name of Plaid Cymru, but it would be 'open to members to undertake a particular "action" when it is a matter of conscience for them to do so'.[73]

This was a necessary accommodation and it prevented the party from splitting in the period immediately after Llangollen. To all intents and purposes, the party was prepared to turn a blind eye to any unlawful acts committed by its members. But there was one condition, that members would not claim to be acting in the name of Plaid Cymru. In keeping with this policy, *Y Ddraig Goch* announced that Emrys Roberts and a number of individual party members ould be fasting in Liverpool at the end of September.[74] But there was a price to be paid for this concession: it made Gwynfor look like a particularly weak President. People did not take him seriously – as happened when Plaid Cymru announced its intention to fight 30 seats at the General Election. The *Western Mail* was especially dismissive of Plaid Cymru's commitment to pacifism and the constitutional route. According to one reporter the pacifist way forward could be described thus:

> ... there will be a 'great march' with banners and slogans – lots of them – and finally, that most devastating of weapons, a Noson Lawen at 6.30 p.m. This is being planned by Misses Cassie Davies and Nel Davies which suggests it will be a most successful night.[75]

On all fronts, Gwynfor was in trouble. By November 1961, even Teledu Cymru, the company that had been a source of such pride, was being used as a stick with which to beat him. The bone of contention was that Teledu Cymru's Welsh-language programmes were not being broadcast at peak times as had originally been promised. For commercial reasons, the company was forced to broadcast its Welsh output in the evenings between 6 and 7 and after 10. 'We are,' Gwynfor said in an attempt at justification, 'a commercial company and have to depend on advertising revenue. The network programmes carry the heaviest advertising. We must make the best of things as they are.'[76] From a business point of view, it made perfect sense, but it was without doubt a U-turn on the company's part. It also betrayed the directors' naivety, as they had promised something that could not be delivered. Although it had been the board's decision to change the scheduling of Welsh programmes, Gwynfor, because of his political connections, suffered the consequences and he was remorselessly attacked by his political enemies for being a hypocrite. Teledu Cymru, according to one of those critics, Iorwerth Peate, was the 'sanctimonious' channel, 'churning out by the yard *Rawhide* and *Maverick* and the innumerable quizzes of commercial television – in the name of nationalism'.[77] The culmination of these assaults was a stinging pamphlet called *Teledu Mamon* ('Mammon Television') by Aneirin Talfan Davies, deputy head of programming at BBC Wales. Writing under the pseudonym '*Sodlau Prysur*' ('Busy Heels'), Talfan Davies called on Gwynfor to resign from the board of Teledu Cymru and remain true to his principles.[78] Gwynfor did not give Talfan Davies's request a moment's consideration, choosing to believe it was a Liberal party plot between Aneirin Talfan Davies and his brother, Alun Talfan Davies, the prospective Liberal candidate in Carmarthenshire. But the damage was done and Gwynfor was concerned that these continual attacks would weaken the faith of 'our people' in the enterprise.[79]

The Teledu Cymru venture was also proof for Gwynfor's critics that he was too ready to compromise and to avoid harsher questions concerning the political vacuum at the heart of Plaid Cymru. The arguments soon began again and Roy Lewis was obliged to use *Y Ddraig Goch* to appeal publicly for a ceasefire between 'those young members who see Plaid paralysed by sentimental dreams about Cymru Fydd' and 'those who despise the liberal and pacifist elements in Plaid Cymru'.[80] It is some indication of the party's crisis that open disputes like these were not regarded as unusual at the beginning of 1962, but such infighting left its mark. The hardest blow to Gwynfor, no doubt, was J E Jones's decision to resign as Plaid Cymru's General Secretary. Explaining his decision in his resignation letter, Jones told Gwynfor that the post was 'a considerable strain' for him.[81] This was only half the truth in fact. Jones had been suffering with nervous problems for years, and the real reason why he was leaving was the constant feuding between him and his deputy, Emrys Roberts, at party headquarters. On everything from organization to ideology, the two were poles apart. Frequently, Emrys Roberts was driven to distraction by Jones's reluctance to move with the times. He tried to explain his position to Elwyn Roberts, a more sympathetic character:

> The truth is that although I respect J E for having devoted his life to Plaid, I have no respect at all for his methods or any trust in them (he is far too inclined to treat people like little children), and he certainly raises the hackles of the lads down here in the south.[82]

A small party like Plaid Cymru could not cope with such tensions, and Gwynfor tried unsuccessfully to save J E Jones by offering to create an office to look after the counties of mid-Wales.

But J E Jones refused to reconsider (or so it appeared at the time – but he did return later as a paid adviser).[83] Then, out of the blue, a difficult situation turned into a nightmare for Gwynfor when Emrys Roberts wrote to him, within a month of J E Jones's resignation in January 1962, to inform him that he too wanted to leave. He complained to Gwynfor that his contribution was 'very small' and that he was being used like 'some sort of little clerk'. The conservatism of the Executive (and Gwynfor) on the matter of reorganization also annoyed him.[84] From an administrative point of view, things were a mess, and it took three months of delicate negotiation before Emrys Roberts could be prevailed upon to stay. He stepped into J E Jones's shoes, but persisted in telling anyone who would listen his complaints about how Gwynfor was running the party. Plaid Cymru, he told one meeting of the Executive, had no 'respect for constitutional methods' and 'often ignored regional and branch officers'.[85] Statements like this eroded Gwynfor's authority. Even so, he thought it worth tolerating Emrys Roberts in order to end the administrative chaos at national headquarters. Gwynfor made a concession to his new and excitable senior officer. He promised Emrys Roberts that a commission would be set up to look at the party's organization – a small concession at the time – but a promise that became a millstone around Gwynfor's neck, as he was the most absolutist of Presidents.

Plaid Cymru was in ferment by 1962, and it was against this background of administrative and ideological confusion that Saunders Lewis decided to 'save' his party from oblivion. On Tuesday 13 February 1962, he broadcast his lecture *Tynged yr Iaith* (The Fate of the Language) – the most important lecture in the history of the Welsh language and also the most misinterpreted. One thing is certain: the lecture did not constitute a call for those who loved the language to form a society to protect its interests: that, given the parlous state of Undeb

Cymru Fydd, was the last thing Saunders Lewis had in mind. The lecture, rather, was a calculated attempt to undermine Gwynfor's whole political strategy, and to bury his passionate commitment to constitutional means. That, without question, was the true significance of *Tynged yr Iaith*. Although Gwynfor is not named, the 'betrayal' of Tryweryn lies at the heart of the lecture, which begins with Lewis's assertion that it was 'dishonest' to blame Henry Brooke, the Welsh Affairs Minister. It was the Welsh people themselves, according to Lewis, who had failed to defend Capel Celyn because they had not followed the example of Irish nationalism, believing that 'Bread before Beauty' was more important than basic principles.[86] A further tragedy, to Lewis's mind, was the brave and unsupported stand made by the Beasleys in Llanelli. He judged that the time was ripe for an organized movement to support the Beasleys and others like them. This, he claimed in his closing peroration, was 'the only political issue' that was 'worth a Welshman taking pains over'. From then on, he hoped to see 'a period of hatred and persecution' – something that was far, far more desirable 'than the pacifist love' that typified Welsh politics in 1962.[87]

Saunders Lewis's message could hardly have been clearer, but this was not his last word on the matter. On Saint David's Day, the BBC broadcast his satirical play, *Excelsior*. Once again, there was an open attack on constitutional politics, and on the foolishness of those who thought Wales could be saved through Westminster. *Excelsior*, like *Tynged yr Iaith*, was an attempt to pull the intellectual rug from under Gwynfor's feet and Lewis was unapologetic. The play had been written the previous autumn in the wake of the Llangollen conference when feelings ran high. As he wrote to his friend, the artist David Jones: 'It [*Excelsior*] is a satirical farce on Welsh MPs and the Welsh Nationalist Party and on Welsh Socialists – the pent-up anger of twenty years'.[88]

According to Lewis, the lecture was 'a five minute stir' but, for others, the experience of hearing it was life-changing.[89] Many misinterpreted its message, but Gwynfor and his circle knew exactly what was intended. Although there is no record of Gwynfor's private response, his closest allies were furious at Saunders Lewis's last significant intervention in public life. Tudur Jones wrote to Gwynfor to tell him it was 'nonsense' to 'set self-government and the fate of the language in opposition to each other'[90] while Jones feared it was dangerous to suggest that political action could be taken only by 'raising the hackles of the other side'.[91] Others, such as Dafydd Orwig, were more openly supportive of Gwynfor's strategy. 'I think,' he wrote to Gwynfor, 'that SL is talking through his hat if he wants Plaid to become a Language Movement.' With support like this, there was never any chance that Lewis's agenda would be accepted by Plaid Cymru. His and his followers' prospects of success were negligible because no credible name was proposed to challenge Gwynfor as President. Even so, Gwynfor did not escape unscathed. Over the following four years, between the publication of *Tynged yr Iaith* and the by-election in Carmarthen, the lecture made his position all the weaker. During that time, it was Saunders Lewis and not Gwynfor who would be the iconic hero of most of the younger generation.

The irony, of course, is that this same generation ignored their hero's wishes by establishing the Welsh Language Society, Cymdeithas yr Iaith Gymraeg. But Saunders Lewis's concern about the future of his party was so deep that he returned to *Tynged yr Iaith* a month after its publication. In a spirited letter to *Y Faner* he expressed regret that 'some people are already misinterpreting' his radio address, adding that he had not said a word about setting up a new movement. He claimed in the same letter that it was 'painfully obvious' that *Tynged yr Iaith* had been 'a direct message for Plaid Cymru' and that it had been written at the same time as *Excelsior* with the same purpose in mind. There was no need to delay for even a week, he asserted. 'All' that was needed was 'a mind and a heart for revolution'. And if such a will did not manifest itself, then Saunders Lewis's advice to his party was that it should 'disappear'.[93]

For some closest to Gwynfor, the letter in *Y Faner* was tantamount to a declaration of war, a re-igniting of the old tribal feud between the Gwynforites and the Saundersites. For one Gwynforite, R Tudur Jones, the 'affected' letter to Gwilym R Jones, editor of *Y Faner*, was a step too far, even by Lewis's standards. It was 'obvious', he told Gwynfor, that 'Saunders is beginning to attack us publicly now – which is a change from attacking us *via* Catherine Daniel and Raymond Edwards. Let us be perfectly clear on this; with all due respect to Saunders and his manifold abilities, if he were at the helm, Plaid would be no more than an insignificant collection of oddities, if it existed at all'.[94] Quite simply, it was a vendetta, but Gwynfor refrained from making any personal attacks on Saunders Lewis.

Two days after the broadcast of *Tynged yr Iaith*, Gwynfor published the first of three articles in *Y Tyst* on the critical state of the Welsh language in Carmarthenshire.[95] Like Saunders Lewis, he called for a speedy change of attitude by the authorities with regard to the language, but this was the only thing they had in common. Rather than calling for sacrifice, Gwynfor appealed for better provision in education and the media, and pleaded with the chapels to show leadership. He was as convinced as ever that it was only a Welsh Parliament, and not a language movement, which would restore the language to its former glory. Gwynfor intended these articles to be an honest contribution to the debate and, shortly afterwards, he published a pamphlet summarizing their main arguments, entitled *Cyfle Olaf yr Iaith Gymraeg* (The Last Chance for the Welsh language).[96] For all his sincerity, Gwynfor's intervention in the language struggle served only to draw attention to his own weakness. Saunders Lewis's lecture was broadcast before the publication of Gwynfor's articles, although he had been working on them since January if not sooner. The clear impression given was that Gwynfor was reacting to events, not moulding them. To make matters worse, Saunders Lewis attacked *Cyfle Olaf yr Iaith Gymraeg* saying that there was no hope for the Welsh language if Wales followed the respectable, chapel-going route proposed by Gwynfor. Now, Saunders Lewis wrote, Plaid Cymru faced a choice: 'is it to be a Welsh branch of the English socialist pacifists, or a Welsh nationalist movement? If the first, then that isn't the party I took part in establishing years ago. There can be more than one form of betrayal'.[97]

That, for the time being, was the last word on *Tynged yr Iaith*. It marked the end of a tempestuous three months for Plaid Cymru and, as things settled, Gwynfor came up with another option. It is not surprising that his proposed remedy was another dose of constitutional political action. Indeed, if anything, *Tynged yr Iaith*, and the clash with Saunders Lewis, made Gwynfor work even harder for parliamentary success. It was his polite way of aggravating Lewis. Despite growing problems with the market gardening business, and his concern that financial problems would force him to leave public life, he devoted himself to an agenda diametrically opposed to *Tynged yr Iaith*. Over a period of six weeks during the spring of 1962, Gwynfor spent just one night at Talar Wen. For the rest of the time, he addressed meetings across Wales and beyond. For Gwynfor, his critics were people 'not acquainted with the work', and although progress was slow, he was certain it was consistent. This, he wrote to Huw T Edwards, was more than could be said of the nationalist movements of 'Scotland, Brittany and Northern Ireland'. The answer, then, was to make the demand for a Parliament a priority for the party 'by concentrating on it and seeking all possible support for that aim in every way'.[98]

It is a testament to Gwynfor's single-mindedness that he undertook this mission so soon after *Tynged yr Iaith* and after his party had suffered another by-election thrashing, this time in Montgomeryshire in May 1962. Although Plaid's candidate there, Islwyn Ffowc Elis, had been routed, Gwynfor believed 'the work, the organization, the publicity, Islwyn himself, the integrity of his message' had all done 'great good'.[99] Gwynfor and his colleagues had also managed to defeat an attempt by Moses Gruffydd – another wise man and close personal friend of Saunders Lewis – to end the policy of fighting by-elections. When his proposal to fight just two or three seats at the General Election was discussed, only five members could be found to support it.[100]

This was the central paradox of Gwynfor's Presidency during this period. Although his hold over his party was pretty much absolute, he was a weak leader. It was one thing to have obsequious friends and staunch allies on the Executive, but altogether another to be able to set a headline-grabbing intellectual agenda. During the summer of 1962, Plaid Cymru's efforts to prevent the building of the dam at Clywedog through buying tracts of land seemed to be falling apart.[101] The party managed eventually to revive the scheme, but members were beginning to look elsewhere for ways to protect Wales. At that year's summer school, some members came together in Pontarddulais to form a Welsh language protection society. It was the beginning of Cymdeithas yr Iaith Gymraeg, although the new society did nothing more than plan and prepare until February of the following year.

The new society's members were not the only people within Plaid Cymru who yearned for the opportunity to break the law in the name of Wales. Shortly after midnight on 23 September 1962, Gwynfor received a phone call from Elystan Morgan to inform him that two Plaid Cymru members had been arrested for causing oil to seep onto an electricity transformer at Tryweryn. The damage caused was substantial but Plaid Cymru was delighted with the action of David Walters and David Pritchard. The general cathartic feeling was that these two non-Welsh-speakers from the Monmouthshire valleys had at last *done* something – even though it was felt that the outcome could have been far greater given that they had been assisted by another four Plaid Cymru members that night. But there were joyous celebrations nevertheless. When their solicitor, Elystan Morgan, met the pair for the first time at the police station in Bala, he joked that he would have joined them 'if I'd known you were going to do this'.[102]

It can now be revealed that Gwynfor knew of the deed in advance, and in some detail too. Before they left for Tryweryn, Gwynfor had met Walters and Pritchard and given the scheme his seal of approval. He did so on one clear condition – that the act must be non-violent. When the news broke, therefore, it was inevitable that Plaid Cymru, from the President down, would be supportive. Despite this, Gwynfor had taken a massive gamble; had the press found out about the meeting between himself, Walters and Pritchard, he might very well have had to surrender the Presidency. It is also possible that the authorities could have charged him with conspiracy. The action certainly created further confusion over Plaid Cymru's attitude to law-breaking. A week after Walters and Pritchard had made their stand, Gwynfor stated that their names would be honoured for ever as Welsh patriots even though, he said, they had contravened party policy.[103] At Gwynfor's request, a letter was sent to Plaid Cymru members asking as many as possible to attend the pair's court appearance in Bala,[104] a decision he made without consulting anyone. It was 'strange thinking', concluded an editorial in the *Western Mail*,[105] and to his opponents his behaviour smacked of hypocrisy. Alun Talfan Davies called it 'deceit', and he was not the only one to think in such terms.[106] Having heard of the President's enthusiasm for law-breaking, the Plaid Cymru student branch in Aberystwyth wrote to party headquarters to express its hope that this act would motivate Plaid Cymru to change its attitude towards direct action.[107] Raymond Edwards from the Edeirnion branch wrote in a similar vein,[108] but the most telling condemnation of this moral ambiguity came from John Daniel, who wrote that 'official statements on this all-important issue have been uncertain and complex; and as a result not even Executive members can give us any authoritative assurance what Plaid Cymru's intention is in this respect'.[109]

There was no third U-turn over Tryweryn. Gwynfor felt that the intellectual compromise he had struck in the Walters and Pritchard case had worked – despite the accusations of hypocrisy. He now felt that his position had been strengthened, and he set about the process of expelling one of his most outspoken – though inconsequential – critics, Neil Jenkins. It is extraordinary that it was the figure of Neil Jenkins, of all people, that brought the spat between Saunders Lewis and Gwynfor to a close, so it is worth examining the background in greater detail. Since early 1962, Neil Jenkins – a teacher of Welsh in Merthyr Tydfil – had been a thorn in Gwynfor's side, writing hostile letters about him and accusing him more than once of being a pacifist coward.[110] The leadership of Plaid Cymru began to keep a watchful eye on him and, according to one official report on his conduct, he had been seen 'laughing and hissing, and booing when the name of the Plaid President is mentioned'. He was also fond, it was noted, of using phrases like 'Merseyside Scum' – much to the chagrin of the party Executive's more respectable members.[111] Armed with a mass of evidence against this enfant terrible, a sub-committee was set up to discuss his case and he was asked to apologize. He refused to do so and his membership of the party became a topic of heated debate between readers of *Cymru Ein Gwlad* and the Gwynforite establishment. Raymond Edwards, editor of *Cymru Ein Gwlad*, for example, held that it was shameful that an impeccable nationalist such as Jenkins should be persecuted. Worse still, he added, Plaid Cymru appeared to be doing nothing to root out the 'Communists and fellow-travellers' in its ranks. Unfairly or otherwise, Jenkins was on the point of expulsion.[112]

On 1 November 1962, the party Executive decided to expel Neil Jenkins by 50 votes to 8.[113] Although Gwynfor did not speak, it was clear he was strongly in favour of throwing Jenkins out, in the hope of silencing an unruly hothead. At this point, Saunders Lewis took to the stage, writing to Gwynfor that the Executive's decision was 'another example of mimicking the English Labour Party'. As a consequence, he informed Gwynfor that he would 'resign publicly unless a statement is made that the expulsion is void'.[114] And so the fireworks began. Gwynfor and J E Jones were terrified that the BBC and Teledu Cymru would get their hands on the story.[115] They managed to keep the dispute out of the press, but Lewis stuck to his guns. A change of tactic was needed and, at Gwynfor and Jones's request, Griffith John Williams, a founder member of Plaid Cymru, visited Saunders Lewis in an effort to silence his old friend. The report Gwynfor received two days after Christmas was bitterly disappointing. Lewis, Williams wrote, was intransigent. Knowing how stubborn Lewis could be, Williams advised Gwynfor to 'show leadership' by ignoring the Neil Jenkins question – as had been done with other disruptive elements, such as Gwerin in 1938, and the Republicans in 1949.[116]

Gwynfor, however, was adamant. Indeed, Saunders Lewis's obstinacy only served to infuriate him. On the day after hearing from Griffith John Williams, Gwynfor wrote to D J Williams to tear a strip off Saunders Lewis for his disloyalty. He wrote that he considered Neil Jenkins to be part of a group 'that had been troublesome' for the past two years and that the root cause was Catholicism. Although Jenkins was not a Catholic, Gwynfor was convinced it was no coincidence that so many of his enemies were and that they had expressed 'impatience with Nonconformist control over Plaid'. 'Just think,' he told D J Williams, 'about Cathrin and John Daniel, Victor Jones, R O F Wynne, O T L Huws, H W J Edwards, Raymond Edwards and his wife (about to join the Church), Miserotti, Peter Hourahane and his sister, Mair S L and Haydn her husband along with Trefor Morgan and Harri Webb.' This group, he believed, had asked Saunders Lewis for his help in defending Neil Jenkins. It was for this reason, according to Gwynfor, that Lewis was now holding 'the pistol of his resignation' to Plaid Cymru's head, in support of 'a nasty boy' like Jenkins. Having fought so many battles over the previous two years, Gwynfor Evans was not about to give in to a man who, in his estimation, had fostered 'disunity' by his 'support for the troublemakers'. But Gwynfor faced a major dilemma. On the one hand, he knew full well that Lewis's resignation would be 'a splendid gift to the *Western Mail*', and to 'all the party's enemies, and the troublemakers within'. On the other, he was afraid that deferring to Saunders Lewis might cause 'even more damage'.[117]

It would also have destroyed Gwynfor's credibility as President. When his allies realized the extent of the crisis, they closed ranks around him in anticipation of the inevitable conflict. Elystan Morgan wrote that there should be no climbdown and that 'the NJ case is just a small part of a conspiracy by scores of malcontents who have ideas completely at variance with those of Plaid'. These 'malcontents', he went on, were either using Plaid Cymru as a vehicle for their 'egotism' or their 'Papism' and it was now 'impossible for Plaid to continue with them as members'.[118] A similar letter arrived from Dafydd Orwig, insisting that Saunders Lewis had been a political 'myth' for a quarter of a century. [119]

This correspondence placated Gwynfor, but the most significant response came from D J Williams. Aware of the potential disaster, he set about saving Gwynfor from what he called a Catholic 'conspiracy' within the party. On New Year's Day 1963, Williams wrote to Saunders Lewis to warn him that the 'Catholic Circle' inside Plaid Cymru was likely to be torn apart by 'the most hypocritical farce' he had ever known 'in all Welsh history'.[120] For at least two days, Williams's words appeared to have no effect on Saunders Lewis who wrote to Gwynfor again begging him not to expel Neil Jenkins, claiming that men such as he 'who do not act in a way that Plaid would call constitutional' were Plaid Cymru's only hope. And he closed with the coup de grâce: '… you know that it is in spite of the Executive's policy that I have remained a member of Plaid. It was Plaid Cymru's Executive that betrayed the cause at Tryweryn. I cannot forget that. Forgive me for troubling you, Saunders.'[121] It was a malicious letter, but the threat to resign was short-lived. Within days Lewis had withdrawn it. But that did not mean he and Gwynfor were reconciled. For all D J Williams's efforts, in 1963 no meeting took place to broker peace between Lewis and Gwynfor.[122] However, even though the threat from Lewis never receded completely, the battle to expel Neil Jenkins was a vital victory for Gwynfor. From January 1963 on, the influence of the Saundersites waned as, by degrees, Plaid Cymru's obsession with an act to rival Penyberth retreated.

Seeing Cymdeithas yr Iaith emerge at last in 1963 also helped to temper Saunders Lewis's influence. Ever since its establishment, back in August 1962, there had been widespread speculation about what exactly it would do and who precisely was involved with this so-called 'militant faction', as the *Western Mail* called it. Gwynfor's honest answer was that he did not know, telling the press he did not take its existence seriously.[123] But when the Society held its first sit-down protest on Trefechan bridge, Aberystwyth, to press its demand for bilingual summonses he sensed correctly that Welsh history had changed. From then on, he felt that the Society would make things that much easier for Plaid Cymru by leaving it free to concentrate on conventional, constitutional politics.

Hours after hearing of the demonstration, Gwynfor wrote to Tedi Millward, the Society's new Secretary, to congratulate him. It was 'so good', he said, to hear of 'a gathering of young people who see so much value in the Welsh language that they are prepared to suffer for it'. Gwynfor believed the sit-down on the bridge had 'inspired friends of the language' and that it would be seen as 'a milestone in the language's history'. In this same revealing yet measured letter, he explained to Tedi Millward why he did not wish to see Plaid Cymru leading any illegal action. The first reason was a lack of human resources. Adopting a policy like that of Cymdeithas yr Iaith Gymraeg required, he said, the readiness of 'scores of members, at least, for a period of years, to face prison for long periods – prison that could destroy their businesses, their careers, their family lives'. In a 'revolutionary situation', Gwynfor believed it could be right 'for a man to sacrifice his family for a great political cause' but there was no 'revolutionary situation' in Wales. Gwynfor was equally certain of his second reason, that a policy of civil disobedience was 'likely to destroy Plaid's constitutional political work'. There was a third reason of which he was not quite so sure. This, he told Millward, was

1950: With his sons Dafydd and Alcwyn Deiniol at Tynllidiart.

Gwynfor addressing the Llandrindod Conference of 1950: This conference was the first credible attempt to put devolution back on the agenda since the days of Cymru Fydd half a century previously.

The 'Nationalist Clark Gable': Gwynfor addressing one of the early meetings of the Parliament for Wales campaign, c.1950.

Sowing the seeds of devolution: Plaid Cymru Summer School, Abergele 1951.

'Soft Soap for the Voters?' Gwynfor addressing the Parliament for Wales rally in Cardiff, November 1953.

The row over 'Gwynfor's squatters' and the Trawsfynydd protests continues: Gwynfor in a radio debate with Iorwerth Thomas, Labour MP for Rhondda West, September 1951.

'*Cofia'n Gwlad, Benllywydd Tirion*' {Dear Lord, Protect our Country}: the second Trawsfynydd protest, September 1951.

The road to conversion: the Pencader rally, September 1952.

Leaving Wernellyn: moving to Talar Wen, 1953.

A new type of campaign: Plaid Cymru's shop window during the Aberdare by-election of October 1954.

Presenting the Parliament for Wales Petition, April 1956: Here Lady Megan Lloyd George is seen receiving the petition from Goronwy Roberts.

Marching through Liverpool protesting against the drowning of Tryweryn: this protest became one of the defining images of nineteen fifties Wales. This is how the Capel Celyn villagers were described by the *Manchester Guardian's* correspondent: 'Small boys in new boots, with the tags sticking out behind: bigger boys in the pride of long trousers: and girls: a group of women in neat winter coats who might have been part of a women's outing; farmers with tweed caps and faces under them tanned to the protuberant bones: a tiny girl with a fur muff staggering slightly.'

MES ARE SAFE
VE OURS
OT DROWN
HOMES
POLICE NOTICE
NO WAITING

'Welcome Home': Gwynfor on his return from his exceptionally successful trip to America. A month later, Gwynfor finally decided that there would be no illegal action by Plaid Cymru to prevent the construction of the Tryweryn dam.

From sect to denomination: an election meeting in Bryn-crug, Merioneth, October 1959.

'Moses' rejected: announcing the Merioneth result in Dolgellau, October 1959.

On the stump in Merioneth during the October 1959 General Election.

Signs of the times: Plaid Cymru posters during the 1959 General Election.

Plaid piracy: producing the illegal radio station, Radio Wales. The young man pictured broadcasting here is Emrys Roberts. He eventually became Plaid Cymru's General Secretary and the subject of bitter in-fighting.

The *Via Media*: R Tudur Jones, *consigliere* to Gwynfor and a key member of the 'Court of Llangadog' is seen on Gwynfor's left. Harri Webb, the man who coined the 'Court of Llangadog' sobriquet is seen on Gwynfor's right.

'that such a policy might distance a large proportion of our nation from our aim, and tear the Welsh hopelessly apart'. Now that Cymdeithas yr Iaith Gymraeg was active, Gwynfor could see a new political horizon ahead of him. From this point onwards, Plaid Cymru would concentrate on 'its political work and on giving moral support to nationalists who use unconstitutional methods'.[124]

Cymdeithas yr Iaith Gymraeg had held its first protest exactly a year after Saunders Lewis's *Tynged yr Iaith* lecture, and Gwynfor used the opportunity to clash with Lewis once more. The difference this time was that it was Gwynfor who struck the first blow and not the Penarth gadfly. In February 1963, Gwynfor wrote a long piece for the newly-launched monthly magazine *Barn*, stating that a policy of adopting Saunders Lewis's methods would 'hasten the end' of the Welsh language, because the Welsh people lived in 'a non-revolutionary situation'. Winning the battle to expel Neil Jenkins had boosted Gwynfor's confidence and he went so far as to predict a Welsh Parliament within twenty years, 'if he were spared'. He added that he would remove himself and his family 'from the old country to New South Wales' unless there were some hope that this would happen.[125] A month later, Gwynfor received an answer from Saunders Lewis, who warned again of 'the dreadful danger that Plaid Cymru could sell out the Welsh language in order to fight elections'.[126]

By this time Lewis had lost some credibility in the eyes of the party leadership, but giving his political opponent a bloody nose was no guarantee that 1963 would be easy for Gwynfor. There were countless problems ahead, some new, others familiar. As ever, there was the problem of new reservoirs and how Plaid Cymru could credibly oppose them without breaking the law. Among the party's rank and file speculation was rife about which valley would be drowned next. *Y Ddraig Goch* in January 1963 claimed there were plans to submerge Cwm Twrch in Montgomeryshire, and that an Indian engineer named 'Mr Panelle' had been excavating there.[127] This was untrue, but it was easy to understand how the nationalist imagination could be overwhelmed by such fears. Cwm Twrch was only a stone's throw from Clywedog where the work of building a reservoir had long since started. There were worries too about the future of the Gwendraeth Fach because Swansea Council had been eyeing the area since 1959. But through it all, it was Tryweryn, as a symbol of Plaid Cymru's impotence and English greed, which preoccupied younger nationalists.

At a quarter to three on the morning of Sunday 10 February 1963, the

Tryweryn saga entered a new, dangerous phase when explosives were used for the first time. Gwynfor's first instinct was to condemn the action while at the same time condemning Liverpool's greed,[128] but when Emyr Llywelyn Jones, a cherubic university student and son of the well-respected author and poet T Llew Jones, was arrested he changed his tack. He asked whether Emyr Llywelyn was a member of Plaid Cymru and when he discovered that he was, the party decided to back him to the hilt.[129] Emyr Llywelyn had been planning the action for at least a year, and the man who supplied him with the explosives was none other than David Pritchard – the Plaid Executive member Gwynfor had defended after the first attack on the site. Pritchard, according to Emyr Llywelyn, was the 'big man'. This was not the only connection with Plaid Cymru. Some leading figures within the party knew that Emyr Llywelyn had been planning a major action. Indeed, some had offered to take part in the enterprise, and Emyr Llywelyn had gone as far as to visit Saunders Lewis to ask for his advice. Lewis, for the record, had told him not to pursue such a tactic, reminding him of the horrors of prison life.[129]

But the act had now taken place, and the 'national movement' was obliged to defend Emyr Llywelyn. When 'Emyr Llew' appeared for the first time before magistrates in Bala, Gwynfor – who was unable to be present – arranged for Plaid Cymru to be officially represented. Then, in the middle of March, Gwynfor held a private meeting with Emyr Llywelyn where they agreed to co-author a pamphlet on the water campaign. Gwynfor arranged for it to be printed 'almost immediately', but Emyr Llywelyn was unable to complete the work.[130] Others wanted to go further. Emrys Roberts wrote to Islwyn Ffowc Elis, for instance, to say that Wales 'needs acts like Emyr Llew's' and that 'Plaid should do things like this officially'.[131] Party policy did not change, but the connections between Plaid Cymru and the 'activists' remained strong when the case came before Carmarthen Assizes. There were cheers and applause when Gwynfor entered the Guildhall, and Plaid Cymru leaflets were distributed among the large crowd on the square.[132] In television and newspaper interviews, Gwynfor refused to condemn Emyr Llywelyn and, in one interview, for the *Gallery* programme on the BBC, he said he had the greatest moral admiration for 'activists' and that he would never throw them out of the party.[133] Indeed, so great was Gwynfor's admiration of Emyr Llywelyn that he considered asking him to stand as a Plaid Cymru candidate in the next General Election.[134]

Gwynfor made further sympathetic statements when two other young men,

John Albert Jones and Owain Williams, were arrested in April 1963 on suspicion of damaging a pylon conveying electricity to Tryweryn. As Plaid Cymru found itself forced to support activists, some nationalists sensed they could change party policy on unlawful action, and some like Kate Roberts and Gwilym R Jones called for a conference on the issue. Emyr Llywelyn, they said in a public statement, had acted 'on their behalf' and what he did was to be 'admired'.[135] But Gwynfor refused to revise his position. With a General Election on the horizon and not a single town or region canvassed, he believed that he and his party had 'far too much work' to do already.[136] In the same vein, he thought it unwise for Plaid Cymru to hold a protest outside Liverpool's Walton Gaol, where Emyr Llywelyn was being held.[137] Gwynfor, it appears, did not want to be associated too closely with Saunders Lewis and R O F Wynne. It was probably for this reason that he refused a request from Wynne and Lewis to formally link himself and his party with the financial appeals of the 'Emyr Llywelyn Jones Fund'.[138]

In the eyes of his political opponents, both inside and outside the nationalist camp, Gwynfor was trying to have it both ways. They regarded it as intellectual fraud that a pacifist and constitutionalist could express sympathy with the person and the motivation, while at the same time condemning the act itself. In that summer's edition of *Cymru Ein Gwlad*, he was roundly attacked for making political capital out of the 'courage' of the three who had planted explosives at Tryweryn.[139] The act was also seen as proof that Gwynfor was losing his grip on Plaid Cymru. According to one critic, Roderic Bowen, the Liberal MP for Cardiganshire, Plaid Cymru now stood at a crossroads 'where they will soon have to decide whether they are to take over the role of the IRA and operate by the bomb or the ballot-box'.[140] This was nonsense, of course, but Gwynfor too was ready to indulge in such claptrap when it suited him.

A few weeks after the explosion at Tryweryn, Gwynfor managed to meet Noel Jerman, a senior civil servant in the Welsh department of the Ministry for Housing and Local Government. Jerman asked Gwynfor what would happen were his personal standing within Plaid Cymru to suffer. Gwynfor's answer, according to Jerman's memorandum for the minister, Keith Joseph, was as follows:

> He did not think that he would lose the leadership or the loyalty of the Party but that he would have to declare his hand and throw in his lot with those who intend more violent action if measures of devolution are not forthcoming.

The civil servant advised his minister that it was important to ensure Plaid Cymru continued as a constitutional party, 'rather than a disintegrating party broken into militant cells'. Jerman was equally unambiguous on Gwynfor's politics: 'It is clear that Evans is anti-Labour and is a Conservative in his party loyalty'. This resulted in the first official meetings between Gwynfor and government ministers.[141] In 1963, Gwynfor met Keith Joseph, the Minister for Welsh Affairs twice, and in 1964 he met Edward Heath, then a Minister for Regional Development. Following his meetings with Joseph, Gwynfor could claim, with little evidence it must be said, that the government had established an economic research unit in Wales because of his influence. The reality, not revealed at the time, was that Joseph was of the opinion that Gwynfor talked through his hat on economic matters.[142]

But ministerial meetings were not the only positive outcome of the explosions from Gwynfor's point of view. Emyr Llywelyn did not want his action to be seen as a personal challenge to Gwynfor. A few days after he went to prison, he insisted in *Y Ddraig Goch* that the activists were not 'inimical to Mr Gwynfor Evans', and that the only intervention made by *Cymru Ein Gwlad* thus far had been 'criticism of Plaid's leadership'.[143] Given Emyr Llywelyn's attitude towards him, it is perhaps understandable why Gwynfor claimed that the explosion had done Plaid Cymru a 'priceless favour' by obliging it to accept that 'political actions' were its modus operandi. The action taken at Tryweryn, according to Gwynfor, had brought to a close 'the schizophrenia that has so divided Plaid for three years or more, making it unsure of itself, a party with no consistent objective'.[144] True enough, but only a select few intellectuals would understand such a sophisticated argument.

Across Wales it was felt that Plaid Cymru was dead as a doornail. At the end of March 1963, on the day Emyr Llywelyn was sentenced, the party suffered another electoral humiliation at the Swansea East by-election. The Plaid Cymru candidate, Chris Rees, scraped together 1,620 votes, but he was pushed into fifth place behind the Reverend Leon Atkin – a maverick with a party which had only two members: himself and his wife. For many in Plaid Cymru, it was an extremely significant result, and several came to the conclusion expressed in *Y Faner* that the whole campaign had been a fiasco.[145] Within days, there were a deluge of calls for Gwynfor to forget his parliamentary ambitions. Moses Gruffydd resigned from the Executive, informing Gwynfor that he had failed to get 'good Welsh people who are sympathetic to Plaid' to contribute financially simply because the party was fighting 'so many' parliamentary elections.[146]

Losing an old-school nationalist like Moses Gruffydd was undoubtedly a blow, but the most significant demand for a change of policy came from Islwyn Ffowc Elis – whose support for Gwynfor had until then been unstinting. In the wake of the Swansea East result, he wrote to Gwynfor confiding his fears regarding the party's prospects. Plaid Cymru, he said, had reached an 'impasse' and he warned Gwynfor that the inevitable outcome of fighting parliamentary elections would be 'a beating in the next General Election' which would be 'worse and more destructive' to the spirit of Plaid Cymru than the 1959 results. With vivid memories of his own electoral disaster in Montgomeryshire in the previous year, he pleaded with Gwynfor to focus Plaid Cymru's electoral energies on local council elections and to refrain from contesting parliamentary seats until around 1974. He insisted that this would be an 'unexpected tactic' which would prevent 'a period of bitter squabbling as happened after 1959'. It would also, he argued, deflect a possible demand for Gwynfor to resign 'from the Presidency' by protecting the unity that he had created 'so bravely and steadfastly' from 'being permanently shattered'. The priority now, he said, was to hold on to 'the strong element among the intelligent young people in Plaid' who disagreed with fighting so many parliamentary elections, and spare them 'a beating which would be harmful'.[147]

Islwyn Ffowc Elis's passionate letter served to underline the depth of the crisis facing Gwynfor – so much so that he felt obliged to send a 'confidential' letter to all Plaid Cymru members arguing that direct action would 'destroy the party'. This letter was his most outspoken defence of the parliamentary strategy and it contained a dire warning that 'by turning its back on parliamentary elections, Plaid Cymru would wither, grow sick and fall apart'.[148] For a President who was so adept at masking the internal tensions within Plaid Cymru, being forced to employ a new tactic like this was demeaning but, even so, his attempt to foster party unity failed. Huw T Edwards, now free from the restraints of the party Executive, called on Plaid Cymru to desist from being a political party and to turn itself into a 'Welsh National Movement', a non-party organization which would concentrate on winning hearts and minds for the idea of a Welsh Parliament. This, he argued, would ensure that 'the personal rifts come together into one forceful stream'.[149] However, as Gwynfor refused to budge, the suggestion only made matters worse.

Plaid Cymru's opponents licked their lips at the party's misfortunes. The

Liberals believed they had a golden opportunity to start a real revival in Wales, as was happening in England under Jo Grimond.[150] Labour, now making a conscious effort to improve its Welsh credentials, was similarly ecstatic and Gwilym Prys Davies wrote to Jim Griffiths expressing his confidence that growing numbers were now aware 'that Plaid Cymru no longer has a potential' and that the day was coming when there would be 'a reconciliation of interest between the Welsh "establishment" and Labour'.[151] The popular press reinforced the idea that Gwynfor's Presidency was in the balance and the *Western Mail* published a series of damaging articles during July 1963 under the title *Crisis in Plaid Cymru*.[152] J Gwyn Griffiths, a Gwynfor loyalist, attempted to prevent publication of the articles on the grounds that they were libellous. Gwynfor himself dismissed them as 'undergraduate gossip', but Peter Kane, the *Western Mail* correspondent, was almost certain that Gwynfor would lose the leadership:

> If the present leadership cannot persuade the rebels to toe the line, it will be swept away and a radically different and more militant party will emerge; or the Plaid will disintegrate into a host of tiny groups, each pursuing their own immediate aims in their own way'.[153]

The low point came with these satirical lines in *Y Ddraig Goch*:

> There's a crisis in the Blaid,
> So they say,
> And Wales is on the slide,
> So they say,
> The arguments and rifts
> Are tearing Plaid to bits
> And Gwynfor's having fits,
> So they say.[154]

This attempt to mock the *Western Mail* served only to strengthen the perception that Plaid Cymru was in crisis and that Gwynfor could no nothing to calm the storm.

The fate of Teledu Cymru in the summer of 1963 also fed the idea that Gwynfor was an ineffectual leader who was squandering his time on irrelevant trivia. Throughout the autumn and winter of 1962-3, Gwynfor and the other directors found themselves in a nightmare as the company began broadcasting and making huge losses. Although some of the output was outstanding, especially the children's programmes and the news under the direction of John Roberts Williams, the company seemed doomed to failure from the outset. It was not the fault of Teledu Cymru that it had so few transmitters, but the decision to begin broadcasting without more was a major error, as was the decision to build an expensive studio on Western Avenue in Cardiff. But the biggest mistake of all was probably the pathological inability of some directors to grasp the idea that money did not grow on trees. Haydn Williams was probably the most culpable in this respect, but Gwynfor was among his keenest supporters. Even after Gwynfor had been warned in February 1963 that Teledu Cymru was in deep trouble,[155] he continued to tell fellow-directors like T H Parry-Williams that 'the outlook is very satisfactory'. T H Parry-Williams rightly judged, however, that 'the company is being run by a small clique' and that their leader, Haydn Williams, was 'too optimistic'.[156] There is further proof of this, if proof were needed, in the company's eventual demise. Although Gwynfor had heard the financial situation was bleak,[157] he still insisted privately that the company would pay its way if it could survive until October 1963.[158]

It was a forlorn hope and, on 17 May 1963, the directors of Teledu Cymru met and concluded that the game was up; on 20 May, it was announced that the company could not continue to produce programmes in Welsh. Although it still produced English programmes, Teledu Cymru had lost its raison d'être and, in September 1963, it was taken over by TWW. This was not only a blow for the Welsh language, it was also a slap in the face for those who had left stable employment to work for the company. Some faced unemployment and debts and, as a consequence, the union leaders at Teledu Cymru blamed the rank amateurism of the directors.[159] The directors faced further censure for having convinced 900 people to invest their savings in a venture which had folded so easily. The 'whole business', as Frank Price Jones wrote in his television column for *Y Faner*, 'stinks'.[160] But although there were nineteen directors on the board, the demise of Teledu Cymru was an especially cruel blow to Gwynfor and Haydn Williams. These two, after all, were the architects of the scheme; it was they who had invested so much time, credibility and hope in the company. Now, at the death, all Gwynfor could do was blame others. In *Y Ddraig Goch*, Teledu Cymru's failure was ascribed to people who wanted to see 'the demise of the language' and although they were not named, it was implied that the culprits were Aneirin Talfan Davies and Iorwerth Peate.[161] Others implicated in what Plaid Cymru chose to portray as a conspiracy were the government, the ITA and commercial companies such as Granada and TWW. This trinity, it was said, had willed the end of Teledu Cymru. The reality, however, was that TWW and (to a lesser extent) the ITA had done all they could to support Teledu Cymru. Nevertheless, Gwynfor persisted to exonerate himself by rewriting history and excusing his role in the whole sorry affair.[162]

Teledu Cymru's disastrous collapse affected Gwynfor for many months to come. Although Saunders Lewis's supporters were by now more measured in their attitude, Gwynfor was far from safe. Around him, the symbols of his failure grew: Tryweryn, Clywedog and, by September, Llangyndeyrn. In the case of Llangyndeyrn, Gwynfor had been warned by the Defence Committee to keep away, so fearful were they that his presence would undermine their battle against Swansea's Labour administration.[163] All that Gwynfor could do, therefore, was to suggest another scheme to meet Swansea's need for water by building a damn at the upper end of the Tywi Valley. This is what eventually happened, and Llangyndeyrn was saved, but Gwynfor did not get the credit he deserved for his behind-the-scenes contribution.[164] But the Clywedog battle was politically even more damaging for Gwynfor. Although hundreds of Plaid Cymru supporters bought strips of land there, Birmingham Corporation knew it was only a matter of time before a compulsory purchase order would force the nationalists to surrender their land.[165] In such an atmosphere, it was evident by the summer of 1963 that indiscipline had infected Plaid Cymru and Gwynfor's appeal for unity had been ignored. The annual conference was marred by more neurotic squabbling about Plaid Cymru's commitment to the Welsh language, and Kate Roberts was seen laying down the law to non-Welsh-speakers from the south-east for having dared to join the party when they did not 'give a hoot' about the language.[166] She threatened to cut Plaid Cymru out of her will if the party, as she said, was going to keep 'Welsh out of its policy as the current organizer [Emrys Roberts] and his followers threaten'.[167]

There was not an ounce of truth in the accusation that Emrys Roberts wanted to omit the Welsh language from Plaid Cymru activities. He was from Leamington Spa, and had learned to speak Welsh fluently, but the ferocity of Kate Roberts's attack was evidence that the presence of young, talented nationalists from the south-east upset the old guard who had founded Plaid Cymru. Emrys Roberts was undoubtedly the unofficial leader of this new generation, and he was supported by gifted people like Phil Williams and Harri Webb, as well as the organizer in the south, Ray Smith. Ever since the disappointment of 1959, several of them had been thinking hard about that perennial question: why had Plaid Cymru achieved so little success, especially in the valleys? For Emrys Roberts and those around him, the answer was that Plaid Cymru should no longer be a party that existed *solely* to save the Welsh language, it should become a party that would campaign for a free, bilingual, socialist Wales. They also looked at the world with secular detachment, and were keen to sever the umbilical connection between Plaid Cymru and the chapel. In essence, their political and social values were remarkably similar to those of the Republicans who had also felt they could reform Plaid Cymru from within. They aimed to save both Plaid Cymru and Gwynfor. Their initial objectives were noble enough but, from the beginning, Gwynfor and those around him were suspicious. For him, reform meant surrendering his absolute power and potentially his Presidency. This, in the autumn of 1963, led to one of the deepest and most enduring schisms in Plaid Cymru's history.

Emrys Roberts's supporters wanted a reorganization and, given the state of Plaid Cymru in 1963, one can well understand their obsession with the party's administration. For one thing, they believed that Gwynfor wielded too much power as President and chair of the Executive – a position exploited to suppress dissent. Their second criticism centred on party organization, and the fact that it had two offices – one in Bangor and the other in Cardiff. The southern office dealt with political matters while the one in the north concerned itself with finance, but this resulted in incredible inefficiency. Signing a substantial cheque required seven signatories, and the cheque would be sent from Cardiff to Bangor, and returned to Cardiff before being sent, via Porthmadog, back to Cardiff again. When a specialist company was asked to look at the party's financial arrangements it refused to undertake the task, knowing it would be a waste of time. The party's head office was chaotic, with senior members of staff like Emrys Roberts and Nans Jones at each other's throats and J E Jones presiding over it all, in some ill-defined advisory capacity. It was, Ray Smith told the Executive, a first-rate mess: 'The impression of the Party which I have gained in the few short months I have worked in Cardiff is that it exists but it does not live: it stands, but it does not move.'[168]

At the end of August 1963, Gwynfor met the 'reformers' for the first time. He promised to set up a committee to discuss reorganization but in reality, he showed very little interest in this vital matter. Gwynfor could have learned much by listening to Emrys Roberts, Ray Smith and others like them, but his worry about the real motives of Roberts and those around him got the better of common sense. And the same tendency was evident among Gwynfor's friends. Roberts and his supporters tried to raise the matter of organization in the Executive once again, but the response as ever was lukewarm. In no time, an atmosphere of watchfulness had become venomous, and Emrys Roberts's group began to meet regularly, calling itself 'The New Nation Group'. The group included Harri Webb, Margaret Tucker, Roger Boore and that right-wing eccentric, John Legonna. As he saw what was happening, R Tudur Jones could not contain himself, describing the new critics in a letter to Emrys Roberts as: 'friends who are emotionally immature and crude in their behaviour – people with a permanent grudge against society'.[169] Elystan Morgan's reaction was similar. Emrys Roberts, he told J E Jones, 'is likely to cause serious harm to Plaid', driving away some of its traditional supporters in Merioneth like Tom Jones, Ifor Owen and Gèrallt Jones. 'These,' he added, 'can't give of their best while they feel that headquarters is being run by people who belittle their efforts.'[170]

As the New Nation grew in strength, Gwynfor attempted to keep a lid on things by emphasizing that the old guard within the party could accommodate the new radicals. He did this in 1964 in his book *Rhagom i Ryddid* ('Forward to Freedom'), an attempt to marry the traditional nationalism of Plaid Cymru with modern ideas. The book was as much a confession of faith as anything and something that Gwynfor had wanted to do for some time. However, his priority in putting pen to paper was offering the party a lead and making peace. He was fully supported by Elwyn Roberts who ensured that some Plaid Cymru stalwarts were on hand to sing the praises of *Rhagom i Ryddid* when it was published. D J Williams announced, 'This is the Book of Exodus for the Welsh' by 'a Moses', while Lewis Valentine described the work as 'a fiery flame'. J E Jones concurred. From now on, he said, it was 'perfectly clear that Plaid Cymru's emphasis, or "philosophy" has a relevance to more than the problem of saving Wales'.[171] But Elwyn Roberts failed to persuade Huw T Edwards to sing from the same hymn-sheet. The latter suggested, spikily, that it would be no bad thing for Gwynfor 'as a Christian... to try to see some good in his opponents' and 'allow them a modicum of honesty'.[172]

Huw T Edwards's letter was a private one but, in early January, he succeeded in ruining Gwynfor's hopes of re-launching his Presidency. In *Y Faner*, he published an article arguing once more that Plaid Cymru should contest only one parliamentary seat and that it would serve the party better to become an apolitical movement to defend Wales.[173] From then on, Gwynfor came to see Huw T Edwards not just an unreliable nuisance but an enemy. His was not a lone voice, however; a similar idea to that propounded by Huw T Edwards came from Alun Talfan Davies, chair of the Liberals in Wales, and from Gwilym Prys Davies of the Labour Party too. That February, Gwynfor wrote to D J Williams to voice his unease: 'Were we to follow him, it would be the end of us. You'll notice the only people who support Huw T are ones like Gwilym Prys, Alun Talfan and Iorwerth Peate, who have all left Plaid. The only winner if we followed H T would be Labour.'[174] Despite this, Gwynfor was concerned about the possible effect of the Welsh-language press. There were several long discussions in the Executive about 'how to kill' the newly-launched Welsh monthly *Barn* and it was only on Gwynfor's casting vote that a decision was taken not to adopt a formal policy of trying to scupper the magazine.[175] It was a little easier to sway editorial opinion in *Y Faner* and Gwynfor wrote to the editor, Gwilym R Jones, asking him not to carry any more controversial pieces on Plaid Cymru's electoral policy. Astonishingly, Gwilym R Jones agreed, promising not to publish a word on the issue until after the election. He also promised that Plaid Cymru would have *Y Faner*'s support 'while I'm here, because I couldn't not support it'.[176] A month later *Y Faner* announced a policy of 'not publishing correspondence on Plaid Cymru election policy' until after the General Election.[177] It was an unusual act of self-censorship, but it smoothed the way for Gwynfor to concentrate on the constituency he had neglected for so long: Carmarthen.

The most striking thing about Gwynfor's position in the months leading up to the October 1964 General Election was the disparity between his local standing and the state of Plaid Cymru more generally in Carmarthenshire. Six months before the election, the party did not have a branch in the town of Carmarthen and, at best, had roughly a hundred active campaigners in the constituency.[178] The contrast between Merioneth and Carmarthen could not have been starker: Merioneth had been reserved for the President and the expectation had been that if he could break through anywhere it would be there. However, Gwynfor had failed, and it was now Elystan Morgan's turn in the county. Gwynfor was left to endure the embarrassment of standing in a completely unwinnable seat.

The most optimistic prediction was that he would keep his deposit and get about 6,000 votes.[179] Fighting Carmarthen for the first time was clearly a disheartening experience for him and it was no coincidence that *Y Ddraig Goch* prepared Gwynfor's supporters for the worst by describing the seat in these terms: 'Political features of the constituency – conservatism; personal loyalty. A very apolitical constituency ... People do not think politically – with a few rare exceptions.'[180] But rather than complain, Gwynfor devoted himself to establishing a party machine in the county. The Carmarthen town branch was relaunched and the young and diligent Cyril Jones was given the task of organising the campaign.

As the seeds of hope were sown in Carmarthenshire, things were going from bad to worse for Plaid Cymru at a national level with factional infighting as bad as ever. Cassie Davies wrote to Emrys Roberts pleading with him to stop his activity with New Nation and to rein in his radical friends. For her, the most visible symbol of the tensions were the Executive Committee's meetings. 'By now,' she said, 'they have deteriorated into constant bickering, taunting and fault-finding, an endless picking on everyone and everything, and this is destructive. There is more tedium than inspiration in them. Indeed, I know that such petty squabbling keeps some of the best people in Wales away and alienates them.'[181] But Emrys Roberts's supporters were unrepentant: they believed reform was necessary to save Plaid Cymru from an inevitable demise. The results in the May 1964 local elections had been deeply disappointing and Owen John Thomas, a young Emrys Roberts loyalist, wrote of a 'virile radical alternative' to fire up a party dying on its feet: '... no spirit of fervour amongst members, and little sign of a battle being fought'.[182]

Emrys Roberts was particularly outspoken in his personal discussions with New Nation members. As Plaid Cymru membership fell, he prepared a memorandum for the group exposing what he considered to be the party's utterly miserable position. According to Plaid Cymru's General Secretary, these were the party's major shortcomings in June 1964:

(1) The party is scarcely known at all.

(2) Where it is known, the image is bad, old-fashioned, puritan, wanting to put the clock back, fanatical, impractical.

(3) It is regarded as being almost synonymous with the Welsh language.

(4) Its aim of self-government and a seat in the UNO seems far too remote from the

> ordinary man to be taken realistically.

Roberts was equally scathing of the 'Court of Llangadog':

> These 'public' weaknesses are caused by the Party's 'private' – i.e. internal, weaknesses. These are: it is amateurish, conservative, lethargic, with no drive or initiative. It is also far too academic.

And despite his position, he did not refrain from making a personal assault on Gwynfor:

> The weaknesses noted appear to be part of the leader's personality – shy, weak, unimaginative, lacking in drive. This is heightened by the fact that the leader's chosen advisers are largely of the same stamp and make things worse rather than better.

In the same document, Emrys Roberts admits that he had considered setting up a new party but had concluded that the answer was: 'a fairly small group, with a number of agreed objectives and an agreed plan of campaign'. And retaining Gwynfor as President was part of the strategy, if he could be changed: 'With good organisation and handling, he [Gwynfor] might develop into a fairly effective front man.' Emrys Roberts's nightmare was that 'Elystan Morgan, Wynne Samuel or someone else like them, worse than Gwynfor' would win the Presidency. But Emrys Roberts was not totally loyal to Gwynfor and was ready to consider someone else, if his 'nightmare' scenario became reality: 'In the fight to establish improved organization, a leader might emerge who would later be able to take over the Presidency, if it were found that Gwynfor still did not measure up to requirements.'[183] A month later, another memorandum written by Emrys Roberts shows there was 'disagreement on our attitude to Gwynfor – whether he should be kicked upstairs, or completely discredited and kicked out'.[184] Even with hindsight, it is remarkable to note that Emrys Roberts, the General Secretary of Plaid Cymru, was part of these discussions.

On the eve of the annual conference, rumours began to circulate that Huw T Edwards was about to re-join Labour. Gwynfor knew nothing about such rumours and was left dangling. 'The last I heard of him,' a baffled Gwynfor told a reporter, 'was that he had promised his full support in our election effort and had offered his house as an office.'[185] Huw T Edwards stayed in Plaid Cymru for another six months before returning to Labour, but the uncertainty fuelled the feeling that the conference would be shambolic. Those who harboured such thoughts were proved right. The chosen theme was meant to be 'the National

Struggle of the Welsh', but the delegates arriving in Fishguard were far readier to struggle among themselves. The race for the Vice-Presidency between Elystan Morgan and Chris Rees became a bitter proxy contest between the supporters of Gwynfor Evans and Emrys Roberts. Although Chris Rees had never shown any sympathy for the New Nation group, the Roberts faction was eager to see him elected as a block to 'Stan' as Elystan Morgan was known to his enemies. Through it all, Gwynfor and Elystan Morgan maintained close contact. Just days before the vote, Morgan wrote to Gwynfor warning him that Plaid Cymru was falling apart:

> ... I feel very angry at this. I think Emrys is perhaps gunning for me as candidate for the vice-Presidency. Poor him!!! I don't give a hoot whether Chris Rees is elected. He's a splendid chap. That's not the issue, but rather the danger that Emrys will ruin the Conference. I think by now that he's spiteful and malicious.[186]

Emrys Roberts had a similar opinion about Elystan Morgan; he claimed to members of New Nation that Elystan Morgan had denigrated him in conference by saying he was having 'a nervous breakdown'.[187]

Whatever the truth regarding these accusations, the tragedy for Gwynfor was that he had lost control of two of the party's most talented young members. When Chris Rees was elected to the Vice-Presidency in August 1964, Elystan Morgan began to entertain serious doubts about why he was persevering with politics under the fractious banner of Plaid Cymru. As he did so, Emrys Roberts and New Nation were growing in confidence. To them, the election of Chris Rees was proof that the Gwynforite ancien régime and the clueless 'Aunties' on the Executive Committee had nearly had their day. But they decided to postpone their constitutional revolution until after the General Election due on 15 October. In the circumstances, it is ironic that Plaid Cymru's election manifesto was entitled *Nerth/Strength*.

The situation had hardly improved when the campaign proper got under way. The broadcasting 'ban' was still in force, forcing Plaid Cymru to make extensive use of Radio Wales to reach the 23 constituencies where it was fielding candidates. Originally, Gwynfor had hoped Plaid Cymru could broadcast on Radio Caroline, the pirate radio station, 'between the pops'.[188] Plaid Cymru and Gwynfor were perfectly candid about this intention and announced that the party had arranged for solicitors in the north to meet representatives of the station that broadcast from a ship anchored off the coast of the Isle of Man. Having gone to all that trouble, Plaid Cymru learned shortly afterwards that Radio Caroline no longer wished to co-operate, and with the grand idea in ruins they had to make do with eight transmitters in the hope this would attract some attention and sympathy, as had happened to an extent in 1959. But this time, the press was far more cynical about the whole affair, and the issue became a 'charade', to quote the *South Wales Evening Post* – especially when the party denied there was any official connection between it and Radio Wales.[189]

Gwynfor also tended to blame the 'ban' for everything, not realizing that his own ideological cupboard was bare. In a year when Wilson would offer a Secretary of State and a technological revolution to Wales, Gwynfor's off-the-peg homilies had become dated. By now, the familiar sermon on the anti-Welsh bias of the Labour Party sounded desperate and uninspired. The slogans being painted up and down Wales by a clandestine group calling itself the Free Wales Army caused another headache and the party was forced more than once to deny any connection. The press were more interested in the FWA's promise of direct action at Tryweryn, than Gwynfor's pronouncements on the Beeching cuts and the broadcasting 'ban'.[190] As the election drew closer, Emrys Roberts bluntly complained to Gwynfor that he had become 'worn out, lifeless and lacking in ideas – doing little more now than keeping things ticking over somehow '.[191]

This was not wholly true. Among fellow-members of New Nation, Emrys Roberts buzzed with ideas and, in mid-campaign, wrote a memorandum expressing his earnest hope that Gwynfor would lose the chairmanship of the party Executive immediately after the election. He, Emrys Roberts, could then occupy the chair before handing it to Ray Smith. He had also worked out a strategy that would see some of his closest friends become 'Directors' of Plaid Cymru. In his vision, John Legonna would be appointed transport director, Meic Stephens would become policy and research director and Harri Webb would take responsibility for publicity and publications, leaving Roger Boore in charge of finance.[192]

Indeed, it could almost be said that Gwynfor's tenacity was the only positive aspect of a defective campaign. In Carmarthen, he addressed at least five public meetings every evening, reminding his audiences time and again that a vote for Plaid Cymru was a moral act.[193] Without doubt the atmosphere there was 'good', and young activists joined the local party in droves.[194] Gwynfor fought hard, but the battle for Carmarthen could not be won; he was up against the appeal and charisma of Labour candidate, Megan Lloyd George, and the presence of a popular Liberal candidate in Alun Talfan Davies made things harder still.

The Carmarthen result was announced at quarter to two in the morning in front of a crowd of several hundred on the Guildhall Square. As expected, Megan Lloyd George was re-elected with Gwynfor in third place with 5,495 votes. From a personal point of view, the result was underwhelming; although he had improved Plaid Cymru's share of the vote from 5.2 per cent to 11.7 per cent, he had failed to keep his deposit and was 500 short of the target he had publicly set for himself. The total was also slightly lower than that of Jennie Eirian Davies in 1957. Gwynfor's rather diplomatic description of the result was 'satisfactory progress'. Nonetheless, Carmarthen was the least of his problems.[195] By the early hours it was clear that Plaid Cymru had performed abysmally across the board. The election was always going to be particularly close between Labour and the Tories, but the return of a Labour government had squeezed the Plaid vote. For the first time in its history, its total vote had fallen: from 77,571 in 1959 to 69,507. Gwynfor's strategy was in ruins. The vultures were circling and he needed a miracle. Within two years, salvation was at hand for Gwynfor Evans – MP.

Chapter 8

A NEW DAWN 1964–66

THE DAY AFTER THE ELECTION, WALES AWOKE to a transformed political landscape. Not only was Harold Wilson Prime Minister but, for the first time, after years of campaigning, Wales had a Secretary of State and a designated Welsh Office. From his first day in Cathays Park, Jim Griffiths started a quiet revolution in the way Wales was governed. The country now had its own fledgling government. The establishment of the Welsh Office was a small step, but a significant one. For the first time, here was a concrete symbol of Labour's readiness to devolve power. There was also a freshness and Welsh flavour to the new government, and a promise that ministers like Cledwyn Hughes and Jim Callaghan would ensure that Wales's voice was heard at the highest level. John Morris, the MP for Aberavon, announced that the Labour Party was now the real party of Wales.[1] The new government, in short, stole Plaid Cymru's thunder. It was a remarkable spectacle to see Gwynfor having to congratulate Labour on keeping its word. 'I warmly welcome its belated arrival,' he said of the Welsh Office, 'because this gets rid of a great block on the road to Welsh self-government.'[2]

The contrast between Labour and Plaid Cymru was stark. As Labour began to govern, Plaid Cymru undertook its most savage post mortem ever. It was almost inevitable that the tensions that had simmered under the surface for so long would boil over. To make matters worse, the SNP – a party which had traditionally been far weaker than Plaid Cymru – had done well. For many members, Plaid Cymru had entered a new and frightening world. At home, Gwynfor felt the force of this perception. In his diary, his son Dafydd wrote that the drop in support for the party had 'put it in a new, strange position' because Plaid Cymru 'had always thought of itself as a growing party'.[3] Like his son, Gwynfor was aware that he was in deep water. One of his first acts after the election was to write to party members to explain why it had fared so badly. The letter was an attempt to calm anxieties, with Gwynfor eager to argue that things could have been worse. Labour had 'revived strongly in Wales'. He put some of the blame too on 'Plaid's unhappy position after the previous election', but still considered the 'ban' as the true reason for the dismal performance. It was the right to broadcast, according to Gwynfor, that had ensured a stable Liberal vote in seats like Anglesey and Merioneth. This was not an excuse, he said, 'but a fact'. His priority from this point onwards would be party discipline, and he closed his letter in his most publicly self-pitying tone ever: 'It is essential for us to move together as a united and disciplined Party. We will certainly lose some of our members; we'll hear again the old cry that we should work through the English Parties and the call for "direct" action. Ours is truly a difficult part to play...'[4] He employed the same appeal to the emotions in press interviews. When he was asked by *Y Cymro* how he could carry on like a John the Baptist in the wilderness, his answer was revealing: 'My life would have no meaning if I gave it up.'[5]

By then, however, some party members, especially those in New Nation, were desperate to see Gwynfor relinquish the Presidency. Three days after the vote, Harri Webb wrote to John Legonna stating that the situation was so bad that 'the very existence of the party [is]... in doubt'. Webb could not understand why Gwynfor was so blind to it: '[Gwynfor] doesn't seem to realise exactly what has happened and the extreme unlikelihood of the party being able to carry on as at present. Still reluctant to recognise the importance of reorganization. Makes excuses. Seems to be utterly obsessed by the effects of the TV ban.'[6] Harri Webb hardly needed to spell it out for John Legonna, because he too was doing all he could to undermine Gwynfor. With that in mind, Legonna urged New Nation to prepare themselves for one final push.

Another section of the party, the Saundersites, came out of hibernation, sensing a new opportunity. Nina Wynne, daughter of R O F Wynne, asked Saunders Lewis whether he would be willing to return as President. It was all pie in the sky, and although he refused the offer, Saunders Lewis urged his supporters to fight again against the policy of contesting parliamentary elections:

> As for the nationalists, I am now (after the election results) quite hopeful, I think the idea that a nationalist movement can succeed by parliamentary elections has now been proved preposterous. So the younger element of Plaid Cymru may drop their socialistic trend and begin again to be nationalistic.[7]

Within a month, the Garthewin Group had announced that as 'a Saturday School of Welsh nationalists' they wished to state 'their faith in the political philosophy of Saunders Lewis as expressed in the radio lecture *Tynged yr Iaith*'.[8] Some leading members of Cymdeithas yr Iaith Gymraeg made similar noises, and a letter was sent in the names of Cynog Dafis and John Davies pleading with Gwynfor to give up fighting elections which they believed would bring the party 'a step closer to destruction and obscurity'. They also promised quite openly that they would '... support another more realistic movement (such as Cymdeithas yr Iaith Gymraeg) and recruit as many members as we can from Plaid into any such movement. This is not a threat but a plain statement of the truth'.[9]

The pressure brought to bear by language nationalists was intense, but the real enmity towards Gwynfor came from New Nation. It had been Gwynfor's original intention to pour oil on troubled waters but there was pressure on him to face down his critics in the south-east, once and for all. On 20 October 1964, R Tudur Jones wrote, pleading with him to act, so 'great' was the concern that 'the movement (especially in Anglesey)... is falling apart'. It was time, in his opinion, to take a stand:

> We must rid the Executive Committee of the discordant elements that have been so prominent within it in the past few years. There was a time when Executive meetings were inspirational and an aid to activity. One would look forward to them. That can hardly be said about these last few years. I have nothing to say about this on paper except to suggest my attitude so that you know I share your concern and that I am eager to help.[10]

The problem for Tudur Jones and Gwynfor, however, was that they had neither the means nor the evidence to destroy these 'discordant elements' but, a few days later, the situation changed.

Tudur Jones was not the only member of Plaid Cymru to put pen to paper that day. In Cardiff, Emrys Roberts was thinking about the future of his party too, even though he had told Gwynfor that he would quit as general secretary as soon as he had another job. On 20 October, Roberts wrote to his colleagues in New Nation, setting out what had been discussed when the group met to analyse Plaid Cymru's condition on 26 September. The minutes show that the group had debated which was better: a Leader or a 'Directorate' for the party. Roberts said he was tired of Gwynfor's excuses: 'Blame the TV and Radio Ban and lack of Plaid coverage on the news. Blame the Liberals, try to get the Home Rule

MPs to put forward a bill of some form of self government – to show their true colours not in expectation of any concrete results.' It was a remarkable letter for any general secretary to send, and his final point proved more damning than any other. Roberts expanded on the familiar call for Plaid Cymru to have a Chair, and explained to his New Nation colleagues exactly how he envisaged the President and the Chair could work together:

> We have to decide whether we are prepared to accept this and let the Chairman fight it out later with the best man coming out on top, or whether we want to put into the constitution a division of responsibility – President over development of policy, Chairman over organisation. This is what we want.[11]

The letter was sent to a handful of New Nation members, but that evening in the Plaid Cymru office in Cardiff, one was read in error by the party secretary, Nans Jones. Office procedure at the time was to register every letter, but Emrys Roberts forgot to seal one of the envelopes containing his explosive memorandum. It proved to be a momentous error. Seeing one of the envelopes open, Nans Jones read the contents, and was astounded. Having regained some of her composure, she tried to speak to Gwynfor. He was not at home at Talar Wen, but she did manage to get hold of Rhiannon. She was just as outraged as Nans Jones and interpreted the letter as a plot against her husband. She asked Nans Jones to copy it and send it to Llangadog immediately.[12] It is impossible to say now what Gwynfor's reaction was when he read it, but that copy – now housed in the National Library of Wales – contains a word in Gwynfor's own hand that sums up his feelings towards Emrys Roberts: 'Bradwr' (Traitor).[13] Days later, Gwynfor wrote to his deputy, Chris Rees, giving a detailed record of his response.

In this letter, written on 1 November 1964, Gwynfor said that 'a most serious situation with Emrys' had developed and that the letter (subsequently known as the 'Judas Letter') was indisputable proof that 'several people are operating as an alliance within Plaid'. He went on to mention two 'especially dreadful' things that had come to light in the wake of the letter. The first was 'that the General Secretary of Plaid is leading a coterie of conspirators within its ranks'. But even worse, in Gwynfor's eyes, was the general secretary's 'treacherous' attitude towards other officers: 'Where there is such abysmal lack of loyalty, no movement can survive.' It is obvious too that it was only after reading Emrys Roberts's letter that Gwynfor began to think of New Nation as a real threat:

> It casts… light on many incidents in the party's history over the previous few years. I was often warned that Emrys was to blame, but I was too innocent to believe it; and I prevailed upon him to stay both times that he resigned, and persuaded him (against the advice of many) to stay on for the election.

By now, the pieces were falling into place, and Gwynfor could see that Emrys Roberts had led a plot to get rid of J E Jones, Nans Jones and Elwyn Roberts. Even so, Gwynfor was unsure how to respond. He comforted himself that 'the trouble revealed in the letter is confined to a relatively small group of people' and that 'the situation in the west is very healthy'.[14]

The crisis deepened when Gwynfor's friends received copies of Emrys Roberts's letter. This letter, D J Williams wrote in his diary, was what 'alarmed me more than anything … revealing a conspiracy to unseat Gwynfor as President of Plaid Cymru'. The same group of friends were told by J E Jones that Emrys Roberts had left his wife for Margaret Tucker, one of the leading lights in the party's youth movement.[15] There is no doubt that this was part of an intentional effort by J E Jones to prepare the ground for the dismissal of Emrys Roberts and, a week later, the story was in the tabloids. It is impossible to say whether J E Jones contacted the *Sunday Mirror*, but seeing the story in print under the headline 'Private Lives Row in Party' was devastating to a chapel-based party like Plaid Cymru.[16] R Tudur Jones spoke for many in the party when he opened his heart to Gwynfor: 'Emrys's family troubles are doing us great harm… Think of all the talk we've heard about Plaid's "image"! We have a really lovely "image" now! And after all our fine talk in the summer school about the Tories "collapsing from scandal to scandal".'[17] The publication of the story was also a shock to Emrys Roberts, who speculated whether Gwynfor himself was responsible for feeding it to the press. 'I have wondered,' he told Harri Webb, 'whether he [Gwynfor] was clever enough in order to weaken my position. I don't really think he would do this, but one never knows.'[18]

Whatever the truth of the matter, Emrys Roberts was fighting for his political life and for the right to leave his post on his own terms. Gwynfor was urged by Tudur Jones to exhibit 'some ferocity with these people' and it is clear that he followed this advice, phoning Emrys Roberts to accuse him of 'personal disloyalty and personal betrayal'.[19] Roberts refused to accept a word of this and, on 13 November, he wrote to Gwynfor insisting that he had never tried to get rid of J E Jones and pointing out that he was fond of Elwyn Roberts. The only member of Plaid Cymru's staff who deserved to be criticised, he said, was Nans Jones. He also denied that New Nation's aim was to gain power. 'It's true,' he told Gwynfor, 'that there is one member of the group who feels that Plaid can only be made to work effectively by doing this – but not so the rest of us.' The greatest betrayal of all, according to Emrys Roberts, was being committed by the party establishment, those people who still saw Gwynfor as 'some sort of Jesus Christ... a man who will carry the whole burden and bear their sins – i.e. do the work for Wales that they should be busy doing themselves'. It was also high time, he said, for Gwynfor to realize that he was not a:

> ... supernatural, infallible, omniscient, all-wise being. Loyalty to Wales is not exactly the same thing as loyalty to you. You could be a first-rate President of a truly effective party if you were content with that instead of thinking that anyone who tries to do something for Plaid with which you do not fully agree is a traitor.

Emrys Roberts closed with this sharp advice to Gwynfor: 'And don't be so ready to use the word traitor in such a childish way.'[20]

Gwynfor's instinct was to avoid an unnecessary clash but, this time, he had no choice. Judging by his correspondence, he clearly discussed the 'treachery of the Cardiff lot' for about a week and a half with R Tudur Jones and Elystan Morgan, before coming to the conclusion that Emrys Roberts had to go. Emrys Roberts's fate was sealed and, on 14 November, Plaid Cymru's executive met at the Belle Vue hotel in Aberystwyth for one of the dirtiest and most shabby meetings in the party's history. Several knew full well what was about to happen, but no one dreamed that a saint like Gwynfor could be so Machiavellian. Vitally, his supporters were all behind him. Indeed, some like Tudur Jones and Elystan Morgan had been dreaming of this moment as Gwynfor began to outline the prosecution case against Emrys Roberts.

In his familiar measured tones, he said that Emrys Roberts would not be allowed, as originally agreed, to continue to work for the party until he found another post. The reason, he said, was 'Emrys's personal and domestic circumstances', and the fact that this had received 'considerable publicity during the fortnight before the Executive Committee'. His concern, he added, was that further publicity 'could do great harm to Plaid were Emrys to stay on as a member of staff'. Because of that, Gwynfor concluded, it would be 'better if Emrys did not continue working in the Office'.[21] The 'Judas Letter' was brought forward as irrefutable evidence of Emrys Roberts's 'treachery'. Then, a vote was held on the issue, but it was touch and go. Although Gwynfor had struck at Emrys Roberts's weakest spot, and although he had packed the executive with his supporters, there was a majority of just seven in favour of sacking Emrys Roberts, with a further seven abstentions.[22]

It was only after the vote had been taken that Emrys Roberts was allowed to address the executive. Once more, he put it to Gwynfor that he was no traitor. He also emphasized that his aim was to ensure a future for the party. However, the game was up. Gwynfor had disposed of the man he considered his most dangerous enemy. Gwynfor's supposition was wrong, nonetheless. Emrys Roberts had never wanted the Presidency; his crime was the woeful naivety of believing that he could get rid of Gwynfor's political allies while remaining General Secretary. For many, the whole affair left a very nasty aftertaste, because Gwynfor had used morality as a political weapon.[23] In private correspondence, Harri Webb described Gwynfor as 'a loathsome stoat' for having hung Emrys Roberts out to dry. This, Webb judged, was 'one of the most horrible scenes I ever want to see'. The fact that he had relied on the support of 'gogs and bogs as rhubarb chorus' – people like Elystan Morgan, Ioan Bowen Rees and Cassie Davies – made an unpleasant situation a thousand times worse.[24]

Sacking Emrys Roberts was also a miserable experience for Gwynfor. A fortnight after the dramatic meeting of the executive, he wrote to D J Williams confessing that he had felt 'hesitant' before opening his mouth at the Belle Vue but he had felt he had no alternative. He did so, he said, mainly because of the General Secretary's marital circumstances: 'The tabloid press could destroy us by building up the story. Every nationalist knows the story of Parnell; the Irish National Party was destroyed by his (brave or stubborn) decision to hang on to his job.' Getting rid of Emrys Roberts was a double-edged sword for Gwynfor. The whole thing was 'a disaster' since Plaid Cymru had never seen 'a more able politician than him' and he admitted that his departure would be 'a great loss' – something, he told D J Williams, that could not be said if others – 'Ray Smith, Boore, Legonna, Tucker etc...' and some of the 'Garthewin people, like the Daniel coterie' – were to leave. But there was one thing he could not forget. There was, he insisted to D J Williams, 'a dangerous edge' to Emrys Roberts's character.[25]

Gwynfor attempted to build bridges with Emrys Roberts and begged him to ensure that there would be no personal 'divorce' between them, but Roberts refused the offer. In a letter, he told him that he did not know Gwynfor well enough for there to be a 'divorce' and that the leadership should be ashamed at having made him a scapegoat. He further accused Gwynfor of giving people a false impression of his private life, adding that Mike Tucker, Margaret Tucker's husband, had never been 'a close friend' of his, as had been suggested to Gwynfor. But Emrys Roberts's chief complaint was that Gwynfor had learned nothing, and that it was time for him to listen to his real friends: 'It's high time you recognized your real friends – those who are likely to help make Plaid effective for Wales – rather than the bunch of toadies you have around you at the moment'.[26]

This episode did not mark the end of the wrangling. Gwynfor was afraid that the situation would continue to be difficult in 'East Glamorgan', and so it proved for another two months. Several members in the south-east threatened to resign over the Emrys Roberts affair and there was a report of 'general unrest amongst our membership here in the south east'.[27] One of his supporters, Owen John Thomas, went so far as to warn Gwynfor that it could open a disastrous rift in Plaid Cymru's ranks. He wrote to Gwynfor: 'When it becomes known that he [Emrys Roberts] is now "On the Dole" after serving our Party (no doubt to the detriment of his own home and family) then the reaction amongst our members can only be one of hostility towards those responsible.'[28] In mid-December, New Nation had publicly announced its existence,[29] egged on by Emrys Roberts who said: 'Don't let the forces of reaction intimidate you or other go-ahead elements into leaving the party. If we stick together, our point of view will win.'[30]

The fury subsided shortly thereafter. Although New Nation began to publish its own magazine, *Cilmeri*, Emrys Roberts's decision to leave Wales for work in Stockton-on-Tees was crucial, and within the year Roberts himself accepted that New Nation was 'pretty ineffective, scattered all over the place, the only thing we've done is produce *Cilmeri* and that's not much'.[31] This statement was true as far as it went, but it was not a particularly generous appraisal, considering the movement's importance. By January 1966, Gwynfor had enacted most of New Nation's recommendations on how Plaid Cymru should be organized and this proved key to the modernization of the party. The New Nation faction was also crucial because it continued the work of the Republicans in promoting the Plaid Cymru message in the south-east. Unlike Gwynfor, New Nation understood the culture and mindset of the working class and with Emrys Roberts in charge it had the perfect ambassador. A Gwynfor and Emrys Roberts combination could have been a dream ticket, but the two men had failed to understand each other. It was a failure which cost Plaid Cymru dear.

As soon as the New Nation revolt had subsided, Gwynfor faced another unexpected crisis. On 5 January 1965, like a bolt from the blue, his trusted aide and favoured successor, Elystan Morgan, announced he was leaving Plaid Cymru for the greener and less acrimonious pastures of the Labour Party. Elystan Morgan explained to Gwynfor that he had come to the conclusion that Plaid Cymru would never win more than 3,000 votes in any seat and that the party had reached a 'plateau'.[32] There were other reasons too. Elystan Morgan was an ambitious young man and 1965 was an exciting time to be a member of the Labour Party. This would be the first proper year of Jim Griffiths's secretaryship, and it was also the beginning of a serious debate within the party on having an elected council for Wales. In the circumstances, it was hardly surprising that a pragmatic patriot like Morgan would be attracted to Labour. Elystan Morgan had also, it is true, had enough of the constant bickering among Plaid Cymru's high command. Even so, the news, when it came, stunned Gwynfor. 'Elystan,' Dafydd Evans wrote in his diary, was 'the blue eyed boy' and 'Daddy' thought it was 'an important crisis'.[33] True enough. So soon after losing Emrys Roberts, the loss of another colleague of Elystan Morgan's standing was heartbreaking. Gwynfor tried everything to persuade Morgan to stay. He went to Wrexham to see him and, by 10 January, he was confident that he had succeeded. But, not for the first time, Gwynfor was wearing rose-tinted spectacles.[34] By February, the rumours were rife that a prominent member of Plaid Cymru was about to join Labour and the press picked up the story. *Y Cymro* wondered aloud who it might be, naming Elystan Morgan, Nefyl Williams, Geraint Williams and Dafydd Alun Jones as the men most likely to defect. Gwynfor denied that he personally knew of anyone who was discontent with Plaid Cymru.[35] Elystan Morgan, too, denied that he wanted to leave, insisting to the *Western Mail* that all the talk about his future was hot air.[36] In private, however, Elystan Morgan was still uncertain. He had spent weeks discussing his future with Gwynfor and the latter had arranged for the veteran Lewis Valentine to give him a little fatherly advice. Elystan Morgan visited Valentine and held a 'wonderful, fraternal discussion' with him and by February 1965 it appeared that Gwynfor's efforts had succeeded. One Sunday evening, Elystan Morgan met Gwynfor at the Metropole in Llandrindod Wells and told him that he would not be joining Labour.[37]

The news was a great relief for Gwynfor, but these events had undoubtedly damaged him. He admitted to his closest political allies that he felt 'quite disconsolate' that his party had 'produced so few leaders who are completely serious'. The few it had, he said, came from the south, but it was the 'rot' in Gwynedd he found most disappointing. There, after forty years of work, he could not think of anyone who acted 'consistently as a public leader. There should be a dozen leaders there today, all working hard and carrying the country with them, but there isn't one'. It was a cri de coeur, but by his own admission, Gwynfor did not have a clue how to attract these potential leaders 'out of their cells' and into the fray. Maybe, he concluded, 'the armchair and the television are too strong for us now, and we'll need to begin again with the younger generation'. In that regard, he could only look with envy at events in Scotland. There, the SNP was thriving under the pragmatic leadership of men like Billy Wolfe and Ian Macdonald and had attracted 6,000 new members since October 1964.[38]

The SNP was also being transformed by a new sense of unity and better organization, but no such development was discernible in Wales.[39] In March, the familiar skirmish with Saunders Lewis surfaced again when the latter argued in *Barn* that members of Plaid Cymru should abandon the parliamentary route. Lewis's intention was to put pressure on the Plaid Cymru membership to enact the recommendations in his *Tynged yr Iaith* lecture and to cease being so meek: 'You cannot make an omelette without breaking eggs. Wales will not be saved with a smile and a request for support in the ballot box.'[40] When the article appeared, Gwynfor and his closest allies feared the worst. J E Jones believed that 'SL is becoming feeble-minded' and they both agreed that Plaid Cymru would have to answer Lewis to ensure that his supporters did not rise up again.[41] It is this concern that explains why Gwynfor and J E Jones used the front page of *Y Ddraig Goch* that month to 'prove' how inconsistent Saunders Lewis could be. The cover was given over almost entirely to quotations from statements made by Lewis during the 'twenties and 'thirties, all of them in favour of contesting parliamentary elections.[42] It is also clear that Gwynfor contacted Saunders Lewis to ask for an explanation. Lewis answered that he had written the piece in *Barn* in an attempt to prevent the creation of movements which would split the party, and offered to meet Gwynfor to discuss their differences.[43] It was an unusually conciliatory offer, but there is no evidence that it was ever taken up. Unsuccessful too were D J Williams's efforts to get Saunders involved once again in party activity. Lewis refused, telling D J Williams that he himself had not changed since they had launched the party together. 'It's Plaid that has changed,' he said.[44]

Gwynfor tried again to consolidate his Presidency during the summer of 1965. There were successful protests at Clywedog and Gwynfor symbolically trespassed on the land where the dam stood.[45] He published a series of articles in the *Western Mail* on devolution which received considerable attention, but before long the situation began to deteriorate once more.[46] In June, Plaid Cymru found itself in financial difficulties and the bank refused to provide any more loans – even for a week. The party was unable to pay its staff and Gwynfor was forced to borrow money from well-wishers such as his brother, Alcwyn, Thomas Parry and Dewi Watkin Powell to avert the crisis.[47] It was a serious position but not as grave as the situation with regard to Elystan Morgan. By the middle of June, he was having doubts again, telling Gwynfor that he was 'limp and exhausted' and that his situation was very different from what it had been four months previously. Gwynfor considered allowing Elystan Morgan to join the Fabians despite the danger that 'he would be played by them like a fish, and hooked in due course'.[48] It was Gwynfor's earnest hope that Elystan Morgan would reconsider but, this time, his mind was made up. On 12 July 1965, J E Jones wrote to Gwynfor informing him that Elystan Morgan was 'determined' to leave.[49] By then, Elystan Morgan had sent a lengthy and impassioned letter to J E Jones explaining why he was changing his party allegiance. The main reason, he told him, was that he anticipated 'a fairly consistent fall' in Plaid's vote and that it had not had 'an ounce of success' as a party that was trying to have an 'authoritative influence'. After much 'meditation and prayer', he had come to the conclusion that 'a small chance is better than the certainty of failure'.[50]

Gwynfor experienced many disappointments during his time in politics, but Elystan Morgan's departure hit him hard. Even before his decision to leave, journalists were asking Gwynfor how on earth he could keep going after twenty years as President. He replied that he had considered his position, but that someone had to undertake the work, however tiring it was.[51] But losing his colleague left him more isolated than ever. Now, there was no one left younger than him to whom he could entrust the succession. And with Emrys Roberts out of the picture, it was clearer than ever that the best talents of Welsh Wales were channelling their energies through Cymdeithas yr Iaith Gymraeg or the Labour Party.

Elystan Morgan had tried to depart as graciously as possible but, unbeknown to him, the news broke on the Thursday of National Eisteddfod week in Newtown – the busiest day of all. Many nationalists believed he had planned this deliberately, and Plaid Cymru and Gwynfor responded with some rancour. Gwynfor chose to ignore the fact that Elystan Morgan's decision was a principled one and implied to the press that it was prompted more by self-interest. 'It is not surprising,' he said, 'that we occasionally lose someone because we are not yet in a position to ensure him a successful career in politics.'[52] In the same vein, Gwynfor wrote to Elystan Morgan to remind him that he was now 'in the same party as Bessie Braddock', the chief assassin of Capel Celyn.[53] It was no surprise either, given how the President felt, that he and J E Jones should sling mud at Elystan Morgan, comparing him to Cledwyn Hughes, another ex-member of Plaid who could not be relied upon.[54] In a piece for *Y Cymro*, J E Jones pointed out that Cledwyn Hughes had been a member of Plaid Cymru. This led to accusations of slander and Cledwyn Hughes denied that he had ever signed up to the nationalist cause. In essence it was the word of one man against another, but Gwynfor was delighted. After the article appeared in *Y Cymro*, Gwynfor wrote to J E Jones to congratulate him:

> Of course, the story paints Cledwyn in an unfavourable light, but the important question for the public is what is the truth? Uncovering the truth is good for the country, and truth will out. You didn't mean to denigrate Cledwyn, but show how it is impossible to be a decent Welsh nationalist within the Labour Party.[55]

Treating Elystan Morgan in this manner offered Gwynfor an escape route from a difficult situation. But as that troublesome summer came to a close, there were no prospects of a holiday. Plaid Cymru's first ever party political broadcasts helped the party to forget the Elystan Morgan saga, even though the government's concession was only five minutes, once a year – after a decade of struggle. The first broadcast was made on 29 September and Gwynfor clearly made an impact. 'We'll Keep a Welcome' was played.[56] The broadcast (arranged by Islwyn Ffowc Elis and directed by the future Tory Minister, Wyn Roberts) also helped Plaid Cymru to convey a constructive message. However, that autumn, the only topic to occupy the minds of nationalists in Wales was the Tryweryn reservoir opening ceremony. Gwynfor had asked the leaders of Liverpool Corporation to stay away from the official opening out of respect for local feeling, but as the designated date of 21 October grew closer, the tension increased.[57] Plaid Cymru decided to organize an official, peaceful protest, but their intentions were undermined by a statement from the FWA that they planned to scupper the event.[58] Gwynfor was blamed roundly (and unfairly) by Frank Cain from Liverpool Corporation for poisoning their 'cordial relations with most people down there', but what worried Plaid Cymru most was the presence of the FWA.[59] J E Jones implored Gwynfor to cancel the party's protest, so great was his fear that 'the Army' would do something 'stupid' and ruin 'Plaid's good name after you have won it so much favour and support'.[60]

Gwynfor chose to ignore J E Jones's advice and the protest went ahead. It was the final sad act in the tragedy of Tryweryn. Gwynfor failed to present a letter to Alderman Sefton, the leader of Liverpool Council, as a crowd of 500 (including three members of the FWA in full uniform) turned the day into a farce.[61] When the great and the good of Liverpool reached the site, some Plaid Cymru activists tried to block their route and pelted their cars with stones. Others attempted to dismantle the marquee where the celebrations were to be held. Gwynfor was asked by the police to intervene to prevent the situation from becoming even more unpleasant. The day ended when Alderman Cain pressed the button which opened the floodgates with a triumphant flourish. But as the water cascaded into the river Tryweryn below, the point had been made. As they headed home, hundreds of nationalists vowed that neither Liverpool nor any other city would ever be allowed to kill a Welsh-speaking community again.

On the following day, Plaid Cymru claimed the credit for having organized the cathartic protest but, just days later, the praise turned to condemnation when it became clear that Gwynfor had been trying to have it both ways. Even as Plaid Cymru had been arranging the protest, Gwynfor had been in contact with Liverpool Corporation, and had agreed to meet Alderman Sefton in one last, utterly naive, attempt to persuade Liverpool to pay for the water.[62] Essentially, it was an effort to revive his *New Proposals* scheme but no one was surprised (apart from Gwynfor perhaps) when Liverpool rejected the offer. He was harshly criticised by some of his most prominent detractors. Kate Roberts could scarcely understand why Gwynfor was talking to Liverpool so late in the day,[63] and Saunders Lewis confessed to her that he was 'seriously' considering writing a pamphlet to discuss the future of a party that made him feel 'physically sick'.[64] In many respects, Gwynfor's last-minute effort sums up his immense but ambiguous struggle to save

Tryweryn. It was a stand which combined passion, over-optimism and uncertainty – three incompatible elements which did him and his party considerable damage between 1955 and 1965.

But even after Capel Celyn had sunk out of sight, Gwynfor could not escape Tryweryn nor the fatigue which was now an integral part of Plaid Cymru's DNA. The year had ended with political commentators making predictions about when the General Election would be called. The Wilson government had a majority of just one by the autumn and as the parties prepared themselves for an election, Gwynfor still found himself having to persuade his party that the battle ahead was worth the effort. Islwyn Ffowc Elis still had deep misgivings, and Gwynfor sought to allay his doubts by saying that Plaid Cymru was 'more of a force when it fights, even for a thousand votes, than when it doesn't fight'.[65] But his words sounded hollow. Islwyn Ffowc Elis chose to ignore Gwynfor and wrote to Elwyn Roberts, the new Plaid Cymru general secretary. He begged for a change of direction because 'if Plaid fights the election... *in the current political climate* it would be plain suicide. Only blind loyalty keeps many good members in Plaid these days, and another bad blow would mean the death of that loyalty'. It is unclear whether or not Gwynfor received a copy, so one can only speculate on how he might have reacted to Islwyn Ffowc Elis's closing remark: 'I am not the only one who thinks this way. Many good and experienced members of Plaid feel as I do. We have kept our opinions to ourselves for fear of hurting Gwynfor and splitting Plaid again.'[66] When those closest to Gwynfor heard this, their conclusion, that the game was up, was a reasonable one. D J Williams wrote in his diary: 'Although I have done everything in my power, as far as I can see there is no prospect of success. Everyone is so indifferent, even Plaid people themselves'.[67]

The nature of Welsh nationalism at the beginning of 1966 also made things difficult for Gwynfor. On the one hand, the leaders of Cymdeithas yr Iaith Gymraeg – people like Cynog Dafis, Gareth Miles and John Davies – had embarked on a series of controversial campaigns to make post offices use more Welsh. The perception that there was a new style of nationalism emerging was confirmed when four members of the society went on hunger strike over the New Year in order to draw attention to the language's inferior status. The *Manchester Guardian* argued that the 'nuisance value' of a protest like this was every bit as influential as any official protest and, as the message spread, it is not surprising that young nationalists were attracted by the campaign.[68] On the other hand, the

Welsh establishment was full of praise for Sir David Hughes Parry's Report on the language, and Jim Griffiths promised to act on it and create a bilingual Wales. These tendencies left Gwynfor in a no-man's-land: he could not speak out in favour of irreverent acts by the younger generation but he also knew that it was unwise to be too kind about any Labour government.

As his hold on the 'national movement' loosened, Gwynfor was further discomforted when the press began to take the FWA seriously. Indeed, one cannot overstate the damage these cranks and pseudo-fascists did to Plaid Cymru from the very outset. By November 1965, their leader, Julian Cayo Evans, was able to state that the 'army' numbered 500 in the west, and that they met and trained regularly. The fact that some of Saunders Lewis's supporters were also vaguely drawn to them lent further 'credibility' to the whole strange mix.[69] As a result, any record of Gwynfor's life must give them due consideration because many people believed that there was a connection between the FWA and Plaid Cymru. No matter how bizarre his statements, Julian Cayo Evans knew how to rile both the British and the Plaid Cymru establishments. This is probably why the FWA sent a teasing letter to Plaid Cymru at around this time offering a coalition:

> Is it not time that the Party faced up to the fact that by the time they get one Member returned to Parliament, Wales will not exist... Time will not stand still to save us, and time is running out fast. Plaid Cymru has the Membership and the potential support which, together with the FWA, could easily win freedom within about four years.[70]

This all happened within weeks of a possible general election, and Harold Wilson's announcement that the poll would be held on 31 March came as a relief to all politicians after many weeks of conjecture. But, for Gwynfor, the timing was dreadful. Financially, Plaid Cymru could hardly afford to pay its office staff let alone fight an election, and Gwynfor was forced to send out an instruction to all party members asking them to keep electoral costs to the bare minimum.[71] Gwynfor also had to reconsider his dream of putting up as many Plaid Cymru candidates as possible as there was only enough money for twenty – three fewer than in 1964. In the circumstances, a gift to the party of £2,000 from D J Williams, the profit from selling his old home at Penrhiw, was invaluable. However, not even this act of generosity escaped criticism. For one prominent member of Cymdeithas yr Iaith Gymraeg, Harri Pritchard Jones, D J Williams's gift was 'sad', and he predicted that the money would pay for 'a little publicity' before Plaid Cymru fell back into the familiar pattern of 'selling more and more potted pickles, taking part in more and more coffee mornings, and organizing jumble sales, all to raise money for the next five-yearly splurge, when for a few weeks before the election the members believe that Plaid counts in the life of the nation'.[72]

Harri Pritchard Jones's criticism also reflected the tension that existed during the election between Cymdeithas yr Iaith Gymraeg and Plaid Cymru. As the months went by, the language activists became increasingly militant and, in April, one of its members, Geraint Jones, was jailed, the first of many. Some members were infuriated by J E Jones's attitude towards them, and the announcement that Saunders Lewis was 'returning to the field of politics' to be President of Cymdeithas yr Iaith Gymraeg was joyously welcomed in some circles. However, it frightened Gwynfor and J E Jones. Indeed, so great was their concern at Saunders Lewis's political return that they asked Lewis Valentine and D J Williams to write to him in the hope that they could persuade him to keep quiet.[73] Mercifully, Saunders Lewis said nothing, but the former party President was not the only one who now had the power to frustrate Gwynfor's ambitions. On 6 March, a bomb exploded near the dam at Clywedog. Almost inevitably, Gwynfor was challenged to condemn the act but he refused to do so, saying that more people would turn to violence if the authorities continued to ignore the constitutional demands of Plaid Cymru.[74] Stranger still, two days after the explosion, the police called at Talar Wen with a cap and scarf they had found near the dam in order to discover whether the cap, quite literally, fitted.[75]

That, however, was about the only thrill the election produced. Nationally, and in the Carmarthen constituency where Gwynfor was standing for a second time, campaigning was lifeless. Every serious commentator predicted an easy Labour win as Wales, like the rest of Britain, enjoyed a period of economic growth and social optimism. There was a Welsh Office, its innate Welshness adding to the feeling of contentment, and the threat from the Conservatives under their new leader, Edward Heath, was minimal. In Carmarthen, it all meant that the election result, given Megan Lloyd George's legendary charisma, was a foregone conclusion. Even so, Gwynfor worked tirelessly to build an election machine there. Young people flocked to help, but it was difficult to build up the enthusiasm and 'hwyl' in the absence of the effervescent Megan herself.[76] As the campaign began, it was announced that she was suffering from a 'virus infection' and that she would be up and about by the final week.[77] As she lay sick in

Cricieth, the burden of the campaign fell to her nephew, Benjy Carey-Evans, and the former Plaid activist, Gwilym Prys Davies. Altogether, things were pretty odd in Carmarthen and, as the date of the poll grew closer, the press began to suspect that something, maybe, was amiss. As the *Western Mail* put it: 'There is something unreal about the Carmarthen fight somehow. It is a listless affair. The reason of course is that it is a remote-control operation for Labour… Lady Megan's absence has robbed the election of any excitement which it might have stimulated.'[78] But no one in the Labour ranks in Carmarthen knew the dreadful truth about Megan Lloyd George, that she was suffering from cancer and that there would be no recovery. It was only after the final election meeting that Gwilym Prys Davies heard from Benjy Carey-Evans that she was dying.[79] It is impossible to know whether Megan Lloyd George deliberately concealed her state of health from the electors of Carmarthen but be that as it may, a few weeks later, her handling of the situation would have far-reaching consequences.

Megan Lloyd George managed to ensure that her secret was not betrayed during the campaign, and the only thing out of the ordinary on the night of the count was that Benjy Carey-Evans stood in for her as the result was declared. As expected, her vote rose substantially, and the only shock, for some at least, was Gwynfor's performance. Plaid Cymru's vote had increased from 5,495 to 7,416, mostly at the expense of the Liberals. The result allowed him to announce to the crowd outside the Guildhall that he would win next time. No one took him seriously – after all, it was April Fools Day – and Gwynfor's comparative success was of only limited interest in the context of Labour's remarkable victory in Wales.[80] The evening saw the high tide of Welsh Labourism as Harold Wilson's party took 32 of the 36 seats in Wales, including Conservative strongholds like Monmouth and Cardiff North. For Plaid Cymru, however, the result was worse than the implosion of 1964, as its vote fell in fifteen constituencies.

For many nationalists, this was irrelevant. There was one result, more than all the others which symbolised their failure. That night, after a century of Liberalism, Elystan Morgan took Cardiganshire for Labour. To add insult to injury, a proud Welshman, Cledwyn Hughes, was made Welsh Secretary. There was also a promise that Wales would have an elected council and an economic plan. Sir Ifan ab Owen Edwards spoke for the majority of Welsh patriots when he wrote to Cledwyn Hughes to congratulate him: 'Among the lessons that this last Election taught us is that the Nationalist Party, given today's conditions, can never succeed as a political party and that Labour is by now the National Party of Wales. It would be wonderful if Gwynfor and one or two like him could be added to swell your ranks.'[81] The response from within Plaid Cymru was equally resigned. There was none of the fire and brimstone of 1959 and 1964; rather, the disappointing outcome was simply accepted. The critics had been routed and Gwynfor continued his leadership unchallenged.

Immediately after the election, Gwynfor and Rhiannon went to Ireland for a few days' well-earned rest before returning to Wales and the familiar grind – work in the gardens and for the party. But by the end of April, the situation was transformed when it was realized that Megan Lloyd George had something far worse than a 'virus infection' and that a by-election was imminent. Unbeknown to Labour, Plaid Cymru in Carmarthen set about their task in an organized (and sensitive) fashion, so that when, on 15 May, the death of 'The First Lady of Wales' was announced, Plaid Cymru was in a strong position.[82] No one could have known it at the time, but her death signalled the end of Welsh Liberalism. Megan Lloyd George's funeral was held on 18 May and, as expected, Gwynfor travelled to Cricieth for the burial. There, at the graveside, surrounded by the mountains of Snowdonia, his thoughts were on the future rather than the past, and his own prospects in the by-election. In his heart, he believed that he could come a good second. On his way back to Llangadog that Wednesday, he called at Tynllidiart, the family's holiday retreat near Dolgellau, and one of his favourite places in Wales. It was there, he wrote in his autobiography, he had the mystical sensation that nature was showing him a change of direction in his own life. In the county that had rejected him, he saw the river Gwynant whiter than usual and the sun shining on the lakes at Crogenan. He felt convinced that Wales was 'breathing quietly' around him.[83]

However, Gwynfor returned to Carmarthen and to uncertainty. It was a confusing sign of Plaid Cymru's weakness (and Gwynfor's personal popularity) that he had to insist to the press that he would not be standing for either Labour or the Liberals in the forthcoming by-election.[84] But timing proved the most difficult issue. Although Cyril Jones and Islwyn Ffowc Elis had drawn up detailed plans for the by-election, it looked increasingly likely that it would be postponed until the autumn. Wisely, Plaid decided to proceed on the principle that the poll could be called at any time and the campaign plans went ahead. For the first time in its history, the Plaid Cymru publicity machine was running smoothly.

For the first time too, the spin doctors were working successfully. Islwyn Ffowc Elis had learned some important lessons from his friend, Willie Kellock, who had transformed the image of the SNP. News about Plaid Cymru began to reach the two local newspapers, but the crucial aspect for Islwyn Ffowc Elis was that every report should contain a reference to Gwynfor so that he was 'consistently in the public eye'. It was a hugely successful strategy. The *Carmarthen Times* was already supportive and now the *Carmarthen Journal* – which had a larger circulation – was also beginning to warm to the Plaid campaign, so much so that its editor attended Gwynfor's adoption meeting.[85]

The decision to continue campaigning was not the only wise decision taken at the time. Between the general election and the by-election, Gwynfor got in touch with Clem Thomas, Megan Lloyd George's former agent and a man who knew the local Labour Party like the back of his hand. During the campaign Clem Thomas had worked for the *Carmarthen Times* but, in spite of his Labour roots, he had become disillusioned with what he regarded as the anti-Welsh Stalinism of the local council. In this spirit, he began to share his inside knowledge of Labour with Gwynfor, urging him to target industrial villages in the anthracite-producing east of the county, where the realization had dawned that Labour was prepared to close pits by the dozen.[86] The strategy paid dividends, but the coalfield was not the only part of the constituency to feel the chill wind of Harold Wilson's second term. Farmers were appalled by the small business taxes, and a seamen's strike put enormous pressure on the pound. And to cap it all, the local council talked of the possible closure of 22 rural schools.

As the Wilson honeymoon – arguably the shortest on record – came to an end the last piece of the electoral jigsaw fell into place when Plaid Cymru heard that Labour's candidate would be Gwilym Prys Davies. In many respects, he was the perfect Labour candidate: young, gifted, and a patriot who could rely on the unswerving support of none other than Jim Griffiths. But Gwilym Prys Davies was also a square peg in a round hole. First, his north Walian roots counted against him – especially so among local Labourites because he had defeated a young local solicitor from Cynwyl Elfed, Denzil Davies, to take the nomination. Secondly, some in the party were suspicious of him because he had left Plaid Cymru for the Republicans before coming to his senses. Plaid Cymru hardly needed reminding to use this against him during the campaign. Gwynfor himself put together a confidential document for distribution among Plaid Cymru canvassers to inform them that Gwilym Prys Davies had left the party because it wasn't 'sufficiently extremist'.[87] Given this ammunition, it is unsurprising that Gwilym Prys Davies was heckled in public meetings during the campaign, and that Plaid Cymru supporters should upbraid him for his 'shameful past'.[88] But perhaps the greatest problem was Gwilym Prys Davies's own personality. Although he was an outstanding policy adviser, his inability to relate to ordinary people – more so even than Gwynfor – often meant that his shyness was misinterpreted as condescension. Given these three factors, the tide could be seen to be turning slowly in Gwynfor's favour when the unexpected announcement was made that the by-election would be held on 14 July. This gave Gwynfor's campaign a further boost, because coming so soon after the March general election, it tended to confirm the popular perception that Labour had not been completely honest about the state of Megan Lloyd George's health.

The campaign lasted just three short weeks but, from the moment it was called on 22 June, the Plaid Cymru electoral machine worked efficiently to achieve its goal of ensuring Gwynfor a respectable second place. Islwyn Ffowc Elis and Cyril Jones worked unstintingly to make 'Gwynfor' – the first time that Gwynfor was used without the Evans – into a man of the people. The county's electors received a 'personal letter' from him, reminding them that his roots were deep in Carmarthenshire. Gwynfor, it said, 'lives in Carmarthenshire' and works 'among his own people'.[89] It was a clear dig at an incomer like Gwilym Prys Davies, but in the eastern coal belt the party's message was rather different. There, an English leaflet was distributed called *Plaid Cymru and You* focusing mainly on the state of the mining industry. It also addressed the Labour chestnut that a vote for Plaid Cymru was a wasted vote: 'Don't make this Government too smug by returning yet another London-Labour M.P. Return a Welsh one and make it jump!' [90] Across the whole county it was difficult to avoid the bright new product, 'Gwynfor' – especially since Plaid Cymru had hired seven massive hoardings on Willie Kellock's advice. His message for Islwyn Ffowc Elis was unmistakable: 'People think that if you APPEAR big, you ARE big.' And as with the leaflets, the two halves of the county had their different slogans. In the patriotic west the message was 'Gwynfor Evans says: 'For a Better Wales, Support Plaid Cymru.' In the socialist east, 'For Work in Wales, Support Plaid Cymru.' But the master stroke was a map of Wales and the English slogan 'Your Hand Can Make History.' This, even though Cymdeithas yr Iaith was unhappy with the predominant use of English, was the most effective aspect of a particularly sophisticated campaign.[91]

Plaid Cymru was also extremely fortunate as regards timing. The by-election was held during a college break, and hundreds of young nationalists flocked to Carmarthen to join in the campaign. The party benefited too from the numbers of local young people who had turned to Plaid Cymru between 1964 and 1966 (against the national trend). It meant that the youth branches in Carmarthen and Ammanford were strong, and ready to do a good day's work when the by-election was called. Luckily for Gwynfor, most of the young people had not been tainted by the infighting of the previous few years. Vast hordes of canvassers were therefore available to Plaid Cymru and, having been warned that on no account were they to wear FWA uniform, they reminded voters of Gwynfor's virtues: 'He is such an able and honest man. Lives and has lived in the County, and has served it so well. Standing as a candidate to serve the County and Wales; not for the job or the status.'[92] Purist nationalism was a secondary issue; there was no mention of having a seat in the United Nations or about academic matters like 'Independence'. The party line was that Gwynfor was a good man and a better Welshman than anyone else. The only one, it appears, who did not share this belief in new hopes and horizons was Saunders Lewis. As the Carmarthen campaign began to warm up, he wrote to Elwyn Roberts mocking the whole enterprise:

> The whole thing's ridiculous; it shows that nationalism is a hobby for them or that they're childishly innocent. I have long since given up writing anything in case it does damage to Plaid, but its behaviour is one of the great disappointments in life for me. And the self-satisfaction of the statements made by some in the leadership is a source of considerable bitterness. Plaid is more like a religious sect than a national political organization. It thinks it can *persuade* people to vote for it and that that is sufficient! [93]

In comparison, Gwilym Prys Davies's campaign never reached third gear. For one thing, the Labour party machinery was not up to the job, having previously depended so much on the personality of Megan Lloyd George to gain votes. Second, it is clear that some party members did not want to work for Gwilym Prys Davies because of his nationalist background. But the main reason, though not the only one, why Labour did so badly was that the by-election happened during one of the most tempestuous periods in the history of any twentieth-century government. A seamen's strike had caused Harold Wilson untold problems for weeks, but the turning-point was the resignation of the Minister for Technology, Frank Cousins, on 3 July. Cousins, a lifelong union baron, decided to go because of Wilson's policy on wages, and this placed immense strain on the money markets. As speculators undermined the value of the pound, the 'Big Three' – Wilson, George Brown and James Callaghan – argued among themselves, giving the impression that the government was divided. By 4 July, Jim Griffiths was so worried that he wrote to Gwilym Prys Davies to offer his sympathy: 'I am sorry that your Campaign has to bear the strain of the rifts and resignations. This is political life – one can never be sure what may happen any day… concentrate on the areas where our vote is strongest to get our full vote there.'[94]

Gwilym Prys Davies soldiered on with his small band of supporters, but to no avail. It was impossible to shift the perception that Harold Wilson's government was in disarray. Even so, with eleven days to go, no one seriously believed that the county really could make history. On that day, *The Guardian*'s reporter commented that Gwilym Prys Davies was bound to be elected and that the outstanding feature was the battle for second place between Gwynfor and his Liberal opponent, Hywel Davies. 'Between them,' he wrote, 'they are fighting over the anti-Labour vote with almost suicidal fervour.' But Gwynfor was making an impression, and the near certainty that he would not win was a disappointment to the *Guardian*'s man on the spot: 'It is unfortunate that in these circumstances victory begins to look assured for the Labour candidate, Gwilym Prys Davies.'[95]

The final week of the campaign began in familiar fashion for Gwilym Prys Davies as Harold Wilson made another public pronouncement on the 'defeatist cries, moaning minnies and wet editorials that were destroying Britain.[96] But, however loud the PM's protests, something strange was afoot in Carmarthen. Gwilym Prys Davies began to sense a coolness towards him on doorsteps where the welcome had once been warm, and some supporters could not look him in the eye. Cledwyn Hughes, visiting Carmarthen, was forced to admit publicly that Labour's vote was likely to fall by 3–4,000.[97] His comment, made on 12 July – two days before the poll – coincided with Gwynfor's royal progress through the constituency. The difference now, and for the first time, was that people wanted to hear what he had to say. 'In the old days,' Gwynfor remarked, 'they wanted to chuck us in the river. But now they're listening to what we have to say. Take this election. At first, we thought it was another uphill battle. But I've never seen anything like it.'[98] Farmers in Llandovery market all pledged their support; in other parts of the constituency, the refuse wagons were plastered with Plaid Cymru stickers and, in Llandeilo, Plaid Cymru paraphernalia adorned the motorbikes of the local 'Teds'.[99] Dafydd, Gwynfor's son, had never seen such a sight, nor had another diarist, D J Williams. On 12 July, canvassing among the upland farms he'd immortalised, he discovered that 'almost everyone is promising to vote for Gwynfor'.[100] No one mentioned Tryweryn or even nationalism; the constant chorus was that Gwynfor was 'a good man' who deserved a chance.[101] Gwynfor, usually so cautious, began to talk of winning the seat.

Plaid Cymru's campaigners redoubled their efforts on the last day before polling, and held a rally at the Lyric cinema in Carmarthen. That night, the other three parties had also arranged public gatherings in the town, with some of the big guns from Westminster in attendance such as Cledwyn Hughes and Alec Douglas-Home. Faced with this, Plaid Cymru's leadership doubted whether a thousand-seat venue was a wise choice. Their fears were unfounded. The cinema was packed; the 'lad from Llanuwchllyn', Dafydd Iwan, led the singing, and the crowd were overwhelmingly supportive of Gwynfor on an emotional evening that has become part of Plaid Cymru folklore.[102] And, for the first time ever, a *crowd,* not a collection of individuals, allowed themselves to believe that Gwynfor could, some day, deliver salvation for Welsh Wales by constitutional means.

After the euphoria and the cheers, Gwynfor and his team woke to a new worry. Although the headlines that day were as helpful as ever – the government was under pressure and there were rumours of a rise in interest rates – Plaid Cymru could see signs that Labour still meant business. Islwyn Ffowc Elis travelled to the village of Red Roses at the far end of the county and noticed that Labour 'had staffed the polling station handsomely'. Gwynfor saw something similar: on a visit to Brynaman he saw that Labour had twenty canvassers for every one that Plaid Cymru could muster.[103] Although Plaid Cymru had a detailed plan to ensure that its supporters turned out, the great day itself was like a cold shower at the end of a long summer. The announcement that interest rates had indeed risen again did nothing to raise spirits, and when the polling stations closed at 9 o'clock that night, a kind of unease gripped Plaid supporters. There was nothing left to do but wait and pray that there would be some good news at least from the Guildhall.

At the count, Gwynfor's agent, Cyril Jones, could soon see that a pattern was emerging and that Gwynfor was ahead. Gwynfor arrived at around midnight and, as he crossed the still empty square, he saw Elwyn Roberts, who brought him incredible news: 'You're in,' he said. 'No,' answered Gwynfor, 'I utterly refuse to believe it,' adding that he would be happy with second place. But as soon as he entered the Guildhall, Gwynfor saw that Elwyn Roberts was right. Elwyn Roberts phoned Talar Wen to share the news with Rhiannon. She, like her husband, refused to accept what was about to happen. Outside on the square, the nationalists were gathering as the pubs closed. Some were singing hymns, some were chanting 'We want Gwynfor', but others were preparing themselves for another disappointment as the rumours started to circulate. Some had heard that it had been a low turnout; others said that a lot of Plaid Cymru supporters were still on holiday; there was another rumour that Labour had done well in the mining areas. 'I'm going out to try and forget it,' Harri Webb announced, and he was not the only one who assumed that Gwynfor had lost. Cliff Phillips, the legendary Press Association reporter, decided not to bother staying in Carmarthen for the result. He called his office in London before the count with the now infamous headline: 'Labour Have It In The Bag'.

Just before one o'clock, the crowd burst into singing 'Hen Wlad fy Nhadau'. Then, as if the whole thing had been stage-managed, there was a movement at the windows of the Guildhall. The result was announced inside the building first and then the clerk came out onto the balcony followed by the four candidates. The historic announcement began. Gwilym Prys Davies was the first name to be read out and when the crowd of two thousand heard that he had polled 13,473, a sigh went up. A disappointing result for Labour could only mean one thing – a win for the Liberal, Hywel Davies. His name was next but when it emerged that he had only received 8,650 votes, the crowd were thrilled. No one paid any attention to the result for the Tory, Simon Day.Then, W S Thomas pronounced those unforgettable words: 'Gwynfor Richard Evans, sixteen thousand...'. The rest was drowned by the roar of unconfined joy.[104]

An euphoric wave swept over the square and a legend was born. It turned into a sea of celebration as the crowd, young and old, greeted their hero. The only one who kept his head that night was Gwynfor, who was paralysed by fear after the victory – fear that he would not be worthy of the occasion, and fear of facing his new job as an MP. But there was no going back now. He came down from the balcony and into the surging, weeping throng; some were shouting 'Gwynfor, Gwynfor' – the chosen son who they believed had led the nation out of exile. For Plaid Cymru's supporters, this was the day that Wales won her freedom, the 'Nationalist Dawn', as the poet Gwenallt called it, a result which guaranteed further freedom.[105] It was a particularly sweet moment for the older members of Plaid Cymru who had been involved in the struggle from the very beginning. J E Jones was in tears that night, while D J Williams wrote in his diary that his greatest wish was 'to die soon' now that hope was alive.[106]

From that day, Gwynfor was an icon for many people. The date itself was significant: 14 July marked the fall of the Bastille in 1789. The by-election was held eighty years to the day since the first election of the Liberal golden boy, Tom Ellis, to Parliament. Gwynfor's result achieved blanket coverage, from the *New York Times* to *Pravda*, but it was the *Daily Mail* that came closest to capturing the euphoria: '1 a.m.: The Welsh Unseat Labour'.[107] He was carried shoulder-high by his young supporters to the tiny Plaid Cymru office in Bridge Street, but there was no sanctuary there. So great was the rejoicing that he had to be 'rescued' for his own good and driven home to Llangadog.[108]

It was a scene of disarray at Talar Wen too; the phone rang all night as the news spread. For Gwynfor, it was an unforgettable experience for all sorts of reasons, not least that he had finally succeeded. However, it was the nature of that success that pleased him most. Plaid Cymru had won through as a constitutional party and on that evening, at long last, it could bury for good any talk of another Penyberth. Now, as he told journalists a few hours after the declaration, the same thing could be achieved in other parts of Wales. On the following day, Gwynfor received hundreds of telegrams, but the most significant of these was the one that reached Talar Wen from Penarth at a quarter past ten that morning: it was from Saunders Lewis. It bore this simple message: 'Congratulations and heartfelt thanks.'[109] It was a generous act but, after Carmarthen, Saunders Lewis finally lost control of the party he had founded. From then on, Plaid Cymru was Gwynfor's party: a (largely) pacifist and constitutional one.

One question remains unanswered. What had happened? Immediately after the result, two explanations were given for the political earthquake. The first – from Labour – was that it was a fluke, a 'freak' result.[110] The second, Gwynfor's own, was that there had been an awakening and that no one should be surprised at this given that Carmarthenshire had been the cradle of the Methodist Revival.[111] The truth lies somewhere in between the two analyses. Gwynfor was undoubtedly very lucky. The election was held at a bad time for Labour and it found itself reliant on a candidate with neither charisma nor an effective electoral machine behind him. He was fortunate in that Megan Lloyd George should never have stood in March. Liberalism was in decline and Carmarthen was a seat with no tradition of Conservative support. And, true, Gwynfor was also fortunate that the by-election had occurred in a seat with an eccentric political history, more interested in the person than party labels. Gwynfor was following in the steps of personalities like Sir Alfred Mond, Sir Rhys Hopkin Morris and Megan Lloyd George. But this is only half an explanation. Gwynfor fully deserved to win the seat because he was the right man in the right place at the right time; it is hard to imagine any other Plaid Cymru candidate who could have done it – even in such favourable circumstances. And Gwynfor deserved to win, too, because he had managed to undermine Welsh Liberalism to such an extent that its foundations were totally unstable. It must be conceded, too, that although comparatively few committed nationalists voted for him, Gwynfor had created a generation of political patriots who regarded a vote for Plaid Cymru as a vote for Wales. These orphans of Welsh Liberalism may not have wanted to see an independent Wales, but the farmers and small businessmen believed that a vote for 'the Blaid' was the right thing to do from a moral perspective. Gwynfor had created this complex nexus through his own unstinting efforts – and he was its first beneficiary. He would experience further success but, now, London was his next destination, and the beginning of an unhappy chapter in his life – Gwynfor's parliamentary purgatory.

Chapter 9

THE MEMBER FOR WALES 1966–70

GWYNFOR WAS IN TOP FORM during the days and months after his Carmarthen triumph. Indeed, as a 'national redeemer', he would never enjoy such prestige again. On the first weekend after the by-election, he witnessed remarkable scenes as his motorcade swept through the constituency. In every village, he was acclaimed as a hero; people rushed from their houses to greet him, flags waved and crowds roared 'Gwynfor, Gwynfor'.[1] The return to Llangadog, under a blanket of mist, was especially touching; there, on the square of his adopted village, a crowd of over a hundred was waiting patiently to welcome him home. And for days on end, the phone calls and the messages continued unabated. Indeed, he received so many telegrams that the post office in Ammanford could not cope.[2] Newspaper men from London arrived in Carmarthenshire to interview the Commons' newest and most unusual member. On the day after the declaration, he met them at Talar Wen where he stated that he intended to speak for Wales in the House: 'Anything that will be of benefit to Wales I shall support. Anything that is destructive to Welsh life I shall have to oppose.'[3] That evening he gave an interview to the BBC's leading current affairs programme, *24 Hours*. The tiresome days of writing pseudonymous letters to the *Western Mail* were well and truly over.

After all the years of conflict, Gwynfor could now also claim that he led a united party. But this unity was not only confined to party-based nationalism. The FWA called a truce (to see what would come of the new nationalist voice at Westminster); similarly, some of the party's black sheep returned meekly to the fold. Neil Jenkins wrote to apologize for past actions, saying that he (Gwynfor) 'was right all along in keeping to constitutional means within Plaid Cymru'.[4]

Cynog Dafis accepted that he had been mistaken, confessing to Gwynfor that he had been proved 'utterly wrong' in his belief that 'Plaid's election policies led to destruction'.[5] Indeed, the victory took the wind out of Cymdeithas yr Iaith Gymraeg's sails for several months. It was not until October 1967, and the disappointment of a new, less respectful generation with that year's Welsh Language Act, that the society emerged again as an active force.[6]

Nevertheless, the greatest impact was, naturally, on Plaid Cymru itself. The result put Welsh nationalism back on the political map for the first time since Penyberth. Plaid Cymru had become a force once more (albeit for only a short while) in British politics. But internally too, the implications of the by-election were electrifying. During the three days after the victory, the party gained seven hundred new members and emergency centres had to be opened for them to collect their membership cards; within a year, Plaid Cymru's membership had almost doubled, increasing from 14,000 to 27,000. It is perhaps not surprising that the biggest growth occurred in the west, in places like Carmarthen and Merioneth, but all across Wales, new blood flowed into the party's veins. The financial gains were just as spectacular: Owen John Thomas remembers a table in the Plaid Cymru office hidden under a mountain of cheques and bankers' orders.[7] The party raised £10,000 more than it had expected that year.[8]

Having struggled to get by for so long, these were heady days for Plaid Cymru, but they came at a price: a personality cult developed around Gwynfor that bordered on the unpleasant, and what was now expected of him as an MP was utterly unreasonable and unfair. Gwynfor was uncomfortable with this idolatry, but had no control over it. Thousands of nationalists believed in Gwynfor's powers as redeemer of the whole nation.[9] This middle-aged teetotaller made an unlikely sixties icon, but, if there were such a thing as a Welsh-medium counter-culture in 1966, then it was Gwynfor, of all people, who embodied it. Part and parcel of this was the belief (to which many intelligent nationalists subscribed) that a revolution had taken place in rural Wales. Over the summer, this assumption gained currency as the press began to take the Gwynfor phenomenon seriously. One 'hearty, bearded nationalist, who keeps a Union Jack in his lavatory' told *The Times* that this was the fourth revolution that Wales had experienced and that it was every bit as significant as the previous three in religion, politics and economics.[10] This was an exaggeration, of course, but a revealing one, which reflected the notion that Gwynfor was the 'Member for Wales'. It had been

Gwynfor's own idea to call himself the 'Member for Wales', but it meant that he carried an intolerable burden. The decision, as will be seen, also unsettled many of his supporters in Carmarthenshire.

But the greatest price he and his family had to pay was his weekly absences in London. This, without doubt, was one of the great ironies of his career: it had been his burning ambition to win a seat in the Commons, but when he achieved it, he hated every second. During that first weekend of celebrations, he was disarmingly candid about his neurosis, telling the *Herald of Wales* that he was terrified by the prospect of going to London: 'The last thing I wanted was to leave Wales, but if it will be for the good of the nation, I must go.'[11] What he did not explain was why he was so terrified. It was only with the publication of his autobiography that he revealed how public speaking shredded his nerves – so much so that he experienced 'frequent nightmares' at the thought. In these nightmares, everything would go 'so disastrously wrong' that he would wake himself with 'alarming shouts'.[12] He had also come to regard Westminster as the most powerful symbol of the sickness he called 'Britishness'.[13] Considering these factors, the strain was immense and Fridays became a blessed relief for him. On the weekly journey home from the station at Neath, for instance, he would insist on breaking the journey on the Black Mountain to breathe in Welsh air. But even so, it is difficult to understand why London should have provoked such agonies. After all, Gwynfor was perfectly familiar with English institutions; ever since his time at Barry County School, he had spent his days surrounded by self-confident people who are so at home in Oxford or Westminster.

But London called, and Gwynfor boarded the 'Evans Express' from Carmarthen on Wednesday, 20 July. As with the royal progress through his constituency the previous weekend, this was a memorable journey: expectant crowds were waiting for him at every station across the south. There were bouquets and posies in Swansea, hymns in Neath and 200 supporters cheering in Cardiff. Rhiannon confessed to the press that she felt she must be on drugs. When she was asked about the significance of the day, she commented: 'I've been a Plaid widow since 1945 when Gwynfor became President of the party, but it's all been worth it.'[14] Night had fallen by the time they reached Paddington, where another 500 were waiting to greet the man of the moment. A porter commented that he had not seen anything like it since the Beatles passed through. However, not even the Fab Four would have had the temerity to say, as Gwynfor did, that they were coming to London to undo the work of Henry Tudor.[15] Then, from Paddington, the Plaid contingent went on to an official reception organized by Dafydd Wigley, where his harpist wife, Elinor Bennett, performed traditional music.

But the day was not over yet: there was still work to do. Before retiring for the night to the Strand Palace hotel, Gwynfor attempted to deal with the greatest problem that faced him in those first days after his victory, the FWA. Ever since he had won the seat, the press had been investigating Welsh nationalism for any possible link between Plaid Cymru, the FWA and the bombing campaign. The evidence, as usual, was pretty thin, but it was Gwynfor's misfortune that the 'Rhymney and Sirhowy Valleys Column' of the FWA chose to tell *The Times* that their very short-lived ceasefire had come to an end on the day that he reached London.[16] The story was nonsense, but it was taken at face value, and on that first evening in London, Gwynfor had to use his statement to the press to scotch the insinuation. He did so, as usual, by making light of the threat: 'I have met all three members of the Free Wales Army,' Gwynfor said. 'They are nice lads, but Plaid Cymru has nothing to do with them.'[17] He had a theory that there was a deliberate smear campaign against him, coordinated from London, and he made a special point of naming Leo Abse, the Labour MP for Pontypool, as the sort of person who might be responsible. This was one battle Gwynfor would lose. Despite his best efforts, the FWA was believed and used by the press and by those in authority who wished to ignore the facts.[18]

The following day, Gwynfor's first task was to meet George Thomas at the Welsh Office. They had a brief chat and then he crossed Parliament Square to enter the Commons for the first time as an MP. He did so without any fuss, in the hope that he could familiarize himself with his new home before his supporters arrived.[19] Parliamentary procedures were explained to him and he learnt how spartan his life would be: plenty of bars (no use to a teetotaller), but no office or phone. This is how it would be for the whole of his first term in Parliament but, on that day, Gwynfor faced a more important question than office accommodation: would he be allowed to take the oath bilingually? Ever since his election, it was this, above all else, which had preoccupied journalists, and some papers predicted that Gwynfor might be thrown out of the Chamber for daring to speak Welsh there.[20] But at least there was huge support for him in London on that first day. When Gwynfor entered Parliament for the second time – the 'official' arrival, as it were – he was greeted by tumultuous scenes. Outside St Stephen's Gate, almost a thousand supporters had gathered in festive mood. The police wanted them to disperse, but they would not budge. Having waited for so long to see Welsh nationalism on the big stage, no one was going to miss the moment. When Gwynfor arrived, the police had to clear a route through the middle of the crowd and do their best to hurry the new MP along it. But Gwynfor wanted to enjoy every second of the occasion and, much to the frustration of the police, he stopped and addressed his supporters from the steps before disappearing into his new universe.

The early signs were promising. At ten past three in the afternoon came the moment he had waited so long for. He stepped up to the Bar of the House to be received as a full member. On either side of him stood his sponsors, Jim Griffiths and S O Davies. In accordance with custom and practice, Gwynfor took the oath in English before challenging it for the first time by sitting on the government front bench. MPs watched aghast, assuming he was confused, but, within a few seconds, they realized what he was doing. From the government bench, Gwynfor asked for the right to take his oath a second time – in Welsh. As expected, the Speaker of the House, Dr Horace King, refused his request, but not before the Leader of the House had promised to re-examine the rules. And King kept his word; by 1970, the rules were changed and Welsh MPs were allowed to take the oath in Welsh. Gwynfor's stand was a clever one, and parliamentarian stalwarts judged that no new member had created such an impression in years.[21] He had succeeded in choosing a small but significant issue to underline the inferior status of Welsh and had united 'Gaels and Celts', as the *Daily Mail* put it, 'in clan-gathering protest'.[22] Several members supported him, but perhaps the most significant support on that first day came from Elystan Morgan – a good friend to Gwynfor until he was appointed a Home Office minister.

As he left the Chamber, Gwynfor could walk with his head held high, so much so that one reporter remarked on the goodwill shown towards him.[23] The goodwill was, however, in short supply. Later that day, he was shown around the House by the redoubtable socialist, Emrys Hughes, MP for South Ayrshire – son-in-law of Keir Hardie and great-grandson of the hymnwriter John Hughes, Pontrobert. Emrys Hughes had also written a guide to Parliament and he showed Gwynfor the ropes. One golden rule was that he should never sit at the Welsh Table in the tea room because of the hostility Labour felt towards him. 'I wouldn't sit there if I were you,' Emrys Hughes told him, 'your name is mud there.' And Gwynfor never did. It was not until the arrival of Dafydd Elis Thomas and Dafydd Wigley in 1974 that he plucked up enough courage to face Labour MPs. There were other manifestations of this hostility: the Labour MP, Donald Coleman, would pointedly refuse to greet him when they both caught the train from Neath on a Monday morning; Ness Edwards did not speak to him, while Goronwy Roberts would not even look at him. Apart from Elystan Morgan, the only two Welsh members to treat him with any decency were Cledwyn Hughes and Michael Foot.[24] Apart from these notable exceptions, the attitude of the Labour MPs towards Gwynfor reflected their tribal immaturity at its worst, and it is worth noting that history repeated itself here. As had happened during his time on Carmarthenshire County Council, Gwynfor again became the saintly hermit – a man too other-worldly to challenge Labour in the way that Winnie Ewing of the SNP, or the two Dafydds, Wigley and Elis Thomas, would do later. In practical terms, it meant that Gwynfor was at a severe disadvantage throughout the whole of his first parliamentary term, but there was worse to come. In due course, the ill-feeling between him and the south Wales socialists became open aggression when they saw that Gwynfor was on friendly terms with leading members of the Conservative Party.

It took some time for this enmity to crystallise, but the political waters got choppier on the day Gwynfor made his maiden speech on 26 July. Traditionally, maiden speeches are meant to be uncontroversial affairs, but his was not; it deserves to be considered the best he ever delivered. It contained the usual Gwynforian touches: an appeal to Christian tradition, allegations of Labour betrayal and a denunciation of the shortcomings of Britishness. But the most striking aspect was that Gwynfor spoke 'for Wales' in the Holiest of Holies. It was 'patronising rubbish,' he said, for Harold Wilson to talk about Wales profiting from Labour rule. 'You will not be able to get away with it much longer because the Welsh are beginning to take their country as seriously as the Danes and the Swedes take their countries.' But the cry from the heart, the closing vision, stood out: 'Looking round the country in which I live, I can see something different from the light of the setting sun. It looks more like the rising of a new dawn. "Westward look, the land is bright".'[25] The political world was amazed by his performance, and commentators believed that Gwynfor had challenged every convention. This, said the *Western Mail*, was 'the most fiery maiden speech of recent years',[26] but there was a downside. Some thought it could have been 'somewhat more gracious' given the 'considerable warmth of the welcome' he had been shown on that first day.[27] From this point onwards, Gwynfor was a target.

He received a hero's welcome at the Plaid Cymru conference in Maesteg at the end of July. As might be expected, it was an outstanding success, and Gwynfor used the occasion to announce that the party would fight every seat in the next general election. This, he said, was an historic decision: 'Historians in the future will study our attitude towards the present challenge.'[28] Quite so; this was the last battle in Gwynfor's constitutional revolution. Nevertheless, despite his influence, the FWA was still a thorn in his side. Its officers sat in the front row at the conference in full uniform, and Gwynfor had to beg the journalists there (especially those from the BBC) not to suggest that there was any connection between the FWA and the party. And the FWA caused Gwynfor other problems too. During August 1966, a statement by the 'Patriotic Front', the (allegedly) political wing of the FWA, came out publicly in favour of 'direct action' and the Front's secretary, Gethin ap Iestyn, claimed that the Front would soon be greater than Plaid Cymru.[29] That autumn, the party generally, and Gwynfor in particular, did all they could to silence them: he arranged for friends to write to the *Welsh Nation* on the topic; he fed stories to the Westgate gossip column in the *Western Mail*; there was even correspondence with A H Llewys, one of the Front's leaders,[30] and he arranged for Plaid's Youth Committee to have a word with the Front.[31]

But all his efforts were to no avail. The FWA and the Patriotic Front were delighted with the new interest shown in Welsh nationalism. Inevitably, the effect on Plaid Cymru was less welcome. The party's Deputy President, Tedi Millward, for instance, had to convince his relatives in England that Gwynfor was not the leader of a terrorist faction.[32] The press tended to believe every pronouncement by Cayo Evans and his colleagues, and the boys in the FWA had a grand time making the chapel-going members of Plaid Cymru squirm. Cayo Evans would often phone the press from pubs in the south of Ceredigion and tell them a pack of barefaced lies, only to see the same nonsense (such as the story of a plot to assassinate Cledwyn Hughes) in print in publications such as *Paris Match*.[33] These erroneous stories became something of an obsession for Gwynfor. But perhaps he had good reason to suspect some journalists as strongly as he did. As Chief Inspector F J Jones of Lampeter police put it: 'In Lampeter and amongst the majority of Welsh people they are objects of ridicule and ... cause for shame. They have been kept alive by the press.'[34]

The struggle against the FWA was also a waste of Gwynfor's valuable time and so opportunities for him to relax that summer were few and far between. The press was as eager for stories as ever; at the end of August, the BBC current affairs programme *Panorama* went to Carmarthen, and journalists arrived from Holland and the *Los Angeles Times* to interview Gwynfor in Llangadog.[35]

Local events also made demands on his time, and he became an expert in what he had once described to D J Williams as the 'summery social life of Carmarthenshire' – 'the shows, country fairs, sheepdog trials, carnivals'.[36] And as if that were not enough, the letters poured in – at the rate of around a hundred and fifty a week – some from constituents, others addressed to 'The Member for Wales' or 'The Unofficial Leader of Wales'. Gwynfor tried to work in the same way as he had done for decades. He himself would answer almost every phone call and letter, and he would never refuse an invitation to address a meeting. But within days of the Carmarthen victory, some colleagues were alarmed at his working methods. One of the first to speak out was Harri Webb, who wrote to Elwyn Roberts insisting that Gwynfor should ensure he did not become Plaid Cymru's first and last MP. He also wanted Gwynfor to cut back on his public activities: 'One of the few criticisms in the past was that he was too readily available. This is now no longer physically possible nor tactically desirable. Henceforward a sense of occasion must invest his appearances outside his own area.'[37] Gwynfor chose to ignore the advice and, in the same way, he ignored T I Ellis's suggestion that he needed a parliamentary secretary.[38] By the end of August, another warning reached him from Islwyn Ffowc Elis, who wrote to say that he and his friends were worried 'in case you push yourself too far'.[39] Emrys Roberts was even more blunt. He warned him that the challenge was not to emulate Dr Robert Macintyre, the SNP's first MP. 'His success,' Emrys Roberts wrote, 'and his subsequent failure and the failure of his party held back the SNP for 15 years.'[40] None of it did any good; Gwynfor would not delegate power or change his approach. It is also possible that he did not want to be a financial drain on his party as staff allowances were unavailable; in the meantime, the 'Help for Gwynfor' discussions went on for months, but in vain.[41] Throughout his time in Parliament, the only help he accepted came from Clem Thomas, who was appointed as a part-time assistant in the constituency. At home in Talar Wen, his daughter, Meleri Mair, also carried out secretarial work for him. Only very occasionally did she travel to London and even then, Gwynfor – without an office – and Meleri were forced to work at one of the benches.[42]

Gwynfor's decision to refuse help had a negative impact on his quality of life, but at least the party's organization was in better shape after the by-election. There was an awareness, as R Tudur Jones remarked, that Plaid Cymru faced an important question: how could it 'shake off those attitudes that were perfectly appropriate in its pioneering years – the amateurism, the tendency to sulk, the endless capacity to find fault with everyone except ourselves – and take itself seriously?'[43] It was decided that Tedi Millward would hold the fort while Gwynfor was in London, but there was an urgent need to professionalize the whole of Plaid Cymru's activities. Fortunately for Gwynfor and Tudur Jones, one of the most able party members of his generation was thinking along exactly the same lines. His name was Dafydd Wigley, a talented technocrat who was working at the time for Ford in Dagenham, Essex. There had been talk since 1965 of creating a 'think-tank' within Plaid Cymru, but no one had pursued the idea. On 12 August, however, Gwynfor received a letter from Dafydd Wigley outlining his scheme to create a Research Group for Plaid Cymru. In his letter, Dafydd Wigley noted that he had already spoken to two scientists who wanted to join him in the enterprise. The first was Dr Gareth Morgan Jones, who had recently returned from Canada; the second was the outstanding Dr Phil Williams of Clare College, Cambridge. They, he wrote, were eager to work jointly with him on two key projects for Gwynfor and Plaid Cymru. The first was to gather facts so that the party would have a ready answer when 'Mr Abse makes some dubious statement on the number of children who want education through the medium of Welsh'. The second was to come up with a system of recording political quotations.[44]

Gwynfor accepted the offer gratefully. Before long, the Research Group had snowballed, attracting talented members such as Eurfyl ap Gwilym, Keith Bush and Roderic Evans. Within a year, around fifteen of the party's brightest young people were meeting every Monday evening in Clerkenwell, south London, to offer vital policy assistance to Gwynfor and Plaid Cymru.[45] They would present their work to Gwynfor on Tuesday evenings and, for the first time since the death of D J Davies a decade earlier, Plaid Cymru at last had a team of economists who could formulate credible policies untouched by Saunders Lewis's influence.

Thus, when Gwynfor returned to Westminster, things were looking up, and for several months he made a big impression as a one-man band among more than 600 other members. With the help of the Research Group, he had come to the conclusion that the best tactic would be to fight a guerrilla war by asking countless questions on the state of Wales. At the time, Wales existed in a statistical vacuum, and he managed to force all sorts of entertaining and revealing figures out of the Wilson government. Gwynfor's enquiries drove the civil service to distraction but, at £14 a time, they were an effective way of reminding people that he had not been lost in the parliamentary crowd. By the end of his first year, he had asked over six hundred questions, subsequently published in three volumes – the *Black Books of Carmarthen*. The tactic was particularly effective during the months after the Aberfan disaster in October 1966. Armed with answers on the coal industry, Gwynfor was able to expose the shabby way in which the NCB and the Wilson government had treated the residents of the valleys. He accused Cledwyn Hughes, The Secretary of State for Wales, of concealing the truth about Aberfan – an accusation which led to heated exchanges.[46] He also acted on behalf of Cymdeithas yr Iaith Gymraeg and, by Christmas 1966, Gwynfor had earned a reputation as 'the stormy petrel of the Welsh benches' – so much so that David Rosser, political editor of the *Western Mail*, asserted that there was never a dull moment 'with Mr Evans in the House'.[47] Gwynfor took full advantage of this, portraying himself as a martyr – a stunt which served only to infuriate Labour members even more. In their eyes, he was a self-righteous prig, and before Christmas Alan Williams issued this warning from the Labour benches: 'If this is the level which he regards as rough, brutal and personal, he will find that his attempts to don the martyr's crown of thorns will not convince the public.'[48]

But Gwynfor was in his element by Christmas 1966. On a personal level, London was a little easier to bear and he had been accepted as a full member of the exclusive (and expensive) Reform Club which would be his home for the next three years.[49] But the most important thing for Gwynfor was the shape of politics back in Wales. Four months on from Carmarthen, many inside and outside Plaid believed that a permanent shift had occurred and that nationalism had begun to put down roots. Frequently, during Gwynfor's visits to Wales, people would turn out in their hundreds to hear him address a meeting. More striking still was the comparison between Labour and Plaid Cymru. As Plaid Cymru basked in its new popularity, the people of Wales turned against Labour. Aberfan became a symbol of that party's failure in the valleys, at a time when unemployment was at its highest since 1948. But the most conspicuous and encouraging aspect for nationalists were the problems Gwynfor was causing Cledwyn Hughes. In his previous post at the Commonwealth Office, Cledwyn Hughes had earned an enviable reputation as a first-class minister, but it was a different story at the Welsh Office.[50] As the cult around Gwynfor grew, Cledwyn Hughes was left in a vacuum: on the one hand, nationalists regarded him as a traitor; on the other, the unionist wing within Labour suspected that he was not doing enough to put the 'Nats' in their place.

The new year brought political changes every bit as dramatic as those of 1966. In January, Jo Grimond resigned as Liberal leader and Jeremy Thorpe succeeded him. Gwynfor hoped that this would split the Liberals.[51] But the main excitement for Plaid Cymru at the beginning of 1967 was the announcement of a by-election in the Rhondda – 'the most socialist valley in the world'. It was a gilt-edged opportunity, but despite the anticipation, Plaid Cymru reacted in a surprisingly listless manner. The sitting MP for Rhondda West, Iori Thomas, died three weeks before Christmas but it took an age before the nationalist campaign was anywhere near ready. Three days into the new year, Phil Williams refused the nomination, telling Gwynfor that he knew virtually nothing about the Rhondda: 'I've hardly been there.'[52] Wynne Samuel also refused it. Vic Davies, the eventual candidate, was the third choice by a significant margin. It was understandable that Plaid Cymru's organizer in the Rhondda, Cennard Davies, felt that he faced an impossible task as the campaign got underway in the biting winds of Clydach Vale.[53]

But as the month went by, there was a change. For one thing, Gwynfor's popularity was having a positive effect; in the middle of January, it was announced that three thousand copies of the first *Black Book* had been sold and, within three months, the party had to print a further five thousand.[54] Rhondda's economic woes also led people to predict great things for Plaid Cymru. Across the two valleys, about nine hundred men were unemployed – the highest percentage for five years. There was also a perception that the Welsh Office had delayed for months in choosing the site of the new Royal Mint. The two sites under consideration in Wales were Bridgend or Llantrisant, the latter being the clear favourite among those who lived in the Rhondda. Indeed, the readiness of civil servants at the Welsh Office even to consider Bridgend was seen in the Rhondda as an affront to their abilities and their economic situation. They were also angry at Cledwyn Hughes's attitude, believing him over-optimistic about the area's economic future. For Plaid Cymru, the icing on the cake was the undemocratic behaviour of some Labour councillors and their fondness for making decisions in private.

The local paper, the *Rhondda Leader*, was against Labour and by the beginning of February, there was something of the Carmarthen spirit in the air.[55] Gwynfor attended Vic Davies's adoption meeting on 11 February, and by then some within the party were starting to talk seriously about the possibility of winning the seat. The crowd that came to hear Gwynfor at Cwmparc Hall confirmed this. Although the candidate was fairly uninspiring, about 400 Rhondda people had come to the meeting in the belief that Plaid Cymru could win with Gwynfor at the helm. Gwynfor returned to Westminster leaving most of the campaign arrangements in the capable hands of the Research Group, but from London he did all he could to steer events. He asked a host of questions on mining issues in the hope of causing embarrassment to Harold Wilson, and when he came back to the Rhondda for the closing rally of the campaign, he could sense that the fire was burning more brightly still.[56] As in Carmarthen, Plaid Cymru hired a huge venue for the final meeting and, once again, the crowds flocked to it. On 8 March, the Park and Dare Hall in Treorchy was full to overflowing. The following day, there was better news still as Plaid Cymru came close to creating the greatest shock in Welsh political history, reducing a Labour majority of 16,888 to just 2,306 votes.

On that same evening, 9 March, the SNP performed noticeably well at a by-election in Glasgow Pollok, and although it did not take the seat (finishing third), the combined effect of the two results was electrifying. There was a third by-election that night, in Nuneaton, which also confirmed the general opinion that the tide was turning against Harold Wilson. But the main question for the press was whether nationalism had really established itself or not. Almost without exception, commentators regarded the Rhondda West result as a protest rather than a nationalist vote. *The Observer* said that Plaid Cymru and the SNP had now taken on 'the traditional Liberal role of safety-valve for people who want to let off steam'.[57] The *Rhondda Leader*'s interpretation was similar: suggesting that it was no coincidence that several ratepayers' and tenants' associations had been established in south Wales during the 'sixties, and noting that these, like Plaid Cymru, had benefited from dissatisfaction with the two main parties.[58] This was also a Welsh protest vote and, for the first time, Rhondda turned to Plaid Cymru and not to the Communists to express their frustration. But there was also a nationalist element to the Rhondda West result, particularly among the younger generation. It is no surprise that Gwynfor ignored the ambiguity of the result, and insisted in all his public statements that the Welsh had, at last, embraced nationalism and that the dawn which had broken over Carmarthen now shone its light into the darkest corners of the country. The goal from now on, he said, was for Plaid Cymru to win sufficient seats in the general election to form 'a party more like the Irish party than the House of Commons has known since 1918'.[59]

During the weekend of rugby that followed the Rhondda result, 'God Save the Queen' was drowned out at the Arms Park by shouts of 'Gwynfor, Gwynfor'. He returned to Westminster believing that 'Rhondda has confirmed Carmarthen in a remarkable way'.[60] And not without good reason. Some elements within Labour were in a panic, and Gwynfor was praised for developments over which he had no direct control. That week, Cledwyn Hughes announced that the government would not pursue its plan to build a new town in mid-Wales. The announcement pleased many Welsh MPs but the decision was ascribed to Gwynfor's influence.[61] Now at the height of his parliamentary powers, Gwynfor was courted by the Tories and, during March 1967, he was in contact with 'many' Conservative leaders on the topic of devolution. He had several conversations with Keith Joseph, after which Joseph would report back to Edward Heath, the Conservative leader. Gwynfor believed that Heath wanted to meet him (although there is no evidence that this ever happened) and he held similar talks on devolution with Enoch Powell, Quintin Hogg and Selwyn Lloyd.[62] More astonishing still, he claimed to D J Williams that George Thomas had approached him, his 'eyes like saucers' to say that Rhondda had changed his mind on devolution: 'Well Gwynfor boy, I must say I am deeply shocked. But the message is loud and clear. We will have to think again.'[63]

It is extremely difficult to believe that George Thomas meant what he said and the likelihood is that Gwynfor misinterpreted him, but whatever the truth, there was a widespread feeling that Plaid Cymru was dictating the political agenda in Wales and in Westminster. When it was announced that there would be no official opening ceremony at Clywedog, some papers like the *Liverpool Daily Post* decided that it was time to take the fight to Plaid Cymru.[64] The same paper wanted to see Jim Griffiths return to the fray, saying that he would have torn

Gwynfor and his twopenny-halfpenny claims apart if he were still in Cathays Park.[65] Some within Labour shared this sentiment; during March 1967, they concluded that there was nothing to be gained by sulking over Gwynfor and that it was time the gloves came off. The end of the month saw this new attitude in action: on the floor of the House, Gwynfor was described as a 'Neo-Nazi' by two prominent Labour members, Merlyn Rees and Ivor Richard.[66] At the beginning of April, the same spirit was at work in Carmarthenshire for the local elections. There, Labour published a leaflet quoting words it attributed to Cayo Evans: 'We must continue to have dedicated leadership to carry on the struggle. Military training and discipline will be tough. We are not revolutionaries and not a political group… recent by-elections have clearly illustrated our success.'[67] In the same leaflet, Labour asked whether Plaid Cymru's candidates supported Cayo Evans's statement or not. It was evident to Gwynfor that Labour wanted to denigrate Plaid Cymru and he was appalled when papers like the *Llanelli Star* delved into the matter in some detail.[68] 'Our alleged connection with the FWA,' he told Harri Webb, 'is the only thing that people in this county are concerned about in relation to Plaid.' Gwynfor also suspected that Cayo Evans was 'in London's pocket' but, without proof, it was impossible to strike back.[69]

To suggest that Plaid Cymru and the FWA were birds of a feather was a crude but highly effective tactic, and Plaid Cymru lost some ground in the local elections as a result. But, unquestionably, Labour's most artful manoeuvre to rein in Gwynfor concerned the Investiture of the Prince of Wales. Since July 1958, it was known that the Queen was to invest Prince Charles in Caernarfon; however, no date had been set. But after the Carmarthen by-election and the Aberfan disaster, the Welsh Office began to press for a swift investiture. Indeed, from December 1966 onwards, Cledwyn Hughes bothered Downing Street and Buckingham Palace for a definite date to such a degree that Harold Wilson had to tell him to calm down.[70] One can only imagine Hughes's joy, therefore, when it was announced on 17 May 1967 that the Investiture would go ahead on 1 July 1969.

In no time, Wales was celebrating the good news. Caradog Prichard wrote in the *Daily Telegraph* that the Investiture would be an opportunity for the Welsh to show that there were no 'divided loyalties' – despite the results in Carmarthen and Rhondda West.[71] I B Griffith, in his column in *Y Cymro*, was equally keen to celebrate the fact that 'a new member of the family is coming to Wales – is coming here to Caernarfon. We shall have a new son, and so let us show him and his mother and father what the family can do'.[72] With Welsh Wales frequently expressing such views, Gwynfor found himself facing a dilemma. Inevitably, the British and international press wanted to know how this Welsh 'rebel' would respond. On the day of the announcement, he confined himself to a bare statement that he was 'unenthusiastic' about the event.[73] But, crucially, Gwynfor (without consulting anyone else in the party) did not oppose the Investiture itself. One good reason – as he saw it – was fear that any outspoken opposition would alienate thousands of his natural supporters. Second, Plaid Cymru's constitutional policy of calling for Commonwealth status also made it clear that the party recognized the Crown. They were not republicans. Faced with such difficulties, Gwynfor sat himself comfortably on the political fence in the hope that remaining silent, as he had during the Coronation in 1953, would see him through.

It took a long time for the Labour-inspired pageantry to take effect, however. After Whitsun, Gwynfor returned to the Commons and his daily routine in good spirits. During the day, he would lay down his questions and contribute to debates before retreating to the Commons Library. There, having read a little and after dealing with his copious correspondence, he would repair to the Reform – unless he had been asked to address some meeting or other in London. It was a secluded life, but he could cope with loneliness. After all, his position of strength was a fair price to pay for the isolation of London. And the interest in him continued as his party now had a strong voice on matters as diverse as Europe (he voted against joining the European Economic Community) or the siting of the Royal Mint (which was located in Llantrisant rather than Bridgend or Scotland).[74] Eirene White, a Welsh Office minister, predicted a winter of discontent for the Wilson government in Wales.[75] Similarly, Cledwyn Hughes begged the Department of Transport to save the mid-Wales line from the Beeching axe because Gwynfor was in a position to provoke a 'dangerous' reaction.[76] Gwynfor was a winner on all counts – except one, perhaps.

It is one of the great paradoxes of Gwynfor's first period as an MP that the growth of nationalism between 1966 and 1967 damaged the argument for an elected body for Wales. Labour had been discussing the idea of such a body since 1965, commending the idea a year later. Those socialists who favoured devolution faced a difficult task but they were confident that they could carry it through.[77] Gwynfor's election, however, became a turning-point, undermining the aspirations of those like Cledwyn Hughes, Elystan Morgan and Gwilym Prys Davies. As Gwynfor fought and won his corner at Westminster, Labour's devolution champions found their position weakened. Comments like those made by Merlyn Rees and Ivor Richard in March 1967 became increasingly common as did the feeling that Gwynfor, to quote Leo Abse, was 'boring' with his incessant interventions from the opposition benches (where the Tories sat).[78] During these months, George Thomas's wing of the Labour Party chose to interpret all things Welsh (such as the elected council and the 1967 Language Act), as concessions to nationalism. There was a similar response in Carmarthenshire as well, where Labour councillors voted against establishing an elected council. In July 1967, the anti-devolutionists won the battle within the party and Cledwyn Hughes's dream of such a council was crushed. In political terms, Gwynfor had been responsible for destroying Cledwyn Hughes's credibility and invoking anti-devolutionist paranoia. It is supremely ironic that Gwynfor's success wrecked the case for devolution until 1973. But he, because of the apparent strength of Welsh nationalism, was blind to the development. At the time, he assumed that the growth of Plaid Cymru was so invincible that he would no longer need to rely on Labour to bring about a devolved Wales. This explains his tendency to mock devolutionists within the Labour Party; 'they', he said, 'have been belittled insufferably by the Government's recent actions'.[79]

Cledwyn Hughes and Elystan Morgan's position was further proof for Gwynfor that only Plaid Cymru could achieve devolution. With this in mind, he set about ridding his party of any elements such as the FWA which might harm his cause. During the spring and early summer of 1967, Gwynfor grew increasingly worried about the FWA and the Patriotic Front. What had happened during the local government elections of 1967 remained indelibly etched in his memory, and although he believed that most of them were 'harmless fools', he also suspected some of them 'more and more'.[80] He had also heard from Elwyn Roberts that the problem of the FWA was not confined to the south, and that canvassers across Wales had been cross-examined on the relationship between Plaid Cymru and the FWA. By July 1967, Gwynfor and Elwyn Roberts regarded the FWA as 'a hostile organisation' and Plaid Cymru consequently passed a resolution during the Eisteddfod at Bala calling for the expulsion of any party member who was also a member of the FWA or the Patriotic Front.[81] Owain Williams, the Tryweryn bomber, was the first to be thrown out and accused of dabbling with the FWA.

Despite the attention his case received that September, Gwynfor saw it as proof that his party had the ability to curb its unruly elements.[82] Similarly, he himself decided not to renew his membership of Cymdeithas yr Iaith Gymraeg saying, some years later, that he had done so because of the society's emphasis on direct action.[83]

It was easy enough to deal with the FWA. A large majority at conference passed a resolution to expel its members, but it proved harder to safeguard the gains made in Carmarthen. Although the number of new members continued to flourish, Gwynfor was worried that there was an 'urgent need' for more staff and offices – especially since the *Welsh Nation* was about to be re-launched again as a weekly.[84] These were not the party's only growing pains. By the summer of 1967, a clear gap had opened between the modernizers in the Research Group and some of the old guard. R Tudur Jones, for instance, expressed regret that there was no mention of Welsh history or 'inspirational lectures' in the summer school. He was sorry too that 'principles and philosophy' were seen as having no place.[85] There were palpable tensions too between new, non-Welsh-speaking members and old stagers like Kate Roberts. Some of the younger element complained to Emrys Roberts, who was back in Wales, that 'many of the older members of Plaid, and the old-fashioned ones, expect new members of Plaid to learn the language first'.[86] Gwynfor had to close this internal cultural rift as well as face external criticism. He was embarrassed by the decision of parents from Aberfan to criticize Plaid Cymru for what they described as the party's failure to ensure a fair share of the fund that had been collected for them. The row culminated in a demonstration in front of Cardiff Castle by parents carrying placards announcing 'Plaid Cymru Has Let Us Down' and 'Plaid Cymru Traitors to Aberfan Dead'.[87] This was a further incentive for Labour to attack Plaid Cymru. Just four days after Gwynfor had attempted to appease the parents of Aberfan, Cledwyn Hughes made his most aggressive speech ever about Plaid Cymru, accusing its leadership of encouraging militant nationalism and of using religion to lend its message an air of respectability. [88]

On top of all this, Gwynfor continued to push himself as relentlessly as ever. Over a period of three weeks in September 1967, he attended 31 meetings, which had an adverse effect on his health. Privately, his friends suggested that he looked awful during his television appearances and he was warned by Elwyn Roberts to reduce his workload.[89] But Roberts was whistling in the wind. Although

Gwynfor and Rhiannon managed a fortnight's holiday in Italy and Yugoslavia at the end of September, he would not change his way of working. If anything, his pace increased as the autumn of 1967 drifted into winter. By then, Gwynfor had to decide on one of the most difficult issues of his Presidency: Plaid Cymru's stance on the Investiture. From the outset, he knew that he would face pressure from both sides, with one faction calling for Plaid Cymru to ignore the whole thing and another wanting the party to announce a boycott. That summer, the latter group had been in the ascendancy and one of their young leaders, Dafydd Elis Thomas, had refused to stand for the Queen when 'God Save the Queen' was played at a graduation ceremony at the University College of North Wales, in Bangor. According to Elis Thomas, he always refused to stand in Wales 'because I do not acknowledge the Queen of England as being the Queen of my country'.[90] A similar protest was held by seven Aberystwyth students, and Cymdeithas yr Iaith Gymraeg announced that it would be 'boycotting the whole frivolous and hypocritical business'.[91]

Anti-royalist sentiments like these were increasingly prevalent within Plaid Cymru and – even worse for Gwynfor – this was a time when bombs were being planted in Wales. On the day after his visit to the Hamilton constituency in Scotland on 31 October, he wrote to Islwyn Ffowc Elis to share his worries. The basic problem, he said, was that prominent party members like Glyn James and Ted Merriman were already displaying 'bluntness' in their anti-royalist statements. What concerned him now, he continued, was that 'the younger element [would be] wilder' still. Within two years, he foresaw a situation where 'feeling will run high in favour of the Investiture' with 'jollity across Wales' and 'a week's tour for Charles' that would attract children to stand on the roadside 'in every county'. Equally worrisome was the prospect of Prince Charles spending a term at the University College of Wales, in Aberystwyth. Although he knew there was an obligation to make the Prince feel 'completely happy and at home', Gwynfor, as he confessed to Islwyn Ffowc Elis, was still unsure 'what instructions to give to party members there'.[92]

Over the coming days, Gwynfor thought hard about this crucial decision, while at the same time Welsh and Scottish nationalism adapted to these new, exciting times. As mentioned, Gwynfor spent three days in Scotland campaigning for the SNP and its candidate, Winnie Ewing, in the Hamilton by-election. She said that Gwynfor's contribution was 'a fantastic boost' for her and, on 2 November, she took the seat. It was interpreted as a victory for both Plaid Cymru and the SNP and the arrival of the fiery Winnie Ewing at Westminster was a source of comfort. On a personal level, the pair were remarkably loyal to each other; when Gwynfor spoke in the chamber, Winnie Ewing would go along to lend moral support. Gwynfor would return the favour when she faced the catcalls from the Labour benches. Indeed, the barracking she faced in the chamber was worse than that experienced by Gwynfor. More often than not, Winnie Ewing would be heckled when she opened her mouth in the chamber, and once described the experience of speaking in the Commons as a crucifixion. One Labour backbencher suggested to her that she should see a psychiatrist, while another went so far as to stalk her.[93] The Scottish press was wholly unsympathetic; in comparison, the *Western Mail* and the *Liverpool Daily Post* treated Gwynfor with unfailing courtesy. Without doubt, it was an unpleasant atmosphere and Winnie Ewing came to despise Parliament almost as much as Gwynfor did. However, Ewing was a solicitor who had served her apprenticeship in the insalubrious surroundings of the magistrates' courts in Glasgow and, as a consequence, had a steeliness that Gwynfor lacked. It was she, more than anyone, who taught him resolve, and together they managed to hold their own and present their efforts as a Celtic 'project' to solve 'a common problem, namely the English Government'.[94]

Even so, and despite the importance of Winnie Ewing's arrival at Westminster – from a both political and personal standpoint – the Investiture cast a shadow over Gwynfor. Two days after Winnie Ewing's victory, he finalised a crucial discussion document for the party executive that formed the basis for debating the Investiture. In it, he argued that the government had set a trap for Plaid Cymru and that the correct response was to 'play it cool'. The guiding principle for Gwynfor was what had happened after the arson at Penyberth, and the damage that had been caused to Plaid Cymru by boycotting the Coronation in 1937: 'All the good that had been done during the previous year was ruthlessly sacrificed and we were thrown back to a position of greater weakness than we had in 1935. We would be foolish indeed to repeat this kind of mistake now.'

Given this, he urged Plaid Cymru's leadership to do two things. The first was to be 'as quiet as possible'. The second was to turn the situation to its own advantage by insisting that the Prince should identify himself with Wales: 'It will be something to have a King of England who speaks Welsh.'[95] It was for this reason that Plaid Cymru allowed its Vice-President, Tedi Millward, to be a Welsh tutor to the Prince. The executive accepted the argument, and it is easy to understand why. Gwynfor was not the only one by any means who remembered how damaging the decision had been to boycott the Coronation and how apparently massive support for the party had evaporated back in 1936–37. Outside Plaid Cymru as well, there was widespread agreement about such an approach. It was, for instance, the view of Alwyn D Rees, charismatic editor of the Welsh monthly *Barn*, and many nationalists agreed with him, that Plaid Cymru should not get caught up in a row over the Investiture.[96] In the long term, however, Gwynfor's policy of studied equivocation proved unsustainable.

Political circumstances also guided Gwynfor's decision to avoid an unnecessary row. During November 1967, many observers believed that Labour was in a serious, if not terminal, crisis in Wales and Scotland. The *New Statesman* described events in Scotland as 'a forest fire certain to consume more'.[97] At the same time, Harold Wilson was being warned by Richard Crossman, Leader of the Commons, how unwise it would be to ignore the 'growing feeling that Wales and Scotland are not getting a fair deal from Whitehall'.[98] Serious discussion of devolution began at Cabinet level again, and the Conservatives in Scotland announced that they were in favour of devolving power – just three days after Winnie Ewing's victory.[99] The miners too were in militant mood and on 21 November the pound was devalued. All things considered, the Wilson government was in turmoil, and Gwynfor began to assert publicly that Plaid Cymru could win a majority of the parliamentary seats in Wales.[100] He also believed (despite the fate of Cledwyn Hughes's elected body) that it was now not a case of whether there would be a parliament for Wales but when.[101]

As the fire of nationalism threatened to consume everything in its path (and with talk of a possible by-election in Llanelli), Gwynfor felt sufficiently confident to undertake a controversial and highly dangerous visit to Vietnam over Christmas. The idea had been mooted in the summer of 1967, and the original, rather vague, scheme had been for Gwynfor to travel there as part of a humanitarian delegation to work in a hospital or as a labourer on a building site. His simple and idealistic goal was to 'do something about the situation rather than talk about it'.[102] But from the outset, there were serious problems with the arrangements being made by his old colleague from the Tryweryn period, the Reverend Michael Scott. Despite months of trying, it proved impossible to secure visas and some of the prospective travellers began to have second thoughts – the most prominent of these being the rugby coach, Carwyn James. Gwynfor was also under enormous pressure to withdraw. His friends feared for his personal safety, and some were convinced that he would be killed. Indeed, the concern was such that Islwyn Ffowc Elis and other Plaid Cymru supporters in Carmarthen wrote a newsletter imploring him to stay at home.[103] The second reason for seeking to postpone the trip was Plaid Cymru's image, and the fear that such a venture would confirm the caricature of the 'Member for Wales' – the absentee member who neglected his constituency to go on globetrotting missions. There was also some concern on the right wing of Plaid Cymru, where it was feared that the party could be accused of supporting communism were the visit to go ahead.[104]

The discussion rambled on for months, but Gwynfor was adamant. Although he believed (according to his son, Dafydd) that he might be killed, he was convinced that going to Vietnam was consistent with Plaid Cymru's pacifist, anti-imperialist principles.[105] The government, too, saw the visit as vaguely useful and Bill Rodgers, a Foreign Office minister, hoped that Gwynfor could use his influence to make enquiries in Hanoi, the capital of North Vietnam, about William Wallis, a British businessman who had gone missing there.[106] On 3 January 1968, Gwynfor and his 25 companions set off for Phnom Penh, the Cambodian capital, hoping to pick up visas there before going on to Hanoi. In Phnom Penh, however, they were disappointed to learn that they could not obtain the necessary visas because the situation was so dangerous there. Meanwhile, Gwynfor and Michael Scott had to content themselves with a visit to Prince Sihanouk, the President of Cambodia. Gwynfor used the rest of his time in the country to investigate the humanitarian situation there. He put a brave face on things, but there was no doubt that the journey was a political failure. Vietnam proved elusive and the Labour Party in Carmarthenshire revelled in Gwynfor's discomfort. Its prospective candidate for the seat, Gwynoro Jones, believed that Gwynfor had made a huge misjudgement. Reports spoke of miners in the Gwendraeth Valley laughing out loud when they heard about prayer meetings at Providence chapel, Llangadog, for Gwynfor's safe return.[107]

Gwynoro Jones attacked him with gusto, mocking the trip as a 'non-event' because he had failed to reach Hanoi. And Gwynoro Jones was not the only one who thought Gwynfor had made a terrible mistake.[108] When Gwynfor returned to Wales, Plaid Cymru's area committee in Carmarthenshire officially censured him. Their minutes show they decided to 'have a word with the MP not to take on too many invitations outside the constituency during these next 18 months, and to devote more time to his own constituency. Everyone was concerned that the MP had to be MP for Wales as well as for Carmarthen'.[109] Gwynfor did himself further harm on his return when he suggested that the NLF, or Vietnamese communists, were fighting a similar battle to that fought by Plaid Cymru.[110] The response to a fund set up by Plaid Cymru to pay for the trip was also poor – much to Elwyn Roberts's chagrin.[111]

But Gwynfor faced an even trickier financial problem on his return – again, partly of his own making. Since the middle of 1967, Plaid Cymru had been discussing the possibility of setting up its own printing press and Gwynfor believed he had found the perfect solution. On a train journey, Gwynfor met an entrepreneur called Brian Kelly, a printer who made promises about a possible partnership with Plaid Cymru. The deal, in short, was this: Plaid Cymru would invest in a press on the understanding that he, Kelly, could use it when time allowed. On paper, it looked like a good bargain and in June 1967 Gwynfor travelled to Bromley in Kent to see Kelly's 'amazing' printing presses in action.[112] As a result, Plaid Cymru and its backers poured £10,000 into the partnership, but unbeknown to Gwynfor and his party, Brian Kelly was not all he seemed.[113]

By the time of Gwynfor's return from Vietnam, it was obvious that Plaid Cymru had still not got the measure of Brian Kelly. The basic problem was that Kelly had used a lot of the money invested in the new company, Gwasg Cymru, to support his own business.[114] Elwyn Roberts was livid, describing the mess to Islwyn Ffowc Elis in these terms: 'We're in deep trouble with Brian Kelly and the press.'[115] But rightly or wrongly, Kelly believed that he had the right to invest money that was lying idle. That in itself was sufficient embarrassment to Gwynfor but, to make matters worse, Emrys Roberts was drawn into the row. He argued that the best way of resolving the situation and defending Plaid Cymru's interests was through co-operation with Brian Kelly. Emrys Roberts also agreed with Kelly's central argument that he had a legal right to invest money resting in the account.[116] During April 1968, Emrys Roberts gave editorial assistance to Gwasg Cymru to publish an unofficial magazine called *Free Nation*, using pieces intended for the *Welsh Nation*. There was a print run of 6,000 copies, but only around 50 were distributed – a messy conclusion which also confirmed many of Emrys Roberts's pretty legitimate doubts about the whole venture. The partnership between Kelly and Emrys Roberts was short-lived and ended abruptly.[117] Looking back at the fiasco, Islwyn Ffowc Elis regretted a situation that could easily have been avoided: 'A lot of good Plaid members have lost money and the whole thing has shaken the movement.'[118]

The Brian Kelly crisis came at a time of considerable political change. Internationally, 1968 was a year of violent upheaval; from Grosvenor Square in London to Paris and the University of Berkeley in California, there were protests and challenges to the status quo, and Wales was no exception. Indeed, nationalism came of age in Wales. From January 1968 on, Cymdeithas yr Iaith began to behave in a more militant fashion over the Investiture as a reaction to the preparations made by the Croeso [Welcome] '69 committee. Gareth Miles, the society's chair, promised a series of protests against the Prince. Plaid Cymru's youth wing was also keen to show its teeth and Dafydd Elis Thomas, its chair, offered this advice to the Prince: 'If you don't want to make a fool of yourself in the greatest farce of Welsh history, don't come to Caernarfon in 1969 – but go back to Cambridge, Charlie boy. Wales has her own leaders and destiny now.'[119] In the same vein, the youth wing's members took their lead from their chair's colourful remarks and displayed car stickers proclaiming 'Parliament not Prince'.

Little by little the political climate in Wales was changing. The correspondence columns of the *Liverpool Daily Post* crackled with dire warnings that Cymdeithas yr Iaith would split Wales in two. The Gittins Report, calling for more bilingualism in schools, raised the temperature too. But the two major events of 1968, which between them transformed Gwynfor's first term in parliament, were the increasing number of explosions, and the decision to sack Cledwyn Hughes as Secretary of State on 5 April. That date marked a turning point in Gwynfor's parliamentary career because Cledwyn Hughes was succeeded by the very different figure of George Thomas. In a sense Gwynfor and George Thomas had quite a lot in common: they were both convinced pacifists, Christians and teetotallers. And when Gwynfor first went to Parliament, George Thomas had written to ask whether he wished to join the Christian Fellowship. But George Thomas also had a vindictive, uncharitable side to his character. According to Richard Crossman, a fellow member of the Cabinet, George Thomas considered Cledwyn Hughes's Welsh version of Labourism to be 'sheer treason'.[120] From his first day, George Thomas did all he could to undermine Gwynfor with a mixture of malice and talent – the weaponry of the most controversial figure ever to serve as Secretary of State for Wales.

Gwynfor and his party were slow to respond to the new threat. On the contrary, Gwynfor chose to concentrate on Cledwyn Hughes's 'failure' and on Elystan Morgan's decision to accept a post as a Home Office minister.[121] Plaid Cymru's continuing success was also a source of satisfaction. At the end of the month, he addressed huge public meetings in Cardiff and Monmouth. He was also cheered when Keith Joseph told him that he was about to present 'a report to Edward Heath' on all the discussions the pair had held.[122] He also met William Whitelaw, the Conservative Chief Whip, and concluded that 'the Tories are now willing to think seriously in terms of a Welsh Parliament'.[123] Similarly, he was excited by a meeting with a tycoon with Plaid sympathies called Lord Arwyn. He was a friend of Harold Wilson, but he also told Gwynfor that he wanted 'to become the Plaid Cymru representative in the Lords'. Gwynfor interpreted this as a sure sign of public support, even though nothing tangible came out of the discussions.[124]

In electoral terms, Gwynfor was overly-confident. During April 1968, he shared a platform for the first time with the Labour prospective parliamentary candidate in Carmarthen, Gwynoro Jones. By that time Gwynoro Jones was doing his utmost to regain the seat for Labour, and spent his time visiting dozens of fairs and carnivals. His activities had been well known since the summer of 1967, but Gwynfor did not take him seriously and this proved to be a costly mistake. As he described him to a friend, Ioan Bowen Rees: 'He is utterly self-confident and painfully "big" and self-important (26 years old), a gifted tub-thumper. So, the best way to deal with him is to get people to laugh at him.'[125] With that in mind, Gwynfor suggested to Ioan Bowen Rees that he should write a satirical letter to the local press attacking his young opponent's boastfulness. On another occasion, Gwynfor drew up a letter (sent to the press under the name of 'a young well-wisher from Llandovery') criticizing Gwynoro Jones and drawing attention 'to grammatical errors that pepper his language and to blatant examples of his unintentional humour. The only thing to do with Gwynoro is to laugh at him. He thinks as highly of himself as do Goronwy Roberts or Harold Wilson. He preaches with the Methodists, and I heard that he began a sermon twice by saying "My name is Gwynoro Jones and I have a degree in economics."'[126] For his own part, Gwynoro Jones could not stomach Gwynfor, seeing him not so much as a saint as a self-satisfied, self-righteous politician. Gwynoro Jones also believed that Gwynfor was only too ready to lead the young to prison while he, the respectable politician, risked nothing.[127]

Gwynfor paid dear for his miscalculation, but both he and his party also suffered as a result of heightened fears about home-grown Welsh terrorism. Although Labour were stumbling from one problem to the next, pit closures and the removal of the tip at Aberfan, the explosions came as something of a salvation for the party. On 25 May 1968, a bomb went off at the Welsh Office in Cardiff and a second device was found, two days later, at the Vyrnwy reservoir. It prompted George Thomas to make his infamous accusation that the nationalists had created a monster they could not control. This, without doubt, was George Thomas's most successful assault. But rather than condemn the use of violence and move on, Gwynfor made matters worse by suggesting that those responsible were agents provocateurs acting on the orders of the security forces. Gwynfor did so despite Dafydd Orwig's wise words warning him that he should not suggest that there was any such organized planning behind the blasts. Gwynfor ignored the advice, and continued to make serious accusations without a shred of evidence.[128] For instance, his response to the *Liverpool Daily Post* after the Welsh Office blast was: 'There are a number of possibilities, one of which is that they are the work of the Secret Service who want to do the maximum damage to Plaid Cymru. This sounds fantastic but should not be ruled out.'[129]

The matter did not end there. On 27 May, Gwynfor was blamed by George Thomas on the floor of the House for implicity encouraging the bombers and for being utterly inconsistent: 'On the last occasion when a man was found guilty and sentenced, the Hon. Member for Carmarthen issued leaflets outside the court in which he said: "Although we do not agree with the action they have taken, we cannot condemn them"'. Gwynfor tried to answer but his voice was drowned out, and the press in Wales condemned him.[130] In the *Caernarvon and Denbigh Herald*, it was suggested that he had read too many books on espionage, while his comments were called 'ridiculous' by the *South Wales Voice*.[131] But George Thomas did not escape unscathed either, and the *South Wales Echo* asked, quite reasonably, 'Who emerges as the saddest figure after the recriminations, Mr Gwynfor Evans or Mr George Thomas? Take your pick.'[132] George Thomas was advised by the *Liverpool Daily Post* to shut up but, by then, the Welsh Secretary was being congratulated by Gwynfor's opponents in Carmarthenshire on his excellent work.[133] Loti and Douglas Rees Hughes, two Labour stalwarts in the county, wrote to George Thomas to express their admiration for 'your great courage in tackling Gwynfor Evans in the House about his frequent utterings in the past which were so irresponsible and merely condoning these acts of violence which must give Wales a bad name. He refused categorically to condemn these people during the Tryweryn episodes'.[134]

Encouraged by the support for Thomas, it became Labour policy to claim that Plaid Cymru had created the conditions in which terrorism could thrive. Indeed, Gwynoro Jones suggested to George Thomas that it would be no bad thing to make capital out of Plaid Cymru's alleged links with the bombers. Under the heading 'Suggestions', Gwynoro Jones listed three items for George Thomas to consider:

> 1 – The continual emphasis of the Nationalists on the 'London' or 'English' Government does create the wrong atmosphere. Such emotive words do not help.
>
> 2 – Use of statements like 'freeing' Wales also lends itself to various interpretations. Especially the words used by Gwynfor Evans after he returned from Cambodia – comparing the NLF to Plaid Cymru 'fighting' for self-government.
>
> 3 – Emphasize that in early 60's there was a definite silence from the Nationalist leaders regarding condemning bomb outrages.[135]

The pronouncements of George Thomas and other Labour politicians did Plaid Cymru untold harm, and it is certain that Welsh nationalism would have been more successful between 1966 and 1970 had it not been for the constant insinuations that the party was, in some indefinable way, responsible for the bombings. The best example of the damage caused happened during the Caerphilly by-election in July 1968. In a sense, these were still heady times for Gwynfor and his party and the campaign had the potential to be 'crucial'.[136] As it began, he addressed a meeting in the constituency with a crowd of 600 supporters present. It was an excellent beginning, arguably better than his experiences in the Rhondda and Carmarthen. The only 'small worry' in Gwynfor's mind was a tendency for the Plaid Cymru candidate, Phil Williams, to be 'so presumptious'.[137] But presumptious or not, young people appeared to be flocking to the party. In Francis Street, Bargoed, the very street where Morgan Phillips, the former general secretary of the Labour Party had been brought up, there were 14 Plaid Cymru posters in the windows.[138] Plaid Cymru, to quote Neil Kinnock, was like 'Hell on Wheels' and Phil Williams came within 1,874 votes of winning the seat.[139]

The result was certainly a boost to Plaid Cymru and even Gwilym Prys Davies feared that Plaid Cymru was now being seen as 'a prophet of justice in the growth areas of the 19th century, a defender of homes and wages, young people and society'.[140] But for all the amazing support, even more might have voted for Plaid Cymru were it not for the bomb blasts and the fact that the campaign had been fought against the backdrop of the greatest campaign of terrorist violence that Wales had ever witnessed. According to the *South Wales Echo*, there were those who believed Plaid Cymru was somehow involved.[141] Worse still was the story doing the rounds in Caerphilly, according to Islwyn Ffowc Elis, Plaid Cymru's publications director, 'that one of Gwynfor's sons is leading the terrorists'.[142] Islwyn Ffowc Elis had no idea how to fight the accusation, and Gwynfor found the whole thing 'terribly' worrying.[143]

For a while, the storm between Gwynfor and George Thomas abated before reigniting in an unlikely location – at that year's National Eisteddfod in Barry. The Gorsedd of Bards managed to upset very many people by electing George Thomas a member, thereby preventing Gwynfor from being President of the Day in his home town. The Eisteddfod Council's argument was that no politician should receive any such honour because it might force them to choose between candidates if more than one were nominated. Worse still, it was Gwynfor's parents who had donated the Crown that year and Plaid Cymru suspected 'an underhand conspiracy' to keep Gwynfor away.[144] It is doubtful whether this was the case, but it was certainly a petty and shabby way to treat a family who had done so much to support all things Welsh in the town. The Archdruid, Gwyndaf, was obliged to apologize publicly for the slight which Gwynfor, 'the most brilliant of Barry's recent sons', had suffered. The apology was well meant, but did little to satisfy anyone or cool tempers.[145]

As the day of the ceremony to install George Thomas approached, the police grew increasingly concerned for the Secretary of State's security on the Eisteddfod field itself. Indeed, so great was the concern that Gwyndaf visited Talar Wen to discuss the matter. He warned Gwynfor that 'a major incident' could do untold damage to the Eisteddfod but that cancelling George Thomas's visit would be even more detrimental. At Gwyndaf's request, Gwynfor agreed to walk alongside George Thomas across the Eisteddfod field. On the day itself, there were 60 policemen in uniform on duty, not to mention secret service agents, as George Thomas entered the lions' den. Even these exceptional precautions did not do much to allay the Welsh Secretary's fears and, as he stood at the entrance to the field, George Thomas confessed to Gwynfor that his knees were 'like jelly'. But the arrangements went smoothly; the pair walked between a phalanx of police officers and the crowd of 50 who had gathered to heckle him was utterly 'baffled'.[146] As they came in sight of the pavilion, George Thomas whispered to his mother: 'It's all right, Mam, Gwynfor is with me.'[147] Some days afterwards, Gwyndaf wrote to Gwynfor to thank him: 'It would have been pointless to appeal for peace without your presence... I am sure that you saved the day on the Field, and scored a fantastic "try" in the process.'[148]

It was a particularly generous gesture from Gwynfor given George Thomas's less than welcoming attitude towards him during his first parliamentary term. The act also succeeded in distracting some attention from an interview Saunders Lewis gave to the BBC in which he said that the only language the 'English Government' understood was 'violence'.[149] But the peace that had reigned during the Eisteddfod was short-lived. After a summer school that Gwynfor judged 'excellent' (discussing how to finance a Free Wales), political life slipped back into its familiar pattern.[150] On 9 September, a bomb exploded at Pembrey, injuring an airman called William Houghton. As expected, Plaid Cymru was roundly condemned for fostering an atmosphere in which violence could thrive. Jim Griffiths, the Labour MP for Llanelli, led the assault: 'If the leaders of Plaid Cymru continue to use such emotive terms as "the London Government" or "the English" or to refer to their opponents as "enemies of Wales", they will reap the whirlwind of Nationalist frenzy.'[151] George Thomas suggested that the explosion was the direct legacy of the fire at Penyberth, and that evening both the BBC (*Week In Week Out)* and ITV (*News at Ten)* broadcast pictures of Saunders Lewis to accompany their reports.[152] It was a familiar accusation, but, this time, a difficult situation was exacerbated by Saunders Lewis and his supporters who expressed total sympathy with violence. On 10 September, Denis Tuohy, presenter of the *24 Hours* programme, asked R O F Wynne whether he would be willing to plant a bomb for Wales. His answer was unambiguous: 'Well, I am getting a bit old for that sort of thing; but I suppose if I felt that it was my duty and that it was necessary, I would have to pull up my socks and do something.'[153]

Saunders Lewis was thrilled when he heard about Wynne's comments and wrote to him to congratulate him on his 'courageous speech'. Plaid Cymru's leadership was less appreciative.[154] Elwyn Roberts asked the BBC for a transcript of the interview; meanwhile, Roberts revealed to Gwynfor that several members of the party had contacted him asking for R O F Wynne to be expelled.[155] There is no doubt that Gwynfor would have been well rid of Wynne, but Elwyn Roberts chose not to reveal that the Plaid Cymru leadership had also received a series of letters imploring the party not to throw him out. One such correspondent was Dafydd Iwan, a leading Cymdeithas yr Iaith activist, who wrote to Elwyn Roberts to argue that the party should 'recognize that an act of violence against property may be a huge fillip for the nationalist cause – under certain circumstances… If he were expelled, it would be a triumph for some in the BBC who want to tear Plaid apart. It would also open the way for scores of Plaid's most faithful members to consider their position, and maybe leave the ranks'.[156] Lewis Valentine wrote in a similar vein to say that he could see 'nothing offensive' in Wynne's ideas.[157] Gwynfor and the party were in a difficult situation and the leadership concluded, after extensive discussion, that it would be impossible to expel Wynne. The Investiture, and the need to avoid unnecessary schisms, made R O F Wynne's situation more delicate still. A week on from the row over Wynne's remarks, the leadership had to seek the approval of conference for its policy of ignoring the Investiture. They did so with some skill, and a resolution calling on Plaid Cymru to disassociate itself from the event was left on the table – but only after emotional speeches by D J Williams and Wynne Samuel.[158] By not having a policy, Gwynfor could maintain party unity and sidestep the tensions that were the undoing of so many other organizations during 1968 – from the Urdd to the Congregationalist Union.

His efforts to control Saunders Lewis during the autumn of 1968 were less successful. The party had already had to beg its ex-leader not to publish an article in the July issue of *Barn* calling for 'responsible violence' in the Dulas valley, then being eyed by the Severn Water Authority.[159] The leadership panicked when it heard about the proposed article and Elwyn Roberts asked Lewis Valentine and D J Williams to bring pressure to bear on Saunders Lewis not to publish in order to avoid a 'split'.[160] Lewis Valentine and D J Williams refused Elwyn Roberts's request, and D J Williams went so far as to assert that the piece would be of benefit to the nationalist cause. In the event, after all the agonizing, the article, to Gwynfor's relief, did not appear. However, Saunders Lewis showed no signs of holding back in the October issue of *Barn*, in which launched a vitriolic attack on Gwynfor's pacifism and blamed him for what he saw as the failures of Tryweryn and Clywedog. The truth of the matter, he said, was that 'Plaid's pointlessness in the Commons and its reverence for England's "constitution" are leading it to its quiet demise'. Damning words, but there was worse to follow. Saunders Lewis went on to say – not for the first time: 'You cannot make an omelette without breaking eggs. Telling the Welsh people that self-government will come through painless voting... is self-deception and an untruth.' The only way forward, he continued, was to make the process of governing Wales 'too expensive and too liable to provoke anger and mockery across the world to continue'.[161] Even by Saunders Lewis's standards, this was a remarkably unguarded outburst and by then the party's former President openly wondered whether Plaid Cymru would expel him. That was never going to happen, but Plaid Cymru was forced to take the highly unusual step of criticizing him publicly for raising the issue 'thereby playing into the hands of its opponents'.[162]

From a political point of view, Saunders Lewis's intervention was unfortunate because it undermined the credibility of a letter Gwynfor had just sent to the Home Secretary Jim Callaghan, calling for the FWA to be proscribed and for an inquiry into the possibility that the government was using agents provocateurs in Wales. In the same letter, Gwynfor accused the government of having 'a political interest in ascribing the explosions to the Welsh Nationalists or to Welsh extremists'.[163] As expected, the suggestion of a conspiracy provoked a furious response from the Home Secretary, and Callaghan's reply spoke of 'ridiculous allegations and no one who is of sober judgement would believe them'.[164] The press concurred, and by making the suggestion without any evidence Gwynfor had only managed to make matters much worse for himself. The accusation of an organized conspiracy also harmed the fragile relationship he had with Labour MPs. A few days after Callaghan's reply, Gwynfor suffered the most sustained attack ever made on him in Parliament. For over six hours during a Welsh debate in October 1968, he was forced to sit in the Commons chamber and listen to endless criticism of his party's inability to control Welsh terrorist activity. By this time, the lack of respect for him on the Labour benches was palpable and some, like the Aberdare MP, Arthur Probert, rushed to congratulate George Thomas for having dismissed 'the infantile utterings of the Hon. Member for Carmarthen, whom I regard, because of his presence in the chamber, as a disgrace to Welsh public opinion'.[165]

The situation did not improve when Gwynfor claimed that he knew who was responsible for one of the blasts. In November 1968, evidence came to light to suggest that a member of the RAF had planted the Pembrey bomb. Gwynfor's source was the young man's vicar, who told him that he had confessed to the action and that he was now being held in a secure psychiatric facility at an RAF hospital. At Gwynfor's request, the legendary detective Jock Wilson, who was in charge of the investigation, came to see him at Talar Wen to discuss the matter. Gwynfor gave Wilson all the details he had, even showing him the vicar's letter, but his efforts were to no avail. Nevertheless Gwynfor persisted in believing that he was right and asked George Thomas to explain in the Commons why the government continued to claim that Welsh nationalists had planted the bomb. George Thomas retorted that the whole thing was 'a monstrous slur' and that the young man in question had already been found not guilty.[166] Following this, the vicar wrote to Gwynfor again repeating his assertion. Whatever the truth of the matter, the unpleasant fact remained that Gwynfor had accused the government of conspiracy on very flimsy evidence.

More astonishing still, the KGB, the Soviet Union's secret police, began to take an interest in Welsh politics and the claims made by Gwynfor. It appears that some KGB spies planned to plant a bomb, set to explode on the eve of the Investiture, on the road between Porthmadog and Caernarfon. Had 'Operation Edding' gone ahead, the Soviets would have sent a letter to Gwynfor warning him that M15 was responsible in the hope that he would then challenge the secret service in Britain. The Soviets' longer-term hope was that this would lead to wider criticism by nationalists like Gwynfor of the way the British secret police operated. Fortunately for Gwynfor (and for the KGB perhaps), the absurd scheme was never implemented because it was considered too dangerous. The details of the plot were not revealed until 1999 when they were discovered deep in the KGB's archives in Moscow.[167]

By the end of 1968, Gwynfor had come to detest the House of Commons, and found little comfort or inspiration in his parliamentary isolation. The bombs worried him, as well as the belief that British secret services were targeting him by attempting to draw him into a sex scandal. On more than one occasion as he walked through parks in London, beautiful young women would try to talk to him.[168] It is impossible to say whether this was merely paranoia on Gwynfor's part, but his concern about 'honeytraps' was a sign of the times. Devolution under Labour appeared as distant as ever, and the announcement that there would be a commission on the constitution made little impression on Gwynfor or his party. The only faint hope, as far as he could see, was the Conservative Party and Keith Joseph's mention in 'very brief, telegraphic notes' that the party was drawing up a policy for Wales. But such glimpses of a brighter future were rare. Another year's work lay ahead of Gwynfor in Westminster, that 'dreadful place', and he longed to return from London to 'life in Carmarthenshire and Wales'. He had, he told Ioan Bowen Rees, had enough and longed for civilized company: 'If there were a few like-minded people about it might be different, but the most friendly ones are "noblemen friends", and there are some from Wales here who make you look over your shoulder wherever you go and whatever you do.'[169]

But things did not improve. 1969 was even more furious on the political front than 1968. On New Year's Day, Cymdeithas yr Iaith embarked on a roadsigns campaign that would come close to painting the whole of Wales green. It was a messy campaign for an important principle but an unpopular one too, and many in Wales considered Gareth Miles and Dafydd Iwan to be unprincipled vandals. At the same time, the preparations for and against the Investiture continued apace throughout January 1969, polarizing Wales more than ever. In Carmarthenshire, 'a first class programme of events' was promised as part of the '69 Welcome;[170] while some nationalists threatened to stand against Plaid Cymru in the forthcoming general election because of its willingness to 'compromise' on the Investiture.[171] By the end of the month, four Aberystwyth students were on hunger strike as a protest against the arrival of the Prince of Wales at the College by the Sea.[172]

The dual effect of these developments was to force the Welsh, especially Welsh-speakers, to choose whether they wanted George Thomas's Wales or the Wales of J R Jones, the most articulate voice of those who opposed the Investiture. Gwynfor was appalled at the predicament and thought privately that J R Jones was doing 'great harm to the nationalist cause' by speaking 'as if the Crown represents the main threat to Welsh existence'. His philosophy, he told Pennar Davies some years after the Investiture, was the product of 'a lack of balance' that led to 'follies'.[173] But follies or not, Wales stood at a crossroads, and Gwynfor faced one of the most difficult decisions of his life. He had already decided that he would not go to Caernarfon; now, he had to consider whether he would meet the Prince in Carmarthen as part of the tour of Wales after the Investiture.

Plaid Cymru's leadership was divided on the issue. Some, like Tudur Jones and

Dafydd Orwig, thought it wisest for Gwynfor to meet the Prince in Carmarthen since he would be doing so as part of his function as an MP, and not as part of the Investiture. Another faction disagreed, including Robyn Léwis, who warned Gwynfor that Owain Williams (the Tryweryn bomber) might stand against the party in a general election were 'the party [to be seen] compromising too much with the Establishment'. He was, he told Gwynfor, alarmed to see so many people in Gwynedd at the rally opposing the Investiture: 'Not young people by any means. Middle-aged ones and older ones as well. Teachers, preachers, lawyers, doctors, businessmen, lorry drivers, labourers and so on.'[174]

It was a particularly tough call for Gwynfor. This, as he warned back in 1967, was the trap that had been set for Welsh nationalism. On the one hand, he knew that 'several young people' whom he respected would be 'displeased' if he were to meet the Prince. At the same time, he knew that staying away could 'create ill feeling… that could adversely effect the result of the next election'. There were other considerations too, as he pointed out to Elwyn Roberts. It was necessary, he said, 'to distinguish between the Investiture itself and the tour through the country that follows'. The problem that was likely to arise were the Queen to visit Carmarthen in future also needed to be discussed. Courtesy was also important to Gwynfor because Charles was 'a distinguished visitor' and he was worried that not meeting him would be 'a personal affront to him'. Gwynfor in this respect remembered the way in which the Congress Party in India drew a distinction between a royal individual and the institution of royalty.[175]

Having weighed up the arguments, Gwynfor decided during February 1969 that he had no choice other than to meet the Prince when he came to Carmarthen. It remained his strategy throughout the Investiture – gaining some advantage for the nationalist movement by treating the Prince with respect while not supporting the event. It was a dangerous strategy but the situation could have been far worse. His positive relationship with Dafydd Iwan, chair of Cymdeithas yr Iaith, proved crucial at the time, and Dafydd Iwan himself was given an undertaking by Gwynfor that he would do all he could to ensure 'support among Welsh nationalists'.[176] Gwynfor believed the society could 'do splendid work' although he did not feel 'completely happy' with its decision to interfere 'in the Investiture issue'.[177] But despite this understanding with Dafydd Iwan, there were many in Cymdeithas yr Iaith who were very unhappy with Plaid Cymru's policy of studied indifference. The most fluent was Gareth Miles, a cerebral radical who thought, with good reason, that Gwynfor was a fence-sitter.[178]

Strangest of all was the situation in Aberystwyth where the former vice-president of Plaid Cymru, Tedi Millward, was the Prince's Welsh tutor for a term – a golden opportunity, as Gwynfor saw it, to steep the heir to the throne in Welsh sensibility. Before Charles reached Aberystwyth, Gwynfor had contacted Tedi Millward to discuss language laboratories and, following a visit in March 1969, Gwynfor was convinced that the Prince could learn the language proficiently in six weeks.[179] Charles arrived in Aberystwyth on 20 April and, as he settled in, Gwynfor wrote to Tedi Millward again, offering a work schedule for the Prince:

> As well as providing your friend with financial, economic and political facts about Wales, it would be a good idea to interest him in its history. In particular, it would be good for him to know something about the efforts of some of the leaders who were true princes in the past. Visits to places of interest, especially if they are in romantic places will help I think. For instance, I wonder whether he has seen Strata Florida where Dafydd ap Gwilym is buried. If he went there with you he could learn a little about the history of our literature and could travel on to Tregaron, home to the monument of Henry Richard who is associated with so much of our recent past as well as being home to Twm Siôn Cati and many of the cultured drovers.[180]

To the extent that it is possible to turn the heir to the Crown into a nationalist, Gwynfor and Tedi Millward's efforts (along with the other Plaid-supporting tutor, Bobi Jones) had some effect. The arch-royalist commentator John Eilian was infuriated at seeing the Prince among a nest of nationalists in the Welsh Department at Aberystwyth. He judged it 'most irresponsible'; George Thomas was angrier still, complaining to Harold Wilson about the underhand way in which the Aberystwyth nationalists were ramming their ideas down Charles's throat.[181] There is some evidence that this happened. Half way through Charles's time at Aberystwyth, Tedi Millward wrote to Gwynfor to provide a confidential report on the Prince's education. Millward commented on his royal pupil as follows: 'His mind is completely free of the political clichés that enslave our "friends" in other parties and there is already considerable common ground between us.' Millward also thought that 'his views on the Welsh language are completely sound; he maintains that it should not be a political issue and that no one should make political capital out of it. He told me that he feels increasingly nationalistic the more he hears talk of internationalism and large units. Today, he received the three *Black Books* and the *Voice of Wales* and the water pamphlet – "I'd better hide them, or people will think I've joined Plaid Cymru". In addition, he says he feels free to say things that a politician cannot say'. Given all this, Millward concluded 'there is hope that the prince will identify – to some extent at least – with the awakening in Wales. I think it is perfectly possible that he will say something in favour of the language, for example, that can do great good. I hope that he will – there will be an opportunity at the Urdd Eisteddfod and he wants to address the nation, in Welsh, on Harlech television. I can only think there is the potential for a very valuable friend'.[182]

Charles was also very aware of Gwynfor's position. Further correspondence between Millward and Gwynfor reveals that one of the questions Charles asked his tutor as he practised his Welsh was: '*Ydy Gwynfor Evans yn mynd i Gaernarfon?* (Is Gwynfor Evans going to Caernarfon?)'[183] Indeed, Charles was not the only one to feel a little awkward with Gwynfor's decision not to attend the Investiture. During May 1969, Thomas Parry, Aberystwyth's principal, attempted to bridge the gulf between Gwynfor and Charles by asking Gwynfor to meet the Prince over dinner. Gwynfor refused 'in case one of our lads heard about it'; he also worried that he would be open to the charge of wanting the best of both worlds. But that was not the end of the matter. Gwynfor made a confidential and highly unusual offer to Thomas Parry: that the Prince could come to Llangadog for supper. At Talar Wen, Gwynfor thought 'he would be sure of a warm welcome and he would have the chance to meet a large Welsh-speaking family including some around his own age. I suggested that a Sunday would be a good time for this'.[184]

Suffice to say that this remarkable offer was not taken up, but the invitation showed Gwynfor's genuine, if not entirely innocent, respect for the Prince. And certainly, during the months prior to the Investiture, Gwynfor believed the party was suffering as a consequence. The bogeyman, time after time, was the FWA. Since the end of February, its leading lights had been in custody on charges of public order offences. This, and the fact that the bombs were continuing to explode, meant that Welsh terrorism was being given blanket coverage in the British press. Gwynfor tried to exert some influence on the course of the full hearing against the FWA when the case began at Swansea by asking the authorities to call John Summers, a freelance journalist, as a witness. Summers had written a controversial article in the *Daily Telegraph* claiming that the FWA's influence was of real significance.[185] Gwynfor was very worried by the piece and attempted to use his own influence not only to undermine Summers as a journalist but also to destroy the credibility of the FWA. Indeed, he confessed to Islwyn Ffowc Elis that he had spent 'some time speaking with people in Swansea so that the defence would call him' but to no avail. Summers was not called because the prosecution, according to Gwynfor, was 'determined not to allow it'.[186]

The waters were stirred up further by Saunders Lewis's interest in the FWA case, who saw a kind of heroism in the way its members had, 'so much fun provoking and outraging the respectable and police-loving grand old men in the respectable movement called Plaid Cymru'.[187] Lewis tried to force Gwynfor to attend the hearing but failed. It would be wrong to conclude, however, that Gwynfor had no sympathy with the young men in the face of such a political case. On the contrary, as he told D J Williams: 'I would be happy to concur because I believe that the lads in the FWA, who are among the stupidest people in the country, have been unfairly treated and continue to be so. The treatment they have received from the moment they were seized is utterly shameful and we will need to say clearly what we think of this in due course.' But for all his obvious sympathy, Gwynfor believed that Saunders Lewis's personal challenge to him was politically idiotic:

> Still, and in all parts of the country, there are people who want to tar us with the same brush. If I went to the trial, as I did to see the lads in Bala [Walters and Pritchard] and Emyr Llew, I fear that it would be an act of folly. The press would seize on it and there would probably be a picture in the paper and the rest of it. I'm sure that dear George in Parliament would refer to the fact that I had been there, however much I would like to go, I cannot afford to be there, for Plaid's sake of course.[188]

At around this time, the relationship between Gwynfor and Saunders Lewis was at its chilliest – so much so that the pair met in an attempt at reconciliation. They came together over dinner in a restaurant owned by Gwynfor's relative, Nesta Howe, in Barry. It was there, Gwynfor says, that Saunders Lewis leapt 'like a deer' when a bottle of Bordeaux '46 was brought to the table as he himself sipped his Jaffa '64 – a light-hearted anecdote about a meeting where the two failed to see eye to eye on the FWA.[189] Saunders Lewis thought that Gwynfor was 'bereft of generosity and munificence' for having failed to attend the trial, and the split between them proved permanent. After Lewis's death, Gwynfor confessed that the old man had never forgiven him for having stayed away from Swansea.[190]

In May 1969, Wales had an opportunity to express its opinion on the political developments of the day in a number of local council elections. Gwynfor sensed that things were still going well for Plaid Cymru with 'Labour as well as the Liberals now falling apart'.[191] Political commentators of the day agreed; Geraint Talfan Davies, correspondent for the *Western Mail*, predicted that Plaid Cymru would make substantial gains since they were fielding almost a hundred candidates – their largest number to date.[192] The party, however, was disappointed: it won just seven seats as the Conservative vote increased. The *Liverpool Daily Post* described the result as a 'catastrophe' for Plaid Cymru and Elwyn Roberts was forced to admit that a combination of the FWA and the roadsigns campaign by Cymdeithas yr Iaith had done them serious damage.[193] Gwynfor received even more depressing reports. According to one, written by two workers at the party's central office, Dr Gareth Morgan Jones and Dafydd Williams: 'In the year of the Investiture, further bomb outrages, the FWA trial, sign-daubing, canvassers from all areas reported that the public raised these matters frequently during the campaign. There can be little doubt that these things affect Plaid Cymru's progress.'[194] A fundraising trip to America – led by Gwynfor – was cancelled because the Investiture had turned so many Welshmen and women living there into ardent royalists. As one Plaid Cymru member in the USA at the time saw it: 'people either do not know what Plaid Cymru means or have a sentimental idealised dream of the old country… they are thrilled with the Investiture'.[195]

The protest held against the Investiture at the Urdd Eisteddfod was a further turning point and, faced with an uncomfortably hot political climate, Gwynfor's closest allies began to fear for his chances of holding on to his Carmarthen seat. At the beginning of June, Islwyn Ffowc Elis wrote to Dafydd Iwan to remind him how vital Gwynfor's seat was both symbolically and in real terms. He warned too of what might happen if Gwynfor were to lose: 'It would lead to bitterness among the young and (this time terminal) dejection among older nationalists who have waited so long for the dawn. And ten or twenty years would go by before another nationalist victory was possible.'[196] The letter was a subtle plea by Islwyn Ffowc Elis for Cymdeithas yr Iaith to turn down the heat but, by June, Plaid Cymru was prey to far stronger and more sinister forces than language activism. Bombs were exploding and, for three days before the Investiture, it was, to quote Saunders Lewis, 'something close to open warfare between the government's police and the young people of Welsh Wales'.[197] On the morning of the Investiture, 1 July, two young men, George Taylor and Alwyn Jones, were killed as they planted an explosive device at Abergele. 'All of Wales Exploded into a Holiday of Song' as the *Sun*'s rather unfortunate headline had it, but nationalists did not concur.[198] On the day of the Investiture, Gwynfor found himself in a three-quarters empty House of Commons asking about the Abergele blast. George Thomas rubbed salt in the wounds by arranging for a junior minister from Scotland to answer his question. Twenty years on, George Thomas conceded that the whole affair was deliberate: 'That was my wheeze... I knew this would irritate Gwynfor more than anything, and I wanted all my junior ministers in Caernarfon.'[199] On the same day, in what can only be described as a prime example of the British establishment's organizational flair, six members of the FWA were found guilty for their part in the movement's 'terrorist' activities.

After the circus in Caernarfon, Charles toured Wales, reaching Carmarthen on 3 July. As anticipated, the meeting between Charles and Gwynfor in Carmarthen Park was a polite and seemly affair; they spoke briefly in Welsh and Gwynfor expressed sympathy with him in his efforts to learn the language. The Prince (now speaking in English) replied: 'The trouble is people don't know what I'm talking about when I talk about mutations.'[200] In one respect, Gwynfor conducted himself with considerable dignity given the pressure he was under, but not everyone shared that view. Several nationalists saw the meeting as a gaffe, and George Thomas wrote in his autobiography that Gwynfor's decision to boycott Caernarfon and then attend the celebrations in Carmarthen was pure 'humbug'.[201] Humbug or not, the week had been a nightmare for Gwynfor. Three days after his meeting with the Prince, a boy was injured by a bomb in Caernarfon. It was further proof for Gwynfor that it was unlawful action, more so than the Investiture, that was making the situation so extremely difficult. He wrote to Islwyn Ffowc Elis:

> The bombs are souring the atmosphere, and as the Establishment creates the temperature that produces them through the press and television, I fear that there are more to come. And they will be mercilessly exploited against us. Look at how Wil Edwards [the Labour MP for Merioneth] and others are criticizing the police in Gwynedd for not having said earlier that the little lad was injured by a bomb.[202]

It would have been reasonable for Gwynfor to conclude that the Investiture had harmed Plaid Cymru. This is certainly the interpretation he gives in his autobiography as he discusses the erosion of support in rural Carmarthenshire, but this was not how Gwynfor interpreted the situation in the summer of 1969.[203] It may be that his tactic was to put a brave face on things, but he was adamant that his absence from Caernarfon had not done 'much damage'. This was the view he expressed to Islwyn Ffowc Elis, for instance, pointing out how prominent members of the Congregationalists, Baptists and the Urdd had also boycotted the Investiture in order to emphasize that what he did was not exceptional.[204] Indeed, after the Investiture, Gwynfor believed his party's priority was to 'take over the Investiture' and create the impression that Plaid Cymru had 'grown hugely in strength'.[205] A fortnight after the Investiture, Gwynfor was clearly sticking to his theory. Writing to Harri Webb, he said he believed 'that we shall see six months down the line that the Investiture has done us more good than harm, especially by the fillip it has given the Welsh language (which is so closely associated with us) and the jolt it has given to the national identity of half-hearted Welshmen'.[206] By the end of July, Gwynfor thought that things were as bright as ever: Cymdeithas yr Iaith's victory in the battle for bilingual road tax discs was proof for him that there was, 'a great move afoot these days, especially as far as the language goes'. Locally too, there were triumphs to savour: it was announced that the Towy was to have a new bridge, and the party did well in the local elections in Carmarthenshire.[207]

With the benefit of hindsight, it can be seen that Gwynfor's attitude towards the Investiture was an eccentric one, but most of the leadership of Plaid Cymru concurred. Robyn Lewis said that he, like Gwynfor, was 'confident that this uncomfortable period will pass'.[208] In the same way, R Tudur Jones claimed that the Investiture had been a big 'flop' in the north but that it had done Plaid Cymru harm in the south because of its popularity. But even there, he perceived signs of hope. In the valleys, Tudur Jones said, in patronizing tones: 'the proletariat there are ready to march with any passing band – voting for Plaid yesterday, waving the Union Jack today. But remember, it will be no great wonder if they vote for Plaid again tomorrow'.[209]

Labour, of course, was happy to exploit Gwynfor's discomfiture. Two days after the Investiture, Gwynoro Jones (now a full-time Labour Party worker) wrote another memorandum for the attention of George Thomas on 'Extremism in Wales'. In it he noted that Plaid Cymru and Gwynfor faced a series of questions following the events of the preceding few months:

> Whilst it is true that the Welsh Nationalist Party have condemned violence and have said that they dissociated themselves from the extremists, the following points must be borne in mind:

> (1) The seeds of discontent and the potential atmosphere for extreme action to take place have already been planted long before last year or so.
>
> (2) I believe that the Welsh Nationalist Party only disowned these extremists from the party some three or four years ago. Why the delay?
>
> (3) Is Saunders Lewis – the founder member of the movement – still in the Party? If so all people who call for extreme action have not been ostracised from the party.[210]

Labour eagerly devoted the following weeks to acting on these comments. At the same time the bombing campaign continued; Cymdeithas yr Iaith proved as militant as ever and Gwynfor still faced Labour accusations that he and his party were, in some mysterious way, responsible for turning up the political heat in Wales.[211]

Nevertheless, the Labour policy of targeting Gwynfor was not wholly negative. More government attention was lavished on Carmarthen than any other Welsh constituency in the post-Investiture period. On 25 July, Harold Wilson and George Thomas came to Carmarthen; two days later George Thomas wrote to Wilson pleading with him not to close the mid-Wales railway line. According to George Thomas: 'Three marginal seats border on this railway, and also Llanelli where we are faced with a strong Welsh Nationalist challenge… The timing of the announcement and then of the closure itself could have catastrophic effects for us.'[212] Within two days, Eirene White, Minister of State at the Welsh Office, wrote to the Prime Minister (as she had done to John Morris two years before): 'The Central Line (Shrewsbury to Llanelli) is a money loser. But it is the one issue, other than water, on which the Welsh Nationalists could really hope to regain the initiative which has been slipping from them.' Closing the line, she told Wilson, would be electoral suicide for her party: 'We should lose Brecon and Radnor and Cardigan and forfeit any hope of defeating Gwynfor in Carmarthen.'[213] Two months later, the announcement came that the line, providentially, would remain open. It was also revealing that George Thomas chose Carmarthen that August to announce that he would allow bilingual road signs if councils wished to make use of the new dispensation.[214]

Labour's dual strategy cast a shadow over all Plaid Cymru's efforts to regain the political high ground. That summer, the party's leadership worked on the evidence it would submit to the Crowther Commission on the Constitution. Their conclusions were presented to the commission that September, the result of many months of detailed discussions, mainly by Gwynfor, Dafydd Wigley and Dewi Watkin Powell. The Research Group continued to flourish too and, in the wake of its annual conference, Plaid Cymru (thanks to Dafydd Wigley and Phil Williams) had a credible policy on the economy for the first time since the days of the TVA – over twenty years before. It was also Gwynfor's hope to make the campaign to save Cwm Dulas his party's focus, but the press insisted on giving publicity to the unholy trinity of paint, bombs and the Prince. Gwynfor could do little about the latter two but, by September 1969, he felt that he needed to do something to rein in Cymdeithas yr Iaith.

At the end of the month, he wrote to Dafydd Iwan asking Cymdeithas yr Iaith to lay down their brushes during a sensitive general election year. The tone of his letter was as friendly as ever but the message it carried was unmistakable:

> It would be a pity to see methods employed during the coming year that could frustrate our progress. As we saw again during the sittings of the Constitutional Commission, almost everything depends on Plaid Cymru's success. Houghton, who is chair of the Parliamentary Labour Party, told me personally that what the Government does depends on the support that Plaid Cymru receives.

Gwynfor's suggestion, therefore, was that members of the society should run 'a countrywide campaign... to try to persuade shopkeepers and other individuals to use the Welsh language publicly. This cannot be done by forcing them, but it can be done through persuasion'.[215] Gwynfor was not the only one among his circle of friends to warn Dafydd Iwan in this manner. He received a similar letter from Cassie Davies informing him that the situation looked bleak in the Tregaron area: 'Between the Investiture protest and the bombs, the atmosphere has changed completely, and Plaid's prospects are low, in my estimation.' The same effect, she said, was evident in Carmarthen: 'Believe you me, the painting in Carmarthenshire is surely going to cost us the only Plaid seat we have in Wales.'[216]

In the middle of November, Gwynfor heard that the society had called a year-long truce in its road signs campaign to allow the authorities to put up bilingual ones.[217] In political terms, this was excellent news for Gwynfor during a miserable month when his mother died. But, despite his personal loss, he was politically heartened when he heard that Jim Griffiths had become seriously ill and that there might be a by-election in Llanelli after Christmas.[218] The Labour patriarch pulled through, however, living on until 1975, and Gwynfor was denied his ideal by-election. In spite of the disappointment, he could state confidently on the eve of 1970 that the 'seventies decade would see Wales gain her freedom and take her seat at the United Nations.[219] The New Year brought better news still. In spite of a flu epidemic, the faithful came in their droves to see D J Williams open Plaid Cymru's new office in Water Street, Carmarthen. Appropriately, it bore the name of the home the author had sold to raise funds for the party: Penrhiw.

It was D J Williams's last public act for the party to which he had devoted his life; just two days after opening Penrhiw, he died in the chapel near his old family home, leaving Gwynfor bereft. For three days, D J Williams's body lay at Talar Wen before burial. The loss for Gwynfor was immense. Of those closest to him, D J Williams was the most important, with his unfailing encouragement and unconditional support. 'I shall miss him more than I can say,' was Gwynfor's tribute to a man he considered akin to a saint.[220] Following such a blow, Gwynfor tried to return to the work of preparing his party for the election, but his friend's death marked the beginning of a period of deep anxiety both for him personally and for his party. It began with the imprisonment of language campaigner Dafydd Iwan on 14 January – an act that led to demonstrations across Wales calling for his release during the rest of the month. But the most striking protest was yet to come. On 4 February, as Gwynfor was leaving the chamber of the House of Commons, the parliamentary press rushed up to him with astonishing news: his daughter Meinir, together with thirteen other members of Cymdeithas yr Iaith, had been jailed for three months for having disturbed the PQ 17 libel trial at the High Court in London. As an act to draw attention to Dafydd Iwan's case, it had succeeded wonderfully. Even so, none of the young protestors could ever have dreamed that they would be treated so severely by the authorities. Their imprisonment received huge publicity mainly because Meinir, an MP's daughter, was under lock and key. Gwynfor strode off towards the Strand to see what was happening and, on his way into court, a BBC reporter asked for his reaction. In an interview which surprised many within Plaid Cymru, Gwynfor said that he was full of admiration for his daughter's bravery and, in other interviews, repeated the message. 'What father,' he asked *The Times*, 'would not be proud of a daughter with such courage and conviction?'[221]

Given how close his party was to a general election, voicing support so openly was a courageous act and he knew the possible consequences. On the following morning, Meinir, the 'blonde student', was big news in the *Sun* and her father was criticized for siding with a bunch of lawbreakers.[222] Over the weekend, Cymdeithas yr Iaith held a protest march against the sentences and Welsh-language services were held at Pentonville and Holloway. On 4 February, however, Gwynfor's priority was securing the release of Meinir and the others. During those few moments he spent with the protestors in the cells at the High Court, he succeeded in convincing them that the wisest course was to appeal against the sentences. Gwynfor left the matter to Dewi Watkin Powell and, a week later, on 11 February, eleven of them were released although three of the men refused to appeal and spent another two months behind bars.

During the appeal, the Master of the Rolls, Lord Denning, said that the protestors had much to commend them. He added (to general astonishment) that Welsh should enjoy the same status as English.[223] But this was a triumph for Cymdeithas yr Iaith, not Plaid Cymru. For weeks on end, Gwynfor faced condemnation over his relationship with Cymdeithas yr Iaith; in the Commons, Gwynfor was accused by George Thomas of having done all within his power 'to stir up members of the Welsh Language Society to the sort of hooligan exercises we have witnessed'.[224] Gwynoro Jones went further, challenging Gwynfor to discipline Saunders Lewis for his remarks on violent action, and to tone down the 'extremist' language he himself was using.[225] These activities would culminate, he said, in creating something akin to Northern Ireland in Wales.[226]

It is indisputable that criticisms like these affected both Plaid Cymru and Gwynfor's popularity. A week after the High Court hearing, the farmers in Cwm Dulas warned that they did not wish to be associated with the 'demo boys', and nationalists generally were asked to keep away from the valley.[227] Gwynfor's friends were concerned about the effect that Cymdeithas yr Iaith might have. Just days after he had secured a successful appeal for Meinir and the rest, Dewi Watkin Powell wrote to Dafydd Iwan pleading with him to recognize that:

> … the reports from the constituencies across Wales show that Cymdeithas yr Iaith's unlawful tactics are more of a hindrance than a help. It would be nothing less than a tragedy to undo the good work done in 1966. There is a need and a demand to channel the energy in Cymdeithas yr Iaith through different, lawful channels… The nationalist movement faces a genuine crisis.[228]

The irony, of course, was that Dafydd Iwan was on the conciliatory wing of Plaid Cymru, but the criticism of Cymdeithas yr Iaith was not restricted to conservative-minded types like Watkin Powell. Dafydd Iwan received a similar communication from Peter Hughes Griffiths, an increasingly influential figure within Plaid Cymru, warning him that 'there is only a small difference between Plaid and Cymdeithas yr Iaith. Almost without exception, most people in the county view the two as ONE'.[229] In the same vein, Dafydd Iwan heard from Cynog Dafis that 'the Society's most recent campaigns have created enmity and anger among the people and are likely to have a detrimental effect on the support Plaid receives in the next election'.[230]

In the wake of these difficulties, Gwynfor tried to ensure that both Plaid Cymru and Cymdeithas yr Iaith could move on. He agreed, at Dewi Watkin Powell's suggestion, that prisoners before the Court of Appeal should not challenge their fines; he accepted this advice in an attempt to bring the matter to a close and shift press attention to constitutional issues.[231] The publication of Plaid Cymru's views on the Welsh constitution during March 1970 was an honest effort to do just that. Gwynfor claimed that Plaid Cymru's detailed analysis of the subject was proof of his party's confidence, but the ill feeling over the Welsh language made any sensible discussion of a new constitution for Wales virtually impossible.[232] Much of the blame for the situation as it developed lay with the *Liverpool Daily Post*, George Thomas's paper in all but name. But other influences were at work too. April 1970 witnessed the hearings for John Jenkins and Frederick Alders, those responsible for the bomb blasts that had scarred Gwynfor's first parliamentary term. Elwyn Roberts wrote to Plaid Cymru members urging them not to attend the court, because it was inevitable that so prominent a case would harm Plaid Cymru. It was revealed in court that Alders was an ex-member of Plaid Cymru, raising again the spectre of an association between the party and the explosions.[233] The improving state of the economy also meant that Labour had regained much of its popularity and, during the local government elections in April, Plaid Cymru's results across the country were particularly disappointing.

By then, all eyes were on the date of that year's general election, but Gwynfor faced a different discomfort. That month saw him undergo a series of X-ray examinations to discover the cause of stomach pains and his yellowish complexion. The search revealed gallstones – a common but painful condition that, at the time, meant surgery and some six months' convalescence. As he waited to go into hospital, Gwynfor was forced to cancel a variety of important meetings, but his main concern was that he would need to 'leak this to the press'.[234] On 28 April, Gwynfor was operated on at the Middlesex Hospital in London but because of his status, it was an illness which received more attention than usual. Plaid Cymru found itself releasing daily bulletins on his condition and the rumour spread that he only had six months to live. The phone in the Plaid Cymru office in Carmarthen rang non-stop as people sought the truth about the story. Others had heard that he was dying of cancer and some Plaid Cymru canvassers suspected that the story was being deliberately put about by Labour to damage him.[235] They were suspicious too that the same party had let it be understood that he was a poor employer at his market garden.[236]

On 18 May, as Harold Wilson announced that the general election would be held exactly a month later, Gwynfor was still confined to bed. Undoubtedly, his campaign had begun badly, with Carmarthen so closely fought and his party contesting every seat in Wales for the first time. It fulfilled a dream for Gwynfor but placed an enormous weight of expectation on his shoulders. Many, in spite of the troubles over the Investiture and the bombs, felt that Welsh nationalism was on the verge of its greatest breakthrough since the demise of Liberalism. For these people, the election of 1970 was an opportunity to prove that the 1966 result was no fluke and that they could build on Carmarthen and take seats in places like Caernarfon and Merioneth.[237] And although Plaid Cymru had a well-argued manifesto that incorporated many of the forward-thinking ideas of men like Dafydd Wigley and Phil Williams, it was Gwynfor who was the focus of attention. His future was the party's future. As Trevor Fishlock, *The Times* correspondent saw it: 'Defeat of Mr Gwynfor Evans, the party's President, would be akin to the toppling of a king.' [238]

Faced with this very unfortunate situation, Gwynfor opted to ignore the advice of his doctors and returned to the fray by the end of the month. In spite of this, the rumours about his illness continued. At its first election meeting, Plaid Cymru emphasized that he was fighting fit.[239] The reality was rather different; Gwynfor was not a well man and as the campaign proceeded Labour made much of Gwynoro Jones's image as young and energetic. Gwynfor's illness also meant that he had a mere three weeks to remind the electors of Carmarthen of what he had done for them during the previous four years: from improving the county's roads to saving the mid-Wales railway line, Gwynfor claimed the credit, and with some justification.[240] The problem, of course, was that these were the Labour government's achievements.

The election campaign was fought in searing temperatures that only added to a general feeling of apathy. With the bookmakers predicting a Labour win, the public responded by showing more interest in the World Cup and the genius of Pélé than the contesting claims of politicians. In addition, Plaid Cymru's campaign was impaired by the sudden death of J E Jones; another setback was the seemingly never-ending struggle to win a fair share of air time for party broadcasts. Eventually, Dewi Watkin Powell had to fight Gwynfor and his party's corner through the High Court and the upper echelons of the BBC in London.[241] He won a partial victory but, in Carmarthen, other factors made life even more difficult for Gwynfor. In the constituency, Gwynoro Jones was pulling out all the stops for a Labour gain. But the crucial factor, the man who made the difference between winning and losing, was the Liberal candidate, Huw Thomas. As a former ITN newsreader, Huw Thomas was a well-known face, but his most prominent feature was an uncompromising attitude towards Gwynfor. Echoing George Thomas, he attacked Gwynfor and Plaid Cymru for the bombing campaign. In private, Huw Thomas was desperate to see the back of Gwynfor, and lent his tacit support to the Gwynoro Jones campaign.[242] The other dangerous factor was the Conservative's so-called 'cuddly candidate', the mild-mannered Lloyd Havard Davies.

Just twenty-four hours before the vote on 18 June *Y Cymro*, and many Welsh speakers, were certain that Gwynfor would win and that Plaid Cymru would take Caernarfon, Merioneth, Ceredigion and Maldwyn.[243] The optimism was fed by Gwynfor himself but, in the event, the count brought a huge disappointment. As his anxious supporters turned out of the pubs and headed for the town square, the press was reporting that Edward Heath would win the general election but that Gwynoro Jones would take Carmarthen. It was a tense evening and at three o'clock in the morning the result was declared: Gwynoro Jones had won by three thousand votes. His acceptance speech was drowned out by cries of 'Gwynfor, Gwynfor'. But although Plaid Cymru enjoyed a clear majority in the crowd, the ballot was unambiguous. Contrary to what had happened at the by-election, Labour had managed to get its vote out while the Liberals and Conservatives had largely returned to their respective folds. For the first time as an MP, Gwynfor had been weighed in the electoral balance and been found wanting – not for any specific reason but as the result of a complex mixture of factors. They included the FWA and Cymdeithas yr Iaith, the Investiture and the bombs. They included too the perception that Gwynfor was the 'Member for Wales', not Carmarthen.

The freak nature of 1966 was also part of the picture and the surprise perhaps is not that Gwynfor lost but that he did so well. The same thing could be said of Plaid Cymru's national performance that night, because its share of the vote almost tripled, increasing from 4.3 per cent to 11.5 per cent. But for all the good results, like Robyn Lewis's in Caernarfon or Phil Williams's in Caerphilly, Carmarthen was *the* seat for Plaid Cymru and now it was lost. Gwynfor had made an impression at Westminster, but it was over. Aged 57, he was back in the wilderness with no money, no job and at the helm of a wounded party.

Chapter 10

THE PARTY'S OVER 1970–74

After the excitement of the electoral battle, Plaid Cymru and Gwynfor were a mass of mixed emotions. On the one hand, there was pride in what had been achieved. Plaid Cymru was now the third party in Wales after the collapse of the Liberal vote. That was important, but the nationalist surge was not restricted to the rural west; in the valleys there was a confidence that firm foundations had been laid and that the decent crop of votes in seats like Aberdare (30 per cent) and Rhondda East (25 per cent) was a sign of better things to come. The rise in the nationalist's share of the vote was also substantially higher in Wales than in Scotland – where there had been no Investiture and no bombing campaign.[1] But, on the other hand, seeing Gwynfor lose his seat had awoken the old woes and warnings that the party was destined to fail. The party's vice-president, Tedi Millward, feared that losing Carmarthen was likely to reignite the familiar concerns which were not voiced during Gwynfor's first period in Parliament. And the neurotic questions continued: was 1966 a one-off? Was Gwynfor the only one who could win for Plaid Cymru? Had there really been a nationalist awakening at all? [2]

The other fear among Gwynfor's allies was that Plaid Cymru would revert to being a protest party. No one was more outspoken than Dafydd Wigley on this point, insisting that the party needed to resist 'the overtures of those who wish to use less moderate methods of changing the status quo… The days of showing the flag are over. There is a battle to be won. Glorious defeats are no substitutes for victory'.[3] Others were anxious about what they saw as a lost opportunity in 1966, and felt that not enough had been done to lay firm foundations. Islwyn Ffowc Elis was commissioned to conduct the post mortem and, in typically courteous fashion, he was nevertheless blunt. His main conclusion was this: Plaid Cymru was not 'ready for the nationalist revival' following the Carmarthen victory that spread throughout the country; nor did he believe that the party was 'prepared for the cold winds that chilled that revival in 1969 and 1970'. The nationalist movement was under pressure, and Islwyn Ffowc Elis concluded that many members had left as a result of 'the painting campaign, the FWA trial and the television election'.[4]

No one was more confused in the days and weeks after the election than Gwynfor himself. In a sense, he was relieved that the purgatory of London was behind him. Indeed, Meinir remembers her father telling her that the defeat had kept him alive, given his worry that another parliamentary term would have been the end of him.[5] But the return to Wales was no easy option; losing his seat meant that Gwynfor had also lost those two all important letters – MP – which had justified his whole strategy. His seat in Parliament had given him the moral high ground over the long-haired radicals of Welsh nationalism. But, now, Gwynfor was in a much weaker position and the central irony of 1970 was that however great the relief at leaving London, Gwynfor knew that he needed to regain the seat – and soon. Within ten minutes of losing, Gwynfor was on the phone organizing the next campaign.[6]

He had good reason to do so. Edward Heath's slim parliamentary majority meant another poll could soon be called. But Gwynfor had financial problems. Losing Carmarthen had been a heavy blow, because the salary of £3,250 had made him financially independent for the first time since his early days as a trainee solicitor. The salary had also made him less reliant on the Dan Evans company. Now, though, his situation was bleaker than ever. The greenhouses were running at a loss, and worse was to come. Just a week after the vote, Elwyn Roberts – who had rescued Plaid Cymru from the bailiffs on more than one occasion – announced his retirement as general secretary. It appeared likely that Gwynfor would have to rely once again on the generosity of the Dan Evans company. Then, within days of losing Carmarthen, Gwynfor heard of a possible solution, a solution that made it possible for him to continue with his work, campaigning, and reinvigorating Plaid Cymru.

Gwynfor and Elwyn Roberts were informed that a wealthy property developer in the north-east called Rhys Davies wanted to support the party. By the end of June Rhys Davies had been in touch with Plaid Cymru and, a few days after their first contact, the party's leadership were confident that salvation was at hand.[7] At the end of June 1970, Rhys Davies offered to make Gwynfor a director of his company, Caergwrle Investments Limited. His fees would be equal to those of an MP. Indeed, Rhys Davies promised that he would support Gwynfor on an MP's salary until he regained his seat.[8] It was remarkable news and Gwynfor was appointed director of C.I.L. on 2 July. However, there was even better news to come. On 17 November 1970, Rhys Davies proposed the setting up of a Bare Trustee Company which would benefit from the development profit for a proposed site at Pen y Cae, Wrexham. Rhys Davies suggested that Plaid Cymru receive 80% of the income and that he would receive 20%. Some days afterwards, Gwynfor wrote to Rhys Davies to express his gratitude and shock:

> The trio who visited you on the 17th have not yet recovered from the impact of the plan you uncovered for helping the national party. We still talk to each other with awe and in hushed whispers about its staggering proportions... November was a historic day for Plaid Cymru.[9]

And Rhys Davies was true to his word. Unlike Hywel Hughes, Bogota – a dreamer who promised more than he ever delivered – Gwynfor was given financial support. Over the next four years, Gwynfor received a substantial income that enabled him to live comfortably. Likewise, money was channelled through the Bare Trust into the party's central coffers thereby keeping financial worries at bay. For obvious reasons, the arrangements were not disclosed to all the party's leaders to prevent the news reaching the ears of the press and the party's political opponents. These developments meant that Dafydd Williams, Elwyn Roberts's young successor, got off to a good start in the role. Altogether, Rhys Davies estimates that he contributed the princely sum of £78,550 to Plaid Cymru over the following years, boosting the party's electoral hopes. When Gwynfor won back the Carmarthen seat in 1974, he wrote to Rhys Davies to thank him sincerely for 'munificence which stands on its own in the history of Welsh nationalism during recent centuries'.[10]

Having resolved his financial worries, Gwynfor still had other bridges to cross before the seat could be his again. The first and most important was Plaid Cymru's strategic direction at a time of uncertainty and change. For some months, he struggled to provide a lead and, curiously, Gwynfor and others in the party felt a certain loss when George Thomas was forced to leave the Welsh Office. George Thomas's great virtue in nationalist eyes was that his constant carping offered a strange sort of continuity. Everyone knew where they stood, and despite the damage he caused, there were advantages to having a bogeyman in charge. Peter

Thomas, the new tenant of Cathays Park, would provide a marked contrast. As a Welsh-speaker (and former member of Plaid Cymru), few expected the new secretary of state to be as strident as George Thomas. Thomas was also on the left of the Conservative party, leading political commentators to predict that Wales would be more peaceful than it had been for years. After three months, the editor of *Y Faner*, for instance, commented that the difference between the two Thomases was enormous: 'The second Mr Thomas employs none of the hysterical language of the Mr Thomas who preceded him – words like "separatists", "extremists", "bombers" etc. are never mentioned.'[11] Publicly, Gwynfor hardly change his tune, attacking the Conservatives and accusing them of being just as bad as Labour. But, privately, Gwynfor's attitude was rather different, and he described Peter Thomas in these terms to Rhys Davies: 'Much as one dislikes a Conservative Government, P. T. is the best man we have had in the Welsh Office: an immeasurable improvement on his immediate predecessor.'[12]

Nevertheless Peter Thomas presented Gwynfor with a problem, and some within Plaid Cymru tried to make capital out of Gwynfor's failure to respond adequately to the new political era. Inevitably, the greatest threat to his hegemony came from the socialist wing and their leader (in all but name), Dr Phil Williams. He, by the autumn of 1970, was Plaid Cymru's new chair and considered it the natural step to lead the party to the left – especially as the miners seemed likely to go on strike. He was also eager to loosen Gwynfor's absolute hold on the party, at a time when the President was celebrating a quarter of a century in charge. As he accepted the party's chair, for instance, Phil Williams told the press that he regarded the leadership from then on as 'a joint one' and that he would represent 'the anglicised industrial area of South-East Wales'.[13] This, he said, was the time for 'new shepherds' to take charge of Plaid Cymru, the time for 'learned men of science, economists and technologists to steer Plaid's policy towards more practicable ideals'.[14] In due course, the relationship between Phil Williams and Gwynfor would go through turbulent times but this was not the only challenge facing Gwynfor. Soon after the 1970 election, he came under pressure to reach an electoral agreement with the Liberals – a deal whereby Plaid Cymru and the Liberals would not oppose one another in those seats where they were strongest. Others wanted to see Plaid Cymru go further and form an alliance with the Liberals,[15] but Gwynfor rejected both schemes, telling his colleagues that 'the cost would be too great' and that 'it could divide Plaid' – particularly as the 'young generation', as he put it, 'was very much against'.[16]

However, the crucial factor during this period was Gwynfor's attitude in relation to Cymdeithas yr Iaith. Contrary to popular expectation, Peter Thomas's honeymoon was short-lived and, by Christmas 1970, the society had begun a series of serious acts of law-breaking on two fronts: broadcasting and roadsigns. By the end of 1971, 300 of its members had appeared before the courts, and 68 had been jailed. It was a highly ambitious strategy on the part of Dafydd Iwan, and it succeeded remarkably in radicalizing young and old as the society reached what its historian, Gwilym Tudur, would later call the high water mark of its 'popular' phase.[17] During December 1970, some of Welsh-speaking Wales's most prominent figures – such as the Archdruid Tilsli, Thomas Parry and Goronwy Daniel – came out in public support. In the wake of this backing, a petition was launched that attracted several thousand names.[18] A new, more respectable organization called '*Cyfeillion yr Iaith Gymraeg*' ('Friends of the Welsh Language') was also established to promote the society's aims; by January 1971, Alwyn D Rees believed that 'the gap between the old Wales and the new' that the philosopher J R Jones sensed so keenly, was closing. From now on, the social conservatives marched with the radicals.[19]

It was a difficult situation for Gwynfor because so many of his natural supporters now seemed to be directing their energies towards Cymdeithas yr Iaith. It was doubly awkward because he also admired the society and shared many of its ideals. During the summer of 1970, for example, he co-published a pamphlet with Alwyn D Rees and Pennar Davies calling on chapels to work harder for the language. The booklet, *Gwerth dy Grys*, also restated Gwynfor's conviction that 'the national language' had grown alongside 'the Christian tradition' in Wales.[20] Similarly, he believed that the arrest of 30 members of Cymdeithas yr Iaith in mid-December 1970 was proof of the willingness of young people to shoulder heavy moral burdens.[21] But even as he spoke, a parliament for Wales was still Gwynfor's real priority. He insisted that Plaid Cymru had to resist the temptation to become a protest party and that the only course left open to it in this new, strange era was to forge ahead with its constitutional programme. He was certain too that Cymdeithas yr Iaith was damaging Plaid Cymru. Many were surprised in March 1971, for instance, when Gwynfor spoke publicly for the first time of his long-held belief, that it was Cymdeithas yr Iaith that had cost him his Carmarthen seat.[22]

After months of tactical delay, he decided that a new petition was needed for a Welsh parliament. His goal, as he explained to the party's executive in early 1971, was to attract those more 'forward-looking' elements in the Labour party – like Gwilym Prys Davies, Tudor Watkins and Lord Maelor – to join him in a shared, principled campaign.[23] His objective in the long term was a popular petition and a national conference presided over by Goronwy Daniel. Gwynfor went so far as to contact Daniel, who agreed with the suggestion. However, the idea provoked a furious response from those who thought that it would essentially drag Plaid Cymru back to the 'fifties. Although Dafydd Wigley and Phil Williams opened negotiations with the Liberals, Emlyn Hooson, their leader in Wales, refused to cooperate.[24] Labour was the key to any petition's success or failure but, after the George Thomas years, no nationalist was in the mood to forgive Labour for what it had done.

Within Plaid Cymru, there was considerable opposition (from those such as Tudur Jones) to any plan which would involve Plaid Cymru asking favours from 'Good Welshmen' in the Labour party such as Elystan Morgan. Tudur Jones made important contributions to the debate and others followed. Even so, it appears that party members in Cardiganshire finally defeated the proposal. There was bitter disappointment in the county with Elystan Morgan's refusal, as the local MP, to support the establishment of a Welsh-medium school in Aberystwyth. It was, without question, Elystan Morgan's biggest political error because the comprehensive school that eventually opened, Ysgol Gyfun Penweddig, proved to be a huge success. The argument had another significant impact too because it was the objection to Elystan Morgan which ensured that the new petition for a parliament never materialized. In February 1971, when the debate over a possible petition was at its most passionate, three of the most prominent nationalists in the county (including Elystan Morgan's brother, Deulwyn) wrote to Elwyn Roberts to remind him and the party of the deceitfulness of those opponents who in the past had been so ready to 'wear the mantle of Welshness and nationalism when it was to their advantage to do so'.[25] In other words, there would be no co-operation and, faced with this tide of antagonism, Gwynfor allowed the matter to drop.

The failure of the parliament campaign was a severe blow to Gwynfor, and it was no coincidence that Cymdeithas yr Iaith did so much to fill the resulting political vacuum at the heart of the 'national movement'. The event that changed everything was the decision of the authorities to arrest eight members of the society (including Dafydd Iwan) on suspicion of conspiracy to destroy road signs.[26] The authorities could scarcely have devised a more political charge to bring against the 'Eight', and it sparked fierce protests. The consequences for Gwynfor were grave; without any political masterplan, and with Cymdeithas yr Iaith the focus of such attention, Plaid Cymru had to step in. As the case began against the eight accused on 3 May, Wales was in ferment, and the expectation was that the defendants would face heavy fines in an effort to destroy the society.

On the first day of the case in Swansea, Meinir, Gwynfor's daughter, was jailed for three months after she tried to address the court from the public gallery. Once again, Gwynfor found himself dragged into the affairs of Cymdeithas yr Iaith. There was no shame at his daughter's actions, however. On the following day, he visited Meinir in prison in Pucklechurch, and was astounded when he was required to speak English to her. He complied for the simple reason that he would otherwise have no chance to talk to her for another month, but he regarded the situation as an outrage. On his return from Pucklechurch, he wrote to Peter Thomas pleading with him to change the prison system, and to establish a commission with powers to assess the whole position of the Welsh language. It would cost, Gwynfor told the Secretary of State witheringly, 'at least 0.25 per cent of the cost of Concorde each year'.[27] His request for a commission was denied, but Gwynfor's efforts for Cymdeithas yr Iaith did not end there. On the day that Meinir was imprisoned, he acted as interpreter in another case involving the society – this time at Carmarthen Magistrates' Court. As he stepped forward to translate on behalf of 17-year-old Cathi McGill, there were cheers and applause in court.[28] Her stand, like that of the eight in Swansea, was typical of what he described to Rhys Davies as the act of 'brilliant young people who are dedicating themselves to the cause'.[29]

Another feature of the Swansea case was the less than sensitive treatment by the police of the hundreds of protesters who had gathered outside the court. Dozens of Cymdeithas yr Iaith supporters were injured as the police broke up peaceful demonstrations with unwarranted force. Gwynfor's family did not escape the truncheons and the boots – leading him to identify even more closely with the society. As he later wrote to Rhys Davies:

> I was present at the open-air meeting in Swansea on Saturday – 1500 present – when the police attacked the demonstrators without the shadow of an excuse. Meleri – one

Gwynfor congratulating David Walters and David Pritchard following their act of sabotage at the Tryweryn reservoir site in September 1962. Elystan Morgan, Walters and Pritchard's lawyer, is seen on the left of the picture. Elystan Morgan was considered the natural heir to Gwynfor. Three years later, he quit Plaid Cymru for the Labour Party.

A relinquished dream: Gwynfor pictured at a testimonial meeting shortly before he abandoned the Merioneth parliamentary nomination in 1962.

Sunday, November 8, 1964

Sunday Mirror

© The Daily Mirror Newspapers, Ltd., 1964

Telephone: FLEet-street 0246

I would like a reunion with my husband, says wife

'PRIVATE LIVES' ROW IN PARTY

'Tame' eagle is shot dead by ex-Commando

A "TAME" East African eagle called Nita was shot dead three hours after escaping from a zoo.

Last night, retired Royal Marine Commando Major H. G. Northcott, of Prestatyn, North Wales, told how he shot the eagle with three blasts from his 12-bore double-barreled shotgun.

He was on his private shoot at Mochdre near Colwyn Bay, with his two teen-aged sons and a new golden retriever called Barney, "when Barney suddenly came running towards me, yelping.

Docile

"About a yard over his head the eagle was flying with its claws up. It was obviously in a position of attack. I fired, it veered overhead, and I shot it again. It fell about a quarter of a mile away. It was injured. We finished it off."

Major Northcott added: "I've had some experience of these birds in Abyssinia. I've seen them break a goat's neck."

Earlier, at the Welsh Mountain Zoo, Colwyn Bay, managing-director Mr. Robert Jackson said Nita was tame and docile.

She had been out of the zoo before, and had done no harm.

Police at Colwyn Bay said: "We are looking into the matter."

Mr. Roberts . . . giving up £1,000-a-year job

Mrs. Tucker . . . youngest election candidate

Woman official leaves home

By RONALD MAXWELL and LYNN LEWIS

CRITICISM of the private lives of some leaders of the Welsh Nationalist movement is threatening to cause a crisis in the Party.

Some members fear the Party will lose prestige because of two events which have happened in the past ten days.

THE FIRST concerned Mrs. Margaret Tucker, 21-year-old secretary of the Party youth committee and the youngest Parliamentary candidate in last month's General Election.

Mrs. Tucker left her husband Mr. Michael Tucker, a member of the party executive, and took their two children with her.

THE SECOND EVENT involved Mr. Emrys Roberts, 32, the party's organising secretary, who was also a General Election candidate.

Mr. Roberts left his wife and their two children.

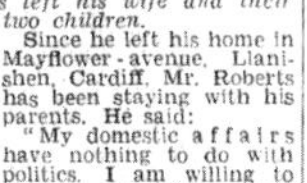

Since he left his home in Mayflower-avenue, Llanishen, Cardiff, Mr. Roberts has been staying with his parents. He said:

"My domestic affairs have nothing to do with politics. I am willing to discuss political matters, but not personal matters."

'Why I Quit'

Mr. Roberts announced two days ago that he was giving up his £1,000 a year job at Party headquarters.

He explained: "This has nothing to do with what has happened. When I took the job I said I would hold it until after the General Election."

Mr. Roberts's wife said of the parting: "Personally I would like a reunion, but Emrys says it is final."

Mrs. Tucker, who has been staying with relatives in Great Yarmouth, is expected to return to Cardiff tomorrow to stay with her mother in Cornwall-street, Grangetown.

Election note: In the election, twenty-one of the Party's twenty-three candidates lost their deposits. These included Mr. Roberts and Mrs. Tucker

Three senior detectives leave the liner Reina del Mar at Southampton.

MURDER NIGHT PARTY IS PROBED

Sunday Mirror Reporter

DETECTIVES probing the Southampton taxi-driver murder were told yesterday of a wild party attended by 14 members of the liner Reina del Mar's crew.

The party took place in Northumberland road, Southampton, near the home of 60-year-old George Newberry, on the night he was found battered to death seven miles away at Chandler's Ford.

Next day the Reina del Mar sailed on a Mediterranean cruise.

When the liner returned yesterday, thirty detectives led by Hampshire CID chief, Detective Chief Superintendent Walter Jones, went aboard.

Fingerprints of all the 401 crew were compared with prints found on the murdered man's car.

Members of the crew who were at the party said there were girls there and that drink flowed.

Most of them remembered very little about it.

A steward on the liner said after the detectives left: "It must have been around three in the morning when we got a taxi back to the ship."

Meanwhile, other detectives searched for a blonde seen getting into Mr. Newberry's cab with a man on what was believed to be his last journey.

NEXT. A STORY OF HOPE

Tabloid terror: this report in the *Sunday Mirror* influenced the way Gwynfor and his circle viewed the domestic affairs of Emrys Roberts, Plaid Cymru General Secretary.

Gwynfor and George Thomas – the polar opposites of 'sixties politics.

The last days of Tryweryn: Gwynfor, alongside Elwyn Roberts (left) and D J Williams (right) at the opening of the Tryweryn reservoir, October 1965.

Tears of joy: Gwynfor with his daughter, Meinir (left), and Lynfa Jones on the night of the by-election.

'The National Dawn'. Announcing the result of the Carmarthen by-election, 15 July 1966.

'1 a.m: The Welsh Unseat Labour.' The crowd on Carmarthen's Guildhall Square react to Gwynfor's by-election victory, 15 July 1966.

The day after: 15 July 1966.

An icon in the making: Gwynfor, Rhiannon and family greeting the crowds, July 1966.

The Member for Wales: Gwynfor being interviewed by the BBC's *Panorama* programme, August 1966.

Ode to joy: celebrations on Guildhall square.

More congratulations: the ‘Evans Express’ reaches Pembrey and Burry Port, July 1966.

Departing for purgatory: Gwynfor and Rhiannon leaving for London, 20 July 1966.

Awaiting the 'Evans Express' in Carmarthen station, 20 July 1966. Islwyn Ffowc Elis, the innovative author who transformed Gwynfor's image is seen alongside him.

Celebrating in Talar Wen: Gwynfor and family embrace the unexpected victory, July 1966.

1967: Gwynfor addressing the Urdd Eisteddfod.

Freedom: Gwynfor greets daughter Meinir on her release from prison, February 1

The hero and the icon: Gwynfor with Carwyn James, the brilliant rugby coach who stood for Plaid Cymru in the Llanelli Parliamentary constituency during the 1970 General Election.

> of my girls – was bruised by being thrown about bodily by the police; Guto was three times dragged by his hair; Alcwyn had his spectacles smashed by a policeman's provocation – this has happened many times; twice in the last fortnight at Carmarthen. When Meinir was dragged from the court gallery (the press report that she 'struggled' is a lie) one policeman said to her 'I have had my eyes on you a long time and I have been dying to lay my hands on you'. They threw her down the stone steps from the gallery and she was almost unconscious at the bottom. She is a small, slight, and pretty girl who, like the others, is conscientiously non-violent. These matters are doing the Blaid a lot of harm just now – at local election time – but they are doing Wales a power of good, and before long the party will benefit.[30]

Gwynfor was not asking for sympathy when he spoke of the harm that the Swansea protest and other similar protests were causing Plaid Cymru – especially in Carmarthenshire. As the trial drew to a close, Labour in Carmarthenshire saw its opportunity, and Gwynoro Jones criticized the ministers of religion who had walked into the police station in Carmarthen to claim responsibility for pulling down English-only road signs.[31] Several of these men were personal friends of Gwynfor and he had to defend their right to protest. Gwynfor believed they were working within the tradition of 'complete commitment' that had prompted radicals like Samuel Roberts or 'S R', Henry Richard and Gwilym Hiraethog to intervene in secular matters.[32] Gwynfor was happy also to appear on television to support their latter-day counterparts. In spite of this, and his pride in showing his loyalty, such statements cannot have done him much good in Carmarthen – a constituency where, even after the 1966 result, there was widespread suspicion of militant nationalism. It gave rise to scathing comments in the local press about who really controlled Plaid Cymru – the language radicals or the more respectable elements. It reopened the debate on Gwynfor's pacifism and one correspondent suggested that Plaid Cymru's support for Cymdeithas yr Iaith was similar in kind to Gwynfor's 'support' for Nazism during the Second World War.[33]

The Swansea trial ended on 14 May, and contrary to popular expectation not one of the eight defendants was sent to prison. Mr Justice Mars-Jones opted, instead, to pass suspended prison sentences on Cymdeithas yr Iaith's leaders – a clever tactic which deflated the society in the long term. But, at the time, the general view among nationalists was that the police had made an enormous mistake by bringing such an obviously political case before the court. Indeed, after the trial, Cymdeithas yr Iaith membership doubled, causing some in Plaid Cymru a measure of anxiety. Some party members called for its supporters to be barred, but Gwynfor clung to the belief that it was his party's duty to support the society, whatever the cost.[34] He would hardly have expressed his opinion with such confidence a decade before but, by 1971, he had learned enough to sense that the activities of Cymdeithas yr Iaith nurtured nationalism in its totality. In the long term, he hoped to see Plaid Cymru benefit as a generation of young people espoused the new radicalism. The clearest symbol of this intellectual shift, in Gwynfor's view, was Dafydd Iwan, a man he considered as 'leader of the young generation'. It was a sign of his respect for Dafydd Iwan that he wrote to congratulate him on his stand and to suggest that the society should campaign to make the education system in Wales more Welsh as well as continuing with the broadcasting campaign.[35] A fortnight later, in June 1971, Plaid Cymru's executive committee voted to put 'all the party's machinery behind the protest meetings' held by the society in the event of Cymdeithas yr Iaith's leadership facing severe punishment in future.[36]

It was easy enough for the party to agree to support the society, but the attention given to it meant that very little thought was given within Plaid Cymru to matters other than the language issue. It can hardly be said, for instance, that there was any considered discussion of such vital issues as the party's attitude towards Europe when a White Paper was published in June 1971. Gwynfor and his party decided to oppose joining the European Economic Community on the grounds that such a body would damage peace and the Welsh economy. However, Gwynfor and his fellow members had reached their decision without having discussed the issue in depth. True, nationalists like Saunders Lewis who took an interest in Europe were exceptions, and he wrote to Gwynfor to complain about the attitude of Phil Williams, chief spokesperson of the anti-European wing of the party.[37] The other exception was Gwynn Matthews, a member of Plaid Cymru's executive and the author of a booklet on the subject – the party's only meaningful publication on Europe. The contrast between Welsh nationalism and the rest of British politics was without doubt striking: in the rest of Britain, Europe was *the* major issue; in Wales, however, the politics of language preoccupied the whole nationalist family, and Gwynfor needed to seek other channels.

It was proving ever harder to gain publicity, and he was forced to seek alternative methods. Over Christmas 1970, he began writing a populist book on Welsh history that he hoped would counter the 'ignorance' that 'weakened the national will'. Gwynfor spent no time whatsoever – by his own admission –

'reading a single ancient manuscript' or 'inhaling the dust from an old document'. Rather, he relied heavily on previous scholarship, but this did not shake his belief that his interpretation of the past was correct. The book, *Aros Mae*, was pure propaganda, not unlike the writings of his hero, O M Edwards, in the popular magazine *Wales*. But, for Gwynfor, the whole point of popular history was to disseminate propaganda and awaken the Welsh to their nation's glorious, uninterrupted heritage. Another influence was Dr Ceinwen Thomas, an academic who also believed that objective history was impossible.[38] *Aros Mae*, then, is a rather crude exercise in missionary work. The first inhabitants of Wales in *Aros Mae* are called Welsh – even though they were really nothing of the sort. But Gwynfor was unrepentant, lambasting academics for peddling 'the pedantry... of giving the Welsh another name early in their history'.[39]

It took him just seven months to complete the hefty volume with Rhiannon doing the typing. And despite the initial doubts of the publishers, John Penry, about the wisdom of such a political work, it sold well.[40] During the National Eisteddfod in Bangor, all the 3,000 copies of the first edition were sold and a second edition was published. The book is immensely readable and, in its own way, is as much a triumph of propaganda as was Churchill's work on English history. But, however popular *Aros Mae*, and the subsequent English translation, *Land of My Fathers*, might have been, professional historians were scathing. The most notable of them, Rees Davies, claimed that some of Gwynfor's comparisons were 'an assault on common sense not to mention history'.[41] But Gwynfor did not seek professional endorsement; what mattered to him was that Welsh-speakers in their thousands were buying the book and learning about their past. To achieve this end, Gwynfor sent the following instruction to his party's central office:

> The main motive for our ensuring wide distribution for the book is... the effect on people's spirits, on their national consciousness, and thus on the politics and prospects of Plaid Cymru. We must get all the Welsh educated classes to read it: teachers, ministers, lawyers, civil servants etc... We must try to reach everyone who has some sort of influence... And we must get the intelligent working people to buy it... As I look at a hundred members in a chapel I'd bet my bottom dollar that I could get ten to buy it, and that's how to go about it.[42]

Aros Mae continued to be popular, and the second edition sold just as quickly as the first. Despite that, it failed in purely political terms, and the autumn brought no real renaissance for Plaid Cymru. Throughout November 1971, Cymdeithas yr Iaith and another trial, this time in Mold, dominated all the national headlines. Three members of the society were jailed for long periods – among them Ffred Ffransis, who would soon become Gwynfor's son-in-law. But, as in Swansea, Gwynfor did not hesitate to show his colours, describing the sentences as malicious.[43] He was also eager to take practical steps, and managed to persuade Sir Goronwy Daniel to chair a campaign committee for a Welsh-language television channel – which Gwynfor considered vital to the wider channel campaign.[44] Gwynfor was also prominent in the efforts made by the University of Wales's Broadcasting Committee (again jointly with Goronwy Daniel)[45] to win the support of the Welsh academic community for the channel. The Welsh-speaking intelligentsia caught the television bug and, by early January, over 300 nationalists (almost all members of Plaid and including public figures like Derec Llwyd Morgan, R Tudur Jones and Harri Pritchard Jones) had announced that they would not be buying a television licence.

Given the context, Gwynfor had little choice but to support the efforts of Cymdeithas yr Iaith but the focus on cultural issues – historical and media-led – prevented him from exercising influence in other areas. For instance, Gwynfor's efforts to identify Plaid Cymru with the miners' strike in January 1972 – the first national strike since 1926 – was an abject failure. Gwynfor wanted his party to do 'everything possible'[46] to support them, and branches were instructed to help with fundraising.[47] The strike lasted for seven weeks, and certain parts of Wales experienced destitution. But although the party, and its President, did what it could to support the miners, some within its ranks felt that it was too little too late – so much so that the secretary of a branch in the south complained that this belated intervention smacked 'of "bandwagoning".'[48]

Without doubt, Gwynfor was caught between a cultural rock and an industrial hard place, and was not sure which way to turn. At the end of January, he wrote to Elwyn Roberts with a stark assessment:

> The work is still very limited compared to the revolution that should be happening now. One way I have of judging it is the number of invitations I receive personally to come to Gwynedd. I haven't received a single one to come to Gwynedd… this year. I would have to go back 30 years to see a similar situation in my diary.[49]

Carmarthenshire was touched by the same lethargy and Gwynoro Jones lost no opportunity to mock Gwynfor as a man whose best days were behind him – an accusation that was partly true. Given the lack of activity, it was no surprise therefore that Gwynfor viewed the appointment of Peter Hughes Griffiths as Plaid Cymru organizer for Dyfed as 'an historic event' when he took up the post in February 1972.[50] Peter Hughes Griffiths was particularly well known as an effective organizer who understood how the county ticked. And set against Gwynfor's paternalistic image, his presence was also vital as Plaid Cymru set about challenging Gwynoro Jones's demagoguery by promoting more populist events like pop concerts and a Welsh Eurovision contest.[51]

But not even a star organiser like Peter Hughes Griffiths could make miracles happen overnight and, as the party sought to shake off its torpor, Gwynfor began to think seriously of retiring from the Presidency by 1975, the party's golden jubilee year.[52] Things hardly improved for Gwynfor and those closest to him when the Merthyr by-election was called in February 1972. It was a seat where the party was expected to do well after what the *Welsh Nation* described as a 'long period of calm' in Welsh constitutional politics.[53] Many were surprised, however, when Emrys Roberts was selected as candidate. Emrys Roberts was a natural choice for such a seat, and Gwynfor was shrewd enough not to oppose his candidacy, but his support was far from wholehearted, and a number of Gwynfor's allies regarded it as an outrageous decision. Islwyn Ffowc Elis wrote to Gwynfor expressing the feelings of many on the traditional wing of the party:

> ... I know that it will be difficult for any member of Plaid from the North, at least, who remembers the ugly conspiracy against you between 1959 and 1964 to lift a finger to help... I can imagine the scheming and·compromise that led to this choice, and I am sure that no blame attaches to you for the step that was taken. I hope that you will not be too despondent.[54]

As it happened, Emrys Roberts achieved an excellent result taking 37 per cent of the vote, coming close to ousting Labour in April. He was helped by Labour divisions over Europe, but Gwynfor chose to ignore this factor. He saw the Merthyr result as a turning point and, like others in his party, misread the signs.[55] Merthyr turned out to be the high water mark of Plaid Cymru's popular support, not a promise of better things to come.

After 1972, Plaid Cymru lost its appeal in the valleys – not least because of energetic young Labour leaders like Elystan Morgan and Gwynoro Jones. But Gwynfor himself did much to hasten the decline by failing to maintain Plaid Cymru support in the valleys between 1967 and 1972, and after Merthyr, Plaid

Cymru did virtually nothing to nurture the south. People like Emrys Roberts and Glyn James, who were genuinely keen to see Plaid Cymru take root there, were rare exceptions.

The opportunity was lost. Plaid Cymru channelled its energies once more into Cymdeithas yr Iaith – a strategy which helped the society but not the party. It was the 'brave leaders' of the society as Gwynfor put it, who benefited most from the relationship, not Plaid Cymru.[56] Rhetoric of this nature from the President was a sign of what amounted to a virtual political marriage between the two organizations after the spring of 1972. During May and June, Plaid Cymru gave its support to magistrates who refused to prosecute the society's protesters and, in Caernarvonshire, there were threats to disrupt the auctions of holiday homes.[57] In a similarly militant move, the party's executive resolved to 'urge party members unofficially' to 'welcome' Lord Hailsham when he came to Bangor, in a protest prompted by Hailsham's comment that it was only a matter of degree that separated the 'baboons' of the IRA from the language protesters.[58]

There were, however, limits to Gwynfor's readiness to see Plaid Cymru side with Cymdeithas yr Iaith. He rejected the recommendation of Clive Betts, editor of the *Welsh Nation*, that the party should officially adopt a policy of refusing to buy television licences.[59] Gwynfor was also sufficiently aware of his duties as a statesman to accept an honorary doctorate from the University of Wales at the same time as William Mars-Jones – who had presided over the Swansea hearing in 1971. Above all it was vital to regain Carmarthen, and for his party to make the most of the recommendations of the Constitution Commission when they appeared. Indeed, Gwynfor had come to believe, from the summer of 1972 on, that the commission (by then chaired by Lord Kilbrandon) was certain to call for an assembly for Wales. Gwynfor's longer-term aim was to make any recommendations the main focus of his party's campaign that winter.[60] He was, however, to be disappointed. In November, the commission announced that the report would not be published until the summer of 1973. It left Gwynfor once more at the mercy of others – particularly Cymdeithas yr Iaith and a commission that was in no hurry to go public. A month later, after a long illness, Dan Evans, Gwynfor's father, died.[61] Gwynfor could comfort himself with the knowledge that he had turned his father into a pacifist and possibly even a nationalist. But losing his father, and seeing Meinir and her boyfriend Ffred back in prison at the same time, marked a depressing end to a grim year.[62]

For a while, from late December 1972 until 1 March 1973, Cymdeithas yr Iaith suspended its campaign for bilingual roadsigns. The intention was to give the government time to respond positively to the Bowen Commission – which had recommended placing Welsh above English. But no such truce was observed in the broadcasting campaign. In the three months between January and March, the society incessantly targeted BBC property. Led by Wynfford James, members occupied buildings and interrupted programmes such as Pete Murray's show on Radio 2.[63] On 2 March, the society recommenced its road signs campaign, thereby ensuring that the politics of language would once again dominate Plaid Cymru's activities. For Gwynfor, the timing was highly unfortunate, because, by March, he was concentrating on elections to the newly-formed Dyfed Council, which included Carmarthenshire. The elections were a test for Plaid Cymru, and Gwynfor hoped to use the creation of Dyfed as an opportunity to make the whole area more consciously Welsh, beginning with the establishment of a bilingual school in Carmarthen. But the strategy was derailed by events in Llangadog, where D T Williams, a fellow-deacon at Providence chapel, stood against Gwynfor for the Liberals. This was in itself remarkable, but just days before the poll, he pulled out and pledged his support to George Morgan, an Independent in name, but a Conservative by instinct. As a result of this move (which caused a split within the chapel), Gwynfor lost Llangadog for the first time since 1949.[64]

Politically, the result came as a shock – especially given that many expected an early general election. The *Carmarthen Times* commented that it marked '*finis*' on Gwynfor's hopes of winning back Carmarthen when the time came.[65] The Welsh-language press sensed too that Gwynfor was a spent force, and that, to quote the *Barn* columnist Viriamu, he had reached his sixtieth year without much to show for his efforts.[66] But on a personal level, the impact on Gwynfor, and particularly on Rhiannon, was devastating. They both felt that Llangadog, their own community, their adopted home, had rejected them. It would rank among the bitterest disappointments of his life – and it was exacerbated by the resulting divisions at Providence.[67] With the chapel split between Gwynfor's supporters and those loyal to George Morgan, Gwynfor and Rhiannon decided to attend nearby Bethlehem instead. They were warmly received, but the row had left its mark. Rhiannon would never regard her neighbours in the same way again.[68]

The Llangadog result, coupled with equally gloomy results across Dyfed, came as a shock to Plaid Cymru. It was the Liberals above all who benefited, but Gwynfor believed that his own failure and the under-achievements of others could be attributed to the actions of Cymdeithas yr Iaith. Five days after the election, he told the constituency committee that Plaid Cymru was far too radical for many, and that the society, 'despite being a strength in Gwynedd is a hindrance in Dyfed'.[69] This was not a desperate search for excuses; before the poll, Plaid Cymru's canvass returns in Carmarthen had shown that Gwynfor's stance regarding Meinir's activities was widely criticized – particularly by the elderly. Rightly or wrongly, it was widely held that Plaid Cymru was the political wing of Cymdeithas yr Iaith. Plaid Cymru's executive saw it in much the same way, and agreed that nationalism was deeper-rooted in Gwynedd than 'in Dyfed where the activities of Cymdeithas yr Iaith are an election issue. It was thought that farmers in Dyfed rejected Plaid's radicalism as well as its nationalism'.[70] As a result, Plaid members in Carmarthen formed a committee to ponder the party's image and ensure that 'this image is wholly clear and independent of the image of Cymdeithas yr Iaith'.[71]

There was little Gwynfor could do, however, to provide the type of leadership his members in Carmarthenshire wanted without causing a split in nationalist ranks. And, in spite of the damage the society was causing, he was still full of admiration for its leaders. When he published his book *Wales Can Win* in June that year, he praised Dafydd Iwan and Ffred Ffransis along with Gronw ap Islwyn.[72] But by degrees, the society was slowly losing ground to Plaid Cymru and constitutional politics, mainly because of two developments, both unconnected with Gwynfor. The first was the publication of favourable reports that oil was likely to be discovered in the Celtic Sea – enough, it was said at the time, to supply twenty million gallons a day.[73] It is hard to overstate the importance of this possible Welsh Eldorado because it strengthened nationalists' belief that they could play – and win – the Westminster game.[74] The second was when the Prime Minister, Edward Heath, gave his opinion on devolution. On 12 May, in a speech at Perth, Heath announced that Scotland would be granted an assembly. A few days later, Dafydd Williams wrote to Heath to congratulate him on his statement.[75] Heath had said nothing about Wales, but Gwynfor was convinced that the Prime Minister would promise a similar body for Wales and that the situation was now 'terrifically exciting'. Gwynfor was equally certain that the Secretary of State for Wales, Peter Thomas and Wyn Roberts, his Parliamentary Private Secretary, favoured such a move.[76]

Early June brought more evidence that Heath was warming to Welsh devolution when he announced that Wales would have control over its own affairs. It was a rather ambiguous, open-ended statement, but Gwynfor was convinced that revolution was in the air.[77] And there was more to come. In early July, Gwynfor received a personal letter from Wyn Roberts saying that Wales would have an assembly. In a letter to Rhys Davies, Gwynfor could barely contain himself:

> Mr Heath's speeches in Scotland and Wales have transformed the prospects for parliamentary self-government. This was confirmed in an amazing way by a letter (not for publication) which I received after a tv programme from Wyn Roberts, M.P. who is Peter Thomas' PPS. We had both been on a programme to discuss Heath's speeches. He had disagreed with my interpretation of them. Within three days he wrote to apologise, and said (in Welsh), 'There is no doubt that Mr Heath intends that Wales shall have a Parliament... Only lack of public support in Wales could prevent this.' He could scarcely have written in his own hand to me, the President of Plaid Cymru, unless he wanted the word to go further.[78]

Unfortunately, Wyn Roberts's letter has not survived, but its implications for Plaid Cymru were far-reaching. Because of the way that Gwynfor interpreted its contents, the party came to assume that devolution was bound to happen. Irrespective of who came to power after the election, Gwynfor regarded 1974 as the year that would 'weight the balance of Wales's fate one way or the other' – the year, as he told Peter Hughes Griffiths, that 'will determine what the next Government does with Kilbrandon'.[79] The first step would be the publication of the report of the Kilbrandon Commission, and although there was still no definite date, Gwynfor insisted that his party was ready. This was the strategy Plaid Cymru pursued throughout the summer of 1973, as the party's membership was informed of the report and prepared for its appearance.[80] At the same time, Gwynfor, Dafydd Wigley and the young barrister Phil Richards planned their response to Kilbrandon. They considered a series of publicity events to mark the occasion – from bonfires to a Miss Kilbrandon contest. [81]

Gwynfor's enthusiasm for Kilbrandon was so infectious that he put the cart before the horse. During August 1973, many at the Summer School were surprised when he announced that Plaid Cymru should not contest parliamentary elections once the Assembly was established. The statement was criticized by some party members concerned that implementing the suggestion would give Labour free rein but, for Gwynfor, there was no doubting that one party or the other would set up an Assembly.[82] The constitutional question now increasingly occupied Plaid Cymru and the language issue faded into the background – especially after the establishment of the Welsh Language Council that September. In the event the council subsequently proved to be little more than a talking shop (even though its members were talented and committed), but fortunately for Gwynfor, it succeeded in distracting attention from language activism and concentrating nationalist minds on constitutional matters.

By the time of Plaid Cymru's annual conference, in late October 1973, Gwynfor was like an excited child on Christmas Eve. With only days to go before the Kilbrandon announcement he felt so confident that he told reporters gathered in Aberystwyth that the next six months would be the most important in the history of Wales.[83] His certainty was shared by the delegates. By an overwhelming majority, they defeated a motion from the Rhiwbina branch expressing grave concern 'at the excessive enthusiasm displayed by Plaid's leadership for the anticipated Welsh Assembly'.[84] Gwynfor could not conceive of any other option: having campaigned so long for a parliament, he saw hair-splitting on such a major issue as idiotic. In the light of such optimism, Gwynfor made known his intention to retire from the Presidency in two years' time, when he reached the age of 63.[85] According to observers, this left three possible successors: Dr Phil Williams, who was the clear favourite, Emrys Roberts and Dafydd Wigley.[86]

Two days after Gwynfor revealed his intention, on 30 October, the Kilbrandon Report was published. Although it was an unsatisfactory report in many ways, Plaid Cymru was delighted by its central conclusion that Wales and Scotland should have their own assemblies. The party ignored the basic dispute in the report over how precisely devolution would work and, almost immediately, Plaid Cymru put its Kilbrandon plan into action by declaring outright that Plaid itself was responsible for the recommendations. Gwynfor was even more heartened by the generally warm welcome given to the report by Edward Heath, as he introduced a White Paper on devolution before the general election.[87] It also seemed likely that the Labour party in Wales would act on Kilbrandon after Michael Foot thought he had succeeded in convincing the parliamentary group of the report's merits. The group included members like Alan Williams, Neil Kinnock and Ted Rowlands, but there were no doubts in the mind of David Rosser, political editor of the *Western Mail*, that even the critics had been appeased: 'At the end of two hours, the Welsh group contained no waverers.'[88] At the end of November, this cautious promise was made good when George Thomas, the Opposition spokesman on Welsh Affairs, announced that Labour would establish an elected Council in Cardiff.[89] Indeed, it was only in the English press – papers like the *Sun*, the *Express* and the *Daily Telegraph* – that those utterly opposed to Kilbrandon received any attention. But little by little, as soon became evident, the grumbles grew into a storm of protest.

In hindsight, it is clear that Plaid Cymru's initial faith in Kilbrandon was almost wholly misplaced but, in the days following the report, there was no organized opposition from either the Labour or the Conservative benches to its recommendations. The oil crisis also aided Plaid Cymru, strengthening its case for the right of any assembly to control the sale of Welsh oil discovered in the Celtic Sea. Gwynfor might be forgiven, then, for his conviction that devolution was on the way and that Kilbrandon had changed the political landscape. In a meeting in Llandeilo in the middle of November, for instance, he claimed that the party had not experienced 'such heady days since the Carmarthen by-election of 1966'.[90] It is harder, however, to understand Gwynfor's attitude from December onwards, when dissent began to stir in Labour ranks. As opposition became more vocal, he concluded that Plaid Cymru would benefit from any Labour split on devolution.[91] The other great advantage of Kilbrandon (although Gwynfor never mentioned it) was that it allowed his party to distance itself from Cymdeithas yr Iaith. The society and its orthodox chair, Emyr Hywel, maintained that Plaid Cymru was fighting for 'a deceptive measure of government that has been recommended... without realizing that years are bound to go by before the English Parliament gives any consideration to the Commission's recommendations'.[92]

Cymdeithas yr Iaith's silence was also a boost on the eve of a probable general election. The most striking symbol of this was the selection of Dafydd Iwan as the Plaid Cymru candidate for Ynys Môn – a decision interpreted by the *Western Mail* as proof that the society was at the crossroads and that the moderate wing was turning to Plaid Cymru.[93] The shift back to constitutional politics coincided with a grave economic situation. The miners' overtime ban coincided with the decision by the Arab oil-producing states to cut production of oil, and increase the price. A State of Emergency was declared in November. There were scenes of panic. Fuel was in short supply, there were frequent power cuts and chapels were ordered not to heat their buildings. By December, Gwynfor could sense that the government was about to fall, and warned his general secretary, Dafydd Williams, that Heath might 'be tempted to go for an election early in the new year' – particularly, he said, 'as he sees the troubles with the railways probably adding to the troubles with the miners'.[94]

January went by amid speculation over the exact date of the election, but it was obviously only a matter of time before Heath's government fell, and the election was called for 28 February. On 4 January, Plaid Cymru approved its manifesto – *A Rich Wales or a Poor Britain* – that attempted to marry Kilbrandon's recommendations with the need to control the new wealth in Wales when the soon-to-be-discovered oil flowed.[95] Influenced by John Osmond and Phil Williams, it was also a particularly left-wing document. But throughout Plaid Cymru more generally there was a feeling that Kilbrandon and the energy crisis had created a 'tailor-made' opportunity, in the words of the *Welsh Nation*'s editor,[96] for electoral success, especially for Dafydd Wigley in Caernarfon – the seat most likely to fall to Plaid Cymru.[97] Gwynfor believed the party could take as many as eight seats and that a 'snap election' could only be a good thing.[98] When the miners voted for a national strike at the end of January, the probability of an early poll increased, and this was confirmed on 7 February, when Edward Heath called for Parliament to be dissolved.

Nationally, Plaid Cymru, after so much speculation about the date, was ready for the election. In Carmarthen – the most interesting of all the Welsh seats – the situation looked promising, and there were high hopes that all the hard work undertaken in the autumn of 1973 by Peter Hughes Griffiths would be rewarded. By dint of his hard work a special leaflet – *Gwynfor Evans and You* – had reached virtually every home in the constituency, and by the time the election was called, much of the spadework had been completed.[99] Peter Hughes Griffiths was also prepared to do Gwynfor's dirty work, and took advantage of every opportunity to portray Gwynoro Jones as a language-hating whitterer with a sentimental attachment to nonconformism.[100] Hughes Griffiths and Gwynfor's agent, Cyril Jones, made sure they had a committed team – men like Alun Lloyd, Aled Gwyn and D O Davies – who knew the county and its people far better than Gwynfor himself. D O Davies was sufficiently plain-speaking to ensure that Carmarthen, and not the rest of Wales, would be Gwynfor's priority and wrote to him in no uncertain terms: 'We cannot afford to allow a lot of nice people to lick their lips while singing Gwynfor's praises and go to sleep dreaming of 1966 with "*Gad fi'n llonydd* " [a popular Dafydd Iwan song at the time] as a bedtime prayer. The heady romance of 1966 will never return.'[101] By the end of the first week, the first canvass had been completed – an immense achievement given the size of the constituency. More astounding still was Gwynfor's energy during the short campaign given that he was now close to pensionable age.

But however splendid the electoral machine, Gwynoro Jones was not an easy man to defeat. The miners' strike caused Plaid Cymru particular problems as it meant that the election was being fought almost entirely on 'British' issues. This election would supposedly determine who ran Britain – the miners or Heath – and Welsh issues tended to be ignored in the crossfire. The strike also meant that Labour was likely to get its vote out, adding to Plaid Cymru's difficulties. Would Plaid, then, fight Labour on the industrial front or would it concentrate on emphasizing its nationalism? As for Gwynoro Jones he had an even greater advantage in that his father was a carpenter at the Cynheidre pit – even though Jones was, in fact, on the right wing of his party and had little sympathy with the NUM leadership. Nevertheless, Gwynoro Jones, as his election literature proclaimed, was 'the collier's friend', a David ready to do battle with the nationalist Goliath, Gwynfor Evans.

It was a difficult situation for Plaid Cymru as it set out its political stall. Nationally, the socialist strategy was the approved course but, in Carmarthen, Gwynfor ignored swathes of his party's manifesto in an effort to garner Liberal votes. After the election, he confided to Rhys Davies how unhappy he had been with many of the ideas developed by Phil Williams, calling his recommendations on workers' control 'half-baked'. He also thought that the party should be 'tentative and experimental' with such concepts. Equally as disappointing, to Gwynfor's way of thinking, was the manifesto's failure to make nationalism the focus of Plaid Cymru's vision:

> There was a general feeling that the impression had been given that we were more socialist (a word that I have always rejected) than nationalist... My own campaign was almost wholly on national political and cultural issues.[102]

Not that Gwynfor did nothing for the miners. It is only fair to mention how often he emphasized that their pay rise was inadequate.[103] Even so, the rhetoric in Carmarthen was very different from the language employed by his party in the rest of Wales – a difference seen at its starkest in Gwynfor's election leaflet on the importance of keeping 'Christian Civilization' alive.[104]

But the real drama came at the count. When the first of the ballot boxes arrived at the Guildhall in Carmarthen, things looked reasonably promising for Gwynfor. The clear impression as the square filled with people was that Plaid Cymru was doing well and, in some places, was ahead of Labour. Then, as more boxes arrived and as the votes were apportioned, it became obvious that the result would be an extremely close one.[105] All eyes then turned to the 97 spoilt papers – a tiny proportion of the 50,000 cast, but enough to make the difference between winning and losing. The tension was electric when it was learned, at ten to three in the morning, that Gwynoro Jones was just ten votes ahead – with 17,205 votes to Gwynfor's 17,195. Plaid Cymru called for a recount. At twenty-five to five in the morning, the gap was even narrower, with Gwynoro Jones's lead down to just three votes. Inevitably, given the circumstances, a second recount followed. By now, many at the count were in a state of nervous exhaustion, none more so than Gwynoro Jones himself, holding the odd ballot paper up to the light to see where the cross had been placed.[106] Plaid's supporters were equally anxious, and Peter Hughes Griffiths confessed that it took 'a heart of steel' to be there at all.[107] Gwynfor withdrew to a side-room and at ten to six in the morning, with the town square invisible under a carpet of fog, the news came that Gwynfor was ahead by four votes and might after all be joining Dafydd Elis Thomas and Dafydd Wigley in the Commons. It then was Labour's turn to ask for a recount; however, because the clerks were exhausted, the returning officer announced that the fourth count would not be held until four o'clock that afternoon.

All eyes were on Carmarthen as the parties reassembled. By then, it was clear that Britain would have a hung parliament – the first since 1929 – making the outcome there even more significant. Three and a half hours later, the scales tipped once more, leaving Labour ahead again – with a majority of just one. The fifth count brought no miracle for Gwynfor. At ten o'clock, Gwynoro Jones was declared three votes ahead. Gwynfor came under immense pressure to demand a sixth count, but wiser counsel prevailed. Gwynfor was advised by Wynne Samuel to accept the result, on the grounds that it was far better to lose by three votes than win by the same margin. With another general election probable within months, Samuel believed that the momentum, not to mention public sympathy, would be behind Gwynfor. He was sensible enough too to ignore the talk of a handful of votes discovered in a rubbish bin. At ten o'clock that evening, it was announced that Gwynfor, much to the disappointment of his supporters in the square below, had accepted defeat.[108]

It brought to an end a legendary day in Welsh politics, but there were mixed emotions within Plaid Cymru. In one respect, there was celebration because for the first time ever, Plaid Cymru had won seats at a general election. Having the 'Two Dafydds' at Westminster meant that Plaid Cymru would have willing hands to carry some of the load Gwynfor had borne alone for so long. But the triumph for Gwynfor was the election of Dafydd Wigley. Now, he knew for certain that there was someone reliable in place who could take the reins within a year. He also knew that Wigley was now sufficiently strong to withstand any possible challenge for the Presidency from Emrys Roberts or Phil Williams. From now on, Gwynedd and Dafydd Wigley, as Gwynfor saw it, would decide the party's direction. Within days of the election, he wrote to Rhys Davies, stating that his legacy was secure with Dafydd Wigley and that those awkward figures in the south would be powerless to destroy it:

> His [Dafydd Wigley] parliamentary position gives him a great advantage; and anyway there has been a massive shift in party leadership from the south to Gwynedd, not only in the parliamentary field but even more in local government. Gwynedd will be setting the pace for years to come; this is the historic bastion of Welsh nationhood.[109]

The Gwynedd results were not Gwynfor's only comfort. In Carmarthen too, hopes were high because Gwynfor's final vote (17,162) was higher than his by-election total. Gwynfor's only worry concerned the county's Liberals, whose vote had held up unexpectedly well after a lacklustre campaign. As he told Rhys Davies: 'If there had been an election at Carmarthen three weeks earlier, we would have won by 10,000 and the Liberals would have lost their deposit.'[110]

At the same time, Plaid Cymru's left wing was disconsolate. Privately, its chief spokesperson, Dr Phil Williams, expressed disappointment that the result confirmed the perception Plaid Cymru was the party of the Welsh-speaking west.[111] In the towns, Plaid Cymru had all but disappeared, and the party's showing in the valleys was also extremely disappointing. If proof were needed that the successes between 1967 and 1972 were a freak, this was it. Nationally, the party had lost ground with the share falling from 11.5 per cent in 1970 to 10.8 per cent. The picture in Scotland was different; there, the SNP share had risen substantially. In short, Plaid Cymru had reached a cultural and electoral impasse; from this point onwards, it would thrive in its heartlands and retreat outside Welsh-speaking Wales. To this extent, Phil Williams's pessimism was well founded.

The post-mortem was brief, however, because there were more important issues to attend to. For some days after the election, there was the intriguing possibility that Edward Heath would try to patch together a coalition government between the Tories, Liberals and even Plaid Cymru. Given the arithmetic – 296 seats for Heath and 301 for Wilson – Plaid Cymru had to decide how to respond to this crucial question, and quickly.[112] On the evening of Sunday, 3 March, Plaid Cymru's leaders met in Dolgellau to discuss the matter. Some feared that Gwynfor would be tempted to negotiate a deal but the possibility was rejected – no real surprise given the connection between Dafydd Elis Thomas and, to a lesser extent, Dafydd Wigley, with Labour's left wing.[113] Two days later Edward Heath was told that Jeremy Thorpe did not favour a marriage of political convenience either. Consequently, Harold Wilson once again stepped through the door of 10 Downing Street.

It marked the end of five extraordinary days in British politics, but Wilson's failure to win a majority had put Plaid Cymru in a commanding position. At Westminster, Labour whips greeted the 'Two Dafydds' like long-lost sons and they were given an impressive office. But the transformation in Wales was more marked still. Completely unexpectedly, it was John Morris, and not George Thomas, who was appointed Welsh Secretary. There was now a keen devolutionist in Cathays Park and, from the very outset, he made it clear that he regarded the implementation of Kilbrandon as a priority.[114] Although some doubted Wilson's sincerity on devolution, no one had any doubts about John Morris – a perception that was confirmed with the appointment of Gwilym Prys Davies as his special adviser. And immediately after the election, there was a heavy hint that Wilson himself wanted to see devolution succeed when he appointed Lord Crowther-Hunt to be his adviser on the issue. It was also promised that Crowther-Hunt would be available to advise Plaid Cymru and the SNP if they wished. Within the month, Crowther-Hunt duly met Wigley and Elis Thomas, praising them in a letter to John Morris for displaying 'a most friendly and co-operative attitude'. On the basis of these confidential discussions, Crowther-Hunt believed that Wigley and Elis Thomas were ready to strike a bargain and accept 'something that fell very short of their long term aims'.[115] Gwynfor could hardly believe the transformation of the political climate when he wrote to Elwyn Roberts:

> Aren't things moving rapidly now? It's obvious that Wilson takes Kilbrandon seriously, even though he may be preparing for an election. It's not likely that he'll go on for a full year, but were he to do so, we might see a bill to establish some sort of elected Assembly for Wales before Parliament this year.[116]

There were some, however, primarily on the left of his party, who doubted the wisdom of such confidence, but Gwynfor made the most of every opportunity to convince ordinary members of Plaid Cymru that changes were afoot within Labour. He also made full use of the 'Two Dafydds' to squeeze all sorts of concessions out of the Labour government. More often than not, therefore, Dafydd Wigley and Phil Williams were the only major figures within Plaid Cymru to question Labour motives, as in the case of the Green Paper on devolution published in June.[117] Gwynfor remained totally silent.

But as Plaid Cymru and Labour grew close at Westminster, it was a vastly different story in Carmarthen. There was now every reason to expect an early election; the atmosphere was more unpleasant than ever and, to all intents and purposes, the electorate was forced to endure a continuous election campaign from February until October 1974. Both sides could take their share of the blame for the childish bickering but, without doubt, Gwynoro Jones, driven into a corner, was the more culpable. He tried to land several blows but to no avail. The turning-point came when he referred to the Second World War and accused Plaid Cymru's leaders of failing to choose between Britain and Hitler. Even by the standards of Carmarthenshire politics, it was a vicious blow. This paragraph by him – quoted in full in a local newspaper – lit the blue touchpaper:

> When the Nationalist Party policy towards the Second World War was NEUTRALITY – i.e. they could not choose between Britain and Hitler – there were sufficient patriots in Wales who fought so that we can enjoy the freedom of speech, religion, etc. today.[118]

If Gwynoro Jones wanted to cause trouble, he succeeded beyond all expectation. For weeks thereafter, the old stories about Gwynfor's pacifism were dragged out once again causing Plaid Cymru to lose considerable momentum.

In addition, Gwynfor was facing personal financial difficulties. At the end of May 1974, it was clear that his business was in serious trouble, and had debts of several thousand pounds. The only logical course was to close, and family members were eager to do so, but the problem was that the business was so widely known in the county as Gwynfor's. There were family rows and Ceridwen was particularly critical of her brother's negligence, writing to complain in strong terms: 'I really cannot understand Gwynfor why all these wonderful opportunities in such a glorious part of Wales are left to rot... If English people bought the farm and glasshouses and made an attractive estate of it, I suppose it would get bashed about.'[119] But however grim the situation, Gwynfor did not dare close the business in case Labour made capital out of the redundancies that would inevitably result. Eventually, it fell to his brother Alcwyn to keep the enterprise afloat until the election. Afterwards, it closed without undue publicity leaving debts of thousands of pounds for the Dan Evans company – debts cleared once again by the reliable Alcwyn.

Alcwyn's support was crucial to Gwynfor, enabling him to campaign without a break (despite his fatigue) throughout the spring and summer of 1974. As he had during the election campaign of February 1974, he relied heavily on Cyril Jones and Peter Hughes Griffiths as Labour poured endless resources into the constituency. In between the two elections, many senior Labour ministers were drafted into Carmarthenshire to boost Gwynoro Jones's campaign. But, this time, many developments favoured Gwynfor, not least the splits within the Carmarthen Labour Party. Since around 1972, Gwynoro Jones had angered some stalwarts because of his support for Europe and his hesitant response to the NUM's pay claims. Even more unpalatable to his opponents, however, was his alignment with Labour's right wing, a faction containing men like Bill Rodgers and Roy Jenkins who would seven years later break away to form the SDP. By the summer of 1974, Labour's left wanted Gwynoro Jones's head on a plate and some of his less loyal supporters began to distance themselves from him.[120] This happened to such an extent that Neil Kinnock, the member for Bedwellty and a prominent figure on the left, could claim with confidence that Gwynoro was: 'a myopic old fool who, by denying the elementary conviction of party has probably committed electoral hara-kiri – so we won't have to worry about him'.[121]

Not for the first time, Neil Kinnock was overstating the case, but his purple prose did have some substance. It is also true that Gwynfor benefited from Cymdeithas yr Iaith's total silence as the fratricidal struggle between Adfer, the hard-line breakaway group, and the society intensified.[122] The strain meant that there was little direct action on their part between the two elections. It also meant an end to the unfavourable headlines that had been such a source of irritation to Plaid Cymru in Carmarthenshire. In the circumstances, the society's decision to reject Plaid Cymru's offer of a truce had little effect.[123] However, the clearest indicator of Gwynfor's tight grip on Welsh nationalism was probably Saunders Lewis's refusal to accept the honorary Presidency of Plaid Cymru. Giving his reasons, Saunders Lewis claimed that Gwynfor's deserved position as leader became 'more evident with every passing year. He has protected the party against immense dangers from within and has earned it fearful respect from without'.[124]

From his position of strength, Gwynfor was free to enjoy the patriotic acclaim that came with the publication of a government White Paper on Welsh and Scottish devolution – the first of its type in British political history. It was, wrote Ann Clwyd, *The Guardian*'s correspondent, 'the most important event since the Act of Union in 1536',[125] even though Gwynfor described it as 'a raspberry'.[126] This would be effectively the last act of the Wilson government. Two days later, on 19 September, Wilson called an election hoping that he could win a clear majority to govern. It left Plaid Cymru well placed; not only did the start of proper campaigning mean the end of weeks of tiresome speculation, calling an election so soon after the publication of the White Paper meant that Plaid Cymru could make the election 'the white paper ballot'. Time and again, Plaid Cymru stressed that only they could make Wilson's promises a reality.

Gwynfor was at his happiest and perhaps his best in such situations – as a pragmatic politician trying to convince Welsh electors that his party could make things happen through Westminster. It was the line he adopted in Carmarthen, where he seized every opportunity to remind voters of what Dafydd Elis Thomas and Dafydd Wigley had achieved since February.[127] There was no mention of Plaid Cymru's supposed socialism in its election literature, and he answered the familiar charge of being a Welsh Tory with the equally familiar riposte that he was a Welsh 'radical'. As it happens Gwynfor did genuinely believe what he said, but being able to appeal to everyone, in particular the Conservative and Liberal farmers of Carmarthenshire, was vital in a contest described in the press as 'Gwynoro v Gwynfor'.[128] The election appeared also to be Gwynfor's last hope of a return to Parliament and, as the campaign drew to a close, there was a clear sense that he would be the victor. At Dai George the bookmaker's in Carmarthen, Gwynfor was the favourite by some way as one of the longest electoral fights in Welsh political history drew to a close. The whole affair made a profound impression on the *Daily Post*'s reporter: Gwynoro Jones 'harassed' and Gwynfor 'calm and confident'.[129]

The confidence was fully justified in the early hours of 11 October as a crowd of three thousand thronged Nott Square to hear the outcome. It was the first time that an election count had been held at St Peter's Hall nearby and, if anything, the expectation was greater than it had traditionally been in Guildhall Square. Almost inevitably, the length and bitterness of the campaign had created an unpleasant atmosphere, and the police feared the worst. However, a nasty situation was saved from complete mayhem by the inspired decision of Chief Inspector Viv Fisher to conduct community singing from the balcony of the hall. Fisher, a giant of a man with a renowned bass voice, started with '*Sosban Fach*' and '*Calon Lân*'. By the time he reached '*Bendigedig fyddo'r Iesu*', the crowd was celebrating Dafydd Elis Thomas's victory in Merioneth. Then, as the Carmarthen count proceeded, the crowd fell quiet as rumours circulated of a recount in Caernarfon. But it was soon followed by a loud cheer as it became apparent that the second Dafydd was back in Westminster.[130]

Only one result remained to be announced and, at half past three in the morning, Gwynfor was declared the winner with 23,325 votes – the highest total ever achieved by any candidate in the history of Plaid Cymru. It was also the only seat that Labour lost that night as thousands of Tories and Liberals joined forces to unseat Gwynoro Jones. It was a totally unique result on an otherwise rather disappointing night for Plaid Cymru. In the valleys, Plaid Cymru was in retreat, but Carmarthen bucked the trend – clear proof that Gwynfor could appeal to nationalists and rural conservatives as effectively as ever. As a result, he was back at Westminster, even though his contempt for the place was undimmed. But, compared to 1966, there was one enormous difference. With Labour in power (with only a majority of three), Plaid Cymru and the SNP were in an apparently ideal position. As he headed for Westminster, Gwynfor believed in all sincerity that an Assembly was imminent and that his life's work would be complete within three years.[131] Scarcely anyone would have guessed that the dream would turn to ashes as it did, but the failure of 1979 was already inevitable. That failure would jeopardise everything that Gwynfor held dear – including his own life.

Chapter 11

DOWNFALL 1974–79

SUPERFICIALLY, THE OCTOBER 1974 RESULT was a substantial victory for Plaid Cymru. According to the party's propaganda, Gwynfor was returning to Westminster despite the best efforts of Carmarthen Labour Party and a nation of cowardly Welshmen and women. He was returning too, it was said, as a redeemer, the man who would transform the white paper on devolution into an Assembly. When he returned to the Commons, he was given a spacious office in the shadow of Big Ben – a small but concrete symbol of Plaid Cymru's status at the heart of the British establishment. There were other signs that times were changing as well. Days after the election, Gwynfor was telephoned by Jeremy Thorpe, the Liberal leader, who suggested that the two parties could come to a mutual understanding. He was not offering a coalition but, certainly, Thorpe considered Plaid Cymru's support to be worth having, considering Harold Wilson's tiny majority. Given his new position of strength, Gwynfor decided to reject Jeremy Thorpe's proposal.[1]

And unlike the situation in 1966, Gwynfor was no longer a one-man band. Now, Plaid Cymru could boast three MPs, a trinity soon immortalized in a photograph popularly known as the 'Father, Son and Holy Ghost'. No one was completely sure who the Son and the Holy Ghost were in this fetching tableau – the important thing was that Gwynfor, Wigley and Elis Thomas were an inseparable trio and about to achieve great things. The hundreds of nationalists who gathered at the gates of Parliament to greet Gwynfor on his first day back thought it was only a matter of time before Wales took its first real steps towards freedom. For Gwynfor personally, the arrival of the two Dafydds and their confident attitude towards Labour members was sufficient – for now – to transform the way he viewed the Commons. The parliamentary nightmare of 1966–70 became a distant memory and, from the moment the 'Two Dafydds' sat at the 'Welsh Table' for the first time, the House now became tolerable. The only apparent difference between him and the 'two Dafydds' was their fondness for socializing with left-wing Labour MPs. In the evenings, they would go for a pint with them, while Gwynfor withdrew to his office to write yet more letters.[2] This was, however, a minor difference; after all, Gwynfor was very close to Wigley and shared a flat in Chelsea with Elis Thomas, enjoying long conversations with the Honourable Member for Merioneth.

But euphoria had blinded some within Plaid Cymru to minor cracks that would, within five years, become deep chasms. The most important and enduring of these was the relationship between Dafydd Elis Thomas and Dafydd Wigley. Between February 1974 and October 1974, Elis Thomas and Wigley evidently worked well together, sharing the parliamentary workload effectively. They may not have been the closest of friends but, certainly, there was no personal enmity between them. They also managed to gloss over their political differences, with Elis Thomas on the left and Wigley more to the centre. But with Gwynfor's arrival, Dafydd Elis Thomas sensed a change, as Wigley tended to side with Gwynfor. Gradually, Elis Thomas would come to feel that his relationship with Wigley was deteriorating, sowing the seeds of the disagreements seen between them by the 'eighties and 'nineties.[3] Wigley was apparently blind to this, and Elis Thomas said nothing about their perceived estrangement. However, Wigley later claimed that it was in the 'eighties that his relationship with Elis Thomas went downhill after the latter began to dabble seriously with the British left.[4] But from Elis Thomas's perspective, the damage had been done long before then, opening a personal and ideological divide. In due course, the split would be only marginally less significant than that between Saunders Lewis and Gwynfor.

This was not the only strained relationship during the Parliament of 1974–79. At the outset, there had been much exaggerated talk of the potential of so many nationalists in the Commons – three Plaid Cymru and eleven SNP MPs. At the very least, it was anticipated that a nationalist group would be formed and there were some, like Gwynfor, who wanted to go further and forge a more formal parliamentary coalition. Indeed, ever since 1938 when Gwynfor first met the SNP, he had longed to see the formation of a pan-Celtic alliance in Parliament. His relationship with Winnie Ewing had also shown how much the two parties could benefit from such an arrangement. On his first day back in Parliament, therefore, Gwynfor stated his goal of a parliamentary coalition between the SNP and Plaid Cymru that would replace the Liberals as a third 'party'.[5] But the waters were muddied almost immediately as Plaid Cymru and the SNP discussed possible ways forward. In essence, the SNP parliamentary representation was a vipers' nest, with little to unite them, neither personally nor ideologically.[6] A further complication was caused by a tendency among some in the SNP to consider their Plaid Cymru counterparts as more conciliatory nationalists than they were – after all SNP's official policy was Scottish independence. Following informal talks between the two parties, it became obvious by late October that any talk of a coalition was a pipe dream. From then on, the policy was to cooperate only as and when co-operation was possible.

There is no doubt that opportunities were missed as a result, but it was certainly not the fault of Gwynfor or Plaid Cymru that the parties failed to form a more powerful bond. However, Gwynfor was responsible for the failure to tackle other urgent problems immediately after the election of October 1974. The first and most serious of these was his inability to formulate a new political agenda in the valleys, where his party had fared so abysmally in the general election. The inadequate response was reflected across the whole party as the membership largely concentrated on the triumph of 'The Three' in the west. Members like Emyr Price who tried to instigate intelligent discussion of the result were rare exceptions. In his own characteristically perceptive way, Emyr Price hit the nail on the head when he observed that Plaid Cymru depended heavily on support from some of the most conservative elements in Wales:

> Indeed, even in the seats that were won, apart perhaps from Merioneth, where Plaid has managed to identify itself with the Labour movement, especially in Blaenau Ffestiniog, it made very little impression on the Labour vote. Is it not a short-term policy, a policy that will be counter-productive and futile, to rely on uncertain support, esoteric, anti-Labour social groups, and reactionary ones in some cases, rather than appeal to the population at large – ordinary working people.[7]

Emyr Price's analysis and his criticism went to the heart of Gwynfor's political shortcomings by October 1974. Gwynfor's basic problem was that his cherished idea of a national movement was more suited to the 'fifties and 'sixties – when Plaid Cymru was seeking a foothold on the political ladder. That had now been achieved and it needed more than the limited cultural agenda of a 'national movement' if Plaid was to break out of its western stronghold. The answer, according to Emyr Price, Dafydd Elis Thomas and Phil Williams – three of the sharpest minds within Plaid Cymru's left wing – was to transform the party into one which would be proud to embrace socialism and which would carry the fight to Labour in the valleys. But, as with Emrys Roberts in the 'sixties, Gwynfor was quick to pour cold water on any such idea. He argued that it would be a colossal mistake to fight the socialists on their own ground. Rather, he claimed that Plaid Cymru's mistake during the election had been to attempt to imitate Labour by saying that they were better socialists than the socialists themselves.[8] Influenced by R Tudur Jones, Gwynfor tried to maintain that the answer was for Plaid Cymru to remain a 'radical' party – one that would marry nationalism and Christianity, as Michael D Jones had done ninety years before. But as Wales grew increasingly secular, it was a distinctly limiting, irrelevant stance. Even so, Gwynfor was confident he could win the battle for hearts and minds, telling Tudur Jones that 'the fact of the matter is that our values are thoroughly Christian and it would be no surprise to find the people of Wales turning almost completely to this way of thinking and acting socially'.[9]

Given the social make-up of south Wales, Gwynfor was foolishly naïve to argue as he did, and it would be fair to conclude that one of the most unfortunate features of his second parliamentary term was his tendency to make light of problems. His goal was to avoid conflict but he undoubtedly damaged his party as a consequence. There is no better example of this political conservatism than his attitude to the reorganization of Plaid Cymru immediately after the election. In November 1974, he received an unsettling letter from John Osmond, the *Western Mail* journalist, and a man on whom he was increasingly reliant for policy advice. The letter warned him that the party's organization was a disaster:

> To the outside casual observer, the immediate impression of the Cardiff Headquarters is 'chaos'. There is a definite lack of professionalism about it. This would not be so bad if it were not reflected in all the incredible filing systems, especially on the finance side… I shouldn't think the SNP work from an HQ that looks like ours. It could do with a coat of paint.

And according to Osmond, the party's unwieldy machine was reflected in its huge deficiencies on the ground – especially in the valleys to the east:

> In many of our key areas in the South-East this has never existed adequately and where it has is coming apart… At present the state of the organisation is appalling. In some areas e.g. Aberdare I think we need an influx from outside of a new energy… I do

> feel very strongly that the leadership needs to take a firm grip now. I sense the sand beginning to slip through our fingers.[10]

John Osmond was not the only important figure to warn Gwynfor that the party was dying on its feet. Indeed, back in 1973, he had received a similar letter from Harri Webb, concerned about the effect that Dafydd Williams's lack of organization was having on his leadership. 'He,' Harri Webb wrote of Dafydd Williams, 'is an exceptionally nice chap, and I couldn't be as unpleasant to him as he deserves. But if he were a member of my own staff, he'd be on the carpet in a big way.'[11] But by the 'seventies Gwynfor was too kind to lay down the law to anyone and, in spite of the warnings, did nothing at the time to re-shape Plaid Cymru. Worse still, the vital relationship between Gwynfor and his chair, Phil Williams, was poor and Gwynfor tended to frown upon Phil Williams not only because of his fiery socialism, but because he was also having an extra-marital affair with a member of the party's staff.[12] However one looks at the situation at the time, it was a mess, and Plaid Cymru would pay dearly for Gwynfor's reluctance to act in the years ahead.

But as well as Gwynfor's personality, the general certainty that devolution was imminent further explains his reluctance to change course. On 5 November, the Labour government declared that it would be putting a devolution Bill before the Commons during that session. This development suggested to Gwynfor that success was at hand. And there were other signs that the devolutionists within Labour would prevail this time. In the same month, Cledwyn Hughes was appointed chair of the Parliamentary Labour Party. There was also an announcement from John Morris that there would be an Assembly sitting in Cardiff during the course of that parliament.[13] To cap it all, there was talk of establishing a Welsh-language television channel – when finances allowed. In the circumstances, there was little reason for Gwynfor to upset anyone in his own party. As he looked forward to 1975, he saw a golden year ahead for Plaid Cymru. This was the theme of nearly all his public pronouncements and his private letters too. After three months back in the Commons, he could tell Elwyn Roberts that 'the impression I had was that the government is serious about Scotland and Wales and that we have had signs that a Parliament on Welsh soil is not an impossibility, with the same status as Scotland within four years'.[14]

The irony, of course, is that devolution would be offered to the people of Wales at a time when nationalism was in decline in Wales and beyond. Private research by the Conservatives, for instance, showed that ordinary people had no interest at all in devolution: 'It was really an in-group subject – the Press, TV and politicians were interested, people were not.'[15] In January 1975, they spotted an opportunity and their spokesperson on Wales, Nicholas Edwards, wrote to Margaret Thatcher, informing her that there was 'growing hostility to an Assembly' evident in Wales.[16] A month later, Margaret Thatcher was elected leader of the opposition and the Conservatives' policy of suspicion turned into an unbending refusal to countenance devolution. However, Plaid Cymru remained as blind as ever to these shifts and was still full of optimism at its annual conference in January 1975 – held four months later than usual because of the election. In vain, Dafydd Wigley warned his fellow-members to avoid being pushed down 'a sterile and time-wasting blind alley'.[17] By then, most Plaid Cymru members believed passionately in the public statements being made by Gwynfor and John Morris. The rank and file and leadership alike were convinced that the long-awaited Assembly was imminent. With everything apparently so promising, Gwynfor was under growing pressure, from the old guard in particular, not to relinquish the Presidency in October 1975. To some of the leading lights, like O M Roberts, 1975 would be 'the worst possible time' for Gwynfor to give up the leadership because the next few months would be 'crucial'. O M Roberts had still more advice for Gwynfor: he also believed that Plaid Cymru could not 'afford a contest between different people for the Presidency' because some of the potential successors might cause 'a rift in Plaid'.[18]

O M Roberts's words were powerful and proved influential because Gwynfor reconsidered his 1973 decision to retire from the Presidency when his term of office ended. However, as the new year dawned, there was an even more important matter than devolution to occupy the minds of Plaid Cymru and the other parties alike. By January 1975, it was public knowledge that there would be a referendum on Europe in June, and Plaid Cymru needed to decide on its tactics – to campaign for continued membership, or to withdraw from the European Economic Community. Ever since 1971, and the publication of the government White Paper on Europe, it had been Plaid Cymru's official policy to oppose membership by arguing that Wales would be disadvantaged by joining an undemocratic, capitalist club of this sort. Gwynfor's own opposition was underpinned by his pacifism because he saw the community as a military power which jeopardized international stability.[19] Plaid Cymru's long-term goal (shared by those on the left of the party, particularly Dafydd Elis Thomas) was to join a European body like EFTA (the European Free Trade Area). This policy was contained in the slogan 'Europe Yes, Common Market, No' and that, when it went to a vote, was the view of most Plaid Cymru members – including Gwynfor. But the policy was only agreed in January 1975 after considerable disagreement. Dafydd Wigley decided to ignore his own party's line, and Saunders Lewis stirred from his slumbers to condemn Plaid Cymru in the *Western Mail* for voting 'in favour of Westminster sovereignty and against Europe'.[20] Privately, the party's ex-president went considerably further, maintaining that 'Plaid's leaders – with the brave and honourable exception of Mr Dafydd Wigley – have betrayed all the fundamental principles of the party on the referendum. Were it not for Mr Wigley… I would not find it hard to sever my connection with Plaid publicly'.[22]

As the referendum campaign gathered pace, Gwynfor feared the worst, warning the party centrally that it should 'prepare for a little difficulty' as the multi-hued factions formed.[22] At one extreme, Dafydd Wigley was campaigning openly for a Yes vote alongside Tories, Labour members and Liberals. At the other, Dafydd Elis Thomas was leading the battle to withdraw, sharing platforms with some of the bright lights of the Labour left – in particular Neil Kinnock. But despite the presence of Kinnock in the No camp, some within Plaid saw a vote against as a means for the Welsh to assert their political identity as distinct from those London-based capitalists who insisted that Wales's proper place was within Europe. Gwynfor largely kept his distance from the referendum battle – his contribution was limited to occasional letters and short articles in the press. With Plaid Cymru and Labour divided on the matter, it was a wise course – particularly when it became evident that Plaid Cymru's policy of withdrawal was generally unpopular. In the Welsh-language press, for example, Geraint Talfan Davies expressed incredulity that Plaid Cymru, of all parties, was campaigning against Europe.[23] In a development of equal significance for Gwynfor, it became apparent that the farmers of Carmarthenshire were delighted with Europe and its generous subsidies. Faced with this, Peter Hughes Griffiths wrote to Dafydd Elis Thomas asking for 'a bit of soft pedal' on the issue because the farmers in the county were 'stupid sods'.[24] It is difficult to say whether Peter Hughes Griffiths was writing on Gwynfor's behalf but, without doubt, his concerns about Elis Thomas's enthusiasm were well founded. Locally, Gwynfor was accused by

Gwynoro Jones of being under Dafydd Elis Thomas's thumb – and he, in turn, Gwynoro Jones claimed, idolized Tony Benn, who was a crank intent on founding a socialist republic.

There is no doubt that was a strange period for politics in Wales and the rest of Britain as Europe dominated everything for six months. When the ballot was held on 5 June, Wales voted by two to one in favour of remaining in the Community. Across Wales, there were clear majorities for Europe, demolishing the credibility of those who had predicted that patriotic Welsh-speakers would vote for a withdrawal. It was obvious, as the *Liverpool Daily Post* remarked, that Plaid Cymru and its President had got it hopelessly wrong: 'The Yes majorities in both Wales and Scotland were a severe rebuff for the Nationalist opponents of the Market. Both Plaid Cymru and the SNP saw the referendum as a fortuitous means of demonstrating that their countries wanted separatism. They too, have been given their verdict.'[25]

After the vote, Gwynfor conceded that Plaid Cymru, like the other parties, had gone through a difficult time and that the history of Britain would never be the same again.[26] He could have added in that interview with the *Carmarthen Journal* that Plaid Cymru's constitutional position had changed irrevocably as well. During the weekend after the poll, the party's leaders met in Dolgellau to discuss the way forward and, within hours, they decided to abandon their opposition to Europe.[27] It was a massive U-turn but was no doubt the sensible, pragmatic thing to do in the face of public opinion. The old policy of opposing Europe was forgotten, and Gwynfor wiped the slate clean, arguing passionately for the new policy. But every bit as important as embracing Europe was the impact on Plaid Cymru's constitution in the long term. After the Dolgellau meeting, the party ditched the goal of attaining Commonwealth (or Dominion as some still called it) status and began to campaign for full national status for Wales, within Europe.

Plaid Cymru managed to live quite happily with this description of its constitutional policy until 2003 – when it voted for independence. However uncontroversial the policy change, the referendum had underlined once more how broad a church Plaid Cymru was. Gwynfor's personality was, largely, the cement which held the random cluster of bricks together and it was therefore no surprise that the demands for him to remain President increased. In July 1975, the executive received a letter from the influential Arfon district calling on him to stay in post.[28] It was an important intervention, but Arfon was pushing at an open door. If the 1975 referendum had taught Gwynfor anything, it was that party unity would be threatened by the left were he to retire.

As a consequence, Gwynfor made a second attempt at bequeathing his party an ideology – the act of a man unwilling to surrender the Presidency. In June 1975, for instance, he wrote to Dafydd Glyn Jones, a leading intellectual, to say that he was 'very eager' to establish the perception that 'we in Plaid Cymru are Welsh radicals and that there is such a thing as Welsh Radicalism that is *sui generis*'. The clear danger, he told Dafydd Glyn Jones, came from the left: 'Being called socialists and seeing so many people calling us socialists is doing us not a little harm.'[29] Gwynfor discussed similar anti-socialist ideas with R Tudur Jones in the same period, telling him that he would rather talk about 'societism' than socialism because it would 'give our people a Welsh ideology'.[30] And he did not confine these ideas to private correspondence. In the July issue of the *Welsh Nation*, Gwynfor was totally frank about whom he considered to be his party's natural supporters: 'As things are, although Plaid Cymru is the most radical Welsh party, the fundamental conservative element in the policy makes it the natural home for those conservative patriots who give their first loyalty to the nation.'[31] By degrees, therefore, Gwynfor was preparing the ground for one of the most spectacular U-turns of his career: to continue in the Presidency until devolution was assured. There was an element of control freakery at the root of his decision not to surrender the Presidency to anyone else, less still to anyone on the left. But the post of President was also more attractive than ever given the tiny Labour majority, and self-preservation was another possible factor. In his autobiography, Gwynfor wrote about how he became 'an important and respectable man' after years of being 'almost anathema'. It meant lavish parliamentary dinners and, on one occasion, an invitation to dine with Wilson, Douglas-Home, Heath and the Duke of Edinburgh. The other guest that evening, Gwynfor added proudly, 'was the Queen'.[32]

There was another major consideration which changed Gwynfor's political position. That summer, the Carmarthen Labour Party's chair, Roger Thomas, announced that he wanted to challenge Gwynoro Jones for the parliamentary nomination. It was a daring bid because Roger Thomas did not believe he had any hope of winning the first round of the selection process. He was right: Gwynoro Jones saw off the challenge with ease.[33] It was at that point Gwynoro Jones made the greatest mistake of his political career: he got angry with Roger

Thomas, and withdrew his own name from the race leaving the field clear for the 51-year-old GP from Garnant. After three months of bitter wrangling, Roger Thomas won the nomination, leaving the local Labour party divided. Gwynoro Jones's decision had been a 'bombshell' for his supporters, but nominating an inexperienced candidate like Roger Thomas was significant for Gwynfor as well.[34] Gwynoro Jones's political demise appeared to make things much easier for him, further increasing the appeal of the Presidency. In the circumstances, he declared he would not retire but would serve as President for a further two years.

It is a sign of Gwynfor's hold on his party that there was no public criticism of his decision, and it was only in retrospect that some realized what a miscalculation it had been for him not to give way to a younger candidate. But Gwynfor by then had only one priority – ensuring devolution for Wales. Another sign of his political bankruptcy was that by the autumn of 1975 all talk, public and private, of establishing 'societism' as an ideology for the party was forgotten. Plaid Cymru's blindness to these critical failures can largely be explained by Gwynfor's personality and his ability to convince his party that he, once again, would be the nationalist Moses who would lead Wales to freedom. Although he was close to retirement age, Gwynfor still had the power to charm and, at the party's annual conference of 1975, hundreds of young people chanted 'Gwynfor, Gwynfor' at the tops of their voices. With idolatry on such a scale to sustain him, he felt no compunction to change course. But by any dispassionate reckoning, devolution was slowly sinking out of sight under the assault of Labour MPs like Donald Anderson and Leo Abse. John Osmond estimated that as many as 10 of the 23 Welsh Labour MPs were opposed to devolution.[35] It was also obvious there were deep disagreements on the issue at Cabinet level, in particular between Cledwyn Hughes and Ted Short, the minister responsible for devolution. In the country too, opposition was growing and a survey for the *Liverpool Daily Post* showed that a majority of electors in the north were against devolution.[36] But only a minority within Plaid Cymru – Phil Williams and Dafydd Wigley in the main – realized that anything was seriously wrong. The rest (including Dafydd Elis Thomas) either misread the signs or were too eager to share Gwynfor's excessive confidence in Labour.

This difference between the way Phil Williams and Dafydd Wigley thought, and the rest, was a substantial tactical divide and in practical terms meant that Labour could rely completely on Plaid Cymru support. At conference, Plaid Cymru resolved to bring down the government if there was any further delay with the White Paper, and passed a resolution to that effect. Dafydd Wigley promised the conference that he would not compromise at all were Labour to hesitate on devolution.[37] But a day after Wigley's threat, the new policy was thoroughly undermined by a confidential memorandum written for party members by Dafydd Elis Thomas and Gwynfor. In the memorandum, *The Latest Situation*, Elis Thomas and Gwynfor painted a very different picture from the stagnation that Wigley had conveyed. Where Wigley saw darkness, Elis Thomas perceived a glimmer in Labour:

> As far as Wales is concerned, the Privy Council Office were not expecting any trouble from the Labour MPs. The Labour Party in Wales has a historic commitment to devolution and the so-called anti-devolutionists were out on a limb, for example, Abse and Anderson… I also detect a far more open attitude among some regional English MPs whom I had considered were opposed to devolution.

But the most interesting aspect of the document, given Gwynfor's numerous statements on the danger of delaying devolution, was that privately he really wanted to see Labour dragging its feet. In an addendum to the Elis Thomas memorandum, Gwynfor added:

> A year's delay in implementing the devolutionary package will be opposed… but in fact it could be a good thing… It will bring disrepute on the Government; will annoy the many people (by no means all Plaid Cymru) whose expectations have been raised high… It could ensure that a General Election for Westminster is held before the Assembly election. This would be the best order for us.[38]

In truth, then, Plaid Cymru – for all its public pronouncements – had no coherent policy on devolution because Gwynfor had unwavering faith in Labour. In his private correspondence, for instance, he told Elwyn Roberts in early November 1975 that there was 'no doubt that a Parliament will come; the only question is the powers it will have'. He still cherished the hope, too, that the decision would be postponed for a year. And that is essentially what happened – causing further problems, as will be seen, for the devolution cause.[39] Even so, Plaid Cymru only had itself to blame for the mess when the White Paper on devolution was published at the end of the month. Although there was nothing unexpected in John Morris's plans, the Assembly he proposed was far weaker than some Plaid members had hoped. The White Paper was also criticized in the press for being a shoddily constructed document – 'more of a liability than an asset', as *The Economist* remarked.[40] The same scepticism was evident in the regional press in Wales as well; from the *Caernarvon and Denbigh Herald* to the *Cambrian News*, no one had a good word to say about John Morris's plans. The general consensus was that Plaid Cymru would oppose the White Paper, but Gwynfor welcomed it without consulting anyone.[41] He, naturally, also demanded fuller powers, but several within the party were surprised that he welcomed Wilson and John Morris's proposals so warmly. Dafydd Wigley judged that Gwynfor was 'politically wrong' even though he also 'respected Gwynfor'.[42] To that end, he wrote to Gwynfor to say he would not stand for an Assembly seat because its powers were so limited .[43]

Dafydd Wigley was not the only one who felt uncomfortable, but Plaid Cymru had to wait until January 1976 before it could begin to undo the confusion caused by its President. By then, the paper had been discussed in the Commons and the vociferous opposition to it from the Labour benches was proof that Gwynfor's confidence was misplaced. The SNP had also angrily responded en bloc to its recommendations, leading ordinary Plaid Cymru members to conclude that their President had made a huge mistake in welcoming the White Paper. These tensions surfaced during a crucial meeting of Plaid Cymru's national council in Llandrindod where a vote was taken (on a motion from Arfon) to reject the White Paper outright.[44] Certainly, passing the resolution was a blow and a personal rebuff to Gwynfor, and his political enemies were quick to spot that Plaid Cymru had clipped Gwynfor's wings for once. Roger Thomas revelled in the nationalists' disarray, mocking Gwynfor in the *Carmarthen Journal*: 'The Gwynfor who composed a Presidential New Year message could hardly have been the same man who agreed to the Plaid National Council's brusque rejection of the same White Paper.'[45]

Gwynfor returned to Westminster somewhat crestfallen but even the ticking-off in Llandrindod was not enough to undermine his faith in Labour. In fact, he soon forgot the incident when the Commons met to discuss devolution in mid-January. The tedious debate went on for four days with the tone of the contributions further proof, if it were needed, that some Labour MPs were ready to dismiss Ted Short and John Morris's plans. But, despite the evidence, Gwynfor was as positive as ever in January 1976 that the Assembly was on its way. His confidence was such that he wrote to Brian Morgan Edwards, the party's deputy treasurer, to voice concern about the money which would be needed to contest a possible referendum on devolution in June that year. The information came, he told Morgan Edwards, 'from a pretty reliable source'.[46] There is no indication who this 'pretty reliable source' was, but Gwynfor's expectant attitude led to a further public rebuke. In the *Welsh Nation*, the editor, Clive Betts, asked whether Plaid Cymru was sleeping in the Commons, given that Wilson had just lost his majority at the height of an economic crisis. Why, the *Welsh Nation*'s leading light wanted to know, was Plaid Cymru 'hanging on to Ted Short's coat-tails, relying on a succession of Labour manifesto promises, and reckoning that all we need to win the battle (as much as we can in the present situation) is Wilson in power for long enough? It is a case of don't rock the boat'.[47]

However, there was no change of policy. Rather than adopt a more militant parliamentary stance, as had the SNP, Gwynfor suggested the best course would be a major campaign to boost support for Plaid Cymru. It was a sound enough idea, but even something as vague as that did not materialize. And there was no community campaigning to speak of either because the party's gaze was continually fixed on the game being played out in the Neo-Gothic corridors of Westminster. Emrys Roberts's valiant attempt to seize control of Merthyr Council was an exception. As for Gwynfor, his only achievement during this period was the publication of another book, *A National Future for Wales* – a polemic for the converted, as the *Daily Post* described it.[48] His instinct was to help Labour, keep his head down and leave the SNP to do the spadework. Privately, he judged 'the Scottish situation near revolutionary' and believed his own party did not need to do too much. But the political sands were shifting quickly.[49] During February and March 1976, ordinary Welshmen and women began to voice the fears that, hitherto, had been expressed so adeptly by Kinnock, Abse and Anderson. Those two months saw a host of councils and public bodies – from the NFU to commercial enterprises in Powys – rushing to reject the government's plans for devolution. Another bitter pill for the nationalists to swallow came with the announcement from the Chancellor, Roy Jenkins, that the government would be postponing the establishment of a Welsh-language television channel because of the economic climate.[50] Within days, Cymdeithas yr Iaith had announced that a law-breaking campaign would be rekindled in order to make the channel a reality.

Given all that, it was no surprise that Dafydd Wigley should reiterate his threat to bring down the government. He was completely fed up with the 'Short

Road' and by now even Gwynfor shared his concern about Labour's sincerity. For the first time since 1974, Gwynfor began to doubt his strategy of trusting Labour and he wrote to Tudur Jones in March 1976 expressing his fear that 'the government will strike some sort of bargain with the powerful opponents on its own back benches. I foresee that they could promise them, if they have their support for the second reading of the Bill, that it will go no further before the next general election'.[51] Devolution, and Gwynfor's credibility, were in crisis but, out of the blue, salvation arrived in the form of Jim Callaghan. At the end of March 1976, Harold Wilson resigned, handing the keys to 10 Downing Street to the Member for Cardiff South East.

It was a stunning decision that had far-reaching consequences for Plaid Cymru and devolution too. Callaghan put Michael Foot, the Leader of the House, in charge of devolution, thereby entirely changing the situation once more given Foot's infectious enthusiasm for devolution. At best, Wilson and Ted Short had felt obliged to bring in devolution because of a past undertaking. But Foot (if not Callaghan) was a very different animal. In his first statement on the matter, he promised there would be no turning back. He was clearly genuine and the nationalists were in raptures when they heard there would be simultaneous translation equipment at the Temple of Peace, the prospective home of the Assembly. In no time, Foot and Gwynfor forged a close personal bond, and over the next three years they became good friends.[52] The icing on the cake was an opinion poll in the *Western Mail* that April which erroneously claimed that two thirds of the people of Wales supported devolution.[53] Gwynfor undoubtedly believed devolution had been snatched from the jaws of death, and he set off for America on a fundraising tour in high spirits. On 20 April, he wrote to Elwyn Roberts to confirm that huge changes were afoot – quite literally: 'You must have seen the encouraging statement made by Michael Foot in Parliament last week. It looks as if the government is quite serious about getting a Bill through before the general election.'[54]

For some inexplicable reason, Gwynfor chose to vehemently deny that fundraising was the aim of his American trip, but despite his protests, the whole venture was plagued by public rows over its purpose. Terry Thomas, the Liberal prospective parliamentary candidate for Carmarthen, wrote to Welsh societies across America urging expatriates not to contribute to Plaid Cymru because Welsh nationalism was so similar to Irish nationalism.[55] Plaid Cymru argued that

Terry Thomas's claim was unfounded and that the journey was not intended to raise money although it was, in fact, Gwynfor's main intention. Since October 1975, the party's executive had considered such a trip as a possible source of financial salvation, and Elwyn Roberts wrote to Colin Edwards, the organizer, to remind him how eager Gwynfor was to meet people 'who are likely to help Plaid Cymru financially'.[56] In the same vein, Plaid Cymru sent a circular to Americans of Welsh descent pleading with the wealthy among them to contribute generously to 'the cause'.[57] In the USA, Gwynfor did not conceal his intentions, but despite his honesty the Welsh Americans were at best lukewarm. Gwynfor returned to Wales on 2 May with $302, hoping that there was more to come, but the expected windfall did not materialise.[58] As he had learned during the 1958 visit to America, romanticizing about Wales did not necessarily manifest itself in a willingness to contribute financially to Plaid Cymru.

Gwynfor's American adventure was not Plaid Cymru's only attempt to raise money during the spring of 1976. There is also evidence that he considered setting up a meat export business in partnership with the government of Libya – a government strongly suspected of having close ties to the IRA. Dr Phil Williams had devised the scheme and his friend, Dafydd Wigley, also thought it was an excellent deal. He told the *Sunday Times* that the Libyans would buy old lamb from Wales 'and at a good price'.[59] However, it was a strange and controversial arrangement. John Powell, the Labour candidate in Ceredigion, made a formal complaint to the Home Secretary, Roy Jenkins, regarding the matter.[60] On the letters page of the *Western Mail*, the arrangement was described by John Roderick Rees, a conservative-minded poet from Pen-uwch, as an example of the political naivety of 'the thrustful new crop of Plaid leaders'. Another correspondent, Hywel S Williams, was more harsh, adjudging the scheme to be further proof of the 'accumulating lunacies' of Dr Phil Williams.[61] The wisdom of such an enterprise worried some in Plaid Cymru too but, even so, the party sent a deputation to Tripoli, the capital of Libya, during April 1976.[62] In a letter to Ahmad Shahmati, Foreign Affairs Secretary of the Union of Socialist Arabs, Dafydd Williams expressed his huge gratitude for 'the splendid hospitality they received during their visit and for the programme that was organized for them. They are all most impressed with what they saw and look forward to very close links between Wales and Libya in the future'.[63] Similarly, a deputation from the Libyan government attended the Plaid Cymru Summer School held in Lampeter that year.[64] One can only speculate on what Gaddafi's officials thought of the town, but one thing is certain – Gwynfor's hold over his party suggests that he must have known about these interesting arrangements and commended them.

It appears that the Libyan connection did not proceed any further, no bad thing given the character of the Libyan dictator. In any event, Gwynfor and his party had other matters to worry about. Gwynfor returned from America on 2 May to the bustle of the local election campaigning – elections that would be a test of Plaid Cymru's popularity under the premiership of Jim Callaghan. Failure would have been a severe blow, but the pessimists were pleasantly surprised. The most impressive result was Emrys Roberts's triumph in winning Merthyr Council, the cradle of Welsh socialism. This victory on 6 May, according to Dafydd Wigley, was Labour's Waterloo and some in Plaid Cymru even claimed it was more important than the Carmarthen by-election win a decade previously.[65] There were other encouraging results too. Plaid Cymru won 23 seats on Rhymney Council and a further six in Arfon, becoming the biggest party there. The picture was equally rosy in Ceredigion, Dwyfor, Montgomeryshire and Anglesey.

Altogether, the party won an additional 81 seats, but this comparatively good showing could scarcely be attributed to any inspired planning on Gwynfor's part – or to the 'Two Dafydds' influence for that matter. More than anyone, it was Emrys Roberts himself and his tireless community-based campaign that had won Merthyr. It is worth adding that Plaid Cymru also benefited from a more general public distaste for the corruption of some Labour councils in the south – the sort of sleaze uncovered by that fearless publication, *Rebecca*. With Labour routed and the Liberals distracted by the Jeremy Thorpe scandal, Plaid Cymru and the Tories could hardly have failed to gain ground at the expense of their rivals. Under the circumstances, however, the result confirmed Gwynfor's perception, and that of Plaid Cymru members, that nationalism was once more a force to be reckoned with. Following the elections, a campaign was launched which would aim, according to Dafydd Williams, to 'grab as much support as possible from Labour and especially the Liberals' and 'peak during May 1977 when the County Council Elections are contested'.[66] The goal was agreed and a budget of £1,000 was confirmed for the 'Fair Play for Wales' campaign. But it made little impression, if any. In the long term, the elections did more harm than good, because the relative success of May 1976 confirmed the misleading picture that Gwynfor and others in his party had painted. Nationalism was certainly a force at Westminster, but this was almost entirely due to the problems faced first by Wilson and, now, by Callaghan. On the contrary, in Wales, nationalism had become increasingly unpopular during early 1976, and Gwynfor and those around him virtually disregarded the fact that Kinnock, Abse and the anti-devolutionists had won over Welsh popular opinion. They may have been demagogues, but the reality was that they understood Wales better than Plaid Cymru did.

During the summer, the two paradoxical trends became more pronounced. At Westminster, Plaid Cymru and the SNP became increasingly more powerful as popular discontent with devolution grew in Wales. At the end of May, Foot agreed to grant more powers to the Welsh Development Agency, and Plaid Cymru, after numerous meetings with the government, succeeded in ensuring that the Bristol Channel Ship Repairers company would not be nationalized. Gwynfor was particularly keen to see the company saved from state control – no great surprise given Dan Evans's past links with the shipping companies of Barry. Gwynfor's friendship with the company's owner, Christopher Bailey, was also a factor, but others in the party – especially Dafydd Elis Thomas – were rather less impressed by Gwynfor's enthusiasm for what appeared to be a right-wing bill. At heart, he felt that his opinion was (not for the first time) being ignored by the President.[67] A similar bargain was struck with the SNP in Scotland to save shipping companies on Clydeside. It would be wrong to think, however, that the nationalists were government lapdogs. Three weeks before the row over the shipping companies, Plaid Cymru voted with the Tories on a motion of no confidence in the government. There was no danger that the government would fall in what was essentially a symbolic vote on 9 June but, across Westminster, political commentators generally acknowledged that nationalism had come of age. David Rosser, for instance, wrote in the *Western Mail* of the salvation of Bristol Channel Ship Repairers: 'A new dimension is appearing at Westminster. The trio of Plaid Cymru MPs are emerging as a pocket power bloc with grim and purposeful determination… Rightly and judiciously too, they are playing the artful dodger to Michael Foot and the Government's other managers to no mean effect.'[68] With the praises of the *Western Mail* ringing in his ears, Gwynfor could celebrate the tenth anniversary of the Carmarthen by-election happy in the knowledge that he was a nationalist hero.

On 10 July, his friend, Pennar Davies, presented him with a biography at a rally in Llangadog – a paean of praise for a hero, telling the story of the inexorable rise of the 'national movement'. It read like the life of a saint, but despite its overly laudatory tone, Gwynfor felt no embarrassment in accepting it and confessed to Islwyn Ffowc Elis that 'books like this are important for Plaid and for the country'.[69] Pennar Davies's book served to strengthen the Gwynfor cult, and any criticism of him tended to be regarded as treason. His word was law – in particular with regard to the party's devolution policy. At the Llangadog rally, and at a host of public meetings during the summer of 1976, Gwynfor asserted his unshakeable faith that Plaid Cymru could not possibly lose, because Callaghan was caught 'on one prong or the other of the nationalist fork'.[70] The crux of Gwynfor's argument was that Plaid Cymru would benefit if Callaghan fulfilled his manifesto commitment, but he was equally convinced that Plaid Cymru would gain if the devolution Bill were defeated in the Commons. Quite simply, Gwynfor believed that defeated Bill would strengthen the party to such an extent that a parliament would follow.[71] His argument was simple and effective and, during a summer of water shortages, those already within the fold believed it passionately, as they were convinced that an Assembly could solve everything including the drought. This simple logic explains why Gwynfor was not overly concerned by the efforts of the anti-devolutionists. It is only with hindsight that the naivety of his position became clear because the end of devolution would also be detrimental to Plaid Cymru.

But during these vital months, as Welsh attitudes on devolution crystallised, most Plaid Cymru members believed that their President was right. Indeed, Gwynfor's only political worry during this time was the predicament of the Welsh language, and the need for Plaid Cymru to draw up a detailed policy in relation to the language. A certain amount of discussion had already taken place but Cymdeithas yr Iaith, for example, complained that the party was spending too much time on devolution, and some prominent Plaid members shared that opinion – including Dafydd Iwan.[72] The journalist Clive Betts went so far as to resign the editorship of the *Welsh Nation* over the issue.[73] On the other hand, others on the executive committee, such as John Dixon, had warned Gwynfor to say nothing, because the 'great danger in a big campaign on the language' was that the party would be accused of 'worrying more about it than about jobs'.[74]

It was a familiar dilemma for Gwynfor but, to his credit, he was eager to see his party campaigning harder on the Welsh language. For one thing, he did not believe the case for devolution could be damaged and, secondly, he felt passionately that the language was in decline. In Llangadog itself, he had observed that 'children and young people only listen to Welsh television for as much as half an hour a week – the majority of them not seeing a single minute of television in Welsh from one week to the next'.[75] The 'crisis', as he told Dafydd Williams, 'was worsening', particularly in local government where no authority took Welsh seriously – apart from Gwynedd. As a result, Gwynfor offered his general secretary a variety of possible plans of action. They included the development of 'theatre and drama'; he also wished to produce an 'effective policy that would bring the Urdd, the Eisteddfod and Merched y Wawr together'. Above all, Gwynfor believed this new campaign should unite Welsh-speakers: 'We would not be giving a lead as political nationalists but rather as individual Welshmen and women who love the language.'[76] It culminated in Gwynfor's gathering a group of prominent people together to draw up a new language policy. But as with so many other Plaid Cymru schemes in the 'seventies, it was short-lived.[77] Nothing came of it because Plaid Cymru had to turn all its attention, once again, to what ordinary people in Wales were by the autumn of 1976 calling 'The Great Devolution Bore'. Indeed, the only significance of Gwynfor's language document, however genuine his motives, was that it ensured a successful conference and avoided the usual domestic squabbles with Cymdeithas yr Iaith.

But if the national conference was a success, there was a discernible change in Gwynfor's political rhetoric. Although he still believed that Plaid Cymru could not lose, and although he congratulated John Morris on choosing the Coal Exchange rather than the Temple of Peace for the new Assembly, there were other worries. As the economic crisis deepened, Callaghan went begging to the IMF. By October, Britain was in ferment. Gwynfor wrote to Tudur Jones to seek his advice on how best to 'develop a Welsh philosophy' that would be 'a source of strength to the National Movement'. However, it was far too late then for Gwynfor to seek enlightenment from his old friend.[79] For the first time in this epic encounter, the Conservatives and the anti-devolutionists sensed that they could win the battle. Somehow or other, Callaghan was expecting Michael Foot to introduce a devolution Bill for Wales and Scotland within a few weeks, without a parliamentary majority and in the middle of the worst economic crisis since the 'thirties.

Privately, Foot feared the worst. Even before the Bill reached the floor of the Commons, he began to prepare for the possibility that the whole thing could be torn apart. He also began to prepare the ground for a possible referendum.[80] Then, in late autumn, the storm broke. As the parliamentary discussions began, there was an 'English Backlash'. The *Sun*, for instance, asked whether the United Kingdom would be torn asunder forever – even though their own opinion poll showed a clear majority against devolution.[81] At the same time, the Conservatives began their campaign against devolution in earnest. Faced with this concerted opposition, Gwynfor moved even closer to Labour, condemning the Conservatives to Dafydd Orwig in no uncertain terms:

> ... when you look at the Tories' record over the past ten years and more, you will find nothing positive that they have done for Wales... They never campaign for anything Welsh, in language or otherwise. Wyn Roberts is one of the worst of the lot, and of course Geraint Morgan says nothing. To all intents and purposes, they represent the English and their membership.[82]

As expected, the devolution Bill was coolly received by from Plaid Cymru when it was published on 30 November. It demanded that it be strengthened and Gwynfor promised that his party would bring down the government unless it kept its promise.[83] It was small comfort for the nationalists that they managed to maintain their internal unity and that there was no fiasco like the one which accompanied the publication of the 1975 White Paper. In fact, there was no real difference between the parliamentary Bill and the White Paper and the more general response did not augur well at all for Gwynfor's hopes of ensuring an Assembly for Wales. On the day following the publication of the Bill, Ioan Evans, the Labour MP for Aberdare, resigned as John Morris's parliamentary secretary. Furthermore, the opinion polls in Wales began to show that the Welsh were very wary of devolution. One revealed that only 27 per cent supported the Bill. The same survey showed that 31 per cent of Plaid Cymru supporters were either indifferent towards the Bill or opposed it outright.

Faced with these trends, some within Plaid doubted the wisdom of giving the Bill any support.[84] Phil Williams, for example, wrote to the Carmarthen district committee to seek their thoughts on devolution. Records confirm that the letter was discussed in a 'long conversation' and that many deep misgivings were expressed.[85] The press was told nothing about the concerns being voiced in Gwynfor's own backyard but it *was* known by the middle of December that the Phil Williams wing of Plaid Cymru wanted to fight one last battle to prevent the party from supporting the Bill.[86] Although these purists were in the minority, it was yet another headache for Gwynfor when the Bill began its journey through the Commons on 13 December. During four days of bitter argument, the debate on devolution for Wales and Scotland generated more heat than light. Although Gwynfor attempted to raise the tone by arguing that devolution was a means of preserving Christian civilization in Wales, the anti-devolutionists won an easy victory.[87] Despite the Bill receiving a second reading, Michael Foot was forced to concede one key point: the government confirmed, after months of trying to skirt the issue, that there would be a referendum on devolution.[88]

This unpleasant debate left its mark on Gwynfor. His working day would often begin at nine in the morning and carry on into the small hours of the following day. The Christmas holidays came as a huge relief and he did as little as possible during this period in a deliberate attempt to conserve his energy for what promised to be a crucial year ahead. As 1977 dawned, he predicted to Elwyn Roberts that the year would see the fulfilment of the aspirations of an entire generation of nationalists:

> There are hard times ahead of us everywhere, including long nights at Westminster and the strain of trying to win some sort of Parliament… This will be the year of a referendum, and maybe a general election. This is how history is made. Plaid has come further than we both thought in our realistic moments.[89]

One can sense the voice of a politician approaching the end of his career in this letter, but after Christmas, Gwynfor had no time to think about his own or indeed Elwyn Roberts's stake in history. The party's priority as 1977 dawned was to decide on its stance on devolution – the prickly issue that Phil Williams persisted in raising. On 31 December, the party's leaders met in Knighton (of all places) to settle the matter. The pilgrimage, as Dafydd Wigley called it, was an exercise in 'Presbyterian self-deprivation'. Even so, the journey proved successful in that Plaid Cymru (in spite of some doubts) agreed with Gwynfor that half a loaf was better than none.[90] From then on, Plaid Cymru decided to support Labour in any referendum.[91] The following day, the members of the National Council struggled through the snow to the same town to approve the policy. With the exception of Phil Williams and one or two others, none opposed Gwynfor and, at last, on the first day of 1977, it appeared that Plaid Cymru had something resembling a united policy on devolution.[92]

With this assurance of Plaid Cymru support, a non-party Yes campaign was formed and the work of preparing for the referendum began.[93] The campaign attracted a mixed bag of celebrities, including the footballer John Toshack, the retired mandarin Goronwy Daniel and the Archbishop of Wales, G O Williams. However, Gwynfor knew full well that such support would do nothing to lighten the load likely to fall on Plaid Cymru, and that his party would have to promote the Labour policy when a referendum came, most probably in October. It was a huge responsibility, and the pressure on Gwynfor became a topic of conversation. By the middle of January, his hair had turned white as the physical and emotional strain became more and more evident.[94] In an address to the Carmarthen constituency executive that month, he spoke candidly about the enormous challenge facing Plaid Cymru. With no meaningful campaign by Labour or the trade unions, he warned some of his closest friends it would be up to them to undertake the thankless task but that even this would need to be largely covert: 'Until the last week of the referendum we must act quietly but effectively. Then in the final fortnight, all the razzmatazz to stir a feeling for Wales in people. Awaken the emotions.'[95]

The minutes of the Carmarthen meeting record how Gwynfor's speech dispelled 'many doubts', but Gwynfor, in fact, was asking his supporters to do the impossible by campaigning for devolution while simultaneously saying nothing about it. Gwynfor could not, however, be blamed for the situation as this was the only avenue open to him. Meanwhile, the atmosphere in the Commons continued to deteriorate. When the House reconvened on 10 January, devolutionists discovered that 300 amendments had been tabled by Tories and Labour rebels. There were the days (and more often than not, nights) of parliamentary filibusters. Although the devolutionists managed to defeat a Conservative attempt to remove Wales from the Bill, Gwynfor and Michael Foot were aware of the painfully slow progress of the debate. By the beginning of February, Gwynfor had begun to doubt the Bill would ever be passed, as only three clauses out of 115 had been discussed. On 3 February, Gwynfor, Dafydd Elis Thomas and Dafydd Wigley wrote to Jim Callaghan pleading with him to speed up the process and expressing, 'our very grave concern at the unconscionably slow progress of the Scotland and Wales Bill... These debates have included no more than one seriously debated issue, that of continued representation at Westminster'.[96] In private, Gwynfor was even more insistent, demanding that Michael Foot discipline the Labour objectors (especially Neil Kinnock). But there was never any prospect of this because Foot himself, as a young politician, had rebelled against his own party on countless occasions.[97]

Callaghan and Foot decided on another strategy, the parliamentary guillotine, to put an end to the prevarication and win the battle. A specified time would be allowed on the floor of the House, but the employment of this procedure proved highly unpopular with Labour, and Gwynfor knew that 'pulling it through the gap of the guillotine' was the all-important step.[98] The vote allowing the guillotine was set for 22 February and Plaid Cymru did all it could to bring pressure to bear on the Labour government. The most significant step was the vote cast on 12 February by Plaid Cymru's executive to bring down the government unless a referendum was forthcoming.[99] Dafydd Williams also busied himself preparing protests and a national rally if the government failed to keep its word. But Labour's rebels were equally determined. In a dramatic and passionate vote, the guillotine motion was lost and the Bill fell. For Gwynfor, it was a crushing blow, as significant to him as 'Labour's betrayal' over Capel Celyn.[100] That evening, in a letter to Dafydd Williams he wrote that parliamentary route was now closed. 'It's obvious,' he said, 'that we shall have to find a way of having an earlier election, alongside the SNP.'[101] Dafydd Wigley agreed and called for a general election. Two days later, the SNP and Plaid Cymru presented a motion of no confidence in the government.[102] Back in Wales, protest meetings were being organized and the party sent a telegram to Callaghan claiming that no Welsh patriot could possibly support Labour, so great was its betrayal.[103] Gwynfor's dream was shattered, but the Bill's defeat was more than a political setback: it was also a deeply personal one, because he had been the man most prepared to lead his party down the parliamentary path. That path was now blocked. Given the circumstances, it was, then, no surprise when Gwynfor began to slide into what can only be described as a bout of depression and physical exhaustion.

Immediately after the vote on the guillotine, he was rushed into hospital 'in a fever and talking a lot of nonsense' due to problems 'on the nervous, constitutional and mental side'. He was looked after by Dr Linford Rees, a well-known psychiatrist and 'good nationalist', who soon discovered there was a lack of 'some special chemical' in Gwynfor's brain.[104] However accurate the diagnosis, Gwynfor remained a sick man. For some weeks, he rested at the home of his sister Ceridwen in the Buckinghamshire countryside. He also spent some time recuperating in Llangadog before receiving further treatment at Glangwili

Hospital in Carmarthen. It fell to Dafydd Elis Thomas and Dafydd Wigley to steer Plaid Cymru through a crucial period. After all, the nationalists had the power and the motivation to call for a general election, if they so wished. On 24 February, Plaid Cymru and the SNP were invited to meet Jim Callaghan and, likewise, Michael Foot wrote to Gwynfor to seek his views on how to achieve greater consensus between the parties on devolution.[105] Having just tabled a motion of no confidence, Plaid Cymru might have been expected to baulk at the invitations. This was Gwynfor's first reaction too, and on 3 March, he wrote to Elwyn Roberts from his hospital bed in Glangwili, saying that 'the great devolution cause is over' and that they would have 'nothing now for some years'. His only comfort was that the 'betrayal' was 'bound to help Plaid'.[106]

But within days, Gwynfor warmed again to the idea of reviving devolution and pragmatism proved stronger than parliamentary rhetoric as Plaid Cymru and the Liberals tried to squeeze what they could out of the ailing government. With this in mind, Gwynfor wrote to Dafydd Williams on 7 March to give his cautious blessing to a joint meeting with Labour: 'It's all right for the boys [Elis Thomas and Wigley] to see what Foot and the others have to say of course, but we shouldn't take part in anything official.'[107] The 'boys' met Callaghan but were not encouraged. The meeting, Dafydd Wigley told Gwynfor, was not 'much good to us' since Callaghan still thought he could win a guillotine vote. The only comfort Dafydd Wigley could offer Gwynfor was 'that [Callaghan] accepts that the way forward means convincing his own people rather than seeking agreement with the Tories'.[108]

Gwynfor, Wigley and Elis Thomas really had no other option. As a result, they began talks with the government in early March 1977. Back in Wales, however, there was a growing perception that the trio in Westminster were playing some elaborate parliamentary game. And much to Gwynfor's alarm, Cymdeithas yr Iaith was now active once again and had done substantial damage to the Blaenplwyf transmitter near Aberystwyth. Privately, Gwynfor was horrified by this upsurge in unconstitutional politics, and wrote to an acquaintance, Professor Dewi Eirug Davies, to share his concern 'about the way Cymdeithas yr Iaith is going about things (although they are preferable to Adfer)'. The sad thing, he added, was that there was 'no possible way for us to control them [Cymdeithas yr Iaith]'.[109] Meanwhile, as constitutional politics lost its relevance, the Plaid Cymru rank and file began to insist that their leaders listened to them. The party's parliamentary whip, Dafydd Elis Thomas, was given a clear warning by Plaid Cymru in Ceredigion. MPs were ordered to 'disassociate' themselves 'from any bill that offers us less as a nation'.[110] Saunders Lewis was even more candid. Writing to the *Western Mail,* he expressed his hope that 'serious Welsh Nationalists' would be as cheered as he was by the failure of the devolution Bill. 'It confirmed,' Saunders Lewis wrote, 'my forecast of many years ago, and I think it is an axiom worth repeating: as long as there is a Welsh Nationalist parliamentary party in the House of Commons there will be no responsible self-government for Wales… only after frantic police activity will the English Parliament pass a measure to recognise and legally establish a Welsh government.'[111]

On the day after the statement, Plaid Cymru's executive met and voted in favour of asking its MPs 'not to carry on further talks with the government'.[112] Saunders Lewis could not have wished for a better outcome but it was another setback for Gwynfor who was still physically and emotionally frail. At the same executive meeting the members also resolved to send a message 'wishing the President well and asking him to take a holiday' but the political disquiet meant there was no time to relax.[113] Gwynfor was forced to postpone surgery because a vote of no confidence in the government had been timetabled for 23 March. With every vote like gold-dust, the political intentions of Plaid Cymru were vital to the political future of Britain. Two days before the vote, Gwynfor, Wigley and Elis Thomas announced they would bring down the government by going through the lobby with the Conservatives. Their justification for doing so, they said, was that both parties were as bad as each other.[114] This policy, nevertheless, was far from popular among Plaid Cymru's grass roots – in particular the socialist nationalists in the valleys.[115] The united statement by the three also disguised the tensions between them because Elis Thomas (despite the public rhetoric) had already told Cledwyn Hughes, chair of the Parliamentary Labour Party, that he would abstain if Labour was in a tight spot.[116] But as time ran out on 23 March, Callaghan was saved when the Liberals agreed to a pact with Labour. That evening, the Plaid Cymru trio voted with the Conservatives, but it was an empty gesture for the nationalists. By the skin of his teeth (and with the support of several ailing members who had been brought to the House by ambulance), Callaghan hung on, still able to claim he now had a parliamentary majority.

It marked the end of four frantic months in Welsh politics – during which time devolution had been destroyed and Plaid Cymru left at the mercy of a divided Labour party. In reality, Plaid Cymru received very little in exchange for its willingness to play the parliamentary numbers game, but Gwynfor paid a very heavy price. Those four months had wrecked his health and undermined his credibility too. From then on, Wigley would be considered the true leader of Plaid Cymru. Gwynfor was more conscious of this than anyone, and accepted the inevitable. Two days after Callaghan had secured his parliamentary survival, Gwynfor wrote to Lewis Valentine and spoke about the end of an era. Now, he sensed that 'Welsh politics has entered another temporary quiet period' as it did not appear probable that there would be 'any sort of elected Assembly in the very near future'.[117]

Gwynfor was being too pessimistic. Devolution returned as suddenly as it had disappeared. In late March 1977, Michael Foot announced his intention to reintroduce devolution in two separate Bills for Wales and Scotland. Within hours, Gwynfor received a letter from Foot promising that the government was still 'fully committed' to devolution.[118] Once more, Gwynfor faced the same nagging question: what would his party do? Would it support a Bill that was likely to be scuppered by Labour rebels or would it remain aloof? It was one of the most perplexing dilemmas Gwynfor would ever face, but a second bite at the cherry proved more attractive than the bitter memory of 1976–77. The party nationally shared the same opinion and that spring there was a willingness to take what was on offer. Even so, the membership was far more wary this time, and the party's MPs were warned in no uncertain terms that they should tread very carefully when bargaining with Labour. These sceptics (led by Phil Williams) also called for a year-long strategy for the party in an attempt to avoid what he termed 'zigzags'. Phil Williams was supported by Dafydd Wigley, who wrote to Gwynfor insisting that Plaid Cymru should 'revise thoroughly' its attitude 'towards devolution and the government's Bill'.[119] On paper, Williams and Wigley had a point, of course, but history was about to repeat itself for Gwynfor in the most unpleasant way. At the end of July, Michael Foot published the White Paper on devolution for Wales, and from that moment on, Plaid Cymru found itself in deep water again. There was, however, one crucial difference. This time, Plaid Cymru had less sway over Labour because Callaghan had a parliamentary majority and no longer needed to indulge nationalist demands. As autumn progressed, only Michael Foot and John Morris's goodwill could ensure that Gwynfor's dream of winning devolution would be realized.

Gwynfor had a very quiet summer and, for some months, Welsh politics was unusually stable. Moreover, since he believed there would be no general election until the spring of 1979, he could sit back and regain his strength. The party followed its President's lead, using the time to raise enough money to move from the infamous Cardiff hovel at 8 Queen Street into more suitable and grander premises on Cathedral Road. The symbolism of the move was hard to ignore as the old guard gave way to the new. It was difficult not to conclude too that Gwynfor's consensus politics of the 'national movement' was utterly irrelevant to those on the increasingly militant left wing of Plaid Cymru. At that year's party conference, a quasi-Marxist resolution calling for 'the social ownership of the instruments of production and distribution' was defeated – but only by 108 votes to 82.[120]

Just days later, on 4 November, the Scotland Bill began its journey through Parliament. Naturally, it was a crucial issue for the Scots but was also vital for Wales, as it was regarded as a dry run for the Wales Bill in a few months' time. Gwynfor watched the Bill's progress with interest, and despite the doubts he had voiced in the spring, it restored his enthusiasm. For one thing, he was convinced that Plaid Cymru could only benefit from the sex scandal surrounding Jeremy Thorpe, the Liberal leader.[121] But the main reason for his new-found zeal was that devolution was back on the political map, and he was cheered more than anything by the fact that Callaghan and John Morris had promised to make devolution a confidence issue. This time, therefore, everything appeared that much easier: if devolution faltered the government would fall. Gwynfor gave the Bill his full support, telling his party there were twelve good reasons to support the Assembly. Several of these were sound administrative ones but the main one, according to Gwynfor, was his love for Wales – the passion that had driven him ever since his conversion back in 1929.[122]

For some weeks, the situation looked promising and there were hints that Michael Foot's tactic of making devolution a matter of confidence was winning hearts and minds. Despite some opposition to the Scotland Bill, it hardly compared to the organized cynicism seen ten months earlier. At last, Gwynfor believed the hour had come and, on 21 November, he wrote confidentially to Michael Foot to thank him for his 'splendid' work in steering the legislation through the shark-infested waters of the Commons. 'I admired,' he told Foot, 'the heroic way in which you sat through the long debates and the way in which you conducted them. This was an extremely difficult task performed with mastery and obvious commitment.' Above all Gwynfor felt the atmosphere was fundamentally different this time:

> I noticed a different spirit in the debates this time and from many parts of Wales. I hear that the spirit too has changed for the better... our people will support it 100 per cent. There would be something very seriously wrong if the Bill failed to get a good majority in Wales where the only organised opposition at present is in the Conservative Party, the National Front and a few Labour mavericks.[123]

He sent a similar private note to Dafydd Wigley suggesting that the Tories were the real problem, and encouraging Wigley to 'attack them continually as a party that has never been of any benefit to Wales. We should focus the attack on the Tories, ignoring the handful of Labour members who are opposed'.[124]

Gwynfor regarded 1978 as 'the most important year in Welsh history, at least for many centuries', but it seemed such confidence was misplaced.[125] Even before Christmas 1977, it had become evident that Labour opposition in the Commons was far more widespread than the 'few Labour mavericks' he had mentioned to Michael Foot. The *Liverpool Daily Post* estimated that as many as 30 Labour MPs were willing to fight to the last against devolution.[126] But, that proved to be a conservative assessment, and when the members returned to the Commons in January 1978, it was obvious that opposition had swept like a plague through the Labour benches. Worse still, it was clear to Gwynfor that the Labour grandees were not prepared to do anything to ensure a Yes vote. On New Year's Day 1978, he decided that Foot needed to hear a few home truths. For the first time, Gwynfor admitted his fear that devolution could fail. For one thing, he wrote to Foot, he had seen:

> ... no speech, statement or letter from your colleagues, either in the Labour Party or the unions... My fear is that if by the summer there has been inadequate counter action, or rather insufficient initiative taken by the Welsh Assembly supporters, the positions taken against it will have hardened too much to change them.

Although he conceded that figures such as Gwilym Prys Davies, Foot himself and John Morris favoured devolution, the basic problem was that 'Labour county councillors seem to be almost *en bloc* in opposition'. Gwynfor attributed this opposition to the councillors' self-interest, and wherever he looked, he could see signs that his analysis was correct. He gave Foot some hard facts:

> In Dyfed, for example, where one would expect a big pro-majority, the Aberystwyth Labour branch voted 20–1 against an Assembly, and the Ceredigion constituency Labour party 14–9 against. The Labour agent and organiser of the Carmarthen constituency has come out strongly against, as has the Labour-controlled Dinfewr District Council and even the Brynaman branch of the party. I have heard no sound in favour from Llanelli and Pembroke or from the neighbouring Swansea constituencies.[127]

But the letter was more than just a reasoned interpretation of how things were on the ground – such an analysis would have been stating the obvious, especially for someone like Michael Foot. Gwynfor's aim was to alarm Labour by threatening Foot with the possible reaction in nationalist circles if the situation were to stay the same:

> ... the nationalists, who are young and vigorous, would direct their criticism at the Labour rather than the Conservative party – who should be the common enemy. The consequences to Labour in Wales could be very damaging, especially if the result were a fiasco and that is not impossible.

What Gwynfor wanted from Foot and the Labour Party, then, was practical assistance. If he was given that assurance, he believed he could avoid this 'black scenario with comparative ease'.[128]

The sought for support, however, was not forthcoming and Plaid Cymru found itself once more at the mercy of Labour. This was nothing new; after all, it had been the case for the last four years, but the big difference now was that the opposition within the Labour Party was much better organized. Led by Robin Cook, the Labour MP for Edinburgh Central, there was bitter opposition to the Scotland Bill, and it reached its zenith, appropriately enough, on 25 January, Burns Night. In what was described as a 'Burns Night Blitz', the anti-devolutionists managed to insert a clause requiring that 40 per cent of all Scotland's electors would have to vote in favour of establishing an Assembly. The amendment tabled by the Labour member, George Cunningham, meant securing a Yes vote would be that much harder; a simple majority would not now be enough.

This was the turning point in the devolution story. It was not without reason that George Cunningham's amendment was described as the most significant act by any backbencher since 1945.[129] On the following day, Welsh anti-devolutionists insisted that a similar amendment should be made to the Wales Bill when it went through the House. Even Emrys Jones, secretary of the Welsh Labour Party, described the move as 'absurd, illogical and unfair'. But the game was up.[130] It was now only a matter of time until a similar threshold was incorporated into the Wales Bill. As expected, Plaid Cymru was furious, and Gwynfor called the new condition wholly undemocratic. Without much conviction, Dafydd Wigley suggested that it would be to Plaid Cymru's advantage and that the party could turn this piece of gamesmanship into 'another Tryweryn'. But these were empty words.[131] Gwynfor had to decide quickly whether to support or oppose the Wales Bill when it came before the House.

It was one of the biggest crises in Plaid Cymru's history, and the party's response during early February was at best confused. For some days, its leaders argued that they would not support a Wales Bill containing a 40 per cent clause, and Dafydd Williams wrote to Callaghan to warn him. Nevertheless, just days later, Gwynfor was hatching a hopeless scheme to make voting compulsory in any forthcoming referendum. The inference was that Gwynfor wanted to accept the Wales Bill even if it included such an impossible clause. However, during this difficult process of consultation, he came under pressure to reject the whole thing. Dafydd Orwig wrote to advise him that it would be more prudent to reject the whole plan with honour as there was no prospect of winning a referendum under such circumstances. He also predicted that 'a militant group [would] act directly' if there were a No vote.[132] The desire to reject Labour's plans grew more evident still when it was announced that Elystan Morgan was to chair the Yes campaign. Nonetheless, with the Wales Bill imminent, Gwynfor came to the inevitable conclusion that he and his party had no alternative but to support it.[133] The party's executive confirmed this view and, on 20 February, Dafydd Orwig's letter showed how powerless Plaid Cymru was by then:

> ... the people of Wales would not understand it at all if we voted against the bill. The government could easily blame us then for defeating it. Nothing would please them more. We all feel furious about the whole thing here but there isn't a lot we can do. I'm sure we must use the opportunity that the referendum campaign gives us to deepen national consciousness and thereby strengthen Plaid Cymru. Somehow or other we must get our people to dedicate themselves completely to the work. Every campaign like this – you may remember the Parliament for Wales campaign in the early 'fifties – is a way of strengthening the will of the Welsh to live like a nation.[134]

In time, some Plaid Cymru leaders like Dafydd Wigley and Phil Richards would view the decision as one of the party's biggest mistakes, but it is difficult to see what other option was open to Gwynfor.[135] The public would not have understood

Plaid Cymru if it had voted against the Wales Bill, after its interminable discussions about devolution for five years. Plaid Cymru could have pulled out of the whole process back in November 1975, but as the Scotland Bill neared the end of its eventful parliamentary passage, there was no real choice. Quite simply, it was too late. The Wales Bill had to be supported – whatever the cost.

The price Plaid Cymru and nationalism would have to pay was obvious from the moment the Bill was presented to the Commons on St David's Day. The previous evening, Gwynfor had written to Cledwyn Hughes to remind him of the 'responsibility of the Bill's Labour friends' and suggested that it would be a good idea 'to arrange for plenty from the back benches to speak on the Welsh Bill'.[137] Cledwyn Hughes was as keen a devolutionist as Gwynfor but, for all his political nous, Labour's devolutionists did not stand a chance. As the days went by, a group of Welsh Labour MPs bared their Unionist teeth. The 'highlight' of the debate was Neil Kinnock's assertion that some schoolchildren in Anglesey were prevented from going to the toilet because they couldn't ask in Welsh.[137] Neil Kinnock was also responsible for the accusation that Plaid Cymru had behaved like Nazis because it had supported the burning of Penyberth,[138] and Leo Abse attacked Gwynfor directly: 'In Pontypool, we need no lectures from you on the Welshness of Pontypool. You have only to look at our rugby team. We know how to express our Welshness in the front line. It is not by returning to the parish pump and becoming Ancient Britons.'[139] The unedifying spectacle continued for weeks and the bitter toilet saga of Anglesey passed into folklore. Buoyed by their success, the anti-devolutionists managed to include a 40 per cent hurdle in the Wales Bill, too.

The Bill completed its passage through the Commons on 25 April. By the time it reached the Lords, however, it was clear that Gwynfor had no stomach for the fight and, in his darkest moments, he still considered destroying the Bill. The following day, he wrote to Cledwyn Hughes attacking Labour, and Callaghan in particular, for their patent lack of enthusiasm. 'When a referendum comes,' he told Cledwyn Hughes, 'we shall lose disastrously… Elystan has given up. Last night on television, John Morris was asked whether we would have devolution; instead of saying, "Of course we shall; we must have it, it's absolutely necessary", he answered "Well, the government has kept its word".'[140] Gwynfor's anger with John Morris was a reflection of the two men's mutual deep incomprehension and it is highly significant that they met only once face to face during the whole of this period to discuss devolution. Gwynfor's criticism of John Morris was, however, unfair given the Secretary of State's record of fighting for a Welsh Assembly. In Gwynfor's estimation, however, Callaghan was most culpable. As he told Cledwyn Hughes, with some justification: 'Unless we have an *assurance* that the Prime Minister is going to give a strong lead, and quickly, my feeling is that we shall have to vote against the Bill and get the SNP to do the same thing.'[141]

Gwynfor was no doubt bluffing because the opportunity to say No had long since passed. Within a fortnight of announcing this empty threat, Gwynfor, 'having thought long and hard', explained to Dafydd Williams how the referendum could be used to best effect. He had, he said, come to the conclusion that using the referendum 'with all our might to further the Nationalist cause by facing people on the doorstep with the question of the life and future of Wales' was the only way of dealing with the inevitable trouncing. The other consolation was this: 'One thing that the Bill has managed to do is to keep the issue of Wales in the public eye for quite a long time.'[142] But the doubts remained, and Gwynfor's rather loosely-planned strategy had little effect on Dafydd Williams. He answered Gwynfor's letter by telling him that the best course would be for Plaid Cymru to defeat the referendum Bill.[143] This hesitancy – from the President down – typified the way the party conducted many of its negotiations over devolution.

Given the weakness of the Plaid leadership throughout May, Dafydd Wigley stepped into the breach and insisted that his party should support the devolution Bill. In a confidential memorandum that pulled no punches, he told some unpalatable truths. Wigley began with the assumption that most Plaid Cymru members wanted to see a Yes vote in any referendum. 'As we face the greatest constitutional leap of faith in Welsh history, the nationalist movement is unsure of itself, fearful and nervous. It is almost like a child about to sit an important exam, but afraid to acknowledge the exam's importance in case it fails.' This attitude stemmed, Wigley argued, from the failure of 'Plaid's leadership to take a sufficiently clear stand for or against the Assembly'. In short, the day of reckoning had come: 'The internal debate must end and we must begin to fight for Wales rather than fighting each other… It isn't enough to pronounce self-righteously after the referendum: "It has failed but our hands are clean, because that's not what we wanted, in any case." Not only will Plaid lose but Wales will too.'[144]

In a sense, Wigley's homily was a severe criticism of Gwynfor's soft leadership style, but it cleared the air, and his plain speaking did the party enormous good. Gwynfor and the rest of the leadership abandoned their legendary caution. This new unity was a comfort to Gwynfor, but the best tonic of all was the announcement by the Liberals that they would not continue with the coalition after the summer recess. The three Plaid MPs were now in a position of strength once more, and they began to play the parliamentary game that had been so familiar to them between 1974 and 1977. But the difference this time was that Callaghan was in such difficulties that they could extract some significant concessions. During June, Callaghan promised to campaign seriously for the Assembly and, days later, he voiced public support for devolution at the annual rally of the Welsh Labour Party. The same month saw Joel Barnett, Chief Secretary to the Treasury, suggest that he would consider Plaid Cymru's request for a tax cut in the budget.

Gwynfor was confident that the 'situation has improved' and that the public now 'see it as a Labour Bill'.[145] But his confidence was again unfounded and there was no real evidence that Callaghan's commitment was any stronger. As a result, the truce called by Wigley buckled and, in early July, Phil Williams resigned from the vice-Presidency of Plaid Cymru. In his letter of resignation to Gwynfor, he blamed the 'clear difference of political philosophy' among the party's leadership. He was also angry that what he considered a small clique, called the 'President's Committee', dictated party strategy 'yet it had no place in the party's Constitution'.[146] With devolution dead, it came as no surprise that many younger nationalists saw greater hope in Cymdeithas yr Iaith than in Plaid Cymru under Gwynfor's leadership. That summer, Rhodri Williams, the society's chair, was regarded as the most charismatic symbol of Welsh nationalism. Dressed in his smart leather coat, he was the 'bogeyman', in the eyes of the *Liverpool Daily Post*, and for days on end the press gave blanket coverage to the conspiracy charges brought against him and Wynfford James at the Crown Court in Carmarthen.[147] The police arrested dozens of the society's members and proceedings in the court were continuously interrupted. Outside, there were unpleasant scenes, and Dafydd Elis Thomas was advised by some of those closest to Gwynfor to stay away in case his presence damaged the election prospects of the member for Carmarthen.[148] In the end, the jury failed to reach a verdict and a second trial was announced – a reminder, for some, of Penyberth.

The parliamentary term ended on 27 July amid these tumultuous events. The Wales Bill had completed its passage but the priority for Gwynfor, like the rest of the party, was the general election that Callaghan would inevitably call that autumn. Gwynfor asked John Osmond to draw up an election strategy, but his assessment was disappointing to both the party and Gwynfor personally. Osmond told Gwynfor that the best Plaid Cymru could hope for was to hold its own:

> In a situation where Labour seems likely to do well in Wales this may be all we can hope for. However, there is the uncertainty of the Liberal vote plus the fact that since 1974 the Blaid must have made a greater impact (though it is probable that the publicity emanating from Westminster, associated particularly with the devolution legislation will benefit Labour since the party will be seen as at least expending time and effort on Welsh problems). Nevertheless, it is reasonable to hope that we could increase our percentage as high as 15 %, plus make a bigger impact in a number of constituencies.[149]

If this was unpromising, Plaid Cymru faced a more specific problem in the Carmarthen constituency. There, the number of people moving in from England had begun to transform the linguistic foundations of the county and Gwynfor was obliged to remind Peter Hughes Griffiths of the need to 'remember the English' because a 'host' of them had come 'into the constituency since the previous election'. 'Given these circumstances,' he said, it was 'all-important to build up the candidate.'[150]

But as these campaign preparations went ahead, there were other, less obvious, developments, which would have a lasting impact on British politics. That summer, Callaghan pondered his approach to the election. After much thought at his farm in Sussex, he felt that he could survive until the spring. Why did he come to that conclusion? According to Callaghan's biographer, K O Morgan, Gwynfor had told John Morris at the end of July that he would not try to bring down the government. Callaghan was also encouraged by the suggestion from the Ulster Unionists that he could count on their support if the province were given more MPs. Above all, Callaghan's often difficult relationship with the trade unions was also improving.[151]

During August, Callaghan set about winning Plaid Cymru's support. As the National Eisteddfod began in Cardiff, Gwynfor and Wigley met Foot at the home of his parliamentary secretary, Caerwyn Roderick, to discuss a bargain that would please both sides.[152] Plaid Cymru's terms were blatantly pragmatic: in exchange for concessions for Wales, they promised they would not try to bring down the government. It appears that Foot and Gwynfor met again that summer,[153] but the crucial meeting was the one held some weeks later on 1 September between Wigley, Elis Thomas and Cledwyn Hughes at the Anglesey Arms, Menai Bridge, where the two Dafydds (having consulted Gwynfor and other party leaders) presented Hughes with what amounted to a wish list of the Welsh legislation they wanted to see in the Queen's Speech.

Cledwyn Hughes promised he would do his best, but Plaid did not harbour high hopes. After all, they, like all informed political journalists, took it for granted that Callaghan would call an election within days. But when the hour of reckoning came on 7 September, Callaghan astounded everyone by announcing there would be no election. It was a remarkable statement and an even greater gamble, but the ramifications for Plaid Cymru and the SNP were serious. In effect, Callaghan was challenging the nationalists to throw him out of office. He knew this was highly improbable given the price they would have to pay. He also knew that Plaid Cymru (with a few exceptions) did not possess the political will to take that step; it was also well known that the SNP was divided on the issue. Gwynfor announced there could be no coalition of any sort between his party and Labour but this was no answer to the key question about Plaid Cymru's stance on any parliamentary bargaining.[154] That came later at the party's national council meeting on 10 September when it was decided that Plaid Cymru should adopt the most pragmatic attitude possible and consider every parliamentary deal on its merits.[155]

Plaid Cymru was well placed: the nationalists would have their referendum and could also insist that Callaghan answered their demands. But the thought of another parliamentary term proved too much for Gwynfor. Two days later, on 12 September, he wrote confidentially to his brother, Alcwyn, telling him he would not stand again at the general election. He confessed that it had been a 'very difficult' decision. Gwynfor also said that he feared his life would be 'very empty' after the election. But despite his concerns, he concluded that he had no other choice because his 'energy continued to wane'. Every morning, he told Alcwyn, he was 'utterly exhausted' – a situation that affected his 'mental and physical energy'. Under the circumstances, he judged that he could not carry out the 'heavy workload' ahead of him and that it would be unfair to Plaid Cymru for him to remain in politics. He warned his brother to keep the secret.[156] Indeed, it appears that not even Rhiannon knew about this letter. However, for some unknown reason, Gwynfor chose to continue as a candidate. It would prove a critical step for both him and his party.

This was not the first time Gwynfor had threatened to stand aside before changing his mind. The same pattern had been seen, as noted, in 1949, 1956, 1961 and 1975. Nevertheless, this time, the decision to remain in frontline Plaid Cymru politics would have immense implications. First, in the early autumn of 1978, the pressure on Gwynfor was arguably heavier than at any time in his political career. After all, there was a referendum pending and the survival of the UK government depended, to a great extent, on Plaid Cymru's leadership. A week after his letter to Alcwyn, Plaid Cymru revealed what it considered to be the acceptable minimum in exchange for keeping Callaghan in power. The Plaid Cymru shopping list contained a demand for more money to alleviate the effects of unemployment, compensation for quarrymen in the north, as well as training grants for teachers.[157] Gwynfor wrote to Cledwyn Hughes to remind him how 'reasonable' these requests were. They were, he said, 'simply extensions of policies already pursued by the government.'[158] But as Plaid Cymru muttered threats about what might happen to Callaghan, the opinion polls began to show that support for the party and for devolution was slipping.[159] Similarly, there was unease about the readiness of those leading Plaid Cymru to be 'bought'. As a result, Dafydd Williams had to release a statement making it clear that the party was not 'For Sale'.[160] Gwynfor suffered in silence before concluding that something had to give. He informed Dafydd Williams that he did not wish to be renominated for the Presidency.[161]

Gwynfor insisted, however, that his decision should not be disclosed until after the referendum. Now, knowing that his workload would eventually be lighter, he tried to whip up his party's enthusiasm for devolution. He told Dafydd Williams that 'the campaign must succeed' and that the referendum was even more important than the general election. He also asked Williams to put together a strategy that would see the 'campaign rising to a crescendo' in the final week. But for some nationalists, talk of winning the referendum was idiotic.[162] On a populist note, the satirical magazine *Lol* referred to Gwynfor as 'Gwynfyd [Paradise] Evans', and at his party's annual conference that year, the referendum debate raised its ugly head once again.[163] A motion was tabled calling on Plaid Cymru to boycott the 'Wales for an Assembly' campaign and it took a barnstorming speech by Emrys Roberts (of all people) for the leadership to carry the day.[164] Even so, the result – 62 votes for and 47 against – was proof of how deep Plaid's misgivings were.[165]

The referendum, however, was not the only bone of contention. Plaid Cymru's relationship with the Callaghan government was also proving problematic. Some prominent Plaid members like Phil Williams and Ted Merriman urged the three MPs to vote against the government and try to bring down Callaghan, if the Queen's Speech were deficient from a Welsh perspective. Gwynfor tried to face up to this, describing the referendum as 'the most considerable improvement in Welsh government that Westminster has ever agreed to'.[166] True enough, but it was impossible to deny what the *Western Mail* had noticed: 'If there was one thing that characterised Plaid Cymru's annual conference it was a feeling of discomfort.'[167]

At the end of October, Gwynfor returned to Westminster to hear the Queen's Speech – the content of which would crucially test his reputation as leader. Some suspected that Plaid Cymru was going to be sold a pup but sceptics like Phil Williams were proved wrong when it transpired that the Speech contained a fair measure of bills relevant to Wales. Indeed, Gwynfor had been given all he could have hoped for – from compensation for the quarrymen to a speedy start for a Welsh-language television channel. A date had also been set for the referendum: Saint David's Day. On the day after the announcement, 1 November, the speech was described by the *Financial Times* as containing 'unprecedented Welsh proposals', while the *Western Mail*'s reporter commented that he had seen nothing like it in his 32 years in the House.[168] No doubt, it was proof to Plaid Cymru members that their leaders could ask for a great deal without asking for the impossible. Following this, Gwynfor stated that his party would not vote against the government in the forthcoming motion of confidence. In practical terms, such a promise was enough, as Margaret Thatcher acknowledged, to ensure there would be no election until the spring.[169]

It was followed by other indications that the partnership was going to succeed. Callaghan promised he would force his ministers to speak in favour of devolution, and Gwynfor secured a meeting with Merlyn Rees, the Home Secretary, to discuss Welsh-medium broadcasting. After the meeting, Gwynfor believed he had secured an early start for the necessary engineering work to set up a Welsh channel.[170] But the channel issue was small change compared to what Gwynfor regarded as a more enduring shift in Welsh politics. By the end of November, he had become convinced that the referendum could be won and that the passionate opposition on the Labour benches was beginning to recede. On 23 November, he wrote to Pennar Davies as if he had experienced a personal renaissance: 'In last night's debate on the Orders for the Assembly referendum those opposed seemed rather dispirited for the first time with their tails between their legs. Their confidence has disappeared. Labour and the unions seem prepared to work.'[171]

Gwynfor stuck to his guns throughout December 1978 despite a statement by a group of Welsh Labour MPs that they would campaign quite openly against devolution. These members formed the 'Gang of 6', but rather than concentrate on the threat from Kinnock and Abse, Gwynfor devoted his attention to the more positive elements within the Labour movement. As the campaigning got under way in the middle of an industrial crisis, Gwynfor reported that the Chancellor, Denis Healey, had enjoyed 'a happy time' at a Yes meeting in Llanelli. Better still, he had spoken 'with several Ministers of the Crown during the same meeting' and heard that people of the calibre of David Owen, Michael Foot and Merlyn Rees were putting their shoulders to the wheel. He had also, he said, spoken to Callaghan and had been promised by him that he would attend 'a special meeting in Swansea and take in a press conference'. Overall, things were looking up 'with Labour and the unions officially zealous for the cause'. He was confident too that the 40 per cent was achievable.[172] As far as Plaid Cymru was concerned, he advised party members not to play too prominent a part in the campaign in case they upset Labour supporters. However, Gwynfor's consistent message was that the referendum could be won – despite the 'cruel' 40 per cent clause.[174]

It is hard to say with any certainty whether Gwynfor's attitude amounted to self-delusion, but there was no denying his sincerity at the end of 1978 when he wrote to Pennar Davies. In spite of this, any evidence to support his confidence was in very short supply. Indeed, the only reasonable conclusion is that Gwynfor had decided that it was by his faith and missionary zeal alone that he could sustain his party, and himself, during the referendum. In brief, he was turning the clock back to his early days on the stump as 1979 dawned amid snow and frost. But even Gwynfor's faith was insufficient protection against the nightmares of that January, as the worst weather in fifteen years mirrored the social unrest that tore Britain apart. Stocks of food and fuel ran low as the effects of widespread strikes and disruption began to bite. But in Wales and Scotland, the bitterness was exacerbated by the devolution debate.

The most obvious split, of course, was between devolutionists and anti-devolutionists, but other tensions too made the situation unbearable for Gwynfor.

Although the Wales for the Assembly Campaign under Elystan Morgan was meant to be non-partisan, it was deafeningly discordant. George Wright, secretary of the Transport Workers' Union, threatened to boycott the official launch in Llandrindod on 6 January were Gwynfor to speak there as well. There was a similar situation in Carmarthen where John Morris, the Welsh Secretary, refused to share a platform with Gwynfor. No doubt, there were tactical reasons for this mutual suspicion between Labour and Plaid Cymru, but there was an unmistakable air of political tribalism at work too. It all made Plaid Cymru look hesitant and uncertain. With a few exceptions (such as Foot, Elystan Morgan and John Morris), it fell to Plaid to do all the campaigning, although Gwynfor could not afford to publicly acknowledge that reality. He confessed to Carwyn James that the campaign was being run 'in fact by Plaid although Labour does not realize it'. 'We,' he added, 'have prepared every leaflet and arranged which speakers go where and organized all the meetings.'[174] The same applied in Carmarthenshire, and when the county's regional committee met on 6 January, it was noted 'that Labour was not doing much at all – the response was disappointing'.[175] As similar reports arrived from across Wales, and with no alternative, it fell to Plaid Cymru to revive a dying campaign.

But in meeting after meeting that January, Gwynfor continued to insist, as he did yet again to his own regional committee, that 'the spirit to win the referendum is excellent'. He also urged nationalists to realize that 'this is an historic opportunity for the people of Wales'.[178] Gwynfor had no other choice but to make utterly baseless statements like these, but they had little effect. During January, nationalists – and in particular language campaigners – began to voice doubts about the campaign quite openly. In *Y Faner*, the Yes campaign was rebuked by the editor, Jennie Eirian Davies, for being 'terribly ambivalent' in its attitude towards the Welsh language. Proof, she said, could be found in its literature with 'no specific and detailed reference to its welfare or its survival'.[177] Jennie Eirian was enough of a pragmatist to know there was no option other than co-operation with the campaign, but others went much further. They included the leaders of Cymdeithas yr Iaith, who decided that the society should not campaign for devolution,[178] partly to protect its independence and partly because members felt that the referendum was a complete waste of time. One of the society's most prominent members, Angharad Tomos, wrote to *Y Cymro* stating that her own intention was to continue 'to interrupt television reception' as part of the broadcasting campaign 'rather than work for a strong vote in favour of a Labour conspiracy to tame Welsh nationalists'.[179] Following this, it was left to Islwyn Ffowc Elis to counter her letter to save Gwynfor's skin. He accused Cymdeithas yr Iaith's leaders of jumping into bed with Kinnock, and he appealed to them to realize the significance of the referendum for Gwynfor's generation: 'If you throw your weight against devolution, you will be playing into your enemies' hands. Moreover, you will let down those like Gwynfor, who have worked hard and made sacrifices for Wales for almost half a century.'[180]

But the biggest concern for Gwynfor was the situation at the University College of North Wales, in Bangor. Years of conflict between the principal, Charles Evans – who had little time for the Welsh language – and the students had reached crisis point. Several students were arrested as the protests continued and three were expelled. These incidents in Bangor received wide coverage, particularly in the north, and the 'hooligans' were given pride of place in the *Liverpool Daily Post*'s rogues' gallery throughout January 1979. The students felt they had no choice but to protest against Charles Evans's regime, but Gwynfor was horrified by their swagger. He wrote to Alwyn Gruffudd, President of the Welsh students' union, Undeb Myfyrwyr Cymraeg Colegau Bangor, pleading with him to rein in the young protesters:

> I am enormously worried by the situation that has been created at University College, Bangor. From what I hear, some who belong to Adfer are willing to take reckless steps such as using dynamite to blow part of the building to bits. Any such action before the referendum and indeed before the general election would do us in Plaid Cymru the greatest possible harm because whatever the members of those movements say everything that Cymdeithas yr Iaith and Adfer do will be closely associated with Plaid Cymru.[181]

Doubtless, Gwynfor was over-reacting and he had obviously been misled by someone. Adfer posed no sort of terrorist threat, but his sensitivity was a reflection of his desire to have complete control over the 'national movement'. He expressed the same frustration with the press, writing a furious letter to Duncan Gardiner, editor of the *Western Mail*, tearing a strip off him for publishing a 'shocker' of an issue on devolution after that first meeting in Llandrindod.[182] In reality, however, Gwynfor had no reason to blame the *Western Mail*. The paper was as supportive of devolution as it had ever been during those years – something which could not be said for a large part of the press in Wales. For the *South Wales Echo*, for instance, devolution was a nationalist plot that had been foisted on a weakened Labour party by John Morris, 'The Voice of Cardigan in South Wales'.[183]

With each passing day, the press, along with anti-devolutionists in the Labour party, managed to feed Welsh fears over the Assembly. They were helped by the Conservatives, some trade unions, and the majority of councils in the south. Support came too from the Federation of Small Businesses – a body represented in 1979 by the 'Tredegar Businessman', Brian Kelly, the printer who had caused Gwynfor so much trouble back in 1968.[184] It was a curious alliance, but the anti-devolutionists' fundamental objection struck a chord across Wales. The cost of the Assembly was also a useful weapon for the No campaign, which succeeded in opening a Pandora's box of prejudices – both geographical and cultural. On top of everything, Callaghan's unpopularity was turning the referendum on devolution into a referendum on the parlous state of his government. Gwynfor tried without success to have Callaghan call a state of emergency in the hope that might limit the damage somewhat. Gwynfor was also worried by a shortage of animal feed, but the Prime Minister stumbled on even though it was obvious his government had long since lost any desire to govern.[185] Given the circumstances, Gwynfor and his colleagues could do nothing more than address meetings and distribute leaflets as the harsh weather continued unabated.

Gwynfor deliberately spent as much time as possible in Wales during February in a last urgent attempt to secure a Yes vote but, if anything, this campaigning seemed to have undermined the devolutionist cause. On 9 February, a BBC Wales poll showed that the proportion of those who supported an assembly had fallen by five per cent since September 1978 – from 38 per cent to 33 per cent.[186] Everywhere, signs of an inevitable rout were becoming increasingly apparent and some government ministers were being treated like lepers. At one meeting in Aberdare, only three people turned up to hear Barry Jones, deputy minister at the Welsh Office, and they were all 'spies' from the No campaign. It is difficult to imagine the impact of such a situation on the Yes campaign, but it was no less deflating than the one faced by the Foreign Office minister, Ted Rowlands. When he returned to address a pro-devolution meeting in his Merthyr constituency, not a single elector could be bothered to attend. John Morris had a similar experience, and the huge meeting in Swansea on 21 February, where Callaghan made his only appearance during the whole campaign, was an exception.[187] He was urged to distance himself from the whole sorry mess and, as the campaign limped into its final few days, those in favour of devolution were seized by panic as they tried to salvage some sort of party pride before their inevitable defeat. George Wright wrote to Dafydd Williams asking for 'a public guarantee' that Plaid Cymru would not bring down the government if there were a No vote.[188] Dafydd Williams refused to agree to anything of the sort, but the nationalists were not blameless either as the rickety wheels came off the devolution bandwagon.[189] With one eye on the general election, Gwynfor telephoned several of his prospective parliamentary candidates asking them to collect evidence of Labour indifference. Full and depressing reports arrived by return. John Rogers, Plaid Cymru's PPC in Flint East, reported that only two Labour councillors in the entire county had done anything to help the Yes campaign.[190] In Wrexham, things were just as bad; the candidate there, Hywel Roberts, wrote that not one Labour member, apart from Wil Edwards and another solitary councillor, had lifted a finger to get the vote out.[191]

Gwynfor, however, did not capitulate until the very end. But, on 28 February, he accepted the grim reality and admitted to the *Liverpool Daily Post* that not enough work had been done on the doorstep and that his dream of a devolved Wales had been shattered. His only consolation, he told his interviewer, was that the campaign had educated the people of Wales about 'the needs of Wales and looking to the future'.[192] The interview was published on the day of the vote, Saint David's Day, but hardly anyone could have predicted the extent of the drubbing as the results began to dribble in from the counties shortly after lunch on 2 March. Beginning with Gwynedd, it was evident that Wales had rejected devolution by a massive majority. There, 66 per cent of the electors had said No, and there was similar opposition in Carmarthenshire, Gwynfor's own county. Seventy-two per cent of voters in Dyfed were against and the national picture was even more grim. By teatime, it was obvious that 80 per cent of the Welsh electorate had rejected self-government. John Morris described the magnitude of the result like having an elephant on the doorstep.[193] It was a memorable statement from a politician who was not famous for his sparkling rhetoric, but John Roberts Williams best summed up the despair of his generation: 'The nation ventured onto the world stage for one brief moment. What did we do? We filled our pants.'[194]

Gwynfor experienced many highs and lows in his career, but this was the nadir. For him and his generation of nationalists, the referendum was more than a ballot on the administration of Wales; the referendum was a vote on the spiritual and existential question of whether Wales existed.[195] After decades of posing the question, Gwynfor had now received an unequivocal answer. He was devastated, not knowing which 'made him feel more sick... Welsh toadyism or Labour deceit and corruption'.[196] His only consolation was what he saw as the heroism of those who had campaigned for devolution. He also hoped that the majority would regret 'that they had voted as they did'.[197] But these were meagre crumbs of comfort. In the days that followed the referendum, Gwynfor witnessed friends, those who had been with him since the 'thirties, lose heart. Another aspect of the disappointment was the blaming and finger-pointing, and Gwynfor was upbraided for having led his party down a blind alley, a nationalist cul-de-sac. Dafydd Elis Thomas was among the first to speak up, condemning the naivety of those who thought that there was 'a short-cut, back-door route to self-government' available 'on the Labour bandwagon'. He was also ready to voice the unpalatable truth that Plaid Cymru had overstated its parliamentary influence between 1974 and 1979 by claiming to have achieved 'things that we really haven't'.[198]

The post mortem would have to wait as Plaid Cymru faced immediate tactical questions. The most important of these was whether Plaid Cymru and the SNP would avenge the government's 'betrayal' by attempting to bring it down. For many in Plaid Cymru, the answer was clear and the leadership was pressured to state unambiguously that Labour would have to pay the ultimate price. However, in Scotland the situation was not so clear-cut. Even though there had been a small majority in favour of devolution, the vote had failed to reach the 40 per cent threshold required in the Cunningham amendment. It left Callaghan treading the 'tartan tightrope' and, in the days immediately following the referendum, the country waited to see whether there was any hope of establishing a Scottish Assembly.[199] The Prime Minister tried to buy time, and when the MPs returned to Westminster on 5 March he suggested cross-party talks to see whether some accord could be found. But this hope faded as soon as it had been articulated and, by 10 March, it was obvious that Callaghan could do nothing to give a Scottish Assembly the kiss of life.

As the information became public, the SNP announced it would table a vote of no confidence in Callaghan's government within a fortnight unless it revived its plans for devolution. Plaid Cymru followed suit, and in a tempestuous meeting of the party's National Council on 10 March, where Gwynfor was roundly criticized for his shortcomings as a leader, a vote was taken to support the SNP's efforts.[200] During that same weekend, a leading SNP MP, George Reid, arrived to discuss tactics with Plaid Cymru. After the meeting, Reid left for Scotland with an unmistakable warning of Celtic unity: 'Time is running out for the Prime Minister... If the Government did not honour its commitment for a Scottish Assembly within two weeks the SNP would go on the offensive.'[201] That weekend proved decisive. The press realized that the nationalists meant business for once and that Callaghan's government could fall before the month was out. On 13 March, Donald Stewart, the SNP's leader in the House, met Callaghan and told him he would table the motion of no confidence unless there was a debate on Scottish devolution. On the basis of the vote by Plaid Cymru's National Council, the SNP believed they could count on Gwynfor, Wigley and Elis Thomas and, on 15 March, Stewart confirmed to the press that Plaid Cymru would also table its own motion in a show of Celtic fraternity.[202]

The effect was electrifying, and a date was set for Judgement Day: 22 March. Donald Stewart could hardly have made it clearer about what would happen next. Stewart was also unequivocal about Plaid Cymru's role in the affair unless the nationalists had their way on devolution, telling the *Western Mail* that 'by next Thursday the SNP will put down a motion of no confidence. A similar motion will be tabled by Plaid Cymru'.[203] Elements within Plaid Cymru agreed with him. The branches in Arfon instructed the three MPs to leave Callaghan for dead. In a similar vein, Dafydd Wigley claimed that a five-year saga was about to end.[204] The Conservatives savoured the approaching parliamentary Armageddon, but Callaghan himself was surprisingly self-assured. After all, it was a miracle that his government had survived for so long and he had a reputation as a political Harry Houdini. On 20 March, five days after the nationalists had announced their timetable, the press reported that Callaghan was convinced they would not topple the government.[205] But the nationalists were determined. A day later, Wigley wrote to Michael Cocks, the chief whip, warning him not to doubt Plaid Cymru's resolve for a moment. He cautioned him too that Elis Thomas and Gwynfor would, like him, support a motion of no confidence unless a Scottish Assembly were established.[206]

Upon receipt of this letter, the government's change of heart was immediate. For the first time during the crisis, Cocks and his experienced team – the men who had kept Callaghan in power thus far – sensed that the Prime Minister's political life was at stake. On 21 March – just a day before the SNP and Plaid Cymru were to table their motions of no confidence – the story broke that the government wanted to make Plaid Cymru an offer it could not refuse.[207] The deal was this: in exchange for swift compensation for some 800 quarrymen suffering from silicosis, Plaid Cymru would support Callaghan in Parliament. In essence, Labour was only promising what it had promised four months earlier in the Queen's Speech. It was the culmination of four years' hard work by Wigley, Elis Thomas and trade unions in Merioneth and Caernarvonshire. Gwynfor's instinct was to reject the offer because he had heard similar promises before. He also wanted revenge for what he saw as Labour's betrayal on devolution. 'I don't think,' he told the press, 'that we can be persuaded with any such late offer to vote for the Government which has done nothing until now.'[208] Elis Thomas was saying the same thing as late as the afternoon of 22 March. But by teatime, all three decided to step back from the brink and refrain from tabling their motion of no confidence. The party wanted to wait and consider any offer made to them but the SNP MPs were furious when they heard. After all, they had been led to believe that there was a formal agreement between the two parties. The *Daily Telegraph* claimed that the nationalists had even decided on the wording of a motion.[209] With some justification, the SNP believed that Plaid Cymru had betrayed them. The Celtic consensus (a fragile and sentimental partnership at best) was in tatters, but the SNP was in no mood to forgive and forget. That evening, they introduced their motion of no confidence in the Callaghan government. Shortly thereafter, at a little after seven o'clock, the Conservatives tabled a similar motion of their own – for discussion on 28 March. The parliamentary drama had reached its final act.

There were two reasons why Plaid Cymru and the SNP found themselves at odds. The first was the nature of their respective parliamentary groups. The SNP MPs (with some exceptions) were far more right-wing than their Plaid Cymru counterparts. The second associated reason was that the SNP depended heavily (for the most part) on conservative votes. Consequently, they believed they could bring down Callaghan without being punished at the polls. Plaid Cymru's position was somewhat different. Wigley and Elis Thomas both relied largely on votes from quarrying areas, and both were naturally left-leaning, Elis Thomas far more so than Wigley. With such a motion before the House, there was little likelihood that Elis Thomas and Wigley would undermine Callaghan. Gwynfor's situation was different, however. Gwynfor had never considered his allegiance to be right or left. His 'Welsh radicalism' was an eclectic mix that made any convenient label impossible. It meant, therefore, that he found it far easier to contemplate voting against the government. His personal experience of Labour was also a factor; he despised the party and, unlike the younger element in Plaid Cymru, he could view the referendum as the latest link in a chain of betrayal that stretched from Carmarthenshire County Council, through Tryweryn and on to the present catastrophe. Finally, both the character of his constituency and the mindset of his supporters were different from those of Elis Thomas and Wigley. If anything, Carmarthen in 1979 was more conservative than it had been in 1966 and, faced with a choice between two evils, many Welsh-speakers and Plaid Cymru supporters would have chosen Margaret Thatcher.

Given these conflicting considerations, the Conservatives were not surprised to discover that they could enlist Gwynfor's support. Just minutes after the Tories had laid down their motion, Nicholas Edwards, the opposition spokesman on Wales, approached Gwynfor on a very specific issue.[210] He proposed to Gwynfor that the Conservatives could introduce as generous a compensation scheme as that proposed by Labour. What Gwynfor said to him that evening is not known, but it is obvious that Edwards was encouraged because he subsequently wrote to him outlining the offer in some detail. In his letter, Edwards confided that Margaret Thatcher had approved the compensation scheme and that it would be settled during the first term of the next parliament.[211] Edwards was not the only one to act as go-between. Gwynfor had two conversations on the same subject with William Whitelaw, Thatcher's deputy.

These offers appealed strongly to Gwynfor. Indeed, they were more powerful than the ambiguous undertakings of the Prime Minister that he would enact 'possible changes which could improve the quality of government in Wales'.[212] The following day, on 24 March, the three MPs met in Aberystwyth to decide finally how they would vote. It had been arranged that they would meet at the Belle Vue hotel, but as there were so many reporters there, they were forced to move to one of the University's halls of residence, Neuadd Pantycelyn, where the warden, John Davies, had set aside a room for them. However, before leaving for Pantycelyn, Wigley spoke briefly to Gwynfor. From the outset, it was obvious that Gwynfor wanted to drive Callaghan from office – a decision Wigley considered 'impetuous'. Wigley also warned him not to act 'in the heat of battle, or out of anger with Labour for having betrayed Wales'. Wigley was also adamant that voting with the Conservatives would damage Plaid Cymru in the valleys, but the prospect of achieving unity on the issue seemed remote.[213] But this wasn't the last word. When Elis Thomas reached the Belle Vue, Wigley insisted that he travel to Pantycelyn with him in his car so that they could have a quick word. During the couple of minutes' drive, Wigley explained to Elis Thomas that Gwynfor wanted to go his own way and vote with the Conservatives – an act that would cause a lasting split in Plaid Cymru's ranks. Faced with this internal crisis, the pair agreed they would have to change Gwynfor's mind – no easy task given his tendency to be stubborn as a mule. As the deliberations got underway, John Davies offered the MPs a bottle of wine and promised a corkscrew 'on condition that they did nothing to support the Tories'. [214] It was a moment of humour during a serious discussion on the future of Britain's government. As usual, Gwynfor did not touch any of John Davies's *Rioja Alavesa* but he was extraordinarily willing to listen. After hours of debate, they came to an agreement: Gwynfor decided not to help bring down the government.

It was a brave, self-sacrificial act, and Gwynfor knew better than anyone how unpopular his decision would be among his supporters in Carmarthen. From that moment, he was in danger of losing his seat, but he decided to back Elis Thomas and Wigley, in order to preserve party unity more than anything. With hindsight, it was a wise course to take, because the SNP subsequently paid dearly for its failure to support the government. Even so, the effects of the decision were far more mixed for Gwynfor given the conservative nature of Carmarthenshire politics. That said, once the Pantycelyn concordat had been agreed, there was no turning back. The following day, the government was informed of Plaid Cymru's exact terms and, on the following Monday morning, they were discussed by ministers. Some Labour MPs felt that Plaid Cymru was blackmailing them and, similarly, Plaid Cymru was accused by trade unionists in Caernarvonshire and Merioneth of making political capital out of the suffering of the quarrymen.[215] But the Callaghan government had no choice given the parliamentary arithmetic. On 27 March, Wigley met Michael Foot and revealed that his party would support the government in exchange for compensation for the quarrymen.[216]

The following day saw the crucial vote of confidence. But even with the support of the Welsh nationalists, Callaghan's government was still far from secure. The confidence debate began at two o'clock that afternoon and Gwynfor explained how he would vote that evening. In essence, he told the House, he had no option but to assist the quarrymen: 'I have seen them struggling painfully step by step up a small incline, having to stop every two or three steps because of the trouble that they have in drawing breath. Sometimes these men are in their thirties and forties.'[217] In was an emotional speech, and would be the last Gwynfor would deliver in the Commons. But for all his rhetoric, it was not Plaid Cymru which attracted the attention of the press. All eyes, rather, were on that eccentric collection of Ulster MPs whose voting intentions were uncertain. As Frank Johnson put it in the *Daily Telegraph*, 'the House thinned but it kept filling up every time some normally obscure Celt rose because it might disclose voting intentions'.[218] Stranger still for the Commons, everyone in the House was fully sober that day simply because the kitchen staff were on strike, though sobriety did nothing to calm the excitement as the vote drew near. At 10.19 p.m. the vote was held, and Callaghan's government fell by one vote – the first time a government had lost a vote of confidence since 1924. The next day, Callaghan announced that an election would be held on 3 May.

Gwynfor returned from Westminster to Carmarthen and into an electoral battle for which he had no stomach, and even less energy. But the fight was on. During what would be a short campaign, he tried to remind his electors of what he had done for them; he was 'Gwynfor Dual Carriageway', the man who had ensured that long stretches of road in the county were being made safer and quicker.[219] His contribution to getting a leisure centre and an old people's centre in Carmarthen were also, his supporters said, evidence of his tireless efforts.[220] The party's national manifesto was written in the same tone. The main thrust of this determinedly apolitical document, containing no real mention of an Assembly, was the benefits that had come to Wales during the hung parliament – from compensation for the quarrymen to the establishment of the WDA, Plaid Cymru took the credit. Altogether, Gwynfor claimed that Plaid Cymru could win five new seats, including Anglesey and Merthyr.[221]

Gwynfor's predictions were pure rhetoric, for he knew his party would do extremely well to keep its three seats. But in these difficult days, rhetoric was the only weapon in his anti-Thatcher armoury. The bitter taste left by the referendum also poisoned nationalist hopes. In Carmarthen, Dr Roger Thomas, the Labour candidate, used the referendum result as a stick with which to beat Gwynfor. 'The people of Wales,' Thomas said, 'spoke very decisively on how much we value being part of the United Kingdom. Here in Carmarthen our flirtation with the separatist party is coming to an end.'[222] He was supported by his faithful party treasurer (and successor in Westminster), Dr Alan Williams. For him, the referendum result was proof of Wales's 'total hostility to nationalism... Gwynfor's vision lies in ruins – his whole life has been dedicated to achieving independence for Wales'.[223] In the heat of battle, the two doctors probably failed to notice the irony of using the failure of a Labour policy to mock Plaid Cymru. Be that as it may, it was clearly part of a strategy to undermine Gwynfor's credibility, further exemplified by another letter to the press by Dr Alan Williams: 'The dignified course of action for Gwynfor now would be to retire at the end of Parliament – at 66 years of age, he has no political future.'[224] As in previous electoral battles, Labour poured as many resources and as much money as they could into the campaign in the hope of regaining Carmarthen. The predictions were that it would again be a tight contest, even though Thomas was a weaker candidate than Gwynoro Jones.

But this time, Gwynfor faced competition from another direction. For the first time since Huw Thomas had stood for the Liberals back in 1970, there was a credible candidate who could win the small c conservative vote on which Gwynfor depended so heavily. The difference now, however, was that the threat came from a Conservative rather than a Liberal: Nigel Thomas, a 27-year-old barrister from St Clears, and an outstanding candidate during the campaign. On 28 April, a *Western Mail* poll predicted that he would perform surprisingly well and that the Conservative share of the vote would rise from the pathetic 6 per cent gained in October 1974 to 23 per cent.[225] His personality was also beginning to dismantle the anti-Labour coalition in Carmarthen, and he benefited from a UK-wide drift to the Conservatives. In comparison, the Plaid Cymru campaign appeared listless and uninspiring.

Gwynfor, on the other hand, already had his share of woes, and was to face an even bigger one. At the height of the campaign, Saunders Lewis, in a letter to *Y Faner* which, even by his standards, was particularly abrasive, criticised Plaid Cymru's decision not to vote with the SNP to bring down the government:

> The opportunity was spurned and Plaid Cymru's votes were sold to the Labour government in a dishonourable deal. It appears to me that Plaid Cymru's days are numbered. Serious Welsh nationalists need to look for leadership from the prisons, which breed honesty, not from Westminster. What a shame that we have lost those upstanding prophets J R Jones and Alwyn D Rees.[226]

It was a familiar enough appeal, but in the prevailing climate, he could scarcely have written a more damaging piece. By return, Gwynfor received a more encouraging letter from Islwyn Ffowc Elis:

> The second childhood of harmless old people arouses one's pity, but the second childhood of a genius is a cause for alarm… There is no doubt that the letter was prompted by jealousy towards you. That is a great pity. SL would be delighted to be in your position, able to bargain with a powerful English government for its very life.[227]

As a rule, Gwynfor would have ignored Lewis's outbursts, but not this time. He, and his brand of Welsh nationalism, were too vulnerable. The following week, Gwynfor answered Lewis's letter in *Y Faner*; it was a bilious masterpiece. Gwynfor voiced the frustration of decades as he attacked 'Plaid's brilliant ex-leader' for having chosen 'to speak his mind in the *Western Mail* and *Y Faner* rather than directly to those who have to decide Plaid's course in difficult circumstances'. Gwynfor went on to remind Lewis of the plight of silicosis sufferers: 'I do not know whether Mr Lewis has seen one of these men racked by silicosis, a young or middle-aged man, perhaps, trying to climb a slight incline, a few steps at a time before stopping to catch his breath; or lying in bed with a huge oxygen cylinder at his side, fighting for enough breath to utter a few hoarse words.' It was a strong, emotional image that echoed his closing speech in Parliament, but he had more to say. Gwynfor ended by doubting 'whether all the brave men and women who sacrificed so much in prison would agree with Mr Lewis's view… I shall finish by saying how sad I find it to have to write this to defend ourselves against an assault by one for whom I have so much respect and to whom I owe so much'.[228]

This unusually public spat occurred as the election campaign drew to a close, but there was worse to come. On 1 May, a BBC Wales opinion poll suggested that Gwynfor was likely to come third behind the Tory candidate in Carmarthen. Plaid Cymru supporters were outraged and utterly convinced that the poll itself and the company which had conducted it had made serious mistakes. However, the damage was done.[229] The opinion poll results were repeated on every Labour loudspeaker in the county and Plaid Cymru suspected that several of its 'natural' supporters switched their allegiance to the Tories as the party best placed to keep Labour out. This in itself was disastrous enough, but no one imagined that Saunders Lewis would do what he did three days later. As the election campaign drew to a close, he wrote another letter to *Y Faner* insisting that neither Gwynfor nor 'anyone else who has no time for me... [should] ever talk again about "the greatest Welshman of the century" or any other such meaningless and degrading nonsense. I am a sinner, an angry, nasty sinner'. True enough, because his letter closed in the most ambiguous way possible: 'I hope that these three [MPs] will have their due on the third of May, but Wales is more important to me than Plaid Cymru, and it is not through that party, with its present leadership, and its present policy, that Wales will have self-government.'[230]

Lewis's letter appeared on 4 May, as the result was declared. Shortly after five o'clock that morning, Gwynfor was given his 'due' by the electors of Carmarthen. Plaid Cymru's majority went almost entirely to the Conservatives. Gwynfor's vote fell from 23,325 to 16,689 as Nigel Thomas's leapt to 12,272. It was a stunning result for the Tories in a constituency with no Conservative tradition, and its impact on Plaid Cymru was devastating. The Tory vote left Gwynfor 1,978 votes behind Dr Roger Thomas. Losing his seat was a cruel blow, but his own result mattered little to Gwynfor in the light of the Wales-wide nationalist meltdown. Plaid Cymru's vote had fallen from 11 per cent to 8 per cent and, overnight, substantial parts of Wales had turned Conservative. Worse still, Gwynfor feared that the Welsh people had exchanged their native radicalism for the bitter pill of British Thatcherism. It was now possible to travel the length of Wales without leaving a Conservative constituency. Devolution was dead in the water, and with Thatcher as Prime Minister, nationalists feared it was only a matter of time before the Welsh language went the same way. Gwynfor was cut to the quick; rejected, he entered his own dark night of the soul.

Chapter 12

ANY OTHER BUSINESS? 1979–83

FOR WEEKS ON END AFTER LOSING CARMARTHEN, Gwynfor reflected incessantly on what had happened and the reasons for the defeat. There were, it is true, some consolations. He took advantage of the new-found freedom to spend more time with Rhiannon; he also helped out around the house for the first time in an age. But the BBC poll still rankled.[1] Indeed, Gwynfor and his supporters became somewhat obsessed by it. A few days after the vote, he insisted in a letter to Pennar Davies that the story he had heard across the constituency was that the poll had caused 'a multitude (especially the farmers) to turn to the Tories… We were well ahead on the postal ballots'.[2] And although he was now drawing his modest parliamentary pension, Gwynfor was in no mood to give up the fight without making a stand. Plaid Cymru issued a press release describing the massive swing in the Conservative vote as the most astounding in the whole of British political history.[3] Similarly, his agent, Peter Hughes Griffiths, called for an inquiry 'by someone of substance' into what had happened. Gwynfor himself sent a peevish letter to the Home Secretary, William Whitelaw, asking him to consider the request,[4] and Owen Edwards, Controller of BBC Wales, was approached on the same issue.[5] No official investigation took place but, in due course, BBC Wales's Broadcasting Council concluded that the poll carried out by Abacus had been 'unacceptably inaccurate'.[6] But even this was only cold comfort; at the time, and for years afterwards, Gwynfor judged that the whole thing had been a calculated act – a 'dirty' trick on behalf of BBC Wales.[7] It was an unfounded, even undignified, assertion, and a clear indication of his belief that the BBC was to blame for his losing Carmarthen. But despite his complaints, the facts remained: his party was on its deathbed and the last rites were about to be administered. Indeed, Plaid Cymru faced its deepest practical and intellectual crisis since the beginning of the Second World War.

The thread which linked these two crises was Gwynfor himself, but with one crucial difference: in 1939, Gwynfor was the redeemer; forty years on, Gwynfor and the innocuous policies of the national movement were the problem. The Gwynforian golden age had lost its lustre. It was a belief shared by many within Plaid Cymru, and it was powerful enough to unite political friend and foe. As far as Gwynfor was concerned, fear and self deception characterised his response to the disaster of 1979. In the first meeting of his regional committee, he claimed that 'this result is temporary'. The simple answer, he said, was 'to work hard between elections to turn Wales from materialism to idealism'. The other great comfort, he told the faithful in Carmarthenshire, was that 'the best people in the nation are with us'.[8]

In his private correspondence, however, another reaction is evident as Gwynfor searched in earnest for something to reignite Welsh nationalism. With devolution dead in the water, he concluded that the Welsh language must be the priority. As the Thatcher revolution got underway, he prided himself on the conservative – with a small c – nature of Plaid Cymru itself. 'I have always maintained,' he told the nationalist-minded Tory, H W J Edwards, 'that Plaid Cymru is the only party in Wales that is truly conservative. We know what we want to conserve and it is something noble. Welsh-speaking Tories only want to conserve their own comfortable positions.'[9] To that end, Gwynfor wanted to see the establishment of an organization to promote the Welsh language along the lines of the New Wales Union. The language was now 'the most important topic in the whole of Wales' for him and his aim was to have 'heartfelt co-operation' across all parties.[10] He tried to enthuse the Conservative MP, Geraint Morgan, and Plaid Cymru's general secretary, Dafydd Williams, about a movement which would co-ordinate the efforts of Merched y Wawr, unions, churches and councils. In essence, Gwynfor had decided that the only strategy for Plaid Cymru was to turn back the clock to the late 'thirties. For his own part, he had reached two conclusions. The first was that he would not contest another election, telling Wyn Thomas, a leading member of Plaid Cymru in Carmarthen, that 'someone younger' was needed. He also believed he had the right man for the job (whom he did not name) in mind.[11] Second, he wanted Plaid Cymru to use him, Gwynfor, as 'a missionary for the national cause'.[12] As he told the *Western Mail*, 'it'll be like the old days for me'.[13]

Talking, as Gwynfor did in May and June, of returning to the good old days was an absurdity. For one thing, Wales was facing the biggest change in its economic and social order since 1945; second, Plaid Cymru was desperate for a more sophisticated response than that offered by Gwynfor. Dafydd Williams merely thanked Gwynfor politely for his idea of a new language movement.[14] Williams did not wish to be negative, but his lukewarm response reflected the fact that Plaid Cymru was now looking for salvation from directions other than Gwynfor. It was also a clear indication that a new era was dawning as the race for the Presidency began in earnest. Gwynfor was becoming increasingly marginal. His most likely successor, Dafydd Wigley, called on Plaid Cymru to rethink almost every aspect of its direction and message because the electoral defeat was 'too significant to be shrugged off or explained away by excuses'. He also believed that Welsh-speakers faced being wiped out like 'the Red Indians' of America.[15] Elis Thomas proffered a quasi-Marxist analysis of Plaid Cymru's problems, but he too was convinced that 'it needs to be less apologetic'. His party and the Welsh people, he said, had had enough of 'the ideology of oppression'.[16]

These were opening salvos by the two Dafydds in the battle for the soul of Plaid Cymru, but one thing was abundantly clear: Plaid Cymru was no longer Gwynfor's party and all the sacred cows faced possible slaughter. There were calls for a more aggressive nationalism during the National Council meeting in June,[17] and a resolution was passed insisting that Plaid Cymru should abolish the 'President's Committee'. There was a general perception too that Gwynfor's secretive and undemocratic administrative methods had to end.[18] This sense of hopelessness was heightened by further electoral failures. On 7 June, Plaid Cymru was humiliated in the first ever election to the European Parliament. Even though its percentage of the national vote – 11.7 per cent – was a little better than it had polled in the general election, it was only in the North Wales constituency that the party and its candidate, Ieuan Wyn Jones, made any impression at all. Worse still, only days later, it was revealed that Plaid Cymru had lost a quarter of its members between 1976 and 1979.[19] In due course, the leadership heard that the party faced debts of £116,897 – a position that Elwyn Roberts, the most experienced of its financial wizards, called 'a very serious crisis'.[20]

The culmination of these tensions was that Plaid Cymru took the advice of its vice-president, Ieuan Wyn Jones, and set up a research commission to establish what had gone wrong. It was a noble aim, but it proved yet another blow to Gwynfor's image; now, a panel of five would hold an inquest not only into the party which he led but also into his political legacy. The commission did not shelter Gwynfor from criticism and, if anything, its work further disrupted Welsh nationalism's internal discipline. Cymdeithas yr Iaith was among the first to maul the party and Cen Llwyd, editor of *Tafod y Ddraig*, used his monthly column to express the hope that:

> ... Plaid Cymru's failure in the last election and the failure of devolution will be... a means to entice back the steady stream of former members who have swum out of Cymdeithas's ranks to work within Plaid over the years. The polling booth route has failed disastrously... [21]

This message was endorsed in the same issue by Rhodri Williams, the society's chair, who asserted that the only way Plaid Cymru could 'keep or regain the respect and support of the younger generation' was by 'placing Welsh and its future at the centre of its politics'.[22]

Statements like these are evidence of the disintegration of both nationalism and the credibility of Gwynfor's legacy during these months, but every bit as important as the growth of language politics was a short-lived revival in republican ideas. The Socialist Republicans, led by Gareth Miles and Robert Griffiths ('Red Rob', the party's research officer), bared their teeth by asking Plaid Cymru to reach out to the working class. Essentially, these republicans were rehashing many of the ideas of their forebears in the 'fifties, but their analysis struck a chord with many Plaid Cymru members who wanted a different brand of nationalism. During the Caernarfon Eisteddfod of 1979, the Gwynforite establishment was rocked by the publication of a highly controversial pamphlet written by Griffiths and Miles called *Sosialaeth i'r Cymry* (Socialism for the Welsh). It called for the political marriage of socialism and the Welsh language, but its most striking feature was its tone. It contained, without doubt, one of the fiercest attacks on Gwynfor ever mounted, voicing the type of criticism that even the republicans and the New Nation group had never dared to air publicly. Better still (from the point of view of its authors), Gwynfor's critics had succeeded in persuading Dafydd Elis Thomas to write the foreword to this challenge to Plaid Cymru orthodoxy. Its fundamental conclusion was as follows:

> It is no surprise that a willingness to compromise, an unwillingness to be adventurous, lack of purpose and cowardice are the main features of the party a large proportion of whose members, including its leaders, are petits bourgeois, Nonconformists and pacifists.[23]

Faced with this criticism, senior courtiers at the Court of Llangadog tried to offer Gwynfor succour and encouragement. He received a letter from Dewi Watkin Powell begging him not to listen to language activists like Meredydd Evans who were calling for a return to unconstitutional methods. Evans, Watkin Powell told him, represented the 'anti-political' tendency in Welsh politics. He also implored Gwynfor to speak to Elis Thomas – whom Watkin Powell admired for his ability, but whom he suspected because of his immaturity and supposed lack of political nous.[24] Watkin Powell's considered advice to Gwynfor was to promote cultural education and harness Welsh identity to solve Wales's problems. It was a safe solution to the difficulties Welsh nationalism faced as it entered a period of uncertainty. Economically, the climate was rougher than ever, clearly exemplified by the decision in July to make 6,300 workers at the steel plant in Shotton on Deeside redundant. Environmentally, the people of mid-Wales were alarmed by explorations for sites suitable for the burial of nuclear waste. The Welsh language also faced what many felt was a bleak future – despite the enlightened policy presented by the new occupants of the Welsh Office of unprecedented funding for the language. There was also a new perceived threat to the language from HTV Wales; by July 1979, it was eager to see Welsh programmes broadcast on two channels rather than the one that had been promised in the Conservatives' general election manifesto.[25] At the same time, the controller of BBC Wales, Owen Edwards, began to express public doubts about where the money to fund the new Welsh channel could be found.[26]

Faced with this situation, the brutal truth was that there was little anyone could have done to raise Gwynfor's spirits. These months intensified his sense of a crisis in Wales, reawakening the feelings he had experienced as a youth in Barry about the death of the nation. A guilty conscience over his political leadership only added to the anguish. But if the nonconformist romanticism of this aesthetic of national death and salvation was a familiar one to him, there was no easy redemption at hand. After all, Gwynfor was the fallen redeemer – the man who had given his all for Wales and 'failed' as abysmally with the referendum as he had with Tryweryn. Now, he was a figure of fun, a man who could be impugned and dismissed. It was out of this despair, with everything torn asunder and all other solutions exhausted, that Gwynfor found one last, shocking idea: he decided the only thing he could now offer to Wales was his own life. In the mid-'eighties, Gwynfor confessed to his son, Dafydd, that he had decided to kill himself at some point in 1979 and lay down his life, his most precious possession, for his country. The act of suicide, he told Dafydd, would have been 'short and swift' and committed on Saint David's Day. It was an incredible plan, even though its political objective was perfectly clear: to blow life into the embers of nationalism and inspire the young people of Wales to fight once more for the nation that had betrayed him.[27]

Gwynfor did not act on his idea because a rather different crisis arose that spared his life – quite literally. On 12 September 1979, the Home Secretary, William Whitelaw, announced in a lecture to the Royal Television Society in Cambridge that the government no longer planned to establish a separate Welsh television channel. Rather, television programmes in Welsh would be broadcast on the BBC and on a new fourth channel, to be called ITV 2. The announcement flew in the face of the clear undertaking made in the Conservatives' election manifesto and was interpreted by almost all nationalists as a devastating betrayal. The reality, however, was that Whitelaw did not consider his announcement to be either underhand or controversial. Indeed, understanding Whitelaw's motives is crucial to the story because it was this pragmatism, in the long run, that saved Gwynfor's life. First, the Conservatives wanted to double the provision by dividing 22 hours of Welsh-language programmes between the BBC and the proposed new channel, ITV 2. This was a slightly lower level of programming than had been anticipated for a single Welsh channel but, to many Tories concerned about the language, Whitelaw's plan seemed a fair and practical way of overcoming the difficulty at a time of financial restraint. After all, the only thing that had been sacrificed, as supporters of the Whitelaw plan saw it, was the principle of placing all Welsh programmes on one channel. Either way, whether on one channel or two, there would be substantially more programmes. The second reason for the U-turn was the pressure placed on Whitelaw by Shirley Littler, the Assistant Under-Secretary of State in the Home Office. It was her, more than anyone, who convinced him that the technical difficulties inherent in creating a new channel were insurmountable. Lastly, those who backed Whitelaw believed that Welsh programmes should appear on 'high-profile' channels and not, as the educationalist Jac L Williams and the *Western Mail* put it, in a Welsh language 'ghetto'.[28]

These, then, were the considerations underlying what came to be known as Whitelaw's 'betrayal'. However, it would be wrong to think that the crisis emanated from Whitehall alone. The second element in the story is that HTV Wales had put Whitelaw under enormous pressure to change his mind. Indeed, very influential figures on the company's board had been lobbying Whitelaw for months, hoping he would get cold feet over the single-channel option. For HTV's directors, like Lord Harlech and Alun Talfan Davies, the plan to place all Welsh programmes on one channel, ITV 2 or S4C (Sianel Pedwar Cymru) as it came to be called, was an utter nuisance. Their great fear (never realized because HTV Wales milked S4C in its infancy) was that they would lose money because the channel would not be controlled by the independent sector under the Independent Broadcasting Authority, or IBA. In June 1979, therefore, HTV decided to act. Between trips to Rhodesia, Lord Harlech, chair of HTV, wrote to William Whitelaw to say that he was 'gravely concerned' with the situation. His great anxiety, he said, was that Welsh programmes would be broadcast in a 'ghetto', 'lumped together on the new 4th channel'.[29] Harlech appears to have met Whitelaw, and his letter and crocodile tears over the fate of the Welsh language were part of a wider campaign by the company to undermine the Conservative manifesto commitment. There is also evidence that HTV and its Welsh chair, Sir Alun Talfan Davies, brought pressure to bear on the IBA to move away from supporting a Welsh channel. These moves were supported by the formidable Lady Plowden, chair of the IBA, who was implacably opposed to a Welsh channel.[30]

The last piece in this jigsaw is the political context. Certainly, neither Whitelaw nor Nicholas Edwards, the Welsh Secretary (later Lord Crickhowell), two Tories so wet that they dripped, did not intend to belittle the Welsh people, but the failure of devolution meant that reneging on the channel was that much easier. The size of the No vote also meant that Welsh Office clout within Whitehall (feeble at best) was by then considerably attenuated. The Home Office's chief concern, however, was that the undertaking to set up a fourth channel in Wales undermined what they saw as the far more pressing scheme to set up Channel 4 in the rest of the UK. Gradually, this constellation of factors came together. In the middle of July, Home Office civil servants drew up a memorandum which envisaged Welsh-language programmes on two channels. It paved the way for the saga of 'betrayal' over the channel. However, in the Welsh Office in Cathays Park, news of the memorandum caused what can best be described as an explosion. R H Jones, a senior civil servant with responsibility for the Welsh language, was livid when he heard, writing to a Welsh Office colleague in strident terms:

> I consider that the Home Office have behaved disgracefully in this matter; for the Secretary of State to be presented with what is virtually a fait accompli is really quite intolerable and to argue that the Secretary of State has no statutory responsibility for broadcasting is no answer… These proposals, if accepted, and I would be very surprised if they are not, will cause considerable embarrassment, not only to the Secretary of State… but also to the Government'.[31]

His assessment of the implications of the decision were completely accurate. It would, nevertheless, be unfair to conclude that Nicholas Edwards was happy with this policy. On the contrary, he was appalled and wrote furiously to Whitelaw insisting that the government should abide by its original policy. 'I was frankly astonished,' Edwards told Whitelaw, 'to receive this paper last night and to see the proposal which it made for the treatment of Welsh Language broadcasting on the fourth channel.' He continued:

> It is not merely that what you now propose will create the most profound political problems in Wales, where as you know, this Government's commitment to the furtherance of the language is already being questioned and a major political row is brewing… What I find unacceptable is that the recommendations in your paper should have emerged in the way that they did one week before they are due to be discussed by colleagues without any prior consultation whatever with me or with my Department… in the meantime the paper which you circulated should be withdrawn until we can, if not agree on proposals to put to colleagues at least produce acceptable options for consideration.[32]

This highly unusual letter was followed by another in the same vein, when Sir Hywel Evans, Permanent Secretary at the Welsh Office, wrote to warn Sir Robert Armstrong, Permanent Secretary at the Home Office, of 'some very ruffled feathers' back in Cardiff.[33]

But for all the sound and fury, politicians and civil servants at the Welsh Office knew they had no hope of success in a straight fight between themselves and the Home Office. It was the natural order of things in the administration of Wales, and Nicholas Edwards was formally advised not to bother with any further opposition. As R H Jones, the civil servant most vocal in his opposition to the policy change put it: 'I do not think that there would be much mileage in advising the Secretary of State to oppose the proposals because, quite clearly, this is the solution which commends itself to the Home Office and to the broadcasting authorities.'[34] His advice was accepted. In his autobiography, Whitelaw writes that Welsh Office ministers did not oppose the suggestion that a Welsh channel should be created.[35] If Nicholas Edwards is to be believed, the Minister of State, Wyn Roberts, along with Sir Hywel Evans, said nothing when they discussed how to proceed. Indeed, Edwards says the deciding factor in his case was hearing the doubts of two proud Welshmen, Roberts and Evans, about the one channel 'solution'. However, his deputy offers a different interpretation.[36] In an interview with the author, Wyn Roberts (later Lord Roberts of Conwy) claimed that the contrary was true and that discussions had become rather 'heated' in his efforts to honour the one channel commitment.[37]

Whatever the truth, one thing was certain: there was to be no separate channel. On 11 September, a day before Whitelaw's Cambridge speech, Wyn Roberts requested a meeting with the Home Secretary because of his genuine fear there would be an 'outcry' in Wales once it became clear that there would be no separate channel. Roberts's objective was to make the best of a difficult situation and ensure optional Welsh-language provision on both channels. Even so, it is clear from the minutes of the meeting that Roberts accepted the principle of broadcasting Welsh-language programmes on two channels. It is clear from the minutes, too, that Whitelaw was not for turning.[38] At the meeting, the Home Secretary confirmed that the Home Office had had reneged on its promise and that the reasonable arrangement now would be to have some 10 hours of Welsh programmes on the BBC and 12 hours on ITV 2. To finalise the deal, the avuncular Home Secretary promised that consultative machinery would be put in place to ensure that the Welsh language was fairly treated.

In retrospect, the whole channel crisis can be seen as a monumental Whitehall cock-up, but that is not how it appeared to many at the time. Many Welsh speakers considered what happened in September 1979 to be part and parcel of a pattern of treachery stretching back to the infamous Blue Books of 1847 and including the referendum. After all, what the Conservatives had originally promised was not particularly radical and the principle of a Welsh-language channel had been confirmed by four official reports: Crawford (1974), Siberry (1975), Annan (1977) and Littler (1978). With the idea of a Welsh channel now as dead as a dodo, Wyn Roberts and Owen Edwards, controller of BBC Wales, both revealed to the author that they considered resigning before deciding that the more honourable course was to stay in post and campaign for a change.[39]

For Welsh nationalists, however, Whitelaw's announcement was more than an administrative failure in broadcasting policy. For one thing, it probably meant more young people would have to undergo periods of imprisonment as had Angharad Tomos and Ffred Ffransis – to name only two of the more prominent members of Cymdeithas yr Iaith. This in itself was enough to provoke an angry reaction but, from the moment he uttered his words in Cambridge, Whitelaw's speech was also interpreted as an expression of the Conservatives' desire to stamp out Welsh identity and deprive the Welsh of their right to create and run an institution of their own. Seeing HTV (a company that some within Plaid Cymru regarded with contempt) caught up in the whole sorry affair confirmed the perception that it was part of a capitalist, anti-Welsh conspiracy.[40] It was a perception shared by civil servants at the Welsh Office too. They had already issued an internal warning of 'a very real danger that this administration may be projecting a somewhat hostile attitude to Welsh cultural matters. This could well bring about a very nasty situation'.[41]

This largely symbolic debate prompted Gwynfor to engage in the most dangerous struggle of his life. It was also, it must be said, an opportunity for him to restore his reputation after the failures of the referendum and Tryweryn. Now he had something worth fighting for. Gwynfor launched himself into the battle for a Welsh channel, but for him it was in reality about something more than that. Personal and political considerations weighed rather more heavily on him than the future of Welsh on television. This was his golden opportunity, the great cause that Gwynfor had waited so long to champion. The day after Whitelaw's announcement, Gwynfor declared that a new chapter had opened in the history of Plaid Cymru. Now, he said, Plaid Cymru must embrace 'other than conventional political methods' faced with a government that had gone back on its promises.[42] These words, delivered in Ystrad Mynach, were more of a U-turn than Whitelaw's decision. They marked the end of the tactical caution and discretion that had typified Gwynfor's conduct over Trawsfynydd and Tryweryn as he returned to the quintessential nationalist principles of Penyberth. There was no more talk of making Plaid Cymru a respectable, constitutional party. Gwynfor's constitutional revolution had run its course and Saunders Lewis's example appeared the more attractive option. Nevertheless, there is no evidence that performing such a volte face on this vital point caused Gwynfor any great difficulty. By then, the failure of nationalism was much greater than his own perceived failure as a politician. He had little time for consistency either, and believed he was perfectly justified in turning the clock back to the 'thirties and the symbolic heroism of Penyberth. From that moment on, Gwynfor knew he would have to be completely sincere in following the path and example of Gandhi.

Whitelaw's pronouncement opened the floodgates to similarly militant reactions from a number of prominent nationalists. Aled Eirug, secretary of Cymdeithas yr Iaith's broadcasting group, claimed that the only option open to the society was a more extreme campaign of unlawful action.[43] Similarly, Angharad Tomos told R Tudur Jones that Welsh nationalism 'is facing another Penyberth or Tryweryn and it is time for dramatic action'.[44] Just days after her comment, Meredydd Evans was busy collecting the names of those who would be prepared to carry out a similar act. Tudur Jones refused to take part, but Pennar Davies, the most revered of the reverends, agreed without hesitation.[45] These unconstitutional steps were mooted within Plaid Cymru as well. Dafydd Elis Thomas undertook not to pay his television licence and, days later, Gwynfor and Dafydd Wigley promised the same. But although Plaid Cymru and Cymdeithas yr Iaith appeared to be in accord, the two camps were far from united. At the outset, the society was distinctly wary of Plaid Cymru. At a meeting three days after the Whitelaw announcement, fears were expressed 'that working too closely with Plaid and others might limit the campaign's potential to act'.[46] A month later, a resolution calling on Cymdeithas yr Iaith to make 'every effort to work alongside Plaid Cymru' was defeated.[47]

It would be wrong to assume too that everyone in Plaid Cymru, and the broader 'national movement', was happy with the decision to turn the party overnight into a quasi unconstitutional body. John Dixon, the Plaid Cymru treasurer, criticized Gwynfor and Elis Thomas's decision to announce a campaign of unlawful action without any sort of consultation. The decision, Dixon said, showed 'that some in Plaid do not respect Plaid's constitution and are not willing to let the most democratic group within Plaid reach a decision'. Dixon's other concern (and a significant one in the view of several Plaid Cymru members) was the attitude of party supporters in anglicized areas where there was less emphasis on the Welsh language.[48] Other nationalists were suspicious of undertaking a campaign of the sort when there was a greater likelihood of success with equally important, if not more important, issues like Welsh-medium education. Harri Pritchard Jones, who had been so keen on direct action over Tryweryn, argued that it would be folly to go 'out into the desert for years, in all our philosophical purity, to try for a Welsh channel when we already have something substantial available here and now'.[49] A statement of the sort by such an inveterate nationalist spoke volumes for the challenge facing those who wanted to win the channel debate. There was one other objection of substance. It came from Jennie Eirian Davies, editor of *Y Faner*, who believed quite sincerely, like the late Jac L Williams, that grouping all Welsh programmes on one channel would be detrimental to the language. For her, Whitelaw's announcement was an opportunity, and she hoped that advantage could be taken of 'the promises given to us, and turn them into a broadcasting service for our nation'.[50]

With the national movement riven by factionalism, Whitelaw's supporters grew in confidence. On 19 September, Sir Brian Young, director general of the IBA, wrote to Alun Talfan Davies to express his delight at the wisdom of Whitelaw's change of heart. 'It looks,' Young wrote, 'as if those of us who have long fought this battle will get more kicks on the shins but now have a decent chance of scoring.'[51] A day later, Cymdeithas yr Iaith began its protest, gluing the locks of BBC vans but, appropriately enough given the campaign's uncertain start, the effect was minimal. A week later, the society attacked the BBC buildings in Bangor but, in reality, it was a disorganized campaign. At heart, Gwynfor was more aware of these shortcomings than anyone. The most compelling evidence of this became apparent on 28 September when Meredydd Evans and his wife, Phyllis Kinney, visited Gwynfor at Talar Wen. Evans's goal was to seek Gwynfor's approval for the action that he, Pennar Davies and Ned Thomas were planning. They intended to switch off the television transmitter at Pencarreg and, as expected, Gwynfor was happy to give his blessing. However, as they were leaving Talar Wen, Evans and his wife were astonished to hear Gwynfor say that he was 'thinking of doing something much more serious'. At the time, Phyllis Kinney thought Gwynfor was considering setting himself on fire as the Czech student, Jan Palach, had done. But the look in his eye was so terrifyingly passionate that both felt it wiser not to ask.[52]

Clearly, then, Gwynfor, as early as September 1979, had aligned his idea of drastic action with the broadcasting campaign. However, it appears that the idea of a fast had not yet taken root. Meanwhile, Plaid Cymru tried to set up its own campaign of refusing to buy licences. On the day after his meeting with Meredydd Evans and Phyllis Kinney, Gwynfor fired the first shot: in a piece for *Y Faner*, he voiced his fervent hope that 'thousands will refuse to pay for television licences'. Indeed Gwynfor wanted 'to see thousands of respectable Welsh people in prison' – an act that would 'shake the government' and 'transform our outlook as a nation'.[53] On 11 October, the Pencarreg transmitter was switched off by three of those respectable Welsh people. The action taken by Meredydd Evans, Pennar Davies and Ned Thomas was a serious one, interpreted as an echo of Penyberth as nationalism moved increasingly in the direction of law-breaking. Plaid Cymru, however, remained divided. Some, in particular those on the left of the party, were cynical about the headlong rush of Gwynforites towards prison cells. As Harri Webb wrote in his diary, for instance:

> 2 of them have shown mettle *déjà*, but Pennar hitherto noted for oversanctimonious posturing and as GE's chaplain and confessor, probably responsible for the fatal volte-face over Tryweryn early 60s. Now trying to make up for it. But the damage has already been done, and the drama of Y Tri [The Three] has already been played.[54]

But three days later, on 14 October, Plaid Cymru's executive voted formally in favour of a non-payment campaign. The following day, from the stage of the cross-party, ad hoc national conference on broadcasting, Gwynfor asked supporters of the channel to pay their television licence fees into a special fund. It was a tried and tested tactic – identical, indeed, to the one the Listeners' Association had used back in 1954 but, this time, the political climate was very different. The basic difference between 1954 and 1979 was that Plaid Cymru's future now depended on this campaign.

Even so, despite the fiery rhetoric and the raw emotion, the campaign was barely stirring. Tom Ellis, the Wrexham Labour MP, and one of the most vocal supporters of Welsh broadcasting, refused to join the national conference. Fundamentally, he believed that victory was impossible. 'We have,' he said, 'to face facts and face up to the situation – just as the Shotton workers have to... The important thing now is to get the BBC and the commercial company to work together.'[55] Such attitudes were echoed by HTV Wales – which had no intention of giving way. During October, it published a booklet arguing precisely why the plans announced by 'Mr William Whitelaw... bode well for exciting developments in television'.[56] Some 5,000 copies of the booklet were distributed, giving rise to harsh criticism from Plaid Cymru and Dafydd Elis Thomas. Elis Thomas was in turn criticized by David Meredith, the Welsh-language spokesman of HTV Wales (and later S4C's head of press relations), for potentially causing 'social divides by locating all Welsh television programmes on one channel'.[57]

The attitudes of 'good Welshmen' like David Meredith also reflected the fact that Plaid Cymru and Cymdeithas yr Iaith were losing the argument. Privately, in a memorandum headed 'Our Critics in Wales' circulated within HTV Wales, Meredith had this to say:

> He [Gwynfor Evans] mentioned to me then that he was prepared to go to prison to further his belief... Dafydd Williams of Plaid Cymru has informed me that although he recognises that the fourth channel has been lost they are determined to continue the struggle in the hope of gains in other directions – e.g. early introduction of the IBA fourth channel in Wales.

Meredith promised that he would do all he could to stay 'one jump ahead of our critics' (in particular Dafydd Elis Thomas), but Dafydd Williams was by no means the only nationalist who believed the campaign was running out of steam.[58] In late October, in his first speech as the new chair of Cymdeithas yr Iaith, Wayne Williams admitted that the channel campaign was dying on its feet.[59] It was in such an atmosphere of conflicting emotions that Plaid Cymru met for its most important annual conference in decades. In one respect, there was a revivalist enthusiasm in the air but given the sense of nationalist betrayal, there was no avoiding the painful awareness that the campaign was not succeeding. Inevitably, the pressure led to tactical errors – most notably perhaps the childish resolution to eject HTV Wales journalists from the conference. Honest brokers like Gwilym Owen and Max Perkins were models of objectivity but, as with so many nationalist campaigns, people were adjudged to be either openly supportive or against. Quite simply, neutrality was impossible in a conference where Gwynfor agreed to serve as President for another year. As Rhoslyn, *Y Cymro*'s political columnist said, it was 'just like being at one of the conferences from the early years'.[60]

But by not giving up the Presidency, and stating from the conference platform that the channel was as important as Tryweryn, Gwynfor was increasing the pressure on himself.[61] After all, he could have surrendered the Presidency at the conference and let someone else, such as Dafydd Wigley or Emrys Roberts, steer Plaid Cymru into calmer waters. Doubtless, the decision to carry on was a brave one because the broadcasting campaign was having virtually no impact on the government. By the end of October, the government began defending its policy more aggressively; Wyn Roberts accused Wigley and Elis Thomas of trying to make political capital out of the Welsh language.[62] Shortly thereafter, a number of local authorities in Wales reconsidered their support for the campaign. At Dyfed Council, on Gwynfor's doorstep, some Plaid Cymru councillors expressed doubts about the channel scheme;[63] by February 1980, only Gwynedd was unequivocally supportive. Several leading broadcasters in Wales began to rethink too; in *Y Faner*, Euryn Ogwen Williams, who would later become S4C's first head of programmes, argued that confining Welsh-language programmes to one channel could make 'more of a contribution to undermining the position of the language than any political decision at Westminster'.[64] Attitudes of the sort also had repercussions within Plaid Cymru itself; as the broadcasting campaign limped on, the republicans grew more vocal and ready to tell Gwynfor some unpalatable truths. As Gareth Miles saw it: '... there is no time. Carmarthen was a fluke; we can't wait for another fluke. Plaid chases its own tail, and Cymdeithas has not established itself as the revolutionary avant garde movement that people were hoping it would be'.[65]

Within a month of these words being written, Plaid Cymru had sacked Robert Griffiths, its research officer. Griffiths's departure was attributed to a lack of funding but, by the turn of the year, Griffiths and Miles had set up the Welsh Socialist Republican Movement, as a party within Plaid Cymru. Nevertheless, sacking a critic like Griffiths was a Pyrrhic victory. The major battle, for the channel, had no direction and several party members were unwilling to commit themselves to it. On 21 November, Dafydd Wigley wrote a crucial letter to Gwynfor telling him that something needed to change – and soon. Wigley in typical fashion, didn't pull any punches:

> I have received a very mixed reaction from friends – some of whom are ardent Plaid supporters, expressing opposition to the policy [of not paying for licences]... if we are to avoid having this campaign fall flat on its face we must act and act quickly as a movement or there's a danger that the whole thing will look pathetic. Our members must get information without *delay*... It is the easiest thing in the world to get steamed up at a conference or a National Council about the need for some campaign or other but it's a very different matter to take on the precise and time-consuming work that's wholly necessary if a political party wants to convey its message in a credible way... I am very worried about the way the campaign has been started.[66]

It was a sobering letter for Gwynfor to receive, but Wigley was not alone in his opinion. In Carmarthenshire too, Gwynfor heard that there was 'dragging of feet over getting people to sign up to withhold the television fee'.[67] The problem there, and in other areas of Wales, was that so many believed that Welsh would be on firmer ground if it were on two channels rather than one. Time and again, the 'Jac L' argument struck a chord with many in Welsh-speaking Wales.

As a result, Plaid Cymru redoubled its efforts. On 11 December, Dafydd Elis Thomas renewed his appeal for friends of the language to withhold their licences fees. His homily coincided with further evidence of decline on the industrial front; on the same day, the British Steel Corporation announced that it was halving its production in Wales. Either Llanwern or Port Talbot would probably be closed, and leading trade unionists like George Wright, secretary of the TUC in Wales, feared that the country was about to experience hardship not seen since the 'thirties.[68] In such a dire situation, and as both cultural and industrial struggles found common cause, some in Wales decided that there was no point in waiting any longer. On 12 December, a day after Dafydd Elis Thomas had attempted to reignite the 'No Channel, No Licence' campaign, a fire was ignited, literally, in Wales. That evening four houses, two on the Llŷn peninsula and two in Pembrokeshire were set on fire; although no one knew it at the time, the Meibion Glyndŵr arson campaign had begun and, by the time it ended in 1991, more than two hundred cottages would have been torched. For Plaid Cymru more than any other party, it was a significant but dangerous development. The arson campaign meant that it would lose some support because of the arsonists, and its opponents would also use the acts to smear Plaid Cymru.

All in all, it was a particularly bleak Christmas for Gwynfor. He was almost at the point of total dejection, but nevertheless, he was still astonished, as he admitted to Lewis Valentine, at 'the work that has been done, much of it cultural' after 'a difficult year for Wales and Plaid'.[69] He also took delight in watching Miss Piggy, star of the *Muppet Show*, on television with his grandchildren. These, however, were merely crumbs of comfort.[70] Around him, he saw a party in turmoil and nationalism in retreat. In Carmarthenshire that Christmas, loyal friends like his son-in-law, Ffred Ffransis, and Peter Hughes Griffiths, tried to give another boost to the broadcasting campaign but with little success. Although Plaid Cymru and Cymdeithas yr Iaith jointly organized several fasts and protests, the numbers who gathered were, in reality, unimpressive. The 'Channel Movement' (a term coined by Peter Hughes Griffiths to create the impression that a powerful body lay behind the campaign) was also forced to cancel some of these protests because of flooding.[71] As the new decade dawned, the press hailed Mrs Thatcher as 'person of the year' and nationalists began to lose heart. Leading figures in Cymdeithas yr Iaith, like Rhodri Williams, spoke of 'being realistic', wondering how they could 'break the news to hopeful Welshmen and women that there would be no Welsh Channel after all'.[72]

Gwynfor, however, was not in a conciliatory mood. For him, 1980 was the year when the Welsh would either 'raise themselves to the level of history' or sink into total oblivion. It left him with only one choice. Faced with this awful challenge, he decided to fast. He did so for sound tactical reasons: he knew full well that he could gain huge sympathy between the beginning of his fast and his probable death. His memory of Gandhi's successful protests during the 'thirties had taught him an important lesson in that respect. Nevertheless, the morality of the action troubled him. He was enormously worried that death by starvation might be interpreted as suicide. Troubled by this thought, and without a word to his family, he went to discuss the matter with Pennar Davies. It was a crucial meeting but it left him in good heart. Davies took the view that it was not Gwynfor who would be responsible for his own death, but the government. Davies also argued that there was no need to worry about the probable violent reaction to his untimely end. Viewed in this way, Gwynfor could think of himself and his action as the behaviour of a soldier on the battlefield.[73]

There was without doubt a large element of self-deception and moral ambiguity in Gwynfor's reasoning, given his reputation as one of the most prominent pacifists in twentieth-century Wales. After all, the success or otherwise of the fast depended on the government's fear of violence. Indeed, it is unquestionable and also deeply ironic that Gwynfor ended his days as a politician using violence as a political weapon – something that Saunders Lewis never did. The unpalatable truth is clear but the crucial issue is that the moral approval he received from Pennar Davies galvanised him for the difficult weeks and months to come. Davies wrote to him shortly afterwards that he should not hesitate to reconsider. But the tactical choice had been made:[74] in the matter of life and death, Gwynfor's views were utterly unyielding and he was willing to fast until the end; all that remained was to tell his family, one by one.

The first to hear was the long-suffering Rhiannon, and although she was horrified by her husband's dramatic intentions, she agreed to support him, albeit against her better judgement. The children reacted in a similar way, with a mixture of admiration for their father's integrity, tempered with tears and dread at his possible death.[75] The next to hear were Peter Hughes Griffiths and Dafydd Williams – those who Gwynfor assumed would be mainly responsible for any campaign arrangements. They were called to Talar Wen to hear the news, spent an entire afternoon with him and, like the family, were dumbstruck. They both opposed the scheme, Williams more so than Hughes Griffiths. Gwynfor, however, was curiously self-possessed; the act was not a fad nor flight of fancy. He saw his decision, rather, as part of a coherent strategy that would breathe new life into Welsh nationalism. And at that meeting, a precise plan for the organisation of the fast was revealed. It would take place at the Plaid Cymru office in Cathedral Road, Cardiff, and it was obvious that everything – when, where and who would do what – had been arranged in detail.[76]

A few days afterwards, on 12 February, Gwynfor wrote to Dafydd Williams to reiterate much of what he had already told him. His letter confirms that his original intention had been to carry out an act, about which he does not elaborate, by Llywelyn's monument at Cilmeri on Saint David's Day. He may be referring to suicide here, but whatever he had in mind, he changed his tactics. His plan now was to fast from October, the month he saw as 'the beginning of Plaid's greatest activity'. The letter committed Williams to complete confidentiality: 'I can now tell you about my intention in strict confidence because Rhiannon has bravely agreed. Without her agreement, it would not be fair for me to carry out the purpose I have in mind.' The letter reveals that purpose in detail; it would not be an exaggeration to claim that it contains his most compelling account of why he chose to act as he did: 'Although I shall be aiming at the government, the impact on the Welsh people will be far more important. I hope that I can urge nationalists to do more determined work, and that it will restore some backbone to other Welshmen and women and focus their minds. The industrial as well as the cultural crisis will be a backdrop.' All things considered, 'because my health is better than it has been for years', he foresaw that he could 'continue for four to five weeks'.[77]

Over the coming weeks, there was a series of further meetings between Gwynfor, Dafydd Williams and Peter Hughes Griffiths to organize the fast. But in the meantime, despite the unstinting efforts of a small band of activists, fears deepened over the people's reluctance to refuse to buy licences. Peter Hughes Griffiths confessed to Wayne Williams, chair of Cymdeithas yr Iaith, that there was 'a big problem in Glamorgan' and that he, along with Dafydd Williams, had had to get in touch with 'several people for the third time of asking' to encourage them to take part.[78] It is also obvious that some nationalists were increasingly critical of Gwynfor's perceived cowardice in not following the example of the Pencarreg three. In a visit to his home in Penarth on 11 January, Meredydd Evans heard Saunders Lewis attack Gwynfor for his failure to act. Gwynfor, the elder statesman of Welsh nationalism claimed, had 'polluted the nationalist struggle'. Worse still, he believed that 'Plaid has been lying for a quarter of a century that Wales can win her freedom by the vote'.[79]

It was all pretty familiar invective, but Lewis's outbursts also indirectly reflected the confidence of the government in early 1980 that it would carry the day. At the end of January, Gwynfor received a copy of a private letter to Dafydd Wigley from Lord Belstead, the Home Office minister with responsibility for broadcasting. The letter made it abundantly clear that the protesters did not have any chance of winning. 'We have already made it clear,' Belstead wrote, 'that Government finance will not be available for the fourth channel.'[80] As he prepared for his fast, the finality of these words must have been crushing for Gwynfor. But Wigley himself had growing doubts about the direction of the campaign. In a letter to Gwynfor dated 22 January, he wrote that it was 'a mistake' to hold a rally on broadcasting in Cardiff 'at a time when we should have been tackling the industrial situation'. It wasn't an argument against the campaign for the channel, he added, but he was convinced that Plaid Cymru had to tailor its activities to the different communities in Wales:

> Men at Llanwern were begging us to fight for them – they said this was the opportunity for Wales to make a stand and for Plaid to make its mark. I think they're right and that there is a danger we'll lose that opportunity unless we respond more actively to the situation… I think the overwhelming majority of people in Cardiff and Glamorgan feel it is rather irrelevant compared to the economic future we face at present.[81]

As he wrote, Wigley knew nothing of Gwynfor's secret, but he was soon to find out. On the evening of Friday, 29 February, Wigley was driving back from a Plaid Cymru meeting in Llanberis with Gwynfor and mentioned some scheme or other he had in the pipeline. As Dafydd Wigley recalled in his autobiography,

Gwynfor's answer in a soft voice was: 'Yes, very good. But I shan't be with you then.' Wigley believed Gwynfor was going to confess to some fatal illness but, by the time they reached Yr Hen Efail, Wigley's home in Bontnewydd, Gwynfor had shared his secret.[82] Wigley was speechless but Gwynfor was insistent. It was 'impossible', he told Wigley, that the government would give way, but he was certain that he needed to do something to 'reignite the flame'. At the time, Wigley was too shaken to say very much, but the more he thought about it, the more he was filled with a mixture of admiration and horror. As he looked back on that meeting, he too saw that the fast was a rather dubious moral course for a pacifist to take. But, for Wigley, it was incontrovertible and final proof that Wales was more important than anything in Gwynfor's eyes: 'Although people think Gwynfor places even more emphasis in his personal creed on pacifism than on nationalism, perhaps when the chips were down, there is more emphasis on Wales and Welsh nationalism than on the ramifications of such an act.'[83]

By St David's Day, therefore, the three men whom Gwynfor considered would be the most important when the time came for his hunger strike knew the facts: the organizer, Peter Hughes Griffiths; the party's head of administration, Dafydd Williams, and Gwynfor's political heir, Dafydd Wigley. All three would need to keep the secret for another couple of months. But although the pieces of the jigsaw were now in place, the broadcasting campaign itself remained in its familiar impotent state. It is true that the number of Welsh-speakers who had promised not to pay their licences was a little higher, a tribute to the tireless efforts of Peter Hughes Griffiths and Dennis Jones of Llanrhaeadr, Denbighshire.[84] Politically, however, Plaid Cymru's power continued to decline. For one thing, Elis Thomas was still out of step, siding with the Socialist Republicans and upsetting many within his own party by claiming that those closest to Gwynfor had switched allegiance to his heir, Dafydd Wigley. Elis Thomas also thought the party's response to the economic crisis had been completely inadequate. Increasingly, Elis Thomas looked to be the favourite to inherit the Presidency – a nightmare scenario for Gwynfor and his supporters. These anxieties deepened in late March when Wigley announced that he would not contest the Presidency because of the ill health of his two sons, Alun and Geraint.[85] It left Gwynfor and those around him in a quandary. With Wigley out of the race and no possibility that Phil Williams and Eurfyl ap Gwilym would stand, it looked as though Emrys Roberts would have to step into the breach, against his will.[86] The alternative was to see Elis Thomas in charge, the very last thing Gwynfor wanted to happen. Indeed, by March 1980, Gwynfor was even willing to countenance his bête noire, Emrys Roberts, as President for a year since it would 'delay the problem of a successor'.[87]

Plaid Cymru was not making any headway, and neither was nationalism more generally. The Republicans and the arson campaign increasingly captured the headlines as Plaid Cymru's leadership crisis deepened. On Palm Sunday, dozens of nationalists were arrested without any discernible reason nor evidence. As a result, some Welsh-speakers came to believe that they themselves, and their way of life, were under siege. This was the great apocalypse for their generation, but Plaid Cymru did not benefit. To further complicate matters, the Conservatives were also ready to strike back and act positively. In Llanrwst on 14 April, Nicholas Edwards delivered the most important speech ever made by a Conservative on the Welsh language, promising to give £1.5 million to Welsh-medium education and laying the intellectual foundations for a policy of generous support and cosy consensus. Over the following two decades, this policy gave the language a substantial fillip, but also succeeded in emasculating language politics.[88] It was no surprise that Dafydd Williams once again begged Gwynfor not to proceed with his fast. At the end of April, he wrote to Gwynfor that he doubted whether the government would 'give way' and that no Welsh television channel, even if it were granted, was likely to have 'the financial resources' it would need.[89]

Others, however, were more positive. On 7 April, on the day his tenth grandchild, Hedd, was born, Gwynfor spoke about his proposed action to the proud father, Ffred Ffransis. Ffransis was supportive and offered practical advice, as one who had probably fasted more often than Gandhi.[90] But support and encouragement from an influential figure like Ffred Ffransis was an exception. Almost everyone else close to Gwynfor was opposed. On May Day, Gwynfor received a letter from Ioan Bowen Rees imploring him to change his mind because 'no television service... is a sufficient matter of principle... to justify a hunger strike'.[91] Four other close friends shared the opinion. On the same day that Bowen Rees's letter arrived, Elwyn Roberts, O M Roberts, Alun Lloyd and R Tudur Jones wrote to say that 'the future of the campaign for political freedom' was more important than television. The crucial thing now, they said, was that Wales had the leadership to achieve it.[92]

But these four, Plaid Cymru stalwarts to a man, should have known better –

Gwynfor had made up his mind. On 3 May, 1980, Gwynfor shared his secret with the world. Plaid Cymru's executive was the first to hear in a dramatic statement. As the executive meeting drew to a close, the chair asked whether there was any other business. Several members of the executive had already left what had been a tedious meeting at Neuadd Pantycelyn, Aberystwyth, and the rest were anxious to leave for home. Then, without warning, Gwynfor raised his hand and said that he did have another matter to discuss. In measured tones, he stated that he would starve himself to death unless a separate Welsh language channel was created. The fast, he stated in a matter of fact way, would begin on 5 October.

It is difficult to convey the chill that enveloped Neuadd Pantycelyn that afternoon. Everyone was, understandably, flabbergasted. Although Gwynfor was notorious for operating behind the scenes and keeping much, too much perhaps, to himself and a favoured band of confidants, this was an entirely different matter. This, quite literally, was a matter of life and death not just for himself, but also for Wales if violence and unrest followed his death. Most members were struck by a blizzard of emotions: respect for the remarkable integrity behind the announcement but horror too at the thought that Gwynfor could be dead by Christmas. As he had stated his intention without warning, members had no choice but to support him.[93] There was, however, no vote to that effect.[94] There was merely a resolution to respect and accept the action. But there was anger too at the wholly undemocratic way in which Plaid Cymru's leader had made them follow him like sheep.

Dafydd Elis Thomas, although he didn't betray his feelings, was particularly irritated and, even in hindsight, that same feeling still prevails. 'Only Gwynfor,' he told the author, 'would have announced this under "any other business".' The way in which the decision to fast was made was a source of annoyance, but what angered Elis Thomas most was his concern that the fast would be 'a huge distraction for Plaid Cymru as a parliamentary party and for Plaid Cymru as a political party attempting to develop a socialist image'. The Member for Merioneth also believed the tactic was naive and 'confused the issue' because it took Plaid Cymru back to the past. Further, he viewed Gwynfor's action as typical of a nationalist party in decline. It was 'fighting battles on its old ground'. Elis Thomas had another reason to feel aggrieved. He did not believe the Whitelaw solution was all that disastrous since he, Elis Thomas, was 'completely certain' there would be sufficient finance for Welsh-language programming on the two channels. And he had in addition 'a fundamental, moral objection' to hunger strikes. His objection stemmed, he said, from the fact that such a course meant 'using the threat of violence against the self as a political weapon'. With violence already a blight on the British landscape, Elis Thomas could only conclude that 'the threat in itself is irresponsible'. Throughout, however, he remained remarkably loyal to Gwynfor and bit his tongue. Even so, he did not hide his feelings, meeting Gwynfor with the express intention of arguing his case, but to no avail.[95]

Elis Thomas knew full well that Gwynfor would not change his mind, but felt strongly that he should hear what he had to say. Gwynfor's sister, Ceridwen, shared his misgivings. On 5 May, the day the official announcement was made, she found out about his intentions on television. Without delay, she wrote a savage letter to her brother insisting that he should refrain from what she considered a foolish act.[96] But Gwynfor did not flinch. The only change he made to his original plan was arranging for the fast to take place at Talar Wen, and not in the Plaid Cymru offices. He did so at the suggestion of Dafydd Wigley in order to avoid 'putting the staff there under immense pressure'.[97] Meanwhile, Gwynfor's apocalyptic vision of Wales found a ready audience with friends like Islwyn Ffowc Elis, who wrote to say that he 'felt that the Third World War is at hand, and it may come upon us before September... That would settle the Welsh Television Channel problem once and for all'.[98]

With such a narrative on national life and death common currency among his friends, it was no surprise that Gwynfor contemplated the impact of probable martyrdom. On the day when the hunger strike was announced, he answered the letter from Elwyn Roberts and the other three who had begged him five days earlier to desist, telling them he had felt 'for a year' that 'the crisis' in Welsh life was such that it demanded that he 'as President of Plaid do something quite major'. By now, his only option was to act as he did because the government had shown its 'contempt for constitutional action by Welsh nationalists'. Gwynfor supposed that the Conservatives had acted in such a 'treacherous' manner following 'the signal that the referendum and Plaid's vote gave it perhaps'. 'Seven months' ago, therefore, he had decided that he would discharge his duty 'in the matter of a Welsh television service' and that his resolve had stiffened in the face of past failures. 'It is obvious,' he wrote, 'that the actions of Cymdeithas yr Iaith and the thousand who refused to pay for licences, and the heroism of Pennar, Ned and Merêd – it is clear that these will exert enough influence.' Gwynfor was now ready to die, and perhaps welcomed martyrdom: 'The first condition of success is a willingness to go to extremes if necessary. Yet going to extremes could prove beneficial. At last someone would have given his life to defend Wales; scores of thousands have given their lives to defend the interests of Britain. It might do a little to promote the struggle for Welsh freedom; it would certainly do a lot more than anything else I could do.'[99]

They were alarming words, underlining his absolute determination. However, not everyone saw the situation in the same light. Initially, some politicians, in particular Conservatives, took the whole thing as a joke. When he heard of the fast, one Tory MP remarked: 'Gwynfor starving himself to death? I'll sponsor him'. It was an attitude shared among the upper echelons of the Welsh Office and, during the first few weeks, it became the stuff of tasteless humour and rumours. One common rumour was the suggestion that Gwynfor was suffering from a terminal illness and that he wanted to turn his death into a final propaganda stunt.[100] But the journalists and politicians who shared this gossip had misjudged the reaction to Gwynfor's announcement across parts of Wales. Despite their doubts, and despite uneasiness about the way in which the announcement had been made, the 'national movement' came together in a way not seen since the arson at Penyberth. From then on, it became a struggle not just to save Gwynfor's life but also to prove that Welsh nationalism itself was still a living force.

Just hours after Gwynfor's statement, campaigners flocked to the ranks of Cymdeithas yr Iaith to protest with renewed vigour. The following day, 6 May, saw society activists disrupting traffic in London. Angharad Tomos was imprisoned for painting Nelson's Column and the protest was carried to the gates of Buckingham Palace. The process of lobbying MPs began too. As the protest gained momentum, Gwynfor came into his own, exhibiting a combination of inner strength and peace of mind. On 15 May, when the licence inspector visited Talar Wen he found the television was in working order but that no one had paid for a licence since February. By this time, several hundred people were following Gwynfor's lead on the issue and, within the week, came the first glimmer of hope for Gwynfor. On 22 May, he heard from Dafydd Wigley that he had spoken to the Welsh Secretary about the hunger strike. It was obvious, Wigley told him, that Nicholas Edwards 'is worried but is saying the usual things about "blackmail"'.[101]

The news drew an increasingly united nationalist response, and some who had been dubious about the cause and the man behind it began to reconsider. Harri Pritchard Jones wrote in *Y Faner*, with echoes of Saunders Lewis's rhetoric a generation and more before, that the only decent thing to do now was to support him: 'Gwynfor Evans, at the height of his leadership, is making a stand, and all of us, commoners and scholars, must stand with him.'[102] Saunders Lewis shared the sentiment. In *Y Cymro*, he revelled in Gwynfor Evans's conversion: 'At last, the answer to the disastrous Welsh Referendum is beginning to form. With Gwynfor Evans, Pennar Davies, Meredydd Evans and Ned Thomas, a new era in the history of nationalism and the history of Wales is opening, an era of tragedy and heroism.'[103]

This unity appeared to unsettle some Welsh Conservative MPs. On 3 June, Keith Best, the Conservative member for Ynys Môn, announced that he found it more and more difficult to support government policy. Some days later, he took the highly unusual step of confirming this in a letter to Elwyn Roberts: 'I am finding increasingly that more and more people, for a variety of different reasons, would wish to see all Welsh Language programmes on one channel.'[104] As the deadline drew closer, journalists too began to take the issue seriously. The *Glasgow Herald* remarked that the Red Lion in Llangadog was already fully booked for the beginning of the fast in October while the village hall had been commandeered for daily news conferences for the assembled hacks.[105] It was also decided to organize a rota of volunteers at the gates of Talar Wen to control the press. Another concern was how to prevent the prying lenses of the television cameras from fixing their gaze on the study where the fast would take place. But these were minor concerns compared to the propaganda war which was beginning to succeed. Although no more than about 600 had refused to pay for their television licences at any point during the campaign, the press lapped up Peter Hughes Griffiths's claims. In June, it was 'confirmed' that 1,500 were willing to face the courts and that the likelihood was that there would be 2,800 names by August.[106] Nonsense, of course, but no one knew this outside the inner circle.

And then there was Gwynfor, the cunning saint. He held the press in the palm of his hand throughout and played the media game to perfection. On 16 June, he gave an interview to the *Western Mail*, stating in the clearest possible terms that the threat to starve was no bluff. Everything, he said, was in place, and he was ready to die: 'My brother-in-law has the farm here in Llangadog. I'm just an old-age pensioner since May last year'. And to support him, there was his family:

Carmarthen, August 1974: Gwynfor, Dafydd Elis Thomas and Dafydd Wigley. Gwynfor regained the seat within two months of this picture being taken despite Dafydd Elis Thomas's taste in ties.

The 'malcontents': Harri Webb and Emrys Roberts.

The Inconstant Gardener: The gardens, in addition to Dan and Alcwyn's money, helped Gwynfor through many difficult times. However, Gwynfor severed his connections with the market gardening business shortly after the General Election of October 1974.

Fundraising for Plaid Cymru: Rhiannon is on Gwynfor's right along with J E Jones, Plaid Cymru General Secretary.

The prolific propagandist: Gwynfor signing his books in Carmarthen Market, August 1974.

Y TRO HWN
THIS TIME
THIS TIME
GWYNFOR EVANS X
Y TRO
GWYNFOR EVANS
GWYNFOR EVANS
Y TRO HWN
GWYNFOR EVANS X
THIS TIME

'Gwynfor Evans This Time': an expectant crowd gathers in Nott Square, Carmarthen to hear the result of the October 1974 General Election.

Return to Westminster: Gwynfor salutes the crowd after regaining the Carmarthen seat in October 1974.

The parliamentary trinity: Gwynfor alongside Dafydd Wigley and Dafydd Elis Thomas in 1974. Dafydd Elis Thomas claimed that his relationship with Dafydd Wigley deteriorated following Gwynfor's return to Parliament during that year.

Ménage à trois? Gwynfor and the 'Two Dafydds' saluting the crowd outside the House of Commons following the General Election of October 1974.

Tea and sympathy: Rhiannon, Gwynfor's wife, was the rock upon which he built his successes.

Gwynfor at the Lliw Valley National Eisteddfod, August 1980. This picture was taken at the the height of the battle over a Welsh language TV channel.

'Any Other Business?': marching through the centre of Cardiff during the television channel campaign, August 1980.

Feteing the U-Turn: This slogan was painted on the Embankment opposite the House of Commons. The man who painted the slogan had to be tied to a rope to enable him to finish his handiwork.

The last electoral stand: Gwynfor on the eve of the 1983 poll.

Verdant Carmarthenshire: although Gwynfor was a newcomer, he came to perceive this Welsh speaking area as 'the real Wales'.

The Old Man of Pencarreg: Gwynfo
in his garden at Talar Wen, Pencarreg
September 199

Journey's end: Gwynfor's funeral, 27 April 2005.

'One of the hardest things is to think of leaving them. That may be easier at the time. I don't know. But I think since we are so close as a family, it won't be too difficult for the children and Rhiannon to stand up by standing together. They have been wonderful, they accept the crisis'. He revealed too that the act itself would take place in the library at Talar Wen where he had six books on Gandhi to offer nourishment for mind and spirit. And, like Gandhi, he had decided to put salt and soda in his drinks to keep him alive for as long as possible. The only unsettling thing in the circumstances would be the smell of cooking drifting from the kitchen – in particular his favourite meal of new potatoes, gammon, pineapple and peas.[107] In another interview, he offered a solution to the effects of his physical deterioration: 'I understand you'll get a bit light-headed. So I'll listen to music on the gramophone… the record player you call it? But then I suppose if I get weaker I'll probably lie on the couch'.[108]

Coming from any other politician, statements like these would have sounded like parody but, increasingly, the Welsh Office realized that it faced a major problem: Gwynfor and what many saw as his beatific qualities. Because he had put what many recognised as his unimpeachable life in the balance, it meant that his statements to the press carried all the more weight. It also meant that his death would be a total tragedy. This, increasingly, became the perceived threat. The *Daily Post* wondered whether the IRA might adopt a similar tactic and, on 17 June, a group of influential Welshmen, including the former Secretary of State, John Morris, wrote to Whitelaw asking him to change course. Two days later, after a Cabinet meeting, Whitelaw and Nicholas Edwards agreed that some kind of compromise was needed. They did so not only because of their growing concern about violence but because Whitelaw had a personal affection for Gwynfor. The first concession was presented to Gwynfor on the evening of 24 June when Whitelaw agreed to review the situation in Wales within a year. Whitelaw claimed that this was a major offer but, in fact, it was no more than a gambit. Unsurprisingly, Gwynfor rejected it out of hand.

Contrary to expectation, therefore, it looked likely that the struggle would reach its endgame. On 28 June, a huge rally was held in Aberystwyth – the first of several – and, on 30 June, *The Times* claimed that the government would probably face a long, hot summer: 'Mr Nicholas Edwards, Secretary of State for Wales, undoubtedly will have advised his colleagues in the Cabinet that Mr Evans is one of the few men from whom such a threat can be taken seriously.'[109] But despite the warning, the government did not want to give ground on the central principle of placing Welsh-language programmes on two channels. In a meeting with Wyn Roberts, Nicholas Edwards insisted that there would be no 'double U-turn' because of the 'extremely awkward practical and political difficulties'.[110] It was a private opinion echoed in the Prime Minister's public conduct. On 10 July, Mrs Thatcher refused to meet Gwynfor and, to reinforce her refusal, she wrote to Dafydd Wigley saying she could see no 'useful purpose' in doing so.[111]

The Prime Minister was eager not to be seen giving in to blackmail but, fortunately for Gwynfor, broadcasting was the brief of the consummate pragmatist, William Whitelaw. Behind the scenes, an escape plan was being hatched. For one thing, Whitelaw had been shaken by Gwynfor's threat and had confessed to Nicholas Edwards that the government had to think of a way out.[112] The Secretary of State for Wales was rapidly coming to the same conclusion. On 7 July, Edwards met Whitelaw and argued that it would be impossible to avoid 'very unpleasant consequences' were Gwynfor to begin his hunger strike. He added that Gwynfor was 'serious, determined and obstinate'.[113] Even so, both men continued to argue that there could be no going back on the two-channel solution. They agreed, rather, that all they could offer Gwynfor was a committee with the power to co-ordinate Welsh programmes between the BBC and the IBA. Three days later, on 10 July, there was an emergency meeting at the Home Office to attempt to solve the Gwynfor 'problem'. The meeting brought together some of the leading figures in British broadcasting: William Whitelaw, Nicholas Edwards, Wyn Roberts, the chairs and senior BBC and IBA managers, and BBC governors. The meeting was also attended by Glyn Tegai Hughes, the Welsh member of the future Channel 4 board. According to Alwyn Roberts, the BBC's Welsh governor, Whitelaw proposed that there should be a committee to co-ordinate the work of Welsh programming on the two channels. And if necessary, he promised to establish one channel if it could be proven that the dual-channel solution was flawed. These proposals were rejected immediately by the Welsh representatives as they did not meet any of Gwynfor's concerns. But for Roberts, the most striking thing was the discussion following the meeting; in informal conversation it became evident that Whitelaw was deeply worried about the effect that the decision to concede would have on the situation in Northern Ireland.[114]

Meanwhile, the government announced its compromise on 16 July. The press reported that Dafydd Wigley had rung Gwynfor in the hope that Whitelaw's bait would be sufficient to bring about a change of heart. But Gwynfor dismissed the idea of a co-ordinating committee simply because he regarded it as too little too late.[115] Furthermore, by then, a 'little' local difficulty over Welsh broadcasting had evolved into a significant crisis for the British body politic. Indeed, as Roberts realized, Gwynfor's situation now jeopardized the stability of the British state. Time was also running out; there were thirteen weeks before the hunger strike would begin, and the ticking clock imbued the protesters with renewed passion. On 18 July, there were unruly scenes in Anglesey during a visit by Mrs Thatcher, where protesters threw themselves in front of the PM's car shouting 'Gwynfor, Gwynfor'.[116] This protest, according to Angharad Tomos, was the 'nearest thing to mass hysteria' that she had ever witnessed in a crowd.[117] On the same day, two explosive devices were left outside Nicholas Edwards's home while he was in London, and Dafydd Wigley interrupted a meeting of the Parliamentary Committee on Welsh Affairs in order, as he told Gwynfor, 'to raise the general temperature so that Nicholas Edwards can tell the Cabinet what sort of direction politics will move to were you to proceed with the hunger strike'.[118] Dafydd Elis Thomas was busy too. More than once, he met the Secretary of State in private in an endeavour to spare Gwynfor and save Plaid Cymru more generally from reverting to being a 'language party'.[119]

On 20 July, another protest greeted Mrs Thatcher when she addressed the Welsh Conservatives in Swansea. There were desperate scenes outside as hundreds of police officers fought with nationalists and trade unionists objecting to redundancies in the steel industry. For one brief moment, it appeared that the long-awaited red-green union between nationalism and socialism had arrived. There would be no real co-operation until the miners' strike, but seeing the two political traditions come together, seemed to many to be significant. After the Swansea protest, there was a strained meeting between Welsh Conservative MPs and Nicholas Edwards where it emerged that several were unhappy with the situation.

As Dafydd Wigley predicted 'insurrection', the Welsh establishment made further efforts to save the day.[120] If Gwynfor is to be believed, Nicholas Edwards arranged for the Archbishop of Wales, G O Williams, Sir Cennydd Traherne and Sir Goronwy Daniel to meet the Prime Minister but the idea did not materialise. Gwynfor's only face-to-face meeting with Nicholas Edwards was equally unpromising. The invitation to Gwynfor came through Cledwyn Hughes, and the two men met on 21 July 1980 at the home of Sir Hywel Evans, permanent secretary at the Welsh Office. In a two-hour meeting, they discussed every aspect of the problem including the cost and technical issues, but to no avail. Gwynfor had the impression that Nicholas Edwards was there 'to lay down the law'.[121] The meeting confirmed everything that Owen Edwards, controller of BBC Wales, had told Gwynfor that morning, that he was not 'hopeful that a change of policy was likely'.[122] Indeed, the meeting was so worthless that Nicholas Edwards forgot all about it until he was reminded of it while reading Gwynfor's autobiography, *Bywyd Cymro*.[123]

Following the meeting, on 22 July, Keith Best wrote what turned out to be a significant letter to Nicholas Edwards warning him that he could no longer support government policy. More significantly still, he claimed that 'a majority of the Conservative backbench members' supported him and that they, like him, wanted the government to change its mind.[124] Labour brought pressure to bear too, with prominent figures like Leo Abse and Ioan Evans calling on Edwards to settle the matter. Their reasoning was rather different to Gwynfor's, as they wanted to get rid of the wretched nuisance of 'Welsh programmes' so that English channels were not cluttered with unintelligible nonsense. However the effect was the same: the government was trapped in a vice. The meeting was also proof that the government, as Gwynfor interpreted it, was 'seriously worried' by the situation it had brought about.[125]

On 31 July 1980, the Select Committee on Welsh Affairs, a new but increasingly influential body, announced that it would undertake an inquiry into broadcasting in Wales. The inquiry was an attempt by the committee's chair, Leo Abse, to ease the situation somewhat but Gwynfor rejected the suggestion out of hand. Welsh MPs, however, were anxious, warning that Wales faced 'serious social disorder'.[126] It was a statement that could not easily be ignored and, on the same day, Dafydd Iwan (by now a central personality in the campaign), was jailed for not having paid his licence. As July slipped into August, and as the most politicized National Eisteddfod in living memory opened in the Lliw Valley, the campaigners mustered for one last stand. With the willing support of the Archdruid, Geraint Bowen, Nicholas Edwards's car was penned in and the HTV Wales and the IBA stands were smashed to smithereens. The protesters were roundly condemned by Sir Alun Talfan Davies (or 'Sir Alun Mammon' as Harri Webb memorably called him) as was anyone who was not part of the movement to keep Gwynfor alive. As *Y Ddraig Goch* commented, Wales was split between the realists and the idealists.[127] Some of the foremost journalists in Wales found themselves caught between these extremes. Jennie Eirian, editor of *Y Faner*, was viciously treated for daring to question the new orthodoxy. The criticism would eventually contribute to her tragic suicide, a huge loss to journalism in Wales.[128] Gwilym Owen, the leading Welsh-language journalist of his generation, was attacked with equal venom as the idolatry of Gwynfor slipped into bigotry.[129] In fact, Gwynfor did very little to calm the situation, merely appealing to his supporters not to turn to violence in the event of his death. He also warned them to guard against agents provocateurs who might try to fan the flames.[130]

The truth was that Gwynfor had very little reason to want to cool the political temperature. After all – and this was the central irony of his act – only the threat of violence and serious social disorder seemed likely to move the government. On a personal level, Gwynfor became the kingpin of nationalism as his critics forgot their bitterness over the referendum. The hunger strike, to quote Saunders Lewis, saved Gwynfor 'as a leader – and provoked the disappointment and anger of that shameful paper, *Y Faner*, that teaches fear and treason to the young girls of Wales'.[131] But as the Gwynfor mania spread, further efforts were made to save him from the situation he had provoked. Even before the confrontation at the Eisteddfod, the Gorsedd Board had discussed the possibility of organizing a deputation to see Whitelaw.[132] There was no longer a moment to be lost and the National Eisteddfod Court arranged that a triumvirate of the great and the good should visit the Home Secretary: Archbishop G O Williams, Cledwyn Hughes and Sir Goronwy Daniel.

Meanwhile, the government's opposition was softening. On 4 August, William Whitelaw wrote privately to the Archbishop of Wales, G O Williams, emphasizing the reasonableness of the concessions he had already made.[133] Two days later, Nicholas Edwards heard that the BBC had written to Whitelaw warning him of 'insurmountable scheduling problems' in relation to the plans to put Welsh-language programmes on two channels.[134] This came as a major blow, but the knockout punch followed on 9 August, when Wyn Roberts informed him that peers of all parties intended to revise the broadcasting legislation when it reached the House of Lords – at the very time when, he feared, Gwynfor would be in the middle of his hunger strike.[135] Days later, the first newspaper report appeared saying that the government was going to concede.

This was followed by an editorial in *The Times* calling on the government to think again.[136] But publicly, at any rate, the government appeared as adamant as ever. Nicholas Edwards used the BBC *Panorama* programme to appeal directly to Gwynfor not to go ahead; similarly, on 19 August, the Secretary of State informed Keith Best publicly that there would be no separate Welsh channel.[137] Whitelaw was also urged not to meet the Eisteddfod delegation by Roger Thomas MP, Gwynfor's successor. On 8 August, he wrote: 'This I feel would be a very unwise move indeed, for I can assure you that the voice of the loud vociferous minority in Wales is no true reflection of the feeling on this matter particularly amongst Welsh speakers. I have questioned hundreds in my own constituency in this matter and Carmarthen has nearly 60 per cent of bilingual people amongst its residents.'[138]

Within Welsh broadcasting circles too, there were corresponding efforts to maintain the same unanimous front. On August 29, Alwyn Roberts received a letter from the Home Office convening the committee that would co-ordinate the work of the two channels.[139] The meeting never took place and the reality was that Nicholas Edwards was by now fighting a losing battle. He lacked supporters and those who did speak for him tended to weaken his case. One memorable example was this gem of a statement from Delwyn Williams, the Conservative MP for Montgomeryshire: 'Mr Gwynfor Evans can only die once. If this Government or any other Government gives in to a threat of suicide by this foolish old man what will be the next cause that he intends to die for?'[140] At the height of the battle, the announcement came that Gwynfor would continue as President for a further year, up until 1981. This had been decided, it was said, to avoid a presidential contest during his hunger strike. It was, doubtless, the sensible thing to do, but the decision would have far-reaching consequences once the channel campaign reached its conclusion.[141]

On 1 September, Gwynfor celebrated his 68th birthday but, under the circumstances, there was little cause for merriment. For family and friends, the real fear was that this would be his last, and Gwynfor sensed that they could be right. 'I cannot see Thatcher yielding on this. I don't see the Government backing down,' he told *The Guardian* on the morning of his birthday. He was also ready to die and craved not so much death itself but the impact his martyrdom would have:

> There are ripple effects everywhere and if I were allowed to die there would be a tremendous upsurge of Welsh nationalism... The odds are that we cannot survive as a nation. Something very big has to happen if we are to live. I can see this fast leading to something very, very big in Wales.[142]

He also hoped (somewhat vaguely) for unity between language nationalists and the working class, and on the day after his interview in *The Guardian*, press-handling arrangements were agreed. At the beginning of the hunger strike, the plan was that he would speak to the press on an almost daily basis and that, as his condition deteriorated, these interviews would be replaced by a daily medical bulletin.[143] On the same day, 2 September, he received a letter from Professor Linford Rees suggesting survival strategies: 'I would recommend that you drink three to four pints of water a day and also take vitamins in the form of Plurivite M, one or two tablets daily and glucose, about 100 gms a day.'[144]

With just a month to go, a series of highly successful rallies was organized to draw attention to the campaign. Here again, the arrangements were precise and there were careful instructions for those introducing Gwynfor:

> The whole purpose of the rallies is to give heart to Plaid and engender hope for the future. It is important to ensure that these meetings do not develop into one big goodbye that will embarrass Gwynfor... For whoever is introducing Gwynfor – he or she should not mention the hunger strike or the possibility of death at all, that is Gwynfor's wish. A joyful and congratulatory introduction – yes, but nothing sad or miserable.[145]

The arrangements were followed to the letter and there were packed meetings in Wales and another in Scotland. The most memorable gathering was in Cardiff on 6 September when more than 2,000 people marched through the capital. This protest was one of the largest nationalist displays since the reaction to the burning of Penyberth in 1937 and a feeling of emotion swept like a wave over Gwynfor's supporters. Saunders Lewis judged that nothing 'in all Welsh history from 1536 to today' had caused the government so much discomfort. In the same article for *Y Faner*, Lewis urged nationalists to use violence if necessary.[146] Lewis Valentine's appeal to Gwynfor was equally as agonized, but more private. On 9 September, he wrote to him:

> I have never found it as hard to write to a friend, and putting off writing has not made the task any easier... I did not imagine that anything like this would happen, and I

> am struck dumb, and tears are easier than words or emotional outbursts... I have very mixed feelings about your sad, splendid resolution – a mixture of guilt and elation. Elation that someone like you has risen among us, and guilt that I and those like me have not been harder on ourselves, and disciplined ourselves more severely to serve our nation in our generation.[147]

The day after he received the letter was the most crucial day in Gwynfor's life: 10 September, when the deputation of Welsh grandees met William Whitelaw. There had already been informal talks between them, and Gwynfor had written to Sir Goronwy Daniel to say he would not give an inch: 'I would be very sorry if you succeeded in getting an agreement, only to find that I could not keep to it... No compromise is possible.'[148] But the truth is that Gwynfor did compromise to a degree by accepting the suggestion made by a friend, Leopold Kohr, that S4C could be tried for two years to see how it performed.[149] It was equally important that the deputation contained men (in particular Cledwyn Hughes and Sir Goronwy Daniel) who possessed considerable diplomatic skills. Before the vital meeting, they gave serious consideration to their tactics. On 26 August, Sir Goronwy wrote to Hughes that they would be as well 'not to go into detail on things like costings or how the channel might be run'. He also believed that Whitelaw had to grasp 'the tendency for more nationalists and socialists to turn to extreme actions'. Sir Goronwy also wanted Whitelaw to appreciate this central point: 'The general respect that Gwynfor enjoys... If Gwynfor dies the emotional impact will be enormous.'[150] Hughes accepted all these arguments but insisted that costs had to be mentioned. After all, Whitelaw had already told Hughes that the change of mind had been prompted by doubts over financing the channel. It was a point well made, and Hughes had another – that they would go to see Whitelaw not as go-betweens from Gwynfor, but as the voice of moderate Welsh-speaking Wales:

> ... Although we must be conscious of Gwynfor's stance and respect it, I do not believe that we should be bound hand and foot by it either. We are not going to Whitelaw as his ambassadors, and if it appears there is an organizational solution... which could be used that would help the government change course, without betraying Gwynfor's principle, it should certainly be considered.[151]

With this plan in mind, the deputation met Whitelaw on the afternoon of Wednesday, 10 September. The minutes show there were six present: the Home Secretary and Welsh Secretary, as well as the three crucial figures named at the outset, the Archbishop of Wales, Cledwyn Hughes and Sir Goronwy Daniel. Last, and not least, was Emyr Jenkins, director of the National Eisteddfod, to whom thanks are due that a full record of the event has survived. Cledwyn Hughes spoke first; in fact, this was Hughes's meeting as he charmed his old friend Whitelaw with homespun wisdom.[152] He began by mentioning the action taken at Pencarreg and the fact that there was 'a developing lack of respect for the democratic processes. The Welsh hitherto have been a law-abiding people'. Inseparably bound up with this was the concern at what would happen were Gwynfor to die. 'If Gwynfor Evans dies,' Cledwyn Hughes said, 'the consequences would be incalculable… One cannot separate the linguistic/cultural side from the economic situation.'

Then there were questions. Whitelaw's anxious enquiry was this: 'Where do Gwynfor Evans's demands end?' He also emphasized that the two main stumbling blocks were finance on the one hand and, on the other, the IBA's unwillingness to forfeit the money they would receive if they ran the new fourth channel, ITV 2. These were important considerations but, in truth, they were minor compared to the flood of questions posed by Nicholas Edwards. He still insisted that programmes in Welsh on two channels was the better solution and that losing Channel 4 to Welsh programming would lead to 'a much larger reaction'. He was also afraid of the impact a Welsh channel would have on HTV: 'If the 4th channel is given to Welsh-language programmes, people will switch aerials to the Mendips thereby depriving HTV of viewers to its present channel.' Last, but not least, Nicholas Edwards stated the government's most fundamental political objection: 'others may follow if he succeeds'. But the 'three' had a ready answer to this pointed question. As the meeting drew to a close after one and a half hours, Cledwyn Hughes proposed the solution, that the Welsh channel could be tried for two years. Doing so would protect the government from any accusation of having given way to blackmail. 'I do not see this as final and irrevocable,' Cledwyn Hughes remarked, 'but as an experimental period which will take the heat out of the situation.'[153]

It was without doubt a masterful performance, but Cledwyn Hughes's intervention is also evidence of his generosity of spirit, especially given Gwynfor's less-than-generous behaviour towards him on various occasions before 1980. After the channel crisis, however, Gwynfor thanked him unreservedly. But on that evening, 10 September, there was no sign that Cledwyn Hughes had saved Gwynfor's life. Alwyn Roberts recalls telephoning two members of the deputation and hearing depressing reports of Whitelaw's and Nicholas Edwards's response.[154] The following day, Sir Goronwy Daniel responded in similar fashion, telephoning Gwynfor to say that the deputation had been politely received but he did not believe the government would concede. Michael Foot had the same impression after he met Whitelaw to discuss the issue. After the meeting, he wrote to Gwynfor with the disappointing news that the government did not look likely to compromise.[155] This was also the impression given by the government's press releases. In an atmosphere of almost unbearable tension, Whitelaw stated that the way forward was for the BBC and HTV to converge their schedules and content. He also announced that Dafydd Jones-Williams would be the new chair of the Welsh Television Committee to co-ordinate the service. Nicholas Edwards appeared equally unenthusiastic. He told the press that he had listened to 'the three' before concluding that one channel would present 'very considerable difficulties'.[156]

But the statements contained a large element of bluff. Although the deputation had pushed the door ajar, the government did not want to give Gwynfor an easy victory. Behind the scenes, however, things were rather different. A matter of hours before the meeting, Nicholas Edwards was advised by his mandarins to give way. On 9 September, a leading civil servant at the Welsh Office wrote to Edwards as follows:

> ... Mr Evans and his friends are mounting a most effective campaign; there are signs that this will continue and it shows every indication of being a skilfully orchestrated exercise. The Government, on the other hand, has had a poor press... the tide of public opinion seems to be running against the Government on this issue... it may be possible for the Government to win the day in Parliament and the country – but this will not stop Gwynfor from seeking the martyr's crown. And I find it very difficult to predict whether it will be possible to isolate the major problems we face in other fields from his campaign on this emotive issue.[157]

As everyone speculated about what the government would do next, more protests followed: an organised trespass took place on the Epynt firing range and groups as diverse as mothers and Congregationalist ministers protested in favour of a Welsh-language channel. It was an enormous effort on the part of a comparatively small number of Cymdeithas yr Iaith and Plaid Cymru activists but, unbeknown to them, the drama was about to end. On 15 September, Nicholas Edwards met Whitelaw. They decided that the only option was to concede.[158] After lunch, they went together to 10 Downing Street to seek the approval of the Prime Minister.

She heard her Home Secretary admit that he and Edwards had been astonished by the response to Gwynfor's threat. Faced with the 'likely consequences', Whitelaw advised the Prime Minister that the wisest course was to accept the inevitable. He was supported by Nicholas Edwards, who told Mrs Thatcher that a Welsh channel had to be established to avoid 'intolerable consequences'. Mrs Thatcher listened and agreed.[159] The Iron Lady was for turning. It was at this historic meeting, following a decade of imprisonments and one man's threat to starve himself to death, that S4C was born.

On the morning of 17 September, when Gwynfor was summonsed for not having bought a licence, some of the London papers reported that the government was going to concede. As the rumour spread, Talar Wen was a hive of activity. Hearing the news, the broadcaster, Emyr Daniel, raced there to get Gwynfor's response. Daniel was there all day and witnessed the varying reactions. Rhiannon was in tears and begged Daniel to urge her husband to give up. Meanwhile, official confirmation came from London and Cardiff that there would indeed be a channel. It was a triumph, but Gwynfor's response could only be described as disappointment, and he questioned Daniel about exact figures on funding for the channel.[160] He had sound reasons to do so; at heart, Gwynfor knew the crisis had ended far too soon and that nationalist fervour would cool. From then on, he knew too that the series of rallies that had been organized by Plaid Cymru would lose their significance. Cymdeithas yr Iaith would also need to abandon its plans to attack television stations across Britain. It had been hoped that it would lead to the jailing of hundreds of people.[161] There was no option but to accept Emyr Daniel's advice and embrace the imperfect triumph that was on offer. Thus, on 17 September, Gwynfor revoked his threat to fast to death.

That evening in Crymych, Gwynfor was hailed as a hero and, for a full five minutes, the sizeable crowd there chanted his name. In London, the most memorable slogan in the history of Welsh nationalism appeared on the Embankment wall, opposite the House of Commons: Gwynfor 1, Whitelaw 0. Gwynfor himself described the victory as the greatest in the history of the Welsh language. Its future was secure, he said. On the following day, he set off on a tour of Wales, beginning in Porthmadog and ending at Melin-y-Wig, the birthplace of J E Jones. There, he unveiled a memorial to his old colleague and, everywhere he went, people rushed up to him to express their gratitude. But these emotional scenes gave a misleading impression of the strength of nationalism. The fact that any sort of battle had been fought was due to the efforts of a tiny handful of people. The campaign's co-architect, Peter Hughes Griffiths, refused to go to Crymych, regarding some of those who attended as hypocrites for not having shown their support much, much earlier. 'I could not,' he said, 'stomach the whole thing.'[162] In hindsight, the victory can be explained in three ways: Gwynfor's willingness to die, the intervention of 'the three' and, finally, the threat of violence. This unpalatable truth perhaps lies at the heart of the campaign: S4C was established partly because of the fear of unrest that would follow in the event of the death of one of Wales's greatest pacifists. As Saunders Lewis told Meredydd Evans just days after the victory: 'the threat was not made by a consistent pacifist. But thank goodness for it'.[163] The truth of Lewis's words was borne out by the fact that the IRA imitated Gwynfor's tactic within a year. According to Michael Pierse, historian of the republican hunger strikes, the Irish were thrilled by what had happened: 'Prisoners in Long Kesh were encouraged in their demands to the IRA's Army Council that they be allowed to begin a hunger strike, strangely through the inspiration of a development in Wales.'[164]

But if the threat to starve to death was morally questionable, the impact on Plaid Cymru was even more mixed. However important the creation of S4C was for Welsh broadcasting, Plaid Cymru in fact gained very little from the successful campaign. It was Gwynfor who received the acclaim and not his party. Indeed, it could be argued that the establishment of S4C, and the growth in broadcasting from Cardiff, harmed Plaid Cymru because the expansion deprived the 'national movement' of many of its natural leaders. From then on, these talented young media people became the 'intellywelshia', indulging themselves in the fashionable suburbs of west Cardiff, rather than leading 'Plaid' back to 'Welsh Wales'. It might be argued too that the channel campaign, important though it was, confirmed the widespread perception among electors that Plaid Cymru was first and foremost a language party.[165] Within Plaid Cymru itself, the victory led to a tendency to intellectual lethargy as some of its leaders dined out on the 'channel miracle'. To quote *The Guardian* some days after Gwynfor's triumph: 'TV Victory leaves Plaid Cymru without a Cause... This week's score may well be Gwynfor 1 Whitelaw 0. But next year, Plaid Cymru may find itself relegated to the bottom division.'[166] Last, but not least, the channel campaign made Plaid Cymru's position as a constitutional party that much harder as well. At the beginning of the 'eighties, for instance, there is evidence that Nicholas

Edwards considered conceding to Plaid Cymru on affordable housing to be 'a further capitulation to violent Nationalist pressure'.[167]

It is fair to argue, too, that the channel campaign muddled voters' perception of Plaid Cymru. After the battle for S4C, it was easy to conclude that Plaid Cymru was the political wing of Cymdeithas yr Iaith rather than a party in its own right. Again, there was confusion over tactics, which reopened the old question of Plaid's raison d'être. What was it, really? A constitutional party or an unconstitutional one? There was, of course, only one answer to that: a constitutional party, now led by the legatees of the Carmarthen by-election victory. Plaid Cymru had, it was true, passed a resolution in its conference of 1980 calling for a campaign of lawbreaking to oppose unemployment, but this was just talk. Although there was a fairly successful campaign of refusing to pay water rates in 1982, one can hardly conclude that breaking the law remained a long-term strategy. To that extent, there was none of the 'readiness… to show the strength of our feelings' that Dafydd Iwan had called for.[168] Another exception to the rule was the unconstitutional battle against the poll tax of which Plaid Cymru was a part in 1991. But the basic fact remains, as his Presidency waned, Gwynfor had turned his back on some of his fundamental principles – before resuming the narrow, constitutional path once more. The channel had been won, but the party suffered.

In fairness to Gwynfor, he tried to move the agenda forward a little. At one of the first rallies following the broadcasting campaign, he promised to do all within his power to alleviate the effects of unemployment in Wales. His evident hope, as Dafydd Wigley put it, was to use his new status to lead a united front against Thatcherite economic policies.[169] To that end, Plaid Cymru set up a fund to raise £50,000 for a campaign, but nothing of substance came of it. The target was never reached and there were tactical errors too. As Emrys Roberts explained a few months later: 'We decided to fight against the plans of the Steel Corporation when the important decisions had already been made and when the trade unions had, more's the pity, accepted them. And we decided to protest against Margaret Thatcher. Everyone enjoys the thrills of a protest. But to what end?'[170]

These shortcomings were exacerbated by a leadership vacuum. It was known by the autumn of 1980 that Gwynfor wanted to relinquish the Presidency within a year and, as a result, a furious (but completely necessary) battle began for the intellectual legacy. There developed a polarization between left and right, but it was essentially a battle of the left, as the party's intellectuals set about dismantling

Gwynfor's idea of a 'national movement'. Cynog Dafis was particularly scathing, arguing in forthright terms that the party had to abandon the old 'idea of Plaid Cymru as a body that brings together under one umbrella people of different political persuasions – left and right – who are agreed that Wales needs to be saved. Because "saving Wales" is an empty concept'.[171] For Cynog Dafis, the answer was socialism, and with Dafydd Elis Thomas elected party vice-president during the 1980 conference, the left-right question became central to the discussion on Plaid Cymru's future. But as the debate took off, Gwynfor argued in *Y Ddraig Goch* that such ideological factionalism was 'a phoney war'. He was sure, he said, that socialism was an 'unclear, misleading, divisive' term. 'It has very little appeal for ordinary people.' No, Gwynfor was far happier with 'the Welsh radical tradition' in which Michael D Jones was the central figure.[172]

That tradition was a chimera by the eve of 1981, however. If the left of the party had learned anything between 1974 and 1979, it was the all-important lesson that Plaid Cymru needed to define exactly where it stood in the political spectrum. This was confirmed by the publication of the Plaid Cymru Research Commission report in January 1981 – a document which, for all its shortcomings, buried some of the ideas that 'the national movement' held most dear. The main thrust of the report, and its 73 proposals, was that Plaid Cymru should combine radicalism, socialism and nationalism under the banner of 'devolved socialism' and avoid what it derided as 'Westminster-based consensus and compromise politics'.[173] Privately, Gwynfor believed the Research Commission report had received a 'fairly kind reception' but the consequences for 'Gwynforism' were far-reaching. The report gave further encouragement to the iconoclasts and their idol, Dafydd Elis Thomas. Gwynfor secretly feared the worst as he contemplated 'Dafydd Êl with his personal campaign' against tradition. Gwynfor was of the opinion that his ideas cut 'across central Plaid policy' [174] and he urged the leading nationalist thinker, Ioan Bowen Rees to tackle what he regarded as Elis Thomas's Marxism.[175] But in vain: Bowen Rees refused, and in any event, the tide by then was too strong.

The only consolation of substance Gwynfor could turn to during these months was the development of S4C. After a slow start, the government had kept its word by ensuring a fair deal for the channel and Gwynfor was delighted to hear that Sir Goronwy Daniel rather than Glyn Tegai Hughes would chair the S4C Authority.[176] It was an excellent choice as Sir Goronwy proved to be both wise and judicious, giving S4C the best possible start. But as the channel flourished, Plaid Cymru's woes intensified while the relationship between Dafydd Elis Thomas and Dafydd Wigley deteriorated. In April 1981, Elis Thomas invited Marcella, the sister of Bobby Sands, and his agent, Owen Carron, to visit Parliament and hold a press conference. It was a brave step for Elis Thomas to take, and in due course it was seen to be fully justified, because the election of Bobby Sands as Sinn Fein MP for Fermanagh and South Tyrone accelerated the peace process. But at the time, Sands was on hunger strike and viewed by many as being beyond the pale. Wigley was horrified and, during these months, Gwynfor acted as a kind of father confessor to him. On the day after the decision to invite Bobby Sands's sister, Wigley wrote to Gwynfor expressing his 'horrified' fear over the direction in which the party was moving.[177] In a further letter, Wigley suggested to Gwynfor that he would have to challenge the new vice-president: 'Obviously, we cannot allow the present slide to continue for any length of time.'[178] Gwynfor also received copies of Wigley's letters to the party's central office, revealing a candid picture of the relationship between Plaid Cymru's two MPs. In one of these letters, Wigley expressed his opinion that Elis Thomas's decision to become involved in Northern Ireland politics had been utterly disastrous: 'The reaction (in the short term at least) to all this has been bad for Plaid. At the Urdd Eisteddfod, at the North Wales Show, as well as in my constituency, I have received a cold and totally negative reaction. *Perhaps* in the long run there will be some justification. But certainly not three weeks before local elections.'[179]

Wigley had good reason to be anxious. In the May 1981 local elections, Plaid Cymru performed surprisingly badly. It lost a third of its seats but the problems were not all of its own making. A new political party – the Social Democratic Party – had been formed. It united left and right in an attempt to win over electors who had grown tired of the ideological extremes of Labour and the Conservatives. The SDP illuminated British political discourse like a shooting star before fading in 1981, but its consensual agenda also threatened to break the mould of Welsh politics. For Plaid Cymru, it posed a particular dilemma given Plaid Cymru's success under Gwynfor in winning over the radical, moderate vote in the west. It was claimed that the SDP was about to gain a foothold in Gwynedd and there were reports of Labour stalwarts in places like Llanberis joining the new party. These stories had very little substance, any more than the rumour that Dafydd Wigley was about to join the SDP. But even having to deny such an absurd assertion was proof of Plaid Cymru's weakness. In was no coincidence, then, that Gwynfor reconsidered his decision not to stand again in Carmarthen.

Wigley had already marked down the Reverend Aled Gwyn as Gwynfor's successor and Gwyn had allowed his name to go forward.[180] Aled Gwyn would certainly have been a worthy candidate because he was popular and knew the county well. But, unbeknown to Gwyn, some Plaid activists in Carmarthen were unwilling to see Gwynfor go. Indeed, within two days of the announcement that Gwynfor would not be standing again, the constituency chair wrote to him stating that party members in the constituency 'implored in desire and hope' that he would think again.[181] Three weeks later, a constituency deputation went to Talar Wen with the same message. They were eager for him to reconsider and, faced with such pressure, Gwynfor vacillated before succumbing to the inevitable. He decided to stand again and, justifying his decision, said his advancing years would not present any problem because it was the age of the veteran after all. 'It is not,' he prophesied in the *Western Mail*, 'the age of the very young any more. The rulers of Russia and China are in their 80s – and look at Ronald Reagan.' It was an absurd comparison. It was also, it later transpired, an act that would harm both Gwynfor and Plaid Cymru in Carmarthen.[182]

Gwynfor's basic problem was his inability to let go with grace. After all, politics was his life, his other interests were few and far between and he had very little to fill the gap that would inevitably come with retirement. In the same way, he insisted in June 1981 that Plaid Cymru's problems were temporary ones, and that the talk of left and right would all be forgotten within a year or two. But, as his political career waned, Gwynfor undoubtedly lost the support of a large section of his own party during the summer of 1981, so much so that some members pleaded with him to continue as President so that the ideological day of reckoning could be postponed.[183] The key event was the decision of Dafydd Elis Thomas and his acolytes such as Aled Eirug and Emyr Wyn Williams to form The National Left. The aim of the organization was to broaden Plaid Cymru's support base by establishing contact with movements and individuals on the left of Welsh politics. It was a group with considerable intellectual clout, and its short-lived presence marked an important step in the process of turning Plaid Cymru into a mature, left-wing party. A similar process was under way in Scotland with the growth of the '79 Group within the SNP; the movement, however, caused a split within the SNP and the same thing was true, to a lesser extent, of the National Left. For many nationalists, the National Left operated as the Militant Tendency of Plaid Cymru, a party within a party with its own membership lists. The Gwynforite establishment was convinced that the National Left was an unholy curse, and immediately after the organization's first public meeting Gwynfor wrote to *The Observer* claiming that Plaid Cymru had always been left wing. This was a pretty dubious claim, as Plaid Cymru had shifted miraculously to the left overnight, but it allowed Gwynfor to portray Elis Thomas and his like as Marxists.[184]

There was certainly the odd pseudo-Marxist (and pseud) associated with the National Left, but Gwynfor's decision to rechristen his party as moderate left was well judged. Saunders Lewis, for instance, was astounded that Plaid Cymru had moved to the left so quickly, but the effect was the same: Gwynfor had succeeded in painting the National Left as extremists.[185] Meanwhile, the speculation continued about who would defend the Gwynfor legacy. Jennie Eirian Davies's observation that the struggle would be a struggle for Plaid Cymru's very 'soul' was characteristically perceptive.[186] A report in *The Guardian* suggested Plaid Cymru was in such deep trouble that Gwynfor himself would need to return to keep his party from falling apart altogether.[187] The article was unfounded, as too was the rumour that Gwynfor was on his way to the House of Lords. But the febrile atmosphere led Plaid Cymru's moderate wing to play its last card: Dafydd Wigley.[188] As has already been seen, Wigley had ruled out running for the Presidency because of family circumstances, but the situation was about to change. After a summer of 'pure enjoyment' at Tynllidiart near Dolgellau, where he read a collection of Saunders Lewis's essays, Gwynfor heard the news he had hoped to hear: Wigley was prepared to contest the Presidency after all.[189] Wigley says that Gwynfor never pressurized him to reconsider, but he did receive his support. And the two had very similar objectives: they were both adamant that the party needed to be 'saved' from Elis Thomas.[190]

The same relief was evident among Gwynfor's family and friends. His son, Guto Prys, wrote rejoicing that Wigley was going to challenge 'Dafydd Êl' – whose judgement he considered 'clouded'.[191] Among Gwynfor's own people, Plaid members in Carmarthenshire, Elis Thomas came at the foot of the poll when a vote was taken on whom they intended to nominate for the Presidency.[192] But the situation was rather different across the rest of Wales as a close and fierce race developed between left and centre. Gwynfor was sufficiently wise and gracious to stay well clear of the battle although he pledged his private support for Wigley.

Until the very last day, Gwynfor remained the quintessential party loyalist: he was 'Plaid' and party unity was paramount. In his final press statement as President, he told the journalists who had flocked to the conference in Carmarthen that there was no real difference between Elis Thomas and Wigley. Elis Thomas, he said, appealed to the working-class majority, whereas Wigley's greatest appeal was to the majority of people, who were working class![193] Nonsense, of course; there were then huge differences between Wigley and Elis Thomas but, for Gwynfor, it was essential to keep such disputes within the walls of the 'national movement'. The last thing he wanted to see was an ideological split such as that between Tony Benn and Denis Healey which had proved so harmful to Labour. When it came to nationalism, Gwynfor could always find a compromise.

A few hours after this statement, Gwynfor showed just how far his pragmatism would go when he voted in favour of a resolution, almost Soviet in nature, calling for 'devolved socialism' to become a party objective. The same resolution also asked for self-government to be rejected as a goal and replaced by a 'devolved socialist state'.[194] It was considered a controversial move, negating decades of party tradition, and a close vote was anticipated. Gwynfor, of all people, was expected to vote against but astounded the conference when he raised his hand in favour. Seeing this, many in the hall followed suit, making the wording part of the party's constitution. His decision remains a mystery and some, like Rhydwen Williams, the editor of *Barn*, have argued that Gwynfor simply made a mistake.[195] Another suggestion from the left is that Gwynfor's support was a sign of desperation.[196] Although one cannot be certain, the most likely explanation is the one given by Gwynfor himself, that the resolution was merely a matter of words on paper because the policies remained unchanged.[197] And Gwynfor was right. With Wigley his likely successor, Gwynfor ensured party unity at the cost of a little pride and a willingness to refrain from hair-splitting.

The following day, Saturday 31 October, Dafydd Wigley was duly elected President of the party, much to Gwynfor's delight. The result, 273 votes for Wigley, 212 for Elis Thomas, was close, but Gwynfor could step down in the knowledge that the 'Merioneth Marxist' had been defeated, the heir had been crowned and his own succession was safe after 36 unbroken years in charge.[198] A few days later, Gwynfor wrote to the colourful nationalist lawyer, Robyn Lewis, stressing Wigley's virtues. 'Dafydd Wigley,' he said, 'will make a first-rate President. He has displayed wisdom and balance throughout and makes every effort to hold Plaid together and promote its unity.' His only concern was Wigley's health due to 'family pressure', but he had promised from the start that he would do what he could 'to protect him from overworking'.[199] Gwynfor, suffice it to say, kept his promise assiduously. At the same conference, he was presented with a Fidelity television set (Made in England), but he had little time to watch it. As he stepped down from the Presidency after such a lengthy period of service, it never crossed Gwynfor's mind not to continue doing what he could to promote the party.

Even so, the party was surprisingly ungrateful for all the time Gwynfor had devoted to it. Following the 1981 conference, a testimonial collection was launched to honour him but the response was disappointing. Elwyn Robers, who organized it, had hoped to raise £18,000 by Christmas but was astounded by the 'pitiful contributions' made by some 'prominent' members. Arfon contributed most (£2,112) but the response in the south was poor: £60 from Merthyr and district, £1,280 from Cardiff and £664 from Swansea. The testimonial was marred by the assumption that Gwynfor was a wealthy man. Even though he had been generously supported by his father and his brother, Alcwyn, it was a relationship founded on dependency, and it could hardly be said that Gwynfor had much money in reserve. Indeed, his financial situation by 1981, as Elwyn Roberts put it, was 'very tight'. Although Gwynfor's debts had been cleared, the money he had inherited after Dan's death had already been spent. In addition, £1,000 was needed for repairs to Talar Wen and he did not have a penny in the bank.[200] Eventually, the target of £18,000 was reached and the money invested in an annuity on his behalf. With this annual sum and a (fairly small) parliamentary pension, Gwynfor managed to get by. Alcwyn continued to be as generous as ever but, even so, Gwynfor did not enjoy a comfortable retirement by any means.

Not that his was a normal retirement. For one thing, his appetite for evangelising was undiminished, and he channelled his energies in various directions: some familiar, others less so. The end of 1981 saw the publication of his polemical *Diwedd Prydeindod*, an attempt to convince a new generation that it was their duty to undertake thankless work for the nation. It was typical Gwynfor, even though the anti-Labour tone was more vitriolic than ever as he contrasted Neil Kinnock and Roy Jenkins's 'faint-hearted servility' with the 'nobility and confidence of figures like Llywelyn the Great and Owain Glyndŵr.[201] In all honesty, *Diwedd Prydeindod* had little new to say and its impact was minimal. Far more substantial, as far as Plaid Cymru was concerned, were Gwynfor's efforts at the time to marry the party to anti-nuclear and environmental movements. They culminated in the successful joint candidacy of Plaid Cymru and the Greens, taking Ceredigion at the general election of 1992, but it was Gwynfor who led Plaid Cymru in that direction. During the summer of 1981, Brig Oubridge, Welsh co-ordinator of the Ecology Party, wrote to Gwynfor suggesting it would be useful for both to exchange ideas. Oubridge's aim was to counterbalance what he described as the 'sky blue-pink' mentality of the three main parties and it appears that Gwynfor – despite the qualms some in Plaid Cymru felt at his consorting with a 'hippy' – warmed to the invitation.[202] That November, Gwynfor and Oubridge met, leading Gwynfor to conclude that the environmental movement not only shared some of his own thoughts – small-scale development, pacifism, environmentalism – but that they offered a solution to the failure of the British left.[203]

Gwynfor also wanted to see Plaid Cymru move once again, as it had done during the Second World War, in the direction of assertive pacifism. Even so, as with so much that Gwynfor did as a politician, his wish combined principles and pragmatism. As far as principle went, there is no doubt that Gwynfor, like many other pacifists, was horrified by the escalation of the arms race. The government's decision to allow Greenham Common in Berkshire to be used as a home for 96 American Cruise missiles prompted thousands of Welsh pacifists to take a stand. Gwynfor also viewed these developments as 'mass murder on a scale hitherto uncontemplated'.[204] As the international situation deteriorated during 1981, it was decided to reinvigorate the Welsh wing of CND which Gwynfor saw as an opportunity not only to promote pacifism but also to strengthen Plaid Cymru. In an echo of the relationship between Plaid Cymru and the Welsh Pacifists forty years earlier, Gwynfor insisted in a letter to Dafydd Williams that his party was 'seizing the lead that is now in English hands because of their commendable commitment'.[205] It was a crude tactic, but it succeeded, and figures like Jill Evans, Dafydd Iwan and Toni Schiavone made a major contribution to CND Cymru in the name of Plaid Cymru.

Gwynfor's other objective in 'reaching out' like this was to bring Welsh and English-speakers closer together after the referendum. To an extent, this happened originally between members of Plaid Cymru and those in the other peace and environmental groups, but in Carmarthenshire itself the situation was rather different. For one thing, Welsh-speakers there were deeply suspicious of the peace movement. When Gwynfor organized a series of meetings in March

1982 to show the anti-war film *The War Game*, only a handful of Welsh-speakers came to see it.[206] Some prominent party members in Carmarthenshire – such as D O Davies – went so far as to warn him to spend less time with peace activists.[207] Gwynfor refused to change course, but the concern of a figure like D O Davies reflected a fear that Gwynfor was neglecting the task of winning back the constituency where politics, and language politics in particular, were as savage as ever and Gwynfor's final years as a public figure were spent in a nasty Carmarthenshire dogfight. At the end of 1981, and throughout 1982, the local press was filled with vituperative salvos against Gwynfor by Dr Alan Williams, the Labour constituency secretary for Carmarthen. After Gwynfor relinquished the Presidency, Williams hurried to remind the people of Carmarthen that the decision to 'force' an old man like Gwynfor to stand again as a candidate was cruel.[208] It would become a familiar theme from Williams until the general election of 1983, and his forte was a relentless attack on Welsh nationalism. Some in Plaid Cymru were convinced that Alan Williams was taking a leaf out of Dr Goebbels's book as he dragged language politics in Carmarthenshire into the gutter.[209] But Alan Williams was a skilled operator, deliberately using the Welsh language (and the holiday homes arson campaign in particular) to denigrate Gwynfor.

Gwynfor tried to respond but his call for Alan Williams to halt his vendetta went unheeded.[210] Williams had an uncanny ability to interpret a variety of developments as part of a nationalist conspiracy, working at the behest of his mentor, Dr Roger Thomas, with great success during what was an exceptionally difficult time for Gwynfor. Privately, Gwynfor's hatred for Labour was such that he longed to see the SDP break the party's hold in Wales.[211] He never mentioned this in public and although he tried to regain some political momentum by drawing attention to local issues such as the poor state of Dinefwr Castle, these efforts were undermined by language politics.[212] Gwynfor was not the only one to suffer during this period. Plaid Cymru was only just able to keep its head above water, and Dafydd Wigley threatened to resign as President unless his fellow-members did more to pay off the party's debts.[213] He did not carry out his threat, but his Presidency was inhibited by his inability to close the divide between left and right and create 'a national movement' as effectively as Gwynfor had done.[214] The Falklands conflict of spring 1982 also had a deep impact, as jingoism swept through Wales. Plaid Cymru looked isolated, albeit principled, as the only major party in Britain to oppose the war. It was in this inhospitable climate in autumn

1982 that Gwynfor began to plan for a general election.

It would be his last electoral fight and he tried to present himself to the people of Carmarthenshire as an experienced politician and not as an old man desperate for a purpose in life. Despite his urgent protestations, however, Gwynfor's political career was approaching its end and his actions betrayed him. In the spring of 1982, he wrote his autobiography, *Bywyd Cymro*, in three short months under the guidance of his editor, Manon Rhys. To complete the work within such a tight schedule was quite an achievement. However, it held up a mirror to his virtues and shortcomings. In *Bywyd Cymro*, there is no middle ground; everyone is either splendid or flawed. The splendid figures, are of course, nationalists; the rest are beyond redemption. The book was notable too for what it said about Gwynfor's interpretation of history. It was certainly not a modest work. Gwynfor seized upon every opportunity to praise himself and his party. It was Plaid Cymru, according to Gwynfor's interpretation of history, that 'saved' the nation – no one else contributed. But what is most striking is what Gwynfor decided to omit from *Bywyd Cymro*. There is hardly any mention of the disputes over Tryweryn or his threat to resign in 1961. There are few references to Saunders Lewis and Emrys Roberts. From cover to cover, the book is a conscious study in political self-aggrandizement.

That said, for all its faults, it is a significant book because it analyses a huge contribution over such a long period. It is also interesting because Gwynfor openly airs his own shortcomings, such as the public nervousness which had plagued him throughout his career. The book sold well, making a not inconsiderable contribution to the canonization of Gwynfor. The first step in that process had been taken when he was made honorary President of Plaid Cymru in December 1982. But between accepting the honour and publishing *Bywyd Cymro*, it had become evident to Gwynfor himself that his political career was effectively over. He became increasingly fascinated by history, publishing a pamphlet on the early ruler Macsen Wledig and the birth of the Welsh nation, in January 1983.[215] He also worked closely with the Cofiwn movement to have Macsen commemorated, leading to the composition of Dafydd Iwan's popular celebratory song, '*Yma o Hyd*'. In due course, it became an anthem of defiance for Welsh-speakers, sung on occasions as varied as football matches and drunken wedding receptions.

These efforts were all praiseworthy and certainly deepened the passion a section of the Welsh people felt for their nation at a time when Welsh consciousness appeared to be fading. However, it is less certain how they benefited Gwynfor's image as a modern politician, especially on the eve of a general election. The Carmarthen result was expected to be close; indeed, the supposition was that boundary changes would work in Gwynfor's favour and that it would be too close to call between himself and the Labour candidate, Roger Thomas.[216] Nigel Thomas, the Tory who had performed so well in 1979, was nowhere to be seen and Plaid Cymru offered a prize to whoever spotted him.[217] Even so, the Plaid Cymru campaign was deficient and Gwynfor's age became a key factor. More than once, he found himself having to assure the press that he was not too old to enter Parliament. In an interview for *The Guardian*, he compared his position with that of Jim Griffiths and Ronald Reagan – who had both remained active in politics well into their seventies.[218] It was an unfortunate comparison given that the first had died and the second was a bogeyman for radical Plaid Cymru pacifists. Doubtless, it was a gaffe, then, but not half as unfortunate as his original decision back in 1981 to stand again.

But the damage had been done. In the early hours of Friday, 10 June, Gwynfor's political career ended with his failure to regain Carmarthen. Dr Roger Thomas held on to the seat with a majority of 1,154, bringing to a close a unique record of political activity stretching back to 1945. Losing was painful but worse, far worse than that, was the experience of coming third behind the Tory, Nigel Thomas. Nationally, the picture was similar as Wales embraced the Thatcher revolution. Plaid Cymru won just eight per cent of the national vote, and some observers feared that nationalism and left-wing politics were mortally wounded. Within days of the poll, Wyn Roberts, Minister of State at the Welsh Office, was urging his master, Nicholas Edwards, to ensure that the Conservative party would become the party of Wales. This Conservatism, Roberts hoped, would also evolve to become a 'native, organic force like some of our best national institutions'.[219] However, as the Conservatives celebrated, Gwynfor responded with alarm as he saw the three things he loved most – the Welsh language, Wales and world peace – in jeopardy. When he was asked what his next step would be, Gwynfor could only express himself with solemn defiance: 'Old soldiers never retire, they gradually fade away. I am not retiring from politics.'[220] But the reality was that a lifetime's work had already drawn to a close, having brought him (with the exception of S4C) precious little success. Now, he and his fellow nationalists faced dark days ahead.

Chapter 13

THE OLD MAN OF PENCARREG 1983–2005

OVER THE NEXT FEW MONTHS, Gwynfor seemed like a wounded animal, troubled in mind and spirit and broken by the events of the previous four years. He could not sleep and refused to see visitors. Above all, he wanted peace, quiet and time to reflect on what had gone wrong in the Carmarthen constituency. He could not understand why nationalism was waning and why S4C had given him such a poor electoral return. Gwynfor was not the only one to suffer: the previous few years had hit Rhiannon hard too. For her, what had happened to Gwynfor in June 1983 was nothing less than a disaster. She could not fathom why the voters of Carmarthen had rejected Gwynfor when he, as Rhiannon saw it, had devoted his life to them.[1] Faced with this situation, the two resolved to seek sanctuary at their family home near Dolgellau. They spent some weeks away from Carmarthenshire with their small grandson, Hedd, for company.[2]

Gwynfor used the time to lick his wounds and attempt to recuperate but, around him, the storm still raged over Plaid Cymru's future direction. The battle between the rival supporters of Elis Thomas and Wigley became, for Gwynfor, a struggle also for his legacy. Given this, he could only feel horrified at Elis Thomas's growing militancy. For Elis Thomas, the disaster of 1983 was further proof, if not *the* unmistakeable proof, that Plaid Cymru needed to escape the dead hand of Gwynfor and his cautious successor, Dafydd Wigley. The priority for Elis Thomas was to transform Plaid Cymru and create nothing less than 'a new political tradition'.[3] It was an ambitious claim, but Elis Thomas was deadly serious. The British right was at the height of its powers and he did not believe Plaid Cymru had any choice. From then on, the National Left became ever more confident, with scant regard for the gradualist approach of Gwynfor, Wigley and their colleagues in the Hydro group, a faction established to 'save' the party from Elis Thomas.[4] The left's development was aided too by the launch of *Radical Wales*, a magazine established and funded by Plaid Cymru, but a mouthpiece for the party's left. For its editors, the key question facing Plaid Cymru in the autumn of 1983 was this: 'Is Plaid Cymru a political party or an extramural branch of Merched y Wawr and Côr Meibion Cwmsgwt?'[5]

It was a central question for many on the left but, as he witnessed this endless questioning, Gwynfor's suspicion of Elis Thomas and his impact on the party grew. In private, Gwynfor tended to despise Elis Thomas, mocking his overweening delight in ideas which, in itself, exposes another irony about Gwynfor. Although he surrounded himself with some of Wales's brightest intellects, like Tudur Jones, Pennar Davies and J Gwyn Griffiths, Gwynfor was never a man of ideas. Indeed, Gwynfor regarded an over-reliance on ideas as a bad thing in politics. Now, however, he was watching an intellectual trying to seize his party in the name of the Welsh left. It explains why he was impatient with Dafydd Elis Thomas the politician, but there are other considerations too. Gwynfor also felt that Elis Thomas was unreliable, a maverick, whose latest 'whim' could not be guessed with any certainty. Would he be a Communist? Would he be an Anarchist? Would he be Green? He also asked whether Elis Thomas had some obsession with gaining personal attention. 'Dafydd Êl' led one to expect the unexpected, and Gwynfor disliked his inconstancy – a tendency that he ascribed to Elis Thomas's allegedly complex relationship with his father.[6]

Gwynfor remained in a depressive state for months but, gradually, with medical help and Rhiannon's love, he emerged in better shape. By Christmas, he was sleeping better and was more willing to see people again.[7] And like a moth to a flame, he returned to politics. The turning point came with an incident in Carmarthen and the shocking news that the local MP, Dr Roger Thomas, had been arrested on suspicion of indecency in a public toilet near Swansea. It was a dreadfully sorry story and Gwynfor expressed full sympathy with what he described as 'a personal tragedy for the MP for Carmarthen'.[8] It was a munificent response considering Roger Thomas's impact on his own life, but Gwynfor knew what the outcome would be – Thomas would have to give up his seat and call a by-election. The promise was made and, without delay, Gwynfor began his search for a candidate. Some commentators mentioned the possibility that Gwynfor himself might return to the fray but, this time, there would be no second thoughts.[9] In time, Hywel Teifi Edwards, a charismatic and gifted academic, was chosen to succeed him as Plaid Cymru's candidate.

Hywel Teifi Edwards decided to accept the nomination at Gwynfor's prompting. But the truth was that Hywel Teifi Edwards was not a natural politician. He agreed to stand against his better judgement and remembers visiting Gwynfor at Talar Wen in a state of uncertainty. He left, however, inspired with the belief that he could become a prime minister within five years![10] Within some sections of Plaid Cymru, Gwynfor still had a strong appeal. But as Gwynfor began his reaquaintance with politics, Rhiannon was eager to leave Llangadog and the county she felt had betrayed her husband. She was sure that the people of Llangadog hated Gwynfor and, eventually, she insisted on going.[11] Ideally, she would have liked to move to Dolgellau or Cardiff. There were other considerations too: Talar Wen was far too large for them and the stairs were becoming vertiginous for both of them. However, Gwynfor wanted to remain in Carmarthenshire and, after a short search, they found a patch of land in the village of Pencarreg, on the northern edge of the county. The news of their departure was announced in March 1984 and a farewell supper was held in Llangadog Hall that July. It was an 'unforgettable' evening, as the community paper reported, as over 200 people paid their respects to a couple who had done so much for all things Welsh in their community for over 45 years.[12] Even so, it was a solemn farewell to their adopted home.

They moved into a new bungalow in Pencarreg in the summer of 1984, hoping that they would end their days in a new Talar Wen. But there was more heartbreak in store. That summer, Rhiannon discovered she had Parkinson's disease, a cruel and demeaning condition. She accepted her fate with stoicism as did Gwynfor who would now, after so many years of loyal care from Rhiannon, dedicate himself to looking after her. But his talents as a cook and cleaner over the coming years were mixed at best. As often as not, he operated on Rhiannon's instructions. Very gradually, however, a domestic regime developed that enabled them to cope with their old age. Their love for each other, as well as the care from their children, made life tolerable.

But Gwynfor's political disappointments continued. In August 1984, Plaid Cymru supporters in Carmarthenshire discovered there would no by-election after all. Labour had wisely decided against, scuppering Plaid Cymru's hopes of benefiting from Neil Kinnock's difficulties in the south Wales coalfield and beyond as the miners' epic strike continued. As Britain split between left and right over the dispute, Plaid Cymru itself shifted inexorably too.

In October 1984, Dafydd Elis Thomas was elected President of Plaid Cymru, defeating Dafydd Iwan, who represented the party's traditionalist wing, by a hair's breadth. It may have been close, but its significance was clear: the Presidency allowed Elis Thomas to build the party in his own image. From then on, Plaid Cymru (if not its traditional supporters) would turn its back on the 'national movement' and seek salvation in the valleys. As the new President put it: 'I doubt if we really appreciate the seriousness of the position... Last year we dropped to 5.6 per cent in the mainly English-speaking areas and 36.5 per cent in the mainly Welsh-speaking areas. We have become more than ever a party of only part of the Welsh nation.'[13] From an electoral perspective, Elis Thomas certainly had a point, but Gwynfor and some of his former colleagues in the leadership felt betrayed by events. Gwynfor heard that Saunders Lewis, now on his deathbed, was appalled by Elis Thomas and feared his influence on 'Plaid'.[14] And essentially, in this respect, Gwynfor fully agreed with Lewis.

Even then, he did not voice his private doubts in public since Gwynfor regarded party discipline as the eleventh commandment – even with 'Dafydd Êl' at the helm. One of the first things that Gwynfor did after moving to Pencarreg was to establish a new Plaid Cymru branch there, Bro Deifi. He chose to exercise his influence in private through the party's internal structures such as the executive and the National Council. And, little by little, Elis Thomas and Gwynfor moved towards an accommodation. Some months after winning the Presidency, Elis Thomas wrote to Gwynfor explaining, if not quite apologizing for, his desire to cause offence: 'As you know I have been angry recently – I feel that I must speak out publicly because Plaid's traditional supporters are in hasty retreat.' Meanwhile, Elis Thomas asked him to defend the party's general secretary, Dafydd Williams, because 'some in Plaid have their knives out for him'.[15]

Gwynfor was not merely motivated by loyalty. As the miners' strike dragged on, he sensed in private that 'things were settling down – D Êl coming to his senses – splendid with the miners'.[16] Without doubt, the strike, and Elis Thomas's prominent role in it, had shown Gwynfor that the talk within the National Left of winning the support of other social groups was not simply hot air. Others of a very different political persuasion saw matters in the same way. As Kim Howells, the NUM's research officer in south Wales put it: 'We discovered old links, *ancestral* links.'[17] The heightened feelings surrounding the strike, Gwynfor could see, were uniting Wales, nationalists and trade unionists alike. As he watched the process unfold, Gwynfor was not slow to sing Elis Thomas's praises. In an important piece for *Y Ddraig Goch*, he stated that nationalists and socialists should come together in the Elis Thomas broad church:

> We must get rid of the image, which I unintentionally created, of rural, nonconformist nationalism, with its whole emphasis on language. We do no good by complaining that this image is a caricature. It exists and it must be got rid of.[18]

It was without doubt a generous statement for Gwynfor to make given the way in which Elis Thomas had set about dismantling all he had achieved for the party. A few days later, a note of thanks arrived from Elis Thomas:

> I have been very worried during these past months about the deliberate efforts to divide us from some quarters. I am certain that the article will be a means to calm the concerns of many who have been alarmed by the change of emphasis.[19]

The miners' strike came to an end in March 1985 but, in the short term, Plaid Cymru enjoyed no return on the support it gave the strikers. If anything, Gwynfor's perception was that the situation had worsened. In July, he spent some days campaigning for the Plaid candidate in the Brecon and Radnor by-election, the most disastrous by-election in the party's history. The campaign was dogged by an appalling lack of organization from first to last. The dreadful result drove Wigley into a paroxysm of anger, blaming the left and Elis Thomas for the 'shambles', as he put it, but Gwynfor remained wholly supportive.[20] Or, to quote his public pronouncement on the fiasco: "My impression was that if we had the Archangel Gabriel as a candidate and the most perfect organisation our resources would not permit success'.[21]

Gwynfor certainly had to tread with care on the political ground that Dafydd Elis Thomas had cultivated. The same desire to maintain party unity was evident when Saunders Lewis died in September 1985. However deep the divide between them, he did not seek to denigrate Lewis the politician, confining himself rather to a subtle remark that there had been differences between them.[22] However, he was not as guarded in his defence of Plaid Cymru's pacifism – an issue that, for Gwynfor, was as vital as nationalism itself. Without warning, he reignited this historic debate during the autumn of 1985 when Phil Williams attempted to convince the party of the need for a Welsh army for a Welsh state. The solution he proposed was a 'citizens' army' armed with a rifle in every home.[23] Several within Plaid Cymru judged it an absurd idea but it was Gwynfor who finally defeated it.[24]

Gwynfor at the time was also vice-president of CND Wales, and involved in the battle to frustrate a controversial scheme by Carmarthen District Council to build a nuclear bunker under the car park of the council headquarters. But Gwynfor's last meaningful act as President of Plaid was not the preservation of past pacifist virtues. It came, rather, during the spring of 1986 when he decided to sit on Plaid Cymru's constitutional sub-committee – a body which, despite its uninspiring name, was vital to the history of devolution. This body put devolution back on the agenda for Plaid Cymru, and met regularly over the next few months. The culmination of their efforts was the National Conference of February 1987, which created a credible foundation for a new Plaid Cymru campaign for a Welsh parliament.[25]

Having now seen devolution being given a new impetus, Gwynfor's level of activity for Plaid Cymru diminished. Although he still addressed countless meetings in the party's name, he channelled his efforts in a more cultural, less overtly political direction. This was the last phase in his life – the age of Gwynfor the mentor, upholding nationalism in its broadest sense. He had already persuaded Professor Geraint Jenkins to undertake the work of editing the outstanding series of essays on Welsh history, *Cof Cenedl*, and in 1986 he published a volume of his own on significant figures in Wales's past, *Seiri Cenedl*.[26] He also corresponded occasionally with the heads of public bodies in Wales to ensure that Welsh heroes received due acknowledgement. In a joint venture with Merched y Wawr, he led the campaign for a worthy memorial to Gwenllïan in Kidwelly. The commission charged with the responsibility for Welsh heritage, CADW, finally unveiled a monument to her in 1991. Owain Glyndŵr's claim to recognition was not ignored either. Gwynfor remained in regular contact with the idealists behind the Glyndŵr Embassy. To the same end, he exercised what influence he had with S4C. On one occasion, a heated exchange took place between him and Owen Edwards, the controller of S4C, when Gwynfor argued that the channel did not devote enough time to history programmes.[27]

But what prompted Gwynfor's last major pronouncement was immigration into rural Wales during the 'eighties. Since 1985, the economic upturn in south-east England had spawned a new social phenomenon, the arrival of the 'yuppie' in Wales. More often than not, these people were young, affluent and had the means to buy endless acres of Welsh land. Gwynfor had spoken on the issue as early as the Fishguard Eisteddfod in 1986, noting the linguistic impact in his own immediate area. It is no understatement to say that Gwynfor was afraid the Welsh language would be submerged unless urgent action were taken to stem the tide. Following this, he issued a robust statement on the matter with Dr Meredydd Evans, revealing the full extent of what, for them, was a portentous situation.[28] In this respect, the majority of Plaid Cymru's members were in agreement but there was considerable difference of opinion over how best to proceed. Some supported the arson campaign; others, like Meredydd Evans, wanted to see strict legislation prohibiting the numbers who could settle in Welsh-speaking areas. A number of language activists regarded this as 'linguistic apartheid', and Meredydd Evans received scant support from Plaid Cymru.[29] In February 1987, he left the party, believing that Dafydd Elis Thomas was not taking the matter seriously.[30] Gwynfor believed that part of the answer was to establish intensive Ulpan Welsh courses in every district to turn 'the English influx' into Welsh-speakers.[31] He also wished to use the main organizations in Wales to highlight the situation but, as in the case of Meredydd Evans, he was to be disappointed. His efforts to persuade the National Eisteddfod Council to campaign on the issue were similarly unsuccessful. He was curtly informed by Bedwyr Lewis Jones, the Council's chair, that such matters were the responsibility of local and central government.[32] Given that Cymdeithas yr Iaith was concentrating on its campaign for a new Language Act and a body to further the development of Welsh-medium education, Gwynfor only had one option – to found a new movement.

And that is precisely what happened in 1988. Aged 75, he set up PONT ('bridge') to span the cultural divide between Welsh-speakers and incomers. Gwynfor had already laid the foundations by setting up a Plaid Cymru branch for non-Welsh speakers in Llanybydder a year before.[33] Even so, he still felt that something more powerful was needed, a partnership, he hoped, 'between the native Welsh and the new Welsh'.[34] Fortunately for him, others, like the young nationalist, Marc Phillips, were in agreement and believed a national movement was required.[35] Doubtless, however, Gwynfor had something ambitious in mind and the work it entailed would have been enough to exhaust a far younger man. In Gwynfor's case, paradoxically, it reinvigorated him. On 9 June 1988, a cross-section of people in the Pencarreg area, incomers and language enthusiasts, were brought together to discuss the way forward. Addressing the inaugural meeting, Gwynfor talked of his vision, stressing it was the Welsh language that had preserved Wales as a nation and without it the nation would cease to exist. But rather than admonish those who did not speak Welsh for having come to Wales, Gwynfor seized upon the opportunity to inculcate a sense of Welshness in the new arrivals through education – for adults as well as children.[36]

The message, curiously, calls to mind Gwynfor's attitude towards the evacuees half a century before, and by embracing it PONT enjoyed modest success. Three weeks later, Gwynfor unveiled his grand plan on inward migration in a major piece for *Y Faner*.[37] By 1989, the movement had three sections and branches in Gwynedd, Clwyd, Dyfed and Cardiff. They held evening classes to steep new arrivals in the language and succeeded in taking some of the heat out of what had threatened to be an unpleasant situation. PONT attracted intellectuals of the status of Professor Gwyn Alf Williams and some financial support from sources such as the Bank of Wales, the Nat West and, of course, Dan Evans's own company. PONT also provided principled opposition to the Education First movement, an organization led by Dr Alan Williams that sought to restrict the growth of Welsh-medium education.[38] However, PONT never became the 'powerful' force that Gwynfor had hoped to create. It was wound up in the mid-nineties due to lack of finances.[39] That said, its activities offered a hint of reconciliation at a time when the debate over migration to Wales was at its most poisonous. When PONT was founded in the spring of 1988, Dafydd Elis Thomas incensed many nationalists by comparing the poet R S Thomas (a supporter of the arson campaign) to the French fascist, Jean-Marie Le Pen.[40] This statement, for some, was the most foolish of a number made by Elis Thomas, and Gwynfor was evidently exasperated by his constant attacks on the arsonists. Gwynfor had already crossed swords with him in private over his reluctance to call himself a nationalist, rebuking him in plain language:

> What is it in Welsh nationalism that you reject so totally that you are unwilling to use the word? I am a nationalist. I had a hand in building a nationalist party of nationalists... What are the great differences between us that lead you to reject nationalism as I and Plaid have understood it? Is it our attitude to class? I see class as an important reality in our society, but I believe that nationhood is more important than society.[41]

This was an early salvo at the beginning of what were to be uncertain months for the Elis Thomas Presidency. At the time, Elis Thomas was attempting to move his party into the Welsh political mainstream, arguing that the only way to put home rule on the agenda was to reject nationalism. A central plank of this agenda was to launch an assault on Meibion Glyndŵr and their shadowy allies such as the Covenanters. For Gwynfor, however, this was a step too far and in October 1988, he wrote to Elis Thomas to remind him of the seriousness of the situation, telling him that 'swamping', contrary to what the Plaid Cymru President claimed, was a fact.[42] But a far more revealing letter was the one Gwynfor sent to Elis Thomas in December 1988. In this letter, written at a time of anxiety over the threat to Welshness in Pencarreg, Gwynfor comes dangerously close to supporting Meibion Glyndŵr, if not their methods:

> You said that the Welsh who are responsible are 'racists concerned with the purity of the nation', and you compare them to the National Front. May I disagree totally? I doubt whether there is anyone in public life, apart from Elwyn Jones [the Conservatives' agent] who agrees that they are 'racists'... Although I condemn their methods, as I condemn all violence, I believe their motives are the same as my own and those of the people of Estonia and the people of the Lake District in opposing mass immigration that denies local communities... Who are the racists? Here in Dyfed, there is not one rural primary school I know of where the Welsh are in a majority. There was not a single English child three years ago at the school in Llanfihangel ar Arth, where Ffred and Meinir send their children; today the English children are the majority... There is not one community left in Dyfed where 80 per cent or more of the people are Welsh-speaking – the necessary figure, sociologists say, to protect Welsh as the main community language to all intents and purposes; there are only three or four communities over 70 per cent... In the balance is the life of a nation. This is what motivates the arsonists, not racism. They want to keep the nation alive, not keep it pure, however perverted their methods.[43]

But for all his unease, Gwynfor did not dare criticize Dafydd Elis Thomas publicly. He knew full well that to do so would split Plaid Cymru irreparably during 1988–89. When he received letters from Dafydd Wigley that spoke of 'massive discontent in Plaid's ranks in Gwynedd', he was fully aware of the implications.[44] Quite simply, there was no need for him to fan the flames.

Throughout the storm created by the issue of migration into Wales, Gwynfor stood by Plaid Cymru, if not by the controversial Presidency of Elis Thomas. He seized every opportunity to evangelize in print. In March 1989, he published his millionth word in his eleventh book, *Pe Bai Cymru'n Rhydd*.[45] Within two years he published another, *Fighting for Wales,* and if any theme unites these volumes, it is the hope that flows from the growth of Europe. For Gwynfor, as for many nationalists, the evolution of Europe in the early 'nineties was a solution to the age-old dilemma about the status of a free Wales. There was now a sanctuary for the smaller nations. With the Soviet Union now breaking up, he sensed that the raison d'être of the British state had been destroyed, leaving it as 'an imperial Victorian relic'.[46]

Dafydd Wigley's return to the Presidency in October 1991 was a further stabilizing force for Welsh nationalism. It brought with it too something of the old Gwynforian pragmatism and spirit of conciliation in the interests of power. A year later, following Cynog Dafis's victory in the 1992 general election, Plaid Cymru had four MPs – its largest number ever. By then, Gwynfor was 80 and ready to admit that the 'loads were being shed' from his shoulders, even though he continued to travel about 15,000 miles a year as the party's honorary President.[47] His level of activity lessened between 1992 and 1997, which were to prove among the most significant years ever for Welsh nationalism. They witnessed the devolutionary wing of the Wales Labour Party taking the initiative under Ron Davies, the opposition spokesman on Wales. As John Major's Conservative government fell apart, it became obvious that Labour would come to power and that they would, despite internal dissent, introduce a Welsh Assembly. Even though it was Labour that carried the plan through to fruition, these developments confirmed Gwynfor's rather one-sided take on Welsh history. Wales, he sensed, had come back from the dead, thanks to 'Plaid'.[48]

The climax of his career was seeing a Yes vote in the second devolution referendum in September 1997. For Gwynfor, the vote vindicated not only everything he stood for but also his personal tactics; here was irrefutable proof that Wales could gain something through parliamentary means. Although the majority in favour of a Yes vote was tiny, the fact that Carmarthenshire was the last to declare on that dramatic night served to enhance the role the county (and he personally) had played as redeemer of the nation. Although the comparison was simplistic, some commentators could not resist drawing attention to the political symmetry between 1997 and 1966. On the following day, television crews poured into Pencarreg to hear the old man's views on what he considered the most important night in Welsh history.[49] For Gwynfor, the significance of the vote was straightforward: the Assembly, he told the leading academic, Bobi Jones, was 'sufficient to safeguard the life of the nation'.[50] Some days later, at Plaid

Cymru's annual conference, Gwynfor was hailed as the man who had achieved the greatest administrative revolution in the entire history of Wales. When 17 Plaid Cymru members were elected to the first Assembly in 1999, Gwynfor saw a bright dawn ahead. It became the major theme of the book he published a year later, *The Fight for Welsh Freedom*. As a new millennium opened, he took pride in the fact that the people of Wales now lived in an 'unusually hopeful period'.[51]

Basically, Gwynfor believed that everyone had his or her 'purpose' on earth and that his own 'purpose', ever since his conversion, was to save Wales. With the nation now safe and his body in swift decline, he concluded that his own earthly purpose was at an end. Although he believed in eternal life, he began to read books on spiritual matters, giving his son, Dafydd, the impression that he was preparing to meet his God. Gwynfor attended the National Eisteddfod in Llanelli in 2000 to receive a 'Wales and the World' award. It would be his last public appearance. Despite the cheers and applause, the wheelchair that had carried him there that day was a clear symbol to all that osteoporosis was destroying his fragile bones.

In March 2001, he took to his bed and remained there for the next four years. Even then, there were certain things he could still do. He attempted to lessen the effects of a row caused by the controversial comments of the then Plaid Cymru councillor, Seimon Glyn, on inward migration.[52] His aim was to save the fragile Presidency of Ieuan Wyn Jones in the new devolved Wales. He also continued his quest to create nationalists, particularly through the book that occupied him intermittently during these years, *Cymru o Hud*.[53] By 2001, he was also suffering from leukaemia but never complained, grateful throughout for the tender care of his nurses and children. Rhiannon received the same care and, during these last years, Talar Wen resembled a nursing home with Gwynfor and Rhiannon increasingly confined to their beds. They continued, however, to maintain their relationship with touching dignity. As often as not, illness prevented them from seeing each other for more than five minutes or so a day, but they used those moments to hold hands and share a kiss. Gwynfor also suffered from deafness, but still took an interest in the wider world, wanting to know about the latest political news from Cardiff Bay. A highlight of his week was David Frost's politics programme on a Sunday. He also watched S4C despite his mild private disappointment with what the channel had achieved.[54] Very occasionally, he also gave interviews. He used his very last one, in November 2004, to launch a scathing attack on Tony Blair and his decision to go to war against Iraq.[55] The interviewer, Martin Shipton, found the experience of meeting the frail Gwynfor for the first time not dissimilar to meeting a visionary.[56]

As 2004 ended, Gwynfor and Rhiannon suffered a steep decline in health. She spent a long period in hospital, causing Gwynfor deep distress. The more he thought of his own personal situation, the more Gwynfor remembered Saunders Lewis's words to him on his own deathbed, that one can live too long. About a fortnight before the end, Gwynfor sensed that time was short: 'I'm ready to go,' he told his carers. On 9 April, he said the same thing to his son, Dafydd: 'I'm dying.' During the following days, he was tortured by sharp pains in his left leg – pains that made the simple act of moving a few inches an agony. Despite this, he remained as content as ever with the idea that he had no reason to stay alive. Days later, he caught pneumonia and gave up eating. Then, in the early hours of Thursday 21 April 2005, he was heard shouting: 'I'm coming, I'm coming.' It is hard to know whom he was addressing, but Gwynfor had nearly reached journey's end. The doctor called at about eleven that morning but there was little he could do. Gwynfor lapsed into a deep sleep and died, an hour later, in the arms of his son, Guto.[57] He was 92. He left a thousand pounds to Plaid Cymru and the rest to Rhiannon. Having lived for so long on a paltry pension, he had precious little to give. However, the real legacy was enormous. That legacy was, and is, modern Wales.

Chapter 14

WHAT REMAINS: THE LEGACY

GWYNFOR'S FUNERAL SIX DAYS LATER on 27 April was utterly in keeping with the man himself; a public ceremony with no barrier between the private and the political. From the pallbearers to those who paid tribute at Seion chapel, Aberystwyth, there could not have been a more political occasion. This funeral, the closest Wales has ever seen to a state occasion since the burial of Lloyd George, was Gwynfor's final great act. Indeed, it was considered so important that S4C broadcast it live. With a general election imminent, many within Plaid hoped the occasion would 'raise the spirits', to quote one of Gwynfor's favourite phrases. The hearse left for Aberystwyth crematorium to cheers of acclaim and a flood of tears. Gwynfor's time on earth had ended. But for those who were there, Gwynfor would live on, albeit as an icon. For Gwynfor, however, there was one last journey: to the Celtic hillfort of Garn Goch, in the Carmarthenshire uplands, where he had asked for his ashes to be scattered. Appropriately enough, he wanted to return to the earth and close the circle because it was there, grounded in Welsh soil, that his story had begun.

Gwynfor's nationalism can be interpreted as an emotional response to the cultural crisis in Europe after 1918. Even before the First World War, European intellectuals found modernism repulsive and regarded its features – crowds, science, urbanization and industrialism – as a sickness. The fashionable term for this social malaise in France at the time was *dégénérescence*.[1] In Wales, the death of Welsh and Welshness were taken to be further symptoms of the modern disease. The events of 1914–18 hastened the perception of decline. In Germany, Oswald Spengler, one of the period's leading intellectuals, argued that civilization itself was rotten. R H Tawney, T S Eliot and others like them embraced similar views in Britain and, as the crisis deepened, thousands of young people began to reconsider how they could defend identity against the modern and the materialistic.[2] Some embraced fascism; others, like Gandhi, Saunders Lewis and De Valera cherished the idea of nationhood. They saw that only in the nation could they seek shelter from the storm and shade from the heat; this is how and why this generation began to dream of dismantling the British Empire.[3] Only with its demise, they believed, could nations and individuals live full lives. It was the only way, quite simply, that they and their economic class, the middle class, could cope with modernity.

The dream of Saunders Lewis and the nationalists who supported him was absurd. In 1918, the British Empire governed twenty per cent of the earth's territory. Britishness, its intellectual foundation, had never been more secure – in spite of the Easter Sunday Rising in Dublin two years before. But the modernist crisis proved too much for Britishness, creating an intellectual vacuum for the more daring ideology of nationalism. Because of this, patriotism metamorphosed into nationalism, and a new generation turned from the consensus politics of the 'little piggers', as the *Western Mail* put it, to the politics of the 'whole hoggers'.[4] Indeed, as the 'twenties galloped towards the disastrous 'thirties, the need for emotional salvation grew ever stronger. For a sensitive child like Gwynfor, patriotism had a particular fascination. Even so, like Gandhi and Saunders Lewis, Gwynfor was a hybrid, a nationalist of the diaspora.[5] In Barry, he was caught between two worlds, English-speaking and Welsh-speaking, modern and pre-modern; and this explains his conversion. It was fed, too, by his melodramatic instinct but, when he crossed the divide, all doubt vanished and he came to see the world in two colours: black and white. It was a simple, romantic vision, but there was nothing sentimental about it; it had the strength of steel. It was the faith of the saved, not unlike a Marxist faith, and it sustained him.

Gwynfor was besotted by Saunders Lewis's dream of a Welsh-speaking, Christian Wales, even though Gwynfor never sought to define precisely what such a Wales might mean. Indeed, it would be fair to say that he was a fairly shallow thinker despite his unsparing efforts to communicate with the Welsh. During the 'forties and 'fifties, his most important period as a public figure, he never offered any real analysis of the Welsh economy or society. There are huge gaps in subjects as diverse as coal, national insurance and housing. South Wales was a complete mystery to him and he confined his core message to the Welsh-speaking, Liberal north and west. It was only with the arrival of Dafydd Wigley and Phil Williams at the end of the 'sixties that Plaid Cymru managed to bury D

J Davies's ideas on co-operatism. Gwynfor's Christianity is a similarly grey area. He never defined his relationship with his Christ and his God. Rather, he spoke in slogans and offered a quite superficial idea of where he, and Wales, stood in the divine plan. The ideology he attempted to bequeath to his party, radicalism, was similarly confused, to say the least. He knew the type of people he represented – the literate, cultured, eisteddfod-loving men and women of Welsh-speaking Wales. He knew, too, what radicalism was not. Above all, he wanted a radicalism which would ensure that workers elsewhere in Wales would not become like the proletariat in the south – a lost territory that he tended to regard as some Welsh Ulster. Beyond that, he had no conception of what radicalism implied.

That said, and for all his faults, Gwynfor is as important as Saunders Lewis in the intellectual development of Plaid Cymru. As he crossed the cultural boundary from Barry to Llangadog, he did not surrender his upbringing entirely, since he retained some of the most important features of his family's Liberalism and the politics of Cymru Fydd. These included the belief that Westminster could bring something to Wales. Other features were gradualism and restraint. Another salient element in the liberal project was international co-operation, and Gwynfor used pacifism to transform Plaid Cymru. He made it a pacifist party, ensuring that neither Plaid Cymru nor Welsh nationalism (with some rare exceptions) would ever employ violence. Gwynfor's pacifism meant that Plaid Cymru would be forever conscious of its international obligations in the twentieth century, the most violent century in human history. But pacifism had more enduring consequences for Wales too. As the idea of revolt was laid to rest, Plaid Cymru had to tread the constitutional path and return, in part, to the days of Cymru Fydd. It was Gwynfor who achieved this (despite the strange episode which conceived S4C) and it was he who ensured a reconciliation between the two major strands of Welsh nationalism. It meant bringing together the ardent patriotism of Emrys ap Iwan and the pragmatism of O M Edwards. Gwynfor was the ultimate embodiment of the new ideology, and his pragmatism led directly to him winning Carmarthen in 1966. The real significance of Carmarthen was that, from then on, Plaid Cymru would live through the electoral system, not through the sacrifice of its own President.

In many ways, Gwynfor betrayed the nationalism of Saunders Lewis but it was a necessary betrayal, as the instinct of most Welsh-speakers was to compromise with Britishness. Nevertheless, the success in Carmarthen in 1966, and in all the other seats won afterwards would not have been possible had it not been for Gwynfor's willingness to persuade a proportion of Welsh people like these. Gwynfor realized that politics is a dialogue between leaders and the public – an utterly alien concept to Saunders Lewis. Similarly, Gwynfor's pragmatism did not mean that his diluted brand of nationalism was any less effective. For one thing, it was Gwynfor who ensured that Plaid Cymru would survive – a far harder task than creating a party. Political history is littered with the corpses of short-lived movements and parties that rose and fell. Far rarer are those that develop into a credible force. Gwynfor won his share of heroism by travelling all those miles, night after night, week after week, to convince the public of his vision for Wales. Although just 11 per cent – at most – ever voted for Plaid Cymru during Gwynfor's Presidency, the party's influence was immeasurably greater than a mere percentage for it was the only party that gave continuous expression to Welshness. By degrees, he managed to convince the Conservative and Labour parties that they had no choice but to devolve power. In this way, gradually and respectfully, the process of creating a Welsh state began. Gwynfor's influence is also just as important in Welsh intellectual history. Indeed, no one did more than he did to ensure that nationalism would be part of Welsh political discourse, and that the Welsh mind could articulate a real sense of otherness within the British isles. No doubt, as Dafydd Glyn Jones has said, the burning of Penyberth was a revolution, but Gwynfor's velvet revolution was far more important.[6] This revolution aimed at changing the structure of Welsh identity, and was aimed at ordinary people, in chapel vestries and jumble sales. By the end of the sixties, thousands of Welsh men and women had come to believe that it was their duty to put Wales first.

And there is more. It was Gwynfor who created the 'national movement' – that loose, ecumenical gathering which sought to ensure that people of all parties did 'the right thing for Wales'. Over the decades, this amorphous movement managed to make swathes of public life in Wales more consciously Welsh in character. Gwynfor was also the founding father of the Parliament for Wales Campaign – the organization that placed devolution on the agenda for the first time in forty years. There is now a lasting memorial to that organization in Cardiff Bay, among the fashionable bars and restaurants. It is the Assembly, the unmistakable symbol, for better or worse, of the desire of people in Wales to live as a democratic nation. The contribution is undoubtedly immense despite the fact that Plaid Cymru suffered because Gwynfor allied his party with the concept of the national movement. At times, Plaid Cymru did not really know what it was: a pressure group or a party. Perhaps the fairest assessment is that the national movement carried the day to the detriment of the party.

Gwynfor's conversion was a lasting one, but even so he did suffer a crisis of faith. He lacked confidence in his own abilities; more than once he threatened to leave the Presidency of his party. At times, this led to clinical depression and hospital treatment. He was shaken too by the indifference of the Welsh people – from those who betrayed the Epynt farmers to the shopkeepers in Bala who supported the drowning of Capel Celyn. And although his conversion was genuine, Gwynfor was no saint. He could be short-tempered, he could be dogmatic, he could be infuriatingly obdurate. As an administrator, he lacked spark and he surrounded himself with too many sycophants. These were the men who created the Gwynfor cult, heaping words of praise rather than offering sound political advice. But Gwynfor with his quasi-messianic perception of himself quite enjoyed that. He undoubtedly damaged his party by remaining its President for far too long, but Gwynfor was, after all, a politician, albeit one who had come to politics in the wake of a conversion.

Gwynfor wanted to return to Garn Goch, to the soil, the land of Wales where his politics had taken root. Nevertheless, as his ashes blow in the wind, his legacy survives. By 'saving' himself from the brutality of Barry, Gwynfor Evans changed the course of Welsh history. From Queensferry to Chepstow, there is a line: to the west of that line the Welsh live, but they were not born Welsh. They are Welsh because they have chosen to be Welsh. True, there are many in the other parties who have played their part, but no one did more than Gwynfor in the twentieth century. It is not the Welsh-speaking Christian Wales that Gwynfor dreamed of, but it is still Wales. Wales, the nation he loved with such passion, has survived, despite it all.

NOTES

CHAPTER 1 – Conversion 1912–1931

[1] 'Barry Since 1939', Peter Stead in *Barry, The Centenary Book*, ed. Donald Moore (Cardiff, 1985), p. 458.
[2] Dai Smith, 'Barry: A Town Out Of Time', *Morgannwg* XXIX, pp. 80–6.
[3] T Robin Chapman, 'Y Llif Wynebau Llwyd: Cymru Ddiwydiannol a'r Adwaith Moesol yn Hanner Cyntaf yr Ugeinfed Garif', *Llên Cymru*, 26, 2003.
[4] Gwynfor Evans, *Western Mail*, Newport Eisteddfod Supplement, August 1988.
[5] 'Ambition, Vice and Virtue: Social Life, 1884–1914', Brian C Luxton in *Barry, The Centenary Book*, op. cit., pp. 271–333.
[6] Elegy by Habacus (Josiah Davies) for James Evans n.d.. I am extremely grateful to Mrs Llywela Evans for showing me this document in addition to many other kindnesses.
[7] J Camwy Evans, *Hanes Eglwys Lloyd Street* (Llanelli, 1937).
[8] *Barry Dock News*, 2 June 1899.
[9] ibid., 2 June 1899.
[10] K O Morgan, *Wales in British Politics, 1868–1922* (fourth edition, Cardiff, 1991), pp.181–98.
[11] Beriah Gwyndaf Evans in *'Yspryd yr Oes'*, volume 2, Number 5, 1905; and *'Cenad Hedd'*, Number 25, 1905 and *'Album Aberhonddu'*, 1888, ed. T Stephens, pp. 306–7.
[12] *Barry Dock News*, 14 August 1905. See also *Y Tyst*, 2 August 1905.
[13] *Barry Herald*, 14 December 1916.
[14] ibid., 14 July 1909.
[15] *Barry Dock News*, 17 November 1905.
[16] *South Wales Spectator*, volume 7, number 51, June 1964.
[17] *Barry Dock News*, 14 January 1910.
[18] Author's interview with Alcwyn Evans.
[19] *Barry and District News*, 22 July 1932.
[20] *South Wales Echo*, 9 February 2005.
[21] Author's interview with Llywela Evans.
[22] Annual Report of Capel Tabernacl y Barri, 1915.
[23] *Barry Herald*, 22 December 1914.
[24] Gwynfor Evans, *Bywyd Cymro* (Caernarfon, 1982), p. 25.
[25] ESE 2/2/1, Gladstone Road School log 1.1.1917, Glamorgan Archives.
[26] PRO ED 21/46358.
[27] Author's interview with Ceridwen Pritchard.
[28] Annual Report of Capel Tabernacl y Barri, 1911.
[29] *Barry Herald*, 7 March 1913.
[30] Pennar Davies, *Gwynfor Evans* (Swansea, 1976), p.14.
[31] *Barry Herald*, 22 February 1924.

[32] ibid., 28 March 1919; ibid., 19 March 1920.
[33] W J Gruffydd, *Owen Morgan Edwards, Cofiant* (Aberystwyth, 1938), p. 1.
[34] *Barry Dock News*, 15 November 1918.
[35] Author's interview with Ceridwen Pritchard.
[36] *Barry and District News*, 2 April 1924.
[37] *Barry Herald*, 1 February 1924; ibid., 4 July 1924.
[38] *The Barrian*, Number 11, 1924.
[39] 'Gogoniant y Werin Gymraeg', Gwynfor Evans, undated newspaper cutting. Gwynfor Evans papers, NLW, uncatalogued.
[40] *The Barrian*, Number 17, 1931.
[41] *Gwynfor yn Bedwar Ugain Oed*, interview with Sulwyn Thomas, BBC Wales, 1992.
[42] Gwynfor Evans, *Bywyd Cymro*, op. cit., p. 37.
[43] Gwynfor Evans to Griffith John Williams, 7.9.1948 (Griffith John Williams papers, NLW).
[44] T Robin Chapman, *Meibion Afradlon a Chymeriadau Eraill*, (Cardiff, 2004), p. 58.
[45] *Western Mail*, 1 March 1929.
[46] Gwynfor Evans, *Wales Can Win* (Llandybïe, 1973), p. 138.
[47] Heini Gruffudd, *Achub Cymru* (Tal-y-bont, 1983), p. 22
[48] *Barry and District News*, 30 September 1938.
[49] Author's interview with Gwynfor Evans.
[50] *The Welsh Nation*, June 1984.
[51] During his first period in the Commons, he would quote from the works of 'social psychiatrists' to prove his argument that a lack of roots causes emotional damage and uncertainty from cradle to grave; see Gwynfor Evans in *Efrydiau Athronyddol*, 31 (1968).
[52] *The Barrian*, Number 18, 1932.
[53] B1/46(3), League of Nations Union Archive, NLW.
[54] *The Barrian*, Number 17, 1931.

CHAPTER 2 – Mission 1931–39

[1] Gwynfor Evans in *Dan Sylw*, ed. Gwyn Erfyl (Llandybïe, 1971), p. 14.
[2] E L Ellis, *The University of Wales, Aberystwyth, 1872–1972* (Cardiff, 1972), pp. 249–51.
[3] *The Welsh Gazette*, 15 October 1931.
[4] Gwynfor Evans, *Bywyd Cymro*, op. cit., p. 39.
[5] *Y Cymro*, 16 November 1976.
[6] *Y Faner*, 23 September 1977.
[7] Pennar Davies, *Gwynfor Evans*, op. cit., p. 18.
[8] *Baner ac Amserau Cymru*, 24 April 1958.
[9] Gwynfor Evans, *Bywyd Cymro*, op. cit., p. 43.
[10] Quoted in D Tecwyn Lloyd, *John Saunders Lewis, Y Gyfrol Gyntaf* (Denbigh, 1988), p. 247.
[11] E L Ellis, *The University of Wales, Aberystwyth, 1872–1972*, op. cit., p. 252.
[12] *The Dragon*, Michaelmas Term, 1932.
[13] *The Welsh Gazette*, 10 November 1932.
[14] ibid., 9 March 1933.
[15] Quoted in Martin Ceadel, *Pacifism in Britain, 1914–1945: The Defining of a Faith* (Oxford, 1980), p. 174.
[16] *The Cambrian News*, 17 November 1933.
[17] D J Davies, *The Economics of Welsh Self-Government* (Caernarfon, 1931).

[18] *Y Ddraig Goch*, March 1934.
[19] Richard Wyn Jones, 'Syniadaeth wleidyddol Gwynfor Evans', *Efrydiau Athronyddol* 63 (2000), pp. 44–63. See also John Davies, *The Green and the Red: Nationalism and Ideology in 20th Century Wales* (Aberystwyth, 1980), p. 30.
[20] *Y Cymro*, 3 November 1934. See also *Y Ddraig Goch*, November 1934.
[21] *Western Mail*, 1 March 1934.
[22] *Y Ddraig Goch*, July 1934.
[23] Cassie Davies, *Hwb i'r Galon* (Swansea, 1973), p. 80.
[24] *Y Ddraig Goch*, March 1927.
[25] *Y Cymro*, 18 August 1934.
[26] Gwynfor Evans to J E Jones, 14.8.1934 (PCP B 84).
[27] *Yr Aradr*, 1993–4, p. 2.
[28] *Isis*, 14 November 1934.
[29] *The Barrian*, 1 May 1935.
[30] ibid.
[31] Harri Williams to J E Jones, 18.2.1935 (PCP B 94).
[32] *Y Cymro*, 26 October 1935.
[33] Mss Welsh d.1/17 and d.1/18, Bodleian Library, University of Oxford.
[34] *Y Brython*, 6 June 1935.
[35] *Western Mail*, 26 August 1935.
[36] *Yr Herald Cymraeg*, 27 April 1936.
[37] *Y Tyst*, 19 March 1936.
[38] *Daily Despatch*, 25 May 1936.
[39] *Isis*, 26 February 1936.
[40] Gwynfor Evans, *Bywyd Cymro*, op. cit., pp. 49–50.
[41] Pennar Davies, *Gwynfor Evans*, op. cit., p. 22.
[42] Author's interview with Gwynfor Evans.
[43] Gwynfor Evans to J E Jones n.d. (PCP B 145).
[44] *Barry and District News*, 3 July 1936.
[45] Dafydd Jenkins, *Tân yn Llŷn* (Caernarfon, 1975) p. 71.
[46] Gwynfor Evans to J E Jones, 9.9.1936 (PCP B 152).
[47] *Y Ddraig Goch*, October 1936. The Bridgend factory was part of the Woolwich Arsenal that was intended to be moved there. The announcement brought 'unbounded joy' to the town's traders. See *Western Mail*, 25 and 27 May 1936.
[48] *Y Ddraig Goch*, January 1937.
[49] D Hywel Davies, *The Welsh Nationalist Party 1925–1945* (Cardiff, 1983) pp. 163–4.
[50] Gwynfor Evans to J E Jones, 26.4.1937 (PCP B 177).
[51] *Barry Herald*, 14 May 1937.
[52] *Western Mail*, 28 April 1937.
[53] Gwynfor Evans to J E Jones, 19.5.1937 (PCP B 179).
[54] D Hywel Davies, *The Welsh Nationalist Party 1925–1945*, op. cit., pp. 73–9.
[55] Gwynfor Evans, *Y Ddraig Goch*, July 1937.
[56] Gwynfor Evans to J E Jones, 25.5.1937 (PCP B 181).
[57] Gwynfor Evans to J E Jones, n.d. (PCP B 182).
[58] *Yr Herald Cymraeg*, 1 February 1937.
[59] See A 20 and A 32 (PCP).
[60] Marion Löffler, 'Cyfraniad y Chwyldroadau Tawel' in Geraint H Jenkins and Mari A Williams (eds.), *'Eu Hiaith a Gadwant? Y Gymraeg yn yr Ugeinfed Ganrif'* (Cardiff, 2000) pp.

96–9.
[61] *Barry Herald*, 1 April 1938.
[62] Gwynfor Evans, *Bywyd Cymro*, op. cit., p. 52.
[63] *Y Ddraig Goch*, February 1982.
[64] Gwynfor Evans, *Bywyd Cymro*, op. cit., pp. 54–55.
[65] *Seren Cymru*, 23 May 1941.
[66] *Y Tyst*, 21 July 1938.
[67] A year before this, in July 1937, the Union passed a resolution calling for special aid to be given to depressed areas in south Wales. See *Western Mail*, 7 July 1937.
[68] *Western Mail*, 13 July 1938.
[69] Private papers held by Alcwyn Evans.
[70] *Western Mail*, 13 September 1937.
[71] *Y Brython*, 24 June 1937.
[72] *Western Mail*, 18 June 1937.
[73] *Baner ac Amserau Cymru*, 23 November 1937.
[74] *Y Cymro*, 16 July 1938.
[75] Gwynfor Evans to J E Jones, 13.5.1938 (PCP B 221).
[76] *Y Ddraig Goch*, September 1938.
[77] *Peace News*, 20 August 1938.
[78] *Y Brython*, 24 November 1938.
[79] *Peace News*, 3 September 1938.
[80] Gwynfor Evans, *Bywyd Cymro*, op. cit., p. 57.
[81] *South Wales Echo*, 1 October 1938.
[82] *Y Cymro*, 1 October 1938.
[83] *Y Brython*, 9 February 1938.
[84] *Y Cymro*, 28 May 1938.
[85] Mark Gilbert, 'Pacifist Attitudes to Nazi Germany, 1936–1945', *Journal of Contemporary History*, 27 (1992), pp. 493–511.
[86] *Yr Herald Cymraeg*, 9 January 1939.
[87] Gwynfor Evans to J E Jones n.d. (PCP B 249).
[88] Gwynfor Evans to J E Jones, 5.4.1939 (PCP B 287).
[89] J E Jones to Gwynfor Evans, 8.5.1939, ibid.
[90] Saunders Lewis to J E Jones 8.5.1939, ibid. See also Saunders Lewis's statement in *Liverpool Daily Post*, 1 May 1939.
[91] *Cymru'n Niwtral* (PCP B 273).
[92] A O H Jarman, 'Y Blaid a'r Ail Ryfel Byd' in John Davies (ed.), *Cymru'n Deffro, Hanes y Blaid Genedlaethol, 1925–1975* (Tal-y-bont, 1981), p. 77.
[93] *The Welsh Nationalist*, August 1939.
[94] Gwynfor Evans, *Bywyd Cymro*, op. cit., p. 61. See also NLW, Ms 22316 D, '*Y Tyrau*', Dan Thomas, pp. 190–1. Dan Thomas is profiled in *Y Ddraig Goch*, October 1936.
[95] Gwynfor Evans to J E Jones, n.d. (PCP B 273).
[96] Hugh Wynne Griffith in *Pathway*, December 1939.
[97] *Baner ac Amserau Cymru*, 30 August 1939. He made the appeal in a letter co-written with George M Ll Davies and Richard Bishop.

CHAPTER 3 – The Great Storm 1939–45

[1] *Y Cymro*, 9 September 1939.
[2] *South Wales Echo*, 4 September 1939.
[3] J E Jones, *Tros Gymru, J E a'r Blaid* (Swansea, 1970), p. 216.
[4] A O H Jarman, *Cymru'n Deffro – Hanes y Blaid Genedlaethol, 1925–1975*, op. cit., p. 74.
[5] Gwynfor Evans to J E Jones, 3.9.1939 (PCP B 294).
[6] Gwynfor Evans to W T (Pennar) Davies, 8.9.1939, (NLW Ms 20784D).
[7] *Amman Valley Chronicle*, 7 September 1939.
[8] *Baner ac Amserau Cymru*, 13 September 1939.
[9] ibid., 20 September 1939.
[10] Saunders Lewis's attitude is quoted in J E Jones to J E Daniel, 12.9.1939 (PCP B 294).
[11] *Manchester Guardian*, 8 September 1939.
[12] Gwynfor Evans to J E Jones, 3.9.1939 (PCP B 294).
[13] *Y Ddraig Goch*, September 1939.
[14] *Y Cymro*, 16 September 1939.
[15] Gwynfor Evans to J E Jones, 15.10.1939 (PCP B 262).
[16] Author's interview with Professor Dafydd Jenkins.
[17] *Barry and District News*, 24 November 1939.
[18] Griff Jones to J E Jones, 17.9.1939 (PCP B 274); see also the minutes of the Welsh Pacifists, Caerphilly branch, private ownership. I wish to thank Vaughan Roderick for allowing me to see these papers.
[19] Interview between Gwynfor Evans and Colin Edwards (Colin Edwards papers, NLW).
[20] *Baner ac Amserau Cymru*, 1 November 1939.
[21] ibid., 25 October 1939.
[22] Saunders Lewis to J E Jones, 21.11.1939 (PCP B 266).
[23] Gwynfor Evans to Pennar Davies, 10.1.1941 (Pennar Davies papers, NLW).
[24] *Baner ac Amserau Cymru*, 27 August 1976.
[25] Gwynfor Evans in *Munudau Cyfiawnder, Cyfrol Goffa Gareth Thomas* (Swansea, 1992), pp. 60–71.
[26] Author's interview with Gareth Howe.
[27] *South Wales Evening Post*, 17 November 1939.
[28] *Y Llenor*, XVIII, number 3, October 1939.
[29] *The Welsh Review*, November 1939.
[30] *South Wales Evening Post*, 10 September 1939.
[31] ibid., 23 September 1939.
[32] *Y Cymro*, 9 December 1939.
[33] Gwynfor Evans to J E Jones, 22.2.1940 (PCP B 303).
[34] Rev. J P Davies to Gwynfor Evans, 8.1.1940 (GE, 1973, D, NLW).
[35] *Y Cymro*, 20 January 1940.
[36] *Baner ac Amserau Cymru*, 31 January 1940.
[37] *Y Llenor*, XX, number 4, Winter 1941.
[38] See note dated 5.3.1940 (Undeb Cymru Fydd papers, Box 6, NLW).
[39] *Y Cymro*, 16 March 1940.
[40] *Baner ac Amserau Cymru*, 20 March 1940.
[41] ibid., 14 April 1940.
[42] Gwynfor Evans to T I Ellis, 15.3.1940 (Undeb Cymru Fydd papers, Box 5, NLW).
[43] Saunders Lewis to J E Jones, 29.3.1940 (PCP B 313).
[44] Gwynfor Evans to T I Ellis, 2.4.1940 (Undeb Cymru Fydd papers, Box 6, NLW).

[45] William Williams to T I Ellis, 2.4.1940, ibid.
[46] William Williams to T I Ellis, 3.4.1940, ibid.
[47] Gwynfor Evans to T I Ellis, 1.5.1940, ibid.
[48] See File 88, 4.4.1940 (Undeb Cymru Fydd papers, NLW). The members were Saunders Lewis, Moses Gruffydd, Dr Gwenan Jones and Sir Ifan ab Owen Edwards.
[49] *Brecon and Radnor Express and County Times,* 2 May 1940.
[50] Ann Gruffydd Rhys, 'Colli Epynt', *Barn*, 366/367, 1993.
[51] I am grateful to Emyr Price, producer of the four programmes under the general title *'Gwynfor',* broadcast by HTV Wales in 1990, for this information.
[52] Gwynfor Evans to J E Jones, 24.4.1940 (PCP B 314).
[53] Gwynfor Evans to J E Jones, 15.5.1940, ibid.
[54] PRO KV 4/122, Report on the 'Celtic Nationalist Movement'.
[55] *Western Mail*, 7 May 1940.
[56] *South Wales Evening Post*, 6 June 1940.
[57] ibid., 8 June 1940.
[58] ibid., 26 June 1940.
[59] *Baner ac Amserau Cymru,* 5 June 1940.
[60] ibid., 29 May 1940.
[61] Gwynfor Evans, *Bywyd Cymro*, op. cit., p. 88.
[62] Idris Evans to Gwynfor Evans, 14.5.1940 (GE, 1973, E, NLW).
[63] Gwynfor Evans to Pennar Davies, 15.5.1940 (Pennar Davies papers, NLW).
[64] PRO HO 262/4, Report 17.5.1940.
[65] Gwynfor Evans, *Bywyd Cymro*, op. cit., p. 79.
[66] Gwynfor Evans to J E Jones, 23.5.1940. (PCP B 318).
Attitudes like these were quite common among Plaid Cymru's leaders. Saunders Lewis wrote as follows: 'I do not care about the outcome as long as England does not win. I am not eager for it to lose outright and catastrophically, but I am eager for it not to win.' See also Saunders Lewis to D J Williams, 12.12.1940 (D J Williams papers, NLW).
[67] *Y Cymro*, 1 June 1940.
[68] *Y Llenor*, XIX, number 2, Summer 1940.
[69] *Y Cymro*, 15 June 1940.
[70] ibid., 22 June 1940.
[71] *Y Tyst*, 27 June 1940.
[72] Gwynfor Evans to J E Jones, 29.7.1940 (PCP B 325).
[73] Gwynfor Evans to J E Jones, 10.7.1940 (PCP B 322).
[74] *Baner ac Amserau Cymru*, 10 July 1940.
[75] Gwynfor Evans to T I Ellis, 23.7.1940 (Undeb Cymru Fydd papers, A 5, NLW).
[76] *Carmarthen Journal*, 19 July 1940.
[77] *Peace News*, 8 December 1939. The percentage being granted unconditional release by tribunals in the north was far higher – some 55 per cent.
[78] Gwynfor Evans to Pennar Davies, 23.8.1940 (Pennar Davies papers, NLW).
[79] George M Ll Davies to Gwynfor Evans, n.d. (GE, 1973, D, NLW).
[80] *Baner ac Amserau Cymru*, 28 August 1940.
[81] *Y Cymro*, 24 August 1940.
[82] Nancy Richardson to Gwynfor Evans, 10.10.1940 (GE, 1973, R, NLW).
[83] PRO KV 4/123, Regional Summary, 13.11.1941. Gwynfor Evans said that 2,920 had decided to stand as conscientious objectors. See Gwynfor Evans, *Heddychiaeth Gristnogol yng Nghymru* (Llangollen, 1991), p. 25.

[84] The Reverend J P Davies to Gwynfor Evans, 6.9.1940 (GE, 1973, D, NLW).
[85] 'Rob' to Gwynfor Evans, 5.12.1940 (GE, 1973, B, NLW).
[86] George M Ll Davies to Gwynfor Evans, n.d. (GE, 1973, D, NLW).
[87] George M Ll Davies to Gwynfor Evans, n.d., ibid.
[88] 'Rob' to Gwynfor Evans, 11.12.1940 (GE, 1973, B, NLW).
[89] *Y Tyst*, 9 January 1941.
[90] ibid., 26 December 1940.
[91] *Amman Valley Chronicle*, 5 December 1940.
[92] Gwynfor Evans to J E Jones, 7.12.1940 (PCP B 335).
[93] *Amman Valley Chronicle*, 16 January 1941.
[94] *Baner ac Amserau Cymru,* 14 and 21 January 1941.
[95] *Carmarthen Journal,* 13 June 1941.
[96] Gwynfor Evans to J E Jones, 28.1.1941 (PCP B 337).
[97] Gwynfor Evans to J E Jones, 21.2.1941 (PCP B 338).
[98] Rhiannon Prys Evans in *Iancs, Conshis a Spam* (Llandybïe, 2002), p. 76.
[99] *Baner ac Amserau Cymru*, 5 March 1940.
[100] Rhiannon Prys Evans in *Iancs, Conshis a Spam*, op. cit., p. 79.
[101] Gwynfor Evans to T I Ellis, 24.5.1941 (Undeb Cymru Fydd papers, A 22, NLW).
[102] George M. Ll Davies to Gwynfor Evans, 31.1.1941 (GE, 1973, D, NLW).
[103] *Baner ac Amserau Cymru*, 8 October 1941.
[104] *Y Dysgedydd*, April 1945.
[105] Waldo Williams to Gwynfor Evans, 27.7.1941 (GE, 1973, W, NLW).
[106] *Peace News*, 17 October 1941.
[107] ibid., 14 November 1941.
[108] George M Ll Davies to Gwynfor Evans, n.d. (GE, 1973, D, NLW).
[109] *Baner ac Amserau Cymru*, 23 July 1941.
[110] ibid., 20 August 1941.
[111] Gwynfor Evans to Pennar Davies, 18.9.1941 (Pennar Davies papers, NLW).
[112] Gwynfor Evans to J E Jones, 5.10.1941 (PCP B 350).
[113] Gwynfor Evans to T I Ellis, 28.10.1941 (Undeb Cymru Fydd papers, A 22, NLW).
[114] Angus Calder, *The People's War* (London, 2003), p. 298.
[115] *Y Tyst,* 25 December 1941.
[116] *Baner ac Amserau Cymru*, 14 January 1942.
[117] ibid., 28 January 1942.
[118] *Y Tyst*, 22 January 1942.
[119] ibid., 5 February and 12 March 1942.
[120] The passage of the years did nothing to lessen Gwynfor's anger at what Llewelyn Evans did. In his autobiography, he scathingly calls Llewelyn Evans and his brother 'warmongers' who made a sacrifice for Britain in wartime by producing food 'at a profit'. See Gwynfor Evans, *Bywyd Cymro,* op. cit., p. 73.
[121] *South Wales Evening Post*, 2 June 1941.
[122] *Carmarthen Journal*, 6 February 1942.
[123] Gwynfor Evans to J E Jones, 18.2.1942 (PCP B 359).
[124] *Amman Valley Chronicle*, 5 March 1942.
[125] *Baner ac Amserau Cymru*, 4 March 1942.
[126] ibid., 21 January 1942.
[127] *South Wales Evening Post*, 28 February 1942.
[128] Gwynfor Evans to T I Ellis, 2.3.1942 (Undeb Cymru Fydd papers, A 16, NLW).

[129] *Carmarthen Journal,* 29 May 1942.
[130] ibid., 10 July 1942.
[131] *Amman Valley Chronicle*, 11 June 1942.
[132] Gwynfor Evans to Pennar Davies, 17.6.1942 (Pennar Davies papers, NLW).
[133] *The Welsh Nationalist*, June 1942.
[134] *Y Traethodydd*, July 1942.
[135] Gwynfor Evans to Rev Gwilym Davies, 6.7.1942 (Gwilym Davies papers, 3/5, NLW). Cathrin Huws, as she was known under her maiden name, was married to J E Daniel, Plaid Cymru's President, 1939–43.
[136] Gwynfor Evans to T I Ellis, 8.7.1942 (Undeb Cymru Fydd papers, A 21, NLW).
[137] *Y Goleuad*, 22 July 1942.
[138] *Western Mail,* 8 August 1942; *Baner ac Amserau Cymru,* 12 August 1942.
[139] Gwynfor Evans to J E Jones, 24.7.1942 (PCP A 43).
[140] *Y Cymro*, 8 August 1942.
[141] *Baner ac Amserau Cymru*, 23 September 1942.
[142] ibid., 2 December 1942.
[143] ibid., 23 December 1942.
[144] ibid., 30 December 1942.
[145] *Amman Valley Chronicle*, 4 January 1943.
[146] Gwynfor Evans to T I Ellis, 3.1.1943 (Undeb Cymru Fydd papers, A 16, NLW).
[147] Gwynfor Evans to Pennar Davies, 15.1.1943 (Pennar Davies papers, NLW).
[148] Gwynfor Evans to J E Jones, 12.1.1943 (PCP B 381).
[149] Gwynfor Evans to J E Jones, 25.2.1943 (PCP B 388).
[150] Gwynfor Evans to J Dyfnallt Owen, 1.2.1943 (J Dyfnallt Owen papers, NLW).
[151] Gwynfor Evans to J Dyfnallt Owen, 8.2.1943, ibid.
[152] *Y Ddraig Goch*, February 1943.
[153] J E Jones to Gwynfor Evans, 16.2.1943 (GE, 1973, J, NLW).
[154] *Baner ac Amserau Cymru*, 17 March 1943.
[155] Gwynfor Evans to J E Jones, 2.4.1943 (PCP B 401).
[156] Mari A Williams, *A Forgotten Army, The Female Munitions Workers of South Wales, 1939–1945* (Cardiff, 2002), pp. 180–4.
[157] *South Wales Evening Post*, 20 April 1943.
[158] *Baner ac Amserau Cymru,* 23 June 1943; *The Welsh Nationalist,* June 1943.
[159] *Amman Valley Chronicle*, 6 May 1943.
[160] James Griffiths to Gwynfor Evans, 9.6.1943 (GE, 1973, G, NLW).
[161] *South Wales Evening Post*, 24 May 1943.
[162] *Western Mail*, 9 May 1945; *Y Cymro*, 18 May 1945.
[163] J E Jones to Gwynfor Evans, 7.5.1943 (GE, 1973, J, NLW).
[164] Gwynfor Evans to Dr D J and Dr Noëlle Davies, 11.6.1943 (Noëlle Davies papers, NLW).
[165] Gwynfor Evans to J E Jones, 9.6.1943 (PCP B 401).
[166] I am grateful to Professor R Geraint Gruffydd for this information.
[167] Gwynfor Evans to J E Jones, 29.6.1943 (PCP B 402).
[168] Dan Evans to Gwynfor Evans, 2.7.1943 (GE, 1973, E, NLW).
[169] Gwynfor Evans to J E Jones, 4.7.1943 (PCP B 402).
[170] *Baner ac Amserau Cymru*, 10 June 1942.
[171] Author's interview with Gwynfor Evans.
[172] *Y Ddraig Goch*, September 1943.
[173] Abi Williams to J E Jones, 10.9.1943 (PCP M 70).

[174] *Y Cymro*, 7 August 1943.
[175] *Baner ac Amserau Cymru*, 4 August 1943.
[176] Gwynfor Evans to J E Jones, 16.9.1943 (PCP B 407).
[177] Correspondence from T Elwyn Griffiths to the author, 20.3.2003. See also the letter by T Elwyn Griffiths, editor of *Seren y Dwyrain*, in the *Amman Valley Chronicle*, 24 February 1944. In several respects, *Seren y Dwyrain* was an imitation of *Cofion Cymru*, the monthly magazine published between 1941 and 1946 that provided news, stories and entertainment in Welsh for Welsh men and women serving in the forces.
[178] T Elwyn Griffiths, *Seren y Dwyrain* (Y Bala, 1955), p. 27.
[179] ibid., p. 1.
[180] Gwynfor Evans to Pennar Davies, 8.1.1944 (Pennar Davies papers, NLW).
[181] *Y Cymro*, 25 March 1944.
[182] Gwynfor Evans to Pennar Davies, 27.9.1944 (Pennar Davies papers, NLW).
[183] *Baner ac Amserau Cymru,* 12 January 1944.
[184] J E Jones to Gwynfor Evans, 28.1.1944 (GE, 1983, J, NLW).
[185] *Y Ddraig Goch*, January 1944.
[186] Gwynfor Evans to J E Jones, 21.1.1944 (PCP B 425).
[187] *Baner ac Amserau Cymru*, 15 March 1944. Plaid Cymru had been divided on the issue for months but Gwynfor – contrary to J E Jones who wanted to see the office in Aberystwyth – insisted that it should be in Cardiff because of his confidence that 'Cardiff will be the Capital of Wales'. The matter was finally settled in 1946, but the 'shadow' President's determination was doubtless crucial in deciding on Cardiff during 1944. See Gwynfor Evans to J E Jones, 12.6.1944 (PCP B 1326).
[188] Saunders Lewis to D J Williams, 20.4.1944 (D J Williams papers, NLW).
[189] Saunders Lewis to D J Williams, 13.12.1944, ibid.
[190] D J Williams's journal, 20.4.1944, ibid.
[191] Gwynfor Evans to D J Williams, 24.4.1944, ibid.
[192] Gwynfor Evans, *Radio in Wales* (Liverpool, 1944); Gwynfor Evans, *They Cry Wolf – Totalitarianism in Wales and The Way Out* (Caernarfon, 1944).
[193] *Baner ac Amserau Cymru*, 12 July 1944.
[194] ibid.
[195] *Plan Electricity for Wales* (London, 1944).
[196] Author's interview with Dewi Watkin Powell.
[197] Gwynfor Evans to J E Jones, 4.9.1944 (PCP B 1326).
[198] Minutes of Plaid Cymru Executive, New Year 1945 (PCP A 36).
[199] Quoted in Pennar Davies, *Gwynfor Evans*, op. cit., p. 34.
[200] R J Edwards to J E Jones, n.d. (PCP B 438).
[201] J E Jones to Saunders Lewis, 25.10.1944 (PCP B 442).
[202] Marion Eames to Gwynfor Evans, 13.11.1944 (GE, 1983, E, NLW).
[203] *Baner ac Amserau Cymru*, 13 December 1944.
[204] ibid., 20 December 1944.
[205] Donald Port to Gwynfor Evans, 21.12.1944 (GE, 1983, P, NLW).
[206] Donald Port to Gwynfor Evans, n.d., ibid.
[207] Donald Port to Gwynfor Evans, 14.3.1945, ibid.
[208] George M Ll Davies to Gwynfor Evans, n.d. (GE, 1973, D, NLW).
[209] Martin Ceadel, *Semi-Detached Idealists*, (Oxford, 2000), p. 422.
[210] *Baner ac Amserau Cymru*, 3 January 1945.
[211] J E Jones to Gwynfor Evans, 31.12.1944 (GE, 1983, J, NLW).

[212] *Baner ac Amserau Cymru*, 17 January 1945.
[213] Gwynfor Evans to Marion Eames, 15.2.1945 (PCP B 463).
[214] *Y Dydd,* 19 January 1945.
[215] *Baner ac Amserau Cymru*, 24 January 1945.
[216] *Western Mail,* 21 April 1945.
[217] *Baner ac Amserau Cymru*, 28 February 1945.
[218] Wmffra James to J E Jones, n.d. (PCP B 481).
[219] Author's interview with Marion Eames.
[220] Author's interview with Ifor Owen.
[221] *Y Dydd*, 22 June 1945; *Y Seren*, 7 July 1945.
[222] Gwynfor Evans to Marion Eames, 19.7.1945, private ownership. I am grateful to Marion Eames for permission to see this letter.
[223] *Y Cymro*, 3 August 1945.
[224] Gwynfor Evans to J E Jones, n.d. (PCP B 1326).

CHAPTER 4 – Stand Your Ground 1945–51

[1] Author's interview with the Reverend Huw Jones.
[2] Author's interview with Marion Eames.
[3] D J Williams's journal, 22.8.1945 (D J Williams papers, NLW).
[4] *Gwynfor*, HTV Wales, 7 October 1990.
[5] Gwynfor Evans to J E Jones, n.d. (PCP B 1326).
[6] *The Welsh Nationalist*, August 1945.
[7] *Baner ac Amserau Cymru*, 1 August 1945.
[8] *Y Ddraig Goch,* October 1945.
[9] Gwynfor Evans to Pennar Davies, 12.9.1945 (Pennar Davies papers, NLW).
[10] *Wales and Monmouthshire, A Summary of Government Action* (Cd. 6938).
[11] Gwynfor Evans to Noëlle and D J Davies, 28.11.1945 (Dr Noëlle Davies papers, 124/13, NLW).
[12] J E Jones to Gwynfor Evans, 16.12.1945 (PCP B 1326).
[13] *Liverpool Daily Post*, 22 November 1945.
[14] J E Jones to Gwynfor Evans, 17.4.1946 (GE, 1973, J, NLW).
[15] *Baner ac Amserau Cymru*, 12 December 1945.
[16] ibid., 2 January 1946.
[17] *Carmarthen Journal*, 15 March 1946.
[18] Gwynfor Evans, *Bywyd Cymro*, op. cit., p. 113.
[19] *The Times*, 9 April 1946.
[20] *Y Cymro*, 15 March 1946.
[21] *Baner ac Amserau Cymru*, 27 March 1946.
[22] J E Jones to Gwynfor Evans, 27.3.1946 (GE, 1973, J, NLW).
[23] Saunders Lewis to D J Williams, 15.7.1946 (D J Williams papers, NLW).
[24] *Baner ac Amserau Cymru*, 17 April 1946.
[25] Dewi Watkin Powell to J E Jones, 12.5.1946, (PCP B 535).
[26] Gwynfor Evans to J E Jones, 20.1.1946, ibid.
[27] *Baner ac Amserau Cymru,* 6 March 1946.
[28] *Y Byd ar Bedwar,* HTV Cymru, 3 March 1990. I am grateful to Aled Eirug for this reference.
[29] Minutes of Plaid Cymru Executive, n.d. (PCP A 37). See also Dr Noëlle Davies papers, 127/1, NLW.

[30] Interview with Yann Fouéré in *Planet,* 66, 1987, pp. 28–36.
[31] Dr Noëlle Davies to Gwynfor Evans, 13.1.1946 (GE, 1973, D, NLW).
[32] PRO FO 371/67702, 17.4.1947.
[33] ibid., 22.4.1947.
[34] *Baner ac Amserau Cymru*, 12 June 1946.
[35] *Y Cymro*, 31 May 1946.
[36] *The Observer*, 16 June 1946.
[37] *Western Mail*, 2 August 1946.
[38] *Y Cymro*, 9 August 1946.
[39] *Liverpool Daily Post*, 22 August 1946.
[40] *The Observer*, 1 September 1946.
[41] Gwynfor Evans to T I Ellis, 28.11.1946 (Undeb Cymru Fydd papers, File 17, NLW).
[42] Gwynfor Evans to J E Jones, 16.11.1946 (PCP B 534). For the reaction in the Preselau region, see *Cardigan and Tivy Side Advertiser*, 6 December 1946.
[43] Gwynfor Evans to J E Jones, n.d. (PCP B 534).
[44] *Western Mail*, 18 December 1946.
[45] For the best account of the initial period of the land battles, see Janet Davies, *Planet,* 58, 1986, pp. 3–9.
[46] *Baner ac Amserau Cymru*, 8 January 1947.
[47] *Yr Herald Cymraeg*, 6 January 1947.
[48] *Baner ac Amserau Cymru*, 1 January 1947.
[49] *Western Mail*, 13 January 1947.
[50] *Y Cymro*, 17 January 1947.
[51] *Picture Post*, 25 January 1947.
[52] *Y Cymro*, 31 January 1947.
[53] *Wales*, Volume 5, Number 4, 1947.
[54] Gwynfor Evans to J E Jones, 20.1.1947 (PCP B 536).
[55] *Y Dydd*, 17 October 1947.
[56] Peter Beresford Ellis, *Celtic Dawn* (Tal-y-bont, 2002), pp. 108–125.
[57] Gwynfor Evans to T I Ellis, 21.1.1947 (Undeb Cymru Fydd papers, File 91, NLW).
[58] *Y Cymro*, 1 February 1947.
[59] ibid., 28 March 1947.
[60] *Y Cymro*, 7 March 1947.
[61] Kate Roberts to T I Ellis, 26.3.1947 (File 18 Undeb Cymru Fydd papers, NLW).
[62] Minutes of Plaid Cymru Executive, 3 April 1947 (PCP A 37).
[63] *Liverpool Daily Post*, 27 May 1947.
[64] *Baner ac Amserau Cymru*, 2 July 1947.
[65] ibid., 6 August 1947.
[66] ibid., 22 October 1947.
[67] PRO BD 28/414, see the note by Trevor Williams, Regional Manager of the Town and Country Planning Ministry.
[68] *Western Mail*, 11 November 1947.
[69] D J Williams's journal, 16.10.1947 (D J Williams papers, NLW).
[70] Minutes of the subcommittee on conscription, n.d. (PCP M 590).
[71] ibid., R Tudur Jones to J E Jones, 4.9.1947.
[72] Gwynfor Evans to Pennar Davies, 19.12.1948 and 25.5.1949 (Pennar Davies papers, NLW).
[73] *Baner ac Amserau Cymru*, 18 June 1947.
[74] Cliff Bere to J E Jones, 29.6.1947 (PCP B 648).

[75] *Baner ac Amserau Cymru*, 2 October 1947.
[76] Gwilym Prys Davies to John Legonna, n.d. (John Legonna papers, File 10, NLW).
[77] Gwynfor Evans to J E Jones, 28.10.1947 (PCP B 550).
[78] Gwynfor Evans to J E Jones, 21.11.1947, ibid.
[79] Gwynfor Evans to J E Jones, 20.11.1947, ibid.
[80] *Welsh Nationalist*, January 1948.
[81] *Western Mail*, 15 November 1947.
[82] Gwynfor Evans to T I Ellis, 12.1.1948 (Undeb Cymru Fydd papers, File 2, NLW).
[83] Gwilym R Jones to J E Jones, 16.1.1948 (PCP M 592).
[84] *Baner ac Amserau Cymru*, 17 March 1948.
[85] *Welsh Nationalist*, April 1948.
[86] *Baner ac Amserau Cymru*, 21 April 1948.
[87] *Y Cymro,* 16 April 1948.
[88] Report of Plaid Cymru finance committee, 14.9.1948 (Dr Noëlle Davies papers, File 11, NLW).
[89] *Y Cymro*, 15 October 1948.
[90] Gwynfor Evans to Dr Gwenan Jones, 20.12.1948 (Dr Gwenan Jones papers, Box 1, NLW).
[91] Gwynfor Evans, '*Eu Hiaith a Gadwant…': A Oes Dyfodol i'r Iaith Gymraeg?* (Cardiff, 1948).
[92] Gwynfor Evans to J E Jones, n.d. (PCP B 564).
[93] Mari Angharad Williams, *'Yr Iaith Gymraeg yn ei Henbydrwydd': Y Gymraeg yn y 1950au* (Aberystwyth, 2001).
[94] Gwynfor Evans to Pennar Davies, 25.5.1949 (Pennar Davies papers, NLW).
[95] On the beginnings of the Parliament for Wales Campaign, see Elwyn Roberts's essay (Elwyn Roberts papers, File 40, NLW).
[96] Gwynfor Evans to Dr D J and Dr Noëlle Davies, 15.3.1949 (Dr Noëlle Davies papers, NLW).
[97] Gwynfor Evans, *Bywyd Cymro*, op. cit., p. 113. See also Ioan Matthews, 'The Carmarthen By-election of 1957', *The Carmarthenshire Antiquary*, Volume XXXIX, 2003. For the broader background, see D M Harries, 'Carmarthen Politics: the struggle between Liberals and Labour 1918–1960', unpublished MA thesis, University of Wales.
[98] Author's interview with Clem Thomas.
[99] *Carmarthen Journal*, 22 April 1949.
[100] *Baner ac Amserau Cymru,* 25 May 1949.
[101] ibid., 8 June 1949.
[102] *Liverpool Daily Post*, 2 May 1949.
[103] Ciff Bere to John Legonna, 11.2.1948 (John Legonna papers, File 11, NLW).
[104] Cliff Bere to John Legonna, 27.2.1948, ibid.
[105] Gwynfor Evans to J E Jones, 18.10.1948 (PCP B 567).
[106] Trefor Morgan to John Legonna, 22.2.1949 (John Legonna papers, File 11, NLW).
[107] Minutes of Plaid Cymru Executive, 13.4.1949 (PCP A 38).
[108] *Baner ac Amserau Cymru*, 4 May 1949.
[109] J E Jones to Gwynfor Evans, 18.5.1949 (GE, J, 1973, NLW).
[110] Saunders Lewis to Gwynfor Evans, 18.5.1949 (GE, 1983, L, NLW).
[111] Minutes of the Plaid Cymru Executive, 10.6.1949 (PCP A 38).
[112] *News Chronicle*, 30 July 1949.
[113] *Liverpool Daily Post*, 8 July 1949.
[114] Gwynfor Evans to D J Williams, 11.6.1949 (D J Williams papers, NLW).
[115] D J Williams to Gwynfor Evans, 17.7.1949 (GE, 1983, W, NLW).

[116] *Liverpool Daily Post*, 2 August 1949.
[117] Author's interview with Lord Gwilym Prys Davies.
[118] Gwynfor Evans to Dr D J and Dr Noëlle Davies, 18.12.1949, (Dr Noëlle Davies papers, 12/27, NLW).
[119] John Davies, *Hanes Cymru* (London, 1990), p. 600. English language version: *A History of Wales* (London, 1993).
[120] *Liverpool Daily Post*, 27 September 1949.
[121] ibid., 3 October 1949.
[122] *News Chronicle*, 11 October 1949.
[123] *Liverpool Daily Post*, 5 January 1950.
[124] Elwyn Roberts in *Cymru'n Deffro*, ed. John Davies, op. cit., pp. 96–7.
[125] ibid., p. 97.
[126] *Baner ac Amserau Cymru*, 4 January 1950.
[127] ibid., 11 January 1950.
[128] *News Chronicle*, 19 January 1950.
[129] *Baner ac Amserau Cymru*, 18 January 1950.
[130] ibid., 25 January 1950.
[131] Saunders Lewis to J E Jones, 6.7.1949 (PCP A 38). Saunders Lewis believed it would be unwise to go into debt given that a recession 'was likely to come'. For the attitudes of R Tudur Jones and D J Davies, see ibid.
[132] *Liverpool Daily Post*, 11 January 1950.
[133] *Y Cyfnod*, 17 February 1950.
[134] Robin Jones to Gwynfor Evans, n.d. (GE, 1983, J, NLW).
[135] *Y Cymro*, 3 February 1950.
[136] Huw Pritchard to Gwynfor Evans, 16.3.1950 (GE, 1983, P, NLW). This criticism was not restricted to Merioneth. In Arfon, there was a perception that those who had the right to address Plaid Cymru meetings were 'Ministers of the Gospel and graduates almost without exception' and that it was just 'the party of intellectuals and the well-read'. See Meurig Roberts in *Baner ac Amserau Cymru*, 8 March 1950.
[137] *Western Mail*, 2 March 1950.
[138] *Y Cymro*, 3 February 1950.
[139] Memorandum *Gwersi'r Etholiad 1950* (PCP A 38).
[140] *Y Ddraig Goch*, March 1950.
[141] *Baner ac Amserau Cymru*, 8 March 1950.
[142] Gwynfor Evans to D J Williams, 27.2.1950 (D J Williams papers, NLW).
[143] Minutes of Plaid Cymru Executive, 14 April 1950 (PCP A 38).
[144] Gwynfor Evans, *Plaid Cymru and Wales* (Llandybïe, 1950).
[145] *Baner ac Amserau Cymru*, 5 April 1950.
[146] ibid., 12 April 1950.
[147] Dan Thomas to Gwynfor Evans, 4.6.1950 (GE, 1983, T, NLW).
[148] D J Williams to Pennar Davies, 4.6.1950 (Pennar Davies papers, NLW).
[149] Author's interview with Dafydd Evans.
[150] Elwyn Roberts's essay, op. cit., p.4 (Elwyn Roberts papers, File 40, NLW).
[151] *Liverpool Daily Post*, 3 July 1950.
[152] Mervyn Jones, *A Radical Life – The Biography of Megan Lloyd George* (London, 1991), p. 232.
[153] *The Welsh Nation*, August 1950.
[154] *Y Ddraig Goch*, January 1950.
[155] Goronwy Roberts to Gwilym Williams, 8.8.1950. (Labour Party archives, GS/WAL/48,

Manchester).
[156] Minutes of the Parliament for Wales Campaign Central Committee, 4.11.1950, private ownership. I am grateful to Bethan Miles for showing me this important collection.
[157] *Baner ac Amserau Cymru*, 28 March 1951.
[158] Emrys Roberts to Gwynfor Evans, 22.9.1951 (GE, 1983, R, NLW). In his letter, Roberts says that he has been 'working for some time to get the Liberals to stand down in the constituencies where the present Members support a Parliament for Wales unequivocally'.
[159] Alan Butt Philip, *The Welsh Question: Nationalism in Welsh Politics, 1945–1970* (Cardiff, 1975), p. 77.
[160] Peter Stead, 'The Labour Party and the Claims of Wales' in John Osmond (ed.), *The National Question Again: Welsh Political Identity in the 1980s* (Llandysul, 1985), p.105.
[161] J E Jones's circular, 9.4.1951 (PCP A 39).
[162] Wynne Samuel to J E Jones, 14.4.1951 (PCP A 39).
[163] Gwynfor Evans to Pennar Davies, 22.4.1951 (Pennar Davies papers, NLW).
[164] *Y Ddraig Goch*, May 1951.
[165] Tecwyn Lloyd Owen to Gwynfor Evans, 6.5.1951 (GE, 1983, O, NLW).
[166] *Y Cymro*, 11 May 1951.
[167] Wynne Samuel to J E Jones, 14.7.1951 (PCP B 583).
[168] *Y Cymro*, 20 July 1951; *Western Mail*, 18 July 1951.
[169] Gwynfor Evans, *Bywyd Cymro*, op. cit., p. 136.
[170] *Western Mail*, 8 December 1955.
[171] *News Chronicle*, 10 August 1951.
[172] *Baner ac Amserau Cymru*, 30 May 1951. At the meeting, Gwynfor linked forestry with the need for a Parliament. It is possibly this that angered Saunders Lewis more than anything.
[173] ibid., 6 June 1951.
[174] ibid., 13 June 1951.
[175] PRO HO 45/25484.
[176] *Baner ac Amserau Cymru,* 18 and 25 July 1951.
[177] Pennar Davies, *Gwynfor Evans*, op. cit., p. 47.
[178] *Baner ac Amserau Cymru*, 5 September 1951.
[179] *Y Faner Newydd*, Issue 21, Summer 2002.
[180] Saunders Lewis to Plaid Cymru, 31.8.1951 (PCP M 592).
[181] Author's interview with the Reverend Huw Jones.
[182] *Liverpool Daily Post*, 5 September 1951.
[183] *Western Mail*, 11 September 1951.
[184] *Baner ac Amserau Cymru*, 19 September 1951.
[185] PRO HO 45/2484.
[186] Gwynfor Evans to J E Jones, 5.9.1951 (PCP M 592).
[187] *Tros Gymru,* J E Jones, op. cit., p. 305.
[188] E G Millward's recollections in *Y Faner Newydd*, op. cit., p. 29.
[189] *Y Dydd*, 5 October 1951.
[190] *Y Goleuad*, 10 October 1951.
[191] *Western Mail*, 30 September 1951. Privately, Gwynfor was more conscious than anyone of the difficulties that arose after the two protests. In October 1951, he wrote to R O F Wynne: 'We thoroughly expected that the authorities would prosecute us after the second visit to Trawsfynydd, but they obviously believe that that would strengthen our case. The Chief Constable argued forcefully with the Home Office against prosecution. If we can, we shall try to do something similar to what you suggest in the Spring; but it is remarkable how much time

goes into organizing something like this.' See Gwynfor Evans to R O F Wynne, 20.10.1951 (File 1135, Garthewin Add., University of Wales, Bangor).
[192] *Baner ac Amserau Cymru*, 31 October 1951.
[193] ibid., 21 November 1951.
[194] Gwynfor Evans to D J Williams, 8.11.1951 (D J Williams papers, NLW).

CHAPTER 5 – 'Soft Soap For the Voters' 1951–55

[1] Dafydd Miles to Cyril Jones, 14.11.1951, private ownership.
[2] J R Jones to Dafydd Miles, 19.11.1951, ibid.
[3] *Liverpool Daily Post*, 3 January 1952.
[4] J Graham Jones, 'The Parliament for Wales Campaign, 1950–1956', *Welsh History Review*, number 2 (1992), pp. 207–36.
[5] Sir Ifan ab Owen Edwards to Dafydd Miles, 8.12.1951, private ownership.
[6] Dafydd Miles's report, 15.12.1951 (Undeb Cymru Fydd papers, File 202, NLW).
[7] Sir Ifan ab Owen Edwards to Gwynfor Evans, 17.1.1952 (GE, E, 1983, NLW). In the long term, however, the stand taken at Rhandirmwyn had a mixed effect. By 1965, the total amount of land sold voluntarily to the Commission was twice as much as the amount of land originally seized by them. See William Linnard, *Welsh Woods and Forests* (Llandysul, 2000), p. 207. See also George Ryle, *Forest Service* (London, 1969), pp. 124–5.
[8] *Y Ddraig Goch*, February 1952.
[9] *Y Cymro*, 29 February 1952.
[10] *Baner ac Amserau Cymru*, 9 January 1952. The Reverend Fred Jones quoted here should not be confused with his namesake, Fred Jones (1877-1948), a prominent Congregationalist Minister and one of the founders of Plaid Cymru.
[11] ibid., 30 January 1952 and 19 March 1952.
[12] ibid., 13 February 1952.
[13] Saunders Lewis to Pennar Davies, 17.2.1952 (Pennar Davies papers, NLW).
[14] Gwynfor Evans to Pennar Davies, 7.2.1952, ibid.
[15] Gwynfor Evans to Pennar Davies, 13.2.1952, ibid.
[16] *Liverpool Daily Post*, 10 March 1952.
[17] Gwynfor Evans to T I Ellis, 2.4.1952 (Undeb Cymru Fydd papers, File 86, NLW).
[18] Gwynfor Evans to T I Ellis, 9.6.1952, File 175, ibid.
[19] *News Chronicle*, 27 September 1952.
[20] *Baner ac Amserau Cymru*, 1 October 1952.
[21] *Y Cymro*, 9 May 1952.
[22] *Western Mail*, 6 May 1952.
[23] *Y Cymro*, 10 October 1952.
[24] Minutes of Plaid Cymru Regional Committee, Merioneth, 11.10.1952 (PCP C 127).
[25] Ambrose Bebb to T I Ellis, 13.2.1953 (Undeb Cymru Fydd papers, File 202, NLW).
[26] *News Chronicle*, 12 December 1952.
[27] Gwynfor Evans to J E Jones, 8.2.1952 (PCP B 605).
[28] *Baner ac Amserau Cymru*, 24 December 1952.
[29] Minutes of Plaid Cymru Executive, 2.1.1953 (PCP A 40).
[30] See letters by David Hughes-Evans and 'Cafan' in *Baner ac Amserau Cymru*, 7 January and 14 January 1953.
[31] ibid., 17 June 1953.
[32] ibid., 2 February 1953.

[33] Gwynfor Evans to J E Jones, 16.1.1953 (PCP B 611).
[34] J E Jones to Gwynfor Evans, 19.1.1953 (PCP B 602).
[35] *Y Ddraig Goch*, September 1953.
[36] PCP B 615.
[37] Author's interview with Dafydd Evans.
[38] Elwyn Roberts in *Cymru'n Deffro*, ed. John Davies, op. cit., pp. 102–3.
[39] *Y Cymro*, 14 August 1953.
[40] *Liverpool Daily Post*, 14 August 1953.
[41] Dewi Prys Thomas to Rhys Devlin, the builder, n.d. The original quote for building Talar Wen was £3,560. By the time the house was ready, the price was more than £1,000 less. (GE, 1983, T, NLW).
[42] Gwynfor Evans sent his two eldest sons, Alcwyn and Dafydd, to Llandovery College.
[43] Robert Griffiths, *S O Davies – A Socialist Faith* (Llandysul, 1983), p. 163.
[44] *Y Ddraig Goch*, November 1953.
[45] *News Chronicle*, 10 October 1953.
[46] *The Observer*, 27 September 1953.
[47] *Liverpool Daily Post*, 31 October 1953.
[48] Cliff Prothero to Morgan Phillips 6.10.1953 (Labour Party Archives, GS/WAL/6/ii, Manchester).
[49] *Liverpool Daily Post*, 9 November 1953.
[50] *Western Mail*, 18 November 1953.
[51] The five were: Cledwyn Hughes, MP for Anglesey; Goronwy Roberts, MP for Caernarfon; Tudor Watkins, MP for Brecon and Radnor; T W Jones, MP for Merioneth; S O Davies, MP for Merthyr Tydfil.
[52] *Liverpool Daily Post*, 16 November 1953.
[53] Gwynfor Evans to Pennar Davies, 30.11.1953 (Pennar Davies papers, NLW).
[54] Gwynfor Evans to D J Williams, 4.12.1953 (D J Williams papers, NLW).
[55] Gwynfor Evans to Huw T Edwards, 7.12.1953 (Huw T Edwards papers, NLW).
[56] *Y Ddraig Goch*, January 1954.
[57] Minutes of Plaid Cymru Executive, 1.1.1954 (PCP A 40). See also D J Williams's journal, 1.1.1954 (D J Williams papers, NLW).
[58] J E Jones to R Tudur Jones, 30.11.1953 (PCP B 620/13).
[59] *Welsh Clarion*, May 1954, issue 1.
[60] *Baner ac Amserau Cymru*, 20 January 1954.
[61] *Liverpool Daily Post*, 31 May 1954.
[62] Gwynfor Evans, *The Labour Party and Welsh Home Rule* (Cardiff, 1954).
[63] *Baner ac Amserau Cymru*, 31 March 1954.
[64] *News Chronicle*, 5 June 1954.
[65] Gwynfor Evans, *Cristnogaeth a'r Gymdeithas Gymreig* (Llanelli, 1954).
[66] *Y Dysgedydd*, August 1954.
[67] *Manchester Guardian*, 27 May 1954.
[68] Minutes of Parliament for Wales Campaign Executive, 16.10.1954 (Undeb Cymru Fydd papers, File 202, NLW).
[69] Gwynfor Evans to D J Williams, 25.7.1954 (D J Williams papers, NLW).
[70] PCP B 640/118. See also Gwynfor Evans to J E Jones, 7.10.1954 (PCP B 642/148).
[71] Saunders Lewis to D J Williams, 17.10.1954 (D J Williams papers, NLW).
[72] *Aberdare Leader*, 30 October 1954.
[73] *Y Ddraig Goch*, November 1954.

[74] *Baner ac Amserau Cymru*, 20 October 1954.
[75] *Y Cymro*, 5 November 1954.
[76] Press release, 27.10.1954 (Labour Party archive, File 29, NLW).
[77] *Daily Express*, 30 October 1954.
[78] *Western Mail*, 30 October 1954.
[79] Gwynfor Evans to D J Williams, 1.11.1954 (D J Williams papers, NLW).
[80] *Western Mail,* 16 September 1954. Labour's argument was that Welsh broadcasts would confuse the electors. See also Cliff Prothero in the *Liverpool Daily Post*, 26 October 1954.
[81] John Davies, *Broadcasting and the BBC in Wales* (Cardiff, 1994), pp. 243–7.
[82] *Baner ac Amserau Cymru*, 15 December 1954.
[83] *The Welsh Nation*, August 1955.
[84] Minutes of Plaid Cymru Executive, New Year 1955 (PCP A 40).
[85] J E Jones to Emrys Bennett Owen, 31.3.1955 (Emrys Bennett Owen papers, NLW).
[86] *Y Cymro*, 14 January 1955.
[87] POST 122/56, Gwilym Lloyd George to Earl de la Warr, 15.3.1955 (Royal Mail Archives, London).
[88] ibid., 11.8.1955.
[89] The improvement could be ascribed to the decision to erect three new VHF transmitters at Penmon, Wenvoe and Blaenplwyf.
[90] Minutes of Parliament for Wales Campaign Executive, 19.3.1955 (Undeb Cymru Fydd papers, File 202, NLW).
[91] *Y Cymro*, 10 March 1955.
[92] *Carmarthen Journal*, 26 June 1955.
[93] Author's interview with Professor Deian Hopkin.
[94] Gwynfor Evans, *Bywyd Cymro*, op. cit., p. 121.
[95] PRO PREM 11/211.
[96] *Baner ac Amserau Cymru*, 27 April 1955.
[97] Gwynfor Evans to J E Jones, 30.3.1955 (PCP B 651).
[98] Elwyn Roberts to D J Williams, 1.7.1955 (D J Williams papers, NLW).
[99] *Y Cymro*, 5 May 1955.
[100] *Baner ac Amserau Cymru*, 4 May 1955.
[101] *Y Dydd*, 6 May 1955.
[102] *Y Cymro*, 21 April 1955.
[103] *Y Cyfnod*, 20 May 1955.
[104] *Baner ac Amserau Cymru*, 25 May 1955.
[105] *The Times,* 25 May 1955.
[106] *Baner ac Amserau Cymru*, 11 May 1955.
[107] *Y Ddraig Goch*, July 1955.
[108] Gwynfor Evans to J E Jones, 29.5.1955 (PCP B 653).
[109] ibid.
[110] The only child whose name is not mentioned in the main body of this biography is Branwen Eluned.

CHAPTER 6 – Tryweryn 1955–59

[1] PRO BD 11/2975.
[2] Gwynfor Evans to J E Jones, 20.8.1955 (PCP B 659).
[3] *Y Cymro*, 22 September 1955.

[4] *Baner ac Amserau Cymru*, 28 September 1955.
[5] PRO BD 11/2975, Blaise Gillie to J H Waddell, 5.10.1955.
[6] Note by Blaise Gillie, 17.12.1955, ibid.
[7] *Baner ac Amserau Cymru*, 4 January 1956.
[8] ibid.
[9] Minutes of Plaid Cymru Executive, 20.12.1955 (PCP A 42). See also Watcyn L Jones, *Cofio Tryweryn* (Llandysul, 1988), p. 174.
[10] Elizabeth Watkin Jones to J E Jones, 13.1.1956 (PCP B 671).
[11] *Y Dydd*, 6 January 1956.
[12] *Baner ac Amserau Cymru*, 4 January 1956.
[13] Lord Maelor, *Fel Hyn y Bu* (Denbigh, 1970), p. 161.
[14] Elizabeth Watkin Jones to J E Jones, 28.3.1956. (PCP B 671).
[15] *Baner ac Amserau Cymru*, 25 January 1956.
[16] ibid.
[17] Gwynfor Evans to the Clerk of Liverpool Corporation, 27.2.1956 (PCP B 672).
[18] *Western Mail*, 7 January 1956.The news conference contained 60 foreign journalists including correspondents from papers as exotic as the Soviet Union's *Izvestia* and Japan's *Asahi Shimbun*. For Plaid Cymru, such attention was like manna from heaven.
[19] Gwynfor Evans to R Tudur Jones, 26.4.1956 (PCP N 35). Gwynfor Evans hoped it would be possible to establish a Welsh commercial television company. He made the effort despite the fact that he found such television 'boring'. The goal was to raise £7,500,000 in capital. Nothing came of the scheme.
[20] Elizabeth Watkin Jones to Gwynfor Evans, 26.4.1956 (GE, 1973, J, NLW).
[21] *Liverpool Daily Post*, 20 January 1956. See letter from General Skaife to the editor.
[22] *Y Cymro*, 29 March 1956.
[23] R T Jenkins to Elizabeth Watkin Jones, 26.4.1956 (GE, 1973, J, NLW).
[24] *Baner ac Amserau Cymru*, 23 May 1956.
[25] *Y Seren*, 7 July 1956.
[26] ibid., 26 May 1956.
[27] Elizabeth Watkin Jones to J E Jones, 20.6.1956 (PCP B 683).
[28] Elizabeth Watkin Jones to J E Jones, 7.6.1956 (PCP B 682).
[29] Minutes of Plaid Cymru Executive, 9.4.1956 (PCP A 43).
[30] PRO BD 11/2975. Blaise Gillie's note.
[31] Minutes of Plaid Cymru Executive, 9.4.1956, loc. cit.
[32] Author's interview with Gwynfor Evans.
[33] Gwynfor Evans to Dr DJ and Dr Noëlle Davies, 30.9.1956 13/30 (Noëlle Davies papers, NLW).
[34] Author's interview with Professor Bobi Jones.
[35] Dafydd Orwig Jones to J E Jones, 10.6.1956 (PCP B 681).
[36] See the correspondence in files PCP M 55 and B 681.
[37] Elwyn Roberts to Gwynfor Evans, 14.8.1956 (PCP N 40).
[38] Elwyn Roberts's note, (PCP M 258).
[39] Gwynfor Evans to Elwyn Roberts, 30.9.1956 (PCP N 30).
[40] Gwynfor Evans to Elwyn Roberts, 15.11.1956, ibid.
[41] Gwynfor Evans to Elwyn Roberts, 16.12.1956 (PCP N 33).
[42] *Baner ac Amserau Cymru*, 3 October 1956.
[43] Watcyn L Jones, *Cofio Tryweryn*, op. cit., p. 190.
[44] *Y Glannau,* June 1956.

[45] Gwynfor Evans to Dr D J and Dr Noëlle Davies, 30.9.1956 (Noëlle Davies papers, NLW).
[46] *Save Cwm Tryweryn for Wales* (Cardiff, 1956).
[47] Wynne Samuel to R Tudur Jones, 3.10.1956 (PCP N 33).
[48] PRO BD 11/2975, memorandum 3.10.1956.
[49] *The Times*, 17 October 1956.
[50] Minutes of Plaid Cymru's Tryweryn Committee, 20.10.1956 (GE, 1973, J, NLW).
[51] Author's interview with Emrys Roberts.
[52] Saunders Lewis's private views are mentioned in Wynne Samuel to D J Williams, 26.10.1963 (D J Williams papers, NLW).
[53] Elizabeth Watkin Jones to T I Ellis, 22.10.1956 (Undeb Cymru Fydd papers, Box 109, NLW).
[54] Quoted in Watcyn L Jones, *Cofio Tryweryn*, op. cit. p. 193.
[55] *Liverpool Echo*, 7 November 1956.
[56] Minutes of Plaid Cymru Executive, 10.11.1956 (PCP A 43).
[57] Elizabeth Watkin Jones to J E Jones, 27.11.1956 (PCP B 687).
[58] *Liverpool Daily Post*, 22 November 1956.
[59] ibid.
[60] *Manchester Guardian*, 22 November 1956.
[61] ibid.
[62] ibid.
[63] *Liverpool Echo*, 21 November 1956.
[64] R Tudur Jones to Gwynfor Evans, 22.11.1956 (GE, 1973, J, NLW).
[65] *Liverpool Daily Post,* 24 November 1956.
[66] Elizabeth Watkin Jones to Gwynfor Evans, 5.12.1956 (GE, 1973, J, NLW).
[67] Dewi Watkin Powell to Gwynfor Evans, 10.12.1956 (PCP N 33).
[68] *Liverpool Daily Post*, 20 December 1956.
[69] Gwynfor Evans to D J Williams, 25.12.1956 (D J Williams papers, NLW).
[70] Minutes of Plaid Cymru Executive, 28.12.1956 (PCP A 43).
[71] *Liverpool Daily Post*, 25 January 1957.
[72] ibid., 3 January 1957.
[73] *Western Mail*, 14 January 1957.
[74] ibid.
[75] Elizabeth Watkin Jones to J E Jones, n.d. (PCP B 689).
[76] Raymond Gower to Gwynfor Evans 23.1.1957 and 14.3.1957 (GE, 1973, G, NLW).
[77] *Y Cymro*, 17 January 1957.
[78] Gwynfor Evans to J E Jones, 10.1.1957 (PCP B 689).
[79] Gwynfor Evans to J E Jones, 4.12.1956 (PCP B 687).
[80] *Western Mail*, 22 February 1957.
[81] ibid., 3 May 1957.
[82] Elizabeth Watkin Jones to Gwynfor Evans, 5.6.1957 (GE, 1973, J, NLW).
[83] Gwynfor Evans to J E Jones, 16.10.1956 (PCP B 685).
[84] Gwynfor Evans to J E Jones, 11.5.1957 (PCP B 696).
[85] Author's interview with Dafydd Evans.
[86] *Liverpool Daily Post*, 9 July 1957.
[87] Emrys Roberts's memorandum (PCP A 44).
[88] Saunders Lewis to D J Williams, 11.6.1957 (D J Williams papers, NLW).
[89] J E Jones to Dewi Watkin Powell, 23.7.1957 (PCP B 698).
[90] Author's interview with Dewi Watkin Powell.

[91] Dewi Watkin Powell to Gwynfor Evans, 28.7.1957 (GE, 1973, P, NLW).
[92] Author's interview with Dewi Watkin Powell.
[93] *Y Cymro*, 8 August 1957.
[94] Gwynfor Evans, *Bywyd Cymro*, op. cit., p. 193.
[95] *Y Dydd*, 9 August 1957.
[96] PRO BD 24/17, Gwynfor Evans to Ernest Roberts, n.d.
[97] ibid., Cledwyn Hughes to William Jones, 24.7.1957.
[98] ibid., T Hywel Thomas to Blaise Gillie, 26.7.1957.
[99] PRO BD 24/17, Blaise Gillie's note, 12.8.1957.
[100] *Liverpool Daily Post*, 8 August 1957.
[101] *South Wales Echo*, 7 August 1957.
[102] D J Williams to Gwynfor Evans, 25.8.1957 (GE, 1973, W, NLW).
[103] *Western Mail*, 7 August 1957.
[104] Minutes of Plaid Cymru Special Executive on Tryweryn, 31.8.1957 (PCP A 44).
[105] Gwynfor Evans to D J Williams, 2.9.1957 (D J Williams papers, NLW).
[106] Gwynfor Evans, *We Learn from Tryweryn* (Dolgellau, 1957), p. 23.
[107] ibid., p. 24. The Welsh verb that was coined was 'Trywerynu'. It was widely used afterwards in Plaid Cymru literature and in popular songs like those of Dafydd Iwan.
[108] Elwyn Roberts to Hywel Hughes, 17.9.1957 (PCP B 1386).
[109] PRO BD 24/2, David Cole to Henry Brooke, 13.10.1957.
[110] PRO CAB 129/90, Henry Brooke's memorandum 15.11.1957.
[111] PRO CAB 129/32, Part 2, 23.10.1958.
[112] *Liverpool Daily Post*, 21 September 1957.
[113] *The Times*, 29 September 1957.
[114] Gwynfor Evans to Pennar Davies, 9.10.1957 (Pennar Davies papers, NLW).
[115] *Western Mail*, 29 October 1957.
[116] ibid., 23 October 1957.
[117] *Y Seren*, 2 November 1957.
[118] *Welsh Nationalist*, November 1957.
[119] Liverpool Corporation's negative response was received on 21 January 1958.
[120] *Liverpool Daily Post*, 24 January 1958.
[121] *Baner ac Amserau Cymru*, 2 January 1958.
[122] For a more detailed discussion see John Davies, *Broadcasting and the BBC in Wales*, op. cit., pp. 214–22.
[123] *Baner ac Amserau Cymru*, April 1959.
[124] Gwynfor Evans and J E Jones, *TV in Wales* (Cardiff, 1958).
[125] R E Griffith to J E Jones, 28.3.1958 (Undeb Cymru Fydd papers, File 186, NLW). See also T I Ellis to J E Jones, 8.7.1958, ibid.
[126] John Davies, *Broadcasting and the BBC in Wales*, op. cit., p. 217.
[127] ibid., p. 218.
[128] PRO HO 256/408.
[129] *Western Mail*, 18 February 1958.
[130] *Y Cymro*, 27 February 1958.
[131] *Baner ac Amserau Cymru*, 24 April 1958.
[132] Nest Lewis Jones to Gwynfor Evans, 14.5.1958 (PCP A 45).
[133] ibid., Minutes of Plaid Cymru Executive, 21.6.1958.
[134] Minutes of 1958 Summer School (PCP G 35).
[135] *Merthyr Express*, 9 August 1958.

[136] *Y Cymro*, 14 August 1958.
[137] Saunders Lewis to D J Williams, 7.10.1958 (D J Williams papers, NLW).
[138] R Tudur Jones to J E Jones, 10.9.1958 (PCP B 731).
[139] *Western Mail*, 16 October 1958.
[140] ibid., 25 October 1958.
[141] ibid., 9 April 1976.
[142] Wynne Samuel to J E Jones, 11.9.1958 (PCP B 730).
[143] PRO BD 25/13.
[144] Gwynfor Evans, *Bywyd Cymro*, op. cit., p. 213.
[145] Gwynfor Evans to J E Jones, 11.11.1958 (PCP B 1377).
[146] *New York Times*, 11 November 1958.
[147] *Washington Post*, 17 November 1958.
[148] *New York Times*, 11 November 1958.
[149] *Western Mail*, 17 November 1958.
[150] PRO BD 25/13, memorandum, 15.4.1958. Later, Peter Brooke became Northern Ireland Secretary during the Conservative administrations of Margaret Thatcher and John Major. Subsequently, he was appointed Heritage Secretary.
[151] Gwynfor Evans to D J Williams, 29.12.1958 (D J Williams papers, NLW).
[152] Gwynfor Evans, *Bywyd Cymro*, op. cit., p. 214.
[153] Islwyn Ffowc Elis to Gwynfor Evans, 21.12.1958 (GE, 1973, E, NLW).
[154] Circular sent to members of the executive, 5.1.1959 (PCP M 387).
[155] Minutes of Plaid Cymru Executive, 2.1.1959 (PCP A 92).
[156] Elwyn Roberts to Publicity Manager at Faber & Faber, 6.1.1959 (PCP N 74). According to Roberts: 'We are in constant touch with him concerning matters common to Mr Scott and to ourselves.' Michael Scott addressed Plaid Cymru's Summer School in August 1958.
[157] Elystan Morgan to J E Jones, n.d. (PCP M 387).
[158] Dewi Watkin Powell to Gwynfor Evans, 21.1.1959 (PCP M 387).
[159] ibid., R Tudur Jones to Gwynfor Evans, 26.1.1959.
[160] Ifor Owen to J E Jones, n.d. (PCP A 46).
[161] Author's interview with Emrys Roberts.
[162] Gwynfor Evans, *Bywyd Cymro*, op. cit., p. 193.
[163] Gwynfor Evans and J E Jones, *Tryweryn – New Proposals* (Cardiff, 1959).
[164] ibid., p. 3.
[165] PRO BD 11/2975, memorandum, 20.11.1959.
[166] Harri Webb to Gwilym Prys Davies, n.d. (G1/4 Harri Webb papers, NLW).
[167] *Western Mail*, 23 March 1959.
[168] Ifor Owen to Emrys Roberts, 6.3.1959 (GE, 1973, N, NLW).
[169] Dafydd Orwig to Emrys Roberts, 7.4.1959 (PCP B 752).
[170] Eileen Beasley to Gwynfor Evans, n.d. (GE, 1973, A, NLW).
[171] Plaid Cymru Annual Conference Agenda 1959 (PCP A 46).
[172] *Y Ddraig Goch*, May 1959.
[173] Saunders Lewis to D J Williams, 29.7.1959, (D J Williams papers, NLW).
[174] Saunders Lewis to D J Williams, 21.11.1959, ibid.
[175] This is mentioned in J E Jones to D J Williams, 2.7.1959, ibid. In his letter, J E Jones writes: 'I know that he [Gwynfor] is worried because there is no greater danger to Wales at present than to open a divide within Plaid over power and the crown'.
[176] *Y Cymro*, 21 May 1959.
[177] *Y Ddraig Goch*, July/August 1959.

[178] Gwynfor Evans to Huw T Edwards, 15.2.1959 (Huw T Edwards papers, A 1/521, NLW).
[179] *Baner ac Amserau Cymru*, 13 August 1959.
[180] *Y Dydd*, 14 August 1959.
[181] *Baner ac Amserau Cymru,* 20 August 1959.
[182] Gwynfor Evans to J E Jones, n.d. (PCP B 760).
[183] *Baner ac Amserau Cymru*, 17 September 1959.
[184] Gwynfor Evans and Plaid Cymru created an impression on the miners of Cwmllynfell following their considerable efforts to save the pit in January 1959. At the time, the miners' struggle was a *cause célèbre*. Plaid Cymru managed to find a market for the pit's output in the Netherlands and Gwynfor went as far as to draw up a plan to stay down the mine with the workers as a protest – see Gwynfor Evans to Emrys Roberts, 24.2.1959 (PCP B 747). However, the co-operative solution was rejected outright by the Coal Board. Only pits with fewer than 30 workers were allowed to operate as private enterprises – and there were over 300 at Cwmllynfell so the scheme would have broken this edict. That said, Gwynfor overstates the case in his autobiography when he writes that the Llanelli Labour MP, Jim Griffiths, killed the idea (see Gwynfor Evans, *Bywyd Cymro*, op. cit., pp.185–6). It was the NCB that shattered the co-operative dream. It rejected a similar request from the miners at Blackhull pit in Northumberland. For the background, see P H G Harries, 'Cwmllynfell Colliery: An Early Attempt To Form A Workers' Co-Operative', *Llafur*, 7/2 (1997), pp. 41–51.
[185] *Western Mail*, 25 September 1959.
[186] PRO HO 255/473, W Goldsmith's memorandum, 26.3.1959.
[187] *Western Mail*, 31 March 1959.
[188] *The Daily Telegraph*, 16 April 1959.
[189] Elystan Morgan begged for a radio and promised he would go 'anywhere in Wales to listen to it' – see Elystan Morgan to Glyn James, n.d. (PCP B 767). For Glyn James of Radio Wales: 'This was a bid for freedom of expression in the best tradition of British democracy.' Quoted in *Aberdare Leader*, 25 April 1959. Despite the authorities' best efforts, no member of Plaid Cymru was prosecuted for broadcasting propaganda on *Radio Wales*.
[190] *The Times*, 2 October 1959.
[191] *Western Mail*, 28 September 1959.
[192] *Y Seren*, 9 October 1959.
[193] *Gwynfor yn Bedwar Ugain Oed*, interview with Sulwyn Thomas, BBC Wales, 1992.
[194] *Y Cymro*, 10 May 1972.
[195] *Liverpool Daily Post*, 10 October 1959.

CHAPTER 7 – Civil War 1959–64

[1] D J Williams's journal, 9.10.1959 (D J Williams papers, NLW).
[2] ibid., Gwynfor Evans to D J Williams, 13.10.1959.
[3] ibid., D J Williams's journal, 24.10.1959.
[4] Memorandum from Plaid Cymru President's Committee, 24.10.1959 (PCP B 774).
[5] *Baner ac Amserau Cymru*, 26 November 1959.
[6] *Liverpool Daily Post*, 4 February 1960.
[7] Emrys Roberts to Pedr Lewis, 20.4.1960 (PCP B 1379).
[8] J I Daniel to J E Jones, 2.2.1960 (PCP B 790).
[9] ibid., J E Jones to J I Daniel, 3.2.1960.
[10] J E Jones's shorthand note on the meeting (PCP B 1380).
[11] ibid., Vernon Jones, Plaid Cymru Correspondence Secretary, Bala branch, to Emrys Roberts,

3.4.1960.
[12] J E Jones's memorandum to Plaid Cymru members, Llanelli, 8.4.1960 (PCP B 798). Over a period of eight years, the Beasleys received twelve summonses.
[13] *Western Mail*, 9 February 1960. The aggressive columns by the 'Junior Member for Treorchy' were a source of continuing concern for Gwynfor Evans.
[14] *Baner ac Amserau Cymru*, 5 May 1960.
[15] ibid., 12 May 1960.
[16] Gwynfor Evans to J E Jones, n.d. (PCP B 802).
[17] *Baner ac Amserau Cymru*, 7 July 1960.
[18] R Tudur Jones to Gwynfor Evans, 9.7.1960 (GE, 1973, J, NLW).
[19] Gwynfor Evans to J E Jones, 11.7.1960 (PCP B 1064).
[20] Gwynfor Evans to Huw T Edwards, 12.7.1960 (Huw T Edwards papers, A1/635, NLW).
[21] Gwynfor Evans to Pennar Davies, 6.6.1960 (Pennar Davies papers, NLW).
[22] Alun Oldfield-Davies to Gwynfor Evans, 11.7.1960 (GE, 1973, D, NLW).
[23] R Tudur Jones to Gwynfor Evans, 10.6.1960 (PCP B 805).
[24] Gwynfor Evans to D J Williams, 17.7.1960 (D J Williams papers, NLW).
[25] *Baner ac Amserau Cymru*, 11 August 1960.
[26] *Welsh Nation*, December 1960.
[27] Cynog Davies to J E Jones, 25.8.1960 (PCP B 811).
[28] Gwynfor Evans, *Self Government for Wales and a Common Market for the Nations of Britain* (Cardiff, 1960). It appears that the only two who knew about the new policy were Ioan Bowen Rees, a leading member of the executive, and Leopold Kohr.
[29] Gwynfor Evans to Ioan Bowen Rees, 19.8.1960, private ownership.
[30] *Y Ddraig Goch*, September 1960.
[31] Michael Tucker's article in the *Welsh Nation*, December 1960.
[32] Harri Webb to John Legonna, 18.8.1960 (John Legonna papers, 724/1, NLW).
[33] PRO BD 25/13, Blaise Gillie to Henry Brooke, 14.10.1960.
[34] *Welsh Nation*, November 1960.
[35] Author's interview with Professor Meic Stephens.
[36] N.V. Notes, Issue 1 (PCP B 814).
[37] Islwyn Ffowc Elis to Emrys Roberts, 3.9.1960 (PCP B 812).
[38] Meirion Lloyd Davies to Emrys Roberts, 9.9.1960, ibid.
[39] Author's interview with Dr Harri Pritchard Jones.
[40] Author's interview with John Daniel.
[41] *Welsh Nation*, January 1962.
[42] Gwynfor Evans to R Tudur Jones, 29.11.1960 (PCP N 47).
[43] Minutes of Plaid Cymru Executive, 30 and 31.12.1960 (PCP A 21).
[44] *Baner ac Amserau Cymru*, 24 November 1960.
[45] *Y Ddraig Goch*, January 1961.
[46] *Western Mail*, 19 September 1959.
[47] Ifan Gwynfil Evans, 'Drunk on Hopes and Ideals: The Failure of Wales Television, 1959–1963', *Llafur* 7/2 (1997), pp. 81–93. For the broader background, see Jamie Medhurst, 'Teledu Cymru: Menter Gyffrous neu Freuddwyd Ffôl', *Cof Cenedl* XVII, ed. Geraint Jenkins (Llandysul, 2002), pp. 165–91.
[48] *Baner ac Amserau Cymru*, 18 August 1960.
[49] Elwyn Roberts's memorandum (PCP M 239).
[50] Gwynfor Evans to Elwyn Roberts, 29.4.1961 (PCP M 650).
[51] D J Williams's journal, 1.1.1961 (D J Williams papers, NLW).

[52] Elwyn Roberts to J E Jones and Gwynfor Evans, 7.2.1961 (PCP B 825).
[53] ibid., Gwynfor Evans to Elwyn Roberts, 7.2.1961.
[54] J E Jones to Elwyn Roberts, 25.10.1960 (PCP B 1064).
[55] *Y Ddraig Goch*, November 1961.
[56] Minutes of Carmarthenshire District Committee, 7.4.1962 (Pol 18, Carmarthenshire County Council Archives).
[57] Emrys Roberts to Gwynfor Evans, 22.2.1961 (PCP B 825).
[58] Emrys Roberts's circular 28.2.1961 (PCP A 93).
[59] Dafydd Orwig to Gwynfor Evans, n.d. (GE, 1973, J, NLW).
[60] *Baner ac Amserau Cymru*, 13 April 1961.
[61] ibid., 27 April 1961.
[62] Emrys Roberts's circular, 21.4.1961 (PCP N 50).
[63] R Tudur Jones to Gwynfor Evans, 25.4.1961 (GE, 1973, J, NLW).
[64] D J Williams's journal, 19.6.1961 (D J Williams papers, NLW).
[65] Gwynfor Evans to Elwyn Roberts, 17.5.1961 (PCP B 1105).
[66] Press release, 3.6.1961, Merioneth District Committee (PCP C 106).
[67] Plaid Cymru press release, n.d. (PCP C 106).
[68] Phil Williams, *A Voice From the Valleys* (Aberystwyth, 1981), pp. 65–6.
[69] *Western Mail*, 8 August 1961.
[70] Author's interview with John Daniel.
[71] Saunders Lewis to D J Williams, 13.8.1961 (D J Williams papers, NLW).
[72] Catherine Daniel to Islwyn Ffowc Elis, 10.11.1961 (PCP B 1063).
[73] *Y Ddraig Goch*, October 1961.
[74] ibid., September 1961. Eventually, Emrys Roberts's plan to go on hunger strike in Liverpool was dropped.
[75] *Western Mail*, 18 September 1961.
[76] ibid., 27 November 1961.
[77] Iorwerth Peate to Frank Price Jones, 19.1.1962 (Frank Price Jones papers, 132/257, NLW).
[78] *Western Mail*, 8 January 1962.
[79] Gwynfor Evans to Elwyn Roberts, 30.11.1961 (PCP B 1063).
[80] *Y Ddraig Goch*, January 1962.
[81] J E Jones to Gwynfor Evans, 10.12.1961 (PCP M 40).
[82] Emrys Roberts to Elwyn Roberts, 2.2.1962 (GE, 1973, R, NLW).
[83] Mentioned in J E Jones to O M Roberts, 10.4.1962 (PCP M 40).
[84] ibid., Emrys Roberts to Gwynfor Evans, 26.1.1962.
[85] Minutes of Plaid Cymru Executive, 28.4.1962 (PCP M 21).
[86] Saunders Lewis, *Tynged yr Iaith* (third ed., Tal-y-bont, 1985), p. 26.
[87] ibid., p. 32.
[88] Saunders Lewis to David Jones, 19.9.1961 (David Jones papers, NLW).
[89] ibid., Saunders Lewis to David Jones, 22.4.1962.
[90] R Tudur Jones to Gwynfor Evans, n.d. (GE, 1973, J, NLW).
[91] J E Jones to Lewis Valentine, 26.2.1962 (PCP B 848).
[92] Dafydd Orwig Jones to Gwynfor Evans, 7.4.1962 (GE, 1973, J, NLW).
[93] *Baner ac Amserau Cymru*, 22 March 1962.
[94] R Tudur Jones to Gwynfor Evans, 28.3.1962 (GE, 1973, J, NLW).
[95] *Y Tyst*, 15, 22 February and 1 March 1962.
[96] Gwynfor Evans, *Cyfle Olaf yr Iaith Gymraeg* (Abertawe, 1962).
[97] *Y Ddraig Goch*, June 1962.

[98] Gwynfor Evans to Huw T Edwards, 7.6.1962 (Huw T Edwards papers, A1/701, NLW).
[99] Gwynfor Evans to Elwyn Roberts, 20.5.1962 (PCP B 1105).
[100] Minutes of Plaid Cymru Executive 28.4.1962 (PCP A 21); See also D J Williams's journal, 28.4.1962 (D J Williams papers, NLW).
[101] Minutes of Plaid Cymru Executive, 3.8.1962 (PCP A 21).
[102] Author's interview with David Walters.
[103] *Y Cymro*, 27 September 1962.
[104] Circular 26.9.1962 (PCP M 467).
[105] *Western Mail*, 4 October 1962.
[106] *Y Cymro*, 25 October 1962.
[107] Geraint Jones and Megan I Davies to Emrys Roberts, 20.11.1962 (PCP M 467).
[108] ibid., Raymond H Edwards to Emrys Roberts, 28.9.1962.
[109] ibid., J I Daniel to Emrys Roberts, 27.9.1962.
[110] See, for example, *Western Mail*, 19 January 1962.
[111] Minutes of Plaid Cymru Executive, 3.9.1962 (PCP A 21).
[112] *Western Mail*, 29 October 1962.
[113] Minutes of Plaid Cymru Executive, 1.11.1962 (PCP A 48).
[114] The original letter to Gwynfor Evans has not survived, but it is quoted in Gwynfor Evans to D J Williams, 28.12.1962 (D J Williams papers, NLW).
[115] Gwynfor Evans to J E Jones, 20.11.1962 (PCP M 40).
[116] Griffith John Williams to Gwynfor Evans, 27.11.1962 (GE, 1973, W, NLW).
[117] Gwynfor Evans to D J Williams, 28.12.1962 (D J Williams papers, NLW).
[118] Elystan Morgan to Gwynfor Evans, 1.1.1963 (GE, 1973, M, NLW).
[119] Dafydd Orwig Jones to Gwynfor Evans, n.d. (GE, 1973, J, NLW).
[120] The letter is mentioned in D J Williams's journal, 1.1.1963 (D J Williams papers, NLW).
[121] Saunders Lewis to Gwynfor Evans, 2.1.1963 (PCP A 48).
[122] D J Williams's journal, 5.1.1963 (D J Williams papers, NLW).
[123] *Western Mail*, 13 October 1962.
[124] Gwynfor Evans to Tedi Millward, 5.2.1963, private ownership.
[125] *Barn*, February 1963.
[126] ibid., March 1963.
[127] *Y Ddraig Goch*, January 1963.
[128] *Liverpool Daily Post*, 11 February 1963.
[129] Author's interview with Emyr Llywelyn.
[130] Gwynfor Evans to Harri Webb, 2.4.1963 (J Gwyn Griffiths papers, NLW).
[131] Emrys Roberts to Islwyn Ffowc Elis, 14.5.1963 (PCP B 870).
[132] Gwynfor Evans to Elwyn Roberts, n.d. (PCP B 867).
[133] *South Wales Evening Post*, 29 March 1963; *Western Mail*, 30 March 1963.
[134] Gwynfor Evans to Emrys Roberts, 28.5.1963 (PCP B 872).
[135] Statement by Flintshire and Denbighshire branches , 26.2.1963 (PCP B 872).
[136] Gwynfor Evans to Elwyn Roberts, 2.5.1963 (PCP B 1105).
[137] Emrys Roberts to John Alban Davies, 16.5.1963 (PCP B 870).
[138] R O F Wynne to Gwynfor Evans, 21.5.1963 (GE, 1973, W, NLW). Gwynfor answered R O F Wynne's letter on 24 May: 'I have great personal sympathy and admiration for the men who have acted as these did in Tryweryn, and therefore feel a considerable embarrassment when I am invited to sign the appeal. The policy of Plaid Cymru must be made clear, and the Party must as a Party dissociate itself from the actions. By attending some of the courts I have laid myself and the Party open to the charge of being two-faced and of accepting responsibility for a

policy which we have rejected. If I signed the appeal there would be far more ground for such a charge. Therefore I have most reluctantly to decline your kind invitation. I enclose a personal donation to the fund, which I wish every success.' See Gwynfor Evans to R O F Wynne, 24.5.1963. (File 1135, Garthewin Add, University of Wales, Bangor). On the discussions between the Squire of Garthewin and Saunders Lewis, see Saunders Lewis to R O F Wynne, 11.5.1963. Quoted in *Saunders Lewis a Theatr Garthewin*, Hazel Walford Davies (Llandysul, 1995), p. 366. The fund raised £569. In the case of Owain Williams, Elwyn Roberts attempted to ensure that he would not suffer any financial hardship because of his imprisonment, see Elwyn Roberts to John Daniel, 6.4.1964 (PCP B 1166).

[139] *Western Mail*, 31 July 1963.

[140] ibid., 2 March 1963.

[141] PRO BD 15/3, H N Jerman to Blaise Gillie, 1.3.1963. The members of the 'Llangadog Court' were delighted with this meeting. Islwyn Ffowc Elis rejoiced that: 'One of the ministers of the Crown is calling in his dilemma for the President of Plaid Cymru, and for Gwynfor Evans in particular, after the long battle.' See Islwyn Ffowc Elis to Gwynfor Evans, 18.3.1963 (GE, 1973, E, NLW).

[142] A year later, Gwynfor had to apologize for having claimed that the government had decided to establish the Economic Research Centre after his first meeting with Keith Joseph. It was a coincidence that the announcement had been made after the first meeting. *Western Mail*, 23 April 1964. Privately, Joseph believed that many of Gwynfor's ideas about economics were absurd. 'He [Gwynfor] never talks of starting or creating any wealth-earning enterprises but only of attracting or introducing industry from somewhere else. He really does present a picture of a parasitic economy – and the analogy with the enterprising, industrially and commercially super-sophisticated Swiss and Swedes is most inapt.' See PRO BD 25/59 Keith Joseph to Lord Brecon, n.d.

[143] *Y Ddraig Goch*, September 1963.

[144] ibid., May 1963.

[145] *Baner ac Amserau Cymru*, 4 April 1963.

[146] Moses Gruffydd to Gwynfor Evans, 9.4.1963 (GE, 1973, G, NLW).

[147] Islwyn Ffowc Elis to Gwynfor Evans, 10.4.1963 (GE, 1973, E, NLW).

[148] Gwynfor Evans's circular, 3.5.1963 (PCP B 870).

[149] *Baner ac Amserau Cymru*, 20 June 1963.

[150] *Western Mail*, 12 February 1963.

[151] Gwilym Prys Davies to Jim Griffiths, 30.6.1963 (James Griffiths papers, NLW).

[152] *Western Mail*, 2, 3, 4, 5, 8, 9 and 10 July 1963.

[153] ibid., 10 July 1963.

[154] *Y Ddraig Goch*, July/August, 1963.

[155] Eric Thomas, Managing Director of Teledu Cymru, to Gwynfor Evans, 20.2.1963 (GE, 1973, T, NLW). The letter contains a clear warning that the number of sets that could receive Teledu Cymru – 103,000 – is a blow, and that the company faces huge debts.

[156] T. H. Parry-Williams to Emrys Roberts, 27.4.1963 (Emrys Roberts papers, File 20, NLW).

[157] ibid., Financial Memorandum, Teledu Cymru Directors, 4.3.1963.

[158] Gwynfor Evans to Elwyn Roberts, 27.4.1963 (PCP B 1105).

[159] *Western Mail*, 21 a 22 July 1963.

[160] *Baner ac Amserau Cymru*, 30 May 1963.

[161] *Y Ddraig Goch*, June 1963.

[162] *Methiannau*, BBC Wales, 1987.

[163] This is mentioned in Emrys Roberts to Mair Edwards, 25.10.1963 (PCP M 490).

[164] Saunders Lewis thought Gwynfor had betrayed the people of Llangyndeyrn. After the villagers had lost their battle, in 1965, he wrote to W M Rees, Secretary of the Defence Committee, saying: 'My only disappointment is that the President of Plaid Cymru, as an Alderman on your County Council, was not leading you in the thick of the battle.' Saunders Lewis to W M Rees, 26.5.1965. Quoted in *Cloi'r Clwydi*, Robert Rhys (second ed., Llandybïe, 1993), p. 70.
[165] *Western Mail*, 25 October 1963.
[166] *Y Ddraig Goch*, November 1963.
[167] Kate Roberts to J E Jones, 27.11.1963 (PCP M 39).
[168] Ray Smith's memorandum to the Plaid Cymru Executive, August 1963 (PCP N 207).
[169] R Tudur Jones to Emrys Roberts, 13.9.1963 (PCP B 885).
[170] Elystan Morgan to J E Jones, 11.1.1964 (PCP M 39).
[171] *Y Ddraig Goch*, May 1964.
[172] Huw T Edwards to Elwyn Roberts, n.d. (PCP N 28).
[173] *Baner ac Amserau Cymru*, 9 January 1964.
[174] Gwynfor Evans to D J Williams, 1.2.1964 (D J Williams papers, NLW).
[175] ibid., J E Jones to D J Williams, 19.2.1964.
[176] Gwilym R. Jones to Gwynfor Evans, 11.2.1964 (GE, 1973, J, NLW).
[177] *Baner ac Amserau Cymru*, 19 March 1964.
[178] Gwynfor Evans to Emrys Roberts, 29.4.1964 (PCP B 898).
[179] *South Wales Evening Post*, 14 October 1964.
[180] *Y Ddraig Goch*, April 1964.
[181] Cassie Davies to Emrys Roberts, 28.6.1964 (PCP B 916).
[182] *Welsh Nation*, June 1964.
[183] 'Plaid Cymru – The State of the Party', Emrys Roberts, 28.6.1964 (Harri Webb papers, G1/31, NLW).
[184] Emrys Roberts's Memorandum, 21.7.1964 (Harri Webb papers, G1/132, NLW).
[185] *Western Mail*, 29 July 1964.
[186] Elystan Morgan to Gwynfor Evans, n.d. (GE, 1973, M, NLW).
[187] Emrys Roberts to members of New Nation, 29.12.1964 (PCP M 38).
[188] *Western Mail*, 9 September 1964.
[189] *South Wales Evening Post*, 11 September 1964.
[190] *Western Mail*, 20 and 31 August 1964.
[191] Emrys Roberts to Gwynfor Evans, 25.9.1964 (PCP B 898).
[192] Emrys Roberts to members of New Nation, 23.9.1964 (Harri Webb papers, G1/131, NLW).
[193] *Carmarthen Journal*, 11 September 1964.
[194] Author's interview with Aled Gwyn.
[195] *South Wales Evening Post*, 16 October 1964.

CHAPTER 8 – A New Dawn 1964–66

[1] See 'Mabon' in *Barn*, November 1964.
[2] *Western Mail*, 19 October 1964.
[3] Dafydd Evans's journal, 3.11.1964, unpublished version, private ownership.
[4] Reproduced in *Y Ddraig Goch*, November 1964.
[5] *Y Cymro*, 22 October 1964.
[6] Harri Webb to John Legonna, 18.10.1964 (John Legonna papers, 839/1, NLW).

[7] Saunders Lewis to Nina Wynne, 16.10.1964. Quoted in *Saunders Lewis a Theatr Garthewin*, Hazel Walford Davies, op. cit., p. 367.
[8] *Baner ac Amserau Cymru*, 10 December 1964.
[9] Cynog Davies and John Davies to Gwynfor Evans, 8.11.1964 (GE, 1973, D, NLW). The letter was also signed by Gareth Miles, John Daniel, T Llew Jones, Emyr Llywelyn and Peter Hourahane. On 14 November, the request was discussed by the executive but was roundly defeated.
[10] R Tudur Jones to Gwynfor Evans, 20.10.1964 (GE, 1973, J, NLW).
[11] Emrys Roberts to members of New Nation, 20.10.1964 (PCP M 211). The six members who received the 'Judas Letter' were: Michael and Margaret Tucker, Ray Smith, Harri Webb, John Legonna and Roger Boore.
[12] Author's interview with Nans Jones.
[13] Copy of Emrys Roberts's letter (GE, 1973, R, NLW).
[14] Gwynfor Evans to Chris Rees, 1.11.1964, private ownership.
[15] D J Williams's journal, 11.11.1964 (D J Williams papers, NLW).
[16] *Sunday Mirror*, 8 November 1964.
[17] R Tudur Jones to Gwynfor Evans, 11.11.1964 (GE, 1973, J, NLW).
[18] Emrys Roberts to Harri Webb, 8.11.1964 (Harri Webb papers, G1/145 iii, NLW).
[19] R Tudur Jones to Gwynfor Evans, 11.11.1964 (GE, 1973, J, NLW).
[20] Emrys Roberts to Gwynfor Evans, 13.11.1964 (GE, 1973, R, NLW).
[21] Minutes of Plaid Cymru Executive, 14.11.1964 (PCP A 51).
[22] There were 22 votes in favour of dismissing Emrys Roberts with 15 against. Seven members of the executive abstained. See D J Williams's journal, 15.11.1964 (D J Williams papers, NLW).
[23] Author's interviews with Owen John Thomas and Dr John Davies.
[24] Harri Webb to John Legonna, 24.11.1964 (John Legonna papers, 848/1, NLW).
[25] Gwynfor Evans to D J Williams, 29.11.1964 (D J Williams papers, NLW).
[26] Emrys Roberts to Gwynfor Evans, n.d. (GE, 1973, R, NLW).
[27] Ray Smith's Memorandum to the 'South Wales East Co-ordinating Committee of Plaid Cymru' (PCP B 1110).
[28] Owen John Thomas to Gwynfor Evans, 18.11.1964 (GE, 1973, T, NLW).
[29] *Western Mail*, 11 December 1964.
[30] Emrys Roberts to members of New Nation, 29.12.1964 (PCP M 38).
[31] Emrys Roberts to Pedr Lewis, 2.1.1966 (PCP B 1102).
[32] Author's interview with Lord Elystan Morgan. It is also worth noting – contrary to Gwynfor Evans's assertion in his autobiography, Gwynfor Evans, *Bywyd Cymro,* op. cit., p. 241, that the MP for Aberavon, John Morris, did not draw Elystan Morgan into the Labour party. The two were childhood friends but there was no organized conspiracy of any kind between them.
[33] Dafydd Evans's journal, 5.1.1965, private ownership.
[34] ibid., 10.1.1965.
[35] *Y Cymro*, 28 January 1965.
[36] *Western Mail*, 2 February 1965.
[37] Author's interview with Lord Elystan Morgan.
[38] *An Extract from the President's Letter*, n.d. (PCP B 1052).
[39] Peter Lynch, *SNP – The History of the Scottish National Party* (Cardiff, 2002), p. 99.
[40] *Barn*, March 1965.
[41] J E Jones to Gwynfor Evans, 15.3.1964 (GE, 1973, J, NLW).
[42] *Y Ddraig Goch*, March 1965.
[43] Saunders Lewis to Gwynfor Evans, 18.3.1964 (GE, 1973, L, NLW).

[44] D J Williams's journal, 28.3.1965 (D J Williams papers, NLW).
[45] *Western Mail*, 15 April 1965.
[46] ibid., 26 and 27 April 1965.
[47] Elwyn Roberts to Gwynfor Evans, 21.6.1965 (GE, 1973, R, NLW).
[48] Gwynfor Evans to Elwyn Roberts, 9.6.1964 (PCP B 1106).
[49] J E Jones to Gwynfor Evans, 12.7.1965 (GE, 1973, J, NLW).
[50] Elystan Morgan to J E Jones, n.d. (PCP M 38).
[51] *Western Mail*, 30 July 1965.
[52] ibid., 4 August 1965.
[53] Author's interview with Lord Elystan Morgan.
[54] J E Jones in the 'Tŵr yr Eryr' column, *Baner ac Amserau Cymru*, 19 August 1965. Cledwyn Hughes denied that he had ever been a member of Plaid Cymru. See ibid., 2 September 1965.
[55] Gwynfor Evans to J E Jones, 27.8.1965 (PCP B 1052).
[56] The first party political radio broadcast was made on 29 September. Gwynfor Evans made the first television broadcast in English on BBC and TWW at 9.30 p.m. Chris Rees was responsible for the radio broadcast in Welsh on the same evening. *Welsh Nation*, November 1965. It was claimed that Gwynfor Evans had gained a thousand new members as a result of the broadcast. *Annual Report*, Plaid Cymru, 1965 (PCP A 53).
[57] Gwynfor Evans to Liverpool Corporation, 7.10.1965 (PCP M 165).
[58] *Western Mail*, 14 October 1965.
[59] ibid., 20 October 1965.
[60] J E Jones to Gwynfor Evans, 18.10.1965 (GE, 1973, J, NLW).
[61] Supporters of the FWA like Mrs R O F Wynne were hugely disappointed by the tiny numbers and their 'feeble and wretched' attitude. Elwyn Roberts's note (PCP M 262).
[62] W H Sefton to Gwynfor Evans, 12.10.1965 (PCP M 165).
[63] Kate Roberts to Saunders Lewis, 28.10.1965, *Annwyl Kate, Annwyl Saunders*, op. cit., p. 218.
[64] Saunders Lewis to Kate Roberts, 15.11.1965, ibid., p.216.
[65] Gwynfor Evans to Islwyn Ffowc Elis, 30.10.1965 (PCP B 1105).
[66] Islwyn Ffowc Elis to Elwyn Roberts, 8.11.1965 (GE, 1973, E, NLW).
[67] D J Williams's journal, 3.12.1965 (D J Williams papers, NLW).
[68] *Manchester Guardian*, 3 January 1966. The four hunger strikers were Emyr Llywelyn, Gareth Miles, John Daniel and Geraint Jones.
[69] *Western Mail*, 4 November 1965. The 'volunteers' named included Mrs Maureen Huws, wife of O T L Huws and his daughter, Non. Gwenllian Wynne, daughter of R O F Wynne, was another name linked with the FWA.
[70] Members of the FWA to Gwynfor Evans, n.d. (PCP B 1052).
[71] Gwynfor Evans to 'A Friend', n.d., ibid.
[72] *Baner ac Amserau Cymru*, 10 March 1966.
[73] J E Jones to D J Williams, 25.3.1966 (D J Williams papers, NLW).
[74] *The Times*, 3 March 1966.
[75] Gwynfor Evans, *Bywyd Cymro,* op. cit., p.273.
[76] Author's interview with Cyril Jones.
[77] *Carmarthen Journal*, 4 March 1966.
[78] *Western Mail*, 24 March 1966.
[79] Gwilym Prys Davies, *Llafur y Blynyddoedd* (Denbigh, 1991), p. 53.
[80] *Carmarthen Journal*, 8 April 1966.
[81] The letter is quoted in *Gwynfor*, 14 October 1990. HTV Wales.
[82] *The Guardian*, 16 May 1966.

[83] Gwynfor Evans, *Bywyd Cymro*, op. cit., p. 246.
[84] *South Wales Evening Post*, 24 May 1966; *Western Mail*, 26 May 1966.
[85] Islwyn Ffowc Elis's memorandum, 6.10.1966 (Harri Webb papers, G 1/23, NLW).
[86] Author's interview with Clem Thomas.
[87] Gwynfor Evans to J E Jones, 16.6.1966 (PCP J 16).
[88] *Western Mail*, 30 June 1966.
[89] Gwynfor Evans's Personal Letter to the Electors of Carmarthenshire (PCP B 943).
[90] *Plaid Cymru and You* (PCP M 170).
[91] Islwyn Ffowc Elis's memorandum , 6.10.1966, loc. cit.
[92] Instruction to Canvassers by D Cyril Jones (PCP J 16). During April 1966, alleged members of the FWA were seen marching in uniform at the procession to commemorate the Easter Rising in Dublin. Their photograph was printed in the *Carmarthen Times*, 29 April 1966.
[93] Saunders Lewis to Elwyn Roberts, 19.5.1966 (PCP B 1210).
[94] Gwilym Prys Davies, *Llafur y Blynyddoedd* (Denbigh, 1991), op. cit., p. 54.
[95] *The Guardian*, 5 July 1966.
[96] *Daily Telegraph*, 13 July 1966.
[97] *The Guardian*, 13 July 1966.
[98] *Western Mail*, 12 July 1966.
[99] Dafydd Evans's journal, 3.7.1966, private ownership.
[100] D J Williams's journal, 12.7.1966 (D J Williams papers, NLW).
[101] Author's interview with Lili Thomas.
[102] *Liverpool Daily Post*, 14 July 1966.
[103] *Gwynfor yn Bedwar Ugain Oed*, Interview with Sulwyn Thomas, BBC Wales, 1992.
[104] Elwyn Roberts's memoirs (PCP B 1210). See Islwyn Ffowc Elis in *Y Ddraig Goch*, August 1966.
[105] From Gwenallt's sonnet, 'Sir Gaerfyrddin', first published in *Y Ddraig Goch*, September 1967.
[106] D J Williams's journal, 25.7.1966 (D J Williams papers, NLW).
[107] *Daily Mail*, 15 July 1966.
[108] *Carmarthen Journal*, 22 July 1966.
[109] Saunders Lewis to Gwynfor Evans, 15.1.1966, private ownership. In a further letter from him – this time to D J Williams, Lewis said that he was pleased for Gwynfor: 'Chiefly for his own sake; he has been repaid for his long years of labour.' However, he still insisted that Gwynfor was leading Plaid Cymru in the wrong direction: 'To teach that constitutional methods are going to win plays straight into the hands of the English government. And that is what Gwynfor and J E are teaching time after time – and doing huge moral harm.' See Saunders Lewis to D J Williams, 8.9.1966 (D J Williams papers, NLW).
[110] *Daily Telegraph*, 16 July 1966.
[111] *Y Cymro*, 21 July 1966.

CHAPTER 9 – The Member for Wales 1966–70

[1] *Carmarthen Journal*, 22 July 1966.
[2] *The Observer*, 17 July 1966.
[3] *South Wales Evening Post*, 15 July 1966.
[4] Neil Jenkins to Gwynfor Evans, 15.7.1966 (GE, 1973, J, NLW).
[5] Cynog Davies to Gwynfor Evans, 27.8.1966 (GE, 1973, D, NLW).
[6] Cynog Davies, 'Cymdeithas yr Iaith Gymraeg' in Meic Stephens (ed.), *The Welsh Language Today* (Llandysul, 1973), p. 256.

[7] Author's interview with Owen John Thomas.
[8] *Plaid Cymru Annual Report*, 1967 (PCP A 2).
[9] Dafydd Evans's journal, 31.10.1966, private ownership: 'I see a tendency in some almost to worship Daddy these days. I think that this is a dangerous thing. Daddy isn't keen at all either.'
[10] *The Times*, 15 July 1966.
[11] *Herald of Wales*, 23 July 1966.
[12] Gwynfor Evans, *Bywyd Cymro*, op. cit., pp. 257–8.
[13] ibid., p. 256.
[14] *Western Mail*, 21 July 1966.
[15] *South Wales Evening Post*, 21 July 1966.
[16] *The Times*, 19 July 1966.
[17] *Liverpool Daily Post,* 21 July 1966.
[18] It is worth noting how dismissive the police in Ceredigion and Carmarthenshire were of the FWA 'threat' in 1966. They considered possible prosecution of the FWA but concluded that a prosecution would be more trouble than it was worth. In the eyes of the police, Cayo Evans was an 'unbalanced personality' and Dennis Coslett, the other leading light in the FWA, had a 'mental age… [of] about 12 years'. Some freelance journalists, upon whom the FWA relied heavily as a conduit, were also considered to be 'thoroughly unreliable' by the police. PRO DPP 2/4455. 20.9.1966.
[19] *Liverpool Daily Post*, 22 July 1966.
[20] *Daily Mail*, 18 July 1966.
[21] *Liverpool Daily Post*, 22 July 1966.
[22] *Daily Mail*, 22 July 1966.
[23] *Liverpool Daily Post*, 22 July 1966.
[24] Gwynfor Evans, *Bywyd Cymro*, op. cit., pp. 253–6.
[25] *Parliamentary Debates* (Hansard), 5th series, vol.762, columns 1494–1504 (26 July 1966).
[26] *Western Mail*, 27 July 1966.
[27] *Liverpool Daily Post*, 27 July 1966.
[28] *South Wales Evening Post*, 1 August 1966.
[29] *The Times,* 29 August 1966.
[30] A H Lewis to Gwynfor Evans, 31.10.1966 (GE, 1973, L, NLW).
[31] Minutes of Plaid Cymru Executive, 10.9.1966 (PCP A 2).
[32] Author's interview with Tedi Millward.
[33] *Western Mail*, 5 August 1966.
[34] PRO DPP 2/4455.
[35] Gwynfor Evans to Harri Webb, 23.8.1966 (Harri Webb papers, G1/29, NLW).
[36] Gwynfor Evans to D J Williams, 20.8.1966 (D J Williams papers, NLW).
[37] Harri Webb to Elwyn Roberts, *Memorandum of Immediate Action*, 17.7.1966. (PCP B 1208).
[38] T I Ellis to Elwyn Roberts, 12.8.1966 (PCP B 1208).
[39] Islwyn Ffowc Elis to Gwynfor Evans, 30.8.1966 (GE, 1973, E, NLW).
[40] Emrys Roberts to Gwynfor Evans, 6.9.1966, Chris Rees papers, private ownership.
[41] Elwyn Roberts to Dewi Watkin Powell, 7.2.1967 (PCP B 1208).
[42] Author's interview with Meleri Mair.
[43] *Y Ddraig Goch*, September 1966.
[44] Dafydd Wigley to Gwynfor Evans, 14.8.1966 (GE, 1973, W, NLW).
[45] For the story behind the establishment of the Research Group, see Dafydd Wigley, *O Ddifri* (Caernarfon, 1992), pp. 65–6.

[46] *Western Mail,* 15, 16 November 1966.
[47] ibid., 12 December 1966.
[48] ibid., 5 December 1966.
[49] His sponsor was the former judge, Sir Alun Pugh. See Sir Alun Pugh to Gwynfor Evans, 14.12.1966 (GE, 1973, P, NLW).
[50] *Liverpool Daily Post*, 28 November 1966.
[51] Gwynfor Evans to Ioan Bowen Rees, 18.1.1967 (Ioan Bowen Rees papers, NLW). I am grateful to Margaret Bowen Rees for letting me see this correspondence.
[52] Phil Williams to Gwynfor Evans, 3.1.1967 (GE, 1983, W, NLW).
[53] For the background to the by-election, see Cennard Davies's piece in *Y Ddraig Goch,* May 1967.
[54] *Liverpool Daily Post*, 1 January 1967, 10 April 1967.
[55] *Rhondda Leader*, 3 and 24 February 1967.
[56] *Western Mail*, 24 February 1967.
[57] *The Observer*, 12 March 1967.
[58] *Rhondda Leader*, 16 March 1967.
[59] *Western Mail*, 17 March 1967.
[60] Gwynfor Evans to Ioan Bowen Rees, 16.3.1967 (Ioan Bowen Rees papers, NLW).
[61] *Liverpool Daily Post*, 16 March 1967.
[62] Gwynfor Evans to Ioan Bowen Rees, 16.3.1967 (Ioan Bowen Rees papers, NLW).
[63] Gwynfor Evans to D J Williams, 27.3.1967 (D J Williams papers, NLW).
[64] *Liverpool Daily Post*, 19 April 1967.
[65] ibid., 15 April 1967.
[66] *Western Mail*, 13, 18 March 1967.
[67] *Y Cymro*, 20 April 1967.
[68] *Llanelli Star*, 15 April 1967. For Gwynfor Evans's response, see ibid. 13 May 1967.
[69] Gwynfor Evans to Harri Webb, 10.4.1967, G1/34 (Harri Webb papers, NLW).
[70] PRO PREM 13/2359, W K Reid, to Sir Burke Trend 22.12.1966: 'Wales and the Prince of Wales. He said that the PM had spoken to the S/S for Wales advising him to soft-pedal for a bit.'
[71] *Daily Telegraph*, 18 May 1967.
[72] *Y Cymro*, 1 June 1967.
[73] *Liverpool Daily Post*, 18 May 1967.
[74] *The Times*, April 26, 1967.
[75] PRO BD 40/97, Eirene White to John Morris (Parliamentary Secretary to the Transport Department), 14.8.1967.
[76] ibid., Cledwyn Hughes to John Morris, 15.9.1967.
[77] Author's interviews with Lords Gwilym Prys Davies and Lord Elystan Morgan. See also Vernon Bogdanor, *Devolution in the United Kingdom* (Oxford, 1999), pp. 162–4.
[78] *Gwynfor*, HTV Cymru, 14 October 1990.
[79] *Y Ddraig Goch*, September 1967.
[80] Gwynfor Evans to Harri Webb, 17.8.1967 (Harri Webb papers, G1/38, NLW).
[81] *Western Mail*, 10 July 1967.
[82] *Liverpool Daily Post*, 20 September 1967. Owain Williams claimed that he had left Plaid Cymru before he was removed.
[83] *Western Mail*, 24 November 1972.
[84] Gwynfor Evans to Colin Edwards, 18.10.1967 (PCP B 1101).
[85] *Y Ddraig Goch*, September 1967.

[86] Emrys Roberts to Islwyn Ffowc Elis, 8.8.1967 (Islwyn Ffowc Elis papers, NLW).
[87] *The Times*, 14 August 1967.
[88] *Liverpool Daily Post*, 18 October 1967.
[89] Elwyn Roberts to Gwynfor Evans, 26.10.1967 (GE, 1973, R, NLW).
[90] *Western Mail*, 25 July 1967.
[91] *Tafod y Ddraig*, October 1967.
[92] Gwynfor Evans to Islwyn Ffowc Elis, 31.10.1967 (Islwyn Ffowc Elis papers, NLW).
[93] Author's interview with Winnie Ewing. See also Winnie Ewing, *Stop the World, The Autobiography of Winnie Ewing* (Edinburgh, 2004), pp. 63–78.
[94] *The Scotsman*, 4 November 1967.
[95] Gwynfor Evans's statement to Plaid Cymru Executive, 4.11.1967 (Ioan Bowen Rees papers, NLW).
[96] *Barn*, December 1967.
[97] *The New Statesman*, 10 November 1967.
[98] PRO PREM 13/2151. Richard Crossman to Harold Wilson, 13.11.1967.
[99] *The Scotsman*, 7 November 1967.
[100] *Y Ddraig Goch*, November 1967.
[101] Gwynfor Evans to D J Williams, 11.12.1967 (D J Williams papers, NLW).
[102] *Y Cymro*, 31 August 1967.
[103] Islwyn Ffowc Elis's circular, 9.12.1967 (PCP B 1044).
[104] Minutes of Plaid Cymru Executive, 9.12.1967 (PCP A 54).
[105] Dafydd Evans's journal, 5.9.1967, private ownership. In the same way, he confided to the *Carmarthen Journal* that he had spent the Christmas of 1967 worrying about how he would cope in a narrow trench as the American bombs rained down on him. See *Carmarthen Journal*, 5 January 1968.
[106] For William Wallis's papers, see PRO PREM 13/2275.
[107] Author's interview with Gwynoro Jones. Every day, Rhiannon and a group of friends would meet at Providence chapel, Llangadog, to pray for her husband and those travelling with him. *Carmarthen Times*, 12 January 1968.
[108] *Carmarthen Journal*, 16 February 1968.
[109] Minutes of Carmarthenshire District Committee, 17.2.1968 (Pol 18, Carmarthenshire County Council Archives).
[110] *Western Mail*, 16 January 1968.
[111] Elwyn Roberts to Islwyn Ffowc Elis, 6.2.1968 (PCP N 206).
[112] Gwynfor Evans to Islwyn Ffowc Elis, 12.6.1967 (Islwyn Ffowc Elis papers, NLW). The machines were 'remarkable' because they used the 'offset-litho' printing method, something – according to Plaid Cymru's publicity for would-be investors – that would be 'an unmixed blessing' for Welsh publishing. See Elwyn Roberts to Dr D H Davies, 21.9.1967 (PCP B 1188).
[113] Author's interview with Hywel Heulyn Roberts.
[114] Gwynfor Evans to Duncan Gardiner, 10.1.1979 (GE, 1988, Box 25, NLW).
[115] Elwyn Roberts to Islwyn Ffowc Elis, 19.4.1968 (PCP N 206).
[116] Emrys Roberts to Harri Webb, 4.4.1968 (Harri Webb papers, G 1, NLW).
[117] *Forward* (Plaid Cymru Branch Bulletin), 9.4.1968.
[118] Islwyn Ffowc Elis to Willie Kellock, 3.5.1968 (Islwyn Ffowc Elis papers, NLW).
[119] *Sunday Express,* 7 January 1968. See also *I'r Gad*, Volume 1, 1968.
[120] Richard Crossman, *The Diaries of a Cabinet Minister*, Volume 2, 1966–8 (London 1976), p. 771.
[121] R Tudur Jones's editorial in *Y Ddraig Goch*, May 1968.

[122] Gwynfor Evans to Ioan Bowen Rees, 23.4.1968 (Ioan Bowen Rees papers, NLW).
[123] Memorandum described as 'Completely Confidential on the meetings between Gwynfor Evans and Whitelaw (Conservative Chief Whip)' (PCP M 259).
[124] Gwynfor Evans to Ioan Bowen Rees, 27.4.1968 (Ioan Bowen Rees papers, NLW).
[125] ibid.
[126] Gwynfor Evans to Harri Webb, 2.1.1969 (Harri Webb papers, G1/42, NLW).
[127] Author's interview with Gwynoro Jones.
[128] Dafydd Orwig to Gwynfor Evans, 9.12.1967 (GE, 1973, J, NLW). In his letter, Dafydd Orwig writes: 'I don't think you should toy too much with the business of supporting the government and the bombing if you don't have secret information. I fear the work is being done by a small group of extremist and determined Welshmen.'
[129] *Liverpool Daily Post*, 27 May 1968.
[130] ibid., 28 May 1968. See also *Parliamentary Debates* (Hansard), 5th series, vol. 765, columns 1229–34 (27 May 1968).
[131] *Caernarvon and Denbigh Herald*, 31 May 1998; *South Wales Voice,* 6 June 1968.
[132] *South Wales Echo*, 27 May 1968.
[133] *Liverpool Daily Post*, 28 May 1968.
[134] Loti Rees Hughes to George Thomas, 22.6.1968 (Viscount Tonypandy papers, File 50, NLW).
[135] Memorandum by Gwynoro Jones, n.d., 'Press Quotations by Nationalists' (File 66, ibid.).
[136] Gwynfor Evans to Ioan Bowen Rees, 6.5.1968 (Ioan Bowen Rees papers, NLW).
[137] ibid., Gwynfor Evans to Ioan Bowen Rees, 1.7.1968.
[138] *South Wales Echo*, 17 July 1968.
[139] Quoted in Martin Westlake, *Kinnock – The Biography* (London, 2000), p. 61.
[140] *Y Cymro*, 25 July 1968.
[141] *South Wales Echo*, 12 July 1968.
[142] Islwyn Ffowc Elis to Robyn Lewis, 3.6.1968 (Islwyn Ffowc Elis papers, NLW).
[143] ibid.
[144] *Y Ddraig Goch*, July/August 1968.
[145] *Liverpool Daily Post,* 7 August 1968.
[146] *Western Mail*, 9 August 1968.
[147] Gwynfor Evans, *Bywyd Cymro*, op. cit., pp. 260–1.
[148] Gwyndaf (Evan Gwyndaf Evans) to Gwynfor Evans, 15.8.1968 (GE, 1973, E, NLW).
[149] Interview between Saunders Lewis and Meirion Edwards, 9 August 1968, BBC Cymru.
[150] Gwynfor Evans to Ioan Bowen Rees, 4.9.1968 (Ioan Bowen Rees papers, NLW).
[151] *Western Mail*, 11 September 1968.
[152] *Y Cymro*, 19 September 1968.
[153] Interview between R O F Wynne and Denis Tuohy, 10 September 1968, *24 Hours*, BBC 1.
[154] Saunders Lewis to R O F Wynne, 18.9.1968. Quoted in Hazel Walford Davies, *Saunders Lewis a Theatr Garthewin*, op. cit., p. 371.
[155] *Liverpool Daily Post*, 12 September 1968.
[156] Dafydd Iwan to Elwyn Roberts, 12.9.1968 (PCP M 191).
[157] ibid., Lewis Valentine to Elwyn Roberts, 12.9.1968.
[158] *Y Cymro*, 26 September 1968.
[159] Saunders Lewis, 'Y Bomiau a Chwm Dulas' (NLW 22726 E); For background to the article, see Menna Baines in *Barn*, July/August 1994.
[160] Elwyn Roberts to D J Williams, 12.9.1968 (D J Williams papers, NLW).
[161] *Barn*, October 1968.

[162] *Liverpool Daily Post*, 11 October 1968.
[163] Gwynfor Evans to James Callaghan, 7.10.1968 (GE, 1973, C, NLW).
[164] James Callaghan to Gwynfor Evans, 12.10.1968 (GE, 1973, C, NLW).
[165] *Parliamentary Debates* (Hansard), 5th series, vol. 770, column 292 (15 October 1968).
[166] ibid., vol. 774, Columns 706–707 (28 November, 1968).
[167] *The Times*, 13 September 1999.
[168] Author's interview with Aled Gwyn.
[169] Gwynfor Evans to Ioan Bowen Rees, 1.12.1968 (Ioan Bowen Rees papers, NLW).
[170] *Carmarthen Journal*, 31 January 1969.
[171] *Y Cymro*, 30 January 1969.
[172] *Western Mail*, 28 January 1969.
[173] Gwynfor Evans to Pennar Davies, 8.7.1974 (Pennar Davies papers, NLW).
[174] Memorandum by Robyn Lewis, '*Cyfarfod y Tywysog*', 13.3.1969 (Islwyn Ffowc Elis papers, NLW).
[175] Gwynfor Evans to Elwyn Roberts, 26.2.1969 (Ioan Bowen Rees papers, NLW).
[176] Dafydd Iwan to Gwynfor Evans, 15.3.1969 (GE, 1973, I, NLW).
[177] Gwynfor Evans to Dafydd Iwan, 12.3.1969 (Dylan Phillips Research Papers, File 7, NLW).
[178] Author's interview with Gareth Miles.
[179] Gwynfor Evans to Tedi Millward, 12.3.1969, private ownership. I wish to thank E G (Tedi) Millward for permission to see these letters.
[180] Gwynfor Evans to Tedi Millward, n.d., ibid.
[181] *Western Mail*, 13 March 1969.
[182] Tedi Millward to Gwynfor Evans, 30.5.1969 (Islwyn Ffowc Elis papers, NLW).
[183] Tedi Millward to Gwynfor Evans, n.d. (GE, 1973, M, NLW). In his letter, Tedi Millward says that he also taught Charles about 'the water problem' and that he was 'interested in the countryside and the threats it faces'.
[184] Gwynfor Evans to Tedi Millward, 6.5.1969, private ownership.
[185] *Daily Telegraph*, 6 September 1968. The author John Aeron Summers of Swansea wishes to make it clear that he is not the John Summers referred to here and in the Welsh-language version of this book.
[186] Gwynfor Evans to Islwyn Ffowc Elis, 7.5.1969 (Islwyn Ffowc Elis papers, NLW).
[187] *Barn*, August 1969.
[188] Gwynfor Evans to D J Williams, 24.4.1969 (D J Williams papers, NLW).
[189] Gwynfor Evans, *Bywyd Cymro*, op. cit., pp. 274–5.
[190] *Barn*, October 1985.
[191] Gwynfor Evans to D J Williams, 24.4.1969, (D J Williams papers, NLW).
[192] *Western Mail*, 16 April 1969.
[193] *Liverpool Daily Post*, 10 May 1969.
[194] Internal report by Dr Gareth Morgan Jones and Dafydd Williams, 20.5.1969 (PCP B 1207).
[195] Quotations from the pathologist Bernard Knight. See Dr Gareth Morgan Jones to Elwyn Roberts, 24.6.1969 (PCP B 1101).
[196] Islwyn Ffowc Elis to Dafydd Iwan, 5.6.1969 (Dylan Phillips Research Papers, File 5, NLW).
[197] *Barn*, August 1969.
[198] *The Sun*, 1 July 1969.
[199] *Western Mail*, 30 June 1989.
[200] *Carmarthen Journal*, 11 July 1969; *Western Mail*, 4 July 1969.
[201] George Thomas, *Mr Speaker – The Memoirs of Viscount Tonypandy* (London, 1985), p. 121.
[202] Gwynfor Evans to Islwyn Ffowc Elis, 9.7.1969 (Islwyn Ffowc Elis papers, NLW).

[203] Gwynfor Evans, *Bywyd Cymro*, op. cit., p. 277.
[204] Gwynfor Evans to Islwyn Ffowc Elis, 9.7.1969, (Islwyn Ffown Elis papers, NLW).
[205] Gwynfor Evans to J E Jones, 15.7.1969 (PCP M 33).
[206] Gwynfor Evans to Harri Webb, 25.7.1969 (Harri Webb papers, G1/48, NLW).
[207] Gwynfor Evans to Alwyn D Rees, 28.7.1969 (Alwyn D Rees papers, CH 9/7/35, NLW).
[208] Robyn Léwis to Dafydd Iwan, 14.7.1969 (Dylan Phillips Research Papers, NLW).
[209] ibid., R Tudur Jones to Dafydd Iwan, 14.7.1969.
[210] Memorandum by Gwynoro Jones, *Extremism in Wales*, 3.7.1969 (Viscount Tonypandy papers, File 86, NLW).
[211] See, for instance, the attack made by Eirene White, Welsh Affairs Minister, on the 'idolatry of the Welsh Language' during the Flint Eisteddfod. *Liverpool Daily Post*, 4 August 1969.
[212] PRO PREM, 13/2996 George Thomas to Harold Wilson, 28.7.1969.
[213] ibid., Eirene White to Harold Wilson, 30.7.1969.
[214] *Liverpool Daily Post*, 29 August 1969.
[215] Gwynfor Evans to Dafydd Iwan, 21.9.1969 (Dylan Phillips Research Papers, File 5, NLW).
[216] ibid., Cassie Davies to Dafydd Iwan, 25.10.1969.
[217] *Baner ac Amserau Cymru*, 13 November 1969.
[218] Gwynfor Evans to D Cyril Jones, 10.11.1969 (GE, 1988, Box 34, NLW).
[219] *Carmarthen Times*, 2 January 1970.
[220] *Carmarthen Journal*, 9 January 1970. Gwynfor's other 'saint' was George M Ll Davies. *Y Ddraig Goch*, February 1970.
[221] Gwynfor Evans, *Bywyd Cymro*, op. cit., pp. 278–9; *The Times*, 5 February 1970.
[222] *The Sun*, 5 and 6 February 1970.
[223] *Liverpool Daily Post*, 12 February 1970.
[224] *Western Mail*, 17 February 1970.
[225] ibid., 25 February 1970.
[226] *Carmarthen Times,* 27 February 1970.
[227] *Liverpool Daily Post,* 23 February 1970. For the previous six weeks, things had been difficult between Plaid Cymru and the farmers of Cwm Dulas – in particular because Plaid Cymru had given some consideration to unlawful methods of saving the valley. But, in September 1969, Plaid Cymru's leadership was warned by Elwyn Roberts that it was 'even more obvious by now that the locals in Dulas – some of them at least – don't want Plaid in the business at all'. See Elwyn Roberts to 'A Friend', 8.9.1969 (PCP M 93).
[228] Dewi Watkin Powell to Dafydd Iwan, 17.2.1970 (GE, 1973, P, NLW).
[229] Peter Hughes Griffiths to Dafydd Iwan, 16.2.1970 (Dylan Phillips Research Papers, File 5, NLW).
[230] ibid., Cynog Dafis to Dafydd Iwan, 15.2.1970.
[231] Gwynfor Evans to Elwyn Roberts, 15.2.1970 (PCP B 1188).
[232] *Western Mail*, 7 March 1970.
[233] *Liverpool Daily Post*, 15 April 1970.
[234] Gwynfor Evans to Elwyn Roberts, 17.4.1970 (PCP B 1188).
[235] Author's interviews with D Cyril Jones and Gwynoro Jones. Gwynoro Jones denies that he authorized anyone to spread the story of Gwynfor Evans's 'cancer'.
[236] After the general election, the workers at the allotments wrote to the local paper (completely independently of Gwynfor) stressing that the suggestion that he was a merciless boss was a lie. *Carmarthen Journal*, 17 July 1970.
[237] See Kenneth O. Morgan, 'Gwleidyddiaeth Cymru yn 1970' in D Ben Rees (ed.), *Arolwg*, Volume 6, 1970 (Tonypandy, 1971), pp. 27–31.

[238] *The Times*, 4 June 1970.
[239] *Carmarthen Journal*, 5 June 1970.
[240] Gwynfor Evans's election leaflet (PCP M 211).
[241] Plaid Cymru's row was not only with the government but also with the BBC in London. Dewi Watkin Powell wrote on behalf of Plaid Cymru to the BBC's chiefs several times to upbraid them for their negative attitude towards the party. In one, he writes: 'Day in day out we are given the unending procession of Wilson-Heath-Thorpe and their assistants which, so far as Wales is concerned, presents a wholly false, misleading and unbalanced picture of the election… At present, it is perilously near to being a cynical disregard of the principle of freedom of expression. This is grave indeed where a state corporation is involved.' See Dewi Watkin Powell to John Crawley, BBC news and current affairs editor, 7.6.1970 (File 1241, BBC Archives, Caversham). It is worth noting, in passing, that the Welsh Secretary, George Thomas, was diametrically opposed to Watkin Powell and Gwynfor, during precisely the same period. Thomas wrote to Harold Wilson to complain that 'The BBC of Wales [is]… firmly in the grip of Welsh Nationalists'. It was a familiar complaint from the Welsh Labour Party and Wilson did not give it a moment's attention. See George Thomas to Harold Wilson, 10.2.1970, PRO PREM 13/3069.
[242] Author's interview with Gwynoro Jones.
[243] *Y Cymro*, 17 June 1970.

CHAPTER 10 – The Party's Over 1970–74

[1] Wales saw an increase of 185 per cent in Plaid Cymru's share of the vote. In Scotland, there was an increase of 134 per cent in the SNP vote.
[2] Author's interview with Tedi Millward.
[3] *Triban*, Volume 4, Issue 2, 1970.
[4] Memorandum from Islwyn Ffowc Elis, *Plaid Cymru, 1970–1974 – Rhai Awgrymiadau at y Dyfodol* (PCP M 231).
[5] Author's interview with Meinir Ffransis.
[6] Author's interview with Eurfyl ap Gwilym.
[7] Author's interview with Rhys Davies.
[8] At the end of 1970, Plaid Cymru had debts of £9,230. See Financial Report 1970 (PCP B 1226).
[9] Gwynfor Evans to Rhys Davies, 24.11.1970, private ownership. I am indebted to Rhys Davies for permission to see this correspondence.
[10] ibid., Gwynfor Evans to Rhys Davies, 18.10.1974.
[11] *Baner ac Amserau Cymru*, 24 September 1970.
[12] Gwynfor Evans to Rhys Davies, 10.8.1970, private ownership.
[13] *Western Mail*, 26 October 1970.
[14] *Baner ac Amserau Cymru*, 5 November 1970.
[15] Peter Hourahane to Gwynfor Evans, 8.8.1970 (GE, 1973, H, NLW).
[16] Minutes of Plaid Cymru Executive, 23.7.1970 (PCP A 57).
[17] See '1971' in Gwilym Tudur (ed.) *Wyt Ti'n Cofio?: Chwarter Canrif o Frwydr yr Iaith* (Tal-y-bont, 1989), p. 83.
[18] *Y Cymro*, 25 November 1970.
[19] *Barn*, January 1970.
[20] *Gwerth dy Grys* (Llandysul, n.d.), p. 4.
[21] Gwynfor Evans to Rhys Davies, 14.12.1970, private ownership.

[22] *Western Mail*, 15 March 1971. For the response to these comments, see Meg Elis in Gwilym Tudur (ed.) *Wyt Ti'n Cofio?: Chwarter Canrif o Frwydr yr Iaith*, op. cit., p. 84.
[23] Minutes of Plaid Cymru Executive, 9.3.1971 (PCP A 6).
[24] Minutes of Plaid Cymru Executive, 13.3.1971 (PCP A 58) and 10.4.1971 (PCP A 17).
[25] Deulwyn Morgan, Peter Hughes Griffiths and Tegwyn Jones to Elwyn Roberts, 12.2.1971 (PCP B 1086).
[26] *Liverpool Daily Post*, 3 February 1971. Seven were arrested and the eighth, Robat Gruffudd, was arrested later.
[27] PRO BD 25/38, Gwynfor Evans to Peter Thomas, 4.5.1971.
[28] *Western Mail*, 4 May 1971; *Carmarthen Times*, 7 May 1971.
[29] Gwynfor Evans to Rhys Davies, 13.5.1971, private ownership.
[30] ibid. Following the protests, an independent inquiry found that the police had been far too heavy-handed during the Swansea case. *Liverpool Daily Post*, 28 August 1971.
[31] *Liverpool Daily Post,* 17 April 1971.
[32] *Carmarthen Times*, 7 May 1971.
[33] ibid., 4 June 1971. One correspondent, Gwyn Charles, was of the opinion that the party could not decide 'whether to support Britain or Hitler'.
[34] Neil Taylor and Graham George's letters in the *Welsh Nation*, July and August 1971.
[35] Gwynfor Evans to Dafydd Iwan, 23.5.1971 (Dylan Phillips Research Papers, NLW).
[36] Minutes of Plaid Cymru Executive, 8.6.1971 (PCP A 58).
[37] Saunders Lewis to Gwynfor Evans, n.d. (GE, 1973, L, NLW). Nationalists with an interest in European affairs, like Saunders Lewis, were the exception. He wrote to Gwynfor to express his 'sadness… that Phil Williams and his gang are always competing with Labour on Labour's ground … Plaid Cymru's story from the outset has been to claim her place in Europe for Wales'.
[38] Pennar Davies, *Gwynfor Evans*, op. cit., p. 73.
[39] *Y Ddraig Goch*, May 1971.
[40] Gwynfor Evans to Harri Webb, 3.9.1971 (Harri Webb papers, G1/52, NLW).
[41] *Y Cymro*, 22 September 1971.
[42] Gwynfor Evans to John Hughes, 1.11.1971 (PCP B 1031).
[43] *Liverpool Daily Post*, 11 November 1971. Myrddin Williams and Goronwy Fellows were jailed along with Ffred Ffransis.
[44] Gwynfor Evans to Rhys Davies, 14.1.1972, private ownership.
[45] Gwynfor Evans to Sir Goronwy Daniel, 15.2.1972 (Sir Goronwy Daniel papers, NLW). Gwynfor's aim was to make the University Committee destroy the argument that a Welsh corporation would cost £38 million. Gwynfor and his fellow-members on the committee thought that a figure of £2.75 million was closer to the mark. On 14 July 1972, the University Court adopted the recommendations of the Broadcasting Committee that a Welsh-language channel should be set up under the control of an Independent Board and its conclusions were sent to the Communications Minister.
[46] Minutes of Plaid Cymru Executive, 8.1.1972 (PCP A 72).
[47] *Welsh Nation*, 18–24 February 1972.
[48] Dick Kennard, secretary of Ton-teg Branch to Dafydd Williams, 23.2.1972 (PCP A 72).
[49] Gwynfor Evans to Elwyn Roberts, 19.1.1972 (PCP B 1105).
[50] Gwynfor Evans to Peter Hughes Griffiths, 21.2.1972 (GE, 1988, Box 34, NLW).
[51] *Liverpool Daily Post*, 17 May 1972.
[52] This is first mentioned in Islwyn Ffowc Elis to Gwynfor Evans, 17.3.1972 (GE, 1983, E,

NLW).
[53] *Welsh Nation*, 24–30 March 1972.
[54] Islwyn Ffowc Elis to Gwynfor Evans, 14.3.1972 (GE, 1983, E, NLW). Before the general election of 1970, the executive succeeded in preventing Emrys Roberts from standing as a candidate.
[55] *Y Ddraig Goch*, May 1972.
[56] ibid., July 1972.
[57] *Liverpool Daily Post*, 26 May, 1 June 1972.
[58] Minutes of Plaid Cymru Executive, 8.7.1972 (PCP A 72).
[59] *Western Mail*, 24 June 1972.
[60] ibid., 5 August 1972.
[61] For Dan Evans's obituary, see *Baner ac Amserau Cymru*, 1 December 1972.
[62] Interview between Gwynfor Evans and Emyr Daniel, *Welshmen of Our Time*, 26 August 1979, BBC Wales.
[63] *Western Mail*, 16 December 1972.
[64] ibid., 13 April 1973. Gwynfor lost his 'Llangadog no. 6' seat comparatively easily. George Morgan received 1,309 votes with 931 for Gwynfor.
[65] *Carmarthen Times*, 13 April 1973.
[66] *Barn*, July 1973.
[67] Author's interview with Meinir Ffransis.
[68] Author's interview with Dafydd Evans.
[69] Minutes of Carmarthenshire District Committee, 17.4.1973 (Pol 18, Carmarthenshire County Council Archives).
[70] Minutes of Plaid Cymru Executive, 14.4.1973 (PCP A 72).
[71] Minutes of Carmarthenshire District Committee, 5.6.1973 (Pol 18, Carmarthenshire County Council Archives).
[72] Gwynfor Evans, *Wales Can Win* (Llandybïe, 1973), p. 145.
[73] *Western Mail*, 1 June 1973.
[74] *The Scotsman*, 14 May 1973.
[75] Dafydd Williams to Edward Heath, 16.5.1973 (PCP M 685).
[76] Minutes of Carmarthenshire District Committee, 15.5.1973 (Pol 18, Carmarthenshire County Council Archives).
[77] *Liverpool Daily Post*, 1 June 1973.
[78] Gwynfor Evans to Rhys Davies, 3.7.1973, private ownership.
[79] Gwynfor Evans to Peter Hughes Griffiths, 17.8.1973 (GE, 1988, Box 34, NLW).
[80] Internal memorandum, n.d. (PCP A 19).
[81] Plaid Cymru memorandum, *Kilbrandon – Forcing the Pace* (PCP M 685).
[82] *Western Mail*, 4 August 1973.
[83] *Liverpool Daily Post,* 26 October 1973.
[84] *Y Cymro*, 3 November 1973.
[85] *The Times*, 24 October 1973. In an interview with the paper's Welsh correspondent, Trevor Fishlock, Gwynfor took pride in what nationalists had achieved: 'Thirty or 40 years ago nobody thought of Wales as an economic or political entity. That has changed. We have changed the way that governments think about Wales and we have got our country recognized.'
[86] *Western Mail*, 29 October 1973.
[87] *The Scotsman*, 1 November 1973.
[88] *Western Mail*, 12 November 1973.
[89] *The Times*, 29 November 1973.

[90] *Carmarthen Times*, 16 November 1973.
[91] Minutes of Carmarthenshire District Committee, 4.12.1973 (Pol 18, Carmarthenshire County Council Archives).
[92] *Tafod y Ddraig*, March 1974.
[93] *Western Mail*, 10 January 1974.
[94] Gwynfor Evans to Dafydd Williams, 4.12.1973 (PCP A 72).
[95] *Liverpool Daily Post*, 5 January 1974.
[96] *Welsh Nation*, 4/10 January 1974.
[97] *Baner ac Amserau Cymru*, 15 February 1974.
[98] Press release, 24.1.1974 (PCP J 235).
[99] Author's interview with Cyril Jones.
[100] *Y Ddraig Goch*, January 1974.
[101] D O Davies to Gwynfor Evans, 28.12.1973 (GE, 1983, D, NLW).
[102] Gwynfor Evans to Rhys Davies, 11.4.1974, private ownership.
[103] *South Wales Guardian*, 10 January 1974.
[104] Gwynfor Evans's election leaflet, *Y Ffordd yng Nghymru* (PCP J 235).
[105] Author's interview with Cyril Jones.
[106] Gwynfor Evans, *Bywyd Cymro*, op. cit., pp. 297–8.
[107] *Y Ddraig Goch*, April 1974.
[108] For detailed reports on the chronology of the evening see *Baner ac Amserau Cymru,* 8 March 1974; *The Times*, 2 March 1974.
[109] Gwynfor Evans to Rhys Davies, 11.4.1974, private ownership.
[110] ibid., Gwynfor Evans to Rhys Davies, 9.3.1974.
[111] Author's interview with Professor Phil Williams.
[112] ibid.
[113] *The Guardian*, 4 March 1974.
[114] *Liverpool Daily Post,* 6 March 1974.
[115] PRO BD 111/21, Lord Crowther-Hunt to John Morris, 17.4.1974.
[116] Gwynfor Evans to Elwyn Roberts, 20.3.1974 (PCP B 1096).
[117] *The Times*, 24 June 1974. Dafydd Wigley, Dafydd Elis Thomas and Dr Phil Williams believed the government's recommendations on devolution were insufficient because they did not give enough powers to a Welsh Assembly. Wigley and Elis Thomas believed they had been shabbily treated by the government and that from then on they would be more 'spiky' in the Commons.
[118] *Carmarthen Times*, 12 April 1974.
[119] Ceridwen Pritchard to Gwynfor Evans, 31.5.1974, private ownership.
[120] Author's interview with Gwynoro Jones.
[121] Neil Kinnock to Sir Archibald Lush, n.d. (Michael Foot papers, Labour Party Archives, C10, Manchester).
[122] *Y Cymro*, 17 September 1974.
[123] It is fair to say that the relationship between Cymdeithas yr Iaith and Plaid Cymru was quite strained at this time. During May 1974, the leaders of both sides met to discuss Gwynfor's request for Cymdeithas 'to refrain from unlawful action' in the Carmarthen constituency during the election. Cymdeithas refused the request and Terwyn Tomos, its secretary, wrote to Gwynfor: 'I have now been asked to state the Senate's unhappiness with the idea that Plaid Cymru has of the function of Cymdeithas yr Iaith… We are not a 'Pressure Group' or even a language wing of Plaid Cymru. That is the main reason for rejecting your request to refrain from action.' Terwyn Tomos to Gwynfor Evans, 25.6.1974 (PCP M 711).

[124] *Baner ac Amserau Cymru*, 7 June 1974.
[125] *The Times*, 18 September 1974.
[126] *The Guardian*, 18 September 1974.
[127] *Pwyntiau i Ganfaswyr Plaid Cymru* (GE, 1988, Box 21, NLW).
[128] *South Wales Guardian*, 10 October 1974.
[129] *Liverpool Daily Post*, 4 October 1974.
[130] *Y Cymro*, 15 October 1974.
[131] Gwynfor Evans to Rhys Davies, 18.10.1974, private ownership.

CHAPTER 11 – Downfall 1974–79

[1] *Liverpool Daily Post*, 15 October 1974.
[2] Author's interviews with Lord Elis-Thomas and Dafydd Wigley.
[3] Author's interview with Lord Elis-Thomas.
[4] Author's interview with Dafydd Wigley.
[5] *Liverpool Daily Post*, 23 October 1974.
[6] Dafydd Wigley, *Dal Ati* (Caernarfon, 1993), p. 51.
[7] *Y Ddraig Goch*, December 1974/January 1975.
[8] *Welsh Nation*, 18/24 October 1974.
[9] Gwynfor Evans to R Tudur Jones, 21.11.1974 (GE, 1979, Box 9, NLW).
[10] John Osmond to Gwynfor Evans, 1.11.1974 (GE, 1983, O, NLW).
[11] Harri Webb to Gwynfor Evans, 11.1.1973 (GE, 1973, W, NLW).
[12] Harri Webb noted: 'Phil's liaison with her... besides being incomprehensible is damaging to him and the party. He is being cold-shouldered by Gwynfor because of it. Sex and the office have been inseparable throughout its history.' Harri Webb's journal, 15.8.1975, private ownership. I am most grateful to Professor Meic Stephens for permission to see these diaries.
[13] *Liverpool Daily Post*, 11 November 1974.
[14] Gwynfor Evans to Elwyn Roberts, 5.12.1974 (PCP B 1106).
[15] Minutes of the Conservative Study Group on Devolution, 16.1.1975 (Lord Crickhowell papers, NLW).
[16] ibid., Nicholas Edwards to Margaret Thatcher, 19.1.1975.
[17] *Western Mail*, 7 January 1975.
[18] O M Roberts to Gwynfor Evans, n.d. (GE, 1983, R, NLW).
[19] *Western Mail*, 2 June 1975.
[20] ibid., 21 January 1975.
[21] Saunders Lewis to Peter Hughes Griffiths, 11.6.1975, private ownership. I am grateful to Peter Hughes Griffiths for permission to see this letter.
[22] Gwynfor Evans to Nans Jones, 19.3.1975 (PCP B 1289).
[23] *Barn*, May 1975.
[24] Peter Hughes Griffiths to Dafydd Elis Thomas, 20.2.1975 (Dafydd Elis Thomas, papers C 1/2, NLW).
[25] *Liverpool Daily Post*, 7 June 1975.
[26] *Carmarthen Journal*, 13 June 1975.
[27] *Western Mail*, 10 June 1975.
[28] This is mentioned in the minutes of the Plaid Cymru Executive, 12.7.1975 (PCP A 62).
[29] Gwynfor Evans to Dafydd Glyn Jones, 12.6.1975 (GE, 1979, Box 9, NLW).
[30] Gwynfor Evans to R Tudur Jones, 3.7.1975, ibid.

[31] *Welsh Nation*, 27 June/3 July 1975.
[32] Gwynfor Evans, *Bywyd Cymro*, p. 305.
[33] Author's interview with Gwynoro Jones.
[34] *Carmarthen Journal*, 5 September 1975.
[35] *Western Mail*, 6 August and 30 October 1975.
[36] *Liverpool Daily Post*, 3 November 1975.
[37] ibid., 28 October 1975.
[38] Memorandum *The Latest Situation*, 29.10.1975 (PCP L 24).
[39] Gwynfor Evans to Elwyn Roberts, 7.11.1975 (GE, 1979, Box 9, NLW).
[40] *The Economist*, 29 November 1975.
[41] *Western Mail*, 28 November 1975.
[42] Author's interview with Dafydd Wigley.
[43] Dafydd Wigley to Gwynfor Evans, 12.12.1975 (GE, 1983, Box W, NLW).
[44] *Liverpool Daily Post*, 5 January 1976.
[45] *Carmarthen Journal*, 9 January 1976.
[46] Gwynfor Evans to Brian Morgan Edwards, 29.1.1976 (PCP A 63).
[47] *Welsh Nation*, 23/29 January 1976.
[48] *Liverpool Daily Post*, 1 March 1976.
[49] Gwynfor Evans to Rhys Davies, 15.2.1976, private ownership.
[50] *Liverpool Daily Post*, 19 February 1976.
[51] Gwynfor Evans to R Tudur Jones, 10.3.1976 (GE, 1979, Box 1, NLW).
[52] Author's interview with Michael Foot.
[53] *Western Mail*, 14 April 1976.
[54] Gwynfor Evans to Elwyn Roberts, 20.4.1976 (PCP M 149).
[55] *Carmarthen Journal*, 7 May 1976.
[56] Elwyn Roberts to Colin Edwards, n.d. (PCP M 149).
[57] ibid., see the circular for the Welsh in America.
[58] ibid., Gwynfor Evans to Elwyn Roberts, 6.5.1976.
[59] *Sunday Times*, 22 August 1976.
[60] *Liverpool Daily Post*, 18 August 1976.
[61] *Western Mail*, 18 August 1976.
[62] Guto ap Gwent to Dafydd Williams, 25.8.1976 (PCP A 72).
[63] Dafydd Williams to Ahmad Shahmati, Foreign Affairs Secretary, Union of Arab Socialists, 28.5.1976 (PCP G 202).
[64] Author's interview with Dafydd Williams.
[65] *Liverpool Daily Post*, 12 May 1976; *Y Cymro*, 11 May 1976.
[66] *Memorandum on Plaid Cymru Strategy*, Dafydd Williams (PCP 72).
[67] Author's interview with Lord Elis Thomas. See also *Western Mail*, 1 July 1976. As well as the meetings with Michael Foot, there were several meetings between Plaid Cymru's MPs and Gerald Kaufman, the Industry Minister.
[68] ibid., 9 July 1976.
[69] Gwynfor Evans to Islwyn Ffowc Elis, 30.8.1976 (Islwyn Ffowc Elis papers, NLW).
[70] *Y Ddraig Goch*, August 1976.
[71] *Carmarthen Journal*, 16 July 1976.
[72] *Baner ac Amserau Cymru*, 26 March 1976.
[73] Clive Betts to Gwynfor Evans, 22.1.1976 (GE, 1979, Box 2, NLW). In his resignation letter, Clive Betts writes: 'My decision to leave Plaid Cymru comes after many months of careful consideration. As a number of people know, I have been deeply dissatisfied with the party's lack

of activity on the language front.'

[74] John Dixon to Gwynfor Evans, 20.4.1976 (GE, 1983, Box D, NLW).

[75] Gwynfor Evans to Jac L Williams, 7.7.1976 (GE, 1979, Box 5, NLW).

[76] Gwynfor Evans to Dafydd Williams, 6.9.1976 (GE, 1979, Box W, NLW).

[77] *Western Mail*, 21 October 1976.

[78] PRO BD 108/292. Gwynfor Evans to John Morris, 26.10.1976. In his letter, Gwynfor tells the Welsh Secretary that the Coal Exchange would be a 'truly wonderful choice, far superior to the Temple of Peace in every way – location, architecture, convenience, acoustics and opportunity for expansion. It will also be a great asset to the City of Cardiff'. This is an official translation of the original letter, now lost. See also *Liverpool Daily Post*, 22 October 1976, for Gwynfor's more cautious attitude towards devolution.

[79] Gwynfor Evans to R Tudur Jones, 4.11.1976 (GE, 1979, Box 3, NLW).

[80] PRO BD 108/27, 'Devolution – A Timetable Motion', 3.9.1976.

[81] *The Sun*, 20 October 1976.

[82] Gwynfor Evans to Dafydd Orwig Jones, 23.11.1976 (GE, 1979, Box 9, NLW).

[83] *The Guardian*, 1 December 1976.

[84] *Western Mail*, 10 December 1976.

[85] Minutes of Carmarthenshire District Committee, 7.12.1976 (Pol 18, Carmarthenshire County Council Archives).

[86] *Western Mail*, 13 December 1976.

[87] *Parliamentary Debates* (Hansard), 5th series, vol. 922, columns 1034–42 (13 December 1976).

[88] *The Guardian*, 17 December 1976. Plaid Cymru agreed with the policy of holding a referendum. Phil Williams claimed that the referendum would be as much an opportunity for Plaid Cymru as was Scottish oil for the SNP. See press release, 23.1.1977 (PCP M 686).

[89] Gwynfor Evans to Elwyn Roberts, 27.12.1976 (PCP B 1096).

[90] *Western Mail*, 3 January 1977.

[91] Minutes of Plaid Cymru Strategy and Policy Committee, 31.12.1976 (PCP A 72).

[92] Minutes of the National Council, 1.1.1977 (PCP A 64).

[93] The uncertainty that led to the Knighton meeting is evident in a memorandum sent by Eurfyl ap Gwilym, Plaid Cymru's chair, to his fellow-officers. He believed the confusion could be beneficial: 'It may well be in the interest of the campaign to continue to give the impression that Plaid Cymru is divided on the question of the way we should campaign in the referendum. Journalists are already aware of the presence of "hard liners" in the leadership who are against Plaid Cymru's "soft" line on the Bill. There is no doubt that we could get considerable mileage out of this if we wish. The danger is that some of our members could be confused. However, to the public at large, the impression that Plaid Cymru is lukewarm in supporting the Assembly needs to be cultivated.' See memorandum *Plaid Cymru and the Referendum* (PCP L 26).

[94] Harri Webb's journal, 13.1.1977, private ownership. Webb says this about Gwynfor: 'Gwynfor's hair has gone quite white, he looks saintly, but rather fragile. I imagine the strain of the present touch-and-go situation is very great. Even Leo [Abse], I think, looked slightly appalled by the point put to him that he and the 6 shits [the Labour rebels] have now got the fate of W[ales] in their hands. He's not wearing too well, either.'

[95] Minutes of Carmarthen constituency executive, 18.1.1977 (Pol 18, Carmarthenshire County Council Archives).

[96] Gwynfor Evans, Dafydd Elis Thomas and Dafydd Wigley to James Callaghan, 3.2.1977 (GE, 1988, Box 11, NLW).

[97] Author's interview with Michael Foot.

[98] *Liverpool Daily Post*, 14 February 1977.

[99] Gwynfor Evans to Dafydd Williams, 10.2.1977 (PCP B 1005).
[100] *Y Ddraig Goch*, April/May 1977.
[101] Gwynfor Evans to Dafydd Williams, 22.2.1977 (GE, 1979, Box 9, NLW).
[102] *Liverpool Daily Post*, 24 February 1977.
[103] ibid.
[104] Gwynfor Evans to Islwyn Ffowc Elis, 8.3.1977 (GE, 1988, Box 31, NLW).
[105] Michael Foot to Gwynfor Evans, 28.2.1977 (GE, 1979, Box 9, NLW).
[106] Gwynfor Evans to Elwyn Roberts, 3.3.1977 (GE, 1988, Box 31, NLW).
[107] ibid., Gwynfor Evans to Dafydd Williams, 7.3.1977.
[108] Dafydd Wigley to Gwynfor Evans, n.d. (GE, 1983, Box W, NLW).
[109] Gwynfor Evans to Professor Dewi Eirug Davies, 7.3.1977 (GE, 1988, Box 31, NLW).
[110] D Philip Davies, Plaid Cymru organizer for Ceredigion, to Dafydd Elis Thomas, 4.3.1977 (Dafydd Elis Thomas papers, NLW).
[111] *Western Mail*, 11 March 1977.
[112] Minutes of Plaid Cymru Executive, 12.3.1977 (PCP A 73).
[113] ibid.
[114] *Liverpool Daily Post*, 22 March 1977.
[115] Harri Webb's journal, 24.3.1977, private ownership.
[116] Lord Cledwyn's journal, 21.3.1977 (Lord Cledwyn papers, A 1, NLW). Cledwyn Hughes writes: 'Dafydd Elis Thomas is particularly upset... He has a better grasp of political realities than his two colleagues although he is the youngest of them.'
[117] Gwynfor Evans to Lewis Valentine, 25.3.1977 (Lewis Valentine papers, 6/2, NLW).
[118] PRO BD 108/290, Michael Foot to Gwynfor Evans, 31.3.1977.
[119] Dafydd Wigley to Gwynfor Evans, 3.6.1977 (GE, 1979, Box 9, NLW).
[120] *Liverpool Daily Post*, 28 October 1977.
[121] Gwynfor Evans to Islwyn Ffowc Elis, 4.11.1977 (Pol 18, Carmarthenshire County Council Archives).
[122] *Y Ddraig Goch*, December 1977.
[123] Gwynfor Evans to Michael Foot, 21.11.1977 (GE, 1988, Box 40, NLW). Gwynfor's only concern at the time was the government's decision to abandon the plan to install a simultaneous translation system in the Assembly. John Morris rejected the scheme because of its political sensitivity. According to a memorandum by the civil servant in charge: 'There was in fact a change of policy. The original intention was to install simultaneous translation facilities (and this was made public) but it was later decided not to provide a full system because of the political sensitivity of so doing.' See PRO BD 108/272. Gwynfor made an official complaint to Michael Foot about this breach of promise. See Gwynfor Evans to Michael Foot, 8.11.1977, ibid.
[124] Gwynfor Evans to Dafydd Wigley, 8.12.1977 (PCP 26).
[125] Gwynfor Evans to Rhys Davies, 5.1.1978, private ownership.
[126] *Liverpool Daily Post*, 14 November 1977.
[127] Gwynfor Evans to Michael Foot, 1.1.1978 (GE, 1983, F, NLW).
[128] ibid.
[129] *Western Mail*, 27 January 1978.
[130] *The Times*, 28 January 1978.
[131] *Liverpool Daily Post*, 2 February 1978.
[132] Dafydd Orwig Jones to Gwynfor Evans, 13.2.1978 (GE, 1979, Box 1, NLW).
[133] *Y Cymro*, 31 January 1978.
[134] Gwynfor Evans to Dafydd Orwig Jones, 20.2.1978 (GE, 1979, Box 1, NLW).
[135] Author's interviews with Dafydd Wigley and Phil Richards.

[136] Gwynfor Evans to Cledwyn Hughes, 28.2.1978 (Lord Cledwyn papers, C 7, NLW).
[137] *Western Mail*, 3 March 1978. Following Neil Kinnock's allegation, Gwynedd Council held an investigation that concluded that his complaint was unfounded. *Liverpool Daily Post*, 6 July 1978.
[138] *Liverpool Daily Post*, 9 March 1978.
[139] *Western Mail*, 2 March 1978. Privately, Cledwyn Hughes thought that Leo Abse had 'a strange inexplicable hostility to Wales, or probably Welsh speaking Wales... Anything outside the anglicised circle of Cardiff is anathema to him'. Lord Cledwyn's journal, 1.3.1978 (Lord Cledwyn papers, A 1, NLW).
[140] Gwynfor Evans to Cledwyn Hughes, 26.4.1978 (PCP L 26).
[141] ibid.
[142] Gwynfor Evans to Dafydd Williams, 3.5.1978 (GE, 1979, Box 1, NLW).
[143] ibid., Dafydd Williams to Gwynfor Evans, 5.5.1978.
[144] Memorandum by Dafydd Wigley, 18.5.1978 (PCP L 26).
[145] Gwynfor Evans to Eurys Rowlands, 4.7.1978 (GE, 1979, Box 1, NLW).
[146] Dr Phil Williams to Gwynfor Evans, 7.7.1978 (GE, 1983, Box W, NLW).
[147] *Liverpool Daily Post*, 17 August 1978.
[148] Author's interview with Lord Elis-Thomas.
[149] John Osmond, *1978 General Election Strategy*, 14.7.1978 (PCP J 236).
[150] Gwynfor Evans to Peter Hughes Griffiths, 21.8.1978 (GE, 1988, Box 41, NLW).
[151] K O Morgan, *Callaghan* (Oxford, 1997), pp. 627–38.
[152] Author's interview with Caerwyn Roderick. See also Dafydd Wigley, *Dal Ati*, op. cit., pp. 39–43.
[153] Gwynfor Evans, *Bywyd Cymro*, op. cit., p. 304.
[154] *Liverpool Daily Post*, 8 September 1978.
[155] *Western Mail*, 11 September 1978.
[156] Gwynfor Evans to Alcwyn Evans, 12.9.1978, private ownership.
[157] *The Guardian*, 19 September 1978.
[158] Gwynfor Evans to Cledwyn Hughes, 13.10.1978 (Lord Cledwyn papers, C7, NLW).
[159] *Western Mail*, 23 September 1978.
[160] *Liverpool Daily Post*, 10 October 1978.
[161] Gwynfor Evans to Dafydd Williams, 5.10.1978 (PCP B 1403).
[162] ibid., Gwynfor Evans to Dafydd Williams, 13.10.1978.
[163] *Lol*, Winter 1978/1979.
[164] *Y Cymro*, 24 October 1978.
[165] *Liverpool Daily Post*, 21 October 1978.
[166] ibid., 23 October 1978.
[167] *Western Mail*, 23 October 1978.
[168] *Financial Times*, 2 November 1978; *Welsh Nation*, December 1978.
[169] *The Times*, 2 November 1978.
[170] Gwynfor Evans to Vernon Howell, secretary of the Union of Welsh Parents, 15.11.1983 (GE, 1988, Box 9, NLW).
[171] Gwynfor Evans to Pennar Davies, 23.11.1978 (Pennar Davies papers, NLW).
[172] Gwynfor Evans, *Gallwn Gyrraedd 40%*, 29.12.1978 (GE, 1988, Box 17, NLW).
[173] *Y Ddraig Goch*, January 1979.
[174] Gwynfor Evans to Carwyn James, 23.1.1979 (GE, 1988, Box 41, NLW).
[175] Minutes of Carmarthen District Committee, 6.1.1979 (Pol 18, Carmarthenshire County Council Archives).

[176] ibid., Minutes of Carmarthen District Committee, 9.1.1979.
[177] *Y Faner*, 12 January 1979.
[178] Minutes of Cymdeithas yr Iaith Gymraeg Parliament, 13.1.1979 (Cymdeithas yr Iaith Gymraeg papers, Box 11, NLW). Tudur Jones, leader of Cymdeithas yr Iaith's Status Group, wrote to Raymond Edwards, organizer of the Wales Assembly Campaign, to rebuke him: 'Calming the fears of those who don't speak Welsh is one thing because of the short-term need for votes, but if we want to ensure a future that's worth fighting for the defensive compromise must stop somewhere.' See Tudur Jones to Raymond Edwards, 2.1.1979 (ibid., File 7/4).
[179] *Y Cymro*, 6 February 1979.
[180] ibid. 20 February 1979.
[181] Gwynfor Evans to Alwyn Gruffudd, 11.1.1979 (GE, 1983, G, NLW).
[182] ibid., Gwynfor Evans to Duncan Gardiner, 10.1.1979.
[183] *South Wales Echo*, 31 January 1979.
[184] ibid., 6, 9 January 1979.
[185] Gwynfor Evans to James Callaghan, 13.1.1979 (PCP 1403).
[186] *Western Mail*, 10 February 1979.
[187] *Liverpool Daily Post*, 16 February 1979.
[188] George Wright to Dafydd Williams, 15.2.1979 (PCP L 35).
[189] ibid., Dafydd Williams to George Wright, 16.2.1979.
[190] ibid., John D Rogers to Dafydd Williams, 25.2.1979.
[191] ibid., Hywel Roberts to Dafydd Williams, 25.2.1979. Although not mentioned here, the local MP, Tom Ellis, was also prominent in the North East Wales Yes campaign.
[192] *Liverpool Daily Post*, 1 March 1979.
[193] *Daily Telegraph*, 3 March 1979.
[194] *Y Cymro*, 6 March 1979.
[195] Author's interview with Gwynfor Evans.
[196] *Y Faner*, 16 March 1979.
[197] Gwynfor Evans to Cassie Davies, 8.3.1979 (GE, 1988, Box 41, NLW).
[198] *Y Faner*, 3 March 1979.
[199] *The Guardian*, 5 March 1979.
[200] *Western Mail*, 12 March 1979.
[201] *Daily Telegraph*, 10 March 1979.
[202] *The Guardian*, 16 March 1979.
[203] *Western Mail*, 16 March 1979.
[204] *Liverpool Daily Post*, 16, 20 March 1979.
[205] ibid., 20 March 1979.
[206] Dafydd Wigley to Michael Cocks, 21.3.1979 (PCP M 676).
[207] *Western Mail*, 22 March 1979.
[208] ibid., 23 March 1979.
[209] *Daily Telegraph*, 23 March 1979.
[210] *The Guardian*, 23 March 1979.
[211] Nicholas Edwards to Gwynfor Evans, 23.3.1979 (PCP M 676).
[212] James Callaghan to Gwynfor Evans, 23.3.1979 (GE, 1983, C, NLW).
[213] Dafydd Wigley, *Dal Ati*, op. cit., pp. 90–2.
[214] John Davies, *Plaid Cymru Oddi Ar 1960* (Aberystwyth), pp. 8–9.
[215] *The Guardian*, 26, 28 March 1979.
[216] *Daily Telegraph*, 28 March 1979.
[217] *Parliamentary Debates* (Hansard), 5ed series, vol. 965, columns 499–500 (28 March 1979).

[218] *Daily Telegraph*, 29 March 1979.
[219] Gwynfor Evans's general election leaflet, 1979 (PCP 1403).
[220] *Carmarthen Journal*, 13 April 1979.
[221] *Liverpool Daily Post*, 19 April 1979.
[222] *Carmarthen Journal*, 13 April 1979.
[223] ibid., 13 April 1979.
[224] *South Wales Guardian*, 8 March 1979.
[225] *Western Mail*, 28 April 1979.
[226] *Y Faner*, 13 April 1979.
[227] Islwyn Ffowc Elis to Gwynfor Evans, 12.4.1979 (GE, 1983, E, NLW).
[228] *Y Faner*, 20 April 1979.
[229] *Western Mail*, 2 May 1979.
[230] *Y Faner*, 4 May 1979.

CHAPTER 12 – Any Other Business? 1979–83

[1] *Western Mail*, 7 May 1979.
[2] Gwynfor Evans to Pennar Davies (Pennar Davies papers, NLW).
[3] Press release, 2.5.1979 (PCP J 235).
[4] Peter Hughes Griffiths to William Whitelaw, n.d. (GE, 1988, Box 9, NLW).
[5] Peter Hughes Griffiths to Owen Edwards, 21.6.1979, ibid. In his letter, Gwynfor's agent writes: 'So many official and unofficial reports that flow into this office and go to Talar Wen make us certain that it was the BBC poll that lost this seat for Gwynfor Evans so that the situation is almost unbearable.'
[6] Peter Hughes Griffiths's report on the inquiry (GE, 1988, Box 2, NLW). The Wales Broadcasting Council's basic conclusion was that the company that had carried out the survey, Abacus, was too inexperienced and the sample of people questioned (400) too small.
[7] *Y Faner*, 18 May 1979. Over twenty years later, he still stuck to the same accusation that BBC Wales's inaccurate poll was intentional. See *Gwynfor yn Bedwar Ugain Oed*, interview with Sulwyn Thomas, BBC Wales 1992.
[8] Minutes of Carmarthen District Committee, 8.5.1979 (Pol 18, Carmarthenshire County Council Archives).
[9] Gwynfor Evans to H W J Edwards, 14.6.1979 (GE, 1979, Box 13, NLW).
[10] ibid., Gwynfor Evans to Geraint Morgan MP, 13.6.1979.
[11] ibid., Gwynfor Evans to Wyn Thomas, 29.6.1979.
[12] ibid., Gwynfor Evans to Gwilym R Jones, 1.6.1979.
[13] *Western Mail*, May 18, 1979.
[14] Dafydd Williams to Gwynfor Evans, 1.6.1979 (GE, 1983, Box W, NLW).
[15] *Liverpool Daily Post*, 9 June 1979.
[16] *Y Cymro*, 22 May 1979.
[17] *Liverpool Daily Post*, 12 June 1979.
[18] Dr Eurfyl ap Gwilym to Gwynfor Evans, 6.6.1979 (GE, 1983, Box G, NLW).
[19] *Western Mail*, 12 June 1979.
[20] Elwyn Roberts to Eurfyl ap Gwilym, 26.8.1979 (PCP B 1422).
[21] *Tafod y Ddraig*, June 1979.
[22] ibid.
[23] *Y Faner*, 7 August 1979.
[24] Dewi Watkin Powell to Gwynfor Evans, 22.8.1979 (GE, 1983, Box P, NLW).

[25] *Liverpool Daily Post*, 21 July 1979.
[26] *Western Mail*, 30 June 1979.
[27] Author's interview with Dafydd Evans.
[28] Author's interview with Lord Roberts of Conwy. It is worth noting that some of the most influential figures in Welsh broadcasting such as Gareth Price, head of programming for BBC Wales, were of like mind. He assumed that a fourth Welsh-language channel was 'doomed to failure… The Welsh language audience will shrink when programmes are put on the channel'. *Western Mail*, 28 March 1979.
[29] David Ormsby-Gore to William Whitelaw, 28.6.1979 (Sir Alun Talfan Davies papers, File 671, NLW).
[30] Robin Reeves to Gwynfor Evans, 16.6.1991 (GE, 2002, NLW). In his letter, Reeves, a member of the IBA's Welsh Advisory Committee, tells Gwynfor: 'At a meeting soon after the 1979 General Election, the committee was urged by both the IBA in London and HTV Wales (there was a letter from Alun Talfan Davies) to drop its support for one channel and adopt the "more realistic option" of the two channel solution, in view of the change in political climate.'
[31] PRO BD 25/327, R H Jones to P J Hosegood, 16.7.1979.
[32] ibid., Nicholas Edwards to William Whitelaw, n.d.
[33] ibid., Sir Hywel Evans to Sir Robert Armstrong, 17.7.1979.
[34] R H Jones to P J Hosegood, loc. cit.
[35] William Whitelaw, *The Whitelaw Memoirs* (York, 1998), p. 220. He writes: 'My colleagues in Wales did not consider that the proportion of Welsh speakers could justify delivering the whole new channel in the Welsh language.'
[36] Author's interview with Lord Crickhowell. The perception that there was 'a good deal of support for, and little argument against the Home Office proposal' is confirmed in Lord Crickhowell's autobiography. Nicholas Edwards, *Westminster, Wales and Water* (Cardiff, 1999), p. 19.
[37] Author's interview with Lord Roberts of Conwy.
[38] Minutes of the Welsh Office on Welsh-medium Broadcasting, 11.9.1979, papers held by the author.
[39] Author's interviews with Lord Roberts of Conwy and Owen Edwards.
[40] Since 1977, Plaid Cymru had enjoyed a fractious relationship with HTV Wales, to say the least. Although the company was responsible for admirable programmes in Welsh such as the news magazine *Y Dydd*, some Plaid Cymru staff and members believed that the company itself was run by people with little sympathy for the language. Dafydd Elis Thomas complained about HTV's attitude frequently and, as late as July 1979, claimed that it deserved to lose its licence because of what he called the 'media imperialism from across the Severn'. *Western Mail*, 23 July 1979.
[41] PRO BD 25/327, Memorandum from R H Jones, 30.8.1979.
[42] ibid., 14 September 1979.
[43] ibid., 15 September 1979.
[44] The conversation is mentioned in R Tudur Jones to Gwynfor Evans, 18.9.1979 (GE, 1983, J, NLW).
[45] ibid., 27.9.1979 (GE, 1983, J, NLW).
[46] Minutes of Cymdeithas yr Iaith Gymraeg Parliament, 15.9.1979 (Cymdeithas yr Iaith Gymraeg papers, Box 11, NLW).
[47] Minutes of General Meeting of Cymdeithas yr Iaith Gymraeg, 19.10.1979 (Cymdeithas yr Iaith Gymraeg papers, Box 20, NLW).
[48] *Y Ddraig Goch*, December 1979.

[49] ibid., October 1979.
[50] *Y Faner*, 21 September 1979.
[51] Sir Brian Young to Alun Talfan Davies, 19.9.1979 (Sir Alun Talfan Davies papers, File 3, NLW).
[52] Author's interview with Dr Meredydd Evans. The date and precise details are taken from Dr Meredydd Evans's journal.
[53] *Y Faner*, 28 September 1979.
[54] Harri Webb's journal, 12.10.1979, private ownership.
[55] *Y Cymro*, 23 October 1979.
[56] HTV Cymru, *Y Bedwaredd Sianel yng Nghymru: Datganiad gan HTV Cymru* (Llandysul), p. 15.
[57] *Y Cymro*, 23 October 1979.
[58] *Our Critics in Wales*, David Meredith's memorandum to Ron Wordley, HTV Wales 22.10.1979 (Sir Alun Talfan Davies papers, File 671, NLW).
[59] *Western Mail*, 20 October 1979.
[60] *Y Cymro*, 6 November 1979.
[61] *Western Mail*, 26 October 1979.
[62] *Liverpool Daily Post*, 29 October 1979.
[63] *Western Mail*, 11 November 1979.
[64] *Y Faner*, 7 December 1979.
[65] *Y Cymro*, 20 November 1979.
[66] Dafydd Wigley to Gwynfor Evans, 21.11.1979 (GE, 1983, W, NLW).
[67] R Maldwyn Jones to members of Plaid Cymru, Carmarthen Region, 9.12.1979 (GE, 1988, Box 20, NLW).
[68] *The Guardian*, 17 December 1979.
[69] Gwynfor Evans to Lewis Valentine, 20.12.1979 (Lewis Valentine papers, File 6/4, NLW).
[70] *Western Mail*, 4 January 1980. Gwynfor Evans was of the opinion that 'Miss Piggy' had remarkable 'sex appeal'.
[71] *S4C: Pwy Dalodd Amdani?* (Neath, 1985), p. 80.
[72] Angharad Tomos, *Cnonyn Aflonydd* (Caernarfon, 2000), p. 89.
[73] *Gwynfor yn Bedwar Ugain Oed*, interview with Sulwyn Thomas, 1992, BBC Wales.
[74] Pennar Davies to Gwynfor Evans, n.d. (Pennar Davies papers, NLW).
[75] Author's interview with Meleri Mair.
[76] Author's interview with Peter Hughes Griffiths.
[77] Gwynfor Evans to Dafydd Williams, 12.2.1980 (PCP B 1403).
[78] Peter Hughes Griffiths to Wayne Williams, 15.2.1980 (Cymdeithas yr Iaith Gymraeg papers, Box 11, NLW).
[79] Author's interview with Meredydd Evans.
[80] Lord Belstead to Dafydd Wigley, 25.1.1980 (GE, 1983, J, NLW).
[81] Dafydd Wigley to Gwynfor Evans, 22.1.1980 (GE, 1983, W, NLW).
[82] Dafydd Wigley, *O Ddifri* (Caernarfon, 1992), pp. 186–7.
[83] Author's interview with Dafydd Wigley.
[84] *S4C: Pwy Dalodd Amdani?* op. cit., p. 81.
[85] *Daily Post*, 29 March 1980.
[86] *Western Mail*, 31 March 1980.
[87] Gwynfor Evans to Dafydd Williams, 24.3.1980 (PCP B 1403).
[88] *Daily Post*, 15 April 1980.
[89] Dafydd Williams to Gwynfor Evans, 22.4.1980 (GE, 1983, W, NLW).
[90] Author's interview with Ffred Ffransis.

[91] Ioan Bowen Rees to Gwynfor Evans, 1.5.1980 (GE, 1983, R, NLW).
[92] R Tudur Jones, O M Roberts, Elwyn Roberts and Alun Lloyd to Gwynfor Evans, 1.5.1980 (GE, 1983, A, NLW).
[93] Author's interview with Dr Eurfyl ap Gwilym.
[94] Author's interview with Dafydd Wigley.
[95] Author's interview with Lord Elis-Thomas.
[96] Author's interview with Ceridwen Pritchard.
[97] Dafydd Wigley to Gwynfor Evans, n.d. (GE, 1983, W, NLW).
[98] Islwyn Ffowc Elis to Gwynfor Evans, 7.5.1980 (GE, 1983, E, NLW).
[99] Gwynfor Evans to Elwyn Roberts and friends, 5.5.1980 (PCP M 507).
[100] Patrick Hannan, 'One Man and His Channel' in Patrick Hannan (ed.), *Wales in Vision* (Llandysul, 1990), pp. 136–45.
[101] Dafydd Wigley to Gwynfor Evans, 22.5.1980 (GE, 1983, W, NLW).
[102] *Y Faner*, 13 June 1980.
[103] *Y Cymro*, 10 June 1980.
[104] Keith Best to Elwyn Roberts, 9.6.1980 (PCP M 507).
[105] *Glasgow Herald*, 16 June 1980.
[106] Author's interview with Peter Hughes Griffiths.
[107] *Western Mail*, 16 June 1980.
[108] *South Wales Echo*, 24 June 1980.
[109] *The Times*, 30 June 1980.
[110] Minutes of the Welsh Office on Welsh-medium Broadcasting, 27.6.1980, papers held by the author.
[111] Margaret Thatcher to Dafydd Wigley, 11.7.1980 (GE, 1983, T, NLW).
[112] Minutes of the Welsh Office on Welsh-medium Broadcasting, 1.7.1980, papers held by the author.
[113] ibid., 7.7.1980.
[114] Alwyn Roberts, 'Some Political Implications of S4C', *Transactions of the Honourable Society of Cymmrodorion*, 1989. pp. 211–19.
[115] *Daily Post*, 17 July 1980.
[116] ibid., 19 July 1980.
[117] Angharad Tomos, *Cnonyn Aflonydd*, op. cit., p. 97.
[118] Dafydd Wigley to Gwynfor Evans, 18.7.1980 (GE, 1983, W, NLW).
[119] Author's interview with Lord Elis-Thomas.
[120] *Western Mail*, 28 July 1980.
[121] Gwynfor Evans, *Bywyd Cymro*, op. cit., p. 315.
[122] Owen Edwards to Gwynfor Evans, 21.7.1980 (GE, 1983, E, NLW).
[123] Nicholas Edwards, *Westminster, Wales and Water*, op. cit., p. 20.
[124] Keith Best to Nicholas Edwards, 22.7.1980, private ownership. I am most grateful to Keith Best for permission to see this letter.
[125] Gwynfor Evans, *Bywyd Cymro*, op. cit., p. 315.
[126] See the note dated 31.7.1980 (Leo Abse papers, D i/7, NLW).
[127] *Y Ddraig Goch*, August 1980.
[128] According to her son, Siôn, Jennie Eirian Davies felt that she had been 'cut off' from Gwynfor Evans's friends. As well as suffering a number of public attacks, she received several threatening letters and telephone calls. It had a lasting effect on her, leading to loss of confidence. This, as well as the unbearable pressure of editing *Y Faner*, proved too much. Jennie Eirian Davies killed herself in May 1982. Author's interview with Siôn Eirian.

[129] Author's interview with Gwilym Owen.
[130] *Western Mail*, 8 August 1980.
[131] Saunders Lewis to Pennar Davies, 21.8.1980 (Pennar Davies papers, NLW).
[132] The original three were Sir Goronwy Daniel, Sir Edmund Davies and Cledwyn Hughes. See James Nicholas, Gorsedd Recorder, to Sir Goronwy Daniel, 26.7.1980 (Sir Goronwy Daniel papers, NLW).
[133] William Whitelaw to the Archbishop of Wales, 4.8.1980 (Lord Cledwyn papers, C 9, NLW).
[134] Minutes of the Welsh Office on Welsh-medium Broadcasting, 6.8.1980, papers held by the author.
[135] ibid., Wyn Roberts to Nicholas Edwards, 9.8.1980.
[136] *The Times*, 12 August, 1980.
[137] *Daily Post,* 27 August 1980.
[138] PRO BD 25/39, Roger Thomas to William Whitelaw, 8.8.1980.
[139] Alwyn Roberts, 'Some Political Implications of S4C', loc. cit., p. 222.
[140] *Daily Post*, 21 August 1980.
[141] *Western Mail*, 22 August 1980.
[142] *The Guardian*, 1 September 1980.
[143] Dafydd Williams to Peter Hughes Griffiths, 2.9.1980 (GE, 1988, Box 23, NLW).
[144] Professor Linford Rees to Gwynfor Evans, 2.9.1980 (GE, 1983, R, NLW).
[145] See PCP B 1405.
[146] *Y Faner*, 5 September 1980.
[147] Lewis Valentine to Gwynfor Evans, 9.9.1980 (GE, 1983, V, NLW).
[148] Gwynfor Evans to Sir Goronwy Daniel, n.d. (Sir Goronwy Daniel papers, NLW).
[149] After the meeting, Sir Goronwy Daniel wrote to Leopold Kohr to thank him: 'Who would have thought that one of the most harrowing problems that Wales has faced would be solved by an Austrian philosopher...Wales has much to be grateful to you for and this is only the latest example.' Sir Goronwy Daniel to Leopold Kohr, 18.9.1980 (GE, 1983, C, NLW).
[150] Sir Goronwy Daniel to Cledwyn Hughes, 26.8.1980 (Lord Cledwyn papers, C 9, NLW).
[151] ibid., Cledwyn Hughes to Sir Goronwy Daniel, 28.8.1980.
[152] ibid., see the note dated 14.8.1980.
[153] ibid., Notes on the meeting held at the Home Office, 10.9.1980.
[154] Alwyn Roberts, 'Some Political Implications of S4C', loc. cit., p. 223.
[155] Michael Foot wrote to Gwynfor Evans on 10 September, 1980. The meeting, and Michael Foot's feelings, are reported in Gwynfor Evans's letter to Dewi Watkin Powell, 3.10.1980 (GE, 1983, P, NLW).
[156] *Daily Post*, 11 September 1980.
[157] PRO BD 25/331, Trevor Hughes to Nicholas Edwards, 9.9.1980.
[158] Minutes of the Welsh Office on Welsh-medium Broadcasting, 15.9.1980, papers held by the author.
[159] ibid.
[160] Author's interview with Emyr Daniel.
[161] *S4C: Pwy Dalodd Amdani?* op. cit., p. 90.
[162] Author's interview with Peter Hughes Griffiths.
[163] Saunders Lewis to Meredydd Evans, 22.9.1980, private ownership.
[164] *An Phoblacht*, 19 October 2000.
[165] Essay by Alan Shore, chair of the Clwyd executive committee, n.d. (PCP A 74). He says: 'It [S4C] confirms the suspicion of many outside the party that it is only the language which

matters to Plaid Cymru. This is certainly the belief of some party members and "supporters" anyway and it is hard to deny with the public face currently presented through national officers'.
[166] *The Guardian*, 20 September 1980.
[167] Minutes of the meeting at the Welsh Office on holiday homes, 1.12.1981. Minutes held by the author.
[168] *Y Cymro*, 28 October 1980.
[169] *Daily Post*, 29 September 1980.
[170] *Y Ddraig Goch*, May 1981.
[171] ibid., October/November 1980.
[172] ibid., December 1980.
[173] *Report of the Plaid Cymru Commission of Inquiry*, 1981, p. iii.
[174] Gwynfor Evans to Ioan Bowen Rees, 28.1.1981 (GE, 1983, R, NLW).
[175] ibid., Gwynfor Evans to Ioan Bowen Rees, 30.1.1981.
[176] *Y Faner*, 20 February 1981.
[177] Dafydd Wigley to Gwynfor Evans, 15.4.1981 (GE, 1983, W, NLW).
[178] ibid., Dafydd Wigley to Gwynfor Evans, n.d.
[179] ibid., Dafydd Wigley to Dafydd Williams, n.d.
[180] Author's interview with Aled Gwyn.
[181] Denley Owen (constituency chair) to Gwynfor Evans, 19.5.1981 (GE, 1983, O, NLW).
[182] *Western Mail*, 6 June 1981.
[183] ibid., 8 June 1981. See also *The Guardian*, 15 June 1981.
[184] *The Observer*, 28 June 1981. There is no doubt that Gwynfor felt very aggrieved at the way he was portrayed by the left of his party. In July 1981, he wrote to the historian Dr John Davies: 'In the eyes of the left I am an arch-bourgeois, and to make things worse, rural and nonconformist! My fellow-deacons have included two railway workers, a worker at the allotment who was a farmhand, a lorry driver, a roadmender, a clerk, a failed weaver, a carpenter and a few farmers. Our branch workers include four poor widows, a roadmender's wife, a lorry driver's wife, a postman, a farm worker, a milk tanker driver etc. I notice that some who mock us are pretty well off and from good backgrounds, some of whom can afford expensive meals, wines etc that are beyond our means.' See Gwynfor Evans to Dr John Davies, 18.9.1981, private ownership. I wish to thank Dr John Davies for permission to see this letter.
[185] Saunders Lewis to Bobi Jones, 12.7.1981 (Bobi Jones papers, File 592, NLW).
[186] *Y Faner*, 24 July 1981.
[187] *The Guardian*, 15 June 1981.
[188] Gwynfor Evans to Dafydd Williams, 25.6.1981 (GE, 1983, W, NLW).
[189] Gwynfor Evans to Saunders Lewis, 25.8.1981 (GE, 1983, L, NLW).
[190] Author's interview with Dafydd Wigley.
[191] Guto Prys ap Gwynfor to Gwynfor Evans, 23.9.1981 (GE, 1983, A, NLW).
[192] *Arcade*, September 18–October 1. Among Plaid members in Carmarthenshire, Wigley received 84 votes, Emrys Roberts 58, Dafydd Iwan 52 and Dafydd Elis Thomas 41.
[193] *Daily Post*, 30 October 1981.
[194] *Western Mail*, 31 October 1981. See also Dafydd Wigley, *Dal Ati*, op. cit., pp. 142–3.
[195] *Barn*, November 1981.
[196] *Gwynfor*, HTV Cymru, 1990. Interview with Robert Griffiths.
[197] Gwynfor Evans, *Bywyd Cymro*, op. cit., pp. 342–3.
[198] *Rebecca*, October 1981.
[199] Gwynfor Evans to Dr Robyn Léwis, 9.11.1981, private ownership. I am grateful to Dr Léwis for permission to see this letter.

[200] Elwyn Roberts to Gareth Evans, 6.12.1981 (PCP F 40).
[201] Gwynfor Evans, *Diwedd Prydeindod* (Tal-y-bont, 1981), p. 12.
[202] Brig Oubridge to Gwynfor Evans, 17.8.1981 (PCP M 711).
[203] Gwynfor Evans to Brig Oubridge, 25.6.1982 (GE, 1983, A, NLW). Having seen the Ecology Party's manifesto, Gwynfor wrote to Oubridge: 'The concensus [*sic*] between the Ecology Party and Plaid Cymru, judging by this statement, is extraordinary. There is no part of this which I could not accept completely. The majority of its points are central to Plaid Cymru policy.'
[204] Press release by Gwynfor Evans, 5.2.1981 (GE, 1983, E, NLW).
[205] Gwynfor Evans to Dafydd Williams, 13.7.1981 (PCP M 708).
[206] Gwynfor Evans, *Diwedd y Byd* (Swansea, 1982), p. 7.
[207] D O Davies to Gwynfor Evans, 7.1.1982 (GE, 1983, D, NLW).
[208] *Carmarthen Journal*, 1 January 1982.
[209] ibid., 8 January 1982.
[210] ibid., 19 February 1982.
[211] Gwynfor Evans to Professor Robert J Alexander, 6.11.1982 (GE, 1983, A, NLW). It is worth adding that Gwynfor had little time for the SDP either, describing it as 'just another British nationalist party'.
[212] *Western Mail*, 21 July 1982. The battle to restore Castell Dinefwr proved to be a long one for Gwynfor. In 1998, Ron Davies, the Welsh Secretary, announced that the Welsh Office would pay for repairs.
[213] *Y Faner*, 11 June 1982.
[214] ibid., 1 November 1982. The Hydro group was formed in late 1982 to ensure that Plaid Cymru did not move any further to the left.
[215] Gwynfor Evans, *Macsen Wledig a Geni'r Genedl Gymreig*, n.d (Swansea).
[216] *Carmarthen Times*, 3 June 1983.
[217] Press release, 26.5.1983 (PCP J 237).
[218] *The Guardian*, 1 June 1983.
[219] Wyn Roberts to Nicholas Edwards, 2.7.1983 (Lord Crickhowell papers, NLW).
[220] *Western Mail*, 11 June 1983.

CHAPTER 13 – The Old Man of Pencarreg 1983–2005

[1] Author's interview with Dafydd Evans.
[2] Author's interview with the Reverend Guto Prys ap Gwynfor.
[3] *Y Faner*, 29 July 1983.
[4] The Hydro Group was established at the Hydro hotel, Llandudno, in October 1982. It attracted a fairly small number of members under the leadership of the highly colourful businessman from the valleys, Clayton Jones. He set out his initial objectives as follows: 'Put pressure on Dafydd Elis Tomos [*sic*]... Get rid of Emyr Williams from Plaid... To show up "loony left" and their policies for what they are'. (PCP, Hydro Group papers, File 1, NLW). When Hydro ceased operations in July 1986, Gwynfor Evans, Ieuan Wyn Jones and Dafydd Wigley were criticized by members of the group for not having said in public 'what they said in private'. *Western Mail*, 15 July 1986.
[5] *Radical Wales*, October 1983.
[6] Author's interview with Dafydd Evans.
[7] Dr Huw Edwards (his psychiatrist) to Gwynfor Evans, 20.12.1983 (GE, 1994, File E, NLW).
[8] Gwynfor Evans to Dafydd Williams, 11.9.1983 (PCP B 1404).
[9] *Carmarthen Journal*, 9 March 1984.

[10] Author's interview with Professor Hywel Teifi Edwards.
[11] Author's interview with Dafydd Evans.
[12] *Y Lloffwr*, October 1984.
[13] Dafydd Elis Thomas won just 188 votes. *Liverpool Daily Post*, 29 October 1984.
[14] Wynne Samuel to Gwynfor Evans, 14.11.1984 (GE, 1994, File S, NLW). In his letter, Samuel says: 'I visited Saunders Lewis in hospital yesterday. He is completely blind now and in a dreadful physical condition. But his mind is as sharp as ever. He is worried about and severely critical of Dafydd Elis. Before the Conference, he and his friends were out and about around a lot of the branches collecting votes for the Plaid Presidency.'
[15] Dafydd Elis Thomas to Gwynfor Evans, n.d. (GE, 1994, File T, NLW).
[16] ibid. This revealing note appears in Gwynfor Evans's hand on a letter he received from Dafydd Elis Thomas.
[17] *Planet*, June/July 1985.
[18] *Y Ddraig Goch*, February/March 1985.
[19] Dafydd Elis Thomas to Gwynfor Evans, 19.2.1985. After this, Elis Thomas began to move from the left to the political centre ground. It is no coincidence that the influence of the Nationalist Left also began to wane. *Western Mail*, 23 September 1986.
[20] *Y Faner*, 17 July 1985. This was borne out by a letter from Dafydd Wigley to the executive. Wigley writes that it is a 'disgrace' for Plaid Cymru to consider not fielding a candidate in order to make things easier for Labour. It was not Plaid Cymru's 'rightful job', he said, 'to ease the way for Neil Kinnock, or any other British politician'. See Dafydd Wigley to Plaid Cymru Executive, 15.7.1985 (PCP E 12).
[21] *Welsh Nation*, August 1985.
[22] *Barn*, October 1985.
[23] *Welsh Nation*, September/October 1985.
[24] ibid., December 1985 and January 1986.
[25] The other members of the sub-committee were Dafydd Elis Thomas, Dafydd Huws, Emyr Wyn Williams and Dr Phil Williams.
[26] *Seiri Cenedl* (Llandysul, 1986).
[27] Gwynfor Evans to Owen Edwards, 9.10.1986 (GE, 2002, NLW).
[28] Gwynfor Evans and Meredydd Evans, *Yr Iaith yn y nawdegau: yr her o'n blaenau.* 1988.
[29] *Western Mail*, 5 , 11 August 1986.
[30] Dr Meredydd Evans to Gwynfor Evans, 3.2.1987 (GE, 1994, File E, NLW).
[31] *Western Mail*, 9 September 1986.
[32] Bedwyr Lewis Jones to Gwynfor Evans, 27.5.1987 (GE, 1994, File J, NLW).
[33] *Cambrian News*, 17 April 1987.
[34] *Barn*, December/January 1989/90.
[35] Author's interview with Marc Phillips.
[36] Minutes PONT (GE, 2002, NLW).
[37] *Y Faner*, 24 June 1988.
[38] *Western Mail*, 24 September 1990.
[39] ibid., 13 June 1988.
[40] Gwynfor Evans to Emyr Humphreys, 4.3.1989 (Emyr Humphreys papers, AI/459, NLW).
[41] Gwynfor Evans to Dafydd Elis Thomas, 7.12.1987 (Dafydd Elis Thomas papers, A3/41, NLW).
[42] ibid., 6.10.1988.
[43] ibid., 13.12.1988.
[44] Dafydd Wigley to Gwynfor Evans, 6.11.1989 (GE, 2002, NLW).

[45] Gwynfor Evans, *Pe Bai Cymru'n Rhydd* (Tal-y-bont, 1989).
[46] Gwynfor Evans, *Fighting for Wales* (Tal-y-bont, 1991), p. 208.
[47] *Gwynfor yn Bedwar Ugain Oed*, interview with Sulwyn Thomas, BBC Wales, 1992.
[48] *Y Ddraig Goch*, April/May 1994.
[49] Author's interview with Gwynfor Evans.
[50] Gwynfor Evans to Professor Bobi Jones, 22.9.1997 (Bobi Jones papers, File 327, NLW).
[51] *The Fight for Welsh Freedom* (Tal-y-bont, 2000), p. 176.
[52] *Golwg*, 30 August 2001. Elin Jones AM, Plaid Cymru's chair, wrote to Gwynfor to express her gratitude because the leadership, she felt, was on 'a merciless rollercoaster with the *Welsh Mirror*, the rest of the press, Labour and our own members tearing us in all directions'. Elin Jones to Gwynfor Evans, 10.9.2001 (GE, 2002, NLW).
[53] *Cymru o Hud* (Tal-y-bont, 2001).
[54] Author's interview with Dafydd Evans.
[55] *Western Mail*, 9 November 2004.
[56] *Gwynfor Evans: The Member for Wales*, BBC Wales, 2005.
[57] Author's interview with the Reverend Guto Prys ap Gwynfor. Rhiannon, Gwynfor's wife, died on 13 January 2006. She was cremated on 19 January 2006 at Aberystwyth crematorium.

CHAPTER 14 – What Remains: The Legacy

[1] Daniel Pick, *Faces of Degeneration, A European Disorder, 1848–1918* (Cambridge, 1989), p. 222.
[2] Peter Watson, *A Terrible Beauty* (London, 2001), p. 186.
[3] Robert Colls, *The Identity of England* (Oxford, 2002), p. 289. See also Grahame Davies, *Sefyll yn y Bwlch* (Cardiff, 1999), pp. 1–17.
[4] *Western Mail*, 1 August 1925.
[5] Robert Young, *Postcolonialism* (Oxford, 2001), p. 316.
[6] Dafydd Glyn Jones, 'His Politics' in *Presenting Saunders Lewis* (Cardiff, 1983), eds. Alun R Jones and Gwyn Thomas, pp. 23–78.

INDEX

Abergavenny 107
Abergeirw 137
Abse, Leo 270, 282, 350, 371, 420, 501, 506
Adfer 338, 364, 380
Air Raid Protection 95
Amman Valley Chronicle 58, 74, 82, 85, 461, 463-5
Amsterdam 55
Anderson, Donald 350
Anglesey 57, 130-1, 138, 182, 242-3, 356, 371, 375, 388, 419, 472
ap Gwilym, Eurfyl 275, 411, 493, 499, 503, 506
ap Iestyn, Gethin 273
ap Iwan, Emrys *see* Jones, Robert Ambrose
ap Siencyn, Neil *see* Jenkins, Neil
Armstrong, Sir Robert 399, 504
Arwyn, Lord 290
Atkin, Leon 228
Attlee, Clement 91, 100, 124, 137
Australia 37, 203
A History of the Madagascar Martyrs 15

Babell chapel, the 64, 66
Baghdad 92
Bailey, Christopher 357
Bala 31, 47-48, 164, 166, 192, 200, 220-1, 226, 282, 302, 456, 465, 478
Baner ac Amserau Cymru 458, 460-74, 476, 478-80, 482-5, 492-3, 495-8
Bank of Wales 447
Baptists 305
Barclay, John 77
Barmouth 99
Barn 225, 235, 250, 286, 295, 327, 434, 462, 481, 483-4, 489-91, 493, 495, 497, 508, 510
Barnett, Joel 373
Barrian, The 39, 40, 458, 459
Barry 14-32, 38, 43, 44, 46, 48-9, 53-5, 57-8, 61, 67-68, 70, 75, 88-9, 120, 151, 174, 293, 302, 357, 396, 453-4, 456, 457
Barry and District News 44, 457-9, 461
Barry Catholic school 17
Barry County School 24, 29, 269
Barry Cymmrodorion 22, 46
Barry Cymmrodorion Tests 22
Barry Docks 18-9
Barry Herald 18, 48, 457-60
Basque Country, the 49
Bath and West Show 37
Beasley, Eileen 193, 201, 477
Beasley, Trefor 121, 193, 201
Bebb, Ambrose 27, 54, 83, 100, 144, 471
Beeching (cuts) 239, 281
Belgium 20
Belle Vue Group, the 206, 212
Belstead, Lord 410, 505
Benn, Tony 348, 434
Bennett, Elinor 270
Bere, Cliff 115-6, 121, 123, 467-8
Best, Keith 416, 420, 422, 506
Betts, Clive 326, 353, 358, 498
Bevan, Aneurin 100, 125, 132, 199
Beveridge, William 86
Bevin, Ernest 86
Bible, the 15
Bishop, Richard 72, 78, 460
Blaenau Ffestiniog 99, 127, 343
Blair, Tony 451
Bonaparte, Napoleon 67
Boone, Ronnie 24
Boore, Roger 234, 239, 484
Bowen, Geraint 420
Bowen, Roderic 227
Bowen Commission 327
Braddock, Bessie 171, 252
Braddock, John 171, 173, 175
Breconshire 63-5, 110
Bristol Channel Ship Repairers 357
British Steel Corporation 407
Bronaber 135
Brooke, Henry 176, 178-9, 181, 188-9, 203-5, 217, 476, 479
Brooke, Peter 189, 477
Brown, George 262
Brynaman 69, 263, 369

Buckingham Palace 280, 415
Bush, Keith 275
Butlin, Billy 106
by-elections: Aberdare (1946) 108, 153; Brecon and Radnor (1985) 444; Caernarfon Boroughs (1945) 98; Caerphilly (1968) 292; Cardigan (1932) 33; Carmarthen 74, (1966) 144, 331, 335, 356-7, 429, (1957) 176, 218, 258-61, 265-8, 275, 280, 468; Ebbw Vale (1960) 207; Glasgow Pollok (1967) 278; Hamilton (1967) 284; Llanelli (1975) 307; Merthyr (1972) 325; Montgomeryshire (1962) 220; Neath 98; Newport (1956) 168; Nuneaton (1967) 278; Ogmore (1946) 109; Rhondda (1967) 277; Swansea East (1963) 228; University of Wales seat (1943) 84

Cadet Corps 82
CADW 445
Caergwrle Investments Limited 315
Caernarvon and Denbigh Herald 291, 352, 490
Caerphilly 292-3, 313, 461
Caeshenkin 16
Cain, Frank 171, 253
Callaghan, James 144, 241, 262, 296, 354, 356, 362, 364, 491, 499, 502
Cambodia 287, 292
Cambrian News 35, 352, 458, 510
Cambridge 275, 289, 397, 400-1, 511
Capel Celyn 161-6, 169-78, 180-2, 185-7, 190-1, 194, 196-7, 200-1, 217, 252, 254, 363, 456
Capel Celyn Defence Committee 165-6, 172-3, 175
Cardiff 11, 13-14, 23, 37, 43, 48, 51-3, 55, 57, 67, 70, 75, 93, 104-5, 107, 112, 117, 141, 145-9, 161, 169, 182-3, 185-6, 193, 204, 231, 233, 243-4, 246, 257, 269, 283, 290-1, 331, 344-5, 354, 367, 374, 399, 409-10, 423, 427-8, 435, 442, 447, 450, 455, 457-9, 464-5, 468, 470, 472-3, 475-7, 479, 484, 499, 501, 504, 511
Carey-Evans, Benjy 257
Carl Rosa Opera Company 18
Carmarthen 31, 47, 70, 74-5, 82, 85, 121, 144, 152, 156-7, 159, 176, 209, 218, 226, 235-6, 239-40, 256-9, 261-9, 274, 276, 278-80, 283, 287-8, 290-2, 296, 298-9, 303-4, 306-8, 311-6, 318, 320-1, 326-8, 331-5, 337-41, 348-9, 352, 354, 356-7, 360, 362, 364, 369, 373-4, 379, 386, 387-93, 406, 422, 429, 432-4, 437, 439, 440-1, 445, 454, 462-4, 466, 468, 473, 483, 485-6, 489, 491-9, 501-3, 505, 509
Carmarthenshire 16, 49, 61, 69, 73-4, 82, 85, 110-1, 119-20, 130, 141, 145, 151, 156, 176, 188, 196, 210, 215, 218, 235-6, 260, 265, 267, 269, 272, 274, 280, 282, 287, 291, 298, 304-5, 307, 321, 324, 327, 328, 337-9, 347, 379, 382, 386, 387, 393, 407, 433, 436-8, 440, 442, 449, 452, 468, 480, 486-7, 489, 495-6, 499-501, 503, 508
Carmarthenshire County Council 145, 272, 386, 480, 489, 495-6, 499-501, 503
Carmarthenshire Education Committee 82
Carmarthen Journal 74, 82, 156, 259, 348, 352, 462-4, 466, 468, 473, 483, 485-6, 489, 491-3, 497-8, 503, 509
Carmarthen Times 259, 327, 486, 489, 492, 494-6, 509
Carron, Owen 431
Catholicism 37, 85-7, 128, 206, 222
Catholics 17, 142
Catholic Herald 100
Cecil, Lord 29
Cerddetwr *see* Griffiths, David Rees
Chamberlain, Neville 53
Chapman, T Robin 11, 15, 457-8
Chicago 14
Christian Alternative to War 27
Churchill, Winston 79, 104, 138, 140, 142, 157, 323
Cilienni 65
Cilmeri (publication) 248
Cilmeri 409
Clwyd Bwlch y Groes 65
Clywedog 210, 213, 220, 225, 232, 251, 256, 279, 296
CND 183, 436, 445
Coal 13-4, 24-5, 79, 95, 260, 276, 453
Cocks, Michael 384, 502
Cofion Cymru 465
Cof Cenedl 445, 479
Cole, David 180-1, 476
Coleman, Donald 272

Colombia 169
Committee for the Defence of Welsh Culture 63, 64
Committee of 100 190
Commonwealth Party 157
Congregationalist Union 35, 49, 79, 295
Conscription 53-4, 105-6, 111-4, 162, 467
Conservative Party, the 272, 298, 368
Cook, Robin 369
Coronation 46, 144-6, 281, 285-6
Corwen 166
Council for Wales and Monmouthshire 117, 141, 187
Cousins, Frank 262
Covenanters, the 119, 448
Crawford Report 400
Cricket 25, 39
Croesor 99
Crossman, Richard 286, 289, 489
Crowther-Hunt, Lord 336, 496
Crwys Road Chapel 75
Cudmore, Lieutenant 136
Cunningham, George 369
CWB exam 26
Cwmllynfell 194, 478
Cwm Cilienni 65
Cwm Dulas 307, 309, 492
Cwm Twrch 225
Cwrtycadno 130
Cyfeillion yr Iaith Gymraeg 318
Cyfres y Fil 40
Cymdeithas yr Iaith Gymraeg (Welsh Language Society) 115, 137, 205, 218, 220, 224-5, 243, 251, 254-6, 260, 268, 276, 283-4, 289, 295, 298-9, 303, 305-9, 318, 320-4, 326-8, 331, 338, 353, 358, 364, 379, 395, 401-3, 405, 408, 410, 414-5, 426, 429, 486, 496, 502, 504-5
Cymro, Y 52, 57, 59, 62, 69, 73, 91, 109, 111-2, 132, 155, 158, 162, 166, 176, 186, 203, 242, 249, 252, 280, 312, 379, 405, 416, 458-9, 460-2, 464-78, 481, 483-4, 486, 488-91, 493-8, 500-3, 505-6, 508
Cymru am Byth 92
Cymru Fydd 78, 89-90, 130, 175, 217, 454, 461-4, 467-8, 471-3, 475-6
Cyprus 166
Cysgod y Cryman 150
Czechoslovakia 51, 53
D-Day 94
Dafis, Cynog 204, 243, 254, 268, 310, 430, 449, 479, 484, 486, 492
Dafydd ap Gwilym Society, the 41
Daily Despatch 43, 459
Daily Express 153, 473
Daily Mail 265, 271, 486-7
Daily Telegraph 280, 301, 331, 385, 388, 478, 486, 488, 491, 502-3
Dalton, Hugh 29, 135
Daniel, Catherine 87, 209-10, 213-4, 218, 480
Daniel, Emyr 427, 495, 507
Daniel, Glyn 24, 26
Daniel, Gwyn 48
Daniel, John 200, 209, 221, 223, 479-80, 482, 484-5
Daniel, J E 57, 59, 66, 69, 84, 87-88, 95, 98, 100, 209, 461, 464
Daniel, Sir Goronwy 324, 419, 421, 424-6, 430, 494, 507
Davies, Sir Alun Talfan 215, 221, 235, 240, 364, 398, 403, 420, 500, 504-5
Davies, Aneirin Talfan 215, 231
Davies, Anthony (Llygad Llwchwr) 125, 148, 151
Davies, Cassie 38, 214, 236, 247, 307, 459, 483, 492, 502
Davies, Cennard 277, 488
Davies, Clement 64
Davies, Cynog, *see* Dafis, Cynog
Davies, David (Llandinam) 14
Davies, Denzil 259
Davies, Dewi Eirug 364, 500
Davies, Dilwyn 38
Davies, D O 332, 437, 496, 509
Davies, Frank 71-2
Davies, Geraint Talfan 303, 347
Davies, Gwilym 29, 35, 82-3, 464
Davies, Gwilym Prys 115, 121, 123-4, 194, 230, 235, 257, 259, 260-2, 264, 282, 293, 319, 336, 368, 468-9, 477, 482-6, 488
Davies, Huw 116, 121, 123
Davies, Hywel 262, 264, 459
Davies, Ithel 113, 123
Davies, Jennie Eirian 145, 176, 240, 379, 403, 421, 433, 506
Davies, Dr John 26, 124, 185, 205, 243, 254, 386-7, 459-60, 469, 472-3, 476, 484, 502, 508

Davies, J P 49, 51, 67, 461, 463
Davies, Kitchener 48, 135
Davies, Lloyd Havard 312
Davies, Meirion Lloyd 206, 479
Davies, Pennar 40, 43, 58, 61, 67, 72, 77, 78, 92-3, 103-4, 119, 142, 149, 182, 298, 318, 357-8, 378, 392, 402-4, 408, 416, 441, 457-9, 461-72, 476, 479, 491, 494, 501, 503, 505, 507
Davies, Rees 323
Davies, Rhys 315
Davies, Ron 449, 509
Davies, Vic 277, 278
Day, Simon 264
Ddraig Goch, Y 33, 36, 44-5, 66, 73, 90, 115, 132, 141, 193, 213-5, 225, 228, 230-1, 236, 250, 421, 430, 444, 459, 460-1, 464-6, 469-73, 477, 479-84, 486-90, 492, 494-8, 500-1, 504, 506, 508, 510-11
Deg Pwynt Polisi 37
Denbighshire County Council 176
Denmark 143
Denning, Lord 309
Department of Transport 281
Derfel, R J 98
Deudraeth Council 182
Development Council for Wales 103
Deyrnas, Y 33, 73
de Valera, Eamon 117
Dinefwr Castle 61, 437
Diphtheria 20
Dixon, John 358, 402, 499
Dolanog 160-3, 166
Dolwar Fach 162
Dolwyn 162
Dominion Status 37, 45, 115, 121, 123
Douglas-Home, Alec 263, 349
Dower, Daï 152
Dragon, The 34, 458
Dr Adam Clarke's Commentary on the Scriptures 15
Dunkirk 68
Dydd, Y 98, 466-7, 470, 473-4, 476, 478, 504

Eames, Marion 96, 99, 465-6
Economics of Welsh Self-Government, The 36, 458
Economist, The 352, 498
Eden, Anthony 160
Education First 447
Edwards, Brian Morgan 352, 498
Edwards, Huw T 93, 116-7, 128, 131, 141, 147, 149, 162, 184, 187-8, 194, 201, 203, 219, 229, 234-5, 237, 472, 478-9, 481, 483
Edwards, Hywel Teifi 442, 510
Edwards, H W J 223, 393, 503
Edwards, Sir Ifan ab Owen 63, 130, 140, 165, 184, 257, 462, 471
Edwards, Jac 36-7
Edwards, Ness 199, 272
Edwards, Nicholas 346, 386, 398-400, 412, 415, 417-22, 425-8, 439, 497, 502, 504, 506-7, 509
Edwards, Owen 63, 130, 140-1, 165, 184, 257, 392, 396, 401, 420, 445, 462, 471, 503, 504, 506, 510
Edwards, O M 26, 28, 323, 454
Edwards, Raymond 206, 218, 221-3, 502
Edwards, Wil 304, 382
Eilian, John *see* Jones, J T
Eirug, Aled 402, 432, 466
Eisenhower, Dwight D 92, 189
Electricity Board for Wales 114
Elfed 133
Eliot, T S 452
Elis, Islwyn Ffowc 136, 150, 175, 189, 203, 206-8, 220, 226, 229, 252, 254, 258-60, 263, 274, 284, 287-9, 293, 302-5, 314-5, 325, 358, 380, 390, 414, 477, 479-82, 485-7, 489-5, 498, 500, 503, 506
Elis-Thomas, Dafydd (Lord) 14, 272, 284, 289, 334, 336-7, 339-44, 347-52, 358, 363, 365-6, 374, 384, 396, 402, 406-8, 413, 419, 430-1, 433, 442, 444-5, 447-9, 497-500, 501, 505-6, 509, 511
Elizabeth II 146
Ellis, Tom (Merioneth MP) 63, 98, 103, 125, 196, 265,
Ellis, Tom (Wrexham MP) 404
Ellis, T I 63-5, 69, 76, 79, 83, 116, 143-4, 274, 461-4, 467-8, 471, 475-6, 487
Epynt 63-6, 78, 164-5, 426, 456, 462
European Economic Community 281, 322, 346

Evans, Alcwyn (brother) 19, 43, 52, 129, 208, 251, 321, 338, 375-6, 435, 457, 460, 472, 501
Evans, Alcwyn Deiniol (son) 81
Evans, Arthen 22
Evans, Ben 15-8, 22
Evans, Beriah Gwynfe 17
Evans, Catherine 75
Evans, Charles 380
Evans, Dafydd 249, 469, 472, 475, 483-4, 486-7, 489, 495, 504, 509-11
Evans, Dan 18-20, 23-4, 46, 49, 62, 67, 315, 326, 338, 357, 447, 464, 495
Evans, Dr Meredydd 396, 402-4, 410, 416, 428, 446, 505, 507, 510
Evans, Ellis Humphrey (Hedd Wyn) 99
Evans, Evan Gwyndaf (Gwyndaf) 293-4, 457, 490
Evans, George 64
Evans, Gwynallt 26
Evans, Gwynfor S 156, 210
Evans, Idris 67, 462
Evans, Ioan 360, 420
Evans, James 15, 457
Evans, Jill 436
Evans, Julian Cayo 255, 273, 280, 487
Evans, Meredydd 396, 402-4, 410, 416, 428, 446, 505, 507, 510
Evans, Oliver 48
Evans, Rhiannon 25, 54-5, 72, 75-6, 108, 129, 146, 167, 196, 244, 258, 264, 269, 284, 323, 327, 375, 392, 408-9, 417, 427, 440-2, 450-1, 463, 489, 511
Evans, Rhys (son) 160
Evans, Roderic 275
Evans, Sir Hywel 399-400, 420, 504
Evans, Tecwyn 62
Evans, Victor 35
Evans, Dan 357, 447, 464, 495
Evans-Jones, Albert (Cynan) 193
Ewing, Winnie 272, 284-6, 342, 489
Excelsior 217-18

Falklands conflict, the 437
Fascism 453
Federation of Small Businesses 381
Fenn, Marjorie 52
Ferris, Paul 148
Ffransis, Ffred 324, 326, 328, 401, 407, 412, 448, 494, 505
Financial Times 377, 501
Fishlock, Trevor 11, 311, 495
Flintshire 90, 208, 481
Foot, Michael 207, 272, 330, 354, 357, 359, 361-2, 364, 366-9, 378, 387, 426, 496, 498-500, 507
Foreign Office, the 108-9, 287, 381
Forestry Commission 130, 134, 141
Fouéré, Yann 108, 467
Francis, W B 43
Free Nation 288
Free Wales 123, 193, 195, 239, 270, 294
Free Wales Army (FWA) 239, 253, 255, 261, 267, 270, 273-4, 280, 282-3, 296, 301-4, 312, 315, 485-7
Frongoch 162
FWA *see* Free Wales Army

Gaddafi, Colonel 356
Gallery 226
Gandhi, Mahatma 43, 51-2, 80, 113, 126, 134, 170, 202, 205, 210, 402, 408, 412, 417, 453
Gardiner, Duncan 380, 489, 502
Garn Goch 61, 452, 456
Garroway Show, the 188
Garthewin Group, the 206, 243, 247, 471, 482, 484, 490
Garth Newydd community house 205-6
Gaumont film studios 18
Gee Press 76
General Election 31, 95-6, 103, 105, 118, 125, 131, 137-8, 146, 153-4, 157, 159, 168, 176, 187, 190, 194, 198, 214, 220, 226-7, 229, 235, 238, 254, 351, 501, 504
Geneva 29-30, 35, 82-83
George, David Lloyd 17, 23, 27, 81, 84, 100, 125, 130, 452
George, Gwilym Lloyd 155, 473
George, Megan Lloyd 130, 138, 140, 148, 157-8, 165, 170, 176, 240, 256-61, 266, 469
George, William 125
George VI 45, 145
Gillie, Blaise 167, 180, 205, 474, 476, 479, 482

Gittins Report 289
Gladstone Road School 457
Glasgow Herald, the 416, 506
Glyn, Seimon 450
Goedwig, y (home) 19
Goleuad, Y 73, 83, 137, 464, 470
Gower, Raymond 174, 176, 185, 475
Gower constituency 159, 174, 176, 185, 475
Granada Television Company 183-4, 232
Grŵp 1942 (1942 Group) 84, 93
Gravelle Choir 61
Griffith, I B (John y Gŵr) 280
Griffith, R E 184, 476
Griffiths, Ann 28, 162, 164
Griffiths, Anthony 18
Griffiths, David Rees (Cerddetwr) 74, 85
Griffiths, Edward 18
Griffiths, James 464, 482
Griffiths, James (Jim) 464, 482
Griffiths, J Gwyn 77, 121, 230, 441, 481
Griffiths, Peter Hughes 310, 325, 329, 332, 334, 338, 347, 374, 392, 407-11, 416, 428, 492, 494-5, 497, 501, 503, 505-7
Griffiths, Robert 395, 406, 472, 508
Griffiths, T Elwyn 92, 465
Grimond, Jo 230, 277
Gruffudd, Alwyn 380, 502
Gruffydd, Moses 88, 220, 228-9, 462, 482
Gruffydd, W J 36, 46-7, 62-3, 69, 84-5, 116, 458
Guernica 49
Gwasg Cymru 288
Gwasg John Penry 323
Gwenallt *see* Jones, David James
Gwerin 47, 50-1, 93, 121-2
Gwyn, Aled 332, 432, 483, 491, 508
Gwynfor Evans and You 332

Hafren 159
Hailsham, Lord 326
Hardie, Keir 36, 54, 114, 150, 271
Harlech, Lord 398
Harris, Oliver 70-1
Haweswater 161
Healey, Denis 378, 434
Heath, Edward 228, 256, 279, 290, 312, 315, 328, 330, 332, 336, 495
Heddychwyr Cymru 50-5, 60, 62, 67, 72-3, 76-7, 89, 97, 101, 436, 461
Henderson, Arthur 150
Henry II 143
Hen Dŷ Fferm 30
Herald Cymraeg, Yr 42, 53, 111, 459-60, 467
Herald of Wales, The 269
Hill, Charles 157
Hirllwyn 65
Hiroshima 103
Hitler, Adolf 34, 37, 42, 45, 52-4, 64, 68, 100-1, 337, 494
Hockey 25, 33, 39
Hogg, Quintin 279
Holland 55, 274
Holton Road, Barry 16, 18
Home Office 67, 185, 271, 290, 397-400, 410, 418, 422, 470, 504, 507
Hoopers ironmongers 16, 18
Hooson, Emlyn 196, 319
Hopkin, Daniel 74
Houghton, William 294
Hourahane, Peter 212, 223, 484, 493
House of Commons, the 98, 117, 174, 279, 297, 304, 308, 365, 427
House of Lords, the 14, 421, 433
HTV Wales 396, 398, 404, 405, 420, 462, 466, 485, 504, 505, 508
Hughes, Cledwyn 129, 131, 138, 144, 148-50, 158, 174-5, 179, 241, 252, 257, 262-3, 272-3, 276-83, 286, 289, 290, 345, 350, 365, 371-2, 375-6, 419, 421, 424-5, 472, 476, 485, 488, 500-1, 507
Hughes, Douglas 119-20
Hughes, Emrys 271-2
Hughes, Glyn Tegai 130, 418, 430
Hughes, Hywel (Bogota) 168-9, 316, 476
Hughes, John 271, 494
Hughes, Loti Rees 490
Hughes, Mathonwy 138
Hughes, Roger 154
Humphreys, E Morgan (Celt) 110
Humphries-Jones, Gwyn 31
Huws, Cathrin *see* Daniel, Catherine 83, 464
Huws, O T L 142, 223, 485
Huxley, Julian 98
Hwntw, *see* Vic Jones 115
Hylton, Jack 184
Hywel, Emyr 331

Independent Broadcasting Authority 398, 403, 405, 418, 420, 425, 504
Iceland 92
ILP (Independent Labour Party) 55, 157
ILP *see* Independent Labour Party 55, 157
Independent Television Authority 208
International Relations Club 34
Investiture of the Prince of Wales 46, 280-1, 284-6, 289, 295, 297-9, 301, 303-7, 311-2, 314
IRA 66, 206, 227, 326, 355, 417, 428
Ireland 14, 38, 46, 53, 60, 108, 115, 132, 206, 219, 258, 309, 418, 431, 477
Isis 39, 43, 459
Israel 144, 202
Italy 22, 91, 284
ITA *see* Independent Television Authority 208, 232
ITV 183, 294, 397-8, 400, 425
ITV 2 397-8, 400, 425
Iwan, Dafydd 263, 295, 298-9, 303, 307-10, 318, 320, 322, 328, 331, 333, 358, 420, 429, 436, 438, 443, 476, 490-2, 494, 508

James, Carwyn 287, 379, 501
James, David 193
James, Glyn 135, 152, 195, 284, 326, 478
James, Walter 22
James, Wmffra 99, 466
James, Wynfford 327, 373
Jarman, A O H 193, 460, 461
Jenkins, Dafydd 47, 459, 461
Jenkins, Geraint 445, 479
Jenkins, John 310
Jenkins, Neil (Neil ap Siencyn) 221-25, 267, 486
Jenkins, R T 84, 166, 474
Jenkins, Warren 184
Jerman, Noel 227
John, Will 64
Johnson, Frank 388
Jones, Alwyn 303
Jones, Bedwyr Lewis 446, 510
Jones, Ben 19
Jones, Ben G 196
Jones, Bobi *see* Jones, Robert Maynard
Jones, Cyril 236, 258, 260, 263, 332, 338, 471, 485-6, 492, 496
Jones, Dafydd Alun 249
Jones, David 217, 480
Jones, David James (Gwenallt) 77, 265, 486
Jones, Dennis 411
Jones, Edwin Pryce 41
Jones, Elizabeth Watkin 163-7, 170, 172, 174-5, 177, 196, 474-5
Jones, Dr Elwynne 170
Jones, Emrys 369
Jones, Emyr Llywelyn 226-8, 481, 484-5
Jones, Frank Price 231, 480
Jones, Fred 141, 471
Jones, Dr Gareth Morgan 275, 303, 491
Jones, Geraint 256, 481, 485
Jones, Gerallt 234
Jones, Griff 48, 461
Jones, Dr Gwenan 33, 118, 131, 207, 462, 468
Jones, Gwilym R (Mignedd) 77, 201, 211, 218, 227, 235, 468, 503
Jones, Gwynoro 287, 290, 292, 305, 309, 311-2, 321, 324-5, 332-4, 337-40, 348-50, 389, 489-90, 492-3, 496, 498
Jones, Harri Pritchard 206, 255-6, 324, 403, 416, 479
Jones, Huw 136, 466, 470
Jones, Ieuan Wyn 394, 395, 450, 509
Jones, John Aelod *see* Williams, John Roberts
Jones, John Albert 227
Jones, Joseph 49
Jones, J E 39, 41, 43-44, 46-47, 53, 58-61, 63, 65-6, 68, 75, 78, 84-6, 88-90, 93, 95-7, 103-6, 110, 112, 116, 122-4, 132, 135, 137-8, 142, 145-6, 149, 158-9, 162, 164, 167-9, 177-9, 184, 186, 192, 200-4, 206, 207, 212, 214-7, 222, 233-4, 245, 250-3, 256, 265, 312, 427, 459-81, 483-6, 492
Jones, J R 40, 140, 298, 318, 389, 471
Jones, J T (Eilian, John) 300
Jones, J W 49
Jones, Major Edgar 24
Jones, Meurig 184
Jones, Michael D 98, 151, 344, 430
Jones, Nans 233, 244-6, 484, 497
Jones, Nest Lewis 186, 476
Jones, Rachel 202-4
Jones, Richard Wyn 37, 459
Jones, Robert Ambrose (Emrys ap Iwan)

144, 454
Jones, Robert Maynard (Bobi) 300, 449, 474, 508, 511
Jones, R H 399, 504
Jones, R Tudur 115, 126, 154, 167, 171, 173, 177, 180, 187, 191, 202-3, 206, 211-2, 218, 234, 243, 245-6, 275, 283, 305, 324, 344, 349, 402, 412, 467, 469, 472, 474-5, 477, 479-80, 483-4, 489, 492, 497-9, 504, 506
Jones, Dr Thomas (councillor for Llangadog) 81, 119
Jones, Tom 167, 191, 211, 234
Jones, Tom (Llanuwchllyn) 167, 191, 211, 234
Jones, T Gwynn 77, 84
Jones, T Llew 226, 484
Jones, T W 138, 149, 164-5, 175, 183, 191, 196, 319, 472, 474
Jones, Vernon 201, 478
Jones, Vic 48, 115
Jones-Williams, Dafydd 426
Jones-Williams, W 136
Jones Michael D 98, 151, 344, 430
Joseph, Keith 227-8, 279, 290, 298, 482

Kagawa 80
Kane, Peter 230
Kellock, Willie 259, 260, 489
Kelly, Brian 288-9, 381
KGB 297
Kidwelly 15, 19, 445
Kilbrandon Commission 329
King, Dr Horace 271
Kinney, Phillys 403, 404
Kinnock, Neil 292, 330, 338, 347, 353, 357, 362, 371, 378, 380, 435, 442, 490, 496, 501, 510
Knighton 361, 499
Kohr, Leopold 424, 479, 507

Labour Party 36, 83, 88, 109, 111, 117-8, 126, 128-9, 131-2, 141, 144, 146-51, 153, 156, 158, 174-5, 198-9, 222, 235, 239, 241, 249, 251-2, 259, 282, 287, 292, 305, 307, 338, 341, 345, 349, 351, 365, 368-9, 373, 449, 469-70, 472-3, 493, 496
League of Nations 27, 29, 34, 42, 458
League of Nations Union 27, 29, 458
Left Book Club 27, 33
Legonna, John 84, 121, 234, 239, 242, 468, 479, 483-4
Levi, Thomas 32
Lewis, Alun 33
Lewis, Anthony (A H Llewys) 273
Lewis, Howell Elvet (Elfed) 133, 259
Lewis, John L 189
Lewis, Pedr 200, 478, 484
Lewis, Robyn 299, 305, 313, 434, 490-1, 492, 508
Lewis, Roy 213, 215
Lewis, Saunders 27, 33, 36-9, 41-2, 44-6, 49, 50-54, 57, 59, 61, 63-6, 70, 74, 79, 81, 83-8, 91-2, 94-6, 98-100, 102-6, 111-4, 116, 118, 120, 122-3, 125-6, 131, 134-6, 142, 144-5, 150, 152, 167, 170, 178-9, 186-7, 193, 201, 206, 209, 213, 216-27, 232, 242-3, 250, 253, 255-6, 261, 265, 275, 294-6, 302-3, 306, 309, 322, 339, 342, 347, 365, 389-91, 401, 408, 410, 416, 421, 423, 428, 433, 438, 443-4, 451, 453-5, 458, 460-2, 465-6, 468-72, 475, 477, 480-6, 490, 494, 497, 507-8, 510-1
Lewis, Vivian 203
Le Pen, Jean-Marie 447
Liberal Party, the 17, 84, 98, 101, 109, 116, 118, 120, 125, 127, 130, 132, 138, 144, 156, 159, 196, 198, 230, 235, 243, 257-8, 277, 303, 312, 317, 319, 327-8, 335-6, 340, 343, 347, 356, 364-5, 373, 389, 468, 470
Libya 355
Lilienthal, David 98
Listeners' Association, the 154, 404
Littler, Shirley 397
Littler report, the 400
Liverpool 55, 62, 70, 160-72, 174-5, 178, 181-3, 186-7, 191-3, 197, 200-1, 210, 214, 226-7, 252-3, 465, 480, 485,
Liverpool Corporation 160-3, 170, 174, 178, 186, 192, 252-3, 474, 476, 485
Liverpool Daily Post 113, 121, 123, 136, 147, 173, 180, 279, 285, 289, 291, 303, 310, 348, 350, 368, 373, 380, 382, 460, 46-76, 478, 481, 486-92, 494-05, 510
Liverpool Echo 171, 475

Llais Llafur 106
Llanbryn-mair 134
Llandaff 74
Llanddewibrefi 130
Llandegfedd 182
Llandeilo 73-4, 263, 331
Llandovery 80, 147, 262, 290, 472
Llandrindod conference 113
Llanelli 16, 87, 120, 138, 149, 155, 201, 217, 280, 286, 294, 306-7, 369, 378, 450, 457, 472, 478-9, 488
Llanelli Star 280, 488
Llanfor 177
Llanfrothen 99
Llangadog 16, 22, 49, 55, 58, 61, 69, 73, 80-1, 85, 88, 97, 105, 108, 112, 119, 120, 143, 155, 211, 237, 244, 258, 265, 267, 274, 287, 301, 327, 357, 358-9, 363, 396, 416, 442, 454, 482, 489, 495
Llangadog, the court of 85, 482
Llangyndeyrn 232, 483
Llanuwchllyn 96, 167, 191-2, 211, 263
Llanwern 181, 407, 410
Llanycil 177
Llenor, Y 62, 69, 461, 462
Llŷn 42, 74, 106, 141, 208, 407, 459
Lloyd, Alun 332, 412, 506
Lloyd, J E 84
Lloyd, Selwyn 279
Lloyd, Tecwyn 93, 132, 458, 470
Lloyd Street chapel 16, 457
Llygad Llwchwr, *see* Davies, Anthony
Llywelyn, Emyr *see* Jones, Emyr Llywelyn
LNU 27, 29-30, 34-35, 38, 42, 44, 50, 82
LNU *see* League of Nations Union
Lol 376, 501
London 18-19, 49, 53, 62, 70, 72, 97, 107-9, 117, 125, 128, 140-1, 174, 180, 192, 260, 264, 266-7, 269-70, 275-6, 278, 280-1, 289, 292, 294, 297-8, 308, 310, 312, 315, 347, 415, 419, 427, 463, 465, 469, 471, 473, 489-91, 493, 504, 511
Los Angeles Times 274

Mabon (William Abraham) 103, 483
Macdonald, Ian 250
Macintyre, Dr Robert 274
Macmillan, Harold 203
Maelor, Lord *see* Jones, T W
Mair, Meleri 4, 275, 487, 505
Makarios, Archbishop 166
Malthouse 48
Manchester 152, 161, 165, 172-3, 254, 461, 470, 472, 475, 485, 496
Manchuria 34
Marks & Spencer 49
Matthews, C F 92, 95
Matthews, Gwynn 322
Maxwell-Fyfe, Sir David 140
McGill, Cathi 320
Meibion Glyndŵr 407, 448
Melin-y-Wig 427
Melincryddan (Siloh church) 16
Merched y Wawr 359, 393, 441, 445
Meredith, David 405, 505
Merriman, Ted 284, 377
Merseyside 59, 163, 169, 173, 222
Merthyr Tydfil 46, 155, 205, 221, 472
MI5 66, 72
Michell, Alan 24, 25, 26
Mignedd, *see* Jones, Gwilym R
Miles, Dafydd 131, 140, 144, 471
Miles, Gareth 193, 209, 254, 289, 298-9, 395, 406, 484-5, 491
Mond, Alfred 266
Monmouthshire 60, 117, 140-1, 157, 182, 187, 220, 466
Montgomeryshire 57, 159, 161, 220, 225, 229, 312, 356, 422
Morgan, Derec Llwyd 266, 324
Morgan, Deulwyn 494
Morgan, Elystan 190, 195, 211, 213, 220, 223, 234-5, 237-8, 246-7, 249, 251-2, 257, 271-2, 282, 290, 319, 325, 370, 379, 477-8, 481, 483-5, 488
Morgan, George 327, 495
Morgan, Geraint 360, 393, 503
Morgan, Gerald 204
Morgan, Gwyneth 154
Morgan, K O 374, 457, 501
Morgan, Trefor 121, 123, 211-2, 223, 468
Morgan, T J 84
Morris, John 241, 306, 336, 345-6, 351-2, 359-60, 366-8, 371-2, 374, 379, 381-2, 417, 484, 488, 496, 499-500
Morris, Rhys Hopkin 81, 176, 266

Morris-Jones, Huw 40, 194, 204
Morrison, Herbert 81, 117, 148-9
Mosley, Oswald 37
Munich (accord) 52-3, 192
Muppet Show, the 407
Murray, Pete 327
Murry, Middleton 93
Mussolini, Benito 37

National Coal Board (NCB) 104
National Eisteddfod 51, 55, 62, 69, 91, 106, 109, 133, 146, 179, 181, 186, 193, 194, 204, 252, 293, 323, 374, 420-1, 425, 446, 450
National Eisteddfod Council 446
National Health Service 104
National Welsh Development Council 37
Nat West Bank 447
NCB, *see* National Coal Board 276, 478
Neath 16, 37, 98, 269, 272, 505
Nerth 238
Netherlands 66, 478
Newport 14, 55, 168, 181, 457
News at Ten 294
News Chronicle 100, 125-6, 144, 148, 151, 468-72
New Nation 234, 236, 238-9, 242-4, 246, 248-9, 395, 483-4
New Statesman 27, 286, 489

Parry, Sir David Hughes 194, 255
Parry, Thomas 180, 251, 301, 318
Parry-Williams, Sir T H 26, 143, 231
Patriotic Front 273, 282
Peace News 51-2, 77, 460, 462-3
Peace of Nations 29
Peace Pledge Union (PPU) 44, 50-1, 53, 66, 72-3, 77-8, 97
Peate, Iorwerth 63, 77, 85, 215, 231, 235, 480
Pencader 72, 78, 143-4
Pencarreg 5, 403-4, 410, 425, 442-3, 446, 448-9, 509
Penllyn 164, 166, 182, 192
Penllyn Rural District Council 182, 192
Penry, John 323
Penuel (chapel) 24
Penweddig Comprehensive School, Aberystwyth 319
Penyberth 42-7, 117-8, 122, 126, 134, 137, 139, 141-2, 168, 180, 187, 191, 213, 224, 265, 268, 285, 294, 371, 373, 401-2, 404, 415, 423, 455
Perkins, Max 405
Phillips, Cliff 264
Phillips, Delwyn 107
Phillips, Marc 446, 510
Phillips, Morgan 148, 292, 472
Phnom Penh 287
Picture Post 112, 467
Pierse, Michael 428

Plaid Cymru and You 260, 486
Plaid Cymru annual conferences 50, 84, 90-1, 114, 121, 133, 180, 186, 193, 204-5, 232, 237, 307, 330, 346, 350, 376-7, 405, 450
Plan Electricity for Wales 95, 465
Plowden, Lady 398
PONT 446-7, 510
Port, Donald 97, 465
Porthmadog 67, 233, 297, 427
Port Talbot 150, 407
Powell, Dewi Watkin 48, 92, 95, 106-7, 123, 145, 155, 157, 174, 179, 181, 190-2, 251, 307, 309-10, 312, 396, 465-6, 475-7, 487, 492-3, 503, 507
Powell, Enoch 279
Powell, John 355
Pravda 265
Price, David 64
Price, Emyr 343, 462
Prichard, Caradog 280
Pritchard, David 212, 220-1, 226
Probert, Arthur 153, 296
Prothero, Cliff 128, 131, 148, 199, 472-3
Providence Chapel 61, 80, 108, 287, 327, 489
Purity and Protective League 23

Radical Wales 441, 509
Radio Caroline 238-9
Radio Corporation 94, 103-4, 106-7
Radio Wales 195, 238-9, 478
Railwaymen's Union 187
Reagan, Ronald 432, 439
Rebecca 117, 356, 508

Reconstruction Ministry 92
Red Roses 263
Rees, Alwyn D 133, 286, 318, 389, 492
Rees, Chris 228, 238, 244, 484-5, 487
Rees, Dr Linford 363
Rees, Ioan Bowen 247, 290, 298, 412, 430, 479, 488-91, 506, 508
Rees, John Roderick 355
Rees, Merlyn 280, 282, 377, 378
Reid, George 384
Reilly, C H 98
Religion 28, 40, 88, 125, 127, 133, 135, 151, 268, 283, 321, 337
Republicans 116, 118, 120-4, 126, 134, 136, 222, 233, 248, 259, 395, 411-2
Rhondda East 100, 314
Rhondda Leader, the 278, 488
Rhondda West 136, 138, 277, 278-9, 280
Rhoslyn 405
Rhys, Keidrych 112
Richard, Elizabeth 19
Richard, Henry 151, 300, 321
Richard, Ivor 280, 282
Richards, Leslie 175
Richards, Leyton 27
Richards, Phil 329, 370, 500
Richardson, Nancy 72, 462
River Severn 181, 295, 504
River Vyrnwy 162
Roberts, Alwyn 418-9, 422, 425, 506-7
Roberts, David 171
Roberts, Elwyn 99, 104, 146, 148, 157, 168-9, 188, 208-9, 211, 216, 234, 245, 254, 261, 263-4, 274, 282-3, 288, 294-5, 299, 303, 310, 315-6, 319, 324, 336, 345, 351, 354-5, 361, 364, 394, 412, 414, 416, 435, 468-9, 472-4, 476-7, 479-83, 485-7, 489-92, 494, 496, 497-500, 503, 506, 509
Roberts, Emrys 52, 100, 127, 131, 138, 170, 178, 192, 200, 206-7, 210-1, 214-6, 232-4, 236-9, 243-9, 251, 274, 283, 288, 325-6, 330, 335, 344, 353, 356, 376, 405, 411-2, 429, 438, 470, 475, 477-84, 487, 489, 495, 508
Roberts, Emrys O (pacifist) 52
Roberts, Goronwy 93, 113, 117, 128-31, 148-9, 158, 174-5, 191, 272, 290, 469, 472
Roberts, Hywel 382, 502
Roberts, Hywel D 36
Roberts, Hywel Heulyn 145, 489
Roberts, Kate 26, 36, 59, 76, 113, 138, 142, 175, 193, 227, 232, 253, 283, 467, 483, 485
Roberts, Mary Silyn 194
Roberts, Samuel 151, 321
Roberts, Wyn 184, 252, 328-9, 360, 400-1, 406, 418, 421, 439, 507, 509
Roderick, Caerwyn 374, 501
Rodgers, Bill 287, 338
Rosser, David 195, 276, 330, 357
Rowlands, Jennie 172
Rowlands, Mary 20
Royal Television Society 397

S4C 398, 405-6, 424, 427-31, 439-40, 445, 450, 452, 454, 505-7
Samuel, Wynne 48, 69, 92, 94, 98, 110, 113-4, 116, 132-3, 152-3, 170, 237, 277, 295, 334, 470, 475, 477, 510
Sands, Bobby 431
Schiavone, Toni 436
SCM (Student Christian Movement) 33
Scott, Reverend Michael 190, 286-7, 477
Scottish National Party 58, 99, 241, 250, 259, 272, 274, 278, 284-5, 335-6, 340, 342-4, 348, 352-3, 357, 363-4, 372, 375, 383-5, 387, 389, 432, 484, 493, 499
SDP (Social Democratic Party) 338, 431, 437, 509
Sefton, W H 485
Seion chapel, Aberystwyth 33, 452
Sennybridge 65
Seren, Y 201, 466, 474, 476, 478
Seren y Dwyrain 92, 465
Seren y Gogledd 92
Shahmati, Ahmad 355, 498
Shipton, Martin 451
Short, Ted 350, 352-4
Shotton 396, 404
Shrewsbury 62, 306
Sianel Pedwar Cymru *see* S4C
Siberry report, the 400
Sihanouk, Prince 287
Simon, Lord 81
Slough 87

Smith, Ray 233-4, 239, 247, 483-4
SNP *see* Scottish National Party
Socialism 39, 47, 50, 93, 115, 126-7, 159, 339, 344-5, 349, 356, 395, 419, 430, 434
Socialist Republicans 395, 411
Socialist Republican Movement 406
Sodlau Prysur *see* Davies, Aneirin Talfan
Somerset Road (Barry) 19, 22
South Wales Echo 57, 291, 293, 380, 457, 460-1, 476, 490, 502, 506
South Wales Evening Post 4, 239, 461-4, 481, 483, 486-7
South Wales Miners' Federation 54, 70
South Wales Voice 291, 490
Spain 25
Spengler, Oswald 452
Stalin (nickname) 48
Stead, Peter 14, 132, 457, 470
Stephens, Isaac 194
Stephens, Meic 4, 11, 239, 479, 486, 497
Stewart, Donald 384
Suez 168, 171
Summers, John 301, 487, 491
Sun, the 304, 308, 331
Sunday closing for pubs 206, 450
Sunday Mirror 245, 484
Sunday Times, the 355, 498
Swaffham 190
Swansea 50-1, 67, 74, 76, 80, 134, 149, 225, 228-9, 232, 269, 301-2, 320-1, 324, 326, 378, 381, 419, 435, 441, 457, 461, 480, 494, 509

Tabernacl Chapel, Barry 16-7, 20-2, 24, 26, 68, 457
Tafod y Ddraig 395, 489, 496, 503
Tawney, R H 452
Taylor, George 303
Teledu Cymru *see* Wales West and North Television
Tennessee Valley Authority 92
Thatcher, Margaret 346, 377, 386, 429, 477, 497, 506
Thomas, Ceinwen 323
Thomas, Clem 259, 274, 468, 486
Thomas, Dafydd Elis *see* Elis-Thomas, Dafydd
Thomas, Dan 54-5, 75, 97, 129, 131, 460, 469
Thomas, David 128, 194
Thomas, Dewi Prys 147, 168, 472
Thomas, Dylan 60, 189
Thomas, D J 100
Thomas, Elizabeth 54, 76
Thomas, George 203, 270, 279, 282, 289, 291-4, 296-8, 300, 304-6, 309-10, 312, 316-7, 319, 331, 336, 490-3
Thomas, Gwilym 120
Thomas, Huw 312, 389
Thomas, Iorwerth 136
Thomas, John 64, 236, 248, 268, 484, 487
Thomas, Ned 403-4, 416
Thomas, Nigel 389, 391, 439
Thomas, Owen John 236, 248, 268, 484, 487
Thomas, Peter 316-8, 320, 328-9, 494
Thomas, Roger 349-50, 352, 388, 391, 422, 437, 439, 441, 507
Thomas, R S 135, 447
Thomas, Terry 354-5
Thomas, Wyn 393, 503
Thomas, W S 264
Thorpe, Jeremy 277, 336, 341, 356, 367
Tilsli, Archdruid (Tilsley, Gwilym R) 318
Times, The 159, 170, 172, 195, 268, 270, 308, 417, 422, 466, 473, 475-6, 478, 485, 487-9, 491-3, 495-7, 500-1, 506-7
Tomos, Angharad 379, 401-2, 415, 419, 505, 506
Toshack, John 362
Traethodydd, Y 82-83, 464
Traherne, Sir Cennydd 419
Trawsfynydd 99, 105, 116-7, 130, 133-5, 137-8, 164-5, 167, 186, 189, 401, 470
Tregaron 31, 114, 300, 307
Trial and Error 119
Tripoli 92, 355
Tryweryn 5, 9, 107, 123, 160-9, 171-2, 174-6, 178-83, 185-7, 189-90, 192-3, 196, 200-1, 204, 206, 209-14, 217, 220-1, 224-8, 232, 239, 252-4, 263, 282, 286, 292, 295, 299, 370, 386, 396, 401-5, 438, 473-7, 481
Tryweryn – New Proposals 192, 194, 200-1, 253, 477
Tucker, Margaret 234, 245, 248, 484
Tucker, Mike 248

TUC Wales 407
Tudur, Gwilym 318, 493, 494
Tuohy, Denis 294, 490
TVA scheme for Wales 92
TWW (Television Wales and the West) 183-4, 231-2, 485
Tynged yr Iaith 134, 216-20, 225, 243, 250, 480
Tynllidiart 55, 76, 258, 433
Tyst, Y 68, 73, 80, 218, 457, 459-60, 462-3, 480
Tystiolaeth y Plant 77

Union of Socialist Arabs 355
United States of America 188, 206
University College of North Wales, Bangor 284, 380
University College of Wales, Aberystwyth 30, 284
University College of Wales, Bangor 30, 193, 284, 380
University of Wales, the 40, 84-5, 98, 324, 326, 458, 468, 471, 482
University of Wales's Broadcasting Committee 324
Urdd Gobaith Cymru 33, 63, 106, 295, 301, 303, 305, 359, 431

Valentine, Lewis 45, 84, 88, 135, 234, 249, 256, 295, 366, 407, 423, 480, 490, 500, 505, 507
Vale of Clwyd, the 113
Vale of Glamorgan, the 16, 26, 44, 48-9
Velindre 15
Versailles 27, 29, 34, 42, 53
Vietnam 286-8
Viriamu 327
Voice of Wales, the 182, 300
von Teffenar, Gerhard 66

Wales 112, 323, 467
Wales Broadcasting Council 154, 184, 195, 503
Wales West and North Television Limited 208, 214-5, 222, 230-2, 479, 482
Wallis, William 287, 489
War Game, The 437
War Office, the 45, 63, 65, 104, 110-11, 114, 116, 133, 137, 141
Washington Post 189, 477
Watkins, Tudor 149, 185, 319, 472
Way of Peace, the 29
Webb, Harri 192, 205, 212-3, 223, 233-4, 239, 242, 245, 247, 264, 274, 280, 305, 345, 404, 420, 477, 479, 481, 483-4, 486-90, 492, 494, 497, 499-500, 505
Week In Week Out 294
Weizman, Chaim 119
Welsh Clarion 150, 472
Welsh Gazette 32, 458
Welsh Labour News 150
Welsh Language Council 330
Welsh Language Petition Committee 47
Welsh Nation 141-2, 168-70, 273, 283, 288, 325-6, 332, 349, 353, 358, 458, 469, 473, 479, 483, 485, 494-8, 501, 510
Welsh Nationalist 44, 52, 54, 59, 65, 71, 109, 112, 114-5, 157, 185, 217, 305-6, 365, 459-60, 464, 466, 468, 476
Welsh Office, the 241, 256, 270, 277, 280-1, 291, 306, 316-7, 381, 396, 398-401, 415, 417, 420, 426, 439, 504, 506-9
Welsh Pacifists 50-5, 60, 62, 67, 72-3, 76-7, 89, 97, 101, 436, 461
Welsh Review, the 62, 461
Welsh Rugby Union 62
Western Command 110-1, 114, 116, 137
Western Mail 23, 49, 52, 54, 73, 82, 89, 98, 111, 114, 136-7, 153, 166, 180, 182, 185, 192, 195, 201, 214, 221, 223-4, 230, 249, 251, 257, 267, 272-3, 276, 285, 303, 330-1, 344, 347, 354-5, 357, 365, 377, 380, 384, 389-90, 394, 397, 416, 432, 453, 457-60, 462, 464, 466-511
Westminster 13, 27, 37, 82, 112, 155-6, 159, 170, 173, 196, 217, 263, 267, 269, 275, 278-9, 282, 285, 298, 313, 328, 335-7, 339-41, 347, 351-3, 357, 361-2, 364, 374, 377, 383, 388-9, 406, 430, 454, 504, 506
White, Eirene 281, 306, 488, 492
Whitelaw, William 290, 386, 392, 397-8, 404, 418, 421, 424, 503-4, 507
Wigley, Dafydd 161, 270, 272, 275, 307, 311, 314, 319, 32-30, 332, 334-7, 339, 342, 346-7, 350-3, 355-6, 361-4, 366, 368, 370, 372, 375, 384, 394, 402, 405-6,

410-11, 414-5, 418-9, 429, 431, 433-4, 437, 440, 448-9, 453, 487, 496-502, 505-6, 508-10
Williams, Jac L 184, 207, 397, 403, 499
Williams, Dafydd 303, 316, 328, 332, 345, 355-6, 359, 363-4, 370, 372, 376, 382, 393-4, 405, 409-12, 436, 443, 491, 494-6, 498-503, 505, 507-9
Williams, Abi 90-1, 96-7, 101, 103, 464
Williams, Alan 276, 330, 389, 437, 447
Williams, Dafydd 303, 316, 328, 332, 345, 355-6, 359, 363-4, 370, 372, 376, 382, 393-4, 405, 409-12, 436, 443, 491, 494-6, 498-503, 505, 507-9
Williams, David 24, 26
Williams, Delwyn 422
Williams, Dr Alan 389, 437, 447
Williams, D J 30, 36, 42, 45, 84, 94, 98, 102, 106, 114, 123, 128-9, 135, 139, 143, 146, 149-50, 153, 174, 178, 180, 187, 198, 208, 212-3, 222-4, 234-5, 245, 247, 250-1, 254-6, 263, 265, 274, 279, 295, 302, 308, 462, 465-9, 471-3, 475-81, 483-91
Williams, D T 327
Williams, Emyr Wyn 432, 510
Williams, Euryn Ogwen 406
Williams, Geraint 249
Williams, Griffith John 193, 222, 458, 481
Williams, Gwyn Alf 447
Williams, G O 40, 362, 419, 421
Williams, Harri 40-1, 459
Williams, Hawys 152
Williams, Haydn 208, 231
Williams, Hywel S 355
Williams, John Roberts (John Aelod Jones) 155, 166, 203, 231, 382
Williams, Llywelyn 103
Williams, Morris 76
Williams, Nefyl 249
Williams, Owain 227, 282, 299, 482, 488
Williams, Phil 213, 233, 275, 277, 292, 307, 311, 313, 317, 319, 322, 330, 332-3, 335-7, 343, 345, 350, 355, 360-1, 366, 373, 377, 411, 444, 453, 480, 488, 494, 496, 499, 501, 510
Williams, Rhodri 373, 395, 408
Williams, Rhydwen 184, 434
Williams, Tudno 41
Williams, Waldo 77, 135, 175, 463
Williams, Wayne 405, 410, 505
Williams, William (farmer) 63, 65-6, 462
Williams, William (Pantycelyn) 28
Williams Wynne, Colonel 208
Wilson, Harold 178, 241, 255, 257, 259, 261-2, 272, 278, 280, 286, 290, 300, 306, 311, 336, 341, 354, 489, 492, 493
Wilson, Jock 297
Wolfe, Billy 250
Wolverhampton 87
World War, the First 20, 34, 54, 60, 70, 73, 158, 452
World War, the Second 49, 111, 321, 337, 393, 436
Wright, George 379, 382, 407, 502
Wyn, Hedd *see* Evans, Ellis Humphrey
Wynne, Nina 242, 484
Wynne, R O F 142, 206, 223, 227, 242, 294-5, 470-1, 481-2, 485, 490

Young, Jubilee 61
Young, Sir Brian 403, 505
Y Traddodiad Heddwch yng Nghymru 77